Local Governance in India

About the Editor

T.M. Joseph is currently Reader and Head, Department of Political Science, Newman College, Thodupuzha, Kerala. He had his doctoral studies at the Institute for Social and Economic Change, Bangalore on the 'Nativist Movement in Bangalore City'. He also had been a Visiting Fellow at Faculty of Law, Kyushu University, Japan from 1998 to 2000. He has to his credit a book titled *Politics of Recruitment: Migration and Ethic Conflict in Urban India* and several research papers published in leading journals. He is the Principal Investigator for the UGC sponsored major research project on "Paradigm Shift in Governance: State-Society Synergy in Rural Kerala with special reference to the *Jalanidhi* Project". He is also a member of Board of Studies and a research guide in Political Science in Mahatma Gandhi University.

Local Governance in India
Ideas, Challenges and Strategies

Edited by
T.M. Joseph

CONCEPT PUBLISHING COMPANY, NEW DELHI-110059

Cataloging in Publication Data—DK
Courtesy: D.K. Agencies (P) Ltd. <docinfo@dkagencies.com>

National Workshop on Decentralised Democracy and Planning (2003 : Thodupuzha, India)
Local governance in India : ideas, challenges and strategies/ edited by T.M. Joseph.
p. cm.
Papers presented at the National Workshop on Decentralised Democracy and Planning, held at Thodupuzha on 19th December 2003.
Includes bibliographical references.
Includes index.
ISBN 8180693643

1. Local government—India—Congresses. 2. Local government—India—Citizen participation—Congresses. 3. Decentralization in government—India—Congresses.
I. Joseph, T. M., 1963- II. Title.

DDC 320.809 54 22

ISBN 81-8069-364-3

First Published 2007

Published and Printed by

Ashok Kumar Mittal
Concept Publishing Company
A/15-16, Commercial Block, Mohan Garden
New Delhi-110059 (India)

Phones: 25351460, 25351794
Fax: 091-11-25357103
E-mail: publishing@conceptpub.com

Dedicated
to the Memory of
Late Prof. Amal Ray

Preface and Acknowledgements

The genesis of this volume is a UGC sponsored national workshop on 'Decentralised Democracy and Planning' held at Newman College, Thodupuzha on December 19, 2003. As it was fairly a good gathering of established scholars and activists in the field, some of the participants suggested that the papers presented in the workshop be compiled in the form of an edited volume. This inspiration helped me to start with this project.

The initiative in this regard from my side has received favourable response from many quarters. The paper writers were quick enough to submit their manuscripts in time. When all the papers presented in the workshop were collected it was thought better to invite some more papers and make the volume comprehensive to the extent possible. Efforts in this direction were also met with reasonable success. Reputed scholars and acknowledged activists in the field have sent in their contributions too. I thank all contributors for generously co-operating with this humble project.

This volume would not have been realized unless my Principal, Rev. Fr. Paul Nedumpurath was kind enough to grant me the necessary freedom and encouragement to hold the workshop and proceed with this publication. I acknowledge the contributions made by all my esteemed teachers especially Dr. S.N. Sangita, Dr. B.S. Bhargava, Dr. K. Raman Pillai and Dr. G. Gopakumar in promoting my academic interests.

My friends Dr. Jos Chathukulam, Dr. M.S. John, Dr. H.S. Shylendra, Dr. Sukhpal Singh, Dr. N. Sivanna, Dr. T.V. Sekher, Dr. S. Rajendran, Dr. V. Venkatakrishnan, Dr. Shaji Varkey, Dr. P.K. Viswanathan and Mr. R.H. Itagi deserve a special mention as their lovely encounters with me always had a boosting effect. My colleagues in the College Dr. P.A. Jose and Dr. Stephen Joseph are also remembered for their constant encouragement and support to this attempt.

My wife, Beena and children, Ajay and Vijay have provided me the much needed moral and other support constantly to sustain my spirit. Last but not the least, I thank Shri Ashok Kumar Mittal, Concept Publishing Company, New Delhi for having brought out this book in quick time.

T.M. Joseph

Contents

SECTION–III

PEOPLE'S PARTICIPATION IN LOCAL GOVERNANCE

SECTION–IV
LOCAL GOVERNANCE AT WORK: DYNAMICS AND CHALLENGES

SECTION–V
THE EMERGING PARADIGM OF LOCAL GOVERNANCE

The Contributors

Boby Mathew

Boby Mathew is a Ph.D. fellow at the Centre for Political Studies in Jawaharlal Nehru University, New Delhi. He has completed M.A. in Political Science from Kerala University. His areas of academic interest include 'social mobility', 'political power' and 'grassroots democracy'.

B.S. Bhargava

B.S. Bhargava is retired Professor and Head, Development Administration Unit, Institute for Social and Economic Change, Bangalore. He is currently Senior Fellow, Institute of Social Sciences, Bangalore. A doyen of Panchayati Raj studies in India for the last four decades. Prof. Bhargava is the recipient of two coveted awards "Panchayat Ratna" and "Smt. Shakuntala Sundarlal Puraskar". He has authored several books and papers on local governments and rural development.

Jos C. Raphael

Jos C. Raphael is the Director of Centre for Community Organisation and Development (CECOD), Trichur, Kerala. He took his master's degree in Economics from Calicut University and furthered skills in Development Planning at School of Development Planning (CDSA, Poona), University of Poona. Dr. Jos holds his doctoral degree in Development Studies from University of Mysore under the guidance of Dr. B.S. Bhargava, Retired Professor ISEC, Bangalore. His subject for thesis was on "Decentralised Planning in India: A Comparative Study of Karnataka and Kerala States". He worked with Kerala Community Irrigation Project, Trichur aided by Dutch Government as Social Scientist of Small Irrigation Sector. Later he joined London School of Economics (University of London) for a practitioner's graduate course in "Social Policy and Planning in Developing Countries". Currently Dr. Jos focuses upon rainwater harvesting and social aspects of water related subjects in Kerala State.

D.V. Gopalappa

D.V. Gopalappa has worked in various capacities at Institute for Social and Economic Change, Bangalore. Currently, he is Reader in Development Studies at University of Mysore and teaches post-graduate students. He has a number of publications in refereed journals to his credit. Dr. Gopalappa has been specialising in Rural Development and Regional Planning. He has been involved in researching more than half a dozen sponsored research projects on issues of contemporary relevance.

K.S. James

K.S. James is currently professor at Population Research Centre, ISEC, Bangalore. Previously he had worked as Deputy Director, Population Research Centre, University of Kerala, Reader at Centre for Economic and Social Studies, Hyderabad and Visiting Fellow at Harvard Centre for Population and Development, USA. His current areas of interest centre around population and health in relation to socio-economic development. He has published several papers in national and international journals and co-edited a book on demographic change, health inequality and human development in India.

Susanta Kumar Jena

Susanta Kumar Jena, is Senior Research Officer, National Disaster Management Authority, Government of India, New Delhi. He did his M.A., M.Phil and Ph.D. from Jawaharlal Nehru University. He presented a paper on "Globalisation and Popular Culture—Reading Advertisements Sociologically" in an International Seminar on Cultural Globalisation at Freiburg University (Germany) in the year 2000. He has also presented a paper on "Local Government in Disaster Preparedness: A Case Study of Orissa" in an International Seminar on "Global Quest for Participatory Democracy" held at New Delhi in the year 2004.

M.S. John

M.S. John is Professor in Politics and Peace Studies, School of Gandhian Thought and Development Studies, Mahatma Gandhi University, Kottayam, Kerala. He was earlier lecturer in politics at St. Joseph's College, Calicut, Kerala. Currently he is engaged in a research project on the role of elected representatives of rural local bodies in conflict management. Areas of concentration are peace studies, new social movements, gender studies, conflict management and decentralised governance.

T.M. Joseph *(Editor)*

T.M. Joseph is currently Reader and Head, Department of Political Science, Newman College, Thodupuzha, Kerala. He had his doctoral studies at the Institute for Social and Economic Change, Bangalore on the 'Nativist Movement in Bangalore City'. He also had been a Visiting Fellow at Faculty of Law, Kyushu University, Japan from 1998 to 2000. Dr. Joseph is the recipient of the Fr. T.A. Mathias National Award for Innovative College Teachers in 2001 instituted by the All India Association for Christian Higher Education. He is interested in studies of decentralisation, ethnic relations, and electoral systems. He has authored a book titled "Politics of Recruitment: Migration and Ethnic Conflict in Urban India" and sereval research papers in leading journals. He is also the Principal Investigator for the UGC Sponsored Major Research Project on "Paradigm Shift in Governance: State-Society Synergy in Rural Kerala with Special reference to the Jalanidhi Project".

George Mathew

George Mathew took his Ph.D. in Sociology from the Jawaharlal Nehru University, New Delhi. His thesis was: 'Secularization and Communalization: Contradiction and Change in the State of Kerala—1890-1980'. He was visiting fellow at the South Asian Studies Centre, University of Chicago (1981-82) and Visiting Professor at University of Padova (1988). He was awarded the Fulbright Fellowship in Summer 1991 for working at the University of Chicago. He has participated and presented papers in international conferences on religion and society, political process and democracy, and human rights. Dr. Mathew is Founder Director, Institute of Social Sciences, New Delhi. Now he is specialising on the local government system (Panchayati Raj), decentralisation and gender equity. He is a regular contributor to national dailies. His major works include: (i) *Communal Road to a Secular Kerala;* (ii) *Panchayati Raj: From Legislation to Movement* and the following edited works: (i) *Shift in Indian Politics*; (ii) *Dignity for All: Essays in Socialism and Democracy;* (iii) *Panchayati Raj in Karnataka Today: Its National Dimensions;* (iv) *Panchayati Raj in Jammu and Kashmir;* (v) *Status of Panchayati Raj in States of India 1994;* and (vi) *Status of Panchayati Raj in the States and Union Territories of India 2000.*

P.M. Mathew

P.M. Mathew, Director, Institute of Small Enterprises and Development, Kochi, has directed over thirty-five research projects, on behalf of several Ministries of the Government of India, other bodies like the Planning Commission, United Nations, Reserve Bank of India, Khadi and Village Industries Commission, development banks, Indian Council of Social Science Research, etc. A consultant to several international institutions, including that of the UN system, he was honoured with the prestigious Oshikawa International Award by the Asian Productivity Organisation (APO), Tokyo, in 1997. Currently, he holds responsible positions in the Government of India, including, as Member, Consultative Group on Unorganised Sector at the Prime Minister's Office, Member of the National High Power Committee on Small Enterprise Development, constituted by the Planning Commission, and the Working Group of the National Sample Survey Organisation (NSSO). A National Consultant to the United Nations Industrial Development Organisation (UNIDO), he is recipient of the Birla National Fellowship in Economics.

Jayaprakash Narayan

Jayaprakash Narayan is a physician by training who went into the Indian Administrative Service in the aftermath of the Emergency and failure of the Janata Experiment. During 16 years of distinguished public service in various capacities, he acquired a formidable reputation in the State of AP. He resigned from Service (IAS) in 1996, and worked with like-minded colleagues for the formation of

Lok Satta and is currently its National Coordinator. *Lok Satta* has now emerged as a leading civil society initiative for governance reforms. Dr Jayaprakash Narayan was honoured with the prestigious Rotary Manav Seva Award 2002 and Yudhvir Memorial Award in 2002.

Pradeep Narayanan

After the completion of MBA from Pune University, Shri Pradeep Narayanan has worked in private and public sector in India and abroad. He later pursued post-graduation from the School of Oriental and African Studies, University of London. He is presently working as Researcher in the Centre for Education and Communication, New Delhi. He has to his credit publications in the *Economic and Political Weekly, The Hindu* and *Labour File.*

Mangala Anant Nayak

Mangaladevi Anant Nayak is a Research Associate at Institute of Social Sciences, Southern Region, Bangalore. She has to her credit, published and presented papers on administrative decentralization and gender studies in several journals and conferences.

Md. Nazrul Islam

Nazrul Islam is a Program Officer in JSI, Bangladesh. He holds a doctorate degree in Political Science from University of Mysore, MSS in Public Administration (University of Dhaka) and MA in Political Science (Bangalore University). He received Indian Council for Cultural Relations (ICCR) Fellowship from the year 1996 to 2003. His research interest includes decentralisation, social capital, transparency and accountability, public health, nursing, and e-governance. His works are published in various professional journals.

G. Palanithurai

Ganapathi Palanithurai is currently heading the Department of Political Science and Development Administration at Gandhigram Rural Institute, Tamil Nadu. He is also the Dean, Faculty of Social Sciences, Member of Syndicate, and Coordinator of Rajiv Gandhi chair at the Institute. He is the Chairman of the Hunger Project in Tamil Nadu.

He has been associating himself with Central Planning Commission, State Planning Commission, State Finance Commission, Population Foundation of India, Ford Foundation, UNICEF, Rajiv Gandhi Foundation, CAPART, Ministry of Rural Areas and Employment and DANIDA (Danish-Indo Development Agency) in specific areas of activities in connection with empowerment of people. He has to his credit several books, articles, working papers, and monographs on three major areas, namely Legislative Behaviour, Ethnicity and Panchayati Raj System. He was a recipient of Fellowship from Sastri Indo-Canadian Institute, New Delhi and World Academy of Art and Science, USA. He has visited the US and Canada on academic assignments. He was a visiting fellow in the McGill University, Canada in 1989.

D. Rajasekhar

D Rajasekhar is Professor and Head, Decentralisation and Development Unit, Institute for Social and Economic Change, Bangalore. He has done his doctoral studies at Centre for Development Studies, Thiruvananthapuram and has authored two books and several papers on decentralization and rural development.

K. Rajasekharan

K Rajasekharan is Librarian, Kerala Institute of Local Administration (KILA), Mulangunnathukavu, Thrissur, Kerala. He has authored a few research papers on decentralisation and local governance.

S. Rajendran

S. Rajendran is an economist, worked with ISEC (Bangalore), CSE (New Delhi) and University of Mysore as Reader in the Department of Economics. He is currently Professor of Economics at Periyar University, Salem. He has rich experience, in teaching, research and extension activities for more than two decades. He has publsihed more than 50 research papers in national and international journals. Dr. Rajendran has visited The Republic of Korea, Canada and Thailand for attending seminars and conferences. His areas of interest include rural development, environment and micro level planning.

Jos Chathukulam

Jos Chathukulam is the Director of Centre for Rural Management, Kottayam, Kerala. After obtaining Ph.D. in Development Administration from Institute for Social and Economic Change Dr. Jos Chathukulam worked for two years as a research associate at School of International Relations, Mahatma Gandhi University, Kottayam. Since the establishment of the Centre for Rural Management in 1990 he has been serving as its Director. Areas of concentration are rural development, rural local government and decentralisation.

P. Sanjay

P. Sanjay is working as an Advocacy Associate with *Lok Satta*. He has a Masters degree in Political Science from University of Hyderabad. He was awarded University medal for having stood first in MA (Political Science).

Sachidananda Satapathy

Mr. Sachidananda Satapathy is a Ph.D. student at Decentralisation and Development Unit, Institute for Social and Economic Change, Nagarabhavi PO, Bangalore-560 072.

T.V. Sekher

T.V. Sekher is Reader International Institute for Population Sciences (IIPS), Deonar, Mumbai. He was Assistant Professor with Population Research Centre, Institute for Social and Economic Change (ISEC), Bangalore. Trained in sociology and demography, his areas of research interest are social demography, reproductive health, migration and health service delivery. During 2003, Dr. Sekher was Visiting Fellow at Wellcome Trust Centre for History of Medicine, University of London and Maison de Sciences La Homme, Paris. He has published many research articles both in national and international journals. He also coordinated two action projects to sensitize the PRIs in Karnataka on health issues.

Sitakanta Sethy

Mr. Sitakanta Sethy is a post-graduate in Rural Development from Xavier Institute, Ranchi during 1991–1993 and as a Junior Research

Fellow (JRF) has completed his Doctoral Research in Development Studies from the Institute for Social and Economic Change, Bangalore. Adding to this, he has around ten years of work experience in the government and non-government development sector and also has published ten articles on participatory development in various refereed journals.

Rashmi Sharma

Ms. Rashmi Sharma is a senior IAS officer of Madhya Pradesh cadre. She has her Master of Public Affairs from Woodraw Wilson School, Princeton University, USA; M.A. and M.Phil. from Delhi University. After holding important administrative positions at state and national governments, Ms. Sharma is currently on deputation to the Centre for Education, Management and Development, New Delhi as resource person. She has written extensively on public policy issues in reputed journals including *Economic and Political Weekly.*

Vandana Shiva

Vandana Shiva is trained as a physicist and did her Ph.D. on the subject "Hidden Variables and Non-locality in Quantum Theory" from the University of Western Ontario. She later shifted to inter-disciplinary research in science, technology and environmental policy, which she carried out at the Indian Institute of Science and the Indian Institute of Management in Bangalore. In 1982, she founded an independent institute, the Research Foundation for Science, Technology and Ecology in Dehra Dun dedicated to high quality and independent research to address the most significant ecological and social issues of our times, in close partnership with local communities and social movements. In 1991, she founded Navdanya, a national movement to protect the diversity and integrity of living resources, the promotion of organic farming and fair trade. In 2004 she started Bija Vidyapeeth, an international college for sustainable living in collaboration with Schumacher College, U.K. Dr. Shiva has contributed in fundamental ways to changing the practice and paradigms of agriculture and food. Her books, *The Violence of Green Revolution* and *Monocultures of the Mind* have become basic challenges to the dominant paradigm of non-sustainable, reductionist Green Revolution Agriculture. Through her books *Biopiracy, Stolen Harvest, Water Wars,* Dr. Shiva has made visible the social, economic and ecological costs of corporate led globalisation. Dr. Shiva combines intellectual enquiry with courageous activism. She is equally at ease working with peasants in rural India and teaching in universities worldwide.

Dr. Shiva has been a visiting professor and lectured at the Universities of Oslo, Norway, Schumacher College, U.K. Mt. Holyoke College, U.S., York University, Canada, University of Lulea, Sweden, University of Victoria, Canada, and organisations and institutions worldwide on ecology, feminism and globalisation.

H.S. Shylendra

H.S. Shylendra is an Associate Professor at Institute for Rural Management, Anand (IRMA). He has done his Ph.D. at Institute for Social and Economic Change, Bangalore. His areas of interest are sustainable rural development, rural livelihood systems, micro/rural finance, and governance. Currently, he teaches courses on Rural Development and Micro-Finance for the students of the Post- Graduate Programme at IRMA. He has co-authored a book titled *Diversification and Sustainable Rural Livelihood* and two monographs titled *Organising for Rural Development* and *Sustainable Livelihood in the Context of Growing Occupational Diversification and Rural-Urban Linkages.* Also, he has some research papers to his credit.

Sukhpal Singh

Sukhpal Singh is Associate Professor, Centre for Management in Agriculture, Indian Institute of Management, Ahmedabad. Dr. Singh has been a visiting fellow at the Institute of Development Studies (IDS) Sussex, Brighton (UK) in 1999 and at the Chulalongkorn University, Bangkok (Thailand) in 2002. He specialises in agribusiness marketing and international agro-trade and teaches courses in agribusiness management and global economic and business environment. He has written widely on the issues of contract farming and the WTO and the SAP regimes in national and international journals and popular press.

K. Subha

K. Subha is the Regional Co-ordinator of Institute of Social Sciences, Bangalore. She holds Ph.D. from the Institute for Social and Economic Change, Bangalore and is interested in the areas of democratic decentralisation and women empowerment. She has published five books and several papers and study reports.

E.M. Thomas

E.M. Thomas, a post-graduate in Economics and a doctorate in the area of economic planning is currently a Reader at the post-graduate department of Economics, Christ College, Irinjalakuda, University of Calicut. He also received special training in economic planning from University of Belgrade (former Yugoslavia) in 1987-88 as part of young Economist's exchange programme between India and former Yugoslavia under the supervision of eminent economists, Prof. Dr. Jovan Tovorovic and Prof. Dr. Alexander Jovanovic. He has to his credit many research papers and articles on various topics in economics including monetary policy and economic planning.

V. Vijayalakshmi

V. Vijayalakshmi is a Ph.D. in Sociology from Institute for Social and Economic Change, Bangalore. She has coordinated a few research projects and published several papers on decentralisation and gender studies.

V. Venkatakrishnan

V. Venkatakrishnan is Joint Director, Panchayati Raj, Centre for World Solidarity, Secunderabad. Dr. Venkatakrishnan has done his Ph.D. in Development Administration at Institute for Social and Economic Change, Bangalore and was later a Research Associate at Institute for Rural Management, Anand, Gujarat.

P.K. Viswanathan

Dr. P.K. Viswanathan is currently a post-doctoral fellow at School of Environment, Resources and Development, Asian Institute of Technology, Bangkok. He was working as Economist at the Rubber Research Institute of India, Kottayam, Kerala after having taken Ph.D. in Economics from Institute for Social and Economic Change, Bangalore. His areas of research interests relate to natural resource economics, institutional aspects of resource management, plantation agriculture, etc.

Introduction

T.M. JOSEPH

The idea that governance should be decentralized is now universally accepted. Cutting across geographical, ideological and disciplinary divides, this idea enjoys support from all walks of life. India is also no exception to the sweep of this idea as the 'decentralisation drive' has already set in place. The epoch making 73rd and 74th Constitutional Amendment Acts intended to strengthen local governments by mandatory transfer of powers and funds to them have been widely appreciated for their democratic content and development potential. The changes that are resultant of these Acts are broadly seen as having the potential of transforming the arena of local governance in India.

However, the idea of 'local governance' involves a much wider meaning than that of local government. Governance refers to the way decisions about public affairs are made in a society and includes a variety of aspects and processes; organizationally therefore, it ranges over a much broader canvas than government entities (Mishra 2004). Therefore, local governance is conceived as not merely a restructuring of local government arrangements, but the sum total of decentralizing moves in India. Mishra believes that in the wake of the emerging paradigms of governance necessitated by the hegemonic ideas of liberalization and privatization, local governance also connotes larger space for private and non-governmental agencies in the local development spectrum.

Arend Lijphart (2001, 326-7) identifies three challenges associated with the sustenance of democratic rule in India. The first is his contention that democracy is impossible in ethnically divided societies like India. The second is the high level of poverty and illiteracy which runs counter to the established linkage between socio-economic development and the maintenance of democratic rule. The third is the contradiction between India's high rate of political violence and its success at maintaining a democratic political system.

In spite of these challenges, India has established itself as a robust democracy which is evidenced in its continued adherence to constitutionalism and rule of law, regular elections, free press, independent and impartial judiciary and assurance of fundamental rights to the citizens. While discussing the degree of democracy in India, what is more important is its extent at the local level.

It is pertinent to start with the origin of the debates on local governments in India. It all began with the Bengal Chowkidari Act of 1870 in the erstwhile Bengal Presidency. A system of policing was established, the cost of which was borne out of the levies and taxes imposed by the local panchayat consisting entirely of nominated members. The passage of Lord Rippon's resolution on local governments in 1882 for the first time paved the way for local boards, consisting predominantly of elected members (Mishra, 2004). Since then, the idea of local governance has slowly set root in India, but its functioning was handicapped by restricted suffrage which was based on status and property holding and due to the continued hegemony of the colonial rule.

In the post-independence period, the discourse started with the constitution-making exercise itself. The Constituent Assembly witnessed heated debates over the status of local governments in the state structure of independent India. The famous Gandhi-Ambedkar arguments were the most prominent among them. Gandhi believed that "independence must begin at the bottom". His concept of village *swaraj* was a complete republic, independent of its neighbours for its own vital wants, and yet interdependent for many others in which dependence is a necessity. He believed that every village should have a Panchayat having full powers including defence. Opposing Gandhi, Ambedkar took a position that any political formation built upon the village is inimical to the interests of the depressed castes who could be subjected to further repression by the high castes in the name of Panchayati Raj.

But finally the Constitution came out with having an advisory provision in the Directive Principles of State Policy that lay unattended till about a decade after independence. In the wake of the poor effectiveness of the community development programmes, the Balwant Rai Mehta Committee in 1957 recommended the resurrection of local bodies. Considering the importance of popular participation in the success of rural development schemes, the committee suggested a three-tier structure for the local governance. These were considered to be the first generation local governments with only the village-level body composed of directly elected members and the other two tiers with indirectly elected and nominated members.

With the advent of Janata Party into power, one more committee was appointed under the chairmanship of Ashok Mehta to look into the issues of local governance. This committee recommended a central legislation to ensure regular and party-based elections so that the local bodies are made political entities and making the district-level government as the basic coordinating and integrating unit of the three-tier local government system. Though the Union government could not act upon such suggestions due to its premature collapse, some state governments tried to pay credence to the recommendations of the Ashok Mehta Committee. Firstly, West Bengal and then Karnataka set up three levels of local governments consisting mainly of directly elected members which played a major role in the successful implementation of various rural development schemes. The governments thus constituted were called the second generation local governments.

Inspired by the West Bengal and Karnataka experiments and on the recommendations of the two committees set up for the purpose, in 1989 the Union government introduced two constitutional amendment bills dealing separately with local government in the rural and urban areas. But the opposition parties saw in the proposals an attempt by the Union government to reach the local governments by-passing the state governments, and therefore, stalled its passing. It was only in 1992, the amendments could pass through providing the much needed legal institutional framework for the third generation local governments; the 73rd Amendment in rural areas and the 74th Amendment for urban areas.

With the 73rd Constitutional Amendment Act of 1992, fully representative local government structures came into effect at three levels for rural areas. The important features of the 73rd Constitutional Amendment are: (1) constitution of Grama Sabha at the village level consisting of all the electors, (2) three levels of directly elected local self-governments for rural areas, (3) regular elections at five-year intervals, (4) reservation of seats for scheduled castes and scheduled tribes in proportion to their population, (5) reservation of one-third of the seats for women, including those of offices of chairpersons at all levels, (6) constitution of State Finance Commissions for considering the financial requirements of the local bodies and making appropriate recommendations to the state governments, and (7) establishment of State Election Commissions for the conduct of local body elections. Ensuring 'maximum democracy and maximum devolution', the 73rd Amendment was considered as a major watershed with respect to local self-government institutions (Bandyopadhyaya, 2002).

It is beyond dispute that the 73rd Amendment has brought in an image of direct democracy at least at the village level, by constitutionally recognizing the institution of Grama Sabha. Along with the reservation of seats for the underprivileged sections such as the scheduled castes and tribes, the reservation of one-third seats for women was a radical break. The inclusion of such underprivileged sections in the institutions of local governance would enable their voices to be heard in a democratic manner. The mandatory conduct of elections in every five years and the creation of special election commission at the state level, led to the expectation of continuity; a guarantee against the premature dissolution or suspension of local governments by the state governments.

As the matter of local governments was listed as a state subject in the constitutional scheme of distribution of powers, the states were required to enact their own laws in conformity with the parent Act. Though all the states did so their degrees of enthusiasm varied.

While some states amended the existing legislations, others went for fresh legislation. Anyhow, the mandatory provisions have succeeded in creating a legal framework for constituting representative local bodies with a credible insurance against their supercession.

It must be recognized that across national contexts, a re-examination of the representative political institutions is underway. This is primarily as a result of seemingly contradictory sentiments of satisfaction and disappointment associated with democratic governments (Mishra, 2004). The moral vindication worldwide of democracy as opposed to other forms of government is a source of satisfaction. Yet, it is also a source of disappointment since, it is becoming increasingly apparent that the systems of government-elected politicians, professional bureaucrats and the variegated apparatus built around them, has failed in delivering the public goods that are so critical for continuation of civic life (*ibid*). The challenge is simple: find institutions that better realize our core democratic values—in particular the fairness, effectiveness and popular determination of public action—than the currently dominant arrangements of electoral representation and technical bureaucracy.

This volume is aimed at a performance appraisal of the local governance mechanism in India for the first ten years of its mandatory existence. It throws light on the ideas behind these institutions, the challenges they face and the strategies to contain them. The volume is spread over five sections, each focusing on a specific theme.

The first section is devoted to understand the very idea of local governance. It starts with the chapter on 'Democracy and Decentralisation' by Jayaprakash Narayan and P. Sanjay which attempts to portray the inadequacies, irregularities and malpractices in the ongoing decentralization drive in India. They are of the view that it is because of the reluctance from the part of the state governments, the 73rd and 74th Amendments did not result in truly empowered and effective local governments. They apprehend that a local legislator whose sole preoccupation is local political patronage often sees the elected local government as a serious rival encroaching into his territory. They argue for citizen centred governance in order to make decentralization effective and meaningful.

In the second chapter on 'Gandhi and the Contemporary Discourse on Decentralization', M.S. John holds the view that the current discourse on decentralization is anchored in a neo-liberal model of development and hence its connections with the Gandhian vision are superficial. Gandhi's views on decentralization were situated in the context of an alternative model of development, one that sought to organize village economy and polity on principles of limitation of wants, self-sufficiency, self-reliance and non-violence.

Md. Nazrul Islam's chapter on 'Decentralised Governance: Looking Back and Forth' tries to understand the concept of decentralization at a theoretical level. The chapter begins with the evolution of the idea of decentralisation and outlines the contemporary global concerns of decentralisation. Further, it attempts to highlight the emerging perspectives on decentralisation. Finally, it describes various enabling factors in the success of decentralised governance and discusses the importance and relevance of decentralised governance for a modern society.

V. Venkatakrishnan in his chapter on the 'Four F's of Decentralisation', gives importance to the fourth 'F'- freedom (autonomy)—in addition to the three F's such as functions, finances and functionaries that are to be endowed with the PRIs for their successful functioning. He regards that necessary freedom to decide the range, quantum and quality of functions, to raise finances such as local taxes and user charges as per the local situation, to engage and have power over the functionaries is the most important condition since lack of freedom (autonomy) in any of the other three F's would seriously hamper the performance of the local government institutions.

G. Palanithurai's chapter titled 'Panchayats, Relevance and Potentials' examines to what extent the newly created institutions have started functioning as expected and whether the leaders who have come to power have performed their functions. Based on his fieldwork in Tamil Nadu, he narrates various success stories where the elected representatives of Grama Panchayats functioned effectively to demonstrate the potential of PRIs. At the same time he reports certain cases where the panchayat leaders are viewed as a threat and a power centre by the bureaucracy and the MLAs and MPs as they are in the community and attend to the needs of the community directly.

Vandana Shiva in her chapter on 'Earth Democracy, Living Democracy: Rebuilding Security in an Age of Insecurity' contends that people's security does not lie in larger military budgets, bigger bombs and stronger police states. It lies in ecological security, in economic security, in cultural and political security at the local level. Rebuilding these multiple securities can recreate peace, justice and sustainability.

The second section gives its attention on how local governance mechanism can bring in social and economic development at the grassroots level. The first chapter in this section is by George Mathew. He talks about how PRIs can foster human rights. His major question was does the decentralisation process and the decentralised institutions increase human rights violations or enhance the possibility for respecting and observing human rights of dalits, tribals, women and the poor? His conclusion is that caste system is the major source of human rights violation in the society and there has been a sharp increase in violent manifestations of casteism in local communities ever since the local government system got strengthened through the constitutional amendments. He illustrates various cases where the human rights of lower castes, tribals, women and poor are grossly violated.

The impact of decentralisation on health care is critically examined by K.S. James in the next chapter. He looks into how far decentralisation has affected the provision of health services and thereby the health status of the poor in the country since the constitutional amendments took effect. His answer is that simplistic analysis of data linking health outcome with decentralisation ignoring several other important factors would be misleading.

T.V. Sekher in his chapter on 'Sensitizing Grassroots Leadership on Health Issues' talks about providing adequate training to the members of PRIs, community leaders and health workers about their new roles and responsibilities through the medium of television. Based on a pilot project in Karnataka, he finds that television could be used as a powerful and effective medium for educating and training grassroots level functionaries all over the state.

The chapter on 'Rural Poverty, Local Democratic Institutions, and Sustainable Development in India under Globalisation' by Sukhpal Singh examines the trends in rural poverty in brief and then goes on to analyse the impact of new economic regime—both domestic and global—on poverty situation. After discussing the relevance of pro-poor growth strategies, it explores the nature of factors which lead to poverty in rural areas. It also examines briefly the World Bank approach to poverty reduction before outlining lessons and strategies for rural poverty reduction. The paper concludes by emphasizing the role of local democratic institutions in reducing poverty which need to be considered for devising strategies for sustainable rural poverty reduction and development.

H.S. Shylendra's chapter on the 'New Governance Paradigm' makes an attempt to examine the nature of the emerging governance paradigm, assess the possible implications of it for tackling the problems of poverty and inequality. The emerging paradigm is that the challenges of development are to be addressed jointly by the State along with market and civil society, instead of being done by the State alone. But this paradigm, according to him, is posing a major challenge for the unfinished agenda of poverty eradication in India.

P.M. Mathew, in his paper on 'Decentralisation, Employment and Enterprises Development' attempts to examine the experience of economic decentralization in Kerala. He focuses upon the conflict between the forces of globalization and localization in relation to the challenges of economic development.

The third section is devoted to understanding the role of people's participation in local governance particularly in the state of Kerala. The first chapter in this section is by Rashmi Sharma who explains how the Kallesseri experiment influenced the People's Plan Campaign in Kerala. The importance of Kallesseri lies in the fact that a process of grassroots planning was developed in this panchayat which became the basis for local planning all over Kerala. The Kallesseri process was initiated by KSSP (Kerala

Shastra Sahitya Parishad), which began primarily as a movement for popularizing science and creating scientific temper among the people in the sixties. Three KSSP projects were important precursors of Kallesseri. The first was 'group farming', aimed at increasing productivity, reducing the cost of cultivation and generating greater and profitable rice production through joint farm operations, water management, plant protection etc. The second important precursor was the state-wide total literacy campaign and the third was the People's Resource Mapping Programme (PRMP). What is examined in her chapter is how the Kallesseri experience was interpreted and adapted in People's Plan Campaign, which leads to the more general question of the dynamics of applying innovative models developed by NGOs in larger governmental contexts.

Boby Mathew's chapter 'Emergence of New Institutions through Participatory Democracy: An Evaluation of Kerala Experiment' attempts to analyse the institutional impact of people's planning programme on various aspects of decentralized development especially during the first phase (1996-2001) under the LDF government. It also takes stock of the situation at the grassroots level after five years of its implementation and provides corrective measures for the forward march of the programme.

The next chapter is by K. Rajasekharan on the problems and prospects of decentralisation in Kerala. He argues that the experiment of decentralisation in Kerala had made drastic changes in the political process, administrative structure, allocation of resources, management of human resources etc. Consolidation of the major problems arising from those changes is the main theme of the paper. The lack of clarity of statutes, problem of departmental integration, absence of management efficiency, ineffective management of transferred institutions, improper record keeping, absence of clear focus on local economic development, public work execution by 'benami contractors' in lieu of beneficiary committees, disinterest of local bodies in mobilizing their own resources, weakness of key institutions such as Grama Sabha, ineffective *ombudsman*, failure in providing proper training etc. are explained duly touching the possible way out. The paper concludes that Kerala had made an excellent beginning and moved much ahead leaving a lot more to do to reach the dawn of a decentralised local government system in the State.

E.M. Thomas in his chapter examines the performance of Grama Sabha in the formation of social capital and empowerment of people. The study is based on the primary data collected from four village panchayats, viz. Alur, Melur, Nattika and Porathissery in Thrissur district of Kerala. Since the attendance ratios in grama sabha meetings fall below the expected levels, he is of the opinion that the success of decentralised planning in generating a sizeable level of social capital for sustainable development of the area is doubtful. The participation rate of male voters in grama sabha meetings declined considerably in all the panchayats, while there is a sizeable increase in the percentage of women's participation in such meetings. He considers it as a clear indication of the formation of social capital and empowerment of women as a result of decentralised planning.

Jos Chathukulam and M.S. John in their chapter based on the evidences from a village panchayat, Chempu, in Kottayam district throw light on the changing contours of social capital in Kerala. They argue that there is no correlation between membership in associations and civic-mindedness. The chapter with convincing reasons proves that higher levels of education and political consciousness need not automatically lead to higher civic mindedness.

The last chapter in this section is 'People's Planning and Kerala's Agriculture: The Missed Linkages' by P.K. Viswanathan. The objective of the paper has been to initiate a discussion on the specific responses of the decentralised planning process towards addressing the persistent impasse confronting Kerala's agriculture sector ever since the mid-1970s, characterised by a paradigm shift in cropping pattern from food to cash crops due to a host of socio-economic, institutional and technological factors. The basic contention here is that the redistributive policies pursued by the state on the agrarian front especially since the late 1960s has invariably increased the risk of farming operations with respect to food crops, while the entire plantation agriculture was kept outside the ambit of ceiling legislations. More precisely, the agrarian impasse as discussed in the chapter is a necessary fallout of the short-sighted agrarian policies pursued by the state and the launching of the peoples' planning programme could have turned out to be a strategic intervention to overcome the stalemate through a host of structural and institutional reforms in agriculture. But he apprehends that the targets and goals of the participatory planning process in Kerala have remained completely devoid of the objectives of growth in material production sectors, especially agriculture.

The fourth section is titled 'Local Governance at Work: Dynamics and Challenges'. The first chapter is 'The Functioning of Grama Panchayats in Karnataka' by D. Rajasekhar and Sachidananda Satapathy. The chapter looks into whether the presidents and secretaries of grama panchayats in Karnataka had undertaken the functions that were constitutionally assigned for them and analyse the factors contributing to their performance or non-performance. The chapter is based on the primary data collected from presidents and secretaries of 74 grama panchayats in six districts (Belgaum, Bellary, Bijapur, Chitradurga, Gulbarga and Kolar) in Karnataka. They have found that the functions that have been constitutionally assigned to GPs have not been fully undertaken by the sample GPs. This implies that there is a gap between the vision of policy makers and the extent to which the vision has been translated into practice.

The second chapter in this section is 'E-governance at the Grassroots: The case of Belandur Grama Panchayat in Karnataka' co-authored by Mangala Nayak, B.S. Bhargava and K. Subha. The chapter tells the story of how a grama panchayat in Karnataka called Belandur, could become a model panchayat through computerisation and efforts made to increase the source of income and became self-sufficient and sustainable. The innovative ideas and practices followed have led the panchayat to maintain its 'accountability and transparency' which are most important for any level of governance. These changes are due to the e-governance at the grassroots that has attempted to transform administration into a people friendly, transparent, efficient and accountable proposition. The chapter contends that e-governance is the best option to remove barriers between the people and the administration to attain good governance at the grassroots.

D.V. Gopalappa has contributed a chapter on the 'Role of Panchayats and Bureaucracy in Rural Development'. The chapter makes an attempt to understand the interface between the elected representatives and the bureaucrats to achieve the goal of rural development. The chapter is based on an intensive fieldwork among the officials of PRIs and elected representatives of three tiers of government in three districts (Mandya, Gulberga and Dakshina Kannada) in Karnataka. The chapter concludes that the power assertion and lack of sincerity on the part of both the officials and representatives are responsible for the ineffective implementation of rural development schemes in selected panchayats.

V. Vijayalakshmi in her chapter on 'Differences and Identities: Women and Political Participation', examines the factors contributing to women's marginalization in the functioning of the Panchayats and why do women support ideologies that sustain their subordination. Her analysis is based on in-depth interviews with elected representatives, members of different communities, and officials from the Gram Panchayats, Taluk Panchayats, and Zilla Panchayats of Mandya and Uduppi districts in Karnataka. She argues that the significance of the 'gender regimes' in the lives of most women has consequences for their political participation. Women's political participation depends on the socio-cultural constraints which were manifested in the gender inequalities, differences among women, and how they deal with their multiple identities. She particularly pointed to the problems of women belonging to disadvantaged caste and class groups. The multiple identities of women and the resulting dilemmas contributed to limiting their participation in panchayats.

The fifth chapter in this section is by S. Rajendran on 'Party Politics and Functioning of PRIs in a Tamil Nadu Village'. Depending on the grassroots level information collected from Nadur—a village panchayat in Thanjavur district of Tamil Nadu—the chapter examines how the inter-party dynamics affect the successful functioning of Panchayati Raj Institutions. He convincingly proves that the political differences between the state government and the local government institutions account for the less successful functioning of PRIs especially on availing grants and sanctioning and executing crucial development projects. He reports that when a particular party governs a state government, it is extremely difficult for the chiefs (belonging to opposition parties) of PRIs to carry on with the development activities.

The concluding section five of this volume is devoted to detail on the new paradigm of governance at the local level. The new paradigm marks a shift from the traditional state sponsored development approach to the new community centric development. The section starts with Pradeep Narayanan's chapter on the 'Panchayat's Raj over Global Capital'. His chapter is written in the background of economic globalization which encourages a cooperation-based relationship between the State and multinational companies in the developing countries for achieving the goals of economic growth and stability. The chapter explores the need and the feasibility of the institutionalization of vulnerable sections of the population in the negotiation process through the platform of the Panchayati Raj Institutions. The case of the agitation by villagers against the Coca Cola Plant at Plachimada in Kerala is presented in the chapter to strengthen the claim that the two main actors cannot ignore the power of the village community and the village Panchayat. Three main issues are highlighted in the chapter. Firstly, since the launch of economic reforms, the relationship between the State and MNCs is gradually emerging into a relationship in which the State's bargaining power appears to be declining. Secondly, the decline of the State's administrative and legislative capacity has an adverse impact on the marginalised sections of the society. Finally, the village Panchayat appears to be in a better position to represent the interests of the community in the negotiation process than the higher levels of government.

The second chapter is titled 'Democratic Institutions in the Water Sector of Kerala' by Jos C. Raphael. The chapter intends to analyse the benefit of participatory approach of irrigation management from KCIP (Kerala Community Irrigation Project) through a micro level study of sample water-user association at Kurumal in Trichur district of Kerala. Empowerment of farmers as managers rather than as beneficiaries is the unique feature of this project. Empowerment of women members into the executive committee with 30 per cent reservation is another landmark seen in the project. The study also focuses on how replicable is the participatory approach adopted in the project for social policy implications in Kerala state.

The next chapter is on the role of local institutions in disaster management in India. In this chapter, Susanta Kumar Jena talks about how best the local governments can prepare for and mitigate the effects of natural disasters. Most of the disaster management programmes have hitherto adopted a top-down approach, with local level involvement serving mainly as an aid to implement such programmes instead of being a part and parcel of the system itself. But the centralised system is increasingly felt inadequate to handle emergency situations because of the necessity to take immediate decisions on the spot as per the circumstances. Therefore, the focus is now shifted towards community participation and the involvement of local level institutions. They are the ideal channels to conduct any disaster management programme, right from relief, recovery and rehabilitation to planning for mitigation and prevention. It is argued in the chapter that the local governmental institutions, with their grassroots level contacts with the common people, can make a substantial contribution to the process by ensuring active people's participation in disaster management activities.

Sitakanta Sethy in his chapter on 'Synergetic Action for Participatory Development' talks about the collaboration among the development agencies, NGOs and government in reducing rural poverty. Synergetic action by the development agencies can be the most effective action towards reducing rural poverty because it can build the poorest of the poor's capacity to fight out poverty. The chapter contends that the government and non-governmental development agencies need to come together and involve the poor in planning and implementation of education, forestry, health, sanitation, credit, asset development, food security and gainful employment programmes in an integrated manner. Partnerships in specific fields that would bring out mutual benefit and maximum utilization of the resources have to be given priority to promote grassroots development.

The last chapter in this volume is co-authored by the editor and Jos Chathukulam. It has been titled as 'New Paradigm of Local Governance: State – Society Synergy in Rural Kerala'. The focus of this chapter is on the emerging pattern of governance in Kerala with special attention on the drinking water sector. It has now been experimented in Kerala to address the drinking water problem with an increased involvement of the people and civil society organizations. The experiment is called Jalanidhi, a project implemented with the support of the World Bank, Village Panchayat, Beneficiary Groups and NGOs. The study has been focused on ascertaining the effectiveness of the synergy between the state and non-state actors as it is an emerging pattern of development governance.

REFERENCES

Bandyopadhyaya, D. (2002): 'Panchayats in Karnataka: Two Steps Back'. *Economic and Political Weekly,* 37(35).

John, M.S. and Jos Chathukulam (2002): 'Building Social Capital through State Initiative: The case of Participatory Planning in Kerala', *Economic and Political Weekly,* 37(20), May 18: 1939-48.

Lijphart, Arend (2001): 'The Puzzle of Indian Democracy: A Constitutional Interpretation', in Niraja Gopal Jayal (Ed), *Democracy in India,* New Delhi: Oxford University Press, New Delhi.

Mishra, Debiprasad (2004): 'Decentralisation and Local Governance' *in Theme Papers, Silver Jubilee Symposium on Governance in Development: Issues, Challenges and Strategies,* Institute of Rural Management, Anand.

SECTION–I

UNDERSTANDING LOCAL GOVERNANCE

1

Democracy and Decentralisation

JAYAPRAKASH NARAYAN AND P. SANJAY

A large-sized district in India is larger than about eighty (80) nation-states in the world in terms of population. Most of our larger states would be among the large nations of the world. Uttar Pradesh, Bihar, Maharashtra and West Bengal—each would be the largest nation in Europe if independent. Even a truncated Uttar Pradesh would be the world's sixth largest nation. Given these mind-boggling demographic realities, coupled with unmatched diversity, our centralized, somewhat imperial style of governance is archaic and ineffective.

An incident during British Raj some 80 years ago illustrates the absurdity of over-centralization in a democratic polity in the 21st century. Chittaranjan Das (C.R. Das), the great Bengali patriot, was elected as Mayor of the newly constituted Calcutta Municipal Corporation in 1924. Das argued with the then British authorities that as the head of the elected local government he should have the right to appoint the chief executive officer (commissioner) of the city government. The British offered him the services of any ICS officer he chose. Das declined and won the right to appoint his own official. He then picked a bright young 27 years old as the commissioner. He was none other than Subhas Chandra Bose!

The story did not end there. Bose did an outstanding job as the city administrator and gained wide recognition in a few months. Several months later, he was arrested as a suspected terrorist and detained in Alipore Jail. C.R. Das again insisted that Bose did a great job, the charges against him were unrelated to his work as the city official, and the elected local government could not be denied his services. Amazingly, the colonial government relented, and directed that Bose should continue as the commissioner even while in custody! Files were sent to him in jail, and his orders were carried out. This extraordinary practice continued until Bose was exiled to Mandalay in Burma. Bose went on to become Mayor of Calcutta in 1930 and later Congress President in 1938 and 1939.

Today the elected local government of even a 'B' grade municipality enjoys no such autonomy, let alone the great metropolis like Kolkata or Mumbai. One of the paradoxes of democratic India is that our governance is far more centralized than in colonial India or communist China.

Distortions of Centralization

This centralized exercise of power led to several inevitable political consequences. At the macro level when we examine a whole state or the country, the electoral verdicts do broadly reflect public opinion. More often than not this verdict is a reflection of the people's anger and frustration and is manifested in the rejection vote, or their support to a leader, promise or platform. However, at the local level, caste or sub-caste, crime, money and muscle power have become the determinants of political power. All parties are compelled to put up candidates who can muster these resources in abundance in order to have a realistic chance of success. While political waves are perceived around the time of election or afterwards, at the time of nomination of candidates, all parties are uncertain about their success and would naturally try to maximize their chances of success at the polls by choosing those candidates who can somehow manipulate or coerce the voters. As a net result, irrespective of which party wins, the nature of political leadership and quality remain largely the same, and the people end up being losers. This is then followed by another rejection vote in the next election and the vicious cycle keeps repeating. Where the candidate cannot muster money or muscle power, he stands little chance of getting elected irrespective of his party's electoral fortunes. Increasingly in several pockets of the country, people are spared even the bother of having to go to the polling station. Organized booth-capturing and rigging are ensuring victory without people's involvement.

There is much that is wrong with our elections. Flawed electoral rolls have become a menace. About 40 per cent errors are noticed in electoral rolls in many urban areas, and bogus voting in towns exceeds 20 per cent, making our elections a mockery. Purchase of votes through money and liquor, preventing poorer sections from voting, large scale impersonation and bogus voting, purchase of agents of opponents, threatening and forcing agents and polling personnel to allow false voting, booth-capturing and large scale rigging, bribing polling staff and police personnel to get favours and to harass opponents, use of violence and criminal gangs, stealing ballot boxes or tampering with the ballot papers, inducing or forcing voters to reveal their voting preferences through various techniques including 'cycling' etc., illegally entering the polling stations and controlling polling process—all these are an integral part of our electoral landscape. No wonder the Election Commission estimate that more than 700 of the 4072 legislators in States have some criminal record against them!

Many scholars wonder how despite massive irregularities the electoral verdicts still seem to largely reflect public opinion, and how parties in power often lose elections. The answers are simple. Happily for us, though parties in power are prone to abusing authority for electoral gains, there has never been any serious state-sponsored rigging in most of India. The irregularities are largely limited to the polling process alone, and most of the pre-polling activities including printing and distribution of ballot papers, and post-polling activities including transport and storage of ballot boxes and counting of ballots are free from any political interference or organized manipulation. That is why parties in power have no decisive advantage in manipulating the polls, and electoral verdicts broadly reflect shifts in public opinion. However, the massive irregularities in polling process make sure that candidates who deploy abnormal money and muscle power have a distinct advantage. Sensing this, most major parties have come to nominate 'winnable' candidates without reference to their ability and integrity. Thus, the use of money power and muscle power are sanctioned by almost all the parties, and often they tend to neutralize each other. The net result is that candidates who do not indulge in any irregularity have very little chance of being elected. Election expenditure—mostly for illegitimate vote buying, hiring of hoodlums and bribing officials—is often ten or twenty times the ceiling permitted by law. Criminals have a decisive or dominant influence on the outcome in many parts of India, and have often become party candidates and won on a large scale.

Why do People Take Money to Vote?

In a large and complex country like India, it is impossible for the national or state legislatures to fairly or effectively represent the people and all shades of public opinion. Given the largeness of constituencies and complexity of elections, there will always be a tendency to abuse public office or resort to vote buying. Even with the best will, and the most comprehensive electoral reforms, in a poor country many voters are often swayed by the inducement of money and liquor. The most credible citizens are discouraged from contesting as long as voters expect money to exercise their franchise. In order to address this question we should first understand why the citizens are selling their vote for money.

This habit of taking money to vote is actually a rational response to an irrational situation. It is often tempting to blame the illiterate and poor citizens for this plight of our democracy. But in reality it is the democratic vigour and enthusiastic participation of the countless poor and illiterate voters, which has sustained our democracy so far. However, most people have realized with experience that the outcome of elections is of little consequence to their lives in the long run. As a net result of several distortions, elections have lost their real meaning as far as the people are concerned. If, by a miracle, all winners in an election lose, and all their immediate rivals are elected instead, there will still be no real improvement in the quality of governance. This remarkable inertia and the seeming intractability of the governance process have convinced citizens that there is no real long-term stake involved in electoral politics. Therefore, many poor citizens are forced to take a rational decision to maximise their short-term gains. As a result the vote has become a purchasable commodity for money or liquor. More often it is a sign of assertion of primordial loyalties of caste, religion, group, ethnicity, region or language. Very often without even any material inducement or emotional outburst based on prejudices, the sheer anger against the dysfunctional governance process makes most voters reject the *status quo*. Often this rejection of the government of the day is indiscriminate and there is no rational evaluation of the alternatives offered. In short, even the illiterate, ordinary voter is making a rational assumption that the vote has no serious long-term consequences and the choice is between Tweedledum and Tweedledee. Therefore, he is attempting to maximise his short-term material or emotional gain.

Link Between Vote and Public Good

This situation can be corrected only when the citizen appreciates the link between his vote and public good. Amartya Sen and Jean Dreze pointed out that the centralized state institutions are unable to meet the basic requirements of the poor people, therefore, there is not only a need to decentralize the administrative apparatus but

Decentralization lowers the cost of raising the income of poor people in South Africa

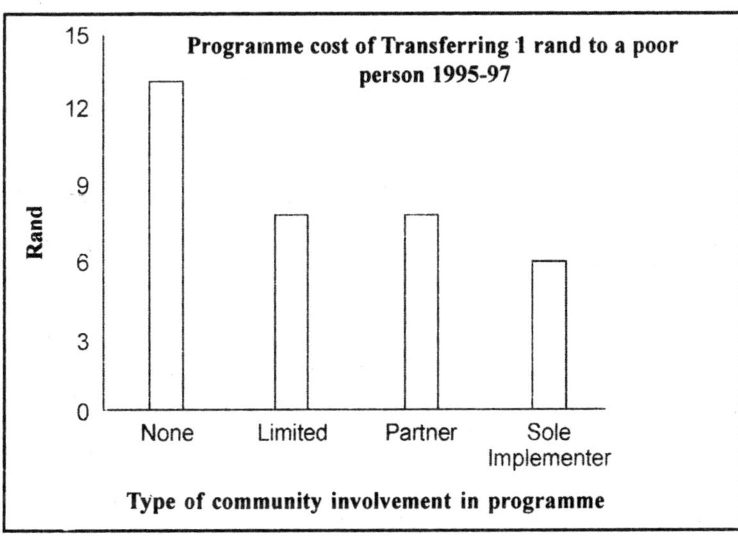

Source: Adato and others 1999.

also empower the local people by strengthening local governments. If the local elected representative has no alibis for non-performance, then vote acquires a new meaning. If the school, road, drain, water supply, traffic regulation, land records, health centre and a myriad other public services are the direct responsibility of the elected government at the local level, then people see that whom they elect has a tremendous bearing on what happens after the elections. Such a situation is possible when the local governments – panchayats or municipalities – are truly empowered, and authority is exercised as close to the citizen as possible in an accountable and transparent manner.

When there is a clear link between their vote and public good, and when tax monies are directly transferred to the public services, then people start using vote as an effective tool to make fine political judgments and elect suitable representatives. There will be greater participation of the people in the decentralized form of governance resulting in empowerment of the poor, as there is easy availability of local information. The availability of local information with the administration also results in better implementation of development policies. For instance in Bolivia decentralization gave communities more power to influence their local governments that the composition of local public expenditure shifted in favour of the poor.[1] This direct and positive relationship between decentralization and economic outcomes is not specific to Bolivia alone.

For instance, many of us admire China's rapid economic growth in recent years. But, we often ignore the fact that the employment and exports in China are powered by the millions of town and village enterprises (TVEs) with the support and active participation of local governments. One of the ironies of contemporary history is that the authoritarian and communist China is far more decentralized than liberal democratic India.

The 73rd and 74th Amendments to the Constitution merely created local governments. It is now mandatory to create panchayats and municipalities, to hold regular elections, to have a State Election Commission and State Finance Commission. However, in the absence of constitutionally mandated entrustment of responsibilities, local governments are at the mercy of the State legislatures. The State governments are often wary of parting with powers and functions. The Eleventh and Twelfth Schedules of the Constitution are merely recommendatory and many State Laws have violated the spirit of the Constitution. These provisions do not have the force of the Seventh Schedule, which clearly demarcates the functional jurisdiction of the Union and States. It is, therefore, necessary to clearly demarcate the functions of local governments constitutionally on par with the Seventh Schedule, and to ensure that the required resources and control of public servants are entrusted to the local governments. Only then can representative government be truly democratic, accountable and effective.

State Legislators *Versus* Local Governments

Another important and unhappy consequence of a parliamentary executive and unaccountable executive power in the hands of State legislators is severe weakening of local governments. A local legislator whose sole preoccupation is local political patronage often sees the elected local government as a serious rival encroaching into his territory. As local governments have been at the mercy of State legislatures until 1993, in most States local governments either did not exist, or when constituted, they tended to be feeble and ineffective. The States rarely showed any degree of commitment to transfer resources, functions and control over functionaries to local governments. As the State's political executive owes its survival entirely to elected legislators' goodwill and support, it is but natural that local governments would not be allowed to take roots against the will of the legislators whose dominance is threatened by empowered local governance. This situation underwent marginal change after 1993, with the advent of the 73rd and 74th Constitutional Amendments. However, given the reluctance of the States, these amendments did not result in truly empowered and effective local governments. The Constitution now only ensures that local governments are constituted, elections are held regularly, panchayats and municipalities are not superceded *en masse*, and independent constitutional bodies are appointed to monitor elections and advise on financial devolution. However, the Eleventh and Twelfth Schedules of the Constitution have no mandatory force and the State legislatures are free to transfer such subjects and powers as they deem fit to local governments. Given the political realities of legislators' unaccountable and disguised executive powers, most States chose not to empower local governments effectively. Even the constitutional obligations of constituting local governments and holding regular and periodic elections are violated with impunity, by employing a variety of disingenuous and undemocratic devices and stratagems.

Model for functional delineation among three-tiers of local government in education sector—Andhra Pradesh
Gram Panchayat Location of school and construction of school should be the function of village level panchayats through the gram sabha. Nutrition programmes should be entirely managed by the village level Panchayats with the help of gram sabha.The gram panchayat should select suitable candidates for Girl's Hostel.
Mandal Parishad Primary education will be transferred to *Mandal Parishads*. As regards vocationalisation of education, *Mandal Parishads* should identify location of work sheds for vocational education. *Mandal Parishad* will decide upon the location of Girl's Hostel.
Zilla Parishad Provision of teaching and training material should be the function of *Zilla Parishads* for which they should identify and promote resource centres. In nutritional programmes *Zilla Parishad* should arrange for linkages in respect of supply of food grains and its transportation. For secondary education regarding Educational Technology and Computer Literacy, *Zilla Parishad* should arrange for the supply of hardware and its maintenance. *Zilla Parishad* should arrange training of teachers in consultation with Directorate of Education and SCERT. For secondary education regarding educational Technology and Computer Literacy, the *Zilla Parishads* should do the selection of teachers. As regards vocationalisation of education, *Zilla Parishad* should carry out the survey with help of District Education Officers. Appointment and training of special teachers for disabled education should be done by the *Zilla Parishad*.

Local Governments in Andhra Pradesh–A Case Study

A close look at the functioning of local governments in Andhra Pradesh will demonstrate the reluctance of state government to empower the local governments effectively. For instance, even the National Commission to Review the Working of the Constitution (NCRWC) has in a consultation paper commented: [2]

> "In Andhra Pradesh...the Gram Panchayats and *Mandal Parishads* are not required to plan for economic development and social justice. All tiers of Panchayat have been assigned with large number of functions. But none of them has financial or administrative resources under their control to execute them. The *Mandal Parishad* has no control over the staff of Development blocks, and the *Zilla Parishad* has no control over the DRDA which controls huge funds over various poverty alleviation programmes."

It is not correct to say that a large number of functions have been given to the local governments in Andhra Pradesh. As per the Eleventh Schedule, 29 subjects can be devolved to the local governments, but the Government of Andhra Pradesh (GOAP) has devolved only 17 subjects and that too without transferring either the funds or functionaries along with the functions. Only advisory and review powers have been transferred. For instance, in the education sector, the GOAP transferred only adult and non-formal education and libraries, but not primary and secondary education. Due to incomplete devolution of powers, the role of local governments has been limited at best to beneficiary selection. District Planning Committees (DPCs) have not been constituted in spite of a clear constitutional mandate to do so. The DPC should prepare a district-level development plan and forward it to the State Government.

Apart from the reluctance to transfer subjects enumerated in the Eleventh Schedule of the Constitution, even in the limited transfer of functions that the GOAP has attempted, it did not transfer either the accompanying functionaries or finances to local governments. The authority of the local governments on the functionaries of various departments carrying out rural development functions is very limited. Elected representatives of local governments cannot take any disciplinary action against any gazetted officer. Representatives of local governments can at the most question the officials in the meetings or request the higher authorities to take appropriate action. Further, even the powers that were given to local governments over some of the functionaries have been withdrawn. For instance, through Government Order (GO no. 358) in 2000, the GOAP vested all powers with regard to teaching and non-teaching staff of schools with the District Education Officer (DEO) removing them from the hands of CEO of *Zilla Parishads*.

The fiscal devolution to local governments has also been very minimal. While Gram Panchayat has taxation powers, *Mandal Parishad* and *Zilla Parishad* tend to depend on the transfers and grants from the state government. In case of Gram Panchayat, the financial resources generated locally are not sufficient to meet its expenses. More often than not, the Gram Panchayats do not have the necessary staff to collect various taxes, propelling them into a vicious circle of fiscal insolvency. The Gram Panchayats do not have resources to employ staff to collect taxes, and inability to employ the staff further exacerbates the financial crunch as the taxes that are levied cannot be collected efficiently. The state government's financial transfers to local governments have been negligible.

The GOAP claims that almost 10.5 per cent of its rural expenditure has been done through local governments. However, a closer examination of facts reveal that a mere 5.3 per cent of its financial resources have been spent through local governments and the remaining 4.7 per cent was from the own financial resources of local governments. There is also absence of accurate fiscal data on the financial devolution to local governments as the World Bank observed in its report: "GOAP figures on the amount transferred to the local governments as "planned" are misleading as *Janmabhoomi*[3] amount is shown as released to the local governments; in reality, it is released directly to the collector, who then releases it to the Nodal Officer"[4]. It is estimated that almost 80 per cent of the meagre financial resources of the local governments is spent on wage bills. As the State government has been complaining, this may be true of the governments own current expenditure. However, in their case, the privilege of employment and powers of supervision and control go with the bill. In the case of local government only the bill bears their name while the power remains with the State government. However, since these are now shown as local government activities, the onus on non-performance falls on them. In the absence of clear functional devolution and control over functionaries, and lack of access to resources the local governments are unable to function in any meaningful manner. The weak local governments and centralization of political power actually dis-empowers State and Union governments, as their policy options will become constrained. This is most evident in the fiscal policies of State and Union governments.

Fiscal Responsibility and Local Governance

It is now common knowledge that India is in the grip of a severe fiscal crisis. The combined fiscal deficit of the Union and State governments is of the order of about 10 per cent of the GDP. As borrowings are diverted to meet the revenue deficits, and as interest burden on the exchequer keeps increasing, the crisis is deepening. While the economic dimensions of the crisis are well understood, it is often not recognized that this is largely a governance crisis. Fiscal deficits can only be addressed by significant increase in revenues or reduction in costs. Revenues can be raised painlessly only by very high, sustained growth rates. As our infrastructure is weak and inadequate, and as the productive potential of the bulk of the population is shackled on account of low levels of literacy and poor health care, there cannot be rapid growth on sustained basis. To overcome these obstacles we need both resources and governance reform to effectively implement policies. The more painful way of increasing revenues is higher taxation. As much of the tax revenue and public expenditure do not result in realizable public goods and services, citizens resist and evade high taxation. With rampant corruption in a centralized governance structure, there cannot be tax compliance in high-tax regime, nor is high taxation politically feasible in a liberal democracy without tangible improvement in public services and community assets. Another way of raising resources is privatizing public undertakings, but our record and the difficulties encountered indicate that it is unlikely that significant revenues can be raised from public sector sales.

There are two ways of reducing public expenditure – reduction of wage bill and elimination of subsidies. Savings through wage reduction or retrenchment of employees are very hard to accomplish. In a centralized governance structure, no government has the power or will to antagonise the vast army of employees. In any case, the problems with public employment are not the excessive number of workers and high wages, but the wrong deployment and lack of accountability. We have too many support staff and too few teachers and health workers, and where public employment is in the right sectors, there is hardly any effective delivery of services. Subsidies cannot be eliminated unless the beneficiaries are satisfied that the money so saved is improving the quality of their lives in some other manner. In centralized structures where such a link is not visible, desubsidization is difficult. All these factors make our fiscal crisis a highly intractable problem in our centralized governance model.

This fiscal crisis can be addressed only through effective and far-reaching decentralization of power and citizen-centred governance. People would elect better representatives and attach value to the vote in a mature and responsible way when their vote is directly and locally linked to public good. We accept tax burden voluntarily only when we see the link between the taxes we pay and the public services we receive locally. Finally, the vast army of employees can be redeployed from areas where they are redundant to sectors where they are needed only in local governance. Once employees are available in the needed sectors and institutions, they perform satisfactorily only when they are accountable to the local people, and when authority and accountability are together.

Citizen Empowerment

All this clearly establishes the need for effective local representation and empowered local governments. We should recognize that all politics is ultimately local, and the citizen is the centre of our political universe. In our democracy the spirit of the Constitution envisages that true sovereignty vests in the citizens. Therefore, citizen-centred governance based on the principle of subsidiarity should be the norm. The fundamental failure of our representation and governance so far has been because of the high degree of centralization delinking the citizen from governance. In a rational and democratic model of representative democracy, it should be recognised that the citizen and his family occupy centre-stage. Most decisions that affect the happiness and well-being of individuals are taken by the citizens and their families. The state comes into picture only when the citizens' actions have a bearing on others' lives, or when common goods and services need to be provided for economies of scale or to harmonize relations between individuals and groups. The first focus of governance in such matters should be the local community of stakeholders who have a common interest in a service or institution. For instance, the parents of children who attend the same school, the farmers whose lands are irrigated by the same source, the consumers who obtain essential commodities from a ration shop, or the producers who sell their product in a market constitute such stakeholders' groups. To the extent feasible, the responsibility for organizing and managing these services should be entrusted to these and other stakeholders' groups.

The Road Ahead

Many public goods and services do not have clearly defined stake-holders. The people at large would need such services from time-to-time. Therefore, such tasks should be entrusted to the local governments. Such local governments should have adequate functions entrusted to them, and commensurate resources should be devolved on them. All the public servants dealing with those functions should be clearly and fully accountable to such local governments. In order to empower the local governments, a few important steps have to be taken:

- Article 243-G and W need to be amended to give explicit authority to local governments. Eleventh and Twelfth schedules of the Constitution should have the same effect as the Seventh Schedule—distributing powers between the Union and States.
- We need to create a single district government for rural and urban areas at the third tier of Panchayats. A district is larger than about 80 nations in the world. The idea of a district Panchayat only for rural areas is outdated.
- All the functions, funds and functionaries pertaining to the subjects enumerated in the Eleventh and Twelfth Schedules should be transferred to local governments with immediate effect. Functional delineation among the three tiers of local governments should mark any such devolution. The process of devolution should be based on the Principle of Subsidiarity, i.e. what can be handled at the local level should be done at that level, and only those that cannot be done locally should be passed on to a higher level, i.e. from the Gram Panchayat to the Mandal Parishad and Zilla Parishad.
- Financial Devolution
  - — The state budget under each head should be divided into: (1) State-wise, (2) District-wise.
  - — Allocating 50 per cent of the total state government plan budget to the local governments.
  - — Savings under non-recurring (capital) items shall not be diverted by local governments for recurring expenditure.
  - — Savings on recurring expenditure can and should be diverted to non-recurring expenditure. This encourages fiscal prudence and savings.
  - — The Zilla Parishad should have the powers for re-appropriating amounts from one item to another within the budgetary allocations for the district,

subject to the conditions that savings under non-recurring or capital items shall not be diverted by local governments for recurring expenditure.

- The functionaries at and below the district level pertaining to all the 29 subjects should work under the control of the local governments. And the officials transferred to the control of Zilla Parishad are to be treated as on deputation. The present service rules governing the functionaries will not be amended. The salaries of the functionaries transferred will be given to local governments as a lump sum grant.
  — The local government will have the power to relocate or re-deploy the functionaries under its control subject to relevant rules on the subject.
  — Once the cadre of the local governments is in place, the state government should constitute a Staff Review Commission to identify the departments and agencies that no longer require recruitment of new officials in each district.
  — Ultimately, the local governments should have their own cadre, consisting of both technical and non-technical officials. The recruiting authority for such cadre can be the Public Service Commission but the appointing authority will be the local government.
- Just as the Union and State governments have accountability mechanisms, similarly, the local governments should also have effective accountability mechanisms. The following measures can be considered for enhancing the accountability in the local governments.
  — *Ombudsmen:* There should be independent Ombudsmen to look into all complaints or grievances related to local governments for every district. The Ombudsman shall have the power to take any action, initiate disciplinary proceedings against any local government representative/employee including removal or dismissal. The government shall have no appeal powers. The appeal will lie with a body of

State-level Ombudsmen. The Ombudsman shall be a person of integrity and reputation in the district, and a committee comprising of the chief minister, chief justice of the high court and leader of the opposition will appoint him.

— *Right to Information* – The state should create effective mechanisms for implementation of the right to information legislation and make them applicable to all branches of state government and local governments. A provision for independent appeal and compensation to the citizen along with penalties for erring employee should be provided.

— *Citizen's Charters* – There is a need to proactively implement the local government citizen charters. The Citizen Charter should clearly outline citizen's entitlements, time frame, and compensation for non-delivery and penalties for the erring employee.

— A District Audit Unit, independent of local and state governments can be constituted to scrutinize the expenditure of local governments, and it should function like the Accountant General's audit

Implementation of the above suggested measures will substantially improve the functioning of local governments in delivery of basic services. This is not to say that the State and Union governments will not have any role in the subjects, which have been devolved to local governments. For instance, in education sector the State and Union governments will still have substantial role in defining school curriculum, evaluation procedures, training for teachers and establishing training institutes. Similarly, even in other devolved subjects the State government will continue to have an important role to play. For instance, in agricultural sector, all the research activities will be carried out by the state and central governments.

Good governance in a democratic society is not possible in centralized structures. Our representative democracy needs to be reorganized facilitating the growth and empowerment of local governments and stakeholders. The insipid uniformity and stultifying central control are inimical to democracy, economic prosperity, releasc of human potential, social justice and good governance. This restructuring demands giving mandatory status to the Eleventh and Twelfth Schedules of the Constitution on par with the Seventh Schedule. We should also evolve mechanisms for devolution of sufficient resources and effective control of employees at each level commensurate with their functions.

NOTES

1. World Bank, "Entering the 21st Century: World Development Report, 1999-2000," (New York: Oxford University Press, 2000), pp. 107-124.
2. National Commission to Review the Working of the Constitution, "Review of the Working of the Constitutional Provisions for Decentralisation (Panchayats)," available at http://lawmin.nic.in/ncrwc/finalreport/v2b2-6.htm.
3. *Janmabhoomi* programme has been suspended recently.
4. World Bank 2000, "Overview of Rural Decentralization in India, Volume II," available at http://www1.worldbank.org/wbiep/decentralization/saslib.

2

Gandhi and the Contemporary Discourse on Decentralisation

M.S. JOHN

Decentralisation has become an evocative word in recent years. Even before the freedom movement, there was some degree of consensus among the key national leaders that Panchayats should have a central place in the post-independent polity of India. While one school was for creating self-government from the above, another group was for doing it from below, relying on the vibrancy of the Indian villages that Metcalfe had described so valiantly. The idea of decentralisation has now become an important governance principle in the transition of a state to a technocratic managerial state. It has now become a "fluid and flexible discourse that can be utilised by different ideological interests" (Mohan and Stokkes 2000: p.250). While the discourse on decentralization evolved in the rest of the world in the context of reform of public administration or for making development and governance participatory and close to the people, Gandhi's advocacy of a decentralised order provided an additional source of legitimacy for decentralisation initiatives in India.

Decentralisation is now a pet theme of a number of groups belonging to different persuasions. Within liberalism, local government was seen as a means for developing a fuller democracy by cultivating Toquevillean values. Reinforced by the contributions of thinkers like J.S. Mill, local government came to be understood as a training ground for political leadership and a means to bring about political equality, accountability, responsiveness and stability.

Beginning with the Catholic notion of subsidiarity, decentralisation has come to be championed by anarchists, social ecologists, feminists, theorists of new social movements, and more recently, even the World Bank. Because of the diversity of the groups recommending decentralisation, some degree of amorphousness has crept into its meaning. Some theorists have made a broad categorization of decentralisation schemes into administrative and political decentralisation, with categories like delegation and deconcentration implied in the former, and devolution in the latter. Although theorists like Cheema and Rondinelli (1983) have suggested privatisation as a category of decentralisation in the context of the rise of neo-liberalism, in addition to the three categories formulated by Maddick (1963), many political scientists are wary of treating it as a form of decentralisation in as much no power sharing between two levels of government takes place in it. Yet, it is perhaps this potential for privatisation and the transfer of service provision to the shoulders of the local bodies to be implemented through private and non-governmental organisations that holds out the promise of decentralisation for agencies like the World Bank. In the scheme proposed by Smith (1985), devolution is another form of delegation. He contemplates the possibility of political decentralisation without democracy, where transfer of power to un-elected traditional elites takes place. Manor (1999) divides decentralisation into administrative, financial and democratic forms. Whatever, may be the name attached to the different forms of decentralisation, there is an underlying thread that connects all of them. The international discourse on decentralisation is primarily a discourse of efficiency couched in instrumental terms rather than looking at it in terms of its intrinsic worth. In contrast, the Gandhian discourse on decentralisation is couched in normative terms, as representing an integral way of life and a worldview.

There is some degree of sentimentality attached to the theme of Panchayati Raj in India, as Maddick (1970) says. The name of Gandhi is often introduced to lend support to Panchayat reforms in India. For example, the most recent round of Panchayat reforms carried out in Madhya Pradesh is titled Gram Swaraj, which has a strong Gandhian flavour. The very same word was used in support of Kerala's decentralised plan campaign. Interestingly, many development reports prepared by the village Panchayats in Central and Southern Kerala carried Gandhi on their cover pages. The views of E.M. Sankaran Namboodiripad (EMS), one of the foremost champions of decentralisation in the post-independence period, are probably a residue of the Gandhian tradition. EMS was found to be radical and consistent in his approach to decentralisation, which obviously contravened the orthodox Marxism that he adhered to and practised throughout his life. One of the major challenges to the Panchayat movement came from Dr. B.R. Ambedkar, an ardent believer in the emancipatory possibilities of modernism, who looked upon any political formation built upon village as inimical to the interests of the depressed castes who could be subjected to further repression by the high castes in the name of Panchayati Raj. Describing the nature of the argument put forward by Ambedkar, Lieten said that "Since India had embarked on the path of modernisation and state building, it was better, the argument continued, to have enlightened intervention by the centralising state. The state has an enlightened and developmental mission, and has to intervene at local levels against the prevailing power structures. If the intervention in hegemonies of high caste landlords, with their bent for archaic cultures and suppressive economies is permissible, decentralisation has to remain guided from above" (2003:21). The same fear was echoed in the report of the Balwant Rai Mehta Committee (Government of India, 1957). This was one of the reasons why it preferred the strengthening of District level Panchayat. Since the District is a larger configuration in spatial terms with a multiplicity of castes, it would prevent the possibility of any one caste monopolising power, it was hoped.

Decentralisation is advocated both by the proponents and opponents of globalisation. Those opposed to it see it as a site of local resistance against globalisation. When participatory planning was introduced in Kerala by the Left Front Government in 1997, it was presented as an anti-globalisation effort. From a Gandhian perspective, this is also one of the grounds why decentralisation is to be favoured. The notion of *Swaraj* means taking control of oneself in every possible sense of the term. By making the locality delinked from the forces of exploitation, Panchayats can have autonomous development. It has also been seen as a means of introducing good governance and of deepening democracies by its neo-liberal advocates. The 73rd and 74th Amendments to the Constitution stated in unambiguous terms that the goal was to usher in self-government and use the local bodies as instruments of social justice and local development. Decentralisation, particularly devolution, and creation of homelands for indigenous communities, is seen as a means of containing conflicts relating to identity issues. In India, the Bhuria Committee recommended a community decentralisation scheme for the tribal areas with considerable powers to the Grama Sabha in such areas, which was later incorporated in the Panchayat Extension to Scheduled Areas Act 1996—a measure that made the Grama Sabha the cornerstone of local tribal governance.

Gandhi was an anarchist. One of the fundamental premises of the anarchists is that human beings are basically good. For anarchists belonging to the Western tradition it is the possession of the rational faculty which lies behind this goodness. But for Gandhi, man is good primarily because he is a spiritual being, and has the element of the divine in him. Since anarchism is in one sense an extreme form of individualism, all forms of control on human beings were looked upon with suspicion. Hence, if power was decentralised, it constituted a significant step towards the creation of the anarchist ideal order.

The concept of a Panchayat had several meanings for Gandhi. Apart from serving as the rural local government, it represented an indigenous way of organizing government as opposed to the British parliamentary system. While the concept of organisation of the Panchayat was a democratic one, it shunned an aggregative approach to politics. This also conformed to his ideal of a non-industrial civilization based on rural values and informed by notions of modern emancipatory consciousness. In other words, he wanted to give primacy to the rural, which has been condemned by both the liberals as well as the Marxists as lacking any potentiality for development or for emancipation. Gandhi also saw Panchayats as a form of government which was least coercive in as much as it represents state in its most deconcentrated form. He also saw the least amount of alienation between the representatives and the people at this level. Since he was opposed to urbanisation and migration of the rural labour force to the urban areas, he did not give much thought to the organisation of urban local government. Gandhi envisioned the evolution of rural Panchayats as crucial to the building of non-violence, which he said cannot be fostered by locating oneself on a factory civilization. For him, the Panchayats represented a post-colonial perspective on polity, which sought to shake off the impact of the colonial administration. His ideas relating to dignity of manual labour, dislike of large-scale machinery, trusteeship and communal harmony were anchored in village life. He believed in the principle of village swaraj or self-sufficiency of villages having a population of approximately 1000 persons. He wanted to convert these villages from 'dung heaps to tiny gardens of Eden'.

Gandhi was opposed to the existence of parties and factions in the villages, which he considered to be derivative of the materialistic values of modern civilisation and reflective of the aggregative politics that it entails. Real freedom comes not by demanding individual rights, and seeking aggregation of such individual needs through competitive party politics, but through the diligent exercise of ones duties by locating oneself in the community. This however, does not mean complete surrender of the individual selfhood, but a new form of selfhood that is not atomistic. Gandhi said that "It is the function of the Panchayats to teach the villagers to avoid disputes, if they have to settle them. That would ensure speedy justice without any expenditure. They would need neither the police nor the military" (Gandhi 1963:.72). In other words, he saw Panchayats as sites for alternative dispute resolution at least in civil matters. Gandhi wanted that the Panchayat had a role in increasing the food production through proper manuring, and milk production through protection of cattle. In other words, the Gandhian Panchayats are not agencies that confine themselves to the narrow realm of governance centred around the performance of civic functions, but would involve in meeting the basic needs of the people by addressing poverty, unemployment, drinking water, and production, among others. By assigning productive functions to the Panchayats, Gandhi assigned it a key economic role. Such a conception makes the institution quite a comprehensive one. In other words, it becomes a central part of the life of the people. While Gandhi was clear on this, critics allege that Gandhi lacked the sociological understanding about the nature of many villages, which have a mixed caste grouping. Another fear was relating to the production relations that existed in the villages , a fear echoed best by Barrington Moore who said that "To democratise the village without altering property relations is simply absurd"(1966:394). However, Gandhi was not unaware of the land problem. Because he was irrepressible optimist, he thought that the land relations could be changed through persuasion rather than force, a project in which the constructive workers of his ideal order would be fully engaged in.

"Independence must begin at the bottom" said Gandhi. Thus every village should have a Panchayat having full powers including defence. "My idea of village swaraj is that it is a complete republic, independent of its neighbours for its own vital wants, and yet interdependent for many others in which dependence is a necessity... the government of the village will be conducted by the Panchayat of five persons, annually elected by the adult villagers, male and female, possessing minimum prescribed qualifications. These will have all the authority and jurisdiction required. Since there will be no system of punishments in the accepted sense, this Panchayat will be the legislature, judiciary and executive combined to operate for the year of office" (Mukherjee 1993: 80). He thought that such village government can be brought into being without looking for governmental approval since most governments do not have any link with the village except for collection of revenue. In other words, such Panchayats have to be evolved at the grass roots by volition and not through state patronage. It must be emphasized here that in the Gandhian scheme the notion of subsidiarity operates in a reverse manner with the local units deciding which all functions are performed best at that level and transferring that which they cannot to the other larger spatial levels. Hence the relations among the different levels are defined in a non-hierarchical manner. It may be noted that some states like Kerala have done away with the principle of hierarchy among the three tiers and opted for the principle of co-responsibility, which has some resemblances with the Gandhian concept. It should also be mentioned here that Gandhi was more concerned with the creation of village Panchayats than Panchayats at larger spatial levels. In many states, village Panchayats are weak and insignificant compared to the other two tiers, a development that could be seen as a distinct contribution of the Balwant Rai Mehta report.

Elaborating the structure of decentralisation, Gandhi said: "In this structure composed of innumerable villages there will be ever-widening, never ascending circles. Life will not be a pyramid with the apex sustained by the bottom. But it will be an oceanic circle whose centre will be the individual, always ready to perish for the village, the latter ready to perish for the circle of villages, till at last the whole becomes ones life composèd of individuals never aggressive in their arrogance but ever humble, sharing the majesty of the oceanic circle of which they are integral units"... "therefore the outermost circumference will not wield power to crush the inner circle but give strength to all within and derive its own from the centre" (Parel 1997:189). In other words, the Panchayat will be the most powerful unit and the other larger geographic levels of government such as District, State and National will exercise powers delegated from this level. It means a sort of reversal of the present system of devolution with the lowest rung becoming the source of all power.

Gandhi's ideas on the practical aspects of organising a Panchayat were contained in his article published in *Young India* in 1931. He objected to the crude attempts to revive Panchayats by giving village elders civil and criminal jurisdiction. He said that such attempts would fail unless they are made scientifically. Hearing about trials of even rape cases carried out by Panchayats and the passing of fantastic judgments in places like Nainital and other parts of Uttar Pradesh, Gandhi laid down a number of guidelines. The first was that every Panchayat should be set-up after getting the sanction of the Provincial Congress Committee. Secondly, a Panchayat should be elected annually at a public meeting called for this purpose. Thirdly, such Panchayat should have no criminal jurisdiction, and civil disputes can be handled by it only if the concerned parties refer such cases to it. In other words, no one should be compelled to refer any matter to the Panchayat. Fourthly, no Panchayat was to have any authority to impose fines; the only sanction behind its civil decrees should be its moral authority. Gandhi was a pragmatist here. He was aware of the many ways in which the Panchayats misused their powers to disadvantage the socially and economically weak. He wanted that only regular Panchayats should come into being. In other words, more than compulsion, the *Panchayat's* decisions should carry a moral force, which alone should be the basis for compliance on the part of the people. Gandhi also envisaged for the Panchayats a key role in local level dispute resolution.

He was opposed to the existence of parties and factionalism. He said "when power politics enter our villages with less thought of the welfare of the villages and more of using them for increasing the parties own power, this becomes a hindrance to the progress of the villagers rather than a help. I would say that whatever may be the consequence, we must make use as much as possible of local help and if we are free from the taint of power politics, we are not likely to go wrong" (Gandhi 1943:234).

In Gandhi's scheme, there is a special place for villages, particularly *charkha* which symbolised the Gandhian model of development and its simplicity, and non-violence. He even equated *charkha* with non-violence. He reiterated that centralisation as a system is the antithesis of non-violence. For Gandhi, a people's planning programme is one that fully utilised the manpower of India —not mere exploitation of raw materials. He said the "the test of orderliness in a country is not the number of millionaires it owns, but the absence of starvation among its masses" (Gandhi, 1963: 35). Obviously Gandhi had wanted that the constructive workers should play a major role for the development of the villages. Constructive work was to become a part and parcel of the Panchayat and he had hoped that some Congress politicians would renounce power politics and engage in social service in the rural areas in a disinterested manner.

In recent years the idea of an invigorated Grama Sabha has been frequently proposed by those belonging to the Gandhian movement in some parts of the country as representing a truly Gandhian vision of Panchayat Raj. This is a gross misrepresentation of Gandhian ideas. Gandhi was aware that no wise outcome can come from such popular assemblies. Instead he wanted that the elected representatives of the people should have the real powers, and the people in turn should trust them. If after six months of assumption of office the Panchayat fails to live up to the expectations of the people, it should be disbanded and another elected in its place. In other words the Gandhian vision of decentralisation is not built on the foundations of the Grama Sabha, but on the role of the village Panchayat, which of course is continuously made accountable to the people. The Diwakar Committee, which made the first countrywide study of the functioning of Gram Sabha, also called for strengthening the Panchayat rather than the Sabha as a first step (Government of India, 1963). While decentralisation places greater emphasis on the elected representatives, the contemporary discourse on natural resource management places the burden primarily on the community. This is based on a notion of dichotomy of interest between the two groups and a belief in the wisdom of community in preserving the commons. Gandhi seeks to bring about a convergence whereby the hiatus between the representatives and the people is reduced to the least possible level. The best servants of the people should form the Panchayat. They should be elected unanimously. Although one may appreciate the changes that have been introduced by the Madhya Pradesh government to shift the locus of power to the Grama Sabha, it will certainly encounter practical difficulties.

As I had hinted earlier, Gandhi's views on decentralisation were situated in the context of an alternative model of development, one that sought to organise village economy and polity on principles of limitation of wants, self-sufficiency, self-reliance and non-violence. Paradoxically, the current discourse on decentralisation is anchored in a neo-liberal model of development and hence its connections with the Gandhian vision are superficial. In other words, the development trajectory that India followed since independence looked upon Panchayats in instrumental terms rather than in terms of their normative implications. The ideal Panchayats of Gandhi's vision can never be realised unless we come to recognise and appreciate post-industrial values. However, considering that Gandhi himself had on several occasions worked in conjunction with existing institutions, taking the decentralization movement forward is certainly a part of the Gandhian agenda.

What then constitutes the Gandhian possibilities in the new Panchayat system? Recognising that Gandhi worked with the existing institutions even when he talked about his ideal ones suggests that the space for Gandhian action in contemporary times is not foreclosed. A Panchayat, which decides to resist the globalising influences, is still thinkable even in the existing system. The recent agitation launched against the Coca Cola company in Plachimada in Palghat District in Kerala with the Panchayat being at the forefront of the effort is certainly a positive development that bears out the possibilities of local resistance against forces of globalization. Instead of creating a hiatus between the people and their representatives, what we need to do is to bridge the gap by electing more disinterested persons. The introduction of an informal system of recall is also thinkable. Redeeming Panchayats from partisan politics and locating them within a politics of social service, which Gandhi often called genuine politics, is also called for. The concept of party politics in the Panchayats is the opposite of the communitarian politics that Sarvodaya thinkers like Jayaprakash Narain advocated. One of the key functions of the Panchayats is to generate enough resources so as to become self-sufficient. Generating resources locally through the spirit of Swadesi is an activity that can be undertaken by the Panchayats instead of being dependent on central grants. Envisaging the Panchayat as a site for local level dispute resolution in civil matters is also an agenda that has strong Gandhian overtones. Even Panchayats that have very little devolved powers can generate enough resources through local effort and sanction and take centre stage in the village polity.

Thus, the name of Gandhi is introduced in the discourse on decentralisation primarily to serve a legitimising function. The "official Gandhism", to borrow the term of Ostergaard (1971), also provides a rationale for future reforms in the field of Panchayat Raj, including the masking of privatisation under the guise of decentralisation. It is, therefore, necessary that the local organisations of the people play a mediating role to ensure that the Panchayat does not become a tool of the market forces and the global players. The Gandhian workers should be in the forefront of such resistance moves.

Gandhi's views on nationalism also synchronized with his views on decentralization. He was opposed to state-building, a pet concern of many nationalist leaders in the post-colonial situation. Instead, his ideas on nationalism did not try to assume any centralizing tendency cantered around the state, which often tends to alienate ethnic and religious minorities. A decentralized polity would make the need for autonomy and separate statehood redundant, and perhaps prevent large-scale mobilization towards this end. Decentralization would enable nationalism to develop in its more cultural foundations rather than assume a political character.

REFERENCES

Cheema, Shabbir G. and Dennis A. Rondinelli (ed) (1983): *Decentralisation and Development: Policy Implementation in Developing Countries*, Beverly Hills, Ca, Sage.

Rondinelli, Dennis A and Shabbir G. Cheema (1983): "Implementing Decentralisation Policies: An Introduction" in Cheema and Rondinelli (ed) *Decentralisation and Development: Policy Implementation in Developing Countries*, Beverly Hills, Ca, Sage, 9-34.

Gandhi , M.K. (1963): *Village Swaraj*, Navajivan, Ahmedabad.

Government of India (1957): *Report of the Team for the Study of Community Projects and National Extension Services*, Vol. 2, Ministry of Community Development, New Delhi.

Government of India (1963): *Report of the Study Team on the Position of Gram Sabha in the Panchayati Raj Movement*, Ministry of Community Development, New Delhi.

Lieten, G.K. (2003): *Power, Politics and Rural Development: Essays on India*, Manohar, New Delhi.

Maddick, Henry (1963): *Democracy, Decentralisation and Development*, Asia Publishing House, Bombay.

—— (1971): *Panchayati Raj: A Study of Rural Local Government in India*, Longman, London.

Manor, James (1999): *The Political Economy of Democratic Decentralization*, World Bank, Washington.

Mohan, Giles and Kristian Stokkes, (2000): "Participatory Development and Empowerment: The Dangers of Localism," *Third World Quarterly*, 21 (2): 247-68.

Moor, Barrington (1966): *Social Origins of Democracy and Dictatorship*, Beacon Press, Boston.

Mukherjee, R. (ed) (1993): *The Penguin Gandhi Reader*, Penguin, London.

Ostergaard, Geofrey (1971): *The Gentle Anarchists: A Study of the Leaders of the Sarvodaya Movement*, Clarendon Press, Oxford.

Parel, Anthony J. (ed) (1997): *Gandhi: Hind Swaraj and other writings*, Cambridge University Press, Cambridge.

Smith, W.C. (1985): *Decentralisation: The Territorial Dimension of the State*, Allen and Unwin, London.

3

Decentralised Governance Looking Back and Forth

MD. NAZRUL ISLAM

Decentralised governance has been conceived as an instrument of local self-government for promoting development in the sectors like health, education, infrastructure etc. It is expected to facilitate effective people's participation, enhance degree of transparency and ensure greater accountability. Decentralised governance is assumed to provide more effective and competitive delivery of services at the grassroots level. Being closer to the people, decentralised governance is assumed to meet the needs and preferences of the people. The services provided by decentralised governance are considered to be cost effective besides helping in the mobilisation of local resources in the form of labour and material. In the developing world, it is seen as a magical elixir to bring about development involving the local citizenry. The present paper attempts to break up the ingredients of this elixir to understand its nuances and cruxes. The paper's sole objective is to understand the concept of decentralisation at a theoretical level. To do this, the paper begins with the evolution of the idea of decentralisation and outlines the contemporary global concerns of decentralisation. Further, it attempts to highlight the emerging perspectives on decentralisation. Finally, it describes various enabling factors in the success of decentralised governance, and discusses the importance and relevance of decentralised governance for a modern society.

I

DECENTRALISED GOVERNANCE: MODERN EMERGENCE OF THE IDEA

First Generation Strategies – Genesis

It is well documented that decentralisation was a well thought and executed style of governance in the ancient world. Further, there are many sophisticated debates on decentralisation in the political literature of the 18th and 19th centuries. Further, self-rule became an issue in moral theory with the rise of modern liberal individualism and the scientific view of the world as devoid of inherent ends and normative laws. The issue was not only how one could be free and subject to political authority, but, more fundamentally, how one could be free and subject to moral obligation. From this backdrop, if we look at decentralised governance we may see the crux of human existence, if we equate political authority to state control and moral obligation to local collective endeavour. This is to say that decentralised governance at the humane and mundane levels makes man free and moral, which a 'state' may not.

Decentralisation emerged as the concept of devolution of power to the people when there was no adult franchise in the western world. The British system of local government found in South Asia, Africa, Australia and North America was conceptualised as a devolved local self-government with characteristics of a representative elected council and citizens' participation, while in Europe, parts of North and West Africa and South America, it is distinguished by deconcentration, executive dominance and rigid hierarchy. Decentralisation is conceptualised as a deconcentrated administrative organ for relieving administrative congregation, since overcentralised governance did not have a way to find out what needs to be done for different places, and what needs and desires of the people are to be met. From this close association with the people of a particular area arose a detailed understanding not only of their needs, but also of the long-term potentialities of that area. The planning of this potential development can be carried out in far greater detail and with a great deal of more understanding by the people of the area who are particularly and primarily concerned with its welfare.

Second Generation Strategies—Middle Era

In 1962, one UN study phrased the problem: 'Decentralisation of government ... relieves members of the legislature and of the national executive from involvement in many purely local issues, frees key officials from onerous and detailed tasks and increases the speed and effectiveness of the administration at all levels; Decentralisation is especially important in developing countries where rapid expansion of public services greatly increases the number of government transactions and consequently the hindrances and wasted efforts resulting from overcentralisation of controls'. Nevertheless, with time and population growth, the state increasingly faced varied problems like widespread unemployment, poverty, and disease, leaving the administration crippled and ineffective because of its inherent maladies. From this backdrop, the scholars of classical public administration sought answers to the following questions:

(1) How can the administration offer more or better services with available resources (effectiveness, efficiency)?
(2) How can administrators maintain their level of services while spending less money (economy)?
(3) How can traditional public administration reorient itself to be relevant to its time?

This new thinking was called New Public Administration as it sought 'to enhance change and change for increasing social equity' which would augment its objectives – relevance, topicality, good management, efficiency, economy, cultivation of virtues, and promotion of social equity. The New Public Administration in its search for a changeable structure tends therefore to modify centralised administration or bureaucratic organisational form with decentralisation, devolution, projects, contracts, sensitivity training, reorganisation, confrontation, and client involvement.

Contemporarily, the new development administration literature talked about ensuring and institutionalising people's participation through the process of decentralisation. Decentralisation, thus results in political elasticity by means of devolution: legal establishment of locally elected political authorities; and deconcentration: transfer of allocative and implementative decisions to local authorities. The erstwhile development administration is understood as the administration of development and development of administration. It connotes planned institutional capacity to accomplish the specific goals of development through the formulation of appropriate policies, programmes and projects and their successful implementation. Participative, responsive, and accountable management constitutes the essence of development administration. However, here popular participation is merely asymmetric partnership with development agencies and development administration was not linked with local area politics, thus preventing allocative decision-making. Development should also mean creating institutional opportunities for power distribution. What kind of development, and for whom and how, are all questions of politics. Development policy formulation and its implementation are vitally connected with the political processes of a society. Hence, to divorce development administration from politics was short-sighted and incomplete.

This new *avatar* of development administration was based on the experiences of such welfare-oriented governments whose development strategies failed miserably. These experiences are:

(1) Governments have limited capacity.
(2) Governments have limited capabilities too. Therefore, people and civil society should be brought in as alternative and complementary institutions/mechanisms for development processes.
(3) Development agencies must capitalise on the pluralistic properties of public administration in particular and political science in general.
(4) Ecological and hermeneutic considerations are vital, when formulating development strategies.

(5) Crisis management should be an integral part of development strategies.
(6) Popular participation must be politically sanctioned; to ensure allocative and implementative decision-making.

In brief, new development administration meant, first, improving the planning and implementation of national development in general and local development in particular and, second, facilitating effective popular participation in the process of development. Therefore, new development administration as a decentralisation dust-up implies giving every citizen an opportunity to actively participate in constructive public work, besides the franchise in a democracy. It also refers to participation in specific action by which the citizen registers her/his involvement in public affairs to achieve a particular objective.

In its initial stage, the reinvented concept of decentralisation was most significant for activating a variety of development functions, ranging from peoples' involvement to better management of grassroots development. The trends, which dominated the thinking and the application aspects, were very crucial in this stage as they were to be the guiding posts for the concerted development of the idea of 'Decentralised governance'. The trends were:

(1) Shift from 'top down' to 'bottom up' approach in development.
(2) Encouraging and ensuring stakeholders' participation in development process.
(3) Institutionalising 'self-reliance' in development strategies.

Third Generation Strategies—Modern Way

In this modern era of the 'administrative state', many writers have voiced concern over the problem of responsiveness of the administrative state to the norms of democratic procedures. To safeguard individual liberties against bureaucratic or arbitrary abuse, an increase in people's vigilance and participation in politics is necessary. Modern states should show 'concern for individual people in the criteria used in making decisions; as an effort to assign each person's needs equal weight in policy deliberations and as an effort to make as broad as feasible the opportunities for people to participate in the decisions that affect them' (Sharkansky, 1991; Bhargava and Rao, 1978).

Political scientists unanimously agree on the fact that the main utility of extensive public participation in politics is to ensure that the stakes of the privileged do not prevail over the interests of the majority. To guard against such possibilities, adequate measures of public accountability and ventilation of public grievances should exist besides avenues of citizens' participation in governance.

Moreover, the contemporary 'communitarian' concerns are also similar. There is an increasing demand to bring in people and local communities for more participatory and direct action-oriented democracy. Communitarians believe that under the new world order of market individualism, social and political power is concentrated even more in those in command of material wealth. What lies at the heart of the communitarian objection to market individualism is the latter's alleged cancerous effect on community life. Human beings who are in control of more economic resources than others are able to set the agenda for everyone from a privileged bargaining position. They can make substantial private 'donations' to those in the government; they can distort public opinion by buying control of the media; they can subdue all those who are dependent on the employment, investment or purchases they offer, by threatening to withdraw them. Selfishness becomes a moral creed. Individuals are encouraged at every turn to put their own interests first, and to demand the freedom to make their own choices regardless of the implications for the civic order.

In order to provide an alternative to individualism and authoritarianism, communitarianism sets out the way in which social and political practices are to be reformed in relation to their contributions to the development of sustainable forms of community life. Such life is fundamentally based upon reformed power relations at every level in society so that all those affected by them can participate as equal citizens in determining how the power in question is to be exercised. This means that questions about the collective action to be taken for the common good are considered through informed community discussions and are not to be left to the political elite, who are rarely answerable to their fellow citizens (Tam, 1998).

Currently, a new rhetoric has also found ground and that is 'Good Governance'. Different scholars look at good governance differently but in general, good governance means that which ensures people's participation, enhances accountability and transparency for effectiveness, efficiency, equity, and capacity building. Decentralisation has become a mechanism through which public goods and services can be distributed effectively and efficiently. In its heyday, many schools observed that decentralisation could reduce the disparities in income and wealth between urban and rural areas and increase productivity and income. Decentralisation is thus a process, which allows peoples' involvement in administration and development programmes. Decentralisation is an instrument to reduce costs, improve outputs, and more effectively utilise human resources to improve efficiency with which demands are locally met. It remains significant for the realisation of people-centred development and therefore, decentralisation is a strategy for enjoying equal rights with the majority population and it is an ability to build the capacity for economic development.

Decentralisation is also seen as a way of reducing the power and size of swollen state bureaucracies and of improving accountability for development planning and spending at a more local level. It will require a responsible, responsive, sensitive and caring public bureaucracy, which is accountable to the community it serves. Decentralisation is more relevant to the issue of accountability because it has contact, which is more direct with the people and is thus more suitable for maintaining public accountability (Joseph, 1997).

II

DECENTRALISED GOVERNANCE: CONCERNS

The idea of decentralised governance is based on the rationale of the known drawbacks of centralised decision-making at the macro governmental level. Being away from the basic spatial units such as hamlets and villages, and with power concentrated at the top of the space in a pyramidal power base, the state and the union government power structures draw representatives from well-endowed sub-regions and weaker sections of the community, leaving the backward regions and backward communities under-represented. This gives rise to the emergence of enclave-type power bases and unequal distribution of power among people. Second, in the centralised system, where there is not much scope for people's participation, the implementation of decisions taken at top government levels becomes weak as it does not inspire or motivate people to extend their cooperation. Therefore, democratic decentralisation has been repeatedly seen as a panacea to ensure grassroots level participation in the nation's development process.

Further, the problem of corruption and leakages are other major areas of concern. It is accepted that corruption builds on the foundation of lack of accountability and procedural opaqueness. The more centralised and concentrated the nature of governance, the more scope for corruption. Democratic decentralisation is the way out for such a state of affairs because access to decision-making by all affected, political as well as financial autonomy for local institutions; and accountability of both elected representatives as well as administrative officials are among the key parameters of decentralised governance. Further, it has been argued that decentralised governance is more cost effective because of its participatory character. The participation of the people in the planning and implementation process will substantially reduce costs normally incurred under the elaborate, perk-galore State machinery. More importantly, people will be careful not to allow mismanagement of funds, and will ensure greater utilisation of resources, technology and wisdom (Sivanna, 1998).

Therefore, direct participation of the people through various democratic decentralised means in the affairs of the governance seems to be the most palatable panacea for controlling corruption, promoting development, and strengthening democracy. The point is to minimise the centralised power accumulation, which alienates people from the state affairs. Much can be said in support of the instrumental values of participatory governance arrangements for both the individual and the organisation. For example, participatory planning arrangements which involve unorganised clientele groups in making decisions about goals, practices, and policies are likely to act as a healthy check on the careerist dimension of professionalism by introducing another perspective into the planning process and by focusing attention on the human consequences of some decisions heretofore regarded as strictly technical (Miller & Rein, 1969).

The prime need to ensure the success of decentralised governance is to bring people, including the poorest of the poor, through active participation into governance institutions to promote transparency and direct accountability and thus ensure visible development. This not only will strengthen democracy but guarantee scrapping of elite-domination in governmental procedures. Further, such participation should include the notions of contributing, influencing, sharing, or redistributing power and of control, resources, benefits, knowledge, and skills to be gained through beneficiary involvement in decision-making. To bring in this type of participation; politicians and administrators have to sacrifice their powers for the general good. The entire state-structure has to be rebuilt. The tragic irony of the modern era is that the institutions like the 'state', which were originally designed to help men master their world, have instead created obstacles to man's endless quest for self-expression, personal efficacy, and human fellowship (Smith, 1971). These three values form the basis of what people have traditionally sought from their social and political institutions—an opportunity for creative development, a means to control their environment, and a sense of community.

It seems to have returned full circle to the philosophy of Aristotle. Effective participation in the life of community institutions is once again believed to be essential to the realisation of a good life, fully lived (Smith, 1971).

III

DECENTRALISED GOVERNANCE: EMERGING PERSPECTIVES

Different schools of thought understand decentralisation in different perspectives. However, the general view is that it is a means of improving the planning and implementation of national development strategies. It is also a way of increasing the effectiveness of development programmes by making them more relevant and responsive to local needs and conditions, allowing greater flexibility in their implementation and proving idle means of coordinating the various agencies involved at the regional or local level (Rondinelli 1981; Conyers 1983; Smith 1985).

Decentralised Governance as a Model of Development

The inversion of European colonial empires and birth of new nation states in Asia, Africa, and Latin America ended in a search for a model of development to change social, political, and economic conditions of those new nations.

During the 1970s and 1980s, many of the new nations fell in serious economic and political crises. Since then, many eminent schools have seen decentralisation as an instrument to achieve a wide-range of development. Alongside, it has been widely advocated by bilateral and international agencies, for instance, US Aid, and many UN agencies. It was justified that decentralisation is a way of managing national, economic, and political development more effectively or efficiently. Decentralisation can provide better services to local preferences, strengthening local accountability and supporting local economic development (Baker, 1997).

Another argument raised by Gerry Stoker (1988) is that a decentralised government has the capacity to win public loyalty. It can better meet local needs and win support for public service provision because it allows choice. It facilitates a matching of local resources and local needs. By making the government less remote and more manageable, makes it more comprehensible, enabling a clear and balanced choice to be made over the extent to which people wish to promote community values.

Decentralised Governance as an Instrument for Peoples' Participation

Decentralisation encourages greater political participation and increased responsiveness on the part of government institutions and in the part of development. It has been emphasised that peoples' active participation in the process of development brings fast socio-economic progress and change. Decentralised governance as a mechanism provides training, ensures people's participation in planning and implementation, therefore, State becomes more participatory more accountable and more effective and efficient (Conyers, 1983; Friedman, 1983; Manor, 1995; Haque, 1997; Sundaram, 1997).

It facilitates the involvement of people in the formulation and implementation of development plans and promotes self-help (Rondinelli & Cheema, 1984). Unless people's involvement in plan formulation and implementation is ensured, it is difficult to say that development achievement will be a progress. Gandhi once stated, "empowerment of people at the grassroots level will go a long way in the development of self-sufficient villages. Decentralised governance is the only way for empowering the grassroots people". Decentralised governance also empowers women and their development; in many a developing country, women constitute nearly forty-eight per cent of country's population and unless their involvement and preferences are explicated in development, it is difficult to foster social change. It is a vehicle for political reform or a way to full democracy. By decentralising, the state apparatus opens new channels for popular participation inside the political system. The idea of decentralisation is closely identified with the creation of democratic units as well as effective and efficient administrative structures at the grassroots levels (Friedman, 1983; Smith, 1985; Haque, 1997; Schonwalder, 1997).

Decentralised Governance as a Process for Innovation

Decentralised governance can lead to more flexible, innovative, and creative administrative set-up. Regional, provincial, district or local level administration units may have greater opportunities to test innovations and to experiment with new policies and programmes in selected areas, without having to justify them to the whole country. If the experiments fail, their impacts are limited to small jurisdictions; if they succeed, they can be replicated in other areas of the country. The ability of a local government to generate innovation, maximise public choice, and promote pluralism and participation is central to development of the locale. Decentralised governance is also an innovation in the field of institution building, perhaps an 'experiment' in institutional building. Fiszbein (1997) stated that decentralisation is an ability to make responsible and innovative leadership.

Decentralised Governance as a Means for Nation-Building, National Integration, Political Stability and Global Cooperation

In different nations or regions of the world, national governments are following decentralised governance as a strategy to strengthen accountability, political skills, and national integration and bringing government closer to the people. This is because of the increased threats from secessionist movements and demand for regional autonomy to reduce socio-economic disparities between places and people, and the pluralistic and multi-ethnic societies laden with particularistic and ascriptive values of the hierarchical class system (Mass, 1959; Smith, 1985).

To Conyers (1983), 'decentralisation is harmonising the interests of both national and local development through both the improved management of rural development which is essential for the well-being of the nation as a whole, as well as the inhabitants of individual rural areas and the achievement of popular participation combined with national unity'. Whereas Smith (1985) looks at decentralisation as a unifying force in the consolidation of new national identities, or a remedy for the ponderous centralised of peripheral states, or a policy that will soften resistance to the inevitable and potentially destabilising social change that 'development' will bring about.

Decentralised governance is an effective media and instrument for meeting peoples' demands and needs. It is working with peoples and priorities, their direct involvement in policy formulation and implementation. It becomes a centre for competition. It is also a pivot for exchanging better experiences with neighbouring governance institutions. UN and other international organisations are also trying to strengthen their capacity to make themselves more responsible to the demands and needs of the global civil society. Recently an international scholar suggested creating a genuine global secretariat, with loyalties to the embryonic world community, socially sensitive and at the same time teaching competence. The secretariats of existing international organisations of the United Nations are not perceived as truly global in their loyalties and commitments. Reforms in recruitment, training and promotion would be needed, and perhaps in the governance and location of these institutions.

IV

DECENTRALISED GOVERNANCE: NECESSARY CONDITIONS

Decentralisation of governance and development has become a major public policy discourse. Decentralisation has been recognised as a progressive strategy to promote development in many developing countries. Decentralisation helps to identify the needs and preferences of people through their direct participation in plan formulation and implementation. It empowers weaker sections and overcomes the domination of the elite to a certain extent (Lieten, 1988; Das, 1999). Decentralisation ensures accountability on the part of the leaders and administrators to the people (Crook & Manor, 1998). Further, decentralisation tends to produce greater transparency. However, some scholars have expressed their doubts about the effective functioning of these institutions (Prud'home, 1995; Tanz, 1995). According to these scholars, decentralisation promotes corruption and inefficiency because of low incomes and a parochial democratic set-up. It is also argued that with the involvement of more people in the planning and implementing process, it contributes more to corruption and wastage. On the contrary, one must not forget that the whole idea of decentralisation is based upon two key concepts of participation and accountability. Prud'home's critique of decentralisation is valid in those regions of the world where poverty and a dysfunctional democracy are rampant for various reasons. Nevertheless, in such societies, civil society groups are assuming far greater roles educating people and ultimately people themselves seek greater fairness from elected and permanent officials to meet their immediate needs. Decentralisation may not be that effective in some parts of the world, but it has indeed paved the way for local citizenry that there is light at the end of the tunnel, if they are active, vigilant, and participative. Many developing countries reveal that the lack of adequate capability at the lower levels to take on all new functions and responsibilities in one go is a serious constraint (Sundaram, 1997). Some countries in the developing world have brought in underprivileged groups into decentralised set-up through positive discrimination. Further, these criticisms may be brushed aside if the following conditions are met before the process of decentralisation starts:

People's Participation, Accountability and Transparency

People's participation, accountability and transparency are often mentioned with a strong consensus to make effective decentralised governance. Local government does not attempt to do everything by itself (Fiszbein, 1997). Successful implementation was always associated with the involvement of someone outside the local administration like the community, an NGO, the private sector or a neighbouring village, or another local government. Participation by the community, individually or collectively, through formal and informal channels – voicing demands, making choices and being involved in projects proved to be as important to sustain capacity, as leadership was in launching it. The presence of an active community increased demands for effective local governments. The individual participation celebrated by Jefferson and De Tocqueville is justified by the fundamental tenet of the republican government that all authority resides in the people; the people should rule (Wolman, 1995). Edmund Burke once suggested that, the well-ordered society must be considered a partnership 'a partnership in all science, a partnership in all art, a partnership in every virtue, and in all perfection'.

Popular movements have been able to increase their own room to maneuver. Arguing that their democratic potential may be best realised not by withdrawing from the institutional space altogether, but by taking advantage of existing possibilities to participate, while maximising their influence and minimising the risk of co-optation by striking alliances with a variety of other actors (Schonwalder, 1997).

Further, there is a need for more information for effective decentralised governance (Sen, 1998). Today, the flow of information in public affairs and services management has become an element of good governance. To access information in decentralised process ensures effective planning and implementation. It helps to invoke knowledge, promoting ideas, strengthening society and societies' lives. It controls misuse and leakages of funds and brings efficiency in the development process.

Transparency can be classified in two ways: external and internal. External transparency helps in knowing locality, local needs, profile of the poor, and the prospective beneficiaries. Internal transparency provides information about the schemes and budget to the people. When both the information is available, then there is less chance for corruption, wastages and leakages (Litvack, *et al* 1998).

Accountability is another crucial caveat for development programmes. It is a system of checks and balances of functioning on the part of leaders and administrators to the people. It can be defined as an explanation of one's actions or responsibility. Accountability can be inter-organisational, as between sub-branches of the government; intra-organisational, as between the supervisor and subordinates; and extra-organisational, as when an organisation and its functionaries answer directly to customers or stakeholders (UNDP, 1990).

Social Capital

Honesty, trust, and law-abidingness can improve the efficiency of decentralised governance by facilitating coordinated actions. One lesson gleaned from Putnam's research is that effective and responsive institutions depend on the language of civic humanism, on republican virtues and practices (Putnam, 1993). When honesty, trust, and law-abidingness are lacking, the outlook for collective action appears bleak. For political stability, for government effectiveness, and even for economic progress social capital may even be more important than physical or human capital. It is true that building social capital will not be easy but it is the key to effective decentralised governance. It is the civic virtue; the people of civic society deal fairly with one another and expect fair dealing in return. They intend their government to follow high standards in terms of all development work and willingly obey and communicate with the government.

Further, social capital is an effective means of achieving objectives of the development vision like improved high performance of services, increased broader participation in both the exchange of information needed for effective plan making and the legitimacy (effective implementation encourages further participation), and enhanced governance responsibility through promoting accountability (functioning according to rule of law) and transparency. It is argued that social capital enhances well-being by making government institutions more democratic and efficient to deliver public goods and services. Thus, it is the most important explanatory of the differential institutional performances in any development field.

There are two dimensions of social capital, namely trust and networks. Trust means a spontaneous relational tie between different actors in society, and networking means establishing a channel of relationships between different actors involved in different actions. Trust and networks enable people to overcome the limits of informal and personal links, and participate in society at large. They provide citizens with confidence and ability to deal with government officials and put pressure on government actions. Trust and networks affect an individual or official to act sincerely, directly, and candidly. These are the crucial qualities of human society, which help in fulfilling the goal of any institution. They ensure a relationship between people, people's leaders and officials for concerted action to avoid overlapping and cross-connections, thus saving on precious resources.

V
CONCLUDING REMARKS

Decentralised governance is not a new phenomenon. The developing world has undergone or is undergoing some form of decentralised governance in line to meet people's demands. It is not merely a moral or rational appeal, but also a demand from the people. It has now been concluded, that bureaucratic administration has failed to meet people's demands (Cheema & Rondinelli, 1984; Wunsch, 1991). Decentralised governance is a wider process than local government which encompasses and enables people, community, community-based organisations (CBOs) or non-governmental organisations (NGOs), public and private agencies to work together and to participate in policy formulation and implementation for effective development, whereas, the local government includes people's representatives (elected by the people or nominated by the local officials) and public agencies who can only take part in policy implementation rather than policy formulation (Bhargava and Rao, 1978). Decentralised governance is thus a process which allows people's involvement in administration and development programmes. It remains significant for the realisation of people-centred development and, therefore, decentralised governance is a strategy for all people to enjoy equal rights, and is an instrument for building the capacity for economic development.

That the process of decentralised governance is a panacea of society can be proved from the case of Korea, Philippines and China. Korea is one of the fastest growing economies of the world along with the Philippines due to governmental commitment to work closely with civil society organisations (Carino, 1996). China is one of the non-democratic countries where the local communist party officials have been quite responsible or accountable to local needs through their local organisation (Bardhan, 1996).

It is very much worthwhile for a country to adopt decentralisation as its development policy. Because a decentralised institution remains significant for the realisation of people-centred development of any nation (Haque, 1997). It is an ideological principle associated with objectives of self-reliance, democratic decision-making, popular participation in government and accountability of public officials to citizens. As such, it has been posed as a desirable development mechanism in itself.

A conclusion that emerges from the discussion is that the goal of realising a modern state and a modern society is greatly dependent upon the establishment of both a stable and cohesive polity and the strengthening of the authoritative structures of the government. For example, in India, it would appear that there has been a decline in the functional capability of both the political and the administrative sectors of the system. A fundamental feature of political development in India is the ineffectiveness of the political system to deal with increasing demands in the shape of providing basic services, maintaining law and order and formulating and executing right policies. Therefore, decentralised governance with its merger feature of politics and administration should accelerate and affect aforesaid requirements and development strategies of modern pluralistic states by way of fostering, nurturing and institutionalising people's participation through efficient and effective decentralisation processes.

REFERENCES

Baker, J. L. (1997): *Poverty Reduction and Human Development in the Caribbean: A Cross-country Study*, World Bank, Washington, DC.

Bardhan, P. (1996): 'Decentralised Development', *Indian Economic Review*, 131 (2): 139–156.

Bhargava, B.S. and Rama Rao (1978): *Indian Local Government: A Study*, Minerva Associates (Publications) Pvt. Ltd., Calcutta.

Carino, Ledivina (1996): 'Development and the Asian States: Providing an Enabling and Facilitating Environment for Decentralised, Participatory and People Centered Development', *Philippine Journal of Public Administration*, 40 (3&4): 165–216.

Conyers, D. (1983): 'Decentralisation: The Latest Fashion in Development Administration?' *Public Administration and Development*, 3 (1): 97–109.

Crook, Richard C. & James Manor (1998): *Democracy and Decentralisation in South Asia and West Africa*, Cambridge University Press, London.

Das, Rekha (1999): 'Decentralisation in India: The Panchayati Raj', in Soren Villadsen (ed), *Good Governance and Decentralisation: Public Sector Reforms in Developing Countries*, Nordic Consulting Group, Gylling.

Fiszbein, Ariel (1997): 'The Emergence of Local Capacity: Lessons from Colombia'. *World Development*, 25 (7): 1029–1043.

Friedman, H. (1983): 'Decentralised Government in Asia: Local Political Alternatives for Decentralised Development', in G.S. Cheema and D. Rondinelli (eds), *Decentralisation and Development*, Sage, Beverly Hills.

Haque, Shamsul (1997): 'Local Governance in Developing Nations: Re-examining the Question of Accountability', *Regional Development Dialogue*, 18 (2) Autumn: 23 (4).

Hicks, K. (1961): *Development from Below: Local Government and Finance in Developing Countries of the Commonwealth*, Oxford University Press, Oxford.

Joseph, Ayee (1997): 'Local Government Reform and Bureaucratic Accountability in Ghana', *Regional Development Dialogue*, 18 (2): Autumn: 86–103.

Lieten, K. (1988): 'Panchayat Leaders in a West Bengal District', *Economic and Political Weekly*, 23 (40): 2069–2073.

Lipton, Michael (1983): *Poverty, Under-nutrition and Hunger*, World Bank, Washington, DC.

Litvack, Jennie, Junaid Ahmed & Richard Bird (1998): *Rethinking Decentralisation in Developing Countries*, World Bank, Washington, DC.

Maddick, Henry (1963): *Democracy, Decentralisation, and Development*, Asia Publishing House, Mumbai.

Manor, J. (1995): Democratic Decentralisation in Africa and Asia, *IDS Bulletin*, 26 (2): 1–2.

Mass, A. (ed) (1959): *Area and Power: A Theory of Local Government*. Glencoe: Free Press, Glencoe.

Miller, John & Martin Rein (1969): 'Civic Participation in Governance Management', *Public Administration Review*, 22 (2): 618–623.

Prud'home, Remy (1995): 'The Dangers of Decentralisation', *World Bank Research Observer*, 10 (2): 89–102.

Putnam, Robert (1993): *Making Democracy Work: Civic Traditions in Modern Italy*, Princeton University Press, Princeton.

Rondinelli, D. & G.S. Cheema (1984): *Decentralisation in Developing Countries: A Review of Recent Experience*, World Bank, Washington, DC.

Rondinelli, D. (1981): 'Government Decentralisation in Comparative Perspective: Theory and Practice in Developing Countries', *International Review of Administrative Science*, 47 (2): 133–145.

Schonwalder, G. (1997): 'New Democratic Spaces at the Grassroots? Popular Participation in Latin American Local Governments', *Development and Change*, 28 (1): 751–769.

Sen, A. (1998): Lead Article, *Panchayati Raj Update*, Institute of Social Sciences, 60 (December): 1–2.

Sharkansky, Ira. (1991): *Public Administration, Policy Making in Government Agencies*, Purples, London.

Sivanna, N. (1998): 'Decentralised Governance and Planning in Karnataka: A Historical Review', *Social Change*, (March): 28–53.

Smith, B. (1985): *Decentralisation: The Territorial Dimension of the State,* George Allen and Unwin, London.

Smith, M. (1971): 'Alienation and Bureaucracy: The Role of Participatory Administration', *Public Administration Review,* 31 (5): 658–664.

Stoker, Gerry (1988): *The Politics of Local Government.* Macmillan, London.

Sundaram, K.V. (1997): *Decentralised Multilevel Planning: Principles and Practices - Asian and African Experiences,* Concept, New Delhi.

Tam, Henry (1998): *Communitarianism: A New Agenda for Politics and Citizenship,* Macmillan, London.

Tanzi, Vito (1995): 'Fiscal Federalism and Decentralisation: A Review of Some Efficiency and Macroeconomic Aspects' in Michael Bruno and Boris Pleskovic (eds), *Annual World Bank Conference on Development Economics,* World Bank, Washington, DC.

UNDP (1990): Website www.undp.org

United Nations (1962): *Decentralisation for National and Local Development,* United Nations, New York.

Wunsch, James (1991): 'Institutional Analysis and Decentralisation: Developing an Analytical Framework for Effective Third World Administrative Reform', *Public Administration and Development,* 11 (5): 431–451.

4

Four Fs of Decentralization

V. VENKATAKRISHNAN

Decentralized governance has been receiving worldwide attention since 1980s. India is one of the leaders in promoting this decentralization. Even though institutions of local governance existed in India for centuries together and were called as 'little republics', the debate on their importance gained momentum very recently. Efforts undertaken by various governments at the national level in the late 1980s and early 1990s to rectify the lacunae of the existing local government system such as absence of regular elections, insufficient devolution of powers, functions and finance and inadequate representation for many sections of the society, have culminated in the 73rd and 74th Amendments to the Constitution, which resulted in a stronger position of rural and urban local governments in India than hitherto available.

Ramification of the Amendment

As a result of the 73rd Amendment, a new beginning had been made in the area of rural local governance in India. There have been diametrically opposing views on the effect of the Amendment. Some scholars feel that the changes effected by the Amendment have neither been radical nor far-reaching. For others, it is a substantial departure from the past as the PRIs have been established with a firm footing than earlier. Nevertheless, it can be noted that in certain areas considerable achievements have been made and in some other areas, there is a gap between the expectations and the reality.

Formation of the PRIs

Though all the States complied with the mandate of the Constitution by enacting a new Act or incorporating the changes in their existing Acts in conformity with the 73rd Amendment, a few States did not form the PRIs. Tamil Nadu had all along maintained that it is not desirable to have Panchayat at district level and instead favoured formation of Panchayat at Village and Block (intermediate) levels only. States like Goa, Manipur and Sikkim opted for Panchayats at village and district levels only. The remaining States, other than those exempted from the part IX, had to form Panchayat at all the three levels. States like Tamil Nadu, Kerala, Karnataka, Jammu & Kashmir and Orissa had postponed the actual formation of the Panchayats by deferring the first elections to PRIs. Some States did not conduct elections immediately after the first term of the PRIs was over. A few States conducted elections for one or two levels of Panchayat and withheld elections for the other levels for some time. The Supreme Court has reportedly observed in its judgment dated 12 August, 1997 in WP (Civil) No.719 of 1995 that '...It is necessary to emphasise that various clauses of Art.243 are to be followed in letter and spirit. The concerned States cannot be permitted to withhold election of Panchayats except in case of genuine supervening difficulties, e.g., unforeseen natural calamities in the State like flood, earthquake, etc., or urgent situation prevailing in the State for which election of the Panchayat cannot be held in time. It will be unfortunate if the concerned States remain insensitive to the Constitutional mandate of holding election of Panchayats in time...'

Even though State Election Commissions are in place in all the States to conduct the elections to Local Government Institutions (LGIs), most of the State Governments have still retained many functions related to conduct of the local elections. Issuance of election notification, delimitation of constituencies, reservation of seats and their rotation and logistic support are some of the areas that remain with many State Governments. In a few cases, the State Election Commissioners (SECs) have been given a shorter tenure than five years and this has also resulted in eroding their autonomy. In Andhra Pradesh, the SEC had to approach the judiciary to overcome the operation of Ordinance promulgated by the State Government to postpone the elections to the intermediate and upper levels of Panchayat. The Central Government also withheld rural development grants to the States, which did not conduct the elections to LGIs, with mixed results. The then Rural Development Minister of the Government of India had admitted that such a disincentive did not yield the desired results. Further, there were criticisms that the people of the States who have already been denied the representation at the local level by the States should not be penalized by the Central Government in this manner. Nonetheless, it has to be noted that many States, which had not conducted the elections to the LGIs for a long period, had ultimately complied with the mandate of the Constitution to hold the elections. The subsequent sections deal with four Fs, such as functions, finances, functionaries and freedom (autonomy) that have to be endowed with the PRIs after their formation, as they are crucial to the success of any organization. This 'Four Fs of decentralization' is an expansion of the existing 'Three Fs concept' used by many others including Planning Commission and Ministry of Rural Development, Government of India.

Four Fs – Functions, Finances, Functionaries and Freedom

Clearly defined functions are the core of any organization. Unless clear-cut demarcations are there between various levels of government such as national, state and local, in their areas of operation, there would be large scope for disputes between them. This might create problems related to accountability too. Thus it is essential to specify unambiguously the functional domain of the LGIs. Once functions are assigned, it is necessary to earmark the finances necessary to carry out them. Powers to enlist the services of functionaries (leaders and personnel) to carryout the tasks assigned to the LGIs is the corollary. Necessary freedom to decide the range, quantum and quality of functions, to raise finances such as local taxes and user charges as per the local situation, to engage and have power over the functionaries is the most important condition since lack of freedom (autonomy) in any of the other three Fs, namely, Functions, Finances and Functionaries would seriously hamper the performance of the LGIs.

Functions

Article 243G of the Constitution stipulates that 'Subject to the provisions of this Constitution, the Legislature of a State may, by law, endow the Panchayats with such powers and authority as may be necessary to enable them to function as institutions of self-government and such law may contain provisions for the devolution of powers and responsibilities upon Panchayats at the appropriate level, subject to such conditions as may be specified therein, with respect to: (a) the preparation of plans for economic development and social justice; (b) the implementation of schemes of economic development and social justice as may be entrusted to them including those in relation to the matters listed in the Eleventh Schedule'. Though the Constitution visualizes the Panchayats as institutions of self-government it has been left to the States (Legislatures) to devolve powers and responsibilities upon Panchayats.

An analysis of the conformity Acts passed by various States after the 73rd Amendment reveals that there is no significant improvement in the status of the PRIs in terms of their functions. For instance, apart from verbatim listing the matters stated in the XI schedule of the Constitution in their respective conformity Acts, many States (barring Kerala to a certain extent) have not clearly delineated the functions of the PRIs. Most states have chosen to retain the PRIs as agents to implement the development functions or schemes designed at State and National levels. Nearly all the schemes are designed at the higher level and PRIs are entrusted with the responsibility of implementing them. This does not give the PRIs scope to prepare the plans for economic development and social justice as specified in Article 243 G (a).

There have been three viewpoints regarding allocation of functions to the PRIs. The first states that while certain areas like defence, foreign affairs, currency, communications, should rest with the Centre, the rest should be transferred to the states and from there to the district and lower levels of elected administrative bodies (Mukarji, 1994). Thus PRIs have been defined as the third stratum of governance along with the Central and State Governments as per this school of thought. This view has led to the demand that there should be a separate Local list in the Constitution similar to that of the Central and State lists. As could be seen from the Conformity Acts passed by the States, none of the States has subscribed to this view since there is no effort to create a separate domain of functions for the PRIs.

It has to be noted that the lists in the Constitution, namely, Union List, State List and Concurrent List relate to the subject matter of laws to be made by the Parliament and by the Legislatures of States as per Article 246. Even after the 73rd Amendment, (a) local government is finding a place in the State list and the entry No.5 of this list is related to Local Government (Local Government, that is to say, the constitution and powers of municipal corporations, improvement trusts, district boards, mining settlement authorities and other local authorities for the purpose of local self-government or village administration) and (b) Article 40 which mentioned that the state shall take steps to organize Village Panchayats and endow them with such powers and authority as may be necessary to enable them to function as units of self-government, has been retained. Thus the subject of 'Local Government', which was under the domain of the States, continues to be a State subject and it is still left to the respective State Legislature to make laws for such States and any part thereof with respect to Local Government. Article 162 of the Constitution mentions that the executive power of a State shall extend to the matters with respect to which the Legislature of the State has power to make laws. Based on this, the executive power of the State extends to the Local Government also. Probably, these are the precise reasons for ratification of the 73rd and 74th Amendments by not less than one-half of the States before they were presented to the President for assent. Thus it can be concluded that the Constitution (as it exists today) envisions PRIs as institutions of governance within the sphere of the State Governments. Though it is difficult to establish one to one correspondence between the matters listed under the Eleventh and Twelfth Schedules related to

Local Governments and the executive and legislative areas of the States and the Union enumerated under the Seventh Schedule of the Constitution, the following generalizations can be thought of.

Firstly, the functional areas of Union, State and Local Governments should not be looked as watertight compartments having no scope for complementing and supplementing. Some of the functions might overlap across all the levels of governance and there are a very few areas which can be classified as exclusive domains for a particular level of government. For instance, even in matters such as defence, war and peace, which are falling under List I – Union List, though the Central Government might be having predominant role, the other levels of governance, State and Local have to join in effectively to supplement. Thus it may be noted that though any particular level of government in a multi-level federal set up may be having overriding powers related to a specific subject matter, it is not possible to exclude the other levels of government totally either from complementing or supplementing. Therefore, even if some functions are traditionally assigned to Local governments, the other levels of government at the Union and States may be having a genuine interest in ensuring the delivery of services at the local level and this should not be called as lack of autonomy or interference from above.

Secondly, there would be certain subject matters where all the levels of government would be having interest, which has to be called as secondary to none. For instance, poverty alleviation programmes need coherent actions of Central, State and Local Governments which have to share different aspects such as formulation of policy, funding, implementation and evaluation to mention a few. This sharing of responsibilities should not dilute the importance to be attached by any level of government to such matters and on the other hand they have to become accountable to each other for actions related to the sub-areas. If such a line of thinking were adopted then there would be the following three categories of functions to be performed by the Local Governments. First of all, the subject matters which are of utmost importance to local level and the planning and implementation of which would be the sole responsibility of the Local Governments. These matters may be termed as 'core areas' or 'devolved functions' of the Local Government and this might be including the civic issues. Secondly, the functions for which the major responsibility rests with higher-level governments but the implementation lies with the Local Government with a lesser degree of decision making at the local level. They may be called as 'delegated functions' wherein the Local Governments might be having operational autonomy depending upon local situation. Finally, there may be a few functions, which Local Governments have to implement as agencies of higher-level governments. The Local Governments will be having a limited role in decision-making as far as these programmes are concerned and hence be labelled as 'deconcentrated functions'.

The demarcation of functions on the above lines is fulfilling the mandates of the Constitution. The 'devolved functions' might be suitable for the preparation of plans for economic development and social justice as mentioned in the Article 243G(a) of the Constitution. The rest, 'delegated functions' and 'deconcentrated functions' would be related to Article 243G(b).

The second viewpoint on allocation of functions to Local Governments contends that when institutions of local government have yet to take firm root, it is important that they win the acceptability and confidence of the people through efficient implementation of development programmes rather than be perceived as organs of state power. It has been suggested that, for the present, Panchayati Raj had better exclusively devote itself to the task of development. Nevertheless, it has been emphasized that the Panchayati Raj Institutions should enjoy as large a measure of autonomy as possible and they should be able to provide responsive administration, which implies a degree of freedom to adjust programmes according to local needs without being hamstrung by detailed government directives (Satish Chandran, 1994). This viewpoint makes a contrast from the earlier viewpoint of 'third level of governance' in the sense that it emphasizes the qualitative aspect of the functional domain the PRIs than mere enlisting of a number of functions. Considering the fact that this viewpoint stresses on the functional autonomy and efficient implementation of the development programmes, it also embodies the concept of self-government to a large extent albeit with less emphasis than that of the 'third stratum of governance'. It may be noted that the second viewpoint has not ruled out devolving more suitable functions and powers at a later point of time. Probably, once the PRIs gain wider acceptability, this might follow.

The third view is that the Local Governments are creations of the State Governments based on the Acts to be passed by them and thus do not have coordinate status with Central Government or State Governments. As per this view they would be under the control of the State Governments and follow the instructions issued from above. Though no scholar has been subscribing to this view, it seems to be the attitude of the most of the State Governments even after the passing of the 73rd and 74th Amendments. It might be noted that before these Amendments, Local Governments were constituted by the Acts passed by the State Governments based on Article 40 and Entry 5 of List II (State List) enumerated under Article 246. Though Local Governments still remain as a State subject, the substantial changes brought out by the Amendments have ensured that Local Governments have been lifted from the morass of total dependence upon the States even for their formation. Nevertheless, barring some changes of window dressing type, there has not been any significant improvement in the functional domain of the Local Governments in most of the States. The following course of action might have to follow if the mandate of the Constitution is adhered to in letter and spirit.

As per the general norms followed globally by multi-level federal systems and according to the principle of subsidiarity, a function should be assigned to the lowest level of government that encompasses all or most of the service benefits provided it can perform the function effectively. This viewpoint has been reflected by a large number of scholars. Oates in his decentralization theorem states that 'each public service should be provided by the jurisdiction having control over the minimum geographic area that would internalize benefits and costs of such a provision'. Satish Chandran while discussing on inter-tier allocation of functions has expressed that 'while accountability is one of the strengths of the local government and efforts should be made to locate an activity at as low a level as possible, there are other aspects to be taken into account: (i) every activity requires a minimum size for functional efficiency and economy: (ii) the area of benefit should not extend beyond the jurisdiction of the Panchayat and (iii) the administrative resources available at the particular level should be capable of handling the activity in a competent manner'. Though Satish Chandran has been focusing on allocations of functions among various tiers of the Panchayati Raj System, these principles are applicable to assignment of functions to various levels of government also. An analysis of matters listed under Eleventh and Twelfth Schedules of the Constitution has to be carried out by each State Government without further delay, keeping in mind the functional efficiency and economy and the area of benefit outlined by Satish Chandran. This has to result in optimal allocation of functions not only between State and Local Governments but also within the various tiers of Panchayati Raj Institutions. In case of non-availability or non-suitability of the administrative resources at a particular level, efforts have to be made either to provide or strengthen them. The lack of personnel should not be cited as the reason for non-sharing of functions between the State and Local Governments since the latter do not have any appreciable manpower as on date.

It might be recalled that preparation of plans for economic development and social justice is an important function assigned to the LGIs by the 73rd and 74th Amendments. Article 243ZD provides for a District Planning Committee (DPC) at the district level to consolidate the plans prepared by the Panchayats and the municipalities in the district and to prepare a draft development plan for the district as a whole. It has been left to the Legislature of the State to make law related to: (a) composition of the District Planning Committees, (b) the manner in which the seats in such Committees shall be filled, (c) the functions relating to district planning which may be assigned to such Committees and (d) the manner in which the Chairpersons of such Committees be chosen. The DPC has to prepare the draft development plan of the district by taking into account the matters of common interest between the Panchayats and the municipalities including spatial planning, sharing of water and other physical and natural resources, the integrated development of infrastructure and environmental conservation and the extent and type of available resources whether financial or otherwise. The DPC may have to consult such institutions and organizations as the Governor may specify. The Chairperson of the DPC has to forward the development plan recommended by the Committee to the State Government.

The creation and functioning of DPCs has been one of the gray areas in the post 73rd and 74th Amendment period. It is reported that many States have not yet constituted the DPC. In some states such as Gujarat, Madhya Pradesh, Maharashtra, Orissa, Tripura and Uttar Pradesh, the State Governments have nominated the Ministers of the State Government as Chairpersons of the DPC. In Tamil Nadu after protests were lodged against making the District Collector as the Chairman of DPC, the Chairperson of the District Panchayat has been made as the Chairperson of the DPC. The experiment of Madhya Pradesh has called the DPCs as 'District Governments' and the powers of the State Government have been delegated to this body headed by a State Minister. There have been criticisms that this move undermines the PRIs. The people's planning campaign through Gram Sabha and other institutions adopted by Kerala seems to be novel and this experiment is worth studying by other States for incorporating the salient features in various States with modifications suited to local needs. By and large, there is not much information on the planning carried out by the DPCs in most of the States.

Thus it can be concluded that PRIs all over the country, barring a few States, have not really blossomed into 'institutions of self-government' as there is an absence of earmarking of functions to be performed by them. In such a case, they may not be in a position to undertake planning for economic development and social justice as envisaged by the Constitution. The next section deals with the corollary to assignment of functions viz, fiscal decentralization.

Finances

Allocation of functions, which can be called as expenditure assignment, has to be followed by revenue assignment. In the absence of a clearly defined set of functions to be performed by the Local Governments, the fiscal decentralization would also be unbalanced. Fiscal decentralization encompasses Local Government finances, budgeting, intergovernmental transfers, borrowing and asset management. Effective functioning of the Local Governments requires a match between the functions and finances allocated to them. In case Local Governments have not been given adequate sources of revenue to perform the functions earmarked for them, the extent to which there is a shortfall might be termed as 'unfunded mandate'. The experience so far in India has been the huge gap between the resources allocated to the PRIs and the responsibilities assigned to them.

Article 243(I) provides for establishment of a Finance Commission by each State within one year from the commencement of the 73rd Amendment and thereafter at the expiration of every fifth year, to review the financial position. This Finance Commission has to make recommendations to the Governor of the State on:

(a) the principles which should govern;
  (i) the distribution between the State and the Panchayats of the net proceeds of the taxes, duties, tolls and fees leviable by the State, which may be divided between them under this part and the allocation between the Panchayats at all levels of their respective shares of such proceeds;
  (ii) the determination of the taxes, duties, tolls and fees which may be assigned to, or appropriated by, the Panchayats;
  (iii) the grants-in-aid to the Panchayats from the Consolidated Fund of the State;
(b) the measures needed to improve the financial position of the Panchayats;
(c) any other matter referred to the Finance Commission by the Governor in the interests of sound finance of the Panchayats.

The composition of the Commission, the qualifications, which shall be required for appointment as members and the manner in which they would be selected, have been left to the State Legislatures. Once the Commission submits the report, it has to be tabled in the Legislature along with the Action Taken Report (ATR).

All the States constituted the State Finance Commission (SFC) in consonance with the Article 243-I after the 73rd Amendment. Most of the SFCs have submitted their reports and a few States have already initiated policy measures based on the recommendations. In some States, no information is available on the action taken over the report of the SFC. It is reported that most of the SFCs were having the dilemma related to the transfer of functions by the State Governments. They were not sure whether to wait for such transfer of functions and assess the funds requirement based on that, as an appropriate assignment of finances could be based only on the functions to be carried out by the Local Governments. Some SFCs have proceeded by identifying the core functions and working out the requirements of the Local Governments on that basis (Srinivasan, 2001).

However, the Eleventh Finance Commission (EFC) constituted by the Centre was having a critical view of the SFCs. It felt that 'Many SFC reports have not addressed the specific terms listed in Articles 243-I and 243Y, nor they have provided a clear idea of the powers, authority and responsibilities actually entrusted to the local bodies' (Report of the Eleventh Finance Commission, Para 8.11.b). First of all, it is the responsibility of the States to delineate the powers and responsibilities of the Panchayats and as the EFC itself has observed, States' legislation merely enumerate the subjects indicated in the two Schedules but do not specify the schemes that have to be implemented by these bodies as contemplated in Articles 243-G and 243-W. It has further noted that the funds and functionaries relating to these schemes continue to remain under the control of the departments of the State Governments (Para 8.28.a). When the States themselves have not performed the duty of delineation of the functions of the Local Governments, it is not right to fault the SFCs, which were at the mercy of the States. In fact, the failure of the States in this context has become a handicap for the SFCs.

Nevertheless, many other observations of the EFC are to be given a serious consideration. For instance, it has pointed out that there is no time limit prescribed either in the Constitution or in the States' legislation for submission of the explanatory memorandum on the action taken by the State Government on the recommendations of the SFCs. It has lamented that even though the reports of the SFCs have been available for a long period, some States have not yet submitted the action taken report (ATR) to their Legislatures. Further, even where some recommendations have been accepted, the implementation has been tardy. Several important recommendations of the SFCs on sharing/transfer of resources are often reported to be under consideration for months and even years (Para 8.11c of the Eleventh Finance Commission Report). These observations have an important bearing on according due importance to the SFC reports.

The EFC was of the opinion that State Governments have to take decisions on the recommendations of the SFCs and place the ATRs on the floor of the State Legislatures within six months from the date of the submission of the report by the SFC. In addition to the placing ATR on the SFC reports, it is suggested that it may be made mandatory for the States to explain why they have not accepted a majority of the SFC recommendations. Similarly, the recommendations, which have been accepted or accepted in principle, should be implemented within a reasonable period of time.

The EFC has further observed that in some States, serving government officers are appointed as chairperson and members of the SFCs and that too in ex-officio capacities limiting the autonomy of the SFCs to recommend in a free and independent manner as has been envisioned in the Constitution. Therefore, it recommended that the chairperson and members of SFCs might be drawn from amongst experts in specific disciplines such as economics, law, public administration and public finance.

A study carried out by the National Institute of Rural Development (NIRD), Hyderabad on behalf of the EFC had found out that few States have been serious in vesting the Panchayats with the necessary powers, funds and staff to enable them to perform the functions assigned to them under the statutes. The

EFC has pointed out that the States' legislations provide for levy and collection of certain taxes, fees and tolls but the rules relating to fixation of rate structure are not periodically done and reviewed.

The EFC with a view to strengthen the resource base of local bodies, in addition to other things, has suggested taxes on land in some form, levy on cess on land based taxes, imposing profession tax, exploiting property tax/house tax to its full potential, replacing octroi with a suitable buoyant tax, revision of user charges to keep pace with the inflation and to recover the cost and providing untied grants to Panchayats and the urban local bodies for maintenance of civic services. It has expressed concern regarding the maintenance of accounts by the local bodies and suggested that the Comptroller and Auditor General (C&AG) should prescribe the format for preparation of budgets and for keeping of accounts for local bodies. Non-availability of data on the finances of local bodies was also an area of concern to the EFC and it felt that in the absence of any reliable financial/budgetary data, no realistic assessment of the needs of the Panchayats and Municipalities for basic civic and development functions can be made. While recommending a grant of Rs. 1,600 crores for the Panchayats and Rs. 400 crores to the municipalities, the EFC indicated that the amounts allocated for maintenance of accounts and audit and for development of data base would be the first charge.

Formation of SFCs has resulted in more attention to the fiscal needs of the PRIs. However, this has not resulted in any dramatic increase in the fiscal autonomy of the PRIs compared to the excitement that was created. Most of the SFCs left the existing tax powers of local bodies unchanged (Jha 2002) and a few SFCs including that of Karnataka (ISFC) did not make any specific recommendation on the taxes of the LGIs. However some of them have tried to rationalize the tax structure. For instance, the first Kerala Finance Commission (1996) has suggested the adoption of plinth area as the basis for tax on buildings, merger of entertainment tax and additional entertainment tax into a single item, doubling of land tax and unification of show tax and surcharge on show tax. Nevertheless, there were a few SFCs such as that of Punjab, which recommended new taxes by village Panchayats such as tax on advertisements and hoardings, tax on brick kilns, rice shellers, stone crushers, petrol pumps, poultry farms, dairy units, etc. (Oommen, 1998).

In terms of distribution between the State and the Panchayats of the net proceeds of the taxes, duties, tolls and fees leviable by the State, many patterns have been recommended by different SFCs. The SFCs of Andhra Pradesh, Karnataka, Kerala, Madhya Pradesh have recommended a share in the tax and non-tax revenue of the State. In case of Tamil Nadu, the SFC suggested share in taxes between the LGIs and the State excluding some taxes such as entertainment tax. Tripura's 1st SFC recommended a share in the state tax receipts (50 per cent commercial taxes, 35 per cent professional tax, 35 per cent of agricultural income tax and land revenue and 15 per cent of forest revenue) as well as in the State's share in the central taxes (10 per cent in State share of Central Taxes) to the local bodies.

Assam's 1st SFC was for a combination of global tax sharing (two per cent of State taxes) and specific tax sharing, i.e. 10 per cent of motor vehicle tax. There are variations in terms of acceptance of the States regarding these recommendations of the SFCs. While Andhra Pradesh 1st SFC recommended 39.24 per cent of the total State revenue, the State Government accepted to 12 per cent of revenue and assigned revenue. In some other States such as Assam (2%), Madhya Pradesh (2.91% share of tax and non-tax revenue) and Rajasthan (2.18% of net State taxes as additional), the recommendations of the SFCs in this regard were accepted by the State Governments. Uttar Pradesh seems to be exception where the 1st SFC recommended 3 per cent of net State taxes and the State increased it to 4 per cent of net taxes. It seems that wherever the shares recommended by the SFCs are relatively high, especially in global sharing, the States have not accepted them fully. When such recommendations were on sharing of a few taxes, such suggestions seem to have been accepted by the States concerned (Srinivasan, 2001).

With regard to grants, which are of two types, general grant or block grant and specific purpose grant or conditional grants, different SFCs have made various suggestions. The former are known as united grants also since they endow the LGIs with sufficient autonomy to spend them. Fiscal decentralization literature justifies grants to overcome vertical and horizontal fiscal imbalances. In addition to making recommendations related to grants to ensure minimum standards in provision of basic services by various LGIs which may not be having sufficient natural resources to raise adequate taxes and non-tax revenues on their own, some SFCs have felt the need for incentive grants to reward better tax collection and utilization of these resources. To what extend the recommendations of the SFCs have been accepted and the degree of actual implementation of them in the ground level are not known in case of most of the SFCs. Moreover, the first generation SFCs faced with many problems such as lack of data related to LGIs revenue and expenditure, absence of proper accounting and auditing procedures and deficiency in knowledge about the functional domain of the LGIs. All these things have to be rectified if the subsequent SFCs were to make an impact on the financial situation of the LGIs. Similarly, in addition to making public the decisions made on the recommendations of the SFC, suitable efforts have to be attempted in implementing the suggestions of the EFC also. The subsequent section is devoted to another equally important 'F', i.e. functionaries (personnel) of the LGIs.

Functionaries

Functionaries of PRIs are those: (a) elected leaders who are involved in the policy formulation and decision making related to the functions of the PRIs and (b) the personnel who are implementing the decisions of the PRIs and assist them in the decision making process. The role of these functionaries in making the PRIs as institutions of self-government is very important and this section is devoted on the developments that have taken place in this area after the Constitutional Amendments.

The 73rd Amendment has been instrumental in conducting the elections to the PRIs more regularly than in the past and it has opened the doors for many persons belonging to hitherto un-represented or under-represented to get elected to these institutions. This has been the case with many of the States, which went for polls to PRIs after the 73rd Amendment. It is reported that in a few cases persons belonging to Scheduled Castes and Scheduled Tribes and Backward Classes could win elections from the general constituencies also.

Nevertheless, there have been reports of killing of Panchayat Presidents belonging to these communities since they dared to challenge the existing social hegemony in these localities by contesting the elections and assuming office on being elected. There has been election related violence during the course of PRI elections covering many of the States ranging from Bihar to Tamil Nadu. However, murder of the President and Vice-President of a village Panchayat belonging to Scheduled Castes of Melavalavu village in Tamil Nadu and the inability of the Tamil Nadu government to hold elections to a few village Panchayats where the positions of Presidents have been reserved for Scheduled Castes since no one is coming forward to file nominations in view of the threats faced from the other castes have served as grim reminders of the undercurrents prevailing in the rural social milieu against the empowering of some sections of the society.

Reservation of seats and chairperson positions in the PRIs for women has also resulted in a large number of women entering into local governance. In some States like Karnataka, where such reservations have been in practice even before the 73rd Amendment, more number of women leaders has assumed office than the minimum of one-third prescribed by the Constitution. Though there have been criticisms that many of these new women leaders are in fact belonging to families which have been well entrenched in the rural power structure for a long period, indications are there to show that there are many first generation leaders. There have been findings to demonstrate that some of these women have been set up as proxies by the persons who have been deprived of leadership positions due to the reservations. In spite of a very high level of illiteracy and division among caste and class lines, many of the women leaders have been functioning effectively in areas of interest to them such as basic health services, primary education and child development to name a few. It is unfair to expect these women leaders to change many ills of the society in a term or two. However, given their various shortcomings in addition to those mentioned above, their performance so far merits appreciation and it is hoped that over a period of time, the women leaders would be making a substantial and positive impact on local governance.

As mentioned earlier many of the elected leaders emerged from hitherto marginalized sections of the society and most of them were first time leaders also. Added to that the 73rd Amendment has brought in new features in rural local governance. Further, many States conducted the elections to PRIs after a long period. Due to this, many persons were not aware of the functioning of the PRIs. All these factors necessitated the imparting of training to the elected representatives on a sustained basis. Efforts have been made by Central Governments, State Governments, many Non-Governmental Organizations and a few international agencies to train these leaders on various aspects of local governance. Majority of these trainings are focused on the conduct of meetings, passing of resolutions, legal provisions, etc. There have been a few attempts in paying special attention to the needs of the women leaders as well. Nevertheless, there is a need to focus the training on various other important aspects such as financial management, planning and social and economic development which have not received due attention. Further, there is a need to continue the training on a regular basis and activate the training institutions, which have become dormant over a period of time.

The personnel working in the PRIs are also forming an important segment of functionaries of the system. In case of the village Panchayats, most of the States have permitted them to engage their personnel. Nevertheless, since the salary levels are very low due to the lack of adequate finances, most of the village Panchayats could employ generally part-time employees. Wherever, the village Panchayats had a viable size of population as in Kerala, they could employ a larger number of full-time employees including the Executive Officer. In a few States like Tamil Nadu, many village Panchayats due to their smaller population size may share the services of the Secretary. Unless their financial position is strengthened by devolving more resources, the Village Panchayats all over the country would not be in a position to shoulder additional responsibilities. Probably, the lack of qualified personnel has also been a bottleneck in levying and collecting of taxes assigned to the village Panchayats. When more functions are transferred to them, they might need to engage more personnel at village level. In such a situation, with a view to endow them with greater autonomy, they might be permitted to engage personnel of their choice and for that devolving sufficient financial resources is a pre-condition.

In case of the middle tier Panchayats, in some States, there are two categories of staff working under them. Majority of them are treated as State Government servants and are either recruited specifically for the Rural Development department of the State Government and posted in the PRIs or deputed from various line departments such as Public Works, Education, Co-operation and Health or a combination of both. The Block Development Officer (BDO), recruited by the State Government functions as the Chief Executive Officer of the middle tier Panchayats in most of the States. These Panchayats might recruit some of the officials like Record Clerk and their salary might be charged to their funds. However, the State Government through its line departments exercises the control over these staff barring the day-to-day supervision by the concerned Panchayats. There were conflicts between the CEO of these Panchayats (generalists) and the officials under deputation from other specialized line departments such as Public Works and Health since some of them might be drawing higher pay than the CEO and technically superior than the CEO. This undermines the functioning of the PRIs.

In case of District Panchayats or Zilla Parishads, in a few States CEOs who hold the *ex-officio* position of Additional District Magistrate are deputed by the State Governments. Various line departments of the State Government depute most of the staff working in these institutions. Though they work under the administrative control of the Zilla Parishad, for their service related issues such as promotion, transfer and seniority they are under the command of their respective departments. This dual control by the Zilla Parishad and the line departments has created innumerable problems of co-ordination at the field level. West Bengal, Kerala and Madhya Pradesh are some of the States having this type of staff pattern. It may be relevant to note that in many states, the District Rural Development Agencies (DRDAs) are still functioning outside the purview of the PRIs with functions overlapping with that of the latter and the officials working in DRDAs in such states are not responsible to PRIs.

Maharashtra has created 'district service' for class III and IV categories of staff and such staff are put under the control of the Zilla Parishads. Nevertheless, the CEO being a senior IAS officer, most of the powers on recruitment, transfer, promotion and day to day supervision have been concentrated in this office and hence the elected representatives do not have any considerable say in their functioning.

As long as the PRIs do not have clearly earmarked functions and finance to perform these functions, the problems pertaining to personnel will continue for many years. Once they are endowed with them, the States may have to transfer a substantial number of their personnel, who are at present performing these functions, to the PRIs. This again might be creating problems since some of the staff may not be interested in working under the PRIs for various reasons such as lack of mobility to other districts and absence of promotional avenues. To overcome this kind of problems, it may be necessary to initially depute these personnel to the PRIs with their existing service conditions. As soon as they retire or opt for some other service with the State Governments, it might be necessary to fill up these positions by recruiting personnel exclusively for the local government service. However, there may have to be some flexibility in appointing for highly specialized positions. Since the number of positions of this nature would be very few in a district, it may not be possible to attract suitably qualified persons for various reasons such as lack of mobility in terms of place and promotion. In such a case, it would be worth exploring the chances of sharing such kind of personnel with State and Central Governments. As the issue is more complex than delineated above, it needs serious thought. Another issue that merits attention in this context is imparting suitable training to the personnel to be deputed to the PRIs since they have to work in a different atmosphere than what they have been used to. Similarly, training the staff who might be recruited exclusively for PRIs in future should also be taken into account.

Even before the 73rd Amendment, there have been reports of conflicts between the elected representatives and the personnel of the PRIs in different States. These conflicts might have been there due to the dual control of the personnel. Both the elected representatives and the personnel of the PRIs have to understand and appreciate each other's role to have a harmonious functioning of these institutions. While the elected representatives may be interested in bringing out substantial change in the development front and demonstrate their performance to their constituency, the personnel possibly will be more interested in complying with the procedures than the outcomes since any deviation from the set processes is likely to be viewed seriously by the higher level bureaucracy irrespective of the results. When the lower level bureaucracy, which was working in the line departments, gets deputed to PRIs in future such conflicts are expected. This would subside when fresh recruitments are exclusively made for the PRIs once those who are under deputation are phased out on their retirement or on their opting for some other service within the State Government. The next section focuses on an equally important aspect of decentralization, namely, freedom (autonomy) enjoyed by the PRIs in decision-making and implementing the functions assigned to them. It might be noted that if any level of government does not have its own independent area and jurisdiction of operation; it cannot be called as self-government.

Freedom (Autonomy)

Freedom in this section does not refer to unfettered independence enjoyed by sovereign States. It however, means the level of autonomy to be endowed with the PRIs in their sphere of governance. To what extend they enjoy the powers to decide about implementing the functions assigned to them, generating resources to fulfil these functions and employing the necessary personnel constitute the discussion on the freedom of PRIs. It may not be possible to think of absolute autonomy to any level of government in terms of the above areas as in multi-tier federal countries, each level of government is dependent on the other for achieving national priorities and objectives.

The Constitution of India terms local governments as 'self-governments' in one hand and on the other, endows the States to enact the legislations to bring the local government into existence. Hence, though the local governments have been historically enjoying certain specific functions related to the civic affairs, for many other functions they had to depend upon the States for assignment of powers and finances. This gives overwhelming position to the States to regulate and control the local governments.

Till recently, even creation of local governments was based on the whims and fancies of the State Governments. The 73rd Amendment has changed this position to large extent by making the elections to local governments mandatory. The constitutional directives that insist that an election to constitute a Panchayat shall be completed (a) before the expiry of its duration; (b) before the expiration of a period of six months from the date of its dissolution has effectively changed the position of local governments at least in terms of their formation notwithstanding the brazen attempts by a few states to breach this condition. Nevertheless, there are many elements in the Acts passed by the states to curtail the autonomy of the Panchayats. For instance, there have been provisions in the Acts of various States to remove an elected member of the PRIs from office or suspend him, nullify the resolutions passed by the PRIs and even supersede the PRIs among many other things. There have been exclusive chapters on 'Control' in the PRI Acts of many States. These undermine the political autonomy of the local government institutions. These methods of subverting the local democracy have to be replaced by a more democratic means such as recall, referendum and by creating institutions such as *Ombudsman* to deal exclusively on local government issues.

With regard to functions, the PRIs, especially the Village Panchayats enjoy autonomy to a large extent in terms of functions, which are historically under their domain such as civic functions. But, in case of development functions, which are entrusted to them, there has been very little scope of autonomy. Detailed guidelines issued from the higher-level governments do not permit the local governments to exercise their wisdom in selection of the schemes and locations in which they can be implemented. Though the higher-level governments, which fund these development functions, are accountable to their electorate for the successful implementation of these schemes, tying down the local governments with various conditions defeats this purpose. While these governments can set broad national priorities to achieve social and economic development, the nitty-gritty of execution of schemes may be best left to the local governments.

Creation of a few parallel bodies such as Water Users Associations, Vanasamrakshana Samiti and Watershed Development Committees have also eroded the functional areas of the PRIs to a large extent. Wherever possible these bodies have to be either integrated with the PRIs or disbanded and their functions handed over to the PRIs.

As it is left to the States to endow the Panchayats with such powers and functions, there is a possibility of withdrawal of many functions, which were entrusted to them based on delegated legislation or by departmental orders. To overcome such an eventuality it might be better to specify the functions of the PRIs in the relevant Acts as withdrawal of any function mentioned in the Acts might need legislative approval.

Similarly, it will be ideal to mention the tax and other resources in the Acts themselves. If the grants are made 'statutory grants' as is the case with a few grants made to the PRIs in Tamil Nadu, the local governments might be assured of a part of their revenue. Many State Governments have made it compulsory for the local governments to seek their approval to impose even the taxes, which are traditionally with the latter. In a few other cases, the States fix the minimum and maximum amount of tax that can be imposed by the PRIs and the periodicity of revision of some important taxes like house tax. Thus the revenue generation abilities of the PRIs have been crippled to some extent.

In case of spending responsibilities also, there have been severe restrictions on PRIs even where they have substantial own revenue sources. In some States, the PRIs have to obtain permission from the State Government to carry out works beyond a fixed financial limit and this applies to the works that may be planned out of their own revenue also. There have been instances wherein the State Governments have exercised their authority through District Collectors to force a few resource rich PRIs to spend their revenues on the schemes of the States.

PRIs do not enjoy much autonomy in matters related to their personnel also. Since most of the staff under PRIs is state government employees who are on deputation or assigned to the former, the PRIs have very little power to manage these employees whose loyalties are with the state governments. Some of the line departments abruptly transfer the officials deputed to the PRIs and this also affects the performance of these institutions. As outlined earlier lack of sufficient revenue does not allow the PRIs to engage personnel exclusively for them. Further, even if a few resource-rich PRIs are capable of employing a few personnel using their own resources, approval of the state governments is necessary in a few cases.

In addition to the above modes of regulating and controlling the PRIs, the State Governments insist on submission of various reports by the PRIs periodically under the disguise of monitoring the development programmes assigned to them. At the same time, it has been found out that in many cases, the funds earmarked for these development works had been released to the PRIs at the fag end of the financial year, leading to frittering away of the scarce resources. All these things have to be overcome if the PRIs have to emerge as 'self-governments'.

Conclusion

The Four Fs of decentralization as delineated above have to be addressed whenever an effort is made to strengthen the local governments in any part of the world. This is more so with the developing world as half-hearted attempts in these regions without an overall picture of decentralization has left them with many hurdles. This has also led to upheavals in certain sections of the society and the rights of these sections got trampled as there were not matching provisions in terms of finances, functionaries and freedom commensurate with the functions earmarked to the local governments. A concerted effort to focus on the Four Fs of decentralization might be the need of hour not only in the newly democratizing countries but also in the countries, which have been federal in nature since long.

REFERENCES

Aiyar, Mani Shankar (2002): 'Panchayati Raj: The Way Forward', *Economic and Political Weekly*, 38 (31), August 3: 3293-3297.

Bandyopadhyay, D. (1997): 'People's Participation in Planning, Kerala Experiment', *Economic and Political Weekly*, 32 (39), September 27: 2450-2454.

Bhargava, B.S. and V. Venkatakrishnan (1992): 'Panchayati Raj in Karnataka—Some Operational Aspects', *Kurukshetra,* 40 (4): 4-7.

Chandran, T.R. Satish (1994): 'Inter-Tier Allocation of Functions', in Amitava Mukherjee (ed), *Decentralisation: Panchayats in the Nineties*, Vikas, New Delhi: 24-36.

Choudhury, R.C. and S.P. Jain (1999): *Patterns of Decentralised Governance in Rural India*, Vols. I and II, National Institute of Rural Development, Hyderabad.

Government of India (2001): 'A Consultation Paper on Review of the Working of the Constitutional Provisions for Decentralization (Panchayats)', National Commission to Review the Working of the Constitution, September, New Delhi.

Government of India (2001): 'Report of the Working Group on Decentralised Planning and Panchayati Raj Institutions', Ministry of Rural Development, November, New Delhi.

Government of India (2001): 'Report of the Task Force on Panchayati Raj Institutions (PRIs)', Planning Commission, December, New Delhi.

Government of India (2002): 'Report of the Eleventh Finance Commission for 2000-2005', Ministry of Finance, New Delhi.

Government of Karnataka (2002): 'Report of the Working Group on Decentralization', Ministry of Rural Development, Bangalore.

Isaac, T.M. Thomas and R.W. Franke (2000): *Local Democracy and Development: People's Campaign for Decentralised Planning in Kerala*, Left Word, New Delhi.

Jha, Shikha (2002): 'Strengthening Local Governments: Rural Fiscal Decentralisation in India', *Economic and Political Weekly*, 37 (26), June

29: 2611-2623.

Manor, James (1995): 'Democratic Decentralization in Africa and Asia', *IDS Bulletin*, 26 (2), April: 81-88.

Mathew, George (2001): 'Panchayat Elections Dismal Record', *Economic and Political Weekly*, 36 (3), January 20: 183-184.

Mukarji, Nirmal (1994): 'The Third Stratum', in Government of India, *Reviewing Local Self-Government in Rural India*, Occasional Paper No.6, Ministry of Rural Development, New Delhi.

National Institute of Rural Development (2001): *India, Panchayati Raj Report, 2001: Four Decades of Decentralized Governance in Rural India*, Vols. I and II, Hyderabad.

Oates, Wallace (1972): *Fiscal Federalism*, Harcourt, Brace Jovanovich, New York.

Oommen, M.A. (1998): *Devolution of Resources to Rural Local Bodies, A comparative study of select state finance commission reports*, Institute of Social Sciences, Occasional Paper Series 21, New Delhi.

Srinivasan, T. (2001): 'Financial Devolution in Panchayati Raj', in NIRD, *India, Panchayati Raj Report, 2001: Four Decades of Decentralized Governance in Rural India*, Vol. II, Hyderabad: 211-224.

World Bank (2000): *Overview of Rural Decentralization in India*, Vol. II, *Approaches to Rural Decentralization in Seven State*, New Delhi.

5

Panchayats: Relevance and Potentials

G. PALANITHURAI

Introduction

In the Indian context, after the enactment of the 73rd Amendment to the Constitution, questions have been raised as to what extent the objectives of decentralization of powers have been realized? If not; why? Whether obstacles and barriers have been identified? If they have been; why they are not removed? Given the background, and the powers and the resources devolved, what changes have been created in governance and in the process of development? For the past one decade discussions have been held in different fora on the powers devolved, functionaries transferred and finances given to the grassroots institutions to achieve what decentralized governance has to achieve in terms of development. Institutions have been created, frameworks for local governance have been evolved through legislation, elections have been conducted, elected representatives are in position and activities are being carried out through these institutions[1]. Against this backdrop one has to visualize to what extent the newly created institutions have started functioning in the way as expected and whether the leaders who have come to power have performed their functions.

For any role to be performed perfectly the role has to be perceived properly by the performer. Further, the same role has to be perceived properly by the clients[2]. In the process of decentralization of powers, one is likely to have a conflicting perception of the role to be performed by the grassroots institutions.

Primarily panchayat institutions are considered an extension of the government and so expected to have the characteristics of the government. There is a counter argument that it is not a government as there is no law making function and the activities listed in the Eleventh Schedule as subjects are not the subjects of the IV list. Further the Panchayat is perceived as an extension of the community and so expected to have flexibility in its functions. As governments failed in delivering the services to the people to their satisfaction, a new mechanism was evolved and it has to deliver the basic essential services to the communities. Thus Panchayati-raj institutions are considered service providers or agents of the both Central and State Governments to carry out the programmes and schemes of the above governments[3]. In the given situation, Panchayati-raj institutions have to work with a variety of strings and obstacles. Panchayat leaders are viewed as a threat and a power centre by the bureaucracy and the MLAs and MPs as they are in the community and attend to the needs of the community directly[4].

As a result, the bureaucracy, the MLAs and the MPs would see to it that adequate powers are not devolved to them. Knowing fully well that these barriers and obstacles would be created in the devolution process, the leaders have to assume responsibility and perform their duties. To work in the disturbed system, the leaders at the grassroots should have the required skill and capability. Otherwise, it will be very difficult to manage the system. People, while electing a leader to the Panchayat, never consider the capacity as a factor and they elect their representative on a different set of considerations. But the elected representatives have to be oriented, sensitized and conscientised on the issues of the society and development[5]. Their skill and capacity have to be enhanced. Panchayat leaders have to build their perspective to manage the system and to work on issues of development. When the above mentioned requirements are fulfilled the system will deliver the goods. Against this background, one has to visualize the potential available in Panchayati-raj institutions for taking initiative for achieving social development based on the experiences of the Panchayats in Tamil Nadu. Before exploring and explaining the potential, it is necessary to have a look at the relevance of such an institution at present to achieve social development.

Relevance

Panchayati-raj institutions have brought people's representatives closer to the people. For the past several years, below the state government there was no representative democratic institution close to the people. Below the state government level it was the rule of the bureaucracy. It is a well known fact that the expansion of the bureaucracy will alienate the people. Middlemen establish links between the people and the bureaucracy and thereby brokerage becomes the accepted formula for all development activities[6]. Now elected representatives are placed in all the areas and people can approach them easily. People will raise questions in the Grama Sabha. If water is not sufficiently available, people can raise the question face to face in the Grama Sabha. If the medical staff from the Primary Health Centre is not visiting villages periodically, people will question the Panchayat leader. Likewise if the primary school teacher is not regular in reaching the school, it can be raised in the Panchayat[7]. When they raise questions, the leaders cannot shirk the responsibility by saying that they have no power or resources. They have to seek power and finance for which they have to work hard and purposefully.

In the whole process, people have developed the attitude that these are the works to be attended to by the government for which the Panchayat leaders have to work. Panchayat leaders have developed the attitude that in the absence of required power and finance to fulfil the needs and demands of the people, people have to be mobilized to exert pressure on the government to get things done for the people. In the whole process, people are being mobilized by the Panchayats. Mobilization is being done in many ways of which the Grama Sabha is one and an important one. No doubt in India people are mobilized for cultural activities, religious activities and political activities periodically by various groups and the political parties. But they are not mobilized for development work. But now Panchayats are mobilizing the people for development activities. It is true that the Panchayat leaders are drawn from the place wherefrom MLAs and MPs are drawn. But MLAs and MPs can keep themselves aloof from the community. Panchayat leaders have to live with the people and in the community and hence they have to be responsible and responsive to the communities. Provision has been made in the structure so that the marginalised and women can find a place legitimately in the institution for governance. Women and *dalits,* who never had any experience in governance, have come to power. They want to be transparent because the community has a hold over them. Hence, there is always a conducive atmosphere for transparent governance by women and dalits which can serve as a model for others[8]. Women have started attending the Grama Sabha meeting. A large number of Self Help Group (SHG) members attend the Grama Sabha meetings and they raise a lot of developmental issues in the meeting as they are oriented in social development activities by the NGOs. As a result, even the process of governance at the grassroots will be changed.

Electing a good leader is in the hands of the electorate. Shaping a leader and making him good lies in the hands of everyone. The leaders at the grassroots have to be conscientised on development and their skill and capacity have to be enhanced for proper management of institutions to achieve development and social justice. Once the leaders are properly trained, they will deliver the goods to the level of the expectations of the masses.

Potential Demonstrated

Leaders come to the Panchayat with different aspirations and levels of commitment. To make the leaders work for the society for its transformation and upliftment, they have to be conscientised on the roles to be performed and sensitized on the real issues of development. To manage the institutions they require management skills. To manage and mobilize the community for development work they need communication skills. To manage development the leaders need constant flow of information on all aspects through all tracks pertinent to development. As communities are uneven in terms of their socio-economic conditions, the leaders have to face several hurdles and, to overcome all those hurdles, they need a supportive structure. When the above requirements are fulfilled, the leaders will achieve what they wanted to achieve and then they will be recognized by the community. Once they win the recognition of the community, the leaders are recognized as path finders. They become visible in the media. They constitute the core group of potential performers[9]. They are visited by Government officials, Panchayat leaders of other districts and leaders of political parties. They spread success stories and they become role models. When MPs and MLAs do not address social development issues who will address them is the main question. It is the Panchayat leaders who are addressing social development issues. Everyone is looking for such kind of Panchayat leaders.

Such Panchayats are now visible in the society though their number is not large. Now the success stories are spreading through media. The media play a predominant role in this regard. From our experience in Tamil Nadu, one would strongly argue that Panchayats are capable of tackling all the social development issues provided the needed support is ensured. Representatives of the people assume responsibilities and perform their role and function. Ten Grama Panchayat Presidents have demonstrated this by their constant attention to the services provided, enrolment of eligible boys and girls in school, reduction of dropouts in schools, ensuring antenatal care and postnatal care, family welfare, adoption of family planning methods, protecting the environment, establishing good sanitary conditions, providing safe drinking water, banning sale of illicit liquor, clearing channels which bring water to drinking water ponds and tanks for irrigation purposes[10]. The above activities were carried out by the Grama Panchayat Presidents with the support of the communities. These activities were the result of the Population Foundation of India project executed in Dindigul district. It was made possible by the continuous training given to the Grama Panchayat Presidents, Vice-Presidents, community leaders and self help groups. The ten Gram Panchayat Presidents visited the Grama Panchayats in Kerala under the interface programme conducted by the Rajiv Gandhi Chair for Panchayati Raj Studies and acquainted themselves with the process of achieving social development. The Kerala visit provided enough input to them to work on social development issues. There are cases where the Panchayat Presidents have taken up the issues pertinent to social development on their own because of the commitment and the continued support of various development agencies.

Ms. Ponni Kailasam first took up the primary health centre (PHC) issue. She made the doctor come regularly and made the paramedical and nursing staff visit the Panchayat. She made the staff of the PHC accountable to the people in the Grama Sabha. She first had a discussion with the doctor and listed the problems and the same was discussed with the District Collector. With the intervention of the District Collector she sorted out the problems in the Primary Health Centre. The doctor recognized her as a leader only after she sorted out the problems faced by the PHC through the intervention of Collector. Further she made the staff affix her signature in the Visitor's Book of Panchayat as evidence to show that she visited the Panchayat area. The PHC was surrounded by an area meant for open air defecation. She took efforts to clean the entire area and removed all the bushes with the help of the youth group and placed the area under the supervision of the same group. Now the PHC is functioning properly. To perform this task she had to struggle. Yet she did it and this brought recognition among the people to the effect that she is capable of doing things. Next, the same leader identified the massive encroachment of common lands and she got orders from the District Collector and removed all the encroachments in the inflow channels of *ooranies* and tanks[11]. After the removal of the encroachment, all the *ooranies* and tanks filled up during the rainy season because all the low channels had been cleared and as a result they brought rain water to the tanks. But she had to face a lot of problems during encroachment removal. She took earnest steps to put an end to the production and sale of illicit liquor in her Panchayat premises. All these activities were carried out with struggles. While experiencing the problems and struggles in the Panchayat activities, she thought that this should not happen to other women leaders. Hence, for collective action, she initiated steps to form a federation of elected women representatives at the Grama Panchayat level as in the other tiers the women necessarily act on behalf of their party. This elected women representatives' federation constantly mobilizes the women leaders to work together to sort out their issues[12]. When they meet periodically they discuss their administrative problems and put them in a petition and submit the same to the Secretary and the Director of Rural Development. After submitting the same they meet the press also. The proceedings of the press meet used to appear in newspapers and hence the officials responded to their request. This outcome makes the federation stronger. Further they started discussing the issues of women in their forum. Thus she was responsible for the critical action initiated at the Panchayat level.

Mr. Panneer Selvam of Keerapalayam Grama Panchayat of Cuddalore District provided toilets to all the households including those of daily wage earners. The entire village is clean and neat. He got several awards. His village is a total sanitation village. He mobilized the people for this public action and the people were sensitized. He was concerned about the utility of such facilities. So he developed a toilet culture in his village. He was supported by the DANIDA. It is an eye opener for many leaders, academics and bureaucrats[13].

Ms. Rani Sathappan, President of K. Rayavaram Grama Panchayat of Pudukkottai District, successfully abolished polythene usage in her village. The Government of Tamil Nadu abolished the use of plastics but revoked the same as there was public pressure. But she did it with the support of the community. The village is clean and neat. With the approval of the community she slapped a ban on the sale and use of polythene in the *Panchayat* area.

Ms. Sahaya Mary, the President of Kakkanur Grama Panchayat established a village based management system for drinking water supply. In fact she collected money from the people to manage the system. Her concept is that water should be given to all and should be brought very near to the people so that women's burden can be reduced. She collected water charges from the public and it is being managed by the people themselves. Her activities were also supported by the DANIDA. She constituted committees to look after the quality of the water supplied to the people. A separate bank account was opened for the management of water supply.

Ms. Jesu Mary of Michealpattinam Grama Panchayat established 100 per cent rainwater harvesting structure in her Panchayat area long before the Government of Tamil Nadu made it mandatory in every house. She was an eye opener for many and especially for the government.

Mr. Irudayam, President of Karisalpatti Gram Panchayat, fought with the community for establishing toilets in the streets for public use and in schools for students' use. There was no scheme at that time. With the help of the nuns who used to undergo internship programme in the convent, he created awareness among the people about the implications of sanitation. The Panchayat president asked the ANM to stay in the sub centre. She did not do so as she has got the support of the local minister. So he passed a resolution in the Grama Sabha and sent the same to the minister. Knowing fully well the implications of the resolution the local minister asked the ANM to obey the order of the Panchayats[14].

Mr. Sreerangam, President of Komberipatti Grama Panchayat eradicated the bad practice of arranging marriage for girls at the age of 14 or 15 in the Kurumbar community. It was an age old practice but it was stopped because of the intervention of the President. He even threatened them that he would inform the police. As a result he was defeated in the next election. He was happy that he stopped the age old practice of a community[15].

Ms. Jamruth Beevi, President of Devipattinam Grama Panchayat in Ramanathapuram district, took a firm decision to kill the pigs in her Panchayat area despite the opposition of hundreds of families who were responsible for rearing pigs. Based on the advice of the doctors and health inspectors, 146 pigs were killed and the Panchayat was made a clean Panchayat. She initiated yet another step to make compost manure out of the waste collected in the village with the help of an NGO. She was responsible for spreading the clean village concept.

Women Grama Panchayat leaders of Tamil Nadu have formed a federation with the objective of highlighting their problems in managing the Panchayats and to take up the issues of women.

This federation is gaining momentum as they adopt a proactive approach. Many of the women leaders in the federation are drawn from self-help groups and hence they are already oriented in social development issues. Whenever conventions are organised, they invite women activists to discuss the issues of women and to evolve strategies to combat the problems faced by the women through the Panchayati Raj. They pass resolutions and declarations for their future action[16]. The women leaders used to invite consumer forum activists to explain to the members of the federation the methodology to be adopted to supervise the service providers. Further, they demand activity charts showing how the service providers could be managed by the local body institutions and what powers the panchayats are enjoying in this regard and, if the service providers do not comply with the request of the leaders what action can be initiated. All these details are discussed in their meeting.

Mr. Ramanathan, President of Naalukkottai Grama Panchayat in Sivagangai district, ensured proper delivery of provisions to the poor through the ration shop by handing over the responsibility of the management of the ration shops to SHGs. It is a well known fact that the ration shop is yet another institution to help the poor by supplying the basic need of food material. It is also true that corruption keeps the poor away from it. He fought with the district administration and got for it a SHG. Now quality products in correct quantity are being supplied to the poor. SHG members are also earning from this service. It has become a role model for others.

Ms. Chinnammal, President of Orathupatti Grama Panchayat, made it clear in her plan document that providing a nail cutter and mats and constructing a baby toilet in the *balwadi* was the priority work. Since the *balwadi* is located in a *dalit* hamlet, she had a vision that all *dalit* children should lead a decent human life, which, she feels, they are not leading now. Further she feels that the school is not clean and neat now. Such conditions have to be changed. Ms. Veera Kalaiarasi, President of Veppankulam Panchayat of Sivagangai district, explained that attending to the needs of the disabled, the destitute, widows and orphans is the priority work as she experienced torture at the hands of her husband and because of poverty. She feels that normally attention is not paid to the above sections. Hence she wants to pay much attention to these segments[17].

The above stated cases demonstrate the potential of the Panchayati-raj institutions. The achievements projected here are the achievements of the leaders. How are these leaders able to achieve such results? They are sensitized, conscientised and capacitated leaders. They establish contact with community, NGOs and government officials. They establish contact with the media also. Government officials are taking these success stories to various places for dissemination. The message they want to spread across the state is that with the limited resources, powers and functionaries, they are able to achieve this much. Why can't others do the same by following these role models? The officials know pretty well that there is no political will and in the absence of political will they want to do something for Panchayats by which the leaders who want to break new ground can get the support of the higher level officials. Many of the higher level officials feel that Panchayats are competent to achieve social development provided needed support is given to the Panchayats[18]. The cases quoted here are a few which have registered remarkable achievements. Likewise Panchayat leaders are breaking new ground in many areas and they are to be documented. Now the Government of Tamil Nadu has decided to form a training team and to conduct training classes for the Panchayat leaders. While sharing their experiences they can motivate others to do such things in the Panchayats. At present these leaders are identified and they are provided needed support individually, not through a system. Panchayat leaders want an activity manual (see Illustration-A). It is very difficult to create political will on the part of the leaders at the state level. But making the leaders perform by assuming responsibilities in achieving social development is possible. When the Government of Tamil Nadu announced a 15-point programme to make Tamil Nadu the number one State in the country, the Women Panchayat Presidents Federation convened a meeting and discussed all the major issues contained in the 15-point programme and they fixed the responsibility of the Panchayats in implementing the 15-point programme in the rural areas. They submitted a memorandum to the Minister, the

Secretary and the Director of Rural Development, Government of Tamil Nadu. By sensitizing the masses through the Grama Sabha about the rights of the people *vis-a-vis* over the service providers, the people were prepared. By doing so people can be mobilized through the panchayats for social development activities. How can the above mentioned activities be done?

Process

The leaders who have broken new grounds had commitment. They were in search of supportive structures. They were supported by many institutions. They enhanced their capacity and fixed targets for accomplishments. They developed their vision regarding the development of the community. They perceived their roles and responsibilities properly as they had undergone training continuously. By putting up exemplary performance they have developed contact with higher level officials. To manage the problems of the middle level officials, they have built an alliance with the media and formed a network with NGOs and other leaders. Because of their achievement the leaders have established strong contact with communities.

Communities are drawn towards the Panchayats by the transparent administration of the Panchayat presidents. They cross the boundaries of caste and political parties for Panchayat work. When their achievements are brought to light they develop their self-esteem. Thus devolution for social development can be achieved through personal evolution. Every village Panchayat is a manageable administrative unit. All social indicators can be achieved at the micro level by enhancing the capacity of the Grama Panchayat leaders. By extending support to such leaders, their achievements will be increased to the next level. Their achievements are brought to light by the media as they are constantly sensitized by The Hunger Project through its media workshop on building the perspective to cover the stories of Panchayats and women's empowerment. Panchayats ensure entitlements. People can claim their rights through Panchayats. By shaping a leader at the micro level, social development can be achieved.

Conclusion

Panchayats are instruments of the people created for governance with the participation of the people to achieve development. Though Panchayat leaders are drawn from the place wherefrom MLAs and MPs are drawn they cannot adopt the attitude and behaviour of the MPs and MLAs as they have to work with the community closely. By increasing their capacity and sensitizing them on developmental issues, Panchayats can be prepared to achieve development and social justice. Capacity building, continuous support extended by the support structure, forming network with the media and NGOs and providing needed information could make them achievers and path finders. If state governments really want to achieve social development, it can be achieved through the Panchayats. People should be mobilized to participate in the development process. In the long run people will assert and claim their rights and entitlements through the Panchayats.

ILLUSTRATION-A

Good Governance and Social Development in Gram Panchayats Indicators

Sl.No.	*Activities*	*Responsibility*	*Outcome*
1.	100% enrolment of eligible children	President, Vice-President, Ward Members, PTA, SHG Members, Youth Clubs, NGO, Retired Officials	Increase in literacy, human resource development
2.	Reduction of Dropouts	President, Vice-President, Ward Members, PTA, SHG Members, Youth Clubs, NGO, Retired Officials	Increase in educational standard
3.	Ensuring protected Drinking Water Supply to School	President, Vice-President, Ward Members, School Teachers	Improvement of students health, reduction of absenteeism of students
4.	Providing toilets to school	President, Vice-President, Ward Members, School Teachers	Increase in health of children
5.	Utilizing the toilets by the school students	President, other members of the Panchayat Council Teachers	Toilet culture developed
6.	Cutting the nails of the students every Monday in *Balwadi* and School	Youth club, SHG, Panchayat Ward Members, School Teachers	Health education, reduction of diseases, improvement of nutrition
7.	Planting of saplings in the school premises	President, teachers, agriculture departments	Environment awareness eco development, income to school
8.	Creating a school garden	President, Teachers PTA, Youth Clubs	Education, increase in nutrition
9.	Keeping the *Balwadi* clean and neat	*Balwadi* teacher, President, Vice-President, Ward Members	Health education, increase in status of health
10.	Providing a toilet in the *Balwadi*	President, Vice President, Ward Members	Education, increase in health status
11.	Bringing a toilet culture among the kids	*Balwadi* teacher	Health education, increase in health status

Contd..

Sl.No.	*Activities*	*Responsibility*	*Outcome*
12.	Adding vegetables to the noon meal by getting donations and getting the vegetables from the school garden	President, Vice-President, Balwadi teacher	Nutritive food for students
13.	Taking steps to prevent the practice of child labour	President, Vice-President, Ward Members, School teachers, PTA, NGO, SHG, Youth Club	School enrolment, literacy, HRD
14.	Cleaning over head tanks	OHT operators, under the instruction of panchayat regularly	Health status, productivity
15.	Creating awareness among the people about the consequence of alcohol and stop brewing and selling the same in the panchayat premises	President, Vice-President, Ward Member, Health Committee, SHG, Youth Club, NGO	Economic status of poor, status of women and children, health of individuals and reduction of social problems
16.	Creating Awareness among the people about family welfare	PHC Staff, President, Vice-President, Ward Members, Health Committee, SHG, Youth Club	Livelihood security
17.	Identify the vulnerable families and ensure food security to them and constantly monitor them with the help of government schemes	President, Vice-President, Ward Members, SHGs	Income generation, reduction of poverty, status of women
18.	Building the skill of the women through training	Presidents, Vice-President, Ward Members, Training institution, Social Welfare Department at the District Women Development Corporation	Income generation, reduction of poverty, status of women
19.	Establish link between the skilled persons and banking sector for the establishment of business venture by the women	President, Vice-President, Ward Members, Planning Committee Members, NGO, Banks, SHG	Development of rural economy, and status of women

Contd..

Sl.No.	*Activities*	*Responsibility*	*Outcome*
20.	Building the skills of the youth through training	President, Vice-President, Ward Members, Training institutions, NYK	Human resource development, economic eevelopment
21.	Establish link between the skilled persons and Banking sector for the establishment of business venture by the youth	President, Vice-President, Ward Member, Planning Committee Members, NGOs, Banks, NYKs	Development of rural economy
22.	Ensuring proper functioning of PDS	President, Vice-President, Ward Members and SHG, officials of Civil Supply	Food security
23.	Prevent open defecation in the villages by creating awareness and constructing toilets in each and every house	President, Vice-President, Ward Members, SHG, Youth Club, NGO, Project Staff, TRSP, Retired Employees	Improvement in health, sanitation environment
24.	Creating awareness about RCH by printing a card and giving it to every family	President, Vice-President, Ward Members, Health Committee, NGO, Staff	Improvement in women and children, health, economic status
25.	Ensure the delivery of services from sub-centre and PHC to the people through the schemes available for prenatal and post-natal care	PHC Staff, President, Vice-President, Ward Members, SHG, NGO, Health Committee	Increase in health status and economic status
26.	Creating awareness about growing medicinal plants and make it a business by involving SHG and Youth Clubs	President, Vice-President, Ward Members, SHG, Planning Committee, Youth Club, NGO	Increase in health, income generation productivity
27.	Creating awareness about the importance of water management	President, Vice-President, Ward Members, Community leaders, Planning Committee Members, NGO	Rational utilization of water

Contd..

Sl.No.	*Activities*	*Responsibility*	*Outcome*
28.	Creating a common burial ground in to grave yard in the villages	President, Vice-President, Ward Members, SHG, Youth Club	Social justice
29	Taking steps to manage the solid waste and earn money from it for panchayats	President, Vice-President, Ward Members, Planning Committee, NGO, SHG	Environment development, income generation, better agricultural practices
30.	Organise workshop for pregnant women to disseminate the needed information akin to ANC PNC	PHC Staff, SHG, President	Increase of health awareness, health status, economic status, Reduction of infant mortality new born babies are in exact weight
31.	Conducting medical camps for poor and school children	President, Vice-President, Ward Members, NGOs, SHG, nearby Rotary and Lions Club	Improved health status
32.	Make the SHG and Youth Clubs to take up Panchayat works instead of employing contractor	President, Vice-President, Ward Members, SHG Youth club, NGO	Employment opportunity, quality of work, reduction of expenditure, local needs
33.	Regularly conducting Grama Sabha meetings.	President, Vice-President, Ward Members	Peoples participation, good governance
34	Ensuring 60 per cent attendance in Grama Sabha meeting.	President, Vice-President, Ward Members, all eligible members, SHG members, NGOs working in the *Panchayats.*	Transparency, accountability of *panchayats*
35.	Ensuring Women/ *dalit* participation 50 per cent of attendance	President, Vice-President, Ward Members, SHG, NGO	Social justice, status of weaker section
36.	Information dissemi-nations, Income/ Expenditure display. Report on schemes implemented display List of schemes proposed to be implemented List of beneficiaries	President and Panchayat Clerk	Transparency, accountability, credibility of Panchayat, better participation

Contd..

Sl.No.	*Activities*	*Responsibility*	*Outcome*
37.	Participatory decision making ● Opportunities for discussion to all communities ● Equal status to all in seating ● Developing consensus	President, Ward Members, community leaders/ retired government officials, school teachers, Planning Committee Members, *Dalit* Leaders, NGOs and other association members	Generation of collective wisdom, social justice
38.	Develop a system of communication to give information about Grama Sabha meeting	President, Clerk, Ward Member, SHG, Youth Clubs, NGOs	Transparency, accountability
39.	Provision of water supply to *dalit* hamlets	President and the concerned Ward Members, Committee for water supply	Communal harmony, status of *Dalit*, productivity of *Dalits*
40.	Removal of untouchability by ● Preventing the two tumbler system ● Participating in temple festival	President, Ward Members, SHG, Youth Clubs, Community Leaders	Social justice, Communal harmony
41.	Training to *dalit* youths in skill development	President, Youth Clubs, NGOs, Education Institutions	Economic development, social justice
42.	Availing THADCO schemes	President, NGOs, Vice-President and Ward Members	Economic development of *Dalits*, social harmony
43.	Identification of all CPR verifying the status of encroachment details	Panchayat President, Vice-President, Ward Members, Government Officials, Police, Department	Environment development social justice, income generation
44.	Removal of encroachments	Panchayat President, Vice-President, (Revenue & Police Department)	Productive use of resources, equity, income generation
45.	Utilizing the common properties and developing the same.	Panchayat president, Ward Members, NGO, SHG, Youth groups	Environment development, income generation

Contd..

Sl.No.	*Activities*	*Responsibility*	*Outcome*
46.	100 per cent house tax collection	President, Clerk, Vice-President, Ward Members, SHG, Youth Club	Financial status of panchayat more government funds
47.	Panchayat functioning as a system	President, Clerk, Vice-President, Ward Members	Integrated development
48.	Records maintenance / transparency	President and Clerk	Good governance
49.	Preparing a perspective plan through village planning forum	President, Ward Members, Planning Committee	Planned development better use of resources
50.	Formation of statutory committees	President	Efficiency of panchayats accountability
51.	Old age, physically and mentally disabled, destitute, orphan and other vulnerable sections	President, Ward Members, SHG, NGO, Government, and Planning Committee	Social security, social harmony

ILLUSTRATION-B

Key Assumptions

— Harmony prevails in Panchayat
— Panchayat is perceived as development space.
— Community supports the Panchayats.
— Panchayat leader has got commitment.
— Panchayat leader has vision.
— Panchayat leader has got skill and capacity.
— Panchayat is not leader centric.
— Panchayat is people and system centric.

NOTES

1. Rajiv Gandhi Foundation (2000): *Panchayati Raj in India: Status Report*, New Delhi.
2. G. Palanithurai (1991): *The Role Perception of Legislatures: A Case Study of Tamil Nadu*, Konark Publications, New Delhi.
3. G. Palanithurai (2003): "Towards Participatory Governance at Grassroots: Synergisation of Rural Communities and Institutions", *South Asian Journal of Socio Political Studies*, 4 (1).
4. Rajiv Gandhi Chair for Panchayati Raj Studies (2000): *Problems faced by the Gram Panchayati Leaders*, Gandhigram.
5. G. Palanithurai (2001): *Capacity Building for Local Body Leaders*, Concept Publishing Company, New Delhi.
6. G. Palanithurai (1996): *New Panchayati Raj System: Status and Prospects*, Kaniska Publications, New Delhi.
7. Rajiv Gandhi Chair for Panchayati Raj Studies (2000): *Functional Efficiency of Gram Sabha: A Report submitted to II State Finance Commission*, Gandhigram.
8. G. Palanithurai (2003): *Evaluation of Process and Performance of Gram Panchayat Women and Dalit Presidents in Tamil Nadu*, Rajiv Gandhi Chair, Gandhigram.
9. Rajiv Gandhi Chair for Panchayati Raj Studies (2003): *The Hunger Project, Report on the Workshop on Panchayati Raj: Trials and Triumphs*, Gandhigram.
10. G. Palanithurai (2003): *Panchayats, Communities and Social Development*, Rajiv Gandhi Chair for Panchayati Raj Studies, Gandhigram.
11. G. Palanithurai (2000): *New Panchayati Raj System at Work: An Evaluation*, Concept Publishing Company, New Delhi.
12. G. Palanithurai (2004): 'Building Alliances and Capabilities among the elected women representatives of Grassroots institutions', *Womens Link*, 10 (1): pp.18-25.
13. Rajiv Gandhi Chair for Panchayati Raj Studies (2004): *Evaluation of Process and Performance of Gram Panchayat Presidents in Tamil Nadu (A Report submitted to UNICEF)*, Gandhigram.
14. *Ibid.*
15. Population Foundation of India (2001): *Empowerment of Panchayati Raj Institutions on Issues Related to Population, Health and Social Development, A Final Report*, New Delhi.

16. When they met on 26th and 27th October in Gandhigram 700 Gram Panchayat Women leaders made a declaration. The following is the declaration:

    We, the elected women representatives who are gathered here at Gandhigram Rural Institute on this 27th day of October 2002, declare that we will address the following issues in the next one year:

(i) All the eligible children (girls and boys) will be enrolled in schools.

(ii) We will strive to remove malnourishment amongst children in the age group of 0-5 years. As elected representatives we shall ensure that no underweight babies are born in our villages. The mothers will be given proper nourishment before and after delivery.

(iii) Better anti-natal and post-natal care will be provided for all the women in our Panchayats.

(iv) Any injustice against women in our Panchayats will be dealt with firmly. As a collective we will fight against domestic violence and also any other form of violence against any women in our Panchayat.

(v) We will ensure that child labour is abolished in our Panchayats.

(vi) We will ensure equitable access to and distribution of Panchayat resources among all the people in the Panchayats and guarantee at least the provision of the basic minimum requirements for the poorest. The PDS system will be improved with our intervention.

(vii) Problems faced by the women Panchayat leaders and women in general will be addressed collectively by making alliance with supportive institutions and organizations.

(viii) The newly implemented sanitary complexes meant for women will be effectively managed by women's groups with the support of the Panchayats.

(ix) Our Panchayats will not suffer from lack of drinking water. Everyone will be entitled to safe drinking water.

(x) We will ensure that Gram Sabhas take place regularly and more and more people take part in these meetings. We will ensure that a minimum of 50 per cent of the total women in the Panchayat attend the meetings and that their issues are properly heard.

(xi) We commit ourselves to the implementation of the 15-point programme prepared by the Tamil Nadu Government and request the state government to devolve necessary powers to the Panchayats and local bodies for the same.

17. G. Palanithurai (2003): *Development Role Reversed: From Government to People*, Rajiv Gandhi Chair for Panchayati Raj Studies, Gandhigram.

18. The higher officials, Director and Secretaries, Government of Tamil Nadu while participating in a workshop on Panchayati Raj: Trials and Triumphs highlighted the potentiality of the Panchayats and indicated the problems faced by them.

6

Earth Democracy, Living Democracy

Rebuilding Security in an Age of Insecurity

VANDANA SHIVA

Humanity seems to be in a free fall towards disaster. The ecological fabric of our existence is being torn apart, as the violence of corporate globalisation combines with the violence of war on a planetary scale. Alternatives beyond war, non-sustainability and social and economic injustice are becoming a survival imperative. These alternatives need to combine our making peace with the planet and our making peace among people from diverse cultures. One is not possible without the other because the roots of terrorism, violence and war lie in environmental and economic exclusion and the insecurity it generates. People's security does not lie in larger military budgets, bigger bombs and stronger police states. It lies in ecological security, in economic security, in cultural and political security. Rebuilding these multiple securities can recreate peace, justice and sustainability.

I

ECONOMIC GLOBALISATION AND THE THREAT TO ECOLOGICAL SECURITY

Climate change, species extinction, the destruction of water resources are threatening the very basis of our existence. Even as we attempt to grapple with the pollution and externalities of the first two industrial revolutions based on fossil fuels and chemicals, in the form of climate change and toxic pollution, new threats of genetic pollution are being unleashed by the third industrial revolution in the form of biotechnology and genetic engineering. The fundamental principles of precaution and polluter pays are being given a go by to rush untested, unnecessary, potentially hazardous GMOs to the market place for release in ecosystems.

It is the poor whose ecological security is most threatened by corporate led globalisation. While an attempt is being made to project resource conservation as anti-poor, it is the poor who pay the highest economic costs for resource destruction and resource privatization.

Globalisation at the most fundamental level, is rewriting our relationship with the earth and her species, alienating land, water and biodiversity from local communities, transforming commons into commodities to be traded freely for profits—with total indifference to the ethical, ecological and economic impacts of this commodification of life.

Globalisation is a break from all earlier stages of human relationships with the earth and her resources.

(1) It is based on enclosures of the remaining ecological commons—biodiversity, water and air, and the destruction of local economies on which people's livelihoods and economic security depends.

(2) The commodification of water and biodiversity is ensured through new property rights built into trade agreements like the WTO which are transforming people's resources into corporate monopolies, viz, TRIPs and trade in environmental goods and services. The corporatisation of food and agriculture is ensured through the WTO. Agreement on Agriculture and Structural Adjustment Programmes of the World Bank.

In Orissa, one of the poorest Indian states, World Bank and DFID are using northern tax payer money to privatize irrigation water which now costs 10 times more and destroying agriculture, the only livelihood of the poor.

In Delhi, a $ 2.5 million World Bank loan for water privatisation has largely financed the consultancy fees for an international accounting firm, Price Waterhouse. In Bolivia, communities resisting water privatisation have been shot at by police. In South Africa, protestors have been arrested.

(3) The transformation of commons and basic needs to commodities is ensured through shifts in governance with decisions moving from communities and countries to global institutions, and rights moving from people to corporations through increasingly centralised and unaccountable states acting on the principle of eminent domain — the absolute sovereignty of the ruler.

This corporate take over of vital resources and vital economic sectors has in turn led to anti-democratic formations and constellations. Instead of acting on the public trust doctrine and principles of democratic accountability and subsidiarity, globalization led to governments usurping power from parliaments, regional and local governments, and local communities.

For example, the TRIPs agreement was shaped by corporations and allows five corporations to control seeds, plants, food and health. It forces Central Government to hijack the rights to biodiversity and knowledge from communities and assign them as exclusive, monopolistic rights to corporations who see a one trillion doller market in seeds. Centralised decision-making is being used by Monsanto to push its GM crops and seeds, bypassing democratic decision-making and all concerns for bio-safety.

The Agreement on Agriculture was shaped by global grain giants like Cargill and is based on taking decisions away from farming communities and regional governments. Governments are being forced to sacrifice their farmers and food security for export led agriculture and dumping of subsidized products on others' markets, creating a regime of mutually assured destruction, instead of systems of food security.

The General Agreement on Trade in Services (GATS) takes decisions and ownership over water from the local and public domain to the privatized, global domain. Water trade is assessed at a trillion doller economy by the World Bank. Water privatisation is carried out through water policies that make water the property of the State. This has happened in the case of India. Land is privatized by using the government's right to acquire land often in violation of the constitutional and community rights as in the case of Bastar.

This undemocratic process of privatisation and deregulation has led to increased political bankruptcy and corruption and economic bankruptcy. It has also led to concentration of power and ownership. Globalisation has relocated sovereignty from people to corporations, through centralising, militarizing states. Rights of people are being appropriated by States to carve out monopoly rights of corporations over our land, our water, our biodiversity, our air. States acting on the principle of eminent domain or absolute sovereignty of the states are undermining people's sovereign rights and their role as trustees of people's resources on the public trust doctrine. State sovereignty, by itself, is therefore not enough to generate countervailing forces and processes to corporate globalisation.

The reinvention of sovereignty has to be based on the reinvention of the state so that the state is made accountable to the people. Sovereignty cannot reside only in centralized state structures, nor does it disappear when the protective functions of the state with respect to its people start to wither away. The new partnership of national sovereignty needs empowered communities which assign functions to the state for their protection. Communities defending themselves always demand such duties and obligations from state structures. On the other hand, TNCs and international agencies promote the separation of the community interests from state interests and the fragmentation and divisiveness of communities.

II

CORPORATE GLOBALIZATION AND THE GROWTH OF ECONOMIC INSECURITY

Both ecology and economics have emerged from the same roots — *"oikos"* — the Greek word for household. As long as economics was focused on the household, it recognized and respected its basis in natural resources, the limits of ecological renewal. It was focused on providing for basic human needs within these limits. Economics as based on the household was women centred.

Today, economics is separated from, and opposed to both ecological processes and basic needs. While the destruction of nature has been justified on grounds of improving human welfare, for the majority of people poverty and dispossession has increased. While being non-sustainable it is also economically unjust. While being promoted as "economic development", it is leading to underdevelopment, while projecting growth; it is causing life threatening destruction.

The dominant model of "economic development" has in fact become anti-life. And it is this non-sustainability model which is being globalised. Corporate globalisation is creating economic insecurity worldwide as livelihoods are destroyed and basic needs are denied to millions.

Globalisation of agriculture has allowed dumping of subsidized artificially cheap products which are robbing small farmers of livelihoods, markets and incomes. Giant corporations controlling production and distribution are using subsidies to push up costs of production and push down prices farmers receive for their products. It is this negative economics that is being globalised by the rules of W.T.O. and the conditionalities of structural adjustment.

The dominant economy is negative both in ecological terms and in financial terms when viewed from the perspective of the poor and women. It is ecologically negative in a dual sense — it is destructive of the resource base of our survival, and it consumes more resources than it produces. The destruction and resource waste is not taken into account, and an essentially unproductive, non-sustainable economy is pushed on grounds of improving welfare.

A usual argument used in promoting industrial agriculture like the Green Revolution earlier and genetic engineering in agriculture now is that only industrial agriculture and industrial breeding can keep up with increased food productivity for feeding a growing population. However, increased mouths to feed imply more efficient resource use so that the same resources can feed more people. Since resources, not labour, are the limiting factor in food production, it is resource productivity, not labour productivity which is the relevant measure. A sixty-fold decrease of food producing capacity in the context of resource use is not an efficient strategy for using limited land, water and biodiversity to feed the world.

Further, since food security is based on food entitlements, and entitlements in peasant societies are based on livelihoods and work, increase in labour productivity based on displacement of farmers cannot reduce hunger. It decreases food entitlements by destruction of livelihoods.

A myth promoted by the one-dimensional monoculture paradigm is that biodiversity reduces yields and productivity, and monocultures increase yields and productivity. However, since yields and productivity are theoretically constructed terms, they change according to the context. Yields usually refer to production per unit area of a single crop. Planting only one crop in the entire field as a monoculture will of course increase its yield. Planting multiple crops in a mixture will have low yields of individual crops, but will have high total output of food.

The negative economy of agriculture destroys biodiversity, soil and water. It also destroys rural livelihoods and creates hunger and starvation. When farmers spend more on production costs than they earn from selling their produce, the economics is negative. It is artificially kept afloat by subsidies. Rich countries give $ 370 billion as subsidies. Corporate farmers of California receive more than $ 500,000 in subsidies. The new farm bill increases U.S. subsidies to agriculture by $ 73.5 billion to $ 180 billion over the next 6 years. This will artificially bring down prices worldwide, destroying millions of peasant livelihoods. It is not efficiency but subsidies which are lowering prices of farm commodities.

It is the poor farmers and small farmers who are destroyed by the globalization of a negative economy. Thousands of Indian peasants have committed suicide because of increasing costs of seeds and chemicals. The poor consumers also suffer, starvation deaths have returned to India for the first time since independence.

As 500 million Indians face starvation, 60 million tonnes are rotting in storage because poor people cannot afford to buy food because of a four fold increase in prices because of removal of food subsidies. Food denied to people is now being exported with subsidies. While the poor in India were paying Rs. 7,000 per tonne of wheat and Rs. 11,300 per tonne of rice because of withdrawal of subsidies, exporters were getting food at a subsidized rate of Rs. 4,300 per tonne and Rs. 5,650 per tonne respectively.

Negative economics push people out of production. They create economic displacement and disposable people, people whose very right to survival is denied. A negative economy is based on pseudo productivity and pseudo surpluses. It is based on an illusion of growth, which hides the poverty and destitution it creates. The growth is of course real for the Monsantos — the seed, chemical and biotechnology industry which have expanding markets even as farmers take their lives, sell their kidneys, or their land. The growth is real for the Cargills who buy cheap from farmers and sell processed food at high cost to consumers. The trade rules are aimed at benefiting the Monsantos and Cargills. An economics for creating scarcity and poverty is transformed into an economics for creating surpluses and growth by a jugglery of statistics. Food output is replaced by "high yield" categories, food security in the household and community is replaced by agricultural trade figures. Yields go up while output goes down; trade goes up while consumption by the poor goes down. Pseudo surpluses hide starvation; super profits hide a crisis of distribution.

The economy that generates super profits for the global corporations also generates ecological poverty for the planet and economic poverty for the poor. It is an economy that produces insecurity for all. And it is this economics of insecurity that is creating politics and culture of insecurity. Globalization is fuelling extremism, terrorism, xenophobia and fundamentalism and deepens destruction of nature, people's rights and democracy.

III

THE GREAT BETRAYAL ROAD FROM WSSD TO W$$D

The World Summit on Sustainable Development (WSSD) organized in Johannesburg from August 26—September 4, 2002 was supposed to have been the Earth Summit II - ten years after the Earth Summit organized in Rio de Janeiro in 1992. But instead of Rio + 10, WSSD became Doha+10. Ten months ago, the Ministerial Meeting of WTO was organized in Doha to salvage the WTO negotiations for a new enlarged round which had failed in Seattle due to citizen protest and a walk out by smaller countries who had been marginalized and excluded in the negotiations. The implementation document of WSSD mentioned Doha and WTO 46 times at one stage and Rio only once. The draft had been introduced undemocratically by the U.S. and E.U., and with minor modifications was reintroduced by South Africa. There was no rebellion by Governments against the surreptitious substitution of the sustainability agenda of Rio with the commercial and corporate agenda of WTO.

While the struggles of the poor in the South are related to their access and rights to natural resources—land, water and biodiversity, and hence are intrinsically environmental and ecological struggles, WSSD was artificially presented as being about 'poverty', not about the 'environment'. Globalisation was then offered as the solution to poverty, and decisions that were aimed at robbing the poor of their remaining resources and hence making them poorer such as privatisation of water, patenting of seeds and alienation of land, were being offered as measures for 'poverty alleviation'. While the landless people and the movements against privatisation marched for environmental and resource rights, globalisation pundits kept repeating the mantra that the poor could not afford the "luxury" of their natural capital—they needed globalisation. Globalisers do not see that globalisation would rob the poor of their resources, make them the property of global corporations who would then sell water and seeds at high cost to the poor thus pushing them deeper into poverty, and over the edge of survival. During PBS/BBC debate in which I participated, industry spokesman clearly said that imposing private property rights to natural resources was their first priority. Globalizing the non-sustainable, unethical, iniquitous systems of ownership, control and use of natural resources was the main agenda at WSSD. The corporate hijack of the Earth Summit was the overall outcome. WSSD had mutated into WSSD.

But the implications go further than the hijack of one summit. These are dangerous trends for democracy. The substitution of multilateral legally binding agreements (Type I outcomes) by so called Type II outcomes in the form of public private partnerships are reflections of the privatization of states and privatization of the UN. The UN of "We the People" was transformed in Johannesburg into the UN of "We the Corporations". It appeared to be an auction house where the Earth herself was being put up for sale. For us in civil society the earth and one world is not for sale. That is why we withdrew our consent to the outcomes.

When I had the opportunity to address the opening of the Civil Society forum with President Mbeki, I talked of how a global apartheid was being created by globalization after South Africa had fought its domestic apartheid. President Mbeki made reference to the "global apartheid" in his draft political declaration at the end of the Summit. He had intended to say:

- From the African continent, the Cradle of Humanity, we declare our responsibility to one another to the greater community of life, and to future generations.
- Meeting in the great African city of Johannesburg, which bears testimony to how industrial activity can change the environment in a matter of decades, we recall the great social and economic divides we have seen.
- This is a mirror of our global existence. If we do nothing, we risk the entrenchment of a form of global apartheid. Unless we act in a manner that fundamentally changes their lives, the poor o the world may lose confidence in the democratic systems to which we are committed seeing their representatives as nothing more than sounding brass or tinkling symbols.

The US forced South Africa to change that text and remove all reference to "global apartheid". It thus contributed to the Summit being nothing more than "sounding brass or tinkling symbols." Only the governments of Norway and Ethiopia spoke up against attempts to make the Multilateral Environment Agreements (MEAs) of Rio subservient to the trade rules of WTO and to dilute the proposals on corporate accountability that the Friends of the Earth campaign had successfully introduced in the text.

The only other 'victory' was the women's alliance of ministers and the women's caucus preventing the removal of language relating to human rights in the context of health. In an age supposedly characterized by a clash of civilizations, the "clashing civilizations" —the US, the Holy See, the Islamic countries were amazingly unified in seeing human rights in health as a threat to all shades and colours of patriarchy. The tragedy was that all "victories" were merely success in preventing further regress—in terms of corporate accountability, multilateral environmental agreements and women's health rights.

Instead of governments committing themselves to conserve water and defend and uphold water rights of all their citizens, they were selling off water in privatization deals, even though water is not the property of the state, but the commons cared for and shared by communities. The privatization of water commons is illegal and illegitimate in common property law, natural law and moral law. This is why there were protests against water privatization through out WSSD. That is why we withdrew our consent from the process. The police attacked one such protest on 24th August with stun bombs, injuring three people. During a TV debate, when a person displaced by a dam in Lesotho to bring water to South Africa's industry and towns called money generated by water privatisation "blood money"—the head of South Africa's water supply said, "I love blood money that creates wealth". Johannesburg made it clear that the real clash of cultures is between cultures of life and cultures of death. The anti-poverty movement, the justice movement, the sustainability movement, the ecology movement are actually one movement, the movement to defend the resources for sustenance and right to sustenance as a natural right—a right that is not given by states and cannot be taken away by greedy corporations. Corrupt deals on pieces of paper cannot extinguish that natural right. This is why in Johannesburg the movements had the moral power, not the corporations or governments.

The moral degradation of the ruling elites was also evident in the privatization of life through biotechnology and patents. Southern Africa has been made a victim of drought and famine under the joint impact of climate change and structural adjustment programmes. The World Bank has forced countries to destroy and dismantle their food security systems. Faced with severe drought, lack of food security is creating conditions of famine. More than 300,000 people face starvation. Famine caused by western powers is now being used to market GMOs through food aid. Zambia, Zimbabwe and Mozambique have refused to accept GMOs in food aid. The WHO was mobilized to force African countries to accept GM food. The US government made the force feeding of Africans with GMOs a major issue. When Colin Powell, representing President Bush kept insisting on African countries importing GM food from US in the closing plenary of the Earth Summit, he was heckled by both NGOs and Governments. African farmers had come to Johannesburg with alternatives—small scale, indigenous-based on farmers' rights to land, water and seed.

The Earth Summit in Johannesburg in 2002, organized 10 years after the Rio Summit which gave us the Convention on Biological Diversity and the Bio-safety Protocol, was also reduced to a marketplace for pushing biotech on Africa. Hundreds of African farmers and government representatives condemned the US pressure to force GM contaminated food aid. As civil society representatives from Africa stated,

> "We, African Civil Society groups, participants to the World Summit on Sustainable Development, composed of more than 45 African countries, join hands with the Zambian and Zimbabwean governments and their people in rejecting GE contaminated food for our starving brothers and sisters:

(1) We refuse to be used as the dumping ground for contaminated food, rejected by the Northern countries; and we are *enraged* by the emotional blackmail of vulnerable people in need, being used in this way.

(2) The starvation period is anticipated to begin early in 2003, so that there is enough time to source uncontaminated food.

(3) There is enough food in the rest of Africa (already offered by Tanzania and Uganda) to provide food for the drought areas.

(4) Our response is to strengthen solidarity and self-reliance with in Africa, in the face of this next wave of colonization, through GE technologies, which aim to control our agricultural systems, through the manipulation of seed by corporations.

(5) We will stand together in preventing our continent from being contaminated by genetically engineered crops, as a responsibility to our future generation.

There was in fact not one Summit but many. There was the hijacked Summit at Sandton, the richest suburb in Johannesburg. To get to the Convention Centre we had to pass a shopping mall. It was an appropriate symbol of a Summit that became a market for the earth resources. There was a limp official NGO gathering at NASREC. At a school, St. Stithians was the celebration of the People's Earth Summit, and in Soweto, children gathered for a Children's Earth Summit. The landless people and the small farmers had their own Summits. The alternative Summits were planning a people-centred, earth-centred agenda for the future. In the midst of corruption, they were creating courage and truth. In the midst of hopelessness they were creating hope. In the midst of violence they were creating non-violence.

When as civil society we walked away from the official process on September 4 and withdrew our consent, we did so in peace, in confidence and joy. We were brutally assaulted by the police of the apartheid era. We remembered Gandhi who was also assaulted on another September 11, and instead of responding to violence with violence, he shaped non-violence into the ultimate power of the weak and excluded. His "Satyagraha", the "force of truth", was a different response from that to the events of the September 11, 2001. His satyagraha is our inspiration. As we said in our statement issued from the People's Earth Summit,

> "We are outraged that the World Summit on Sustainable Development, instead of being an Earth Summit, which reinforced the commitments made in 1992 in Rio de Janeiro to protect the Earth and strengthen the rights of the poor has been subverted by governments and corporations for their own ends at the expense of civil society and the Earth. We refuse to collaborate with laws and systems of governance that deny the most fundamental birthrights of people and our responsibilities within the Earth Community and future generations."

Our collective civil society statement issued on September 4, when we disassociated ourselves with deep concern from the outcomes of the World Summit on Sustainable Development was simultaneously and declaration of our resolve and commitment.

> "We celebrate our common resolve to strengthen the diversity of human cultures and the integrity of our Planet Earth.
> We reaffirm that 'another world is possible' and we shall make it happen."

IV

GLOBALISATION, THE DECAY OF DEMOCRACY AND THE RISE OF TERRORISM, FUNDAMENTALISM AND POLICE STATES

An economics of exclusion creates a political culture of exclusion. Non-democratic economic systems that centralise control over decision-making and resources and displace people from productive employment and livelihoods create a culture of insecurity. Fundamentalist, extremist and excluding politics emerges to fill the void left by the collapse of economic democracy and the growth of economic security. Instead of identifying the root causes of economic insecurity in the global economy, every policy decision is translated into the politics of "we" and "they". "We" have been unjustly treated, while "they" have gained privileges. Globalisation is creating a global culture of insecurity and insecure people can be made afraid of the "other" more easily.

Destruction of resource rights and erosion of democratic control of natural resources, the economy, and means of production undermine cultural identity. With identity no longer coming from the positive experience of being a farmer, a craftsperson, a teacher, or a nurse or from the security of national sovereignty, culture is reduced to a negative shell where one identity is in competition with the "other" over scarce resources that define economic and political power. Positive identities mutate into negative identities— "I" am not the "other" and annihilation and extinction of the other is necessary for my security and survival. Politics emptied of an economics of welfare becomes a negative political and hatred and division on basis of race, caste and religion.

The rise of Jean Marie LePen in France is an illustration of how the culture of insecurity created by globalization fuels xenophobia. LePen has a slogan of "French First" and he sees insecurity as the most severe problem, but he does not identify the erosion of French security with globalization as Jose Bove does. Instead his attempt is to "link insecurity and immigration." It is not the removal of borders for foreign investment, foreign corporations which he sees as creating threats to French identity, culture and jobs. His exclusive focus is on immigrants. If barriers against people are not erected, according to LePen France will be submerged, it will disappear.

It is the WTOs and World Banks that create the LePens in France, Fortuyns in Netherlands, Haiders in Austria and the Narendra Modis in India. There is in fact a comfortable partnership between the supporters of globalization and the promoters of the politics of hate. By keeping people's energies diverted from issues of basic needs and economic democracy, xenophobia and communalism help keep an unjust and inequitable economic order in place. During the worst violence since India's Independence, both GM crops and a new Patent Act were cleared. Corporations gain from globalization and its fall out in terms of social disintegration.

I believe a new politics of hatred and intolerance is arising from the growing economic insecurity and a sense of shrinking space for survival. Simultaneously, representative democracy is loosing its base in economic democracy as decisions move out of countries into global institutions like World Bank, IMF and WTO and boardrooms of global corporations. Politicians committed to ensure people's basic needs are moving to political agendas of exclusion to garner votes and stay in power. People's economic security and democracy are both being systematically killed by the forces unleashed by globalization. Democracy emptied of economic freedom and ecological freedom becomes a potent breeding ground for fundamentalism and terrorism.

Over the past two decades, I have witnessed conflicts over development and conflicts over natural resources mutate into communal conflicts, culminating in extremism and terrorism. My book *Violence of the Green Revolution* was an attempt to understand the ecology of terrorism. "The Harvest of Rage" drew similar links between the Oklahoma bombing and the U.S. farm crisis, and how it creates fertile ground for extremist fundamentalist ideologies and actions. Our international solidarities, our national sovereignties are evaporating and being replaced by the narrowest conceivable sense of who we are.

Centralized economic systems also erode the democratic base of politics. In a democracy, the economic agenda is the political agenda. When the former is hijacked by the World Bank, the IMF, or the WTO, democracy is decimated. The only cards left in the hands of politicians eager to garner votes are those of race, religion, and ethnicity, which subsequently give rise to fundamentalism. And fundamentalism effectively fills the vacuum left by a decaying democracy. Economic globalization is fuelling economic insecurity, eroding cultural diversity and identity, and assaulting the political freedoms of citizens. It is providing fertile ground for the cultivation of fundamentalism and terrorism. Instead of integrating people, corporate globalization is tearing apart communities.

Globalization is creating negative economies, negative politics and negative identities. Rejuvenating, deepening, widening democracy has become a survival imperative for the human species. Reinvention of freedom in our times requires freedom from fear, freedom from violence, freedom from denial of basic needs, freedom from non-sustainable and unethical production, trade and consumption patterns. It requires a shift from negative economies, politics and culture to positive life enhancing positive economies, positive politics and positive identities.

Instead of addressing the root causes of terrorism and fundamentalism in the growth economic insecurity and collapse of economic democracy by ensuring people's needs are met and their livelihoods protected, states across the world are equipping themselves with laws to shut down democracy and freedom in the name of fighting terror.

Whether it is the Patriot Act in the US, Prevention of Terrorism Act in India (POTA), or the Anti-Terrorism, Crime and Society Act (ATCSA) of the UK, new laws created after September 11, 2001 are not just laws against terrorists — they are also laws against citizens' democratic defence of their fundamental freedoms that are being trampled upon by the forces of globalization.

Fear and violence are currently the dominant forms of human expression. Rule through fear and violence are becoming the dominant mechanism for governance. In another period, it would have been described as the rise of fascism and totalitarianism with the totalitarianism of corporate control over markets combining with totalitarianism of militarized states, taking away from people their fundamental rights and freedoms.

Earth Democracy

From Life Destroying to Life Preserving Cultures

Why are we as a species destroying the very basis of our survival and existence? Why has insecurity been the result of every attempt to build security? How can we as members of the earth community reinvent security to ensure the survival of all species and the survival and future of diverse cultures? How do we make a shift from life annihilating tendencies to life preserving processes? How do we from the ruins of the dominance of culture of death and destruction build cultures that sustain and celebrate life?

A major source of threat to our ecological survival and growing culture of insecurity is the rule and domination by abstract constructions, and a denial of the real, the concrete, the life giving. This "escape" from our biological species being is historically rooted in the Cartesian/Newtonian divide between mind and matter, between objective and subjective, between primary and secondary qualities. In the reductionist mechanistic world view, the constructed has primacy and is more real than reality itself. This domination of abstract construction over lived reality is based on division and separation, decontextualization and disembeddedness and blindness to the disintegration that result from separation of that which is interconnected. Atomization has become the dominant thought and dominant practice. The false assumption of separability based on abstraction allows the emergence of life threatening technologies like genetic engineering, and terminator seeds. It allows the dominance of corporations, a legal fiction, over the lives of real people and citizens. It allows the destruction of real wealth such as soil, water, biodiversity, good food, rich cultures for the creation of fictitious wealth of more than three trillion dollars a day which is nearly a hundred fold more than the real goods and services it can command.

Closely linked to the rule and reification of abstraction are dominant traits which threaten life in its diversity, self-organisation and self-renewal—the monoculture of the mind and the law of the excluded middle. The monoculture of the mind pushes to oblivion and extinction of biological and cultural diversity which are the very preconditions of ecological and cultural security. The law of the excluded middle becomes the basis of the legitimization of exclusion of ecocide and genocide. It shuts out in between species in nature and culture. It denies the existence of biodiversity on farms, and food from forests.

Once we break free of the mental prison of separation and exclusion and see the world in its interconnectedness and non-separability, new alternatives emerge. Despair turns to hope. Violence gives way to non-violence. Scarcity transforms into abundance and insecurity to security. Globalization has shrunk our humanity. It has replaced the diverse cultures of conservation and compassion with a global monoculture of consumerism. It has pitted community against community, neighbour against neighbour, and faith against faith. Globalization, a paradigm based on competition and war, has created a world of many wars and multiple conflicts.

We need once more to feel at home on the earth and with each other. We need a new paradigm to respond to the fragmentation caused by various forms of fundamentalism. We need a new movement which allows us to move from the dominant and pervasive culture of violence, destruction and death to a culture of non-violence, creative peace and life. That is why in India we started the Earth democracy movement.

Earth democracy is based on creating living economies that protect life on earth and provide basic needs and economic security to all. It is based on living democracy which is inclusive. The Earth Democracy Movement is a commitment to go beyond the triple crisis of economic injustice and inequality, ecological non-sustainability and the decay of democracy and the rise of terrorism.

Earth democracy provides an alternative worldview in which humans are embedded in the Earth family, we are connected to each other through love, compassion, not hatred and violence and ecological responsibility and economic justice replaces greed, consumerism and competition as objectives of human life.

In earth democracy economy, politics and society move from negative systems that benefit a few in the short run to positive systems which ensure that the fundamental right to life of all species and all peoples are defended and guaranteed. The maintenance of life in its diversity and integrity rather than limitless extraction of profits through monopolies over biodiversity and water and all vital resources is the basis of relationships in Earth democracy.

Earth democracy transforms our mind and our actions, and liberates us from patterns of thought and paradigms which have pushed us to our contemporary predicament. It helps address the common roots of problems that are defined separately as economic, ecological and political. Exclusivist monocultural modes of dominant thinking are leading to:

(1) the destruction of resources and the creation of monopolies over land, biodiversity, water and food;
(2) the deepening of poverty and the exclusion of millions from livelihoods and economic security; and
(3) the destruction of democracy, peace and cultural diversity.

Earth democracy enables us to make mind shifts that are conducive to our meeting our needs without destroying other species and improving human welfare while ensuring welfare of all beings. In India, we pray: "Let all beings be happy".

Earth democracy embodies principles that enable us to transcend the polarization, divisions and exclusions that are putting the economy against ecology, development against environment, people against the planet and against one another in a new culture of hate. It is symbolized in Hindus visiting a Muslim shrine on their pilgrimage to Sabarimala, and Wasiffudin Dagar a Muslim singer praying to Durga and Shiva, keeping the ancient Dhrupad tradition alive for a composite culture. It is symbolized in farms rejuvenating biodiversity, and species acting in mutuality to benefit one another.

Earth democracy recontextualises humans as one member of the Earth family (*Vasudhaiva Kutumbkam*), and diverse cultures in the mosaic of cultural diversity which enriches our lives. Reembedding humans in the ecological matrix of biological and cultural diversity reopens spaces for sustainability, justice and peace by reorganizing relationships restructuring constellations of power and revitalizing freedom and democracy.

We are being ruled by terror and greed, fear and insecurity. As we face the double closure of spaces by corporate globalization and militarized police states, by economic fascism aided by political fascism, our challenge is to reclaim our freedoms and the freedoms of our fellow beings. Reclaiming and recreating the indivisible freedom of all species is the aim of the Earth Democracy Movement. The Earth Democracy Movement embodies two indivisibilities and continuums. The first is the continuum of freedom for all life on earth, and all humans without discrimination on the basis on gender, race, religion, class and species. The second is the continuum between and indivisibility of justice, peace and sustainability — without sustainability and just share of the earth's bounties there is no justice, and without justice there can be no peace.

Corporate globalization ruptures these continuities. It establishes corporate rule through a divide and rule policy, and creates competition and conflict between different species and peoples and between different aims. It transforms diversity and multiplicity into oppositional differences both by breeding fundamentalisms through spreading insecurity and then using these fundamentalisms to shift humanity, focus and preoccupation from sustainability and justice and peace to ethnic and religious conflict and violence.

Earth democracy is the democracy of all life, not just humans, definitely not just humans privileged through class, race, gender and religion. Since other species do not vote, they cannot lobby, and they have no purchasing power in the market place, earth democracy creates an obligation on us as humans to take their well being into account. As His Holiness the Dalai Lama said on his 60th birthday, "all beings have a right to well-being and happiness. We have a duty to ensure their well-being". This creates human responsibility as trustees and stewards, instead of the dominant notion of mastery, control and ownership.

Earth democracy privileges diversity in nature and society in form and in function. When the intrinsic worth and value of every life form and even human is recognized, biological diversity and cultural diversity flourish. Monocultures result from exclusion and dominance of species, one variety, one race, one religion. Monocultures are an indication of coercion and loss of freedom. Freedom implies diversity. Diversity signifies freedom.

Earth democracy also nourishes diversity by going beyond the logic of exclusion of apartheid, of "us" and "them" of either/or, of the law of the excluded middle. It is in the included middle that diversity and creativity flourishes in nature and in culture. The law of the included middle also implies multifunctionality, the logic of "and" of inclusion. It transcends the false polarization of wild *vs* cultivated, nature *vs* culture, or even the false clash of cultures. It allows for the forest farm and the farmed forest, it recognizes that biodiversity can be preserved and also support human needs.

Through diversity replacing monocultures, and multi-dimensionality replacing one dimensional system, the negative economics of scarcity creation can be replaced by the positive economics of mutually shared abundance and guaranteed provision of basic needs and access to vital resources. Gandhi's concept of *Swadeshi*—of economic freedom and economic democracy is at the core of Earth democracy.

Earth democracy puts responsibility and duties at the core of our relationships, with rights flowing from responsibility instead of dominant paradigm of rights without responsibility and responsibility without rights. The separation of rights and responsibility is at the root of ecological devastation and gender, class inequality. Corporations that earn profits from chemical industry or from genetic pollution resulting from GM crops do not have to bear the burden of that pollution. The social and ecological costs are externalized and borne by others who are excluded from decisions and from benefits.

Earth democracy is based on those who pay the price having a say and those who carry responsibility having the rights. This creates the need for direct or basic democracy. On the one hand this implies decisions moving downwards, from global institutions and centralized governments to local communities. On the other hand it implies a shift in our interpretation of sovereignty.

Rights to natural resources for maintaining life are natural rights. They are not given by States, nor can they be extinguished by States, the WTO or by corporations, even though under globalization, attempts are being made to alienate people's rights to vital resources of land water and biodiversity.

Earth democracy shifts the constellation of power from corporations to people, and rebalances the role and functions of the state which is increasingly taking on undemocratic forms. In the dominant constellation, non-sustainable and unjust economics are being kept in place by undemocratic governments. The erosion of economic and political democracy is giving rise to fundamentalist cultures: Old divisions between have and have nots are mutating into new polarizations of the "lives and live nots", as millions are robbed of their very right to stay alive. The economic "apartheid" between the "lives and live nots" is being translated into the genocidal tendencies of ethnic cleansing.

Earth democracy creates sustainable and just economics, governed by democratic and accountable systems. Cultural and biological diversity is protected. Earth democracy is about life, and natural rights to the conditions of staying alive. It is everyday life and decisions and freedoms related to everyday living — the food we eat the clothes we wear, the water we drink. It is not just about elections and casting votes once in 3 or 4 or 5 years. It is a permanently vibrant democracy. It combines economic democracy with political democracy and ecological democracy. It creates positive economies, positive politics, and positive identities. It creates security, and hence the conditions of peace.

Earth democracy is not dead, it is alive. Under globalization, democracy even of the shallow representative kind is dying. Governments everywhere are betraying the mandates that brought them to power. They are centralizing authority and power, both by subverting democratic structures of Constitutions and by promulgating ordinances that stifle civil liberties. The September 11 tragedy has become a convenient excuse for anti-people legislation worldwide. Politicians everywhere are turning to xenophobic and fundamentalist agendas to get votes in a period when economic agenda have been taken away from national levels and are being set by World Bank, IMF, WTO and global corporations, and parties loose elections because of the economic betrayal of their people.

The Earth democracy movement is about living rather than dead democracy. Democracy is dead when gcvernments no longer reflect the will of the people but are reduced to anti-democratic unaccountable instruments of corporate rule under the constellation of corporate globalization as the Enron and Chiquita case make so evident. Corporate globalization is centred on corporate profits.

Earth democracy is based on maintaining life on earth and freedom for all species and people. Corporate globalisation is based on privileging the logic of competition. Earth democracy is based on cooperation. Corporate globalization operates to create rules for the global, national and local markets which privilege global corporations and threaten diverse species, the livelihoods of the poor and small, local producers and businesses.

Earth democracy operates according to the ecological laws of nature, and limits commercial activity to prevent harm to other species and to people. Corporate globalization creates poverty and threatens peace. Earth democracy creates an inclusive prosperity and through it creates peace. Corporate globalization destroys cultural and biological diversity. Earth democracy is the protection of diversity in nature and society.

Corporate globalization is exercised through centralising, destructive power. Earth democracy is exercised through decentralized power and peaceful coexistence. Corporate globalization globalizes greed and consumerism. Earth democracy globalizes compassion, caring and sharing.

This shift is also an ecological imperative. As members of the earth family, *Vasudhaiva Kutumbakam*, we have a share in the earth's resources. Rights to natural resources for needs of sustenance are natural rights. They are not given or assigned. They are recognized or ignored. The eminent domain principle inevitably leads to the situation of "all for some"—corporate monopolies over biodiversity through patents, corporate monopolies on water through privatisation and corporate monopolies over food through free trade.

The most basic right we have as a species is survival, the right to life. Survival requires guaranteed access to resources. Commons provide that guarantee. Privatization and enclosures destroy it. Localization is necessary for recovery of the commons. And Earth democracy is the movement to relocate our minds, our production systems and consumption patterns from the poverty creating global markets to the sustainability and sharing of the earth community. This shift from global markets to earth citizenship is a shift of focus from globalization to localization of power from corporations to citizens.

Resisting the privatisation of biodiversity through IPRs, the privatisation of water through structural adjustment programmes and trade in services and corporatisation of food and agriculture needs a combination of strategies at local, national and global levels and a shift in the constellation of the power and rights of states, corporations and citizens.

Privatisation based on exclusive rights of corporations to vital resources like biodiversity and water is an enclosure of the commons. Reversal of these enclosures requires a recovery of the commons through a combination of actions at their levels.

(1) At the local level, the recovery of the commons needs the strengthening and assertion of local community rights and people's sovereign and natural rights to vital resources such as water and biodiversity.

(2) At the national level, the recovery of the commons requires recognition of local community rights and a reinvention of sovereignty, and a shift from the state functioning on the doctrine of eminent domain to states functioning on the public trust doctrine.

(3) At the global level, the recovery of the commons requires a movement of people to keep water and biodiversity beyond monopoly, ownership and commodification, which in turn prevents patenting of life forms and privatisation of water. These principles need to be enshrined in international law and policy. They become the source of popular democratic pressure reform WTO and the World Bank—to implement the review of TRIPs in which countries of the South are calling for an exclusion of life forms from patentability and to review structural adjustment programmes which impose export led agricultural strategies and policies of water privatisation.

The citizen treaties to defend water and biodiversity as commons will have democratic power and substance to the extent they reflect the recognition and strengthen local community rights at the global level. Global commons not built from or based on local commons is an ecologically and democratically fraudulent category. The global commons is merely a recognition and reinforcement for local community rights. It is not the level at which rights are exercised or assigned.

Since sovereignty based on the doctrine of eminent domain is becoming the conduit for global usurpation of people's resources, and undermining of people's sovereign rights, reclaiming the biodiversity and water commons must go hand in hand with reclaiming sovereignty, and redefining a new partnership between people and governments on the basis of subsidiarity and the public

	Commons	*Privatisation Regimes*
Global	Treaties on commons reflect commitment to share, recognition of local community rights as highest level of rights to water and biodiversity. Reform of TRIPs, GATS and WTO to ensure the people's sovereignty over biodiversity, food and water.	TRIPs for privatisation of biodiversity, GATS and SAPs for privatisation of water. Private monopoly rights of corporations as highest level of rights. No recognition of community rights
National	States function on the doctrine of public trust. Respect and recognize local communities as the highest competent authority, recognize community rights and people's sovereignty.	States function on doctrine of eminent domain. Transfer common property resources to corporations through privatisation laws and policies.
Local	Local communities have sovereign rights conserve, share and sustainably use commons, excluding no one, letting no one exclude. Localization of economics improves livelihood security and ecological security.	Local communities left politically, ecologically and economically disenfranchised and their access to their own resources block by IPRs and privatisation regimes.

trust doctrine. The reclamation of sovereignty embodies Gandhi's concept of *Swaraj* or self-rule.

The economic, ecological and social crises resulting from corporate globalisation are inviting a new way of thinking and being on this planet. A new worldview in which it is not greed but compassion which is globalised, a new consciousness in which we are not reduced to consumers of globally traded commodities if we are privileged and to narrow fragmented one-dimensional identities based on colour, religion or ethnicity, but experience our lives as planetary beings with planetary consciousness, mindful and aware of what our actions, our consumption cost other humans, other species and future generations and connected to all in a common fabric of life.

	Corporate Globalization	*Earth Democracy*
Aim of Human life	Profits, Accumulation, Consumerism.	Maintenance of life on earth, now and in the future. Improvement of well-being and happiness of all beings.
Axis of Global Integration	Global Markets	Ecological processes. Our common humanity and planetary consciousness.
What Disintegrates as a result	Disintegration of local economies, local cultures, ecosystems, ethical basis of life.	Unjust rule, non-sustainable lifestyles.
Security	Military	Ecological, economic, social and cultural.
Dominant Tendencies	Cruelty Greed Fear of everything alive and autonomous ownership. Control of everything and everyone. Exclusion Exploitation Live and live not Monocultures Monopolies Separation Fascism of market and fundamentalism.	Compassion Giving Love for everything alive Belonging, not owning Inclusion Conservation Live and let live Diversity Sharing Inter-relationship Earth democracy

Beginning with people's everyday actions Earth democracy offers a potential for changing the way governments, intergovernmental organizations and corporations operate. It creates a new paradigm for global governance while empowering local communities. It creates the possibility of strengthening ecological security while improving economic security. And on the foundations of ecological and economic security it makes societies immune to the virus of communal hatred and fear.

Earth democracy offers a new way of seeing in which everything is not at war with everything else but through which we can cooperate to create peace, sustainability and justice in our violent and volatile times.

EARTH DEMOCRACY PRINCIPLES OF JUSTICE, SUSTAINABILITY AND PEACE

Ecological Democracy—Democracy of all Life

We are all members of the Earth Community. We all have the duty to protect the rights and welfare of all species and all people. No humans have the right to encroach on the ecological space of other species and other people, or treat them with cruelty and violence.

Intrinsic Worth of all Species and Peoples

All species, humans and cultures have intrinsic worth. They are subjects, not objects of manipulation or ownership. No humans have the right to own other species, other people or the knowledge of other cultures through patents and other intellectual property rights.

Diversity in Nature and Culture

Defending biological and cultural diversity is a duty of all people. Diversity is an end in itself, a value, a source of richness both material and cultural.

Natural Rights to Sustenance

All members of the Earth Community including all humans have the right to sustenance—to food and water, to safe and clean habitat, to security of ecological space. These rights are natural rights, they are birth rights given by the fact of existence on earth and are best protected through community rights and commons. They are not given by states or corporations, nor can they be extinguished by state or corporate action. No state or corporation has the right to erode or undermine these natural rights or enclose the commons that sustain all through privatisation or monopoly control.

Earth Economy is Based on Economic Democracy and Living Economy

Earth democracy is based on economic democracy. Economic systems in Earth democracy protect ecosystems and their integrity; they protect people's livelihoods and provide basic needs to all. In the earth economy there are no disposable or dispensable species or people. The earth economy is a living economy. It is based on sustainable, diverse, pluralistic systems that protect nature and people, are chosen by people, for the benefit of the common good.

Living Economies are Built on Local Economies

Conservation of the earth's resources and creation of sustainable and satisfying livelihoods is most caringly, creatively and efficiently and equitably achieved at the local level. Localization of economics is social and ecological imperative. Only goods and services that cannot be produced locally, using local resources, local knowledge should be produced non-locally and traded long distance. Earth democracy is based on vibrant, resilient local economies, which support national and global economies. The global economy does not crush and destroy local economies.

Living Democracy

Earth democracy is based on local living democracy with local communities, organised on principles of inclusion and diversity and ecological and social responsibility having the highest authority on decisions related to the environment and natural resources and to the sustenance and livelihoods of people. Authority is delegated to more distant levels of governance on the principle of subsidiarity. Earth democracy is living democracy.

Living Knowledge

Earth democracy is based on earth centered and community centred knowledge systems. Living knowledge is knowledge that maintains and renews living processes and contributes to health of the planet and people. It is also living knowledge in that it is embedded in nature and society, is not abstract, reductionist and anti-life. Living knowledge is a commons, it belongs collectively to communities that create it and keep it alive. All humans have a duty to share knowledge. No person or corporation has a right to enclose monopolize patent or exclusively own as intellectual property living knowledge.

Balancing Rights with Responsibility

In Earth democracy, rights are derived from and balanced with responsibility. Those who bear the consequences of decisions and actions are the decision-makers.

Globalizing Peace, Care and Compassion

Earth democracy connects people in circles of care, cooperation and compassion instead of dividing them through competition and conflict. Earth democracy globalizes compassion, not greed, and peace, not war.

SECTION–II

DECENTRALISATION AND DEVELOPMENT

Living Democracy

Earth democracy is based on local living democracy with local communities, organised on principles of inclusion and diversity and ecological and social responsibility having the highest authority on decisions related to the environment and natural resources and to the sustenance and livelihoods of people. Authority is delegated to more distant levels of governance on the principle of subsidiarity. Earth democracy is living democracy.

Living Knowledge

Earth democracy is based on earth centered and community centred knowledge systems. Living knowledge is knowledge that maintains and renews living processes and contributes to health of the planet and people. It is also living knowledge in that it is embedded in nature and society, is not abstract, reductionist and anti-life. Living knowledge is a commons, it belongs collectively to communities that create it and keep it alive. All humans have a duty to share knowledge. No person or corporation has a right to enclose monopolize patent or exclusively own as intellectual property living knowledge.

Balancing Rights with Responsibility

In Earth democracy, rights are derived from and balanced with responsibility. Those who bear the consequences of decisions and actions are the decision-makers.

Globalizing Peace, Care and Compassion

Earth democracy connects people in circles of care, cooperation and compassion instead of dividing them through competition and conflict. Earth democracy globalizes compassion, not greed, and peace, not war.

7

Panchayati Raj Institutions and Human Rights in India

GEORGE MATHEW

Introduction

India had, from ancient times, developed a number of systems of community-based management of local affairs. In most of the country these institutions were known as panchayats, which means, literally, a council of five persons. Their functions bordered on local governance akin to what was developed in other countries during their agrarian phases like the Russian *mir*, German *mark* and the medieval *manor* of England. However, in most parts of India, the panchayat system was based on the age-old caste system, social status and family. During British rule in India, in the latter part of 19th century the local self-government concept was introduced first in the town areas and later in the villages.[1] Since then, it took more than hundred years for the local self-government bodies to become part of the Indian Constitution. These bodies are termed panchayats,[2] but are now democratic institutions with new content. With the coming into being of the new generation of panchayats from the early 90s it is widely believed that tremendous possibilities have been opened up in the areas of decentralization, development, social justice, people's participation and grassroots democracy. How does the new phase of decentralization affect the human rights situation in India?

Human rights cover a broad spectrum of ideas and concepts, which are predominantly rooted in western political thought. There are numerous charters and agreements that have been signed by nations to protect the rights of the citizens of their respective countries. According to the Universal Declaration of Human Rights, human rights constitute both civil and political rights (Articles 1 to 21) and economic, social and cultural rights (Articles 22 to 28). In fact, the Universal Declaration reflected the immediate post-war consensus about human rights based on what President Roosevelt described as four freedoms—including the freedom from want—which he wanted to be incorporated in an International Bill of Rights. There was also a consensus in Vienna at the Second United Nations World Conference on Human Rights in 1993, where the "right to development" was recognized as a universal and inalienable right and an integral part of fundamental human rights.[3] But these did not have any significant impact on the character of the Indian state for some time.

In India human rights has to be studied at three levels: *first*, state violations of human rights; *second*, socio-economic factors which work against the rights of the people; and *third*, denial of the right to livelihood and decent living conditions leading to indignity and lack of self-respect for a majority of the people. In more than one sense the new phase of the village councils in India has attracted in one way or the other human rights questions at all the above three levels. Therefore an attempt is made in this paper to analyze all these aspects with the available data and also eliciting views of human rights activists and experts in decentralization and panchayat studies. Although an all-India perspective is taken for this paper, it may be mentioned here that the availability of data from all the states is not uniform.

Significance of the 1992 Constitution Amendment

Although the Indian independence movement, under the leadership of Mahatma Gandhi, had villages and their self-governing system at the centre, when the Constitution of Independent India was written they did not get a place in its main body; only a reference in the Directive Principles of State Policy.[4] Therefore, the states did not take both the urban and rural local bodies seriously. The Indian state was functioning as a federation only at two levels — Union and the States.[5] Administrative units below the district (today India has 594 districts) were not considered a federal tier. Over the years it was felt that without taking the local communities seriously and devolving powers to them, neither the development of the people nor their governance was possible. As a result of campaigns by civil society organizations, intellectuals and progressive political leaders, the Parliament passed on 22nd and 23rd December 1992 two amendments to the Constitution—73rd Constitution Amendment for rural local bodies (panchayats) and 74th Constitution Amendment for urban local bodies (municipalities) making them "institutions of self-governance".[6] Within a year all the states passed their own acts in conformity to the amended constitutional provisions.

As a result of these constitutional steps taken by the Union and State governments, India has moved towards what has been described as 'multi-level federalism', and more significantly, it has widened the democratic base of the Indian polity. Before the Amendments, the Indian democratic structure through elected representatives was restricted to the two Houses of Parliament, 25 State Assemblies[7] and two assemblies of Union Territories (Delhi and Pondicherry). And they had just 4,963 elected members.

Now there are nearly 600 district panchayats, about 6000 block panchayats at the intermediate level and 250,000 gram panchayats in rural India where 72.2 per cent of India's population lives. Urban India, with 27.8 per cent population, has 96 city corporations, 1700 town municipalities and 1900 *nagar* (town) panchayats. Today, every five years, about 3.4 million representatives are elected by the people through the democratic process, out of whom one million are women. Women head about 175 district panchayats, more than 2000 block panchayats and about 85,000 gram panchayats. Likewise, more than 30 city corporations and about 600 town municipalities have women chairpersons. A large number of excluded groups and communities are now included in these decision-making bodies. As the Indian population has 14.3 per cent Scheduled Castes (SC) and 8 per cent Scheduled Tribes (ST), about 660,000 elected members, i.e., 22.5 per cent of the total membership in the rural and urban local bodies will be from scheduled castes and tribes.

Salient Features of the New Local Government

In order to give the local government institutions the necessary status and dignity, certain basic and essential features were enshrined in the Constitution. They pertain mainly to regular elections, representation of weaker and hitherto excluded sections like scheduled castes, scheduled tribes, women, devolution of powers and financial resources aimed at imparting certainty, continuity and strength to them.[8] The main features are: provision for a *Grama Sabha* (village assembly) for each village or a group of villages comprising all the adult members registered as voters; not less than one-third of the total number of seats and posts of chairpersons reserved for women; reservation of seats and offices of the chairpersons for scheduled castes (SCs) and scheduled tribes (STs) in proportion to their population (in this one-third should be women); liberty to the state legislatures to provide reservation of seats and offices of chairpersons in favour of backward classes; specific responsibilities to prepare plans for economic development and social justice in respect of the subjects listed in the Eleventh Schedule;[9] constitution of State Finance Commissions and Election Commissions to ensure financial devolution and elections respectively. The term of the panchayats is five years.

The Argument

After the new generation of panchayats has started functioning several issues have come to the fore, which have a bearing on human rights. The important factor which has contributed to the human rights situation *vis-a-vis* the panchayat system is the nature of Indian society which of course determines the nature of the state. The Indian society is known for its inequality, social hierarchy and the rich and poor divide. The social hierarchy is the result of the caste system, which is unique to India. Therefore, caste and class are the two factors, which deserve attention in this context. At another level it is essential to look into the question: who are the victims of the social system? Who are the victims of the nature (and character) of the state? They are the former untouchables (who now call themselves dalits, which means 'oppressed'), tribal people, women, and the poor. How can the process of decentralization through strengthening the democratically elected local bodies tackle the above human rights issues? Does the decentralization process and the decentralized institutions increase human rights violations or enhance the possibility for respecting and observing human rights? This paper investigates first the social factors as well as denial of the rights to livelihood then those who are at the receiving end and finally the response of the state. In the unique situation of India, caste and class factors are specially taken up for discussion. The paper concludes with an analysis of the present human rights situation in the context of decentralization raising some questions as to what it holds for the future.

Caste

Caste in India is a social phenomenon that is extraordinarily difficult to define because of the diversity of its nature. In the villages the caste system is deep rooted and life is widely affected by it, as caste is "rooted in the religious order and may be thought of as a hierarchy of hereditary, endogamous, occupational groups with positions fixed and mobility barred by ritual distance between each caste".[10] For this paper we take the approach developed by Louis Dumont on the caste system. Dumont considers caste to be integrally connected with Hinduism and which is inconceivable apart from the Hindu context that provides the basic ideological base to its understanding. For Dumont, caste is a stable and powerful social system presenting a value system, which is based on hierarchy and religiously sanctioned concepts of purity and pollution.[11]

How does caste affect human rights? The human rights activist and scholar R.M. Pal observes that the caste system has created impregnable walls between groups of human beings where birth solely determines the social position in society.[12] This social position is whereby one is born into a certain caste because of his/her doings in the previous life. In his view, the caste system is one of the worst forms of societal violations of human rights in India even today. Pal argues that the Manusmriti or the 'Laws of Manu'[13] from where the caste system takes its roots is the most deprecating aspect of Indian tradition. It advocates that the position of women in society can never be independent of men. More so, the caste system denies basic education to the lower castes and women. This ancient tradition has been passed on down the ages and it has a significant impact on the life of the rural people even today. People belonging to the lower castes are forced to live separately, away from the upper castes, mostly in the outskirts of villages. They are often denied the right to vote and they are also forced to work without any remuneration and treated as bonded labourers.[14] Therefore, what one sees is the age-old caste system which is still being practised in its most humiliating form on the one hand and the Constitution of India which provides equality before the law based on democratic principles on the other. Ramendra, a human rights activist and scholar is of the view that the reality lies somewhere between the above two extremes and reiterates that the caste system is a major source of human rights violation in the society.[15] There has been a sharp increase in violent manifestations of casteism in local communities ever since the local government system got strengthened through the Constitution amendments. When the panchayati raj institutions have been seen by the upper castes as the tool for the lower castes to assert their right as individuals living in a democratic polity the latter have become targets of caste based discrimination and violence. This rising unrest at the local level has become a common phenomenon.

It is evident that the upper castes that have been controlling the affairs of the village and the community and the rural economy cannot tolerate the changes that are being brought about by the decentralized democratic institutions. Therefore, from the beginning of the implementation of the panchayat system, tensions, violence and killings have taken place in order to resist the transformation.

The elections to the local government bodies have been the first and foremost point of attack by the casteist groups. From the very first election under the new system, the rights of the lower castes to participate in the democratic process and hold positions were questioned by the upper castes. The classic case is that of a village in Madurai district of Tamil Nadu, a southern state in India.

In Melavalavu, the dominant castes of the area murdered the panchayat president and the vice-president who both belonged to a lower caste, merely because they dared to fight the panchayat elections. When Melavalavu was declared a panchayat reserved for the lower castes in the October 1996 local body elections, the dominant castes resented this and the polls could not be held. The second attempt to hold elections was also foiled by violence and booth capturing. Finally, when the elections were held on December 30, 1996, the upper castes boycotted it. Members of the lower caste were elected as president and vice-president amongst others despite stiff resistance from the upper castes, but they were never permitted by the dominant caste to enter the new panchayat office. Finally on June 30, 1997, the president and vice-president along with three others were murdered in broad daylight; their only crime was that they had been elected through the democratic process. [16]

These kinds of violations continue unabated even today. In the recent local body election in the same state the upper castes are still suppressing the rights of the lower castes to exercise their franchise.[17] Similar incidents have occurred in most of the states. The northern states, which are prone to more caste conflicts, are witnessing human rights violations after the introduction of the new phase of panchayats. There are a number of instances indicating the presence of powerful caste elites that continue to thwart attempts for a constitutional resolution of social justice issues at the village level.[18] The frequent reports on the killings of low caste men, women and children are not only restricted to backward states, where the process of decentralization of power to the local level has not really taken off. Caste violence is part of the social reality in other states as well except in West Bengal, Tripura and Kerala where political consciousness is high.

In the recent panchayat elections in Bihar, over 96 people including a magistrate and several candidates were killed during the polling and more than 40 candidates were murdered in different districts between notification of polling and filing of nominations. Studies have shown that most of these killings were the result of 'caste war'.[19]

Even after duly getting elected, the lower castes are not getting the power and status they deserve. They are made to sit outside the panchayat offices, on the floor while the traditional village headmen occupy the chairs. Even when upper caste groups are committing atrocities against the lower castes, the latter do not have a supportive redress mechanism. It may also be mentioned that the police (law and order machinery) is not under the authority of panchayats. The people belonging to the lower castes are being subjected to unabated atrocities particularly through the connivance and collusion of the state administration and the local police. In many instances, cases are not even registered against the perpetrators (who are mainly the upper castes) by the police who are greatly influenced by the upper castes or majority of whom belong to the upper castes.[20] Therefore, the fact finding report of the collective of concerned writers and intellectuals of Tamil Nadu on the caste riots in Rajapalayam area of Kamarajar district, 1997 has recommended that at least one third of the officials of various ranks in both revenue and police departments must be from the affected sections.

The new era of decentralization is still grappling with caste tensions that exist in its most crude form in the rural areas. Atrocities and human rights violations against the lower castes can be controlled only through a culture of equality of human beings. This can be achieved by human rights education and eradication of illiteracy. The panchayats have a crucial role in this.

The Economic Factor

Poverty is the denial and absence of human dignity.[21] In India nearly 300 million live below the poverty line in appalling conditions of extreme deprivation. Pervasive poverty that is widespread in India is in sharp contrast to the ideals of solidarity, social justice and equity that are embodied in the Constitution of India. Despite the presence of a number of schemes for the upliftment of the rural poor, there has not been much change in poverty levels, over the years. Recent estimates of rural poverty levels show that 26.1 per cent are below poverty line, out of this 27.1 per cent are in rural areas and 23.6 per cent in urban. Nearly half the rural population is still illiterate (50.56%). The illiteracy among rural women is 60 per cent. The literacy rate among the women belonging to the scheduled tribes is 24 per cent as against 45.72 per cent for the all India women's average (2001 Census). On the health front, the situation is far worse. The infant mortality rate is 63.19 per thousand live births and under 5 mortality rate is 98 per thousand live births. The underweight children are 53 per cent. Population with access to sanitation is only 31 per cent. More than half of the children between one to five years in rural areas are under-nourished and 60 per cent of the rural households do not have electricity connection.

According to Alan G. Smith "the laws of choice suffered by the rural poor at the village level, in which uncertainty of attaining even minimal food and health is intertwined with the deprivation of significant choice, has not been the subject of an integrated human rights assessment."[22] This is true of India more than any other democratic country although India took a radical step towards the realization of democratic ideals in 1950, along with addressing "the need to promote a wide range of social opportunities".[23] According to Amartya Sen and Jean Dreze, in fact, the "directive principles of state policy", which supplement hard legislation, go much further than the strict legal provisions. For instance, they urge the state "to secure a social order for the promotion of welfare of the people" as well as to uphold a range of more specific entitlements, from the "right to an adequate means of livelihood" and "free legal aid" to "free and compulsory education for all children" and "the right to work".[24] The local government system was aimed at bridging the widening gap between the constitutional provisions and the economic realities. However, this is not happening the way it should have.

In the initial years of the introduction of the new Panchayati-raj system, the poor in India have become vulnerable to violence and exploitation. However, there are exceptions. In some states like West Bengal, Karnataka and Kerala the issue of poverty has increasingly become a human rights issue and decentralization is seen as an effective tool to address this problem.

In the subjects listed under the Eleventh Schedule pertaining to the panchayats, majority of the 29 subjects are related to economic development. For instance, agriculture, land improvement, minor irrigation and water management, dairy, fisheries, social forestry, small-scale industries, rural housing, fuel and fodder, roads, ferries and waterways, rural electrification, poverty alleviation programmes and so on.

In the Indian context broadly, caste is co-terminus with class. The lower castes and the outcastes are the poorest. Since in the lowest rung, the social and economic factors are intertwined in the community life they face multi-pronged attacks on their rights.

It has become well known that the programmes and development measures handled by the local governments do not reach the poor as the rich and the powerful corner most of it. Corruption in the decentralized institutions has been attracting attention of civil society organizations and the state. Although there is a check and balance system and social audit, the rich corner the benefits and the poor remain where they are. A number of such instances have come to light. Although corruption is prevalent at the higher levels, when it happens at the grassroots level its impact is felt more on the poor and their right to livelihood. Cases of punishing chairpersons of panchayats for mis-appropriation of development funds (Andhra Pradesh), officials for showing huge expenditure under different development schemes in agricultural sector but the targeted beneficiaries never receiving the funds (Assam), suspension of presidents for financial irregularities like spending huge amounts on purchases without proper procedures (Haryana) and massive graft in civic bodies by awarding contract of construction works (Karnataka), are some of the examples reported in 2001.[25] Field studies in one of the advanced states--Maharashtra—has shown that huge sums of money allocated for poverty eradication and rural development are pocketed by the officials and the politically powerful.[26] Thus the poor remain where they are and in some cases their condition deteriorates becoming more vulnerable to human rights violations.

Dalits

In the traditional *varna* system mentioned above, the fifth category is the untouchable or outcaste. Mahatma Gandhi gave them the name *Harijans* which means 'Children of God'. But after independence, members of the group prefer to call themselves *dalits*, meaning oppressed. Constitutionally, they have special rights and today they are known as Scheduled Castes.[27] In fact after the decentralization through the Constitutional Amendment they were at the receiving end more than anyone else. The father of the Constitution of India, B.R. Ambedkar, himself a member of an untouchable caste, had stated that the villages were the ruination of India because a village in India is a den of ignorance, communalism and corruption. What he said fifty years ago is still valid in most of India even after the new panchayat system has been introduced. After the elections, reports from states showed that the human rights of the *dalits* were violated in more than one sense even after strengthening of the local bodies.

The democratic process at the village level in many cases has not given the strength and power to the participants of that process, namely the deprived castes. A study conducted after the 1993 elections in Madhya Pradesh on the beating up of a dalit panchayat member by the police at a meeting where the Chief Executive of the district was present revealed that the Chief Executive Officer (CEO) visited the villages after a case was filed on the event with the Human Rights Commission. It was stated that he asked people not to appear as witness in favour of the *dalit* member. The people were frightened to comment on the issue, as they were afraid of being harassed by the authorities.[28]

The local bodies' elections were a nightmarish experience for the *dalits*. Elections could not be held in four gram panchayats reserved for *dalits* in some districts of Tamil Nadu—because not a single nomination paper could be filed in the face of threats from upper-caste people in these villages. In many areas, *dalit* candidates are still living in terror, because they defied the dominant caste of their villages by filing their nomination papers for different posts in the village councils. *Dalit* voters were prevented from voting in many panchayats. A number of houses and colonies were attacked to intimidate them.

It should be noted that empowering *dalits* and marginalized groups through ensuring their participation in the decentralized mechanism was one of the stated objectives of the Central Act. However, the ground reality reflects some negative trends too. It was observed that high caste Hindu groups resorted to various measures to dilute or sabotage the attempts to empower marginalized groups especially *dalits*. There are instances where high caste groups challenge the reservation for scheduled caste and scheduled tribes in the court of law, and when this attempt fails they announce a boycott of elections. There are also numerous cases of violence against *dalits* to prevent them from contesting elections or to influence them to favour other interest groups. If these efforts also fail and elections do take place, they look for candidates who can be coaxed to carry out the whims and fancies of the dominant castes. On the other hand if somebody out of favour of the dominant caste manages to get elected, they do not cooperate with the person concerned.[29]

Even after coming to positions of power, *dalit* elected representatives are restricted in effective exercise of their leadership. This is more in the case of women *dalit* members who have to face double oppression. Instances are not uncommon where the women *dalit* Sarpanches sit on the floor during the course of the panchayat meetings while the male upper caste members sit on the chairs. Problems also arise when the *Grama Sachiv* (Panchayat Secretary) happens to be from the upper caste. On the positive side it was observed that the presence of a *dalit* sarpanch or *dalit* ward member has greatly contributed to the participation of greater numbers of the *dalit* community in gram sabha meetings. Disillusionment arises when the dalit sarpanches are forced to give priority to activities favouring the upper caste members.

Tribals

The Scheduled Tribes[30] or *Adivasis* (original inhabitants) include around 400 aboriginal communities, mainly inhabiting remote and forested areas of India. They constitute 7.8 per cent of India's population. The 73rd Constitution Amendment's importance was that it aimed at achieving grassroots democracy guaranteeing adequate representation to the marginalized groups like the scheduled castes, the scheduled tribes and women. However, the 73rd Amendment was not automatically applicable to the scheduled areas (geographical area where the *adivasis* are concentrated) because of their unique characteristics and special needs. An amendment act was subsequently enacted in December 1996 titled, 'The Provisions of the Panchayat (Extension to the scheduled areas) Act, 1996'. The scheduled areas and the tribal Areas are specified in accordance with the provisions of Article 244 and Vth and VIth Schedules of the Indian Constitution.[31] The Extension Act is one of the potent legislative measures of recent times, which recognizes the tribal peoples' mode of living, aspirations, their culture and traditions. However, studies to assess the implementation of the Extension Act and to examine as to what extent the 1996 Act was able to establish grassroots democracy in scheduled areas in accordance with the ethos of the tribal people reveal that nothing notable has taken place in these areas and that the condition of the tribals remain more or less what it was before.

It is a sad commentary on the political will of the state leadership that several states, e.g., Rajasthan did not amend their Acts according to the 1996 amendment Act even after the stipulated time. A brief survey of the state Acts shows that the states have tried to fulfil the constitutional mandate half-heartedly and not in its letter and spirit.[32] Some State Acts do not deal sufficiently with important provisions of the Extension Act like ownership of minor forest produce, prevention of alienation of land, control over natural resource, etc. This shows widespread apathy on the part of the state government towards the tribal areas and their resistance to give so much power to the tribals. On the other hand violations of tribal rights take place at regular intervals. In December 2001 in the state of Madhya Pradesh, tribals who were relying on fishing for their livelihood in a reservoir as their sole means of subsistence were up in arms against the state government as they feared that steps were being taken to deny them the right to market their produce.[33] In Gujarat, more blatant violations have taken place recently when the government denied reservation to tribals just 48 hours before the village council elections were announced.[34]

Scheduled tribe men and women who get elected to office are not allowed to function in the decentralized institutions of self-government. Just like the scheduled castes, the tribals also are not treated with dignity by the panchayat bureaucracy. Elected tribal women members face violence and rape if they dare to challenge the authority of the officials or the powerful.

A tribal woman sarpanch was stripped naked while unfurling the national flag on 15th August 1998 (Independence Day) in a district of Rajasthan. In another case a tribal woman *sarpanch* in Madhya Pradesh was stripped naked in a grama sabha meeting because she was not consulting the leader of the dominant caste.[35] Such violations of human rights are everyday occurrence in the tribal areas of India, in spite of powerful legislations for decentralized governance.

Women

When India was under colonial rule it was only the restricted male members who could vote and contest elections while women were totally absent from the political scene. For instance, the Bombay Village Panchayat Act, 1920 categorically stipulated that no person could become an elected member who was a female and that the election was to be held in each village by the adult male residents at a meeting presided over by the assistant or Deputy Collector.[36] Even after independence the Constitution of India did not mention or specifically provide reservation for women's representation in the Parliament or state assemblies.[37] It took nearly forty years for women to find political representation in the formal political institutions. As stated earlier, this was made possible through the 73rd Constitution Amendment Act, which had the landmark provision of reserving not less than one-third of the total number of seats in the local bodies for women. It provided the much needed opportunity for women to actively participate in the decision-making processes of their locality through the political right that was conferred on them through the Central Act. In this new era of

Panchayati Raj, there are now more than one million women representatives elected to the three tiers of panchayats who give more meaning for democratic representation as they become spokespersons of the local community.

Women's political empowerment in the last nine years through the Constitution Amendments has exploded several myths, like the belief that they are passive and disinterested in political institutions; only the well to do, upper strata women will come through reservation; only the kin of powerful politicians will enter panchayats through political connectivity to keep the seats for them; and lastly, most importantly, women are only proxy— 'namesake'—members and they do not participate in the panchayats. Without discounting the existence in panchayats of some women who do fit into this patriarchally oriented framework, one can say that these myths have now been buried.[38] Today the buzzword is that women can do it.

It is widely recognized that decentralization of power to the local bodies and women's proactive participation on a large scale (in the state of Karnataka women's representation in the local bodies has reached 43 per cent and the time is not too far when women may capture 50 per cent of seats) in the management of the local affairs in the villages has enhanced their status and rights. In many states there is greater awareness about gender equality and women's rights through the work of women's organizations and especially where human rights initiatives have taken it as a challenge to protect the interests of women in society.

It has also been proved that wherever women hold positions in local bodies there is greater efficiency and transparency in the running of public affairs. Ms. Gangamma Jayker, president of a gram panchayat in Malgudi district in the state of Karnataka, is a product of reservations in the Panchayati Raj system. She belongs to the scheduled caste category and had the privilege of completing her primary schooling. She was very keen on promoting education and has been running literacy classes for women in the village. On hearing of the Government programme for girls' education, she got the details of the scheme, and followed the procedures to get a school opened in her village.[39]

The State governments and civil society organizations are today recognizing the outstanding women leaders in the *panchayats* by instituting yearly awards.[40] However, there are serious backlashes too from the male dominated patriarchal Indian society. Elected women have become the victims of exploitation, violence and harassment. There are stories from all over the country of the violations of their rights despite the constitutional provisions. The case of a woman councillor of a city corporation in the state of Tamil Nadu is a case in point. The people of Villapuram had no permanent water supply facility and were totally dependent on water that was brought by the corporation tankers. Moreover, this water was sold to the people for a fee that was levied by the local henchmen. Attempts to provide water pipes from a water source to Villapuram were scuttled as the mafia saw the above arrangement more profitable for them. Leelavathy had campaigned during the elections for the sole mission of bringing drinking water to her constituency. With her unstinted pressure on the local bureaucracy, this was almost a reality. But three days after a trial run, armed men murdered her in broad daylight. Leelavathy came to be known as a symbol of the people's struggle for water.[41]

Initially, women were hesitant to enter this whole new political arena, political parties and vested interest groups took advantage of the situation and proxy rule prevailed. Thus the power remained in the hands of the traditionally powerful groups. A new class of *sarpanch patis* also emerged where the husband of the women *sarpanch* managed the affairs of the panchayat, while the women acted only as a rubber stamp. A study in the state of Karnataka has shown that many women elected to the local bodies/panchayats are surrogates for husbands and fathers who could not contest because of reservation. Some were put in place by the wealthy and powerful, for their malleability—a kind of puppet to serve the vested interests while appearing to be an elected representative.[42] A major concern of human rights activists is the prevalence of the two-child norm as a criterion for contesting elections, especially in the states of Haryana, Madhya Pradesh, Rajasthan and Himachal Pradesh, where this rule has come into force. It should be noted here that early child bearing is the norm in rural India, which means that the fertility rate is also high. This restricts many women from coming into the political fray.

Even after being given the space in a democratic process, women belonging to traditionally marginalized groups were at the receiving end of upper caste atrocities. After more than a year of the elections to the panchayats in Madhya Pradesh, there were reports from four districts—Raigarh, Chhatarpur, Raisen and East Nimar—of a lady *sarpanch* being stripped naked, another lady *sarpanch* being gang raped, an *upa-sarpanch* (deputy president) being tortured and a *dalit* panchayat member being beaten up.[43]

The State Response

The nature of a society is reflected in the character of the state. Although the Constitution of India has the ideal of equality and social justice enshrined in it, the ground reality is altogether different. The nature of the ruling party and the coalition also determine policies regarding decentralization and transfer of power to the people at the village level. The experience shows that the constitutional mandate is not implemented in letter and spirit, especially regarding the panchayats and municipalities.

The first instance is postponing panchayat elections on one pretext or the other. Several state governments have not taken the provision of the Constitution to hold elections on the expiry of the five-year term of the panchayats seriously. Article 243-B of the Constitution of India is categorical that there shall be in every State, panchayats at the village, block and district levels and that (i) every Panchayat shall continue for five years from the date appointed for its first meeting and no longer, and (ii) election to constitute a panchayat shall be completed before the expiry of its five year duration or within six months of its dissolution [Article 243 E (1) and (3)]. Political parties are keen to capture the panchayats from the village level itself and the ruling party in the states are afraid of facing the people either midway or at the fag end of their term. It must, however, be said to the credit of India's maturing democracy that every election is unpredictable and the political parties can no longer take the people for granted.

In most cases the opposition parties also join hands with the ruling party to postpone elections because of their fear of facing the panchayat electorate. Political leaders belonging to the opposition parties are vocal about giving powers to the local bodies, but it has been observed that once they are in power, they change colour. In some cases they indirectly sponsor writ petitions in the High Courts to obtain injunctions on the holding of elections. This is a very important aspect of the formal institutions of government themselves denying the people the opportunity to elect their representatives.

The panchayat elections have been completed in all states except in Jharkhand, Arunachal Pradesh, Punjab and Pondicherry, this too after prolonged battles in the courts and successful interventions by civil society organizations. The problem is that the State Election Commissions in some of the states are succumbing to the pressures of the state governments in this regard. However, there have also been exceptions like the states of Orissa and *Andhra Pradesh,* where the State Election Commissions have successfully withstood undue pressure and discharged their constitutional obligations.

The second instance of the state trying to delimit the powers of the panchayats is the emergence of bodies functioning parallel to Panchayati Raj Institutions. In this aspect both the Central and the State governments seem to be competing with each other in creating or promoting parallel bodies. Funds are placed under the disposal of these registered bodies by ministries and departments. The line ministries at the Centre and the line departments in the States also undertake many centrally sponsored or state-sponsored schemes ignoring the panchayats.

An instance of State government manipulating the democratic process was reflected in the scheme called the *Samras Gram* (harmonious village), by the government of Gujarat, under which incentives up to Rs.100,000 will be given to those gram panchayats whose members are elected without contest. Another instance was that of auctioning of seats, where the highest bidder gets the seat. Once this is decided, nobody can oppose him by contesting against him. If anyone defies this, he is likely to suffer physical violence or social ostracism. In a village in Madurai district of Tamil Nadu, a candidate secured the post of panchayat president by bidding for Rs. 560,000. Bidding started from Rs. 10,000 for the post of a ward member. The auction money is usually used at local festivals and on similar occasions.

Such attempts by state governments only weaken the local democratic processes or rather they make a mockery of the whole process. On the one hand they provide an opportunity for the dominant classes/communities to take charge of the whole affairs of the village and on the other hand they deny the opportunity for women, *dalits*, tribals and other marginalized groups to be active participants of the local decision-making processes.

The right of the people to participate in the decision-making processes of their locality is legally mandated as per the 73rd Constitutional Amendment, through the Grama Sabha (village council). On the one hand Grama Sabha is a forum for people in the locality to discuss their local development needs and problems and be an integral part of the planning process. On the other, it also provides a forum for people to monitor the functioning of their representatives, whom they elected to the panchayats, thus ensuring accountability and transparency in panchayat affairs. A major lacuna is that the 73rd Constitutional Amendment while providing for the constitution of Grama Sabhas, fails to detail out the powers and functions of Grama Sabha. This has been left to the respective state governments. This provision has not really empowered the Grama Sabhas, so as to make them significant and efficient. Policies crafted on a foundation of human rights give primacy to participation and empowerment of the poor.

Human Rights, Panchayat Institutions Interface—An Analysis

The decentralization process that has gathered momentum in India in the last one decade or so has deep implications for human rights situation in India. This is particularly so for the villages in rural India. The democratic process has brought people closer in the villages, and they could now take part in the local election every five years and assert their right to vote. The elections in India are a big education process. The rights of the excluded people had been violated over the years owing to lack of democratic system of governance at the community level where they could participate effectively. The system of local self-government as manifested in the Panchayati Raj institutions has taken a leap forward in guaranteeing a life of dignity and respect to the citizen at the local village level. Ideals of social justice based on gender equality and liberty are best pursued at the local level.

In a formal sense, all the States have conformed to the constitutional requirement of ensuring the participation in the PRIs to the hitherto excluded groups (women, *dalits* and *adivasis*) through the system of reservation. The problems of the poor have been sought to be addressed by transferring some of the poverty alleviation and development programs to the panchayats due to the constitutional obligation. By and large women have found representation in the panchayats through the one-third reservations of seats. The *dalits* and *adivasis* have been represented to the extent of their share in the population.

Evidently, formal representation need not necessarily be an indication of participation. Since the new phase of decentralization, there is evidence that some of the worst forms of exclusion that plagued the rural society in India are no longer practiced in a number of states. Elected members sit together and discuss issues in formal and informal meetings. A symbolic participation of all in the village, including the *dalits* and *adivasis* and women does take place at least as a constitutional requirement. This is due to the slow but sure changes in the larger political landscape in India.

Social transformation through a democratic process is not peaceful in India. Therefore, on the other side after India has taken bold steps to strengthen decentralization and local governance system the human rights violations at all levels have gone up. The main reason is that all those who were enjoying the powers and privileges so far are trying to subvert the constitutional mandate overtly or covertly.

This has to be seen from another angle too. In a traditional society any change that has structural implications involves conflict. The conflict of interests is so powerful that it leads to violence, bloodshed and loss of life. Ever since India got independence this has been happening but it did not take on a prolonged bloody character because of the developing democratic system in the country.

Since 1993, in the new generation of panchayats, at least two rounds of elections have been held except in a couple of states. It is ironical that elections in India become an occasion for serious human rights violations. During the election period, the rich try to dominate the poor by buying their votes or keeping the poor as 'vote banks'. In many cases the upper castes stop the lower castes from exercising their democratic rights if they come to know that the poor and disadvantaged will exercise their votes independently. In the process violent incidents take place with many losing their lives. Although it happens even during elections to the State Assemblies and Lok Sabha the violence is more in the local elections as the polling percentage is higher at this level.

Violence has increased at the village levels as political power is the most important instrument that exists at the local level and everyone wants to wield it. Therefore, tensions that have existed earlier mount when those who aspire for power come up against those who resist giving it up. Muscle, money and caste power are worse at the local level during elections. An analysis of this violence shows that whenever political consciousness is low and development is relatively backward the people in those areas are more prone to violence.

It may be stated here that there are no consistent and systematic attempts with a political will to combat casteism. The implementation of the legal provisions has been minimal and utterly insufficient and often the violators go unpunished. The members of the Indian Parliament belonging to the scheduled castes publicly acknowledged the Government of India's unwillingness to enforce legal sanctions against casteism and the continued abuse of lower caste people. They said, "It is a shameful tragedy and irony of fate for the hapless Indians belonging to the scheduled castes and scheduled tribes that inhuman and barbaric treatment is meted out to them by their own countrymen. Sometimes, their women are paraded naked in streets and their children butchered like animals, their hearths and homes are burnt at whim destroying their meagre source of livelihood. The State and its machinery play at best, a helpless mute witness or indifferent analyst or still worse active collaborator."[44]

State Scheduled Castes/Scheduled Tribes Commissions have been set up following the Scheduled Castes and Scheduled Tribes (Prevention of Atrocities) Act of 1989, but the victims are afraid to report caste atrocities for fear of retribution, despite the protection and monetary compensation that the Commissions promise.

Panchayats have, all the same, opened possibilities for bringing to surface most of the things previously swept under the carpet. No more it is hidden or secret. Although Grama Sabha and Grama Panchayat are hotbeds of manipulative politics, they provide a democratic forum to grapple with social and political issues in the open.[45] Such a forum is now available, for the first time, with the constitutional backing.

Here the role of political parties is crucial. The earlier concept of consensus (in effect, consent to whatever the powerful was saying or doing) is giving way to people aligning on party lines to call into question every action that is less than transparent. If one political party becomes protector of the oppressed for whatever reason, another party becomes the guardian of the oppressor. In the local situation, state politics or national level ideology is of little consequence. As of now, open participation of political parties in the panchayat elections is the best way to challenge the age-old autocracy of caste or family.

The mass media, communication technology and spatial mobility have broken the isolation of villages. Incidents even in remote village panchayats are thrown up promptly at the state and national level. The new panchayat system, with all its current weaknesses, has helped to weave the village into the broader social fabric.

The silver lining on the otherwise dark horizon is positive intervention of judiciary upholding the human rights of the downtrodden at the local level. Although, Indian judiciary is notoriously slow, the public interest litigation has been a successful tool to give meaning and content to the local bodies' legislations. There was an instance where a woman belonging to a *dalit* community who was elected as the head of the panchayat had to face retribution by the defeated candidates belonging to the upper caste. The First Information Report (FIR) lodged with the police station by the *dalit* woman president stated that the miscreants looted her house and abused her using derogatory language. A case was filed in the court. The high court refused to quash the FIR and observed that " the caste system in India, based on the feudal occupational division of labour in the past, is today totally outmoded and is a great hindrance to the nation's progress...no doubt, the word *chamar* is a word denoting a certain caste, but the said word is also used in a derogatory sense for persons who are regarded as inferior by the so-called upper caste, and, therefore, it should not be used by the members of the so called upper castes or OBCs [Other Backward Castes] as it hurts the feelings of the *dalits*."[46]

Several elections more to the local bodies are a necessary condition to create a culture of genuine democracy and political participation. There is no doubt that the local governments based on vibrant democracy at the local government level with the support of civil society organization will protect the human rights of the people at all levels. But in a traditional society like India this will take time through the democratic process.

Note : This paper forms part of a larger study: "Decentralisation, local government and human rights: A survey of the issues" by International Council on Human Rights Policy, Geneva. I am grateful to David Petrasek, Coordinator of this international study involving India, Philippines, Burkina Faso, Mali, Chile, Russian Federation and Uganda, for his comments and encouragement to work on this subject.

NOTES

1. Around the trading centers the British rulers constituted municipal corporations as early as 1687 (Madras) and in 1870 Lord Mayo got a resolution passed by his council for decentralization of power to bring administrative efficiency. During Lord Ripon's Viceroyship in 1882, the Government resolution providing for local boards with elected representatives was the watershed.

2. On 22-23 December, 1992, the Parliament of India passed two Constitution Amendments (73rd and 74th) and on 24 April, 1993 they were incorporated as Part IX for the Panchayats and Part IX-A for Municipalities. In December 1996 the Parliament extended the 73rd Amendment to the Schedule V Areas where tribal populations pre-dominate. Gram Panchayats constitute the lowest level in the three-tier local government system. The Panchayat at the village level covers about 2000-5000 population in north India and in southern states 10,000—15,000. The next level is the intermediate (block/tehsil/mandal) Panchayat, constituted at the sub-district level, corresponding to between 40 and 45gram panchayats on an average. The highest level is district or Zilla Panchayat.
3. Arjun Sengupta, 'Right to Development as a Human Right', *Economic and Political Weekly*, July 7, 2001, p. 2527.
4. The Directive Principles of State Policy are not justiciable. Article 40 of the Constitution of India says, "The State should take steps to organize village panchayats and endow them with such power and authority as may be necessary to enable them to function as units of self-government." No State Government took Article 40 seriously.
5. The Constitution of India says that India is a Union of States. The Constitution adopted by the Constituent Assembly on 26 November 1949 envisaged a strong Centre.
6. Article 243 says, 'Panchayat' means an institution of self-government. And 243 G entrusts the State legislatures to "endow the panchayats with such powers and authority as may be necessary to enable them to function as institutions of self-government. It also says that "such law may contain provisions for the devolution of powers and responsibilities upon panchayats" for preparation of plans and their implementation for economic development and social justice.
7. In October 2000 three new states were created making it a total of 28 states today. The new states are Jharkhand, Uttaranchal and Chhattisgarh.
8. See Article 243-A to 243-O and Article 243-P to 243-ZF in Part IX and Part IX-A of the Constitution of India respectively.
9. There are 29 subjects in the Eleventh Schedule applicable for the Panchayats and 18 subjects in the Twelfth Schedule for the Municipalities. They include subjects ranging from education, agriculture, drinking water, rural housing, health and sanitation to poverty alleviation programs, family welfare, small-scale industries etc.
10. Duncanted G. Mitchell, 1979, *A New Dictionary of Sociology*, London and Henley: Routledge & Kegan Paul.
11. See Duncan B Forrester, 1980 *Caste and Christianity* London, Curzon Press, pp. 1-4. On the other hand F.G. Bailey, a noted scholar considers caste as a rigid and extreme form of social stratification. He defines caste as an exclusive, exhaustive and ranked group system, which are closed, and relations, which are organized by the summation of roles; cooperate and do not compete. Bailey looks at caste without attaching any ideological

strings to it and sees no necessary connection with Hinduism or with ideas directly derived from Hinduism.

12. R.M. Pal, "The Caste System and Human Rights Violations", *PUCL Bulletin*, XII, 10:2-4, 1992.
13. Manu according to ancient legacy is known as a lawgiver, lived 3000 years ago.
14. The institution of a *begar* (a labourer from the lower castes, being forced to work without any remuneration) is sanctioned by the *Manusmriti*.
15. Ramendra, "Human Rights and Caste system", *PUCL Bulletin*, January 1993, pp.8-10.
16. George Mathew, "The Meaning of Melavalavu", *The Hindu*, 30 September 1997.
17. *Panchayati Raj Update*, Institute of Social Sciences; Vol.VIII. No.10, October 2001, p.3
18. G.K. Lieten and Ravi Srivastava, *Unequal Partners – Power Relations, Devolution and Development in Uttar Pradesh*, New Delhi, Sage Publications, 1999; pp. 105-141.
19. *Panchayati Raj Update*, Institute of Social Sciences, Vol. VIII, April 2001.
20. Human Rights Watch; *Broken People-Caste Violence Against India's "Untouchables"*; 1999.
21. *Human Rights and Poverty Eradication – A Talisman for the Commonwealth*; 2001, Commonwealth Human Rights Initiative, New Delhi, p. 6.
22. Alan G Smith; Human Rights and Choice in *Poverty--Food Security, Dependency, and Human Rights-Based Development Aid for the Third World Rural Poor*; Praeger Publishers, 1997, vii.
23. Jean Dreze and Amartya Sen, *Democratic Practice and Social Inequality*, Institute of Social Sciences Occasional Series, New Delhi: 2002.
24. *Ibid.*
25. *Panchayati Raj Update*, January-December, 2001.
26. George Mathew, "Maharashtra's Gram Sevak Raj", *The Hindu*, 13 August 2001.
27. The President of India is empowered to draw up a list of castes for special provisions for the protection of their interest. They are called Scheduled Caste (SC).
28. George Mathew and Ramesh Nayak; "Panchayats at Work; What it means for the Oppressed?"; 6 July 1996; *Economic and Political Weekly, Bombay*.pp. 1765-1771
29. *Frontline*, October 26, 2001, pp. 34-35
30. Just as in the case of lower castes, for tribals also, the President of India is empowered to draw up a list for special provisions to protect their interest. They are Scheduled Tribes (STs).
31. The criteria generally followed to specify the Scheduled Areas are; preponderance of scheduled tribes, geographical isolation and general backwardness. The ten states that have been prescribed as scheduled areas are; Andhra Pradesh, Bihar, Jharkhand, Gujarat, Himachal Pradesh, Madhya

Pradesh, Chhattisgarh, Orissa and Rajasthan. The Tribal Areas specified are in Assam, Meghalaya, Mizoram and Tripura.

32. In the Andhra Pradesh Act some of the mandated provisions envisaged in the Extension Act have not been incorporated. The State Act has endowed the intermediate tier with more powers whereas the Extension Act lays down a more vigorous role for the Gram Sabha.
33. *The Hindu*, 14 December 2001
34. The Gujarat government issued a two-part notification amending the Gujarat Panchayat's Act, 1993 dated 23 November 2000 lays down that provisions of sub-clause (a) of sub section 5 of Section 9 of the Panchayat's Act shall not apply to the gram panchayats in the Fifth Schedule areas, where the population of the Scheduled Tribes is less than 25 per cent of the total population of a gram panchayat. The original sub clause provides reservation of panchayat seats for the STs and SCs in proportion of their population to the total population of the village. When this notification is given effect to, reservations for the STs in gram panchayats having less than 25 per cent ST population will be curtailed or even scrapped.
35. Reported in *Panchayati Raj Update,* June and August 1998.
36. Nirmala Buch; "Panchayats and Women", in *Status of Panchayats in the States and Union Territories of India 2000*; New Delhi, Institute of Social Sciences; 2000; p. 34.
37. It should be noted that the percentage of women in the State Assemblies and Parliament of India is very low. The percentage of women in the Parliament is around 8 per cent however; one cannot also assume that this percentage represents the whole women community.
38. Nirmala Buch, *op.cit.* pp. 34-35.
39. Vinod Vyasulu and Poornima; Women in Panchayati Raj: Grassroots Democracy in India? Experience from Malgudi; March 1999.
40. Some of the awardees have done excellent work in raising women's economic status, took campaigns against child marriage, child labour, bringing piped water supply, building health centres, strengthening primary schools and self-help groups and so on.
41. Mythily Sivaraman, "Blow to Goodness", *The Hindu*, May 18, 1997.
42. Vinod Vyasulu and Poornima, *op. cit.*
43. George Mathew and Ramesh Nayak, *op cit.*
44. South Asia Human Rights Documentation Centre (SAHRDC); *Racial Discrimination: The Record of India*, September 2001, pp. 36-37.
45. For details see George Mathew and Ramesh Nayak; *op.cit.*
46. *Panchayati Raj Update*, Februrary 2001.

8

Decentralisation and its Impact on Health in India:
A Review of Evidence

K.S. JAMES

Introduction

There is high level of expectation from the decentralised bodies in India primarily in improving the provision of health services. The provision of public services in general and health in particular has been dismal in the country due to a number of factors such as non-accountability, insensitivity to local needs, corruption etc. Lack of staff and medicine are the common complaint noted from public health centres in the country. Perhaps some of these ill-effects are due to extreme centralisation of the health departments in every state. A decentralised system of government is expected to do better in the provision of these services. Therefore, decentralisation is a welcome change that has taken place in the 1990s through 73rd and 74th Amendments as far as health is concerned.

It is, however, not clear how far decentralisation has affected the provision of health services and thereby the health status of the poor in the country during the last one decade. No serious attempt has been made as yet to systematically document such changes and evaluate their implications on health care. The purpose of this paper is to fill this gap by systematically reviewing the studies on the impact of decentralisation and economic reforms on health.

One of the serious problems in the discussion of health in relation to policy measures is that often this relationship is considered in a very simplistic form and conclusions are drawn on an inadequate scientific basis. Understanding the linkages between sectoral policy reforms and their outcomes on living conditions of the people is very difficult. It is not easy to successfully isolate the effect of policy changes at the household level from a host of other historical and contemporary factors. Shortage of reliable data too adds to this lack of clarity. As a result studies are reduced to mere descriptions. It is, therefore, necessary to bring out the relevance of existing frameworks for analysing the relationship between complex issues like impact of policy measures on health care.

The objective of this paper is to review the broader literature on decentralisation and health care in India. However, in the beginning we will also critically look at the relevance of existing framework to analyse this relationship particularly in the case of decentralisation.

Decentralisation in Health: Concept and International Experience

The rationale for decentralization in health services is that the programmes can be designed with knowledge of the local culture and circumstances. Conceptually, decentralisation is expected to alter the mode of decision-making and address the local complaints effectively because it

- Increases responsiveness to local needs.
- Facilitates mobilization of the underprivileged and community participation.
- Improves the access of the poor to public goods and services (Collins and Greens 1994).

It is important to remember that there is no standard definition of decentralisation in the health sector. Privatisation and transfer of responsibilities to NGOs in health sector are conceptually considered as decentralisation (Qadeer, 2001). Unlike in India, in several countries decentralisation in health sector came on its own and not as an overall package of political decentralisation.

The underpinning principle in providing primary health care was decentralization. Although purely administrative in nature, an element of decentralisation is expected to be an ingredient of the health system in countries, which are part of the Alma-Ata declaration of "Health for all by 2000". In reality, however, health departments have the reputation of being extremely bureaucratic and inefficiently managed in most developing countries (Pokharel, 2000). There are numerous complaints about the health sector like poor service quality, absence of doctors and para-medical staff, unavailability of medicine etc. These complaints are partly due to a very high level of management centralisation and consequent inefficiency.

The available studies evaluating the impact of decentralisation on health across countries provide mixed results (Nayar, 2001; Robalino, *et al.* 2001). Inadequate human resources due to lack of strengthening in lower level management capacity, inadequacy of financial resources at the bottom, poor local administrative capacities, increase in regional disparities etc. are some of the notable drawbacks of decentralisation drawn out of experience from different countries (Collins and Green, 1994; Robalino, *et al.* 2001). According to Standing (1997) there are three major concerns about the decentralisation process: (1) It can increase regional inequality as the wealthier regions are able to get more funds than the poor regions. Evidence from Zambia suggests such a possibility. (2) The transfer of power takes place from the centre to regional elites. (3) The Central Government evades responsibilities by transferring the burden of financing development activities to the local community.

There are several disappointing country experiences on decentralisation (Araujo and Luiz, 1997; Collins and Green, 1994; Standing, 1997). Chinese decentralisation led to market penetration into health services while in Zambia inter-regional disparities widened. In yet another African country, Senegal, the cost of primary care went up substantially after decentralisation. Araujo and Luiz (1997) observed based on the evidence from Brazil that there are three major obstacles in effective implementation of decentralisation policies: (1) The common centralist culture and tradition, (2) the normal staff resistance, and (3) the lack of skills and other weakness of local governments. He found that in the case of Brazil the majority of the local governments were too weak to overcome these three barriers.

The real question, however, is how far these failures are due to failure of decentralisation or due to its tardy implementation? These weaknesses should be attributed to the implementation difficulties in decentralisation rather than the concept *per se*. Bossert and Beauvais (2002) argued that the issue is not whether or not to decentralise but rather how to design and implement better decentralisation policies to achieve national health policy objectives. According to them there were breakdown in decentralisation when poorly designed not because of the failure of the concept *per se*.

Quest for an Analytical Framework

The major lacuna in decentralisation studies relating to health has been the lack of a standard framework to analyse such a relationship. When decentralisation is not specified and understood only in generality, it admits and involves too many possibilities extending at one extreme up to privatisation and thus lacks sufficient clarity. Often the two terms centralisation and decentralisation were discussed as if they were well defined and binary opposites. Although the quest for an appropriate analytical framework to understand the effect of decentralisation in health had long been felt, it was only in the 1990s that some work addressed this issue in greater detail.

WHO Framework

One of the important breakthroughs in understanding the relationship between decentralisation and health was the publication by WHO clarifying the different meanings of decentralisation and their implication for the organisation of health system (Mills, *et al.* 1990). The framework draws largely from the large body of literature on decentralisation that existed in the field of public administration. This study divided decentralisation into four main categories: (1) deconcentration, (2) delegation, (3) devolution, and (4) privatisation.

Deconcentration implies delegation of authority to regional or district offices within the structure. Thus it is only handing over some authority to locally based offices. *Devolution*, on the other hand, takes place by creating or strengthening a sub-national level of government. It involves well-defined geographical boundaries with legal status and with several functions to perform. *Delegation* is transferring responsibility and functions to organisations outside the government structure and indirectly controlled by the government. In some countries, for instance, control of some teaching hospitals is being shifted as part of a separate board although the government will indirectly control the board. *Privatisation* is the other extreme of decentralisation involving transfer of functions to voluntary organisations and both private, profit making and non-profit making enterprises.

Devolution thus implies a much more radical form of decentralisation than other forms, especially deconcentration. It demands not merely the transfer of powers to local level but through a proper political process also. Democratic participation is an inbuilt characteristic of devolution while deconcentration takes place without democratic functioning. Mill, *et al.* (1990) also provided several interesting case studies drawn from different countries. The country experiences revealed that each country had its own experiments with decentralisation which had evolved within a particular historical context. Most of the countries, however, in different times, felt the need to institute organisational reforms favouring one or other forms of decentralisation.

Going by such a classification, many of the nodal experiments, which are often credited as successful decentralisation experiments in India, are either deconcentration or privatisation. Mostly, they are confined to giving more autonomy to hospitals and some sectors (Durgaprasad, *et al.* 2001; Kumar, 2001; Mohanty, 2000; Sen, 2001). Many World Bank funded projects insist on a participatory and client based approach involving both private sector and Non-Governmental Organisations (NGOs) (Gupta and Gumber, 1999). Thus, NGOs had significantly come into the forefront of health provision in many states in India in the 1990s and government had often handed over many hospitals to be run by NGOs.

Recently Karnataka State's health department has initiated a scheme that will involve private medical colleges, voluntary organisations and charitable trusts in the management of primary health centres (*The Hindu* 2002). The experiment in Madhya Pradesh, Rogi Kalyan Samiti, is also known for its community management of a public hospital. In Andhra Pradesh, although no major component of health sector has been handed over to Panchayats based on 73rd Amendment, there had been initiatives to decentralise health care administration and management (Chatterjee, 2001). Various local level committees were constituted to monitor and supervise delivery of health services like Advisory Committees for Primary Health Centres, Hospital Development Committees for Secondary Level Hospitals and Hospital Development Societies for tertiary hospitals.

Although such experiments are often lauded for its successes, it should be considered as an inferior form of decentralisation. Given the fact that Constitution demands delivery of health services in India through the Panchayats and as the elected bodies are already in existence, decentralisation of administration bypassing these bodies cannot be exalted for their mere success. There are criticisms on the ground that such attempts are merely to obtain public support to the idea of user-fee in public hospitals. Many of these decentralised hospitals introduced user-charges with the support of the committees and in many instances the committee manages and utilises these funds for the development of the hospitals.

The WHO framework thus gives a better way of looking at decentralisation in health sector than earlier. However, although the framework brought out the institutional mechanism of decentralisation, it is not in a position to find out its likely impact on health sector. Thus the value is limited to understanding decentralisation process in health than its benefits as such. The framework is only useful for a country comparison. However, in situations like India where political decentralisation has taken place nearly uniformly across states, the framework fails to give any further insights on the decentralisation process and its impact on health. As this framework looks at issues in such generality, no guidance is provided on the kind of tasks that are transferred from one institutional entity to another (Bossert, 1988).

Decision Space Framework

Bossert (1998) proposed an alternative analytical frame expanding the principal-agent framework. The principal-agent framework developed by economists examines the choices made by managers and private corporations. This theory proposes a principal with specific objectives, and agents who are needed to implement activities to achieve them. The principal uses various mechanism of control to ensure that the agents work towards achieving those objectives. Bossert extended this framework using a concept called "decision space". It is a range of effective choice that is allowed by the central authorities (the principal) to be utilised by the local authorities (agents). Decision space is defined for various functions and activities over which local authorities will have increased choice. The choice is measured in a range from narrow to wide.

The functional areas are classified as: (1) finance, (2) service organisation, (3) human resources, (4) access rules, and (5) governance rules. In each of these areas the decision space is characterised by a range—narrow, moderate and broad. The range of choice in each of these functional areas is determined considering different activities. The functional areas and the activities that determine the range of choice is presented in Table 8.1.

This framework had been applied in the case of several countries (Bossert, 1998; Bossert, 2000; Bossert, *et al.* 2000; Bossert and Beauvais, 2002; Bossert and Kumar, 2002). The case studies revealed the extent of choice granted to the local administration in each of these countries. For instance, in a study of four countries, Ghana, Zambia, Uganda and Philippines, the range of choice in most of the activities were narrow in the case of Ghana. Philippines in comparison represented the case of having greatest range of local decision space followed by Uganda and Zambia (Bossert and Beauvais, 2002). Similar studies also were conducted in Latin America (Bossert, 2000) and in Andhra Pradesh (Bossert and Kumar, 2002). The Andhra Pradesh study brought out the low levels of decision space existing in the state at all levels.

Table 8.1: The Functions and Range of Decision Space

Functions	*Range of Choice*		
	Narrow	*Moderate*	*Broad*
Finance Source of revenue Allocation of expenditures Income from fees and contracts			
Service Organisations Hospital autonomy Insurance plans Payment mechanisms Contracts with private providers Required programmes/norms			
Human Resources Salaries Contracts Civil Rules			
Access Rules Targeting			
Governance Rules Facility board Health offices Community participation			

Source: Bossert (1998).

Once the range of choice is given the next question is how it impacts on equity, efficiency, quality and financial soundness. Bossert (2000) also examined this question using data from Latin American countries. The study found that although radical improvements in health system is unlikely through decentralisation process, certain forms of decentralisation would ensure greater equity and better utilisation of services.

The major weakness of this framework is that, unlike in WHO framework, it does not distinguish between different forms of decentralisation. Thus it gives equal weight to all forms of decentralisation even when it is undemocratic. Second, there is lot of subjectivity involved in the analysis. To cite an example, according to this framework if more and more resources are garnered from the local area itself, it is considered as a superior form of decentralisation having wide decision space and higher weight is assigned. In the Indian contexts, regions which are extremely poor have only limited scope for generating resources. They have to depend upon the state government to transfer most of the fund for the health sector. Against this any attempt to impose resources mobilisation strategy would only result in creating higher regional inequality. Finally, although this framework gives a good ground for comparing the performance of different decentralised form of government even quantitatively, it does not tell about the impact of a better decentralised system on the health delivery and outcome. Instead, Bossert (1998) assumed that a better implemented decentralised system improves the health delivery and outcome as well.

Other Frameworks[1]

Other than the two analytical frameworks discussed here there are several other frameworks although not as comprehensive. Economists look at decentralisation mainly in terms of intergovernmental fiscal transfer (Musgrave and Musgrave, 1989). This framework is also applied in the case of health sector (Jack, 2000). The social capital approach developed by Putnam also provides insights on the decentralisation process, in particular, in the geographical and historical context (Putnam, 1993; Bossert, 1998).

Impact of Decentralisation on Health

In the Indian context decentralisation emerged as a political process and was not specific to health sector. Hence the objective is more political than managerial (Nayar, 2001). In India, health is in the purview of state responsibility although there are a number of vertical programmes handled by the Central government. Most of the policy decisions, therefore, take place at the state level. Under the 73rd and 74th Amendments of the Constitution of India, a set of items including health and sanitation (hospitals, primary health centres, dispensaries, family welfare, housing, drinking water etc.) may be entrusted to local self-government bodies. These institutions should also receive funds to carry out these functions. Two important questions, thus, come out of such an exercise: (1) To what extent have various state governments transferred powers and money to the local bodies in India? (2) What is the impact of this decentralisation on heath delivery and health outcome? We will examine both these issues in order.

The Extent of Health Decentralisation in India

Barring a few exceptions, decentralisation process had been weak in India prior to 73rd and 74th Amendments. The available evidences suggest that decentralisation did not embrace the health area significantly even in those states with better track record of decentralisation (Chandran, 1993; Dutta, 1993).

It is deplorable to note that even a decade after 73rd and 74th Amendments, the extent of sectoral and financial decentralisation has been weak in the country. No significant decentralisation of powers has taken place in health sector as well. The amendment thus far helped in providing an effective political decentralisation. The election to the local bodies was held in most of the states with reservation for socially backward section of the society and women. But the success towards effective decentralisation of administrative powers, functions and finances was limited.

It should be remembered that while retaining the discretionary powers of the state government in the devolution of powers and responsibilities to Panchayats, the constitution also demands the states to endeavour Panchayats with such powers and authority as may be necessary to enable them to function as institutions of self-government (Ministry of Rural Development 2001). Though not mandatory, the constitutional amendment also specified 29 subjects including health in respect of which specific schemes along with resources are expected to be transferred to the domain of Panchayats. However, the performance of the state government in transferring powers and resources has been thus far dismal. In those cases where there was a transfer of power, adequate funds and functionaries did not match it. The number of subjects and funds transferred out of the 29 listed in the Constitution by each state is presented in Table 8.2.

Table 8.2: Number of Subjects and Resources out of 29, Transferred to Panchayats by State Governments in India

States	*No. of Subjects Transferred with*	
	Funds	*Functions*
Andhra Pradesh	05	13
Arunachal Pradesh	—	—
Assam	—	—
Bihar	—	—
Jharkhand	—	—
Goa	—	—
Gujarat	—	—
Haryana	—	16
Himachal Pradesh	2	23
Karnataka	29	29
Kerala	15	29
Madhya Pradesh	10	23
Chhattisgarh	10	23
Maharashtra	18	18
Manipur	—	22
Orissa	5	25
Punjab	—	7
Rajasthan	—	29
Sikkim	29	29
Tamil Nadu	—	29
Tripura	—	12
Uttar Pradesh	12	13
Uttaranchal	12	13
West Bengal	12	13

Source: Ministry of Rural Development (2001).

It is clear from the table that even after a decade of decentralisation, many state governments are yet to transfer functions in general and funds in particular to the Panchayats. The exceptions may be the states of Karnataka and Sikkim, which has transferred all the 29 listed subjects and adequate funds to the Panchayats. Maharashtra and Kerala also made significant progress. However, the progress was tardy in many big states in the country.

It should be pointed out that it is highly difficult to pin-pointedly assess the degree of decentralisation taken place in various state government departments merely on the basis of number of subjects transferred. It is the duty of the state governments to ensure that powers are spelt out clearly with specific activities and function under each of these subjects. Thus the above list provides only a general guideline. It is possible that even after the governmental order the line departments exercise considerable powers of supervision and control over the schemes transferred to the Panchayats (Ministry of Rural Development 2001).

For instance, a review of various state acts on the devolution of powers to Panchayats showed that only in Karnataka, Kerala and Madhya Pradesh some attempt is made to ensure Panchayats as self-governing institutions (National Commission to Review the Working of the Constitution 2001). Special efforts are made in these states to eliminate bureaucratic control over Panchayats' functioning. But in states like, Andhra Pradesh, Gujarat, Maharashtra, Orissa, Tamil Nadu and Uttar Pradesh, there were several loopholes and still considerable bureaucratic control exists in the functioning of the Panchayats.

A recent study by the World Bank (2000) on rural decentralisation showed that sectoral decentralization, despite claims by the state governments, is weak in the country. The study looked at five major sectors—primary education, primary healthcare, rural roads maintenance, rural water supply, and agriculture extension—in seven states of India. The states covered in the study are: Andhra Pradesh, Karnataka, Kerala, Madhya Pradesh, Maharashtra, Rajasthan and Uttar Pradesh. Thus all major states having good track record of decentralisation in India in the 1990s except Gujarat and West Bengal are included in the study.

The study found that some schemes in each of these five sectors are implemented with involvement of the Panchayati Raj Institutions (PRI) in these seven states. However, no states have made effective sharing of powers and finances. The study computed a sectoral decentralization index based on a set of questions which were designed to reveal who makes the real decisions in the above 5 key sectors. Figure 8.1 presents the score of seven states in India in order on a scale of 10 and clearly shows that the Indian states perform poorly. Rajasthan has the lowest score while Kerala has performed the best. In between in the order fall the five states of Maharashtra, Andhra Pradesh, Madhya Pradesh, Karnataka and Uttar Pradesh. As all the major states with good track record of decentralisation except Gujarat and West Bengal are included in this study, one would imagine that the performance of other states would be even worse. The study also found a similar picture as far as financial devolution is concerned.

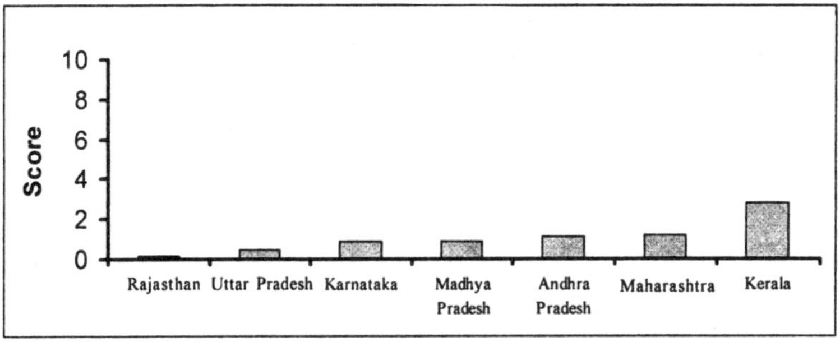

Fig. 8.1: Extent of Sectoral Decentralisation in Seven States in India

Source: World Bank (2000).

A comparison of Indian states with a few other countries depicted Indian states in poor light as far as sectoral and financial decentralisation are concerned (World Bank, 2000). Similar methodology is used to estimate the score. The scores were above five in Philippines, China, Poland, Brazil, and Colombia. Even the neighbouring country like Bangladesh had a better sectoral decentralisation score than many Indian states. On the contrary, the Indian states far exceeded in the political decentralisation compared to many of these countries.

Against this background, it is unlikely that any states in India made significant improvement in the delivery of health services due to decentralisation in the 1990s. Further, the process of devolution of powers had been gradual in many states and occurred only in the second half of the 1990s. Therefore, it is premature to expect any miracle as far as health status is concerned. However, it is possible to make improvement in the delivery of services even during a short period. It would be interesting to look at how far those states which have had better decentralised planning system could benefit in terms of health delivery. The impact of decentralisation in health can be tested by examining its effect either (a) health outcome or (b) health delivery. We will examine both these aspects in relation to decentralisation.

Impact on Health Outcome

Although there are compelling arguments in favour of decentralisation, it is not yet very clear how far such attempts will improve the health status of the people. Ultimately, one of the important objectives of the decentralisation in health sector is to attain a better health status. But studies scarcely address this issue in a serious manner. The qualitative studies, which are commonly undertaken in evaluating decentralisation have helped to understand the pros and cons of decentralization. The magnitude of its impact on health outcomes, however, remains un-quantified.

It is also important to note that health status of the people in a particular region is the result of number of complex historical and contemporary factors. Therefore, it will be misleading to conclude on the effect of decentralisation on health ignoring the historicity of the region. For instance, in the case of Kerala, Soman and Panikar (1993) argued that the power primarily remained centralised till early 1990s. Despite this Kerala achieved a remarkable health status mainly due to equitable distribution of health facilities. This ensured essential health services even to the rural poor in the state. Contrary to this Karnataka and West Bengal were the frontrunners in decentralisation prior to 73rd Amendment. But these states enjoyed much lower health status than in Kerala.

As already pointed out the progress of sectoral decentralisation was uneven across states in India. Some states like Kerala, Karnataka and Madhya Pradesh are known to have made significant progress. Hence, it would be interesting to look at the progress in health indicators of these states in the 1990s. We have presented two health outcome variables infant mortality and immunisation, to get a broad idea on how far states with better decentralised governance performed as far as health status is concerned. The progress of infant mortality rate is considered for the period between 1993-95 and 1998-2000 and immunisation for the period between 1992-93 and 1998-99. The selection of the years is primarily governed by the availability of data. Table 8.3 presents the progress of the states in terms of the two outcome variables infant mortality rate and immunisation of children.

Table 8.3: Infant Mortality and Percentage of Immunised Children in the 1990s in Different States in India.

States	*Infant Mortality*			*All Immunisation*		
	1998-2000 (1)	*1993-1995 (2)*	*Difference 3=(2)-(1)*	*1998-99 (4)*	*1992-93 (5)*	*Different 6=(4)-(5)*
Andhra Pradesh	75	71	-4	59.0	45.0	14.0
Arunachal Pradesh	45	54	9	20.5	22.5	-2.0
Assam	79	80	1	17.0	19.4	-2.4
Bihar	65	72	7	11.0	10.7	0.3
Goa	24	30	6	82.6	74.9	7.7
Gujarat	70	68	-2	53.0	49.8	3.2
Haryana	70	70	0	63.0	53.5	9.5
Himachal Pradesh	64	63	-1	83.4	62.9	20.5
Karnataka	69	74	5	60.0	52.2	7.8
Kerala	14	16	2	80.0	54.4	25.6
Madhya Pradesh	98	107	9	22.0	29.2	-7.2
Maharashtra	58	66	8	78.0	64.1	13.9
Manipur	24	28	4	42.3	29.1	13.2
Orissa	100	110	10	44.0	36.1	7.9
Punjab	57	59	2	72.0	61.9	10.1
Rajasthan	85	89	4	17.0	21.1	-4.1
Sikkim	50	48	-2	—	—	—
Tamil Nadu	58	64	6	89.0	64.9	24.1
Tripura	45	47	2	—	—	—
Uttar Pradesh	88	93	5	21.0	19.8	1.2
West Bengal	55	63	8	44.0	34.2	9.8

Note: All immunisation refers to BCG, measles and three doses each of DPT and polio vaccines. It includes only surviving children in the age group 12-23 months.

Source: Infant mortality rate is taken from various Sample Registration Bulletins and Immunisation is taken from National Family Health Survey (1995) and (2000).

No particular pattern is emerging from the data. Those states with poor instance of decentralisation like Arunachal Pradesh, Bihar and Goa have also recorded good amount of decline in Infant Mortality Rate (IMR). Kerala had a very low level of IMR even by the mid 1990s and expectedly further decline was marginal. In the case of immunisation a better decentralised state, Madhya Pradesh, recorded a decline to the tune of 7 per cent in the 1990s. On the other hand, Kerala, Tamil Nadu and Himachal Pradesh present significant improvement in immunisation indicating no clear relationship with decentralisation.

On the whole, it may be concluded that such simplistic analysis of data linking health outcome with decentralisation ignoring several other important factors would be misleading. Therefore, these results are to be interpreted with extreme caution. Better statistical tools are necessary in linking complex issues like decentralisation and heath outcome. Studies carried out with better statistical techniques revealed a positive impact of decentralisation on health outcome.

The attempt by Mahal *et al.* (2000) using data from a sample of villages in India noted the significant impact of decentralisation on health outcomes. The data used for the study was taken from a survey of human development indicators conducted by the National Council of Applied Economic Research (NCAER) in 1994.Two proxy variables were constructed to measure decentralisation, *viz.*, average annual frequency of local body election in different Indian states during three decades and a dummy variable for states that are known to have made progress towards decentralisation during the period 1970-94. Both these variables had a significant impact on the level of child immunisation and in reducing infant and child mortality rate.

Another attempt to find out the impact of decentralization on health outcome was made by Robalino *et al.* (2001). They tried to measure the impact of decentralization on health in a cross country analysis using infant mortality as the outcome variable. The effect of decentralisation is measured as the ratio between expenditures managed by local government and expenditures managed by Central Government. The panel data used for the analysis included data from both low and high income countries covering the period

1970-95. It is not clear from the report whether India is also included in the study. The result of the analysis revealed a significant positive impact of decentralisation in improving health outcome.

Empirical analysis on the impact of decentralisation on health outcome is not easy, as it demands extensive data requirements and complex statistical tools. This may be the reason for rarity of such analysis. The above studies conceptualised decentralisation in a very narrow sense of political decentralisation. The measurement of decentralisation was using instrumental variables. The former study by Mahal *et al.* (2000) concerning specifically to India was carried out using data for the year 1994. This was the early years after the new initiatives of decentralisation in the country. Even then, curiously, the study found significant positive impact of decentralisation on health.

Although plausible, linking decentralisation efforts to health outcome are difficult due to several reasons. First as noted above health is also a function of several other factors. Controlling these factors statistically, some of which are historical in nature, would be difficult in any analysis. Second, the measurement of decentralisation is troublesome and the dummy variables included in the model give only an indication but not the magnitude of influence. Thirdly, such analysis also demands extensive data requirements. Thus, the findings of the above studies, although relevant, need to be interpreted cautiously.

Impact on Health Delivery

Perhaps, an assessment on the impact of decentralisation on health delivery is comparatively easy. One of the major arguments in favour of health sector decentralisation has been to increase the efficiency of health delivery system. It is implicit that a good delivery system helps to attain better health status for the people in general.

As already noted, since 1977 there had been interest in decentralisation in India. A few states in India made considerable progress toward decentralisation in the 1980s. Of these Karnataka and West Bengal deserve particular mention. Panchayati Raj system was effectively implemented in West Bengal since 1977 and in Karnataka by early 1980s.

A study by Dutta (1993) for West Bengal, however, found that Panchayats could not play a proper role in the health sector as: (1) they were not asked to do so, (2) political leaders suffered from a conceptual lacunae regarding health sector as they considered health care only as a static treatment, and (3) planning in health care was done by medical elites who never wanted to give up that responsibility. As a result health care was not given adequate priority by the local level leaders and politicians. This resulted in lack of success in health care although West Bengal succeeded in the effective implementation of several other development programmes through decentralisation.

Even in Karnataka there was no visible change in the performance of health services after decentralisation (Chandran, 1993). There had been several transitional difficulties and friction arose between state and local bodies particularly in the area of recruitment, transfer and disciplinary control over staff. At the same time, there were instances of some local bodies producing commendable results. In particular, accountability of medical personnel, greater rationality in their posting, purchase of medicines etc. were the areas which became better with the decentralisation process (Srinivas, 1993)

After the 73rd and 74th Amendments, it is already observed that the extent of administrative and financial decentralisation is minimal even in the 1990s. It is not strange that most of the studies evaluating the impact of decentralisation in the 1990s focused on the lacunae in the decentralisation process rather than analysing their impact on health delivery (Durgaprasad, *et al.* 2001; Gupta and Gumber, 1999; Jafri, 2001; Nayar, 2001; Pokharel, 2000; Sen, 2001).

The study by Durgaprasad, *et al.* 2001 in two states, Andhra Pradesh and Gujarat did not consider the impact issue but rather concentrated on the extent of devolution and the areas to be devolved to improve the delivery of health services. The study observed significant decentralisation in Gujarat in the health and family welfare activities and argued that it had a positive impact on rural health scenario. Contrary to this in Andhra Pradesh health is not yet transferred to Panchayati Raj Institutions.

Gupta and Gumber (1999) also argued from the experience of four states in India that Panchayati Raj Institutions (PRI) have a definite role in improving the quality of health care services ensuring better attendance of health care functionaries. They can also play an important role in preventive health care. They have also listed a number of areas where better coordination between PRI and different state agencies will result in better health outcome.

Similar findings are also observed from other studies conducted in different parts of the country (Jafri, 2001; Pokharel, 2000; Sen, 2001; Singh and Jayalakshmi, 1997). The conclusions of these studies are mere guess on the condition that once sectoral and financial decentralisation takes place with obvious co-ordination with the health department it would result in better delivery of health services. However, proof for such findings is scarcely found in the country.

In general the studies conducted in the post 73rd and 74th Amendment phase have been unanimous that decentralised governance contributes substantially to improving health care especially in ensuring the quality of services including better attendance of health care functionaries, improving the supplies of drugs and equipment and also better implementation of preventive health care. Concern was raised on the tardy implementation of decentralisation in different states resulting in a poorer than expected outcome. Therefore, studies came out with number of suggestions for better decentralisation and coordination.

Though the conclusions of these evaluation studies are quite relevant there are inherent weaknesses that limit the value of these studies. First, there is no standard framework adopted in studying the decentralisation process and therefore, most of the conclusions are often subjective qualitative assessments. Second, decentralisation is often defined in loose terms including transfer of strengthening of health system at the lower level or strengthening NGOs etc. and not necessarily strengthening elected local bodies institutions. Thirdly, the analysis was often restricted to the degree of decentralisation and concluded without adequate scientific basis that the health sector would perform better if more powers were transferred to the decentralised system.

Conclusion

Decentralisation of powers is taking place in India with much more vigour since the early 1990s as compared to the earlier decades. There is a need to evaluate its likely impact on the outcome variables. For the social sector in general and particularly in health sector, decentralisation measures are expected to have significant positive impact. But the studies, thus far could not give any conclusive evidence on this. Most of the studies did not try to establish the linkages, but concentrated rather on the forms of decentralisation taking place and the improvement required to achieve better outcomes. However, the recent developments in the methods of analysis provide greater scope for understanding this relationship.

Perhaps, it would be possible to remould some of these studies in the context of the new framework available to understand the relationship between decentralisation and health care. Such attempt is essential to take any relevant policy conclusions on decentralisation and health outcome.

It is imperative that decentralisation is considered in a normative sense in the present review. There are large number of other arguments in favour of decentralisation both direct and indirect. Hence, the attempt, in a sense, is not to argue against decentralisation but rather caution about the high expectation on the impact of decentralisation on health delivery and outcome.

NOTES

1. Bossert (1988) presents a review of all available analytical frameworks on decentralisation and health.

REFERENCES

Araujo, J. and Luiz, A.C. (1997): 'Attempts to Decentralise in Recent Brazilian Health Policy: Issues and Problem 1988-1994', *International Journal of Health Services*, 27 (1): 109-24.

Bossert, Thomas (1998): 'Analysing the decentralization of health system in developing countries: decision space, innovation and performance', *Social Science and Medicine*, 47: 537-21.

Bossert, Thomas (2000): *Methodological Guidelines for Applied Research on Decentralisation of Health Systems in Latin America*, LACHSR Health Sector Initiative, Harvard School of Public Health, Cambridge.

Bossert, Thomas, Joel Beauvais and Diana Bowser (2000): *Decentralisation of Health Systems: Preliminary Review of Four Country Case Studies*, Major Applied Research 6, Technical Report 1, Partnership for Health Reforms, Abt Associates Inc., Maryland.

Bossert, Thomas and Joel C Beauvals (2002): 'Decentralization of health systems in Ghana, Zambia, Uganda and the Philippines: A comparative analysis of decision space', *Health Policy and Planning*, 17 (1):14-31.

Bossert, T. and Shiv Kumar (2002): *Annex 4, Report of Decentralization Team on Development of a Medium Term Health Sector Strategy and Expenditure Framework for Andhra Pradesh*, International Health Group, Harvard School of Public Health, Harvard.

Chandran, T.R. Satish (1993): 'Panchayati Raj and Health Care: The Karnataka Experience', in N.H. Antia and Kavita Bhatia (eds) *People's Health in People's Hand: A Model for Panchayati Raj*, The Foundations for Research in Community Health, Bombay.

Chatterjee, Rachel (2001): 'Health Systems in Andhra Pradesh', in Mishra, Rajeev, Rachel Chatterjee and Sujatha Rao (eds) Changing the Indian Health System: Current Issues, Future Directions, Appendices, Indian Council for Research on International Economic Relations, New Delhi (Unpublished Manuscript).

Collins, C. and A. Green (1994): 'Decentralization and primary health care: some negative implications in developing countries', *International Journal of Health Services*, 24: 459-75.

Durgaprasad, P.S. Srinivasan, and K. Jayalakshmi (2001): *Policy Options for Decentralised Panchayati Raj Health Management and Reorganization of District Health Care System*, Centre for Human Resource Development, National Institute of Rural Development, Hyderabad.

Dutta, Gouri Pada (1993): 'The Effect of Panchayati Raj on the Health Care System in West Bengal', in N.H. Antia and Kavita Bhatia (eds) *People's Health in People's Hand: A model for Panchayati Raj*, The Foundations for Research in Community Health, Bombay.

Gupta, Devender B. and Anil Gumber (1999): 'Decentralization: Some Initiatives in Health Sector', *Economic and Political Weekly*, February 6.

Jafri, Anwar (2001): 'Promise and Problems of Panchayati Raj: Experience from Madhya Pradesh', in Imrana Qadeer, Kasturi Sen and K.R. Nayar (eds) *Public Health and the Poverty of Reforms: The South Asian Predicament*, Sage Publications, New Delhi.

Kumar, C. P. Udaya (2001): 'Decentralising of Health Policy and Planning Using Participatory Rural Appraisal, Global Development Network' (www.gdnet.org).

Mahal, Ajay, Vivek Srivastava and Deepak Sanan (2000): 'Decentralization and its impact on public service provision in the health and education sectors: the case of India.' in J. Dethier (ed.) *Governance, Decentralization and Reform in China, India and Russia,* Kluwer Academic Publishers, London.

Mill, Anne, J. Patrick Vaughan, Duane L. Smith Iraj Tabibzadeh (eds) (1990): *Health System Decentralisation, Concepts, Issues and Country Experience*, World Health Organsiation, Geneva.

Ministry of Rural Development (2001): 'Report of the Working Group on Decentralised Planning and Panchayati Raj Institutions for the Tenth Five Year Plan', Ministry of Rural Development, Government of India, November, New Delhi.

Mohanty, S.R. (2000): 'Rogi Kalyan Samiti: Management of public hospitals through community participation', Global Development Network (www. Gdnnet.org).

National Commission to Review the Working of the Constitution (2001): 'A Consultation Paper on Review of the Working of the Constitutional Provisions for Decentralisation (Panchayats)', November, New Delhi.

Nayar, K.R. (1999): 'Old Priorities and New Agenda of Public Health in India: Is there a mismatch?', *CMJ Online*, 39 (3).

Nayar, K.R. (2001): 'Politics of Decentralisation: Lessons from Kerala', in Imrana Qadeer, Kasturi Sen and K.R. Nayar (eds) *Public Health and the Poverty of Reforms: The South Asian Predicament*, Sage Publications, New Delhi.

Pokharel, Bhojraj (2000): 'Decentralisation of Health Services, Assignment Report', World Health Organisation, Regional Office for South-East Asia, New Delhi.

Qadeer, Imrana, Kasturi Sen and K.R. Nayar (eds) (2001): *Public Health and the Poverty of Reforms: The South Asian Predicament*, Sage Publications, New Delhi.

Robalino, Ravid A., Oscar F. Picazo and Albertus Voetberg (2001): *Does Fiscal Decentralization Improve Health Outcomes?, Evidence from a Cross – Country Analysis*, Policy Research Working Paper 2565, World Bank, Washington, D.C.

Sen, Binayak (2001): 'People's Health Care Initiatives in Chhattisgarh Districts, Madhya Pradesh', in Imrana Qadeer, Kasturi Sen and K.R. Nayar (eds) *Public Health and the Poverty of Reforms: The South Asian Predicament*, Sage Publications, New Delhi.

Singh, Varinder and K. Jayalakshmi (1997): 'Role of Local Government in Tuberculosis Control Programme in Andhra Pradesh', Report Submitted to Department for International Development, British High Commission, July, New Delhi.

Soman, C.R. and P.G.K. Panikar (1993): 'Decentralisation in Health Care: The Kerala Experience', in N.H. Antia and Kavita Bhatia (eds) *People's Health in People's Hand: A Model for Panchayati Raj*, Bombay: The Foundations for Research in Community Health, Bombay.

Srinivas, M.N. (1993): 'Decentralised Health Care: A sociologist's view', in N.H. Antia and Kavita Bhatia (eds) *People's Health in People's Hand: A Model for Panchayati Raj*, The Foundations for Research in Community Health, Bombay.

Standing, H. (1997): 'Gender and Equity in Health Sector Reform Programmes, A Review', *Health Policy and Planning*, 12 (1):1-18.

The Hindu (2002): Karnataka entrusts primary health centres to voluntary organisations, *The Hindu daily*, October: 14, Chennai.

World Bank (2000): Overview of Rural Decentralisation in India, Vol 1, World Bank, September, Washington, D.C.

9

Sensitizing Grassroots Leadership on Health Issues

Experiences of a Pilot TV Project

T.V. SEKHER

Introduction

Decentralization is widely viewed as a way to make government more efficient and responsive to people's needs in the delivery of public services. Such a people-centered grassroots level development process not only needs devolution of powers to the rural masses but also involves sensitizing them, particularly the leaders, towards activating them for their own common weal. Sensitizing people at the grassroots level on development issues is, thus, an integral instrument of the development process adopted to design and execute welfare activities by the people, for the people. Rightly, the 73rd Constitutional Amendment offered the much needed impetous for local government through the three-tier system of governance with Zilla Panchayat at the district level, Taluk Panchayat or Block Panchayat at the intermediary level and Grama Panchayat at the village level. The members to these bodies are elected directly by the people with one-third of seats reserved for women, and another third for the members of the weaker sections such that all sections of the people are given an opportunity to participate in planning their own development. Thus, a great aspiration and expectation is laid on their functioning effectively.

Need for Sensitizing Elected Representatives

The elections for Panchayati Raj Institutions (PRIs) are regularly held at stipulated intervals with around three million elected members in Panchayats (Rural Self-Governments) and Nagarpalikas (Urban Municipal Bodies) in India. Among them, one-third elected members would be women and another one-third the weaker sections. The policy of reservation has provided a unique opportunity to the weaker sections, particularly women, for political participation and decision-making in the local governance process. Most of these members are taking up the role of decision-makers for the first time and they need to be educated, motivated and trained about their rights and responsibilities. Considering, the wide divergences and the element of heterogeneity in their social, economic and educational backgrounds, it may turn out to be a difficult task. Given the relatively lower educational attainments of panchayat members, lack of exposure to any kind of governance outside (an overwhelming majority of the women members are housewives and belong to deprived communities) and political inexperience, their participation in the PRI system and ability to discharge their responsibilities would not be very effective. Therefore, in order to make decentralized democratic planning effective and functional, it is imperative to sensitize these grassroots level leaders about their new roles and responsibilities through motivation and education.

The devolution of powers to plan development has automatically placed a great responsibility on the panchayats in prioritizing, planning and implementing the social development programmes. At the same time, it calls for a certain level of expertise and skills which the new members may not possess. The task of training and reorienting the large number of the panchayat members may, thus, require innovative approaches to support them to function effectively. In 1993, the Government of India appointed an expert group, under the chairmanship of Dr. M.S. Swaminathan, to draft a national population policy. The group suggested a paradigm shift and conceptualized population policies within the context of overall social and economic development agenda with greater devolution of authority and responsibilities to the panchayats. The expert group pointed out that development strategies must address the totality of the way people live, think and work. People must have a central role in deciding how they live. Population policies should, therefore, be viewed in the broader context of social development. The expert group suggested that it is necessary to adopt the principle of "think, plan and act locally and support nationally". The New National Population Policy (2000) reiterates the crucial role of panchayats in planning and implementation of health and family welfare programmes. The National Health Policy (2002) further highlights the need for devolving programmes and funds in the health sector through different levels of the Panchayati Raj Institutions.

The planning tool recommended by the Expert Group for grass-roots level social development is a Socio-Demographic Charter (SDC), to be used at the village, town or city level. This tool helps the elected members of the local bodies to prioritize their basic minimum needs and develop feasible strategies for fulfilling such needs within a stipulated time. The grassroots level socio-demographic charter is to be based on a "pro-nature, pro-poor, pro-women and pro-democratic choice" orientation to developmental planning.

The major aim of the socio-demographic charter is to assist the local communities to develop an action plan that will help in continuously improve the quality of life while living within the carrying capacity of the supporting ecosystems. The Group also felt that particular attention should be given to the basic minimum needs in the areas of primary education, primary health care, reproductive health, environmental hygiene, safe drinking water and household nutrition security.

In India, there exist significant inequities between states and regions within the states with regard to health care facilities. To overcome these imbalances, the Government of India has established national health norms and directly funds many health and family welfare programmes. Despite the existence of an extensive rural health infrastructure, a vast majority of rural population in India have no access to basic health care facilities. For example, with regard to many health and demographic indicators, considerable regional disparities exist in Karnataka

(Sekher, *et al.*, 2001). In this context, decentralised planning assumes importance in addressing issues like regional disparities in health care facilities (World Bank, 1993).

Comprehensive health care cannot be provided through public sector health services alone. Experiences all over the world suggest that one pre-condition for enhancing health status is community participation. This, to a great extent, can be ensured through the active involvement of democratically elected local leaders in health programmes. The involvement of Panchayati Raj Institutions in the implementation and management of health services would facilitate focused attention on vulnerable social groups, more emphasis on preventive measures, and the programmes can be reoriented to meet the specific local needs. Any meaningful involvement of grassroots level leaders can only be made possible by creating awareness in them and training them about their duties and responsibilities in the provision of primary health care in their communities.

The ICSSR/ICMR report of 1981 categorically states that the overall improvement in health conditions is only possible under the Panchayati Raj Institutions. This would rightly entrust the health and illness care to the people who understand the needs of their communities much better than anybody else. In Karnataka, there is an overall improvement in mobilizing local resources for strengthening the health infrastructure and greater accountability of health workers under the decentralised set up (Satishchandran, 1993; Sekher, 2001a). In an analysis of decentralized health planning in two districts, Murthy (1998) argues that even within the existing administrative structures, the district health planning can be made meaningful by focusing on the implementation constraints of service delivery and meeting the needs of the communities. In fact, most of the health problems can be resolved at the local level by imparting health education and by providing primary health care within a relatively affordable cost (Antia and Bhatia, 1993).

The major pillars of health care are education, water supply, sanitation, hygiene, environment and availability of nutritious food. There is, therefore, a need to develop an integrated action plan at the local level on health, nutrition, hygiene, environment and education with sensitivity to gender and population issues. Accordingly, the elected members of the local bodies have to be trained so as to ensure their participation in the process of social development. This training will help the elected members to develop an understanding of the specific needs of their communities and prepare a socio-demographic charter on the lines of the Five Year Plan at the Central and State governments. This charter will help the elected members of local bodies to prioritise their basic minimum needs and develop a feasible strategy for implementing them within a stipulated time frame. In Karnataka, the Task Force on Health and Family Welfare has emphasized the necessity to orient the elected members to formulate model health plans and village health committees (Govt. of Karnataka, 2001).

In view of the foregoing discussion, a need was felt to evolve suitable methodologies for the training of the panchayat members including the development of training materials. Reportedly, all the state governments have set up training institutes for panchayat members. Presumably, their number, capacity to handle a large group, training content and methodologies, and professional competence is inadequate to undertake such a task. Generally, the training institutions under the Government are bureaucratized whereas the need is for it to be innovative and flexible. Moreover, the number of panchayat members in every state would be far greater than the capacity and network of training institutions to handle such a large training load. In a situation like this, where we have to train a large number of elected representatives in each district (preferably during the first three months of their tenure), the government alone cannot handle this task. It is, therefore, imperative to look for more effective, acceptable, participatory and less time-consuming training methodologies at the grassroots level.

The Karnataka Experiment

The first phase of the training and orientation of panchayat members on health issues in Karnataka was started in 1998 when the Institute for Social and Economic Change (ISEC), Bangalore, undertook a pilot training project in Chitradurga district of the state on issues related to social development. By using the locally available resource persons and specially developed training modules and video documentaries, a new training methodology was evolved with the co-operation of the local NGOs. The training, arranged in an informal atmosphere of the villages, facilitated greater participation of local leaders. The local volunteers, who imparted the training, were familiar with the local situations. It gave an added advantage to the training exercise and ensured that their services would be available to the elected members any time in future. The involvement of voluntary organizations in this innovative programme ensured better participation of the representatives of the local bodies. It also facilitated a convergence of expertise and skills of government and non-governmental sectors for a better and a more effective training exercise at the grassroots level. The "Chitradurga Experiment" received wide acclaim from trainers and the government. The methodology was found to be participatory and less time-consuming. The post-training evaluation revealed that the training contributed significantly not only towards enhancing the level of awareness and self-confidence among the local leaders, but also towards improving their performance with regard to the provision of basic health care (Sekher, 2001b).

Considering the initial Chitradurga experience and the necessity to train grassroots level leaders, a need was felt to evolve suitable strategies and methodologies for training the Grama Panchayat members. It is pertinent to mention at this stage that the primary focus of the training programmes has to be on empowerment of the Panchayat members to enable them to perform their role effectively rather than on training of the individuals. Besides, the methods of training also needed to ensure long term sustainability of the programme that can be achieved through effective follow-up and evaluation mechanisms. More specifically, there is an urgent need to inform, train and motivate the members on issues related to female literacy, public health, sanitation, nutrition, family planning and women's status.

In this context and keeping in view its earlier experience in developing a suitable training methodology in Chitradurga district, a follow-up pilot training project for Grama Panchayat members to create awareness about Reproductive and Child Health (RCH) issues using the electronic mass media was undertaken by the ISEC at the request of the Population Foundation of India. Mass media, despite the initial costs of production, usually reach a large audience at a relatively low cost per person. Television is a very popular form of mass media and has a vast reach across all the categories of population. According to National Family Health Survey (NFHS-2), at the national level, 46 per cent of the women watch television at least once a week. Six years back, the figure was just 32 per cent. The rapid increase in exposure to television has been accompanied by decrease in exposure to radio and visits to cinema halls. In Karnataka, 58 per cent of the women are regularly exposed to television. In a country like India, where a significant proportion of population are illiterate or have little formal education, informal channels such as television can play an important role in bringing about changes in their attitudes and behaviour. The role of video films is very crucial in communicating with the semi-literate and illiterate panchayat members (Bose, 2000).

Accordingly, the main objective of the exercise was to train the members of the Panchayati Raj Institutions, Community Leaders and Health Workers through the medium of television. Its aim was to educate and sensitize the Panchayat members and service providers towards health and population issues (Empowerment of Women, Literacy and Education, Communicable Diseases, Reproductive and Child Health, Family Planning Methods and Population and Development) and about their roles and responsibilities.

Training Methodology Adopted

As a first step, a need was felt for a comprehensive handbook or reference manual on reproductive and child health issues (RCH) for the State. There are a few government publications, but, they generally focus only on one or two aspects of RCH. Many field level staff of the government, particularly ANMs and *Anganwadi* workers, are not familiar with various components of the RCH. They are also not in a position to clarify the doubts raised by villagers on various health problems. In this context, the ISEC project team, in collaboration with the Department of Health and Family Welfare, Government of Karnataka, prepared a comprehensive handbook on Reproductive and Child Health for the use of the field staff, NGOs and Panchayats in Karnataka. The Handbook was prepared in consultation with leading health-education and medical experts of Karnataka. A one day workshop was organized at Bangalore to discuss the contents and presentation of the Handbook. About 25 ANMs and 20 *Anganwadi* workers from various districts of Karnataka were invited to the workshop to present their views and suggestions. Besides the consultants, a panel of medical and health education experts interacted with the participants to understand their requirements at the grassroots level so that the Handbook could address the issues more specifically. The Handbook, that was subsequently prepared, contains 13 chapters covering — adolescent health and personal hygiene, age at marriage and importance of womens' education, pregnancy and pregnancy care, delivery and postnatal care, care of new-born babies, importance of breast milk and supplementary feeding, children's immunization, diarrhoea and respiratory infections in children, family welfare, abortion and post-abortion care, reproductive tract infections, nutritious food and iron deficiency anaemia. This multi-colour, 132 pages Handbook in Kannada also gives pictorial illustrations and examples in a lucid language for ready reference of the grass-root level service providers. The Government of Karnataka has printed and distributed 47,000 copies of the Handbook to all ANMs and *Anganwadi* workers in the state. The copies of the Handbook have been sent to the individual workers at their address. The health training institutions and NGOs in the state use this Handbook as a standard reference material for training field workers. ISEC has received wide appreciation for the Handbook from NGOs, health workers and *Anganwadi* workers from all over Karnataka on the accuracy of information, besides its high quality and user friendly presentation. This Handbook served as an important reference material for NGO volunteers in this training project to clarify the doubts raised by Panchayat members after viewing the TV programmes.

Secondly, keeping in view the wide coverage throughout the state, it was decided that Doordarshan may be the most appropriate medium to reach out to the rural leaders and field workers. It was, therefore, decided to prepare health education programmes for telecast through Doordarshan. Once again, besides the earlier collaboration to prepare the Handbook on RCH, ISEC collaborated with the State Health Department in the production of a TV serial on health issues. As a part of this collaboration the Department of Health and Family Welfare, Government of Karnataka, funded the production of a TV serial on health education and empowerment as an activity under the Information Education Communication (IEC) component of the India Population Project (IPP) - IX. Titled as *Thiliyavva Thangi,* the serial covered various aspects of RCH. This TV serial was used for educating and orienting Grama Panchayat members in this training project. ISEC approached Bangalore Doordarshan Kendra for re-telecasting the serial for this purpose and an agreement was reached with the Prasar Bharathi Corporation in this regard.

Considering the convenience for the panchayat members to assemble in a common place in their village wherever television sets are available, it was decided to schedule the telecast in the evenings between 6.00 to 6.30 pm. on Thursdays during June-September 2002. As per the agreement twelve episodes were telecast during this period. Sufficient publicity was given before the commencement of the project through Doordarshan, NGOs and Primary Health Centres.

Thirdly, for a successful implementation of the project, it was felt that the training programme for the Panchayat members should be carried out by a lead voluntary organization working in the district. This was perceived as having the following advantages — (a) generally, NGOs work and live closely with the people and they would have greater ability to perceive and internalise the felt needs, and greater appreciation of the interests and attitudes of the people in their respective areas; (b) it was considered that the NGOs can evolve an appropriate training methodology for the purpose as well as ensure the participation of all concerned; (c) the expertise of NGOs in conducting such training programmes and their familiarity with local conditions, was perceived as the positive aspects of this type of methodology. Accordingly, it was decided to implement the training project in six districts of Karnataka selected on the basis of their various socio-economic characteristics, health and development indicators and geographical locations. The six selected districts were Gulbarga, Dharwad, Mysore, Bidar, Bangalore Rural, and Bijapur.

Based on their experience in providing health care services and their expertise in imparting health education, the following six voluntary organizations were selected for the project implementation in the six selected districts:

- Family Planning Association of India, Dharwad Branch (Dharwad District).
- Swami Vivekananda Youth Movement, H.D. Kote (Mysore District).
- Jayanthi Grama Women and Children Welfare Association (Bijapur District).
- Grameena Abyudaya Seva Samstha, Doddaballapur (Bangalore Rural District).
- Family Planning Association of India, Bidar Branch (Bidar District).
- Action for Rural Reconstruction Movement, Shorapur (Gulbarga District).

A two-day workshop was organised in May 2002 at ISEC to design the strategies for project implementation. Selected NGO personnel, health education and media experts, and government officials participated in the workshop at which the modalities for implementation of the project were finalised. A one-day orientation programme to sensitize the volunteers of the six NGOs on the following issues was also organised at the headquarters of the NGO concerned:

- to discuss the modalities to bring the Panchayat members to the TV viewing sessions in each village;

- to familiarize the volunteers about the contents of each TV episode;
- to organize a meeting of all gram panchayat presidents and secretaries to finalise the venue for group viewing and making necessary arrangements before the telecast of the first programme. The idea was to seek their cooperation and active involvement as well as to give sufficient publicity for the programme;
- to brief volunteers to make necessary arrangements for group viewing, arranging discussions and clarifying the doubts raised by panchayat members after every episode of the TV serial;
- to enable them to organize a pre and post-telecast evaluation by administering a well-designed questionnaire supplied by the ISEC; and
- to supervise the implementation of all aspects of the programme in the project areas (selected Gram Panchayats in six districts).

The volunteers of selected NGOs were trained in various aspects of health care and health education and each one was entrusted with the responsibility of bringing PRI members to the TV viewing sessions for group viewing and facilitate discussions in each village. This new training methodology was appreciated by both panchayat members and volunteers. This programme also facilitated creation of a pool of trained and committed volunteers in the villages and their availability for future health care programmes.

In the districts, the respective NGO convened a meeting of all the Gram Panchayat Presidents and Secretaries to discuss the modalities of organizing the group viewing sessions. Considering the convenience of local leaders, the venues were decided and a time schedule of the telecast and contents of each TV episode were distributed to them well in advance. Through this process, the NGO and the volunteers were able to establish good rapport with the grassroots level functionaries.

The fourth step involved the telecasting of the health programmes. After completing the orientation programme for NGO volunteers and discussions with Gram Panchayat Presidents and Secretaries, the arrangements for group viewing were finalised by the volunteers in their respective villages. The schedule of the telecasting and a summary of each episode were given to the volunteers and panchayat members well in advance. Doordarshan also made all efforts in giving maximum publicity for the programme. The first episode was telecasted on Thursday, 20th June 2002. The active involvement of volunteers and constant supervision by NGO leaders helped in ensuring the participation of a majority of gram panchayat members from the project areas. Altogether 110 Gram Panchayats from 6 districts were covered in the programme.

Though the TV programmes received appreciation from panchayat members, volunteers, health workers and general public, few practical operational difficulties were encountered —.

(a) Many times there was no power supply to operate the TV sets. The frequent power failures in some areas caused inconvenience to the viewers.
(b) In a few villages, TV sets were not available. Even where available, the reception was not very good.
(c) In some areas, where the villages were scattered (particularly in tribal areas like the H.D. Kote taluk in Mysore district), it was extremely difficult for members from different places to assémble at one place for group viewing, that too in the evenings.
(d) A reluctance on the part of Panchayat members belonging to different castes to assemble in one place was observed in one or two villages.
(e) In some villages which had access to cable TV, DD-1 channel was not relayed at all.

To understand the level of awareness (among the panchayat members), about various health problems, a questionnaire was canvassed prior to the telecast of the programme. The same questionnaire was administered again after the telecast of the episode to the Panchayat members who had gathered to watch the TV programme. The questions were related to the particular episode telecast. Individual questionnaire for each episode was prepared and distributed by the ISEC to the NGOs. The local NGO volunteers were given the responsibility of administering the questionnaires (both pre and post-telecast) in their villages. An analysis of the pre and post-telecasts was carried out by the ISEC and it shows very interesting observations and findings:

(a) It was found that the awareness level was quite low among the panchayat members about certain health aspects like care to be taken during pregnancy, problems of adolescent girls, high-risk pregnancy and delivery care, iron-deficiency anaemia, and immunization schedule for children.
(b) The level of awareness and knowledge increased significantly after viewing the TV episode. In some cases, it increased by about 50 per cent.
(c) Based on the analysis, it was observed that a majority of the members were able to grasp the messages from each episode easily.
(d) A good number of panchayat members had wrong notions about various health aspects relating to breast feeding, family planning methods and adolescent health problems. After viewing the TV programmes, these misconceptions were corrected to a large extent.
(e) It was found that the awareness level was comparatively low among the members belonging to scheduled caste/ Scheduled tribe category. On most of the health issues, the level of awareness among female members was slightly better than male members of the similar socio-economic background.

By and large, the TV serial received good viewership from the general public in the project areas. Particularly, in villages where the local NGO volunteers took the initiative, the response was overwhelming. Where combined efforts were put in by NGO volunteers and the local ANM, excellent participation of villagers was observed. But in certain areas it was found that the public were not aware of the programme. Villages where cable connections were available and people had access to many private channels, the Doordarshan programmes received little attention.

In order to increase the viewership, ISEC introduced a cash award of Rs. 500 each to five respondents, to be picked up out of those who gave correct answer to the question that was announced after the telecast of the episode every week. Viewers from all over Karnataka, including Panchayat members, responded to these questions by sending their answers in post cards. The names of the recipients of cash awards were announced during the telecast of the subsequent episode.

Programme Evaluation

After the completion of the telecast, it was decided to evaluate the effectiveness of the training methodology and its impact on Panchayat members. This was expected to help identifying the strengths and weaknesses of the project and lessons to be learnt. It was also felt that the insights drawn from the evaluation exercise would provide useful inputs for formulating training programmes in future and its successful replication elsewhere.

In order to examine the effectiveness of this training methodology and its acceptability among the Panchayat members and volunteers, a field level evaluation was carried out during November-December 2002. The number of Gram Panchayat members who were randomly selected was 117 and structured questionnaires were administered. For this purpose, five grama panchayat members each from 24 villages, spread across six districts, were contacted. Their experiences, opinions and suggestions were recorded.

Using a structured questionnaire, 54 volunteers from six voluntary organizations were interviewed and their experiences and suggestions were elicited. Apart from this, detailed discussions were held with the NGO office-bearers and health departmental officials. Local functionaries like ANMs and *Anganwadi* workers were also contacted at the time of evaluation to seek their opinions.

Based on the analysis of the information gathered from panchayat members, the following observations were drawn:

(1) Television can be used as a powerful medium for orienting panchayat members as it provides audio-visual effects. A majority of the panchayat members felt that it was very effective in conveying desired messages.

(2) Television sets are available in almost all the villages and the per cent of population frequently viewing the TV programmes irrespective of social, economic and gender background is increasing day by day.

(3) The local volunteers persuaded many panchayat members to view the TV programmes on a regular basis and this was appreciated by all.

(4) Almost all panchayat members felt that the TV programmes were very informative, useful and helped them in discharging their responsibilities effectively as community leaders.

(5) The telecast helped in overcoming certain practices and superstitious beliefs, particularly with regard to puberty, breast-feeding and immunization.

(6) Eighty per cent of the panchayat members stated that the timing of the telecast was convenient for them. However, among the members who owned TV set, a good number of them mentioned that anytime after 7 pm was more convenient for them to view.

(7) Ninety-two per cent of the panchayat members interviewed stated that they received information about the TV programme on RCH well in advance and the local volunteer informed him/her personally. Most of them mentioned that if there was no communication by the volunteer, they might not have known about the programme.

(8) In many cases, a group discussion was conducted after watching the programme. Local volunteers were able to clarify the doubts raised by the panchayat members. But, in some occasions, there was no group discussion and members left the place immediately after the telecast.

(9) Since the volunteer was most often from the same village, he/she was familiar with the panchayat members. Interestingly, after this project, panchayat leaders continued to consult and involve the volunteer in all the health related activities and programmes in their respective areas.

(10) Some panchayat members stated that the NGOs arranged video presentation of the serial in their villages. This was done mostly with the help of the Gram Panchayat President and Secretary.

(11) Ninety-five per cent of the respondents stated that they wanted the TV serial on RCH to be re-telecast. Some of them suggested that instead of Doordarshan, even private Kannada channels could be used for this purpose.

The information gathered from the local volunteers and discussions with the NGO office-bearers provided the following broad conclusions—

(1) Eighty-seven per cent of the local volunteers involved in the project had some previous experience in implementing the NGO programmes on health. Most of them had undergone training on RCH issues either organized by the NGO or the government, at some time or the other.

(2) All the volunteers felt that the Handbook on RCH provided to them in this project was very comprehensive, lucid and helpful in understanding various components.

(3) All the volunteers involved in this project attended the one-day orientation programme organized by the NGO. They had also seen the TV serial before the actual telecast of the programme and were familiar with the contents of each episode.

(4) Seventy-three per cent of the volunteers stated that they got good support and co-operation from the panchayat presidents and members for arranging group viewing in villages. But a few also reported the indifferent attitude

of some panchayat leaders towards health education programmes.

(5) In some areas, the group viewing was arranged in the panchayat offices. But in other cases, it was arranged in a convenient location, either in the house of a member or any other person.

(6) The evaluation revealed that though the panchayat office-bearers co-operated well with the volunteers, similar response was not forthcoming from the Primary Health Centres. However, in a few villages, where they co-operated, the response and the impact were tremendous.

(7) In some areas, the local volunteers were able to involve the *Anganwadi* workers in the programme.

(8) The monitoring and the supervision of the programme by the NGO were reasonably good. However, the evaluation indicated that better supervision would have yielded more positive responses from volunteers and Panchayat members.

(9) Ninety-three per cent of the local volunteers stated that they were ready to help the panchayat members and were willing to undertake similar training programmes in the future.

(10) Some volunteers also suggested that the subject coverage of the TV programme could be expanded by incorporating topics like sexually transmitted diseases, AIDS, etc.

(11) It was found that in a few villages the private cable connection networks were not telecasting the Doordarshan channel. This adversely affected the project in some villages.

(12) It was also observed that in few villages (in H.D. Kote taluk in Mysore district), the panchayat members at their own initiative, hired the antenna to view the TV serial on RCH.

(13) In some villages, the volunteers mobilized the support of women self-help groups and Mahila Mandals in arranging and viewing the programme. Their participation generated lively discussion after viewing the TV serial.

A few cases illustrating the impact of the TV serial on viewers (Panchayat members) in the project areas have been presented here:

(1) After viewing the programme on age at marriage (episode no. 3), a discussion was followed in the Hosahalli Gram Panchayat in Doddaballapur Taluk. One member raised the issue of the marriage of a girl aged 12 years in the village to be shortly conducted. The Grama Panchayat members decided to persuade the parents not to go ahead with the marriage. After much persuasion and some sort of threat then the matter could be brought to the attention of the police, the parents agreed to postpone the marriage and allow the girl to continue her schooling.

(2) One women Grama Panchayat president in Dharwad taluk stated that she had no idea of how to breast-feed her twins. After watching the serial on breast-feeding, she understood the method of breast-feeding the twins.

(3) The orientation had a positive impact on the functioning of PHCs and sub-centres. It was observed that the panchayat members started monitoring the attendance of doctors and para-medical staff in some areas.

(4) The panchayat members started persuading the untrained *dais* in their villages to undergo the training at the PHCs.

(5) In a few villages, it was observed that the panchayat members had started monitoring the functioning of the *Anganwadi* centres (ICDS).

(6) During the training programme, the panchayat members learnt that oral rehydration salt (ORS) packets could be acquired and stored by them for emergency use. Many members collected ORS packets from the health centres and started distributing them to their community members.

Lessons Learnt

To discuss the outcome of the project and lessons learnt, a state level workshop was organized at Bangalore on 24th January, 2003. The representatives of the Population Foundation of India, State Health Department, State Institute of Health and Family Welfare, ISEC, six collaborating NGOs and Health Education and Communication Experts participated in it. The findings of the evaluation of the project, carried out by the ISEC, were presented for discussion. The participants appreciated the excellent co-ordination of the project which involved NGOs, Doordarshan, Health Department and ISEC. The project demonstrated that television could be used as a powerful and effective medium for educating and training grassroots level functionaries spread all over the state. However, the mere telecasting of the programme would not yield the expected results. This should be combined with grassroots level efforts by the NGOs and field workers to inform and motivate the panchayat members about the advantages of the programme.

Another workshop was organized at Dharwad on 25th January, 2003 in collaboration with the Family Planning Association of India. The opinions and suggestions of the volunteers involved in the project and the panchayat members participated in the programme were discussed in this workshop. 25 volunteers and 40 Panchayat members participated in the discussions along with the representatives of the NGO, ISEC, and PFI. The overwhelming response from the panchayat members show that they wanted the telecast to continue and also suggested incorporation of some more health issues in the TV serial. The panchayat members also agreed that they would organize video shows of this programme in their villages using the video cassettes supplied by the ISEC. In some villages, the video shows were already arranged not only for the panchayat members but also for the public. This TV programme undoubtedly had some impact on the attitudinal and behaviour pattern of elected members. It was really a learning experience for some of them since this was the first training in health issues for a majority of them. They acquired knowledge on various health issues and governmental programmes, irrespective of their educational and occupational backgrounds. Our field visits revealed that some of the panchayat members had already started putting their newly acquired knowledge into practice.

It was found that the women panchayat members expressed more interest and willingness to view the TV programme. They felt that regular health education programmes should be arranged for women. In rural areas, it is a well-known fact that women and children are the main victims of lack of food, nutrition and health care. Many members expressed the feeling that in most cases the health needs of women got neglected and were attended to only when it reached a crisis. They realized that timely advice and treatment could save the lives of many pregnant women and infants. Some women members asked the health workers to regularly visit their villages for providing ante-natal care.

The volunteers were able to acquire the requisite knowledge and organizing skills which helped in the successful implementation of the project. Most of the volunteers had some previous experience in organizing training and imparting health education. This helped them undertake the prescribed task in a relatively easy manner. They were constantly in touch with the panchayat members in their areas and were also invited and consulted on many occasions. They stated that the Handbook on RCH was very helpful in explaining many health problems. The volunteers also felt that in some areas the panchayat members had a good understanding of health problems and actively participated in the discussions after viewing the TV serial. The volunteers opined that the active involvement of health department staff in the training was required for better outcome. Our evaluation shows that the project was able to create a pool of trained volunteers who were willing to help the panchayat members and were available in local areas.

Recommendations

In India, we have to train a large number of elected representatives of panchayats and create awareness about various developmental issues and programmes. State governments and a few training institutions alone cannot handle this gigantic task. It is, therefore, imperative to look for more effective and acceptable methodologies for orientation, including use of the powerful electronic media and involvement of voluntary organizations. This action project in Karnataka was an innovative effort towards this end. The following are some broad recommendations based on the Karnataka experiment:

(1) There is a unanimous view that this kind of health education programme should continue and extend to all parts of the state.

(2) Broadcasting casting of health education serials should be considered as an effective alternative for the Doordarshan in view of its low cost and easy and sustained implementation.

(3) In view of the spread of multiple private entertainment channels even in remote villages, the cable operators in most of the villages are not telecasting Doordarshan programmes which are affecting most of the governmental initiative in carrying the message to the people. The Prasar Bharati Act prohibits the non-inclusion of DD channels by private operators. Steps should be taken to ensure that the cable operators compulsorily beam DD channels as per the Act.

(4) All the State Ministries of Panchayati Raj should be persuaded to issue directions to all the Panchayati Raj Institutions in their jurisdictions to participate in the developmental education programmes organized by various departments and agencies from time to time.

(5) The Department of Health and Family Welfare in the states should take an active role in such programmes by directing the functionaries from PHCs to sub-centres to actively participate in such programmes and to lend technical and other necessary support to make such programmes a success. It should be realized that this will also help the Health Department to implement their own programmes much more effectively as their participation in such programmes will build up the

required support from all sections of the society at the grassroots level.

(6) The governmental efforts alone in health education have been found severely limited. The experience gained in this programme suggests that several NGOs do have the capability and expertise which may be utilized to supplement the governmental efforts in health education and programme implementation.

Note : This study was undertaken by the Institute for Social and Economic Change, Bangalore, and sponsored by the Population Foundation of India, New Delhi. The guidance and support of M. Govinda Rao, K. Srinivasan, Gopal K. Kadekodi, A.R. Nanda, G.V. Krishna Rau and M. Ramakrishna Reddy are gratefully acknowledged. I am also thankful to the support extended by India Population Project-IX, Government of Karnataka, Sir Ratan Tata Trust, Mumbai, Bangalore Doordarshan Kendra and six Voluntary Organizations of Karnataka at various stages of the implementation of this action project. This paper was originally published in *Economic and Political Weekly*, Vol. xxxviii, No. 46, November 15, 2003.

REFERENCES

Antia, N.H. and K. Bhatia (eds.) (1993): *People's Health in People's Hands.* The Foundation for Research in Community Health, Mumbai.

Bose, Ashish (2000): " Empowerment of Women: How and When?" *Economic and Political Weekly,* 35(34): 3005-07.

Govt. of India (2000): *National Population Policy - 2000,* Ministry of Health and Family Welfare, New Delhi.

Govt. of India (2002): *National Health Policy - 2002.* Ministry of Health and Family Welfare, New Delhi.

Government of Karnataka (2001): *Karnataka Towards Equity, Quality and Integrity in Health,* Final Report of the Task Force on Health and Family Welfare, Bangalore.

IIPS and ORC Macro (2000): *National Family Health Survey (NFHS-2),* New Delhi.

ICSSR and ICMR (1981): *Health for All: An Alternative Strategy,* Indian Institute of Education, Pune.

Murthy, Nirmala (1998): 'Decentralised Health Planning: Lessons from Two Districts in India', *Journal of Health and Population in Developing Countries,* 1(2):1-10.

Satish Chandran, T.R (1993): 'Panchayati Raj and Health Care: The Karnataka Experience' In N.H. Anita and K. Bhatia (eds.), *People's Health in People's Hands,* FRCH, Mumbai.

Sekher, T.V. (2001a): *Functional Review of Department of Health and Family Welfare in Karnataka* in Govt. of Karnataka *Functional Review Reports,* Karnataka Administrative Reforms Commission, Bangalore.

Sekher, T.V. (2001b): *Empowerment of Grassroots Leadership in Health and Population: A Training Experiment in Karnataka, ISEC Working Paper No. 80,* Institute for Social and Economic Change, Bangalore.

Sekher, T.V., K.N.M. Raju and M.N. Shivakumar (2001): 'Fertility Transition in Karnataka: Levels, Trends and Implications', *Economic and Political Weekly,* 36(51): 4742-52.

World Bank (1993): *World Development Report, 1993. Investing in Health.* Oxford University Press, New York.

10

Rural Poverty, Local Democratic Institutions, and Sustainable Development in India under Globalisation

Issues and Strategies

SUKHPAL SINGH

Introduction

Poverty alleviation refers to the eradication of absolute poverty and the reduction of relative poverty as defined in the Manila Declaration for Action on Social Development in the UNESCAP region. Absolute poverty refers to a condition of a family below the threshold while relative poverty refers to the gap between the rich and the poor. Poverty has four dimensions, i.e. social equity, economic prosperity, ecological security, and responsible and responsive governance (Cousart, 1999). Similarly, sustainability comprises economic efficiency, equity, indigenous technology, and ecological sustainability.

Sustainable development involves many things including local institutions and organisations. The local institutions are important for sustainable development as they not only mobilise local resources and regulate their use in a most efficient and sustainable manner, but also encourage people to take a longer-term view by creating common expectations and a basis of cooperation that goes beyond individual interest. However, it should be recognized that local institutions and groups can also produce practices which do not favour sustainability (Uphoff, 1992). Also, it is important to recognize the difference between organizations and institutions. Whereas an institution is a complex of norms and behaviours that persist overtime by serving some socially valued purpose, an organization is a structure of recognized and accepted roles. However, institutions can be organizations and *vice versa* (Uphoff, 1993). But one can only create organizations which, if they effectively meet people's needs and expectations, become institutions as well. Though there could be many levels of decision-making for a particular activity, but three of them—localities, communities, and groups should be considered local as they have face-to-face inter-personnel relationships in all of them which are more frequent and intense within groups. The fact that people know each other creates opportunities for collective action and mutual assistance and for mobilizing and managing resources on a self-directed and self-sustaining basis. In such communities, monitoring is easier, and the social sanctions are easier to implement through reputation mechanisms and multiplex relationships of face-to-face communities (Bardhan, 1993).

For sustainable development, it is not institutions and organizations which are important *per se*, but sustainability of these mechanisms of development. The sustainability of a local institution can be judged by its (a) financial autonomy in terms of whether it is able to stand on its own feet financially; (b) administrative autonomy defined as the capacity of its leaders and members to determine and decide by themselves on the long-term and short-term objectives of the institution and the direction to achieve these objectives; and (c) managerial autonomy in terms of their capacity to manage their day-to-day operations by themselves (Verhagen, 1987). According to Shah (1993), a local institution can be sustainable only if it serves purposes important to its members. He cites many examples of successful and failed co-operatives in various commodity sectors in India to prove this point. Therefore, he distinguishes between co-operatives which have come up on the values-first model like credit and farming co-operatives emphasising purposes important to the state and those which emerged and work in terms of member-first model like dairy and sugar co-operatives in Gujarat and

Maharashtra, and farmer groups in north Gujarat in tubewell irrigation, which serve purposes important to their members on a priority basis and always try to serve them better. These co-operatives survive and grow till they are found useful by their members and perceived to be better than existing or potential alternatives.

This paper examines the trends in rural poverty in brief and the likely impact of new economic regime—both domestic and global—on poverty situation in Section 2. The concept of pro-poor growth is discussed in Section 3. Section 4 discusses the reasons which lead rural households into or out of poverty. Section 5 outlines some of the lessons and strategies including the World Bank approach to rural poverty reduction. The paper concludes by emphasizing the institutional factors in reducing poverty in terms of strategies which need to be considered for sustainable poverty reduction and rural development (Section 6).

Rural Poverty in India

Many village studies find that rural poverty in India declined during the 1970s and 1980s though the progress had been slow and irregular, and that, inequalities within villages had persisted. These continued inequalities could constrain both the scope for further poverty reduction through economic growth, and the impact of policy interventions. Even in the presence of a general declining trend in poverty, certain subgroups of population like women faced a high risk of impoverishment through illness, accidents or life cycle events (Jayaraman and Lanjouw, 1999). It is true that poverty is concentrated in rural areas, and within agriculture, it is related to access to land (Vyas, 2002). The poverty is also found to be higher and more widespread in those areas where the local resource base particularly land, water and forest has become degraded, neglected or subjected to over exploitation and/or natural disasters (Misra, 1999).

A study of poverty during the 1990s found that poverty situation worsened during 1993-94 to 1999-2000 in the states of Assam, Madhya Pradesh and Orissa whereas in other 12 states, there was distinct improvement on the poverty front in terms of absolute size of the poor population (Sundaram and Tendulkar, 2003). Although the incidence of rural poverty has always been higher than that of urban poverty, the differences have been smaller than in most other Asian countries. The gap declined upto the late 80s but increased in the 1990s (IFAD, 2002). In the case of targeted poverty alleviation programmes ranging from wage/self-employment, food and nutrition programmes to land reforms, there had been exclusion and inclusion errors in targeting (Dev, 2000).

Globalisation and Rural Poverty

Globalisation may affect the welfare of the rural poor through productivity, growth, income distribution, technologies, security of livelihoods, and policies. Though there are large potential benefits from higher growth due to globalisation, there is also the real danger that rural poor may be left behind in the process due to lack of access to knowledge and other assets required for success in a commercialized economy. The factors which constraint rural poor from participating in globalised markets include lack of access to education, land, water, credit, and health services. The welfare of rural poor is likely to be more closely linked to general growth of the economy, rural non-farm sector, and efficient labour markets (Killick, 2001).

So far as the impact of trade liberalization on poverty is concerned, it is important to consider that though growth is a necessary condition for sustained reduction in poverty, it is equally important to incorporate distribution aspects. It is also important to remember that the greater the inequality, the less the poverty-reducing effect of growth (IFAD, 2002). The exact impact of trade liberalization depends on how it impacts not only growth, but also the distribution of growth between poor and non-poor. Therefore, trade liberalization should be accompanied by other policies to ensure that a country is successful in integrating with the world in a manner that is favourable to growth and poverty reduction. These policies include sound macro economy, strong institutions, and a favourable investment climate. But, the external shocks and disturbances due to openness could increase the probability of a household falling into poverty (Rajan, 2002).

There is no doubt that trade favours economic growth but its role should not be overstated. That global integration during the 1990s has led to substantial poverty reduction in India is shown by evidence clearly (World Bank, 2002). But, the cost of adjustment, due to globalisation and trade liberalization, to poor people becomes substantial when markets do not work very well. Market failure can happen due to many reasons like lack of basic information, dominance of the markets by a few key players, weak economic governance or poor enforcement of the law (Curtis, 2001).

There is no doubt that higher growth rate can be an important source of poverty reduction. There have been cases of high growth being achieved with the higher expansion of rural economy than the urban economy in countries like Chile. This is due to the fact that the opportunity cost of labour and other mobile factors of production owned by the rural poor increases rapidly in a growing economy. In fact, a more balanced growth that promotes rapid expansion of rural economy reduces rural poverty as well as provides greater incentive for the poor to protect their environmental resources (Lopez, 1997). The rural poverty alleviation has been more impressive when initial conditions in terms of socio-economic structure, level of physical infrastructure and human development were favourable or were given priority. In South East Asian region, the role of the state, land reforms, agricultural growth and diversification towards rural non-farm employment have been important factors in poverty reduction. The macro factors like political stability, enforcement of law and order and quality of governance significantly affect the level of rural poverty through economic growth and allocation of public expenditures (World Bank, 2000).

But, it is also possible that high economic growth may increase poverty. A recent analysis of Indian poverty situation revealed that in the 1990s, the rate of reduction in poverty level came down though the GDP growth rate increased significantly. Further, though urban poverty had been showing a downward trend, the poverty in rural areas worsened (Kashyap, 2000). It is important to realize that the composition of growth is as important as growth *per se* because it also impacts poverty. Higher agricultural productivity is a key factor in rural poverty reduction, especially in situations where agricultural producers are small. In the non-farm sector, a pro-poor process of growth requires better rural and human resource development. For this, higher public spending on basic health and education is must and this can bring large gains to the poor. Agricultural growth also fosters the conditions for pro-poor growth in the non-farm sector (Ravallion, 2000).

Pro-poor Growth

Growth is pro-poor when it is labour absorbing and accompanied by policies and programmes that mitigate inequalities and facilitate income and employment generation for the poor, particularly women and other traditionally excluded groups. In other words, pro-poor growth enables the poor to actively participate in and significantly benefit from economic activities. Promoting pro-poor growth requires a strategy that is deliberately biased in favour of the poor so that they benefit proportionately more than the rich. Such a strategy entails the removal of institutional and policy induced biases against the poor as well as the adoption of direct pro-poor policies. The first kind of constraints relates to social and macro policy related aspects of the economies while the later ones comprise those related to public spending on education, health, credit and small and medium enterprises, besides the tax system (Kakwani and Pernia, 2000).

An empirical investigation of growth and inequality effects on poverty reduction in three countries of south-east Asia revealed that whereas in the Lao PDR, economic growth during the 1990s was slightly pro-poor, increasing inequality reduced the impact of growth on poverty, in Thailand high economic growth in the 1980s and the early 1990s led to a rapid decline in the incidence of poverty. In fact, the pace of poverty reduction would have been much faster, if income distribution had not worsened during the later part of the 1990s. The economic crisis adversely affected the poor proportionally more than the non-poor. In the case of Korea, which had rapid economic growth, low inequality and almost full employment, the incidence of poverty declined from almost 40 per cent in 1990 to less than 8 per cent in 1997. Though it jumped back to 19 per cent in 1998 due to the economic crisis, there is no doubt that economic growth in Korea has generally been highly pro-poor. The implication of this analysis is that poverty reduction would have been even faster if the governments in Thailand and Lao PDR had followed pro-poor policies or avoided policies with adverse consequences on income distribution. In fact, growth in rural areas has been more pro-poor than that in urban areas (Kakwani and Pernia, 2000).

Another study of Thailand reveals that during the boom, the incidence of absolute poverty fell dramatically but relative inequality increased. But, the economic crisis of 1997 reversed this trend when the poor became significantly worse off in an absolute sense, but proportionately less so than the rich implying that inequality declined. In Thailand, growth can be said to be bad for the poor only if one evaluates the economic conditions of poor people solely in comparison with those of the rich which, in fact, is not justified. Though the rich benefited disproportionately more from the growth in the pre-crisis period, the fact remains that, in spite of this, the growth enabled very large number of poor people to improve their material condition substantially. Poverty fell in Thailand because of increased demand for the resource from which poor derived most of their income, i.e. their labour. Economic growth led to many existing and new social and environmental problems in Thailand, but it also created millions of better paying jobs for low income people even in the poorest parts of the country expanding the range of economic opportunities available to them (Warr, 2000).

What makes Rural People Poor?

Before discussing strategies for rural poverty reduction, it is important to understand what makes poor people poor. This can guide in framing better policies and programmes. In a recent study in India (rural Rajasthan), it was found that while some households moved out of poverty, simultaneously some others fell into poverty.

The main factors in escape from poverty were found to be diversification of income sources, irrigation facility, and information provision to the rural people. The programmes of direct assistance for poverty reduction had only marginal impact though this might have made poverty more tolerable. On the other hand, the factors associated with becoming poor were quite different and included poor health, large expenses on poor quality health care, and social functions associated with death and marriages, and high interest loans taken from private sources to meet these unaffordable and crippling expenses (Krishna, 2003). Another set of village studies also pointed to considerable movement in and out of poverty by the households due to fluctuations in agricultural incomes, and natural calamities. Only low caste status and agricultural wage labour were associated with long-term poverty (Jayaraman and Lanjouw, 1999).

So far as credit is concerned, the problem is that most poor people do not have any asset to offer as collateral and, as a result, many potentially viable projects are not financed and the poor remain trapped in poverty. The access to inputs and technology is also severely limited in the case of the poor. The constraints include lack of information about markets, lack of business and negotiating experience and lack of a collective organization which deprive them from interacting on equal terms with the other market participants or market intermediaries (IFAD, 2002). Another aspect of rural economy which has hit hard the interest of the rural poor is the depletion and marketisation of common property resources. It is a well-known fact that the rural poor depend to a great extent on these resources for their livelihoods (Bardhan, 2001). The livelihood studies in Orissa reinforced that poverty is fundamentally an institutional issue and is linked closely to power relations and entitlement to different forms of capital. More specifically, it meant high rates of interest leading to indebtedness and landlessness, control over seasonal migration to urban areas by a few powerful people, long history of dependence of people on government relief intervention, wide gap between allocation to the poor and actual deliveries, and little accountability of the local institutions (Turton and Farrington, 1999).

Lessons and Strategies for Poverty Reduction and Sustainable Development

The poorest places are generally resource constrained like hilly areas, marginal and degraded lands, rainfed areas and coastal regions. Within poor, some people like female-headed households, landless, marginal farmers and tenants, indigenous people, socially excluded like scheduled caste, pastoralists and coastal fishermen are more vulnerable (IFAD, 2002).

Strategy for poverty reduction articulated by the World Development Report 2000-2001 focuses on promoting opportunity, facilitating empowerment and enhancing security. Opportunity promotion involves making markets work for poor people and build their assets by encouraging effective private investments, expansion into international markets, building of assets of poor people, addressing asset inequalities across gender, ethnic, racial, and social divides and getting infrastructure and knowledge into poor areas. Empowerment involves laying the political legal basis for more inclusive development, creation of public administration that promote growth and equity, promoting inclusive decentralization and community development and gender equity, besides tackling social barriers and supporting poor people's social capital. The security dimension involves formulating an approach to help poor people manage risk, developing national programmes to prevent, prepare for, and respond to financial and natural shocks, designing national systems of social risk management which are also pro-growth, and addressing civil conflicts (World Bank, 2001). World Development Report 2000-2001 emphasised the vulnerability of poor people and explicitly focused on an obligation to protect the poor including losers from globalisation. It recognized the role of the state in both poverty reduction and rural development. In this context, a successful rural development strategy should recognize the great diversity of rural situations, be consistent with poverty reduction and decentralization policy, and make the case for productive sectors in rural development (Ashley and Maxwell, 2001).

In the approaches to rural poverty reduction, there has not been enough emphasis on environment, risk management and safety net, private sector roles, gender, education and health, agricultural policy framework, and governance. Even the aspects of income sources, assets, production, and market participation have been omitted in rural poverty diagnosis. In fact, the rural included only agriculture and natural resources in rural space (Cord, 2002). But, agribusiness sector is much larger than just farm production and other allied activities. This approach can help examine many possibilities in the off-farm parts of the agribusiness chains to involve poor people gainfully. This is also important from the point of view of value addition. A recent study of rural poor revealed that diversification of livelihood, interaction with markets on more beneficial terms and managing risks associated with commodity prices are important elements to be incorporated in poverty reduction strategies (Turk, 2002).

Though there has been plenty of successful intermediation in primary production by state and NGOs, much more of it is needed in agro-processing, credit, market access, information, and technology to enable small farmers to reap enhanced competitive benefits offered by free market. Though land reforms are needed, they will not help make a dent on poverty, if not accompanied by marketing links for small farmers who are more efficient and more valuable as they are labour intensive. Poor need access to markets as well as assets to get out of poverty. In this, land reforms should be part of overall reform agenda. Intermediation is required for small farmers to link them up with global markets in processing and marketing (Lipton, 2002).

In order to link poor rural producers with international markets, the International Trade Centre (ITC) of the UNCTAD/WTO has launched an export-led poverty reduction programme (EPRP) aimed at empowering poor people to generate higher income by establishing links between market-oriented production and overseas buyers. This programme is based on 10 building blocks of analysis, operations, support environment, and social concerns which include identifying products and markets, identifying producers and matching product markets and producers under analysis, developing the products and human resources under operations, providing micro finance and other support services under support environment, and finally, incorporating gender and environment as important social concerns (ITC Website, 2002).

Important lessons from poverty alleviation programmes in South Asia include treating poverty in a comprehensive way by incorporating health care, education and nutrition, giving adequate attention to the preservation and enhancement of natural resources and environmental hygiene to make poverty eradication programme sustainable, and appropriate targeting of programmes (Vyas, 1997). What is required to make a dent on poverty is to provide proper health care, information about markets and connection with the world outside, besides provision of credit on affordable terms (Jayaraman and Lanjouw, 1999). Redistributive policies that expand the access of poor to credit can be of great help enabling them to invest in education to get out of poverty and expand their scale of production or take up more high return-high risk projects or occupational choices which were out of their reach earlier. Similarly, there is a need to bring better redistributive justice in education and health (Bardhan, 2001). Further, it is required to increase women's ownership and control of property, reform the property rights of the indigenous and marginalized people, and expand the capabilities of the poor and vulnerable through greater access to self-help development, new skills, and technologies (IFAD, 2002). In India, the weaknesses of the earlier programmes like DWCRA, PDS and IRDP have led to redesign of these programmes to promote people's participation through Panchayati Raj institutions, voluntary and community organizations and promotion of linkages with sectoral programmes for productive employment (Dev, 2000).

Conclusions

What is required for pro-poor growth and reduction of rural poverty is supporting institutions of rural communities and providing legal title to land and other resources to communities or individuals. There is a need to examine the issue of evolution of rural institutions and their consequences for the poor and the environment. In fact, the same institution can have dramatically different impacts on poverty and the environment depending on the adjustment mechanism followed. This necessitates research on explaining the dynamics of adjustment rather than focusing on institutional variety (Lopez, 1997).

However, all this is not to say that the local institutions are easy to evolve and panacea for all ills of rural society. It is only that they, if evolved, are the most suitable organizations for doing development in rural areas as they are based on local traditions and institutions. Co-operation in a more formal sense can emerge from such experiences of informal co-operation; it can rarely generate this experience. Therefore, in the environment of expanding markets and diminishing states, what is required is "assisted self help groups" which represents a pump priming approach to mobilizing local resources in a positive way with external funds and technical assistance offered on acceptable matching bases.

The issues which emerge from many studies of local institutions and organisations are: How to promote and help such local institutions through formal agencies? How far a legal recognition to these kinds of institutions could help building up of developmental linkages? How to devise mechanisms of helping them without imposing negative external effects? Besides, most of these groups are dependent on Self Help Promotion Institutions (SHPIs) in many ways. This raises questions about their sustainability in the absence of this support.

The creation of sustainable local institutions involves participatory approach to such initiatives wherein approaches like participatory appraisal and problem identification can be carried out with the communities and groups as a starting point. However, it is not sufficient *per se*. It is important to have an appropriate philosophy and approach to development since local people form quick, and usually correct, opinions about outsiders' initiatives. Therefore, they are to be regarded as partners in development rather than beneficiaries or target groups. The process of building local institutions starts with identification of partner population and their economic activities through participatory appraisal, research and planning. This then requires resource mobilization of various types like financial, physical, and human in terms of mutual training and education. This is followed by linkage building with third parties which involves obtaining the support of external agencies like banks, government departments, private organizations, and other groups and bodies which are part of the external environment amenable to change, as against the larger economic, political, and socio-cultural environment within which a self-help group has to function.

Some of the areas where private sector can participate in poverty reduction are: economic growth, human resource development, community empowerment and basic service delivery, direct provision of social services and advocacy and social mobilization (Cousart 1999). But, for the private sector, the task of poverty reduction is not attractive, as economic returns are not directly visible. However, it is important to realize that poverty itself becomes a barrier to economic growth in terms of limited markets for the private sector products and services. Therefore, with enlightened self-interest, the private sector should strive to reduce poverty.

REFERENCES

Bardhan, P. (1993): 'Analytics of the Institutions of Informal Co-operation in Rural Development', *World Development*, 21(4), 633-639.

Bardhan, P. (2001): 'Social Justice in the Global Economy', *Economic and Political Weekly*, 36 (5 & 6), February 3-10: 467-480.

Cord, L. (2002): 'Integrating the Rural Dimension into PRS', Paper presented at the Global Distance Learning Course *Reaching the Rural Poor: Strategies for Rural Development for the East Asia Region*, Bangkok, June 3-6.

Cousart, E.A. (1999): 'Poverty Alleviation in the Philippines: The Social Reform Agenda and Role of the Private Sector', *Regional Development Dialogue*, 20(1), Spring, 79-95.

Curtis, M. (2001): *Trade for Life: Making Trade Work for Poor People*, Christian Aid, London.

Dev, M. S. (2000): 'Public Intervention for Poverty Reduction in Asia: Macro Policies and Direct Programmes', Keynote Address presented in Plenary Session on Institutional Changes in Asian Agriculture at the *Third Asian Conference of Agricultural Economists*, October 18-20, Jaipur.

IFAD (2002): *Assessment of Rural Poverty – Asia and the Pacific*, IFAD (International Fund for Agricultural Development), January, Rome.

ITC (International Trade Centre) (2002): *Export-led Poverty Reduction Programme - Linking Poor Producers to International Markets*, http://www.intracen.org/eprp.

Jayaraman, R. and P. Lanjouw (1999): 'The Evolution of Poverty and Inequality in Indian Villages', *The World Bank Research Observer*, 14 (1), February, 1-30.

Kakwani, N. and E.M. Pernia (2000): 'What is Pro-Poor Growth?', *Asian Development Review*, 18(1), 1-16.

Kashyap, S.P. (2000): 'Food Security and Livelihood Security Concerns for Rural India', Keynote Address presented in Plenary Session on Poverty and Food & Nutrition Security in Asia at the *Third Asian Conference of Agricultural Economists*, October 18-20, Jaipur.

Killick, T. (2001): 'Globalisation and the Rural Poor', *Development Policy Review*, 19 (2), 155-180.

Krishna, A. (2003): 'Falling into Poverty—Other Side of Poverty Reduction', *Economic and Political Weekly*, 38(6), February 8: 533-542.

Lipton, M (2002): 'Access to Assets and Land in the Context of Poverty Reduction and Economic Development in Asia', Paper presented at the Global Distance Learning Course *Reaching the Rural Poor: Strategies for Rural Development for the East Asia Region,* June 3-6, Bangkok.

Lopez, R.E. (1997): 'Where Development Can or Cannot Go: The Role of Poverty-Environment Linkages', *Annual World Bank Conference on Development Economics,* The World Bank, Washington D.C, 285-306.

Maler, K. (1997): 'Environment, Poverty, and Economic Growth', *Annual World Bank Conference on Development Economics*, World Bank, Washington D.C, 251-270.

Misra, B. (1999): 'Are we Over-estimating the Possible Role of the Private Sector in Rural Poverty Alleviation? An Analysis of the India Situation and Experience', *Regional Development Dialogue*, 20(1), Spring, 55-72.

Rajan, R.S. (2002): 'Trade Liberalisation and Poverty: Revisiting the Age-old Debate', *Economic and Political Weekly*, 37(49), December 7: 4941–46.

Ravallion, M. (2000): 'What is Needed for a More Pro Poor Growth Process in India?' *Economic and Political Weekly*, 35 (13), March 25: 1089-93.

Shah, T. (1993): 'Institutional Dimensions of Agricultural and Rural Development in India', *Working Paper No.42*, Anand, Institute of Rural Management (IRMA), August.

Sundaram, K. and S.D. Tendulkar (2003): 'Poverty in India in the 1990s: An Analysis of Changes in 15 Major States', *Economic and Political Weekly*, 38 (14), April 5: 1385-93.

Turk, C. (2002): 'Integrating the Rural Dimension into the Comprehensive Poverty Reduction and Growth Strategy (CPRGS)', Paper presented at the Global Distance Learning Course *Reaching the Rural Poor: Strategies for Rural Development for the East Asia Region* held in Bangkok June 3-6.

Turton, C. and J. Farrington (1999): 'Bringing a Poverty Focus to the Sustainable Rural Livelihoods Approach: Experiences from Western Orissa', Paper presented at *Sustainable Livelihoods Workshop*, June 28th, IDS, Sussex, Brighton (U.K).

Uphoff, N. (1993): 'Grassroots Organisations and NGOs in Rural Development: Opportunities with Diminishing States and Expanding Markets', *World Development*, 21(4), 607-622.

Uphoff, N. (1992): 'Local Institutions and Participation for Sustainable Development', *IIED Gatekeeper Series, No. 31*, International Institute for Environment and Development (IIED), London.

Verhagen, K. (1987): *Self-Help Promotion – a challenge to the NGO community*, Royal Tropical Institute, Amsterdom.

Vyas, V.S. (1997): 'Poverty Alleviation and Nutrition Enhancement in South Asia: The Missing Links', *Asian Journal of Agricultural Economics*, 2(2): 101-108.

Warr, P.G. (2000): 'Is Growth Good for the Poor? Thailand's Boom and Bust', *International Journal of Social Economics*, 27 (7/8/9/10), 862-877.

World Bank (2000): 'Attacking the Rural Poverty: Strategy and Public Action', *Rural Development Note No. 6*, December, Washington D.C.

World Bank (2001): *World Development Report 2000-2001 – Attacking Poverty*, OUP, London.

World Bank (2002): *Globalisation, Growth, and Poverty – Building an Inclusive World Economy*, World Bank and OUP, Washington D.C.

11

The New Governance Paradigm

Its Meaning and Some Implications for Development

H.S. SHYLENDRA

Introduction

Even as alleviating poverty and inequality remains a major developmental challenge, the nation is experiencing a transition into a new governance paradigm prescriptively being referred to as good governance. The *dirigiste* regime (Patnaik and Patnaik, 2001) is giving way to a new system of governance characterised by increasing trend towards globalisation, privatisation and liberalisation which is making the state loose its pre-eminence as an agency for development. The new system unfolding in the nation in the last one decade or so entails following new and previously uncharted paths for realising our developmental goals. The thrust of the new approach appears to be one of maximising the growth potential by unleashing outward looking and market driven forces by making necessary adjustments in the structure of the economy and the manner of exercise of control over power and resources (Government of India, 2002). These adjustments have necessitated introducing or adopting a new set of conducive economic and other policies under the broad rubric of good governance. As the outcomes of the new approach still remain ambivalent needing a clear assessment, serious concerns have been expressed about the possible negative consequences of the new approach for the unfinished agenda of eradicating mass poverty (Ghosh, 2002). The present paper, based on a review of available literature, makes an attempt to examine the nature of the emerging governance paradigm, and assess the possible implications of it for tackling the problems of poverty and inequality.

The New Governance Paradigm

In this section, an attempt is made to look at the meaning and nature of the new governance paradigm. The initial discourse on the new governance paradigm is characterised to a certain extent by lack of clarity both in the conceptualisation and operationalisation of the phenomenon. Though the essence of the phenomenon could be seen in the efforts made in the west to dismantle the welfare state in the 1980s, the clear conceptualisation and articulation of the phenomenon emerged much later. Further, the complexity of the phenomenon due to its multi-dimensional and multi-layered nature further added to the difficulty in the clear conceptualisation. However, the growing literature along with the increased efforts towards advocating the concept by various agencies in the last few years has brought in some amount of clarity about its meaning in the ongoing discourse.

The new governance paradigm is being seen and analysed both in the descriptive and prescriptive sense (Chandhoke, 2003). In the descriptive sense, governance is being seen as a phenomenon which is emerging in response to the changing role of state due to various reasons both in the developed and developing countries. In the developed countries of the west, the role of welfare state has been declining under the influence of the neo liberal Reagan-Thatcher ideology, which advocates a drastic cut in the public spending on welfare activities. In the developing countries, the state is being forced to give more scope for other actors in development with the introduction of globalisation and structural adjustment programmes. As a result, there is a growing pluralisation of state with multiple actors or agencies spread over from local to global level trying to both supplement and supplant the conventional state in its basic role of development.

In the prescriptive sense, there are two approaches to governance, a narrow and a broader approach. In the narrow approach, it is mainly about enabling the right manner of exercise of power for attaining better economic development in a country as prescribed by the World Bank (World Bank, 1994). In the broader sense, it is both about the right manner of exercise of power for economic development as well as simultaneously enhancing the scope for promoting participation and even democratic processes as being advocated by bilateral or official aid agencies like DFID, USAID and OECD. In the prescriptive sense, governance is even known or being advocated as good or effective governance. For a better understanding of the concept of governance, it is essential that both types of conceptualisation, descriptive and prescriptive, are taken into account for the concept is evolving in both the senses.

The pluralisation of the state for development is the major feature when governance is seen from the descriptive point of view. Development is to be delivered by multiple agencies including the state. Pluralisation of state basically means the pre-eminence or even centrality of the state is lost. The state has to limit itself or contract its role so that other players like market and civil society are given adequate space and scope to contribute for development. The pluralisation has been necessitated as the state alone cannot respond to the diverse needs of development. The different actors who come into the picture for development include: under state, local and national governments, and multilateral agencies; under market, local traders, national and multinational companies; and under civil society, citizens, community based organisations (CBOs), and national and international NGOs (Table 11.1). Thus, governance as a paradigm includes real multiplicity or plurality of institutions which are supposed to be acting in unison to influence development at and from different levels. All these actors are to co-ordinate and network with each other more through horizontal linkages which are both non-hierarchical and non-bureaucratic (Chandhoke, 2003). Through such a linkage, the sharp difference between the state and non-state is to be blurred or rendered irrelevant for development.

Table 11.1: Actors in Development under Governance Paradigm

Reach/ Jurisdiction	*State*	*Market*	*Civil Society*
Global	Multilateral Agencies (UN, WB, WTO etc.)	Multi-National Companies (MNCs)	International NGOs
National	National/ Regional Governments	Domestic Companies/ MNC Branches	National/ Regional NGOs
Local	Local self-government	Local Traders/ Businessmen	Local NGOs/ CBOs/Citizens

In terms of linking governance paradigm to development policy and practice, it is the prescriptive approach of governance which becomes more important. The prescriptive approach of governance becomes visible in the approaches advocated by multilateral agencies like World Bank, UNDP and official aid agencies like DFID and USAID. It was the World Bank which for the first time tried to define as well as link up governance issues to development (World Bank, 1994). Governance was defined by World Bank as 'the manner in which power is exercised in the management of a country's economic and social resources for development' (*ibid.*). The prime concern of the World Bank in emphasising the role of governance emerged from its interest in ensuring the sustainability of World Bank funded projects which needed promoting good governance through a predictable and transparent framework of rules and institutions for the co-existence of private and public business. To World Bank, good governance is characterised by 'predictable, open and enlightened policy-making; a bureaucracy imbued with a professional ethos; an executive arm of government accountable for its actions and a strong civil society participating in public affairs; and all behaving under the rule of law' (World Bank, 1994). Thus, good governance as per World Bank's prescription has to be brought in within the existing political system. Given its mandate, World Bank has confined advocating good governance only to bring about sustainable socio-economic development. It is governance for better economic management rather than for changing the form of political system. The four major areas of concern, identified by the World Bank to be addressed in achieving good governance are: (i) improving public sector management; (ii) ensuring accountability of public and private sectors, (iii) creating and appropriate legal framework for development, and (iv) promoting transparency and information. All these four dimensions are to work in a mutually reinforcing way leading to establishment of good governance.

The concept of good or effective governance as advocated by World Bank is broadened by official aid agencies which support poverty alleviation programmes of developing countries through development co-operation (Currie, 2001; World Bank, 1994). The approach of many of these aid agencies tries to broaden the concept of governance by integrating political dimensions into the World Bank's concept of good governance. The broadening is done mainly by emphasising that good governance goes along with participatory development and democracy. A democratic system which encourages inclusive and participatory institutions and promotes transparent and accountable societies is a major requirement for good governance. Thus, both the legitimacy and capacity of governance are considered important for attaining various goals of sustainable development.

A major aspect in the emergence of good governance for development is the contextualisation of the phenomenon that seems to be taking place to suit the specific needs of each nation. Even the concept of corporate governance being propagated appears to be the logical extension of such contextualisation of governance to corporate entities. It is here that the recent recognition and articulation on governance paradigm by Government of India becomes relevant (Government of India, 2002). Government of India has come out with its approach to governance under the framework developed for implementation of the Tenth Five Year Plan (2002-07) in the country.

For Government of India, the governance paradigm is more of a prescriptive phenomenon which becomes evident from the fact that there is a clear acknowledgement of the universally accepted features of good governance like the legitimate exercise of political power along with creating administration which is transparent, equitable, participatory and accountable. Given these universal goals, the thrust is on contextualising them to the emerging needs of the country. 'Governance', to Government of India, 'relates to the management of all such processes that in any society, define the environment which permits and enables individuals to raise their capability levels, on the one hand, and to provide to realise their potential and enlarge the set of available choices, on the other' (Government of India, 2002:177). Thus, the proclaimed goal of governance is to bring about human development. The processes of governance are managed by multiple institutions or agencies consisting of the state, market and the civil society; each playing a specific and a critical role in the process. Acceptance of plurality of actors is the key feature of the new governance for development.

In the same vein, an attempt also has been made to operationalise the concept. Given the multiplicity of actors, working towards a common goal requires that a harmonious relationship exists among and between them. The diverse players and also their constantly changing needs and context require that rules of interplay are evolved and harmonised through continuous adaptation.

The three key elements of governance that are identified by Government of India in determining the harmonious interplay are the institutions, both formal and informal, the delivery mechanism and the legal framework. Though both formal and informal arrangements are considered under the institutional structure, it is mostly the formal institutions like parliament and judiciary having a broader developmental goal which have been identified for the purpose. These institutions use the delivery mechanism which is the apparatus run by government, non-government and market institutions for implementing the agenda of development. The delivery mechanism includes apparatus like law courts, hospitals, schools, and police stations providing various services. An appropriate legal framework (laws, rules, and procedures) has to be evolved to help the institutions realize their objectives through the delivery mechanism. The three elements have to adapt to each other suitably so that ultimately the broader goals of the institutions are realised. Bringing about such harmonisation becomes the major requirement under governance to ensure predictability, stability, and efficiency in all the transactions or interactions, be it political or social or economic that may take place among the three actors of development.

In contextualising governance, the Government of India goes further and has identified specific operational strategies that are to be implemented for realising good governance for development. These strategies include: improved people's participation by way of effective decentralisation through local self-governments and involving civil society and voluntary organisations to accelerate socio-economic development; ensuring right to information for transparency; reforming civil service to improve accountability and efficiency; administrative procedural reforms for a hassle free public-government interface; improving the fiscal health of government by improving the resource mobilisation through a transparent and equitable tax-administration and by correcting the subsidy and pricing system of various public services; reforming the judicial system for a speedy delivery of justice; improving the co-ordination between different public agencies and departments involved in development for a better synergy and efficiency; systematic and professional programme/project formulation, implementation and monitoring; empowering the marginal and the excluded to equip them to act as pressure groups to resist bad governance and exploitation by vested interests; and using information technology for a transparent and efficient administration (Government of India, 2002).

Taking into consideration both the descriptive and the prescriptive dimensions of governance as well as its contextualisation, the following key elements emerge which are also summarised in Table 11.2.

(i) The role and responsibilities of the state for development are to be handled by multiple actors like state, civil society, and market institutions whose reach may extend from global to local level, and who may interact with each other more in a non-hierarchical way. Development is no longer the sole prerogative of the state.

Table 11.2: Comparative Features of the Existing and New Governance Paradigm

Features	*Existing Paradigm*	*New Paradigm*
Goal	Economic Development	Human Development
Political System	Democratic or non-democratic	Democratic and Participatory
Actors in Development	State or Market with or without Civil Society	State, Market and Civil Society
Legal framework	Favouring State or Market	Suitable for the co-existence of all three actors
Outcome of various Transactions	Non-predictable	Predictable
Reach/Jurisdiction of Actors	National / Local	Global, National and Local
Source of Mandate for Actors	National / Local	Global, National and Local
Relationship between Actors	Bureaucratic and Hierarchical	Horizontal/ Non-bureaucratic
Purpose of Relationship	Control by State or Market	Co-ordination/ Networking
Delivery Mechanism	Government agencies and/ or Private firms, and/ or NGOs	Government agencies, Private firms and NGOs

(ii) The ultimate goal of governance paradigm is to bring about human development which is to be achieved through the contribution of multiple actors. Efficiency, equity and accountability are the major ways for attaining the goal. While efficiency is to be attained through market mechanisms and administrative reforms; equity is to be ensured through growth and by enlarging choice and opportunities for all sections. Accountability for delivering development is to be brought about through democratic, transparent and participatory decision-making processes.

(iii) Harmonising the relations between multiple actors is the major essence of the new governance paradigm. Different actors and elements of governance are to adapt to the scenario of plurality in order to evolve a system with harmonious interactions. Making the system more predictable and stable through suitable institutional and legal arrangements is the key for such a harmony.

Possible Implications of New Governance for Development

While to the Planning Commission of India 'good governance is one of the most crucial factors, if the targets of Tenth Five Pear Plan are to be achieved' (Government of India, 2002); going by the broader connotations and the potential of the concept for unfolding paradigmatic changes, the concept of governance is likely to have major consequences on the whole developmental process. Since governance as is emerging has a crucial bearing on the manner of exercise of power and control over societal resources, its implications are also immense for tackling the problems of poverty and inequality. However, predicting the real outcomes of the phenomenon is problematic. As such, there is no clear experience of any country which has gone through the new paradigm with all its features. Moreover, the paradigm is still evolving. Hence, the emerging results or outcomes of the new approach are uncertain and ambivalent (Jayal and Pai 2001). This could be a cause of concern for those countries including India which still have a long way to go in eradicating poverty. However, the major concern comes from the argument that the new paradigm of governance being advocated is basically an instrument for pushing forward the western neo-liberal economic ideology which supports capitalistic mode of development using market as the dominant agency of development (Jayal and Pai, 2001). Hence, there is also an argument that the governance paradigm itself needs to be assessed before all its ramifications could be analysed (Chandhoke, 2003).

The pluralisation of state apparently has many implications for development. On the positive side, it means that development which is a complex problem can be tackled in a more efficient and effective manner by combining the strengths of all the diverse players who have been given due space. On the negative side, the major implication of such plurality is how and on whom to fix the clear responsibility and accountability for tackling the problems like poverty alleviation. Further, the relationship between different agencies involved under governance has to be harmonious and predictable. If such a harmonious and predictable relationship cannot be evolved or ensured, potentially there could be a scenario of conflict rather than one of smooth co-ordination among the actors. Such a scenario of conflict may pose difficulties for realising the synergy for development expected of the plurality.

Conclusion

A new paradigm of governance is thus emerging posing a major challenge for the unfinished agenda of poverty eradication. Pluralisation of state for development is the major feature of the new governance. Development is no longer the sole responsibility of the state. The challenges of development are to be addressed jointly by state along with market and civil society. All the three agencies are to act in unison for attaining development and change. A key requirement for the new governance to work is the harmonising of the relationship between different actors so that the common goals could be attained smoothly without any conflict of interests. Creating suitable environment for all the three actors to co-exist so that all the processes of interplay are transparent and outcomes predictable is the major task under the harmonisation process.

The new paradigm appears to be emerging as a result of the changing role of state taking place both in the developed and developing countries. For the developing countries like India, the paradigm is also emerging in the prescriptive form of good governance through the process of conditional development aid and globalisation of trade.

While the new paradigm is yet to emerge in its fullest form of pluralisation, but there are both scepticism and optimism about its possible outcomes for issues like poverty alleviation and equity.

There is a fear that the new paradigm is serving as an instrument or facade for thrusting upon the capitalist and neo-liberal order on developing countries with a potential to reverse the past achievements of the *dirigiste* or the state led developmental regime. The other view is that the new (good) governance paradigm is a need of the hour for making amends in the past failures of the state-led development for achieving higher economic and human development (Government of India, 2002a). Hence, there is a need to look at the real nature of governance phenomenon along with its possible implications for the crucial issue of poverty eradication and equity.

The following are some of the major issues which need to be examined in the light of the emerging paradigm for development in general and poverty alleviation and equity in particular:

(i) Can the new paradigm with multiple actors generate the right kind of synergy which can help address squarely the problems of poverty and inequality? How far the real nature of the new governance about which there is no clear unanimity would help in achieving the much-needed synergy?

(ii) How exactly a harmony can be brought about in the goals and mechanisms of state, market and civil society institutions? What type of systems and processes of interplay between different actors need to be established for such harmonisation?

(iii) What safeguards are needed to avoid the 'governance failure'? The new governance concept is being advocated as a means to overcome both the state and market failures. Can the elements of good governance ensure that the 'governance failure' does not occur for the poor? The 'governance failure' could occur when the actors of governance do not respond to the needs of the poor or conflict of interests between the three actors may lead to adverse fallouts on poverty and inequality. How to avoid or reverse such pitfalls under the new governance? How to make all the actors accountable for poverty alleviation and equity?

(iv) What has been the impact of the changing role of state, civil society and markets observed under the emerging paradigm for poverty alleviation and equity? What should be the ideal role for state under the new governance? How the market should be governed under the new governance? How to tap the strengths of civil society for poverty alleviation?

REFERENCES

Chandhoke, Neera (2003): 'Governance and the Pluralisation of the State: Implications for Democratic Citizenship', *Economic and Political Weekly,* 38(28): 2957-68.

Currie, Bob (2001): 'Political Authority, Public Deliberation, and the Politics of Poverty Reduction', in Niraja Gopal Jayal and Sudha Pai (eds.) *Democratic Governance in India: Challenges of Poverty, Development, and Identity,* Sage, New Delhi.

Ghosh, Jayati (2002): 'Economic Reforms and Globalisation: Country Case Studies', in *Human Development in South Asia 2001*, Mahbub Haq Human Development Centre, Oxford, Karachi.

Government of India (2002): *Tenth Five Year Plan (2002-2007): Dimensions and Strategies,* Vol. I. Planning Commission, New Delhi.

Jayal, Niraja Gopal and Sudha Pai (eds) (2001): *Democratic Governance in India: Challenges of Poverty, Development, and Identity,* New Delhi: Sage, New Delhi:

Patnaik, Utsa and Prabhat Patnaik (2001): 'The State, Poverty, and Development in India', in Niraja Gopal Jayal and Sudha Pai (eds), *Democratic Governance in India: Challenges of Poverty, Development, and Identity,* Sage, New Delhi.

World Bank (1994): *Governance: The World Bank's Experience,* World Bank, Washington D.C.

12

Decentralisation, Employment and Enterprises Development

Some Issues in the Context of Kerala

P.M. MATHEW

Local Economic Development: Theoretical Background

The economic rationale for decentralised governance is embedded in the 'balanced regional development' argument. In India, this argument is as old as the planning era. One of the major arguments for development planning, as a whole, is the need to achieve some level of balanced regional development (See Myrdal, Nurkse, Lewis etc.) The 1980s witnessed a new interest in institutions, largely from the micro-economic angle. This may be explained in terms of two major developments; one relating to economic theory, and the other to organisation theory. The old discussion of 'state *versus* market' was settled by a new theoretical intervention: the theory of New Institutional Economics (NIE).

NIE is a body of economic theory, which ascribes an important role to ideas and ideologies, and is assessable to other social scientists, seeming to open up the terrain of genuinely interdisciplinary enquiries (Harriss, *et al.* 1997). NIE starts from the reality that information is rarely complete, and therefore, transactions have costs associated with them, which are assumed not to exist in the neo-classical model. Since institutions are broadly defined as means of reducing information and transactions costs, such as, that of finding out the relevant prices, of negotiating and of concluding contracts, and then of monitoring and enforcing them.

Under this theoretical paradigm, "institutions provide the mechanisms, whereby rational individuals can transcend social dilemmas". According to Toy, social dilemmas are those kinds of problems which arise when choices made by rational individuals yield outcomes that are socially irrational.

The above theoretical paradigm positions institutions as a cost-reducing and efficiency enhancing instrument which work between the extremes of state and the market. At the more micro-level, organisation theory applies the basic principles of institutions such as 'trust' and 'networking' to the context of interim relationships. According to Campbell (1992), a new type of industrial organisation, somewhere between 'markets' and 'hierarchies' is emerging since 1980s. This new form of inter-firm organisation, also called 'quasi-market', is characterised by growing trust, co-operation and longer-term ties among nominally independent economic units. The theory of 'flexible specialization' and the present-day operational strategy of clusters and networks are based on these theoretical premises.

In the modern times, this argument has appeared in a different form, in the debate on 'industrial districts'. While, the early arguments for decentralisation were largely in the context of developing countries, the period since late 1980s witnessed such a strong argument in the case of industrialised countries. The theory of 'flexible specialisation' and 'industrial districts' focuses on the economics of decentralisation. It states that, there is substantial scope for developing a pattern of decentralised or cluster-based industrial development with the active support of the local government. While, poverty is not the rationale behind such argument, it is deeply rooted in the need for employment creation of a substantial scale.

In the late-1990s, the argument for decentralisation has been strongly anchored on the concept of 'social capital'. The concept of social capital, developed by Robert Putnam (1993), implies "features of social organisation such as networks, norms, and trust that facilitate co-ordination and co-operation for mutual benefit". The theory of social capital states that, even though identical policies aimed at promoting democracy and development may be undertaken, the degree of success in realising these goals is determined by the fecundity of social capital in individual contexts. Social capital thus, fosters reciprocity, facilitates information flows for mutual benefit, and creates trust. Once these are in place, they tend to be self-generative, as future generations are inducted into these norms through socialisation. According to Putnam, "social capital enhances the benefits of investment in physical and human capital" (Putnam, 1993).

Duality of Decentralisation in Kerala

The decentralization debate in India, over the last several decades, has dealt with basically its politics. The situation continues to be the same, even under the pressures of globalisation and mounting problems like youth unemployment. In Kerala, there have been two basic ideological positions, which underlie the process of economic development. The conventional perception is that, private investments should increasingly take place, and for that, there should be a flexible labour market, the market signals should be adequate and appropriate. Another paradigm to the contrary is that, private investments are generally against the interests of social choice, and the focus should be on collective initiatives, where the element of private profit motive is absent. It is an articulation on these lines that made Kerala the home of various forms of collective organizations like self-help groups, micro credit institutions and co-operatives. Hence the ideology of decentralization at the operational level was too confusing in the Kerala context.

But none of these interventions were based on a clear perception of the role of public policy in the day to day economic activities. This state of flux was capitalized by vested interests: (1) state became too rigid and dictatorial in economic policy matters, (2) interest groups became increasingly exploitative as against the interests of the majority who are practically unorganized.

The stringent ideological positions, as above continued until mid-1990s. But, it led more to policy ambivalence than to a pro-active public policy. It was the serious development crisis of the State which provoked thinking on the economic aspects of decentralization. While, public investments have proved to be less productive and stagnant, and private sector being a factor which needs to be scared away, there has been an enhanced focus on social capital. "Energising the productive forces" was argued as the case for decentralization. But what was done to energise it? The answer was too ambiguous. In fact, the net result was a total inertia. In the 1960s and 1970s, cooperatives and public sector were the answers. In the new century, it is social capital.

While Robert Putnam's conceptualization of social capital is relevant, based on the practical experience of developing countries, Scholars like John Harriss raised some fundamental issues regarding its intentions. In this paper, however, it is not intended to dwell into these theoretical debates. On the contrary, our attempt is to examine the experience of economic decentralization in Kerala in the recent past, and to raise a few issues for discussion.

Focusing Social Capital means Escapism

The conventional theories of capital have undergone major changes during the past two decades. Various scholars have shown that, social connections, or social capital, mean a lot in the process of income generation. The basic definition of capital is of "a stock of assets, which can produce a flow of income". Does social capital, and public policy initiatives for its development, add to Kerala's economic development?

Let us examine the experience of Kerala's macro economy. Average SDP growth in Kerala during 1994-95 was 8.6 per cent, it has come down to 4.7 per cent in 2001-02. The disaggregated data again show an alarming picture. While the tertiary sector has been highlighted as the mainstay of the Kerala model of development, this sector too shows a declining trend. Capital expenditure, which essentially means capital formation in the economy, has declined significantly from 16.82 per cent in the 1970s to an average level of 3.56 per cent during the period 1996-2000. Going by Putnam's logic, the surge of social capital formation in the form of SHGs and large programmes like *Kudumbashree*, should have got reflected in SDP as well as capital expenditure. Theoretically, capital is an asset which can produce income. Does social capital in Kerala actually contribute to the process of income generation in the State? It is this question that everybody should ponder when considering decentralization as an engine of economic development.

Kerala's domestic economy is stagnating over time in overall terms. Even the tertiary sector growth, which is considered to be the backbone of the Kerala model of development, is on shaky ground. Why does this phenomenon take place? Capital formation is declining significantly. On the other hand, the rise in revenue expenditure year-by-year is helping to activate the commercial orientation of the economy. Even in this role, the economy does not perform very well.

Why does this happen? The commercial orientation of the economy is pervasive, because the commercial-orientation of entrepreneurship itself is high. In simple language, it means that the economic base of the Kerala society is tuned in such a way as not to promote worthwhile entrepreneurial activity. What is being officially promoted as 'entrepreneurship' is rent-seeking activities, which actually help to weaken the productive forces. Therefore, in Kerala, where public policy speaks of entrepreneurship, it essentially means anti-entrepreneurship.

Economic decentralization is superimposed on this weak base of public policy. Economic decentralization for employment generation and enterprise development should essentially mean an opportunity to provide economic justice to the majority of the people. Economic justice, essentially means anything between basic needs to '*Anthyodaya*'. In a democratic system, which we have, the basic assumption is that every citizen is an economic decision-maker, driven by private economic interests. But how can these private interests be tailored to the needs of regional economic development? This question has not been properly addressed in the context of Kerala so far. Instead of addressing this core issue, it is the PRIs and the so-called expert committees who decide what the entrepreneurs should do.

A conflict between private interest and social interest is typical of any society. The question, therefore, is how to resolve these conflicts. Kerala has not succeeded in understanding the nature and depth of this conflict.

What is a social interest? How is it shaped? "A higher level of living for all, and rising expectations for millions", is the usual answer. But how can the level of such expectations be determined? Here is the conflict between globalization and localization. For the ordinary Keralite the situation is conflicting, but for the multinational companies, it is not. In the context of an industrialized economy such as the USA or Europe, the so-called 'localization of competitive advantage' is a reality (Enright, 2001). But how far is it relevant for an ordinary Keralite?

Crucial Issues

The above discussion leads us to the following crucial issues:

(1) Role of industrial capital and commercial capital in Kerala's economy,
(2) Identification of social groups in terms of their contribution to the economy,
(3) The support base of the political system,
(4) The distribution of power among different social sub-groups,
(5) The pattern of appropriation of surpluses.

While in the context of a highly industrialized economy, the conflict between globalisation and localisation is minimal, in a region like Kerala, such conflicts are substantial. In addition to being part of the Indian economy, which has undergone the globalisation and liberalization process over the last one decade, Kerala's added dimension relates to its significant international linkages through migration. These two factors have significantly triggered an international demonstration effect in Kerala's economy. Globalisation does not automatically mean an opening up of markets. Such opening up takes place through a circuitous process where culture plays a significant role. Kentucky chicken is sold in India, not simply because it is available here, but because the middle class which consider it as prestigious, has grown in our country. How has this middle class grown? It is through a change in the culture and value system, which globalisation brought in. But is globalisation the sole culprit? No, our political parties, religious groups, educational system etc. have been nurturing and promoting such a culture for quite some time (see, for example, how the problems of the NRIs get much greater attention among the political parties than the agricultural labourer!)

If the culture of the Kerala middle class has changed significantly in favour of a variety of imported products, then why should swadeshi soaps and match boxes be manufactured at all? Going by the principles of competition, no entrepreneur will find it viable.

The investment approach, as advocated by many, is often labour-displacing. The thrust on social capital means the opposite extreme of employment fundamentalism. But in any society *employment* is the prime goal, which can create some minimum level of consensus in society in favour of the same economic policies. It will raise issues on competitiveness of firms, employability of labour and the basic foundation of public policy as such. If so, public policy will focus on effective labour market intervention, which Kerala does not do now. It is this common agenda, that can swing Kerala society into action.

REFERENCES

Campbell, O. (1992): *Is the Small Firm Vanishing?*, International Institute of Labour Studies, Geneva.

Enright, Michael J. (2001): *Local Partnership*, Clusters and SME Globalisation.

Harriss, John (2000): *Social Capital*, Left Word, New Delhi.

Harriss, John *et al*. (1997): *New Institutional Economics*, Routledge, London.

Heller, Patrick (1996): 'Social Capital as a Product of Class Mobilisation and State Intervention: Industrial Workers in Kerala, India', *World Development*, 24 (6): 1055-71.

Mathew, P.M. (1997): *Parentage and Entrepreneurial Performance*, Indian Council of Social Science Research, New Delhi.

Mathew, P.M. (2000): *Small Enterprise Development: The Experience of the North and South*, Oxford, New Delhi.

Mathew, P.M. (ed) (2002): 'Database of the Kerala Economy'. *Proceedings of the ISED-State Planning Board Conference on Database of the Kerala Economy*, State Planning Board, Cochin.

Mathew, P.M. (2000): *Decentralised Planning for Small Enterprise Development*, Indian Council of Social Science Research, New Delhi.

Mathew, P.M. (1990): *Understanding Informalism: An Enquiry into Some Aspects of the Industrial Development of Kerala,* Institute of Small Enterprises and Development, Cochin.

Mathew, P.M. *et al*. (2003): *Globalisation and SMEs in India, Interim Report of the Programme on Globalisation and SMEs,* Institute of Small Enterprises and Development, Cochin.

Putnam, R. (1993): *Making Democracy Work: Civic Traditions in Modern Italy,* Princeton University Press, Princeton.

SECTION–III

PEOPLE'S PARTICIPATION IN LOCAL GOVERNANCE

13

From Kallesseri to the People's Plan Campaign

Issues in Governance

RASHMI SHARMA

This chapter may be viewed as an exploration of the 'high-end' of governance and policy-making in India. In the recent wave of decentralization in the country, the process set off in Kerala through the People's Plan Campaign (PPC) has been the most extensive in terms of powers and funds devolved, and also most intensive in terms of processes developed (Jha, 2002; World Bank, 2000). PPC in Kerala drew substantially from the experiences of Kerala Shastra Sahitya Parishad (KSSP) especially that of developing a grassroots planning process. Simultaneously, as the Kerala government planned and steered PPC, a high degree of motivation and commitment was visible (Parameswaran, 1998; Isaac, 2000).

The Kerala experience, therefore, in contrast to the story of grudging and haphazard decentralization characteristic in many Indian states, provides an opportunity to analyze those key issues of policy-making and governance that remain unclear where government initiative is weak. In the latter sort of cases the focus necessarily shifts to the paucity of the initiative. But where, as in the case of Kerala, strong processes are in fact put in place, it becomes possible to understand a different dynamic: what are the issues that arise when governments try to adapt intelligent processes developed by NGOs? This is the question that this chapter addresses.

It needs to be stated at the outset that the analysis attempted is limited to the process of adaptation. There is no attempt to comment on the intrinsic value of the Kallesseri experience and whether or not decentralization was the appropriate policy choice. What is examined is how the Kallesseri experience was interpreted and adapted in PPC, which leads to the more general question of the dynamics of applying innovative processes in larger, governmental contexts. This is an area of policy making that is becoming increasingly important in India as in many sectors governments attempt to adapt models developed by NGOs.

This chapter begins by a brief account of the Kallesseri and PPC experiences, highlighting the similarities and differences. This is followed by an analysis of why these similarities and differences arose and what this means for policy.

The Kallesseri Experience

The importance of Kallesseri lies in the fact that a process of grassroots planning was developed in this panchayat and became the basis for local planning all over Kerala. The Kallesseri process was initiated by KSSP, which began primarily as a movement for popularizing science and creating scientific temper among the people in the sixties. The goal was to empower backward communities and oppressed illiterates, and this empowerment was expected to prepare the ground for democracy and development. In the seventies KSSP extended its activities to optimal utilization of local resources and later became active in building an environmental critique of developmental projects. These concerns led to the realization of the importance of decentralization for appropriate planning. By 1989, KSSP had begun to demand genuine decentralization and strengthening of village level capabilities for self-reliant growth (Isaac, *et al.* 1995).

Three KSSP projects were important precursors of Kallesseri. The first was 'group farming', aimed at increasing productivity, reducing the cost of cultivation and generating greater and profitable rice production through joint farm operations, water management, plant protection etc. As a government initiative, group farming had some initial success, but ran into problems over time. The second important precursor was the state-wide total literacy campaign, again with mixed success (Kumar, 1993, Tornquist and Tharakan, 1996). The third precursor was the People's Resource Mapping Programme (PRMP), a collaborative effort between Centre for Earth Science Studies, the Land Use Board and KSSP, modelled on the literacy campaign and aimed at supplementing group farming towards more radical development in rural areas. For KSSP, PRMP represented a shift from 'alphabet literacy' to 'development literacy'. PRMP was based on the premise that to make local planning a reality, a comprehensive data-base, mass participation as well as development of local expertise were the key. The central activity of PRMP was the preparation of an 'Environmental Appraisal Map' that could be used to identify different soil types, areas susceptible to soil erosion, potential areas of water availability, conservation efforts needed to stem environmental degradation and hazards related to mining, quarrying, inappropriate agricultural practices etc. The mapping exercise included public participation as well as scientific and technical inputs. PRMP was begun in 25 panchayats, including Kallesseri, and later extended to all panchayats (Isaac, 2000; Isaac, *et al.* 1995).

In Kallesseri panchayat, a CPM[1] stronghold with a long tradition of mass movements, it became possible to move ahead with the formulation and implementation of a local action plan. The basic premise was that even though economic self-sufficiency was not possible, the panchayat could aspire for fullest utilization of its internal growth potential, and that public action, that had changed village life for the better in the past, should be the vehicle of further development. A detailed and exhaustive planning exercise was undertaken, initiated with the development of an Environmental Appraisal Map and augmented with a socio-economic survey. Various facets of development in Kallesseri were analyzed. The analysis showed that agrarian reforms had improved the quality of life for the poor and there had been remarkable increase in literacy. Two other exogenous developments, remittances of gulf migrants and the growth of the small-scale sector near Kallesseri, which provided employment to many inhabitants, had improved the standard of living. Yet there was agrarian stagnation, growing unemployment and deterioration of the quality of health and education services. Fragmentation of land did not allow for scientific land and water management or economies of scale. Moreover, these land holdings were inadequate to meet even the subsistence requirements of the landholders, so that non-agricultural activities provided the main source of income. Consequently, land-holders did not try to maximize production. Scarcity of agricultural labour compounded the problem as the better-educated younger generation withdrew from farm work. Agricultural practices too were unsatisfactory. Thus the full possibilities within agriculture for better income and unemployment remained untapped. Issues related to industry, energy, employment, health and education were similarly analyzed (Isaac, *et al*. 1995).

These findings were discussed with people, officials and experts and resulted in an outline of an action programme and identification of issues on which more detailed studies were needed. These included demand survey for vegetables and eggs, survey of educational institutions, survey and mapping of drainage channels, power line mapping, total energy survey, an engineering survey of marshy land for aqua culture and a hydrological survey for the watershed programme. Thus planning in Kallesseri was based not only upon the felt needs of the people, which tended to be heavily biased towards roads, schools etc., but also on an assessment of the resource endowments of the village, a socio-economic survey and technical studies to prepare schemes. There was significant contribution by experts within and outside Kerala. The plan relied heavily on voluntary labour, of which the panchayat had a history. Most of the volunteers were members of mass organizations such as trade unions and various wings of political parties. The village panchayat president was enthusiastic about the exercise. In spite of these strengths, a comprehensive village plan took a long while to be worked out and was in fact viewed by some as an esoteric exercise. As the delays in the completion of studies lengthened, some components were taken up simultaneously for implementation (Isaac, *et al*. 1995).

Given the very limited financial and other powers of the Grama Panchayat at that time (in 1991-92), a new development institution, the Kallesseri Development Society (KDS), with the panchayat president as ex-officio chairman, was formed. All development activities were carried out under the banner of KDS. It had a General Body of 200 persons comprising an elected representative for every 25 households, elected panchayat representatives and government officials. Elections to the KDS were usually based on consensus and voting rarely became necessary. KDS was headed by a Working Committee, which was responsible for the day-to-day functions and also set the agenda, as discussions of the General Body normally took place around a document presented by the Working Committee. The Working Committee comprised panchayat elected representatives, technical experts, a representative from KSSP and officials. There were also eight sub-committees dealing with agriculture, fisheries, animal husbandry, irrigation, energy, education, health and communication (Isaac, *et al.* 1995).

Three projects implemented by KDS, i.e. the construction of a new canal, the repair of an old one, and the construction of a road were highly successful, eliciting speedy completion with the help of voluntary labour and contribution. Government support was also forthcoming. A vegetable cultivation scheme, motivated by its self-employment potential in the given agricultural scenario of Kallesseri, was also implemented. Unemployed youth were organized for vegetable cultivation on fallow land, while seeds were supplied at subsidized rates. Problems arose in providing irrigation facilities on time, and appropriation of high quality seeds. The issue of marketing was not addressed, and as a result, when the harvest came, prices plummeted to one third of the level of the planting season, and the expected profits did not materialize. During the second year, many groups dropped out and the programme was reoriented to promote vegetables for the self-consumption of homestead labour. In all schemes, co-operation of land-holders was a problem, especially if they themselves did not benefit. Owners were often reluctant to allow vegetable cultivation on their land, and give relinquishment statements for construction of canals etc.

These difficulties were overcome by the inter-mediation of the sponsoring institutions and panchayat representatives, by incorporating members of landholders' households into the vegetable cultivation group and in some cases work was carried out in spite of their protest. A project for developing the Panchayat School Complex had a mixed success. Numerous educational activities were taken up and community participation in running of the schools increased, though the issue of quality could not be probed in depth and the panchayat did not achieve self-sufficiency in resource persons. KDS also implemented some schemes in collaboration with government agencies in minor irrigation, rural energy, soil conservation, health awareness, floriculture and fisheries. The experience was mostly unsatisfactory. There were problems of flexibility, delays, and the departments were not interested (Isaac, *et al*. 1995).

People's Plan Campaign

In 1996, as the Left Democratic Front[2] came to power in Kerala, it decided to devolve substantial funds[3] to the Grama Panchayats and also foster local level planning in all panchayats of the state[4] through the People's Plan Campaign[5]. Among the many grassroots experiences that PPC drew from, Kallesseri was central. The State Planning Board (SPB) steered the whole exercise while creating mechanisms to collaborate with experts and KSSP activists. PPC drew heavily on voluntary resource persons, mobilizing and training around 100,000 people, who conducted training camps, facilitated discussions among the community, and provided feedback to SPB for mid-course corrections. PPC was organized in six phases, spanning a range of activities from mobilization to plan preparation (*Economic Review*, 2000; Isaac, 2000). These phases, described below, are instructive in their successes and failures.

The first phase began with mobilisation of people, the tone being set by science and arts theatrical processions on the theme of power to the people all over Kerala. Subsequently Grama Sabhas (people's bodies) met to discuss local developmental problems, their causes and solutions. A broad structure of these meetings was developed at the state level, to facilitate discussions in small groups to ensure that ordinary people would not be intimidated in speaking up in large gatherings. Focus was provided through a model agenda and trained resource persons to lead the discussions. In general, the Grama Sabhas were a huge success and generated public debate on development all over Kerala. However, participation in the Grama Sabha varied widely, increasing where commitment and interest of elected representatives was high, as well as in LDF-led panchayats. Participation of women, scheduled castes and tribes was not satisfactory. While the campaign was well able to use the experience of public mobilization in Kallesseri, the opposition criticized the use of resource persons on the grounds that they created a hierarchical structure parallel to the elected bodies (*Economic Review,* 2000, Isaac, 2000).

In the second phase development seminars were organized in every Grama Panchayat, and development reports were formulated. These reports were to make a list of recommendations on the basis of an objective assessment of the resource potential and problems. However, only a 100 panchayats had completed the PRMP exercise, and a socio-economic survey, as undertaken in Kallesseri, was thought to be too time consuming. Consequently, an attempt was made to map the resources of panchayats through the method of a "transect walk" by appraisal teams consisting of experts in agricultural engineering etc. and to facilitate the use of secondary data. But though all local bodies collected data, and nearly all carried out the transect walk, only 50 per cent actually compiled the data or identified eco zones. Actual utilization of findings was rare. Consequently, development reports were based largely on discussions in the Grama Sabhas. This was a major departure from the Kallesseri process. The limitations of resource persons at the local level were a major hurdle, while the panchayat representatives, officials and the community were not clear about the concept of resource based planning. Yet this phase did succeed in fostering discussion on development all over Kerala and for the first time in the state's (or the country's) history, Grama Panchayats prepared local development reports. Around 5 lakh persons including Grama Sabha representatives, local political leaders, officials and local experts participated in the seminars. But the development reports that resulted proved to be of varying quality. The best analysis tended to be for agriculture, followed by education, for which many school teachers provided support. Chapters on industry, energy and resource mobilisation were the weakest. Many Grama Panchayats now began to lag behind (Chattopadhyaya, *et al.* 1999, *Economic Review,* 2000; Isaac, 2000).

The third phase involved preparation of detailed project proposals to carry out these recommendations. Support was provided from the state level through a handbook and the design of a project format. At the Grama Panchayat level sector-wise task forces, with an elected representative as chairperson and local official as convenor, were constituted to prepare projects. Twelve thousand task forces all over Kerala prepared around one lakh projects. At this stage, it was realized that greater participation from officials and experts within government was necessary, and training camps were organized to orient them. But this training was not as successful as the previous ones and resource persons did not develop the confidence to organize local training programmes. A review by SPB showed that the task forces did not function as effectively as expected. The projects tended to imitate model projects given in the handbook or adopt on-going schemes of the departments. Financial and technical analysis, especially of production related projects, was weak. Here again, in the weakness of the task forces and projects, PPC departed significantly from Kallesseri. Thomas Isaac (2000) identifies three reasons for the failure: the uncooperative and negative attitude of officials, the inability of resource persons to deal with issues raised during training and the fact that some districts had not completed the development seminars. An attempt was then made to revitalize the task forces. Workshops were organized to examine project proposals and rectify mistakes, Grama Panchayats were encouraged to co-opt new members and that failing, a core team of active members could prepare projects. But the preparation of projects remained problematic: 34 per cent projects were written by a core group of members and only in 12 per cent of the panchayats were all the task forces fully active (*Economic Review,* 2000; Isaac, 2000).

In the fourth phase projects were to be prioritized and incorporated into plans. Every Grama Panchayat was expected to have a shelf of projects ready, but because of the problems that cropped up in formulating projects, this was not the case. Subsequently, plan formulation ran concurrently with the preparation of projects. In spite of more large scale orientation and training, drawing up the plan documents proved to be difficult and only a handful of Grama Panchayats finalized their plans by the due date. The local activists found the statistical statements required in the plan documents difficult, and there was much confusion about concepts. Some MLAs remained lukewarm or hostile. The fifth phase, in which higher tier panchayat prepared plans, problems arose in integrating schemes duplication of planning activities, and also critical gaps (*Economic Review,* 2000; Isaac, 2000).

When the plan campaign was launched, only five phases were visualized, but the experience with project preparation showed the technical soundness of projects to be a problem. Consequently, a new, sixth phase for technical and financial appraisal of projects was now added. Retired technical experts and professionals were encouraged to appraise the projects and rectify the technical and financial mistakes. Later, teams of officials and non-officials worked together to scrutinize the projects and mechanisms for approving plans were developed. This completed the first round of planning by local bodies. The first release of funds to a Grama Panchayat took place after a year and a half of discussion and planning and for a majority of the panchayats much later (*Economic Review,* 2000; Isaac, 2000).

To sum up, the major successes of PPC were in fostering public discussion about development and providing a framework in which plans could be articulated through participatory planning. On these counts, PPC was fairly successful in replicating what was achieved in Kallesseri. But it could not enable panchayats to do resource surveys, identify key strategies to achieve developmental goals and convert them into viable projects[6] (Sharma, 2003). The question here, in terms of governance and policy making is, why and how did PPC succeed in replicating some effects of the Kallesseri experience and not others?

The Process of Adaptation

Two sets of issues emerge regarding the process by which PPC built upon the Kallesseri experience. The first set concerns the adequacy of the analysis of the Kallesseri experience itself before it was taken state-wide. First, the process of plan preparation was so lengthy and demanding that it was difficult to complete even in Kallesseri. There were many technical snags, in spite of the enormous technical expertise available. Moreover, despite the existence of highly motivated activists, attendance in the KDS General Body declined over time. Additionally, in the productive sector, success was tenuous to say the least and it was clear that extremely complex issues were involved. What was genuinely successful was the construction of dams and roads with public participation. Given these issues in Kallesseri, what could logically have been expected was a re-articulation of the planning process in terms of do-ability, re-strategizing for the productive sector and a more realistic assessment about sustaining public participation, which was not evident. Second, it was evident in Kallesseri itself that projects that were taken up with government departments tended to become problematic. Huge questions obviously existed about the functioning of government departments, and these needed to be probed in depth. The untested assumption seems to have been that local control would solve these problems, but as we have seen, the issue turned out to be far more complex. Finally, in Kallesseri there was no institutional resolution of problems that arose when private interests clashed with the developmental goals of the panchayat and this lack of clarity was carried on in PPC. Thus there were important issues in the Kallesseri experience that had not been resolved before PPC was launched.

The second set of issues concern the departures from the Kallesseri processes that PPC necessarily had to make, because it was a government programme, on scale, that had to be conducted within a set of rules of government functioning. As a process, PPC differed from Kallesseri on three broad fronts that may be categorized as follows:

	Kallesseri	*People's Plan Campaign (PPP)*
Political	There was strong political support for planning in terms of an LDF panchayat with a big majority and little scope for fractious politics, an enthusiastic panchayat president, a strong history of people's mobilization, and many committed political workers.	Panchayats varied widely in terms of political composition, people's mobilization, motivation of panchayat president and existence of committed political workers. There were differences among and within political parties on the issue of decentralization.
Expertise oriented	Local resource persons were well trained and several had been part of the panchayat resource mapping exercise. There were many experts from various technical institutes who supported the initiative. Studies and surveys formed the bedrock of the exercise.	Technical support was erratic. Resource persons were of uneven calibre and in many areas adequate numbers were not available. Officials were distanced from the exercise. Studies and surveys were not usually completed and used for planning.
Organizational	The Grama Panchayat was not empowered. The main implementing body was KDS, that had the following characteristics: • In the General Body, members were elected by consensus, not party politics. • The Working Committee was responsible for agenda setting and day to day functioning. • In KDS, elected representatives, officials and resource persons came together in the General Body and working committee. • Activists and resource persons played a leading role. • There was no need to get plans approved or fit into a larger structure. Funds included large shares of voluntary contributions.	The main implementing body is the grama panchayat with the following characteristics: • Panchayat representatives provided leadership and they were elected through keenly fought elections along political party lines. • Officials, though not key in planning, had a major role in implementation, management of finances etc. • The role of resource persons was not well defined. They provided support to the planning exercise, but were also viewed as 'parallel structure' by the opposition. • Plans had to be approved and scrutinized and approved by various committees. The state government provided most of the funds. Public accountability, especially of finances was a must.

As we compare the political, organizational and expertise oriented contexts of Kallesseri and PPC, wide differences are visible. Surprisingly, these differences appear to be most bridgeable in the political sphere, not because the Kallesseri situation could be replicated, but because a political strategy appropriate in the larger context, of empowering Grama Panchayats, was adopted. Or, an institutional solution was put in place. Few panchayats had as cohesive a political environment as Kallesseri, but differences within and among political parties on the issue of decentralization are undercut by the fact that all grama panchayat presidents are likely to be in favour of decentralization and local action. Further, the existence of some workers of the ruling political party everywhere ensured that some support was forthcoming. Not surprisingly, PPC did well in its mobilization phase, though the voluntary contributions that had been elicited in Kallesseri, because of its tradition of voluntary service and mass mobilization, were more difficult to replicate.

The picture changes substantially if one looks at the technical and expertise oriented aspects. Kallesseri was far richer in technical expertise, from within and outside the panchayat than the average Grama Panchayat in PPC. Weak technical capacities meant that resource mapping, surveys and studies could not be taken up as envisaged. Consequently, in most Grama Panchayats, plans were based largely on Grama Sabha discussions. This subverted the whole planning process, which was not meant to be a wish-list, but was also to be based on a scientific survey of resources. Formulation of appropriate projects was even more difficult. PPC remained ambivalent about involving officials who usually perform such roles in government, and the officials in turn did not want to contribute. But an adequate alternative channel did not exist either, for the task forces in PPC, unlike their counterparts in Kallesseri, simply did not have the same kinds of skills.

The organizational structure posed still more problems. The main agent in Kallesseri i.e. KDS appears to have been a fairly cohesive body, led by experts and committed activists in the Working Committee. A notable feature is that in the KDS General Body members were elected by consensus. It is likely, that as KDS was not a vehicle of financial or other local power, everyone may have been content with the selection of hardworking and motivated representatives. The dominance of one party in the area would have made this consensus easier. The panchayats in contrast, were far from cohesive either in the political or organizational sense. The elected representatives and the bureaucracy were fairly separate, while resource persons did not enjoy the same position as they did in KDS. The bureaucracy, which had proved to be hindrance in Kallesseri, remained the key player for many aspects of PPC.

Thus what was attempted in PPC was the adaptation of certain processes developed in Kallesseri when the political, organizational and expert structures in the two cases were not comparable at all. Notably, by empowering Grama Panchayats, a strategy that did not exist in Kallesseri, it was possible to obtain a Kallesseri like effect in terms of people's participation and focus on local issues. But as far as the organizational and expertise spheres were concerned, PPC did not adequately transform the Kallesseri processes to suit its own context. This meant that in terms of strategic planning and project formulation much of the essence and effect of the Kallesseri experience was lost, even though the process was retained. Thus, though governments tend to 'adapt' processes from innovations, what is really needed is a re-invention to produce a parallel effect in a different context. In India this transformation is made difficult by the fact that bureaucracies are not oriented towards such re-inventions, and those who innovate resent substantial changes in their innovations, especially by the bureaucracy. Paradoxically, if innovations are not re-invented in a different context, they can lose their meaning.

How Kallesseri could have been better transformed into a large-scale government programme to retain the effect rather than the processes is the next logical question, but one that needs a much wider analysis than is possible in this paper. However, one issue stands out. In Kallesseri, it was possible to ignore the bureaucracy and rely instead on voluntary expertise for planning and project formulation. Given its scale and the issue of government accountability, the same was not possible in PPC and the campaign had to depend on the bureaucracy for some key tasks. Yet, PPC did not give priority to upgrading the skills and changing the mode of functioning of government departments and it did not try to create KDS-like agents within government. What might have happened had this been attempted can only be a matter of speculation. But the journey form Kallesseri to PPC does indicate the importance of reforming government institutions, even when governments attempt to adapt processes from elsewhere. To quote Peter Evans:

> "Robust, sophisticated public institutions are an advantage both in the formation of local social capital and in the pursuit of developmental ends, not because they are instruments of centralization but because they are capable of formulating more nuanced way of distributing power and therefore of supporting decentralisation and openness to local self-organisations". (1995: 1126)

NOTES

1. Communist Party of India (Marxist).
2. Left Democratic Front: an alliance of Left parties led by the CPM.
3. 35-40 per cent state plan funds.
4. There are 990 Gram Panchayats, 52 municipalities, 5 municipal corporations, 152 block panchayats and 14 district panchayats in Kerala.
5. Described in detail by Thomas Isaac (2000)
6. Since PPC many processes have been changed and refined, and several developments have taken place. These are not discussed in this chapter.

REFERENCES

Chattopadhyaya, S. P., Krishna Kumar and K. Rajalakshami (1999): *Panchayat Resource Mapping to Panchayat Level Planning in Kerala*, Kerala Research Programme on Local Level Development, Centre for Development Studies, Thiruvananthapuram.

Economic Review, Government of Kerala, various years.

Evans, Peter (1996): 'Government Actions, Social Capital and Development', *World Development*, 24 (6): 1119-32.

Jha, S. (2002): 'Strengthening Local Governments: Rural Fiscal Decentralization in India', *Economic and Political Weekly*, June 29: 2611-12.

Kumar, Mohana S. (1993): 'Literacy Movement in Kerala: One Step Forward, Two Steps Backwards', *Economic and Political Weekly*, October 9.

Parameswaran, M.P. (1998): 'Kerala "Model" – What Does it Signify?' *Bulletin of Concerned Asian Scholars,* 30 (4).

Sharma, R. (2003): 'Kerala's Decentralization: Idea in Practice', *Economic and Political Weekly,* 37 (36), September 6.

Thomas, Isaac T.M. with Richard W. Frank (2000): *Local Democracy and Development: People's Campaign for Decentralized Planning in Kerala,* Left Word Books.

Thomas, Isaac *et al.* (1995): *Kallesseri Experiment in Local Level Planning,* Integrated Rural Technology Centre Mundur, Palakkad.

Tornquist, O. and P.K. Michael Tharakan (1996): 'Democratization and Attempts to Renew the Radical Political Development Project: Case of Kerala', *Economic and Political Weekly*, 30 (20 & 27), July 13.

World Bank (2000): *Overview of Rural Decentralization in India*, World Bank, Washington D.C.

14

Emergence of New Institutions Through Participatory Democracy

An Evaluation of Kerala Experiment

BOBY MATHEW

Introduction

Democratic decentralisation is the process of devolving functions and resources of state from the centre to the elected representatives at the lower levels, so as to facilitate greater direct participation of people in governance. A major drawback of Indian democracy has been that the participation of citizens in governance was more or less limited to periodic exercise of franchise to elect representatives to the centre and state governments. The centralised planning launched soon after independence turned out to be redundant as there was much scope for leakages, corruption etc. (Nair, 1999 : 256). In addition to that the centralised planning mechanism both at the centre and state levels could not address the local specific needs in a proper way. The centralised planning was seen as 'planning for the people' whereas people's planning is characterised by 'planning by the people'. Democratic decentralisation process in Kerala is known as People's Planning Programme (during Ninth Plan period). In order to generate people's participation both at the level of plan formulation and implementation, Kerala has put into practice the idea of people's planning programme.

One of the objectives behind the launching of people's plan campaign is to provide a solution for the economic crisis of the state manifested in the form of slow growth rate of economy, stagnation in industrial and agricultural sector, high rate of unemployment and declining expenditure on welfare measures. In this background while inaugurating the International Congress on Kerala Studies EMS Namboodiripad said (1994:5):

> Within the limitations imposed by the global and national structures, we will have to find a practical solution to reach a consensus as to what measures are to be adopted to accelerate economic growth without scarifying the welfare gains and democratic achievements of the past. Institutions and social mechanism have to be developed to ensure that the toilers get their due share from the increased production. I must emphasise the importance of democratic decentralisation in this context.

The partial experiment conducted at the local level prior to the implementation of People's Planning Programme (PPP) such as people's vegetable cultivation programme in Kanjikuzhy, people's health programme in Thanalur, drinking water scheme of the Olavanna model, the total literacy campaign of the Kalliasseri experiment etc. gave much impetus for the launching of people's planning programme (Isaac and Franke, 2000 : 54-74). The people's planning programme tries to replicate the success achieved in the above mentioned experiments in Kerala as a whole. Kerala's trajectory of development marked by redistributive reform and determined public action (Heller, 1999:237) has taken a new dimension with introduction of People's Plan Campaign (PPC).

Though people's planning programme was launched with much expectation, in the process of implementation it deviated from the established rules and procedures at many places. This article attempts to analyse the institutional impact of people's planning programme on various aspects of decentralised development especially during the first phase [1996-2001, under the Left Democratic Front (LDF) government]. The relevance of this article lies in the fact that after implementation of five years of decentralised planning, it is high time to take stock of the situation at the ground level and to provide corrective measures for the forward march of the programme.

Grama Sabha and People's Participation

Due to high population of the panchayats in Kerala, grama Sabhas are convened for each ward of a panchayat. The elected member who represents a constituency is the convenor in conducting its meetings. Grama Sabha has to be convened once in three months and its quorum shall not be less than 10 per cent of the voters of the ward (Panchayatraj, 2003:41). Group discussions were not effective in most of the panchayats. In many places the discussions lapsed into mere listing of local demands rather than analysing the problems and prioritizing the needs. In addition to that, a lack of capability among the local level resource persons resulted in fruitless discussions (Vijayachandran, 1999a : 6). The participation of middle class and those in upper strata of society was very little (Chathukulam and John, 2002 : 4922), as they considered it altogether to be an affair of poor people to become beneficiaries of different projects.[1] Another constraint on the quality of deliberations was the lack of adequate time for transactions. In most places the majority of participants were from the party of the elected representative of the ward. The initial enthusiasm shown by the people in the participation of Grama Sabhas is on the wane. There are many instances even that of award winning panchayats in which Grama Sabha meeting could not be conducted for want of quorum (Das, 2000 : 4302). There were many complaints from the aggrieved citizens against gram panchayats, which attempted to subvert beneficiary lists prepared in respective Grama Sabhas.

Training Programme Under People's Plan

The experience of people's plan campaign has underlined the vital importance of detailed preparation and training in ensuring the success of local level planning. Extensive and multi-layered training programmes for officials, elected representatives and resource persons were carried out at state, district and block levels.[2] The training programme was inadequate: inadequate attention to particular sectoral problems, insufficient involvement of officials and ineffective monitoring (Isaac and Franke, 2000 : 300). The various training institutes in the state such as Institute of Management in Government (IMG), Kerala Institute of Local Administration (KILA), State Institute of Rural Development (SIRD) and other departmental training institutes were handicapped by non-availability of sufficient number of trainers (Integrated Report, 2003:26). A large number of persons were to be trained under people's plan hence it did not succeed in training them within a stipulated time. The immediate aim of the training programme was to prepare these people for both plan formulation and implementation of various stages of people's planning programme. As a result the main emphasis was on orientation programme rather than empowerment.

Debureaucratisation Through People's Planning and the Bureaucratic Attitude Towards it

With the introduction of new panchayati raj system the role and status of elected representatives has become more significant. At the same time the role and status of officials have also changed to tender technical and administrative support to Panchayati Raj institutions (Leelakumari, 2001:33). The decision-making power has come to the hands of elected representatives. Debureaucratisation has taken place at the Local Self-Government Institutions (LSGIs) through the following ways. Firstly people can decide their needs and priorities through Grama Sabhas. In the earlier Panchayati Raj system everything was decided at the bureaucratic level and in that process people had no role at all, whereas in people's planning, participation of people is ensured not only at the plan formulation level but also at the implementation level. Through beneficiary committees people became the part and parcel of implementation process. Further, through different subject committees in the Grama Sabha and even through voluntary technical corps people can prepare the projects. Here debureaucratisation does not mean that the whole process is undertaken by people themselves. It ensured participation of the people at the local level and bureaucracy is subordinated to the elected representatives (Kerala State Planning Board, 2000a:21).

While examining to what extent bureaucracy cooperates with new system, the following can be said. When planning process was undertaken at the local level, it automatically led to the increasing work load of bureaucracy. Even after the implementation of people's planning programme redeployment of employees did not take place proportionate to the work at the local level (Vijayachandran, 1999b:13), which was emphasized by the 'Sen Committee Report'. With the advent of new Panchayati Raj and people's plan campaign, a number of department schemes like social welfare, pension, unemployment allowance etc., and plan programmes like planning and implementation of projects, integration of activities of various departments, distribution of funds, maintenance of accounts etc. were transferred to the panchayats. The gram panchayats were loaded with additional responsibilities such as the management of *krishibhavans*, veterinary hospitals, primary schools etc. Further, there was also a dearth of staff having technical knowhow, which adversely affected the timely implementation of development programmes (Sahayi, 2000:34).

When debureaucratisation took place at the local level, some of the officials showed reluctance to accept the power of elected representatives who were elected for the first time especially in the scheduled caste and women quota reservation (Leelakumari, 2001:34-38). Obstacles such as the old model of hierarchy, departmental exclusiveness, obsession with precedents and lack of transparency etc. prevented the effort to overhaul it. Some of the bureaucrats were apparently attempting to preserve the so called autonomy of departments. For example, two orders of the Director of Agriculture to the agricultural department employees restricted them from participating in the people's planning programme[3] (Puthiyavila, 1999:19). The issue of dual control did not attract any serious attention of the proponents of people's plan campaign. The LDF government which initiated people's planning programme did not give due emphasis for the redeployment of bureaucracy and yielded to its pressure.

Voluntary Technical Corps

A review of the projects prepared by the local bodies revealed that, substantial modification is needed in most of the projects to ensure their technical soundness and viability before they were approved for implementation.[4] Due to inadequate employees in the LSGIs, the campaign sought the services of retired officials and experts in different fields so as to overcome the difficulty faced. This led to the formation of Voluntary Technical Corps (VTC), (Puthiyavila, 2000:32), which was later renamed as Expert Committees. The Expert Committees were permitted to issue technical sanction to the various projects of local bodies. They have no power to change the priorities set by the local bodies. Contrary to this, most of the panchayats alleged that they were forced to make major modifications in the projects by the expert committees in the name of ensuring feasibility of the projects (Sahayi, 2000:70). Most of the elected representatives considered VTC as an anti-democratic infringement on their powers[5]. One of the coalition partners in the LDF, i.e., CPI defended the earliest dissolution of VTC. Their main argument was that "conceptually, the expert committee went against the grain of people's plan in that a non-elective quasi-official body was given the power to scrutiny, even scuttle plans and programmes prepared and passed by the elected representatives" (Das, 2000 : 4302). Opposition parties also expressed doubt regarding the genuineness of expert committees.[6]

Reconstitution of Committees by the United Democratic Front (UDF) Government

When UDF came to power in May 2001, a number of changes were introduced in the people's planning programme. Instead of expert committees, the new government formed technical advisory committees at block and district level to vet the projects.[7] By reconstituting the expert committee and task force into technical advisory committee and sectoral committee (Prasad, 2000:36), the UDF tried to eliminate the earlier controversies regarding the constitution of VTC. The other modifications were: (i) introduction of an MLA Fund, (ii) separation of Rural Development Department from Panchayati Raj system, (iii) transfer of Tribal Sub-plan to Tribal Development Department from panchayats, and (iv) change of name from 'people's planning' to 'Kerala Development Programme'.

Beneficiary Committees and its Relevance under People's Plan

In order to avoid the contractor based system and to eliminate corruption at the implementation of public works, the people's planning programme introduced the idea of beneficiary committees (BCs). The public work rules for LSGIs issued in 1997 stated that LSGIs might utilise the services of contractors only as a last resort i.e. if no beneficiary committee is willing to undertake the responsibility and LSGIs cannot directly execute the work (Kerala State Planning Board, 1999:4). The BCs were to be given 25 per cent of the estimated amount subject to the maximum of one lakh as advance. Apart from that the works undertaken by BCs were also exempted from tax (Chathukulam and John, 2002:4920). At some places the meeting in which constitution of BC takes place is so manipulated that a *benami* contractor or his nominee finally grabs the post of the Chairman or convenor of the committee.[8] An assessment made by the VTC members found that nearly one fourth of the BCs were fake and were headed by contractor or his nominees (Pillai, 2000:3). In many cases BCs found themselves working with grossly undervalued estimates done purposefully by the engineers hostile to the new system. The BCs also experienced difficulty in procuring materials and machinery for construction and equipment and skilled labourers in time. In order to show that considerable amounts of extra resource mobilisation has taken place, unrealistic voluntary and beneficiary contributions were shown in the estimated projects which in turn failed to materialise at the time of implementation. All these hurdles in a way prevented more BCs to come forward to undertake public works under panchayats.

Monitoring and Social Auditing

Monitoring of the projects was not given much importance during the first four years of people's planning programme. Though the projects clearly mentioned setting up of monitoring system, an operational mechanism could not be evolved in more than 75 per cent of the local bodies (Kerala State Planning Board, 2000b:243). There can be no better forum to undertake social audit than Grama Sabha. The Kerala Panchayati-raj Act, 1994 stipulates that the expenditure, the annual financial statement of accounts etc. should be tabled before for its approval. But in actual practice important documents such as annual financial statement, performance audit report and local fund audit report are rarely placed before Grama Sabhas. Initially it was expected that Grama Sabhas would ensure transparency in the dealings of LSGIs and facilitate continuous social audit. But in actual practice it did not take place. Moreover, adequate time and opportunities are not given to the people for deliberation. Thus monitoring and social auditing failed miserably under people's planning programme.

The Issue of Corruption

One of the allegations raised against the people's planning programme throughout the campaign period is the issue of corruption. In people's planning programme chances of corruption exist in two important domains. The first one is in the domain of public works and second one is in the selection of beneficiaries and distribution of things (Prabash, 2001:22). There were allegations of nepotism and corruption and complaints about the beneficiary selection procedure in a number of local bodies. One of the leading dailies of Kerala has conducted a study before the Assembly polls in 2001 among a random sample of people throughout Kerala which confirmed the idea that along with decentralisation of power, decentralisation of corruption has also taken place[9] (*Mathrubhumi*, 2001:1 and 11). As a result of people's planning programme, majority of the people are in a position to know the development activities that are taking place in their panchayats. This is vindicated through large number of complaints against people's planning programme during its implementation.

Performance Audit

Performance audit is a system of auditing to check whether the powers and responsibilities vested with panchayats are exercised according to rules and regulations. And if any irregularities have taken place, the system of auditing is expected to bring it to the concerned local bodies with suggestions for appropriate corrective measures (Mohanan, 1998:258). But the government failed to carry it out during the first four years and the first performance audit in a systematic way was conducted only in 2001 January. The major findings brought out by performance audit are: deviations from the guidelines, wastage of money, duplication of work, misutilisation of resources, unexpected delay in the works undertaken by LSGIs, loss incurred due to unscientific decisions, unreasonable and non-transparent expenditures, failures in achieving the objectives set out in the project and lack of proper record on the implementation of the work[10] (Government of Kerala, 2003a:3). One argument put forward for the above-mentioned deviations is that there were no earlier experiences or models to be emulated by people's planning programme. But, since the government failed to effectively carry out different kinds of audit, a measure which was set out by itself to check any flaw in implementing the programme, the above argument becomes invalid.

Ombudsman and Panchayati Raj Institutions

As per the provision of Kerala Panchayati Raj Act, 1994 (271G, Act No. 13 of 1994) government has constituted Ombudsman for LSGIs with effect from 29th May, 2000 (Government of Kerala, 2003b:2). It is a state level quasi-judicial institution established for conducting investigation and/or enquiry in respect of any action involving corruption, maladministration or irregularities in the discharge of administrative functions by LSGIs in Kerala[11]. It is more easily and economically accessible to ordinary citizen rather than judicial courts because it does not prescribe any fee other than the court fee stamp of Rs. 10 to be pasted on the application (Sukumarykutty 2003:3). The number of complaints filed before the Ombudsman in each year shows that, corrupt practices are still prevailing at the local level. For examples in the year 2000 it received 1322 complaints out of which 1200 cases were disposed. In 2001 of the total 2893 complaints, 2200 were disposed. In 2003 and 2004 out of 670 and 700 complaints it received, 400 and 250 were disposed respectively.[12] An examination of the nature of these complaints reveals that most of them are related to corrupt practices involved in the execution of projects and consequently denying benefits to the people. To cite an example the recent judgement of Ombudsman in a case field by 'Chempakachal Damodaran', reached to the conclusion that 'Padinjaraythara' Grama Panchayat has misutilised the fund in Chempakachal road taring (*Mathrubhumi,* 2004a:8). The past three years of experience reveals that Ombudsman provides an opportunity to the people to realise the corrupt practices in their panchayats and they can approach Ombudsman to minimize this evil practices to a certain extent. However, the backlog of cases due to single man system of Ombudsman[13] and lack of its own investigation team can considered to be a serious handicap.

Emergence of Local Level Leadership

The emergence of new layer of leadership at the local level, especially after the implementation of people's planning programme shows a shift from pre-people's planning period. Increasing frequency and intensity of electoral politics as well as various local level initiatives brought new groups in political competition. This is indicated by influx of candidates for civic elections.[14] Different phases of planning process such as theme based discussion in the Grama Sabhas, sectoral committees, beneficiary committees, neighbourhood groups etc. created a favourable environment for the emergence of local level leadership. There is an increase in women representation between 1995 and 2000 elections held to LSGIs. Out of the total elected representatives, 35.8 per cent were women in 1995 which reached up to 38 per cent in 2000 (Seema, *et al.*, 2000:56). If we analyse the emergence of women to the leadership level on community basis, the success achieved by Muslim women (particularly in Malappuram district) is praise-worthy. Two important reasons can be pointed for this. Firstly, due to reservation they were also forced to come to the public sphere. Earlier, their presence in the political sphere was comparatively less when compared to the rest of the communities in Kerala. Secondly, the implementation of Community Development Society (CDS) programme in Malappuram district (Oommen, 1999) and migration of male members to the gulf countries have also partially contributed to this phenomenon.[15] A recent example of successful panchayat leadership is that of 'Perumatty' and 'Puthussery' panchayats when they took action against multinational corporations such as Coca Cola and Pepsi to stop the over exploitation of ground water resources of their villages.[16]

Plan Implementation

The success of every plan depends upon how effective its implementation. Kerala's experiment with decentralised planning will be at cross roads, unless the plans are also implemented effectively. The first three years of people's planning programme experienced serious delay in plan formulation, its implementation and in the transfer of credit mechanism. Implementation of various projects was also adversely affected due to frequent closure of treasuries in the year 2000-01. The failure at the implementation stage was partially contributed by delayed allocation of funds to the panchayats and the failure from the part of the government to completely release the promised amount.[17]

Selected Physical Achievements of Local Governments in the Ninth Plan period (1997-2002)

Sl. No.	*Items*	*Units*	*Total Numbers*
1.	Beneficiaries of seeds/fertilizers/pesticides	No.	5356480
2.	Tillers/Tractors supplied	"	75148
3.	Cattles distributed	"	323766
4.	Poultry distributed	"	2153184
5.	Cattle sheds	"	106281
6.	Sewing machines	"	61230
7.	Persons trained	"	174398
8.	House sites allotted	"	31847
9.	Houses constructed	"	570582
10.	Houses repaired	"	186404
11.	Toilets constructed	"	571145
12.	Wells dug	"	1287875
13.	Water taps installed	"	97893
14.	Pump sets supplied	"	85401
15.	Roads constructed	"	48735
16.	Length of roads	Km	185113
17.	Culverts constructed	No.	12271
18.	Bridges constructed	"	4383
19.	Co-operatives formed	"	7310
20.	New schools built (area)	m.sq.	180680
21.	Hospital buildings (area)	m.sq.	140671
22.	Offices built (area)	m.sq.	249155
23.	Marketing complexes built (area)	m.sq.	133479
24.	Additional area under cultivation (gross)	Acre	552599

Source: Economic Review, 2002, pp. 376 -377.

When compared to the Eighth Five Year Plan the achievements of LSGIs are far better. All the housing agencies of the state government together constructed 2,69,988 houses only during the entire course of Eighth Five Year Plan as against 5,70,582 in the Ninth Five Year Plan. While 1.25 lakhs latrines were constructed during the Eighth Five Year Plan, the LSGIs constructed 5,71,145 during the Ninth Plan. When compared to the Eighth Five Year Plan there is a three fold increase in the length of roads constructed during the Ninth Plan period. In addition to that 75,148 tillers/tractors were supplied, 1,28,875 wells dug, 97,893 water taps installed, 3,23,766 cattle distributed, 21,53,184 poultry distributed and 1,06,281 cattle sheds constructed. While comparing the achievements of people's planning programme with Eighth Five Year Plan we have to take into consideration that the grant in aid to LSGIs were very less during the Eighth Plan period. The achievements of people's planning programme are more in social and infrastructural sectors than in productive sector. One of the basic objectives behind the launching of people's planning programme was to find a solution to the sustainability crisis in agriculture and industrial sector. But people's planning programme could not make headway in these sectors (Parayil and Sree Kumar, 2003:477). One of the reasons behind this is that most of the demands in the Grama Sabhas were related to infrastructural development. Secondly, most of the local political elites were interested in selecting individual beneficiary projects such as distribution of cattle, sewing machines, etc. on the assumption that it will increase their political clout among the local people. Thus they failed to prepare plans on a long-term perspective. On the other hand people's planning programme succeeded in providing basic amenities to the people such as housing, sanitation, drinking water and rural infrastructure.

A stock taking of people's planning programme reveals that it could demystify governance at the local level. If we analyse the socio-economic profile of beneficiaries of the people's plan campaign, we can see that most of them are from lower economic strata of society (Chathukulam and John, 2002:4924). A number of panchayats have taken up the experiment quite seriously and brought about tremendous changes as envisaged under people's plan. The success of these panchayats can be attributed to individual leadership, which is successful in organising people beyond political, social and economic divisions to discuss and make them participate in development process[18] (Das, 2000:4303). These success stories have to be repeated in other panchayats, and they have to prepare plans on a long-term perspective.

On the other hand majority of panchayats failed to select projects which provided employment opportunities or skill development[19]. They instead followed the conventional route of expenditure. If we analyse the impact of people's planning programme in Kerala as a whole it did not succeed in solving the basic issues such as poverty, unemployment, industrial and agricultural stagnation. Further, it did not have a long-term perspective, was unable to give due emphasis on productive sectors and there have been no forward and backward linkages in majority of the projects (Integrated Report, 2003:45).

Conclusion

On the whole a qualitative shift has been evident from the very inception of people's planning programme. The success of the plan depends upon participation of the people, transparency and above all political will to support it. Continuous effort should be taken to rejuvenate and regain the lost enthusiasm of people in decentralisation process. The onward march of people's planning programme depends to a great extent on consistent efforts to rectify the past mistakes and political will to address basic issues such as poverty, unemployment, stagnation in agriculture and industry. It is also an imperative that the Kerala Society undergoes a cultural metamorphosis by addressing the question of patriarchy, caste and religion for the economic progress as a corollary through institutional interventions such as people's planning programme.

NOTES

1. A study in Thrissur district during the initial years of people's planning programme reveals that the number of participants in the grama sabhas is less. Majority of the participants in the grama sabhas are from below poverty line families and their main objective is to become beneficiaries of the programme (Prakash, 1999:8). Another study has been conducted in 'Vallikunnam' Panchayat of Alapuzha district which was awarded the second best panchayat in 1997-98 and the best panchayat in 1998-99 for implementing people's planning programme in an innovative way. The study reveals that 22 per cent of the respondents did not participate in grama sabha since they could not get any direct benefit. The discussions in the grama sabhas were over politicised so as the whole issue was reduced to the question of whom to be given patronage (Prabash, 2001:20-23).
2. As part of institutionalisation process, a project known as 'capacity development for decentralization in Kerala' has been under implementation since 1999 through Kerala Institute of Local Administration with the financial support of a Swiss Agency for Development and Co-operation. The project has utilised Rs. 8.09 crore in the last four years (*Economic Review*, 2002:385).
3. According to him, the officials from agricultural department can participate in people's planning programme only after completing their work in the agricultural department. According to another circular issued by the Agricultural Director, the work entrusted to the employees of the agricultural department can be undertaken, if it is in their view, related to their department or to their technical experiences or else they can put forward the matter to the director of agricultural department. (Circular No. T1 (J) 72068), (Puthiyavila, 1999:19). During the initial years around Rs. 160 crores of agricultural programme came to a stand still due to the negative attitude of the Agricultural Department (James, 2001:41)
4. The local bodies can start the implementation of the projects only after getting the approval of the District Planning Committee (DPC). The DPC approves the projects of local bodies on the basis of recommendations of expert committees at block and district levels. The DPC forwards the integrated development plan of each district to the State Planning Board. The State Planning Board is the state level coordinating agency.
5. A study pointed out that majority of people in Kerala had a negative feedback on VTC. For details see (Dev, 2001:14-16).
6. One of the agenda of United Democratic Front (UDF) manifesto for civic polls in 2000 was disbanding of expert committees, implementation committee and panel of resource persons. When the UDF came to power in 2001 they implemented the above promise made in the manifesto for civic elections (Biju, 2000:90).
7. UDF included most of the members of the expert committees in the new Technical Advisory Committee. In expert committees the rule was that its convenor should be a bureaucrat and its chair a non-official expert whereas

in the newly formed Technical Advisory Committee both these positions are occupied by bureaucrats. The task force had a chairman, a vice-chairman, a convenor and a joint convenor apart from members of different subject groups. The chairman's position should be occupied by an elected representative whereas convenor should be a related official. The vice chairman was a non-official expert and joint convenor should be a district level resource person. Now instead of task force new sectoral committees came into force. In the newly formed sectoral committees there is no place for vice-chairman and joint convenor. In each sectoral committee, the chairperson will be a member of the panchayat and the convenor, now designated as secretary, will be the concerned official dealing with that subject (Prasad, 2001:36).

8. The distinction between real BCs and *benami* committees begins from the character of the meeting for the Formation of BCs. According to the rules the meeting for the formation of BCs should be convened by giving a notice three days in advance. In the meeting the implementation officer or ward member should explain the details of the project. After that they can elect members of the implementation committee. If the meeting for the constitution of BC is held without the knowledge of majority of beneficiaries in the area, it may result in selecting benami or contractor as the chairman or convenor.

9. The study conducted by the *Mathrubhumi* reveals the following. While 67 per cent of the sampled population opined that people's planning programme could achieve various merits, 25.3 per cent disagreed with this opinion. 56 per cent of the sampled population thought that there is truth in the allegation that corruption has taken place through people's planning. Another 56 per cent of the sampled population also believed that there is political discrimination in the distribution of various aids through people's planning programme. Also see (Kannan, 2000:94).

10. At the Grama Panchayat level itself, during the past five years, around Rs. 66.76 crores were deposited in different institutions without even spending a single penny till now. In majority of the panchayats there were no reconciliation between the accounts of the treasury and the accounts of the panchayats. At the Grama Panchayat level itself, the works which are in an abandoned stage even amounted to Rs. 15.5 crores. For details see Performance Audit reports of Grama, Block and District Panchayats, 2003a.

11. The Ombudsman can also enquire into any allegation against a public servant including president, all members, secretaries and other staff of the local governments including the officials transferred to LSGIs. (Rajasekharan, 2001:25).

12. Data collected from the office of the Ombudsman at Barton Hill in Thiruvananthapuram on 2nd January 2004.

13. Originally the Ombudsman consisted of seven members. The UDF Government issued an order (*vide* S.R.O. No.1105/2001 dated 11-12-

2001) in December 2001 to reduce the number of members from seven to one in the name of reduction of expenditure.

14. For details see (Biju, 2000:90).
15. A comparative study on Malappuram and Kannur districts shows that despite all the limitations like backwardness in education, employment, poor economic conditions, patriarchal and religious restrictions, women in Malappuram have been performing better in people's planning programme than their counterparts in Kannur where women are comparatively better placed. Thus the relative lower socio economic status of women in Malappuram co-exists with their higher rate of political participation at the local level (Siddique, 2002).
16. For details see (Krishna Kumar, 2004:38) and also see (*Mathurbhumi*, 2004b:1).
17. The government is supposed to release the funds allocated for local bodies in four instalments. However during 2002-03, it did not release the fourth instalment. The LSGIs received the third instalment in April, well after the financial year was closed (*The Hindu*, 2003:12).
18. In 'Maravanthuruth' Panchayat people united to overcome the problem of drinking water. They have cleared four kilometre long canal to bring water from Muvattupuzha to the panchayat (*Mathrubhumi*, 2004c:8). Also see Franke and Chasin (1997:3061-3068) on Chapprapadavu panchayat, and Kurudath (1998:14-16) on Pathenpara panchayat.
19. According to Kannan only 10 per cent of the panchayats have succeeded in implementing the people's planning programme in an innovative way. In around 30-40 per cent of panchayats, the implementation of people's planning programme was on an average level. The rest 50 per cent of the panchayats failed miserably in the implementation (Kannan, 2000:97).

REFERENCES

Biju, M.R. (2000): 'Local Body Polls in Kerala-2000: Warning signs for the Left', *South Asian Journal of Socio-Political Studies*, 1 (2), June – December: 87-105.

Chathukulam, Jos and M.S. John (2002): 'Five years of participatory planning in Kerala: Rhetoric and Reality', *Economic and Political Weekly*, 37 (49), December 7: 4917-24.

Chathukulam, Jos and M.S. John (2002): 'Building Social Capital through State Initiative: The Case of Participatory Planning in Kerala', *Economic and Political Weekly*, 37 (20), May18: 1939-48.

Das, M.K. (2000): 'Kerala's Decentralised Planning: Floundering Experiment', *Economic and Political Weekly*, 35 (4), December 2: 4300-03.

Dev, P.M. (2001): 'Role and Performance of Expert Committees in Kerala', Participation and Governance, *PRIYA*. 7 (21), July: 14-16.

Franke, Richard W. and Barbara H. Chasin (1997): 'Power to the Malayalee People', *Economic and Political Weekly*,, 32 (48), November 29: 3061-68.

Government of Kerala (2001): *Economic Review-2000*, Kerala State Planning Board, Thiruvananthapuram.

Government of Kerala (2003): *Economic Review-2002*, Kerala State Planning Board, Thiruvananthapuram.

Government of Kerala (2003a): *Performance Audit Report – Grama, Block and District Panchayats from 1997 –98 to 2001-02*, Government Central Press, Thiruvananthapuram.

Government of Kerala (2003b): *Annual Report of Ombudsman for Local Self Government Institutions for the Period 1-4-2001 to 31-3-2002*, Government Central Press, Thiruvananthapuram.

Heller, Patrick (1999): *The Labour Development: Workers and Transformation of Capitalism in Kerala, India*, Cornell University Press, Ithaca.

Heller, Patrick (2001): 'Moving the State: The Politics of Democratic Decentralisation in Kerala, South Africa and Porto Alegre' *Politics and Society*, 29 (1), March: 131-163.

Integrated Report (2003): Prepared by DSP Team from IRMA, IMG and KILA, Kerala Decentralisation Support Programme-Phase I.

Isaac, T.M. Thomas with Richard W. Franke (2000): *Local Democracy and Development: People's Campaign for Decentralised Planning in Kerala*, Leftword Books, New Delhi.

Israyel, T.M. (2001): 'Janapradhinithikalum Udyogastharum' (Malayalam), *Panchayatraj*, 41 (3), June: 18.

James, Saji (2001): 'Janakeeyasuthranam attimarikkappedumo?' (Malayalam), *Samakalika Malayalam Varika*, 4 (35), January 5: 41.

John, M.S. (2000): 'Decentralised Planning and Employment Generation: Case Study of a Village Panchayat in Kerala', *Kurukshetra*, 48 (7): 32-38.

John, Oommen (2000): 'Strengthening of Panchayati-raj Finance in Kerala – A New Phase', *The Indian Journal of Public Administration*, 46 (4), October-December.

Kannan, K.P. (2000): 'People's Planning, Kerala's Dilemma', *Seminar* (485), January: 92-97.

Kerala State Planning Board (1999): *'People's Plan Campaign: Guidelines for Beneficiary Committees*, Thiruvananthapuram.

Kerala State Planning Board (2000a): *Janakeeyasuthranam Oru Kaippusthakam*, (Malayalam) Kerala State Audio Visual and Reprographic Centre, Thiruvananthapuram.

Kerala State Planning Board (2000b): 'Monitoring', in *Janakeeyasuthranam: Oru Padapusthakam*, Thiruvananthapuram.

Krishnakumar, R. (2000): 'Democratic Decentralisation: A People's Movement', *Frontline*, 17 (12), June 23.

Krishnakumar, R. (2004): 'Resistance in Kerala', *Frontline*, 21 (3), February13.

Kurian, Luciamma (2001): *The Structure and Functioning of Gramsabha: A Study Focused on the District of Kottayam*, Unpublished Ph.D. Thesis, Mahatma Gandhi University, (Gandhian Studies Centre), Kottayam.

Kurudath, Anil (1998): 'Viaksanathin Janakeeya Mathrikakal' (Malayalam), *Madhyamam Azchapadipp*, 1 (16), June 12: 14-16.

Leelakumari (2001): 'Interpersonal Relationship between Officials and Elected Representatives in the present panchayati-raj system', *ISDA Journal*, 11 (1), January – March.

Mahipal (1997): 'People's Campaign in Decentralised Planning: Strengths and Weaknesses', *Mainstream*, 35 (26), June 7.

Mathrubhumi (2001): '*Janakeeyasuthranathilude Neattam Kaivarikkan Kazhinju: Azhimathi Nilanilkkunnu*', April 4, Thrissur.

Mathrubhumi (2004a): January 6, Mumbai, p.8.

Mathrubhumi (2004b): January 25, Mumbai, p.1

Mathrubhumi (2004c): '*Vellamethikkan Janakeeyakuttayma*' (Malayalam), March 14, Mumbai, p.8.

Mohanan, B. (1998): 'Controlling Corruption at the Grassroots: Lessons from a Decentralised and Participatory Development Administration', *ISDA Journal*, April-December.

Nair, V. Rajendran (1999): 'Empowerment of Community through panchayati-raj institutions: The Kerala Experiment', *ISDA Journal*, 9 (3 and 4), July-December: 252-285.

Namboodiripad, EMS (1994): *International Congress on Kerala Studies*, AKG Centre for Research Studies, Thiruvananthapuram.

Oommen, M.A. (1999): *Community Development Society of Kerala: An Impact Study*, Institute of Social Sciences, New Delhi.

Panchayatraj (2003): 43 (9), December, p.41.

Parayil, Govindan and T.T. Sreekumar (2003): 'Kerala's Experience of Development and Change', *Journal of Contemporary Asia*, 33 (4): 465-482.

Pillai, A.R.V., N. Jayaprakash and Ajith Bhaskaran (2000): 'Beneficiaries Committees: An Experiment under People's Plan', *International Conference on Democratic Decentralisation*, Kerala State Planning Board, May 23-28, Thiruvananthapuram: 1-10.

Prabash, J. (2001): 'Oru gramathinte Thirichariev' (Malayalam), *Samakalika Malayalam Varika*, April 20: 20-23.

Prakash, B.A. (1999): 'Janakeeyasuthranam enganea vazhi thetti' (Malayalam), *Malayalamanorama*, January 5-6, Thiruvananthapuram.

Prasad, P.S. (2001): 'Janakeeyasuthranam Udyogastha Kendrikrathamakunnu', *Madhyamam Azchapadipp*, 4 (35), August 31, p.36.

Puthiyavila, Manoj K. (1999): 'Janakeeyasuthranam Krishi Vakup Attimarikunnu', *Samakalika Malayalam Varika*, 3 (19), September 17, p. 19.

Puthiyavila, Manoj K. (2000): 'Oru Puthiya Vikasanasamskaram, *Samakalika Malayalam Varika*, June, p.32.

Rajasekharan, K. (2001): 'Ombudsman for Local Governments in Kerala', *Kurukshetra*, 49 (7), April, p.25.

Sahayi (2000): *Status of PRIs in Kerala: An Appraisal 1995-2000*, Centre for Collective Action and Learning, Thiruvananthapuram: 15-80.

Seema, T.N. *et al.* (2000): *Janakeeyasuthranavum Sthree Munneattavum*, Kerala Basha Institute, Thiruvananthapuram.

Sharma, Rashmi (2003): 'Kerala's Decentralisation; Idea in Practice', *Economic and Political Weekly,* 38 (36), September 6: 3832-50.

Siddique, P.A. (2002): *Empowerment of Women through Panchayati Raj Institutions,* Unpublished M. Phil Thesis, Centre for Studies in Social Systems, Jawaharlal Nehru University.

Suhruthkumar, A. (2000): 'Janakeeyasuthranavum bureaucratic samvidhanavum' in E.M. Sreedharan *et al.* (eds.), *Janakeeyasuthrakar: Oru Swayam Vilayiruthal*, Kerala State Planning Board, Thiruvananthapuram.

Sukumarykutty Amma, S. (2003): *Thadesha Swayambharana Sthapanagalkkuventiyulla Ombudsman Samvidhanam: Oru Mukhavura*, Government Central Press, Thiruvananthapuram.

The Hindu (2003): July 21, New Delhi, p. 12.

Vijayachandran, K. (1999a): 'Janakeeyasuthranam Maravippikkanam', *Malayala Manorama*, Thiruvananthapuram, January, p.6.

Vijayachandran, K. (1999b): 'Janakeeyasuthranam: Thuglug paripady', *Samakalika Malayalam Varika*, 2(46), 19 March, p. 13.

15

Decentralisation in Kerala

Problems and Prospects

K. Rajasekharan

Introduction

Decentralisation is a very complex activity of devolution of political, administrative and fiscal responsibilities to the local elected governments. Decentralisation aims at establishing accountable, efficient, accessible and transparent local governance. Consolidation of major problems arising out during those changes is the main theme of this paper.

Kerala, the tiny state in the southernmost part of India, has the fertile preconditions such as traditional community life, land reforms, high literacy and education, qualitative health indicators, powerful grassroots institutions, vibrating civil society and sharp political affinities among people, for creating vibrant local government institutions. In decentralisation, the State had a long history of half-hearted reforms characterised by partial successes and blatant reversals right from its creation in 1957. Kerala, with appreciative development indicators comparable to developed countries, has been experimenting with decentralisation and participatory local democracy, ultimately aimed at realization of the constitutional goal of establishing genuine "institutions of local self-government" since the enactment of Kerala Panchayati Raj Act and the Kerala Municipality Act in the year 1994.

Decentralisation process necessitates a large number of changes to be made in the political process, administrative structure, distribution of powers and responsibilities, allocation of resources, management of human resources and in the degree of autonomy in each tier of government.

Brief History of Decentralisation in Kerala

The enactment of Kerala Panchayati Raj Act and the Kerala Municipality Act in the year 1994, in tune with the constitutional changes made in 1993, was the first step in the recent history of decentralisation in Kerala and the acts incorporated the bare minimum mandatory constitutional requirement. The Act enlisted both mandatory and sectoral responsibilities and institutional structures of the local government system in Kerala.

The functional areas of local governments are made distinctly clearer by transferring a number of institutions and staff positions to the local governments, in September, 1995, following the principle 'work and worker going together'. With this transfer, local governments in Kerala got the services of fairly senior professional officers on health, agriculture, animal husbandry, rural development, social welfare, scheduled caste development, Education etc. They are designated *ex-officio* secretaries with all powers and responsibilities of the secretary, in their sector.

The State budget of Government of Kerala, presented in February, 1996 was the next milestone in the history of decentralisation in the state, which set apart a small amount of untied funds to draw local plan projects by the local governments. This paved the way for legislative approval of resource allocation to local governments through a very unique budgetary process.

The process of decentralisation was pushed further forward in 1996 by introducing the participatory bottom-up planning process in a campaign mode namely People's Plan Campaign (PPC). The campaign initiated by the transfer of one-third plan resources of the state to the local governments in the Ninth Five Year plan, really infused life into decentralisation in the state. "The campaign had succeeded in deepening the process of decentralisation, bringing about qualitative changes in planning and implementation and altering of the mindset about participatory development." (Government of Kerala, 1999). The availability of enormous resources entitled the local governments to realise their functional responsibilities assigned by the new legislation. As well, the transfer of a lot of responsibilities and funds to local governments mounted pressure on the State Government to ensure that the responsibilities are carried out effectively and funds are utilized properly. Because of the heavy transfer of funds, it has become the responsibility of the State Government to ensure that decentralisation works well.

Kerala adopted a 'big bang' approach towards decentralisation, in 'reversal'[1] of the traditional approaches to transfer funds, functions and functionaries to local governments in one go and later made attempts to build up the capacity of the local governments to undertake the transferred tasks.

The Peoples' Plan Campaign, consisted of a series of phases[2], had been taken as an entry point in achieving a high degree of decentralisation in the state. The campaign could establish *ad hoc* systems and procedures, which were later corrected or were attempted to correct on trial and error basis. The campaign could succeed in setting the agenda of decentralisation and push its pace to a great extent.

The decentralisation efforts were expected to move from an experimentation, corrective and consolidation phase to an institutional phase. But the campaign could not go much ahead in transforming the existing administrative operating systems of local governments to the needs of decentralisation, with local political process, good local financial management, excellent procurement system and meaningful relation between elected and appointed functionaries. The interim systems strenuously made during the campaign could not be institutionalised or made sustainable. The expectation of the campaign was that it would accelerate economic growth and create new model of growth with equity in Kerala. (Isaac and Franke, 2000)

The amendment made to the Kerala Panchayat Raj and Municipality Acts in 1999, consequent to the recommendation of the Committee on Decentralisation of Powers (Sen Committee), had transformed the acts proactive to the needs of decentralisation to a very great extend. The recent initiative to institutionalise the good features of learning from Peoples' Plan Campaign, in the ongoing tenth five-year planning process was a good beginning, but the institutionalisation process had left much to be desired.

Decentralisation in Kerala, as in other countries is proven to be a very difficult process for three obvious reasons. The most obvious reason is that many powerful forces influencing the state have little interest in decentralisation. The second is that there is much institutional inertia to overcome. The third is that even when state elites commit themselves to decentralisation, the task of institutional building such as enacting new laws and regulations, redeploying personnel, rechanneling personnel, building up local administrative capacities etc. is herculean. But Kerala has a long and celebrated history of social mobilization and a dense and vibrant civil society, which make the task slightly easier than everywhere else. (Heller, 2000:7)

In spite of many debilitating factors, the decentralisation process in Kerala has become almost irreversible and concrete steps are being made to institutionalise the decentralised governance in the State. (Government of Kerala, 2003)

But whether decentralisation will deliver good or bad is still a debatable question. On the one hand, there has been a growing criticism that in the name of decentralisation, democratically elected governments are urged to abandon social welfare responsibilities and local communities are urged to take up more responsibilities, forcibly dictated by undemocratic international lending agencies. On the other hand, decentralisation can be a way to achieve more quality in the content of democracy.

Kerala shows that democratic decentralisation strongly buttressed by state support can be an effective strategy for reducing inequality in living standards. (Franke and Chasin, 2000).

Major Problems

Refining Legislative Framework

Decentralisation in Kerala is a process launched by legislative enactments and framing of Kerala Panchayat Raj Act and The Kerala Municipality Act and associated rules in accordance with the constitutional amendment and not by any political or social movement. Continuous refinement of legislative framework, in tune with the discernible political reality, is essential for promoting decentralisation. The contradictions, lack of clarity, possibility of multiple interpretations, critical grey areas of silence etc. in the provisions of the statutes, rules and orders, make the decentralisation initiatives very slow, cumbersome or difficult.

The issuance of numerous government orders to address ever emerging problems without considering the holistic perspective, the delay in or absence of communicating the government orders to the field level functionaries and the difficulty in ascertaining the correct interpretation of defective statutes or orders, create a lot of confusion in the minds of practitioners of decentralisation process in Kerala. Unless efforts are made to communicate the government decisions in time, to the field functionaries, with absolute clarity, decentralisation in Kerala cannot march ahead.

An advisory legal cell for continuous examination of statutes, rules and orders and for submitting the possible policy options to the Government should be established as part of academic institutions like Kerala Institute of Local Administration (KILA), to make a refined and meaningful legislative framework for decentralisation. Instantaneous communication of statutes, rules and orders to the field functionaries could be possible by uploading them in a website regularly and the documents thus uploaded can be made accessible to the functionaries through the commercial internet kiosks without lapse of time.

Problem of Departmental Integration

Decentralisation was expected to bring about all developmental programmes earlier run by Rural Development Department (Government of Kerala) to the local government institutions. The existence of Rural Development Department in addition to the Local Self-Government department with almost similar functions, the existence of District Rural Developmental Agency (DRDA) separate from District Panchayat with same functions, emergence of MP/MLA Local Area Development as a separate programme outside local government system, the separation of a part of Tribal Sub-Plan (TSP) from the local government realm, the existence of many state level Corporation or Boards in areas devolved to local governments and existence of many agencies like Urban Development Authorities and the difficulty in integrating all activities of sectoral departments horizontally at local body level, results in duplication of activities, programmes and projects, thereby weakening the decentralisation process through absolute lack of integration.

The existence of parallel organisations such as DRDA which were originally set up to enhance people's participation and flexibility in implementation of projects, weakens the domain of local governments and empowers the bureaucracy in handling local affairs.

The existence of Urban Development Authorities, which were created when local governments were weak, to plan and implement the provisions in the Town Planning Act, have failed in their original intention and majority of them are now taking up road construction and shopping complex construction etc. They are also conflicting with the local governments.

The existence of such parallel structures, surviving as creator of bureaucratic powers, lead to unhealthy competition for space and even pose a challenge to legitimate activity of elected local governments. They need to be disbanded or harmonized with local governments.

Absence of horizontal and vertical integration is another problem. All the functions of the departments and agencies coming under the 29 items of functions constitutionally earmarked to local government institutions as per the Eleventh Schedule of the Constitution should have been horizontally integrated at the district and lower level with the local government institutions, without retaining the department or agency identity as far as possible. Similarly, the vertical integration of plans of all tiers of local governments under the multi-level planning is another requirement. The existence of many Corporations/Boards, as centralized structures, established for professional attention and operational efficiency should not have been allowed to continue. The District

Planning Committee (DPC), working in the manner of a Standing Committee of a district panchayat, at present, should be strengthened to enable them to integrate the rural and urban local body plans at the district level more rigorously. The MP and MLA Local Area Development funds, which should have gone to local governments otherwise, should be wound up/merged with local development plans, so as to avoid the ineffective and wasteful utilization of resources earmarked for the purpose.

Absence of Managerial Efficiency

The recent decentralisation efforts in Kerala veered round People's Plan Campaign (PPC) activities even though the former is a more comprehensive concept touching a broad spectrum of areas than the latter. The management functions in local bodies, which follow traditional administrative practices, remained almost ignored or unattended from any improvement. "There has been no improvement in areas like budget preparation, office management including records maintenance, control over staff, procedures relating to meetings of panchayat committees including sub-committees and so on" (Chathukulam and John, 2002:4917-26). There is urgent need to explore the possibility to develop efficient management systems and new office procedures relating to maintenance of files, flow of files for decision making, storing and retrieving of data or files, providing feedback to elected representatives and establishing public procedures with elements of professionalism in our local bodies. It appears that there is no systematic way of preparing timely agenda notes, accurate recordings of minutes and drafting of speaking resolutions in the meetings of the local governments. For increasing managerial efficiency elaborate management manuals for office administration and for the management of each sectoral institution coming under local governance, on the lines of election manual, need to be prepared as envisaged in the Report of the Committee on Decentralisation of Powers. The manual should contain all the mandatory obligations as well as suggest ideas to be followed by the local government with reference to that particular function.

The manual should provide guidelines for smooth control of day-to-day work in the local governments. The number of registers maintained in local governments would be reduced to an optimum level to avoid unnecessary duplication and easy maintenance. Newly inducted staff need to be given induction training. The practice of non-maintenance of proper records regarding collection of taxes and issuance of certificates needs to be corrected.

Ineffective distribution of work, absence of job description, dual control of officers by sectoral departments and local governments, location of several wings in different places with weak links between those units, lack of supervision and lack of relevant well identified operational practices, are other essential managerial issues. The present day local government offices are characterised by inefficiency, corruption and nepotism, to a large extent .The old office procedures have deteriorated due to pressure of work, imprecise instructions from above, untrained staff, ineffective supervision, imperfect procedures and corrupt motives. Establishment of scientific management based on 'system approach' and simplicity coupled with continuous training and social control, is the only way out. The use of e-governance to simplify the management of offices should also be explored.

Kerala's decentralisation has made possible clear distinction in delineating the functional domain of each tier of local bodies. It has been found that "it is easier to define the functions in the management of institutions, creation of infrastructure and provision of services but when it came to the question of defining the functional areas in sectors like agriculture and industries there is bound to be certain overlaps, and only based on several years' experience can the comparative advantage of each tier in performing various functions would be known early"(Vijayanand, 2001). Thus overlap in the demarcation of functions in the sectors like agriculture, industry etc. remains as a difficult task.

Lack of clear demarcation of functional responsibilities exists among the three tiers of local governments and between state government and local governments in economic development sectors such as agriculture and allied activities, rural industries, poverty reduction etc. lead to duplication of efforts, waste of resources and unnecessary conflict over identification of localities and persons to be benefited.

Ineffective Management of Transferred Institutions

Most of the institutions at the district and lower levels like hospitals, schools, *anganwadies*, hostels, farms, agricultural offices etc. providing important services to less privileged people have been transferred to local governments. The local governments have not been very effective in managing the transferred institutions and professionals, except in improving the infrastructure, particularly in education and health sectors. This is a major area of concern as the efficiency of these institutions is dependent on the manner in which they are managed by the local governments.

Improvement of healthcare and educational institutions is a serious problem area, which needs attention. The local bodies are unable to formulate good projects for sustainable development in those sectors except by creation of infrastructure. Serious efforts are needed for local assessment of problems and finding local solutions in those sectors, which constitute the core of Kerala's development paradigm. Local governments need to manage professionals and run institutions and to enhance quality of services and efficiency of institutions in both the sectors in a better way. The support of officials and the state government departments in those sectors are lukewarm. As well, planning and development in health and education is more complicated than in other sectors.

Lack of clarity on the role of elected local government in the management of these institutions, absence of positive working relationship between the professionals managing these institutions and the elected local governments, dual control of these institutions by the state government departments and local governments, focus on improving infrastructure rather than on quality of services and weak capacity on the part of elected functionaries to manage these institutions are the reasons for such a sorry state of affairs.

Human Resource Management: A Neglected Issue

Decentralization process in Kerala envisaged that the excess staff in various state government departments which devolved functions to local governments, when transferred, would meet the shortage of staff in local governments and the local bodies would discharge those functions more effectively than earlier, while allowing the staff to retain the cadre conditions to allow their career prospect to grow. The local governments are expected to have administrative control over the transferred staff while the department would have professional control over them. In the case of officers transferred to local governments, their professional power and responsibility increases whereas their administrative power remains more or less the same. The transferred officers, who are the *de facto* secretaries to local government in their respective sectors, need to be equipped to play their new role and can no longer remain as a mere implementer of programmes. This system has created dual control, mutual distrust and misgivings resulting in poor performance. Unless this complex issue is solved reasonably, we cannot push the decentralisation further forward.

The lower status of non-gazetted Grama Panchayat secretaries, in comparison to many gazetted sectoral officers, makes it difficult for them to play the role of first among equals to co-ordinate the officers in the senior management and that also poses a serious problem in providing stable leadership in many local bodies. The secretary should be the chief executive with sufficient capacity, motivation and status to provide the administrative leadership, the failure of which would lead to harmful tendencies.

One major deficiency of Kerala decentralisation is that it failed to forge a senior management system in the local governments by integrating the functionaries drawn from different departments. Many of these officers have strongly retained their department identity and have very weak bonds with local government, without having any organic relation among them.

New Purchase Procedure—an Urgent Need

The financial transactions in local bodies, due to heavy transfer of funds, have increased manifold. Similarly, the volume of transactions related to purchase and storage has made the governments a major purchaser of goods and services. But the purchases are made in accordance with the cumbersome government purchase procedure outlined in stores purchase rules basically designed for centralised services which do not allow transparency and social audit. There is urgent need to formulate new purchase procedures and management of stocks in accordance with the changing times.

Effective Account Keeping—Another Need

Account keeping is an identified problem area in local governance, which needs correction. The multiplicity of around 150 registers or documents, poor management of them including asset registers, problem of reconciliation among them, lack of accounting skills among the staff and insufficiency of staff in comparison to workload etc. are the problems in accounting. The account formats containing columns for all the activities connected with the newer role of local bodies are approved recently and the switch over to the new format has been made. The functionaries should be well trained to keep accounts properly. Unless well-stabilized account keeping is established in local governments, decentralisation will be a story of failures. Continuous qualitative training of all practitioners is the urgent need of the hour to have a smooth switch over to the new accounting system.

Auditing as a Control Measure

Subsequent to launching of decentralisation, enormous function and funds were devolved to local governments with unlimited autonomy, but with reduced control by government. So a new system of checks and balances is essential, to have 'fairness in decision, propriety in expenditure, legality in actions and legitimacy in policy'. Audit examination is an important control mechanism to keep the local governance in order.

The local fund audit, performance audit, Accountant General's audit and audit of the Chartered Accountant are prevalent in local bodies. These audits are conducted at various points of time and the duration of auditing also varies. The multiplicity and duplication of audit at varying periodicity ranging from once in a quarter to once in an year at different points of time dilute the professionalism of auditing itself and waste the time of auditor and local body functionaries, forcing the functionaries to compromise on delivery of local government services.

There has been considerable delay and dilution in quality of audit. The routine form of audit, ongoing as of now, does not attempt towards system improvement or enable deterrent penal action on derailed attempts made by the local government functionaries.

The contradiction of findings in audit reports, unscientific performance auditing and delay in non-compliance of audit reports etc. make the audit process a time-wasting exercise, doing more harm rather than good. The auditing should be revamped to ensure financial accountability by the functionaries of local governments. Creation of an autonomous Audit Commission headed by experts independent of government control, to function on the lines of the Controller and Auditor General of India as already suggested need to be established.

As well, social audit formally through monitoring committee and informally through Grama Sabha or committees of the local bodies or community organisations, should form a main deterrent against possible waywardness of local governments. There is urgent need to redefine the role of various types of audits by developing detailed audit manuals and by training audit teams about the new perspectives on decentralisation, to address the issue.

Problems in Local Economic Development

People's planning was set to overcome the stagnation in the productive sectors, reverse the decline in the quality of services and to maximize the use of assets in the social sectors.

Preparation of plans for the development of the concerned area with focus on productivity-increase on the one hand and reduction in beneficiary oriented schemes on the other hand is the major responsibility of the local governments. The plans produced by the local bodies now do not qualify to be called plans, but a bundle of unintegrated projects. Many of the projects were modified versions of standardized department projects, without any meaningful backward and forward linkages and overall thrust on material production. There has been a tendency to mechanically allocate funds on ward basis and prepare projects in response to the preferences of 'vote banks' in each constituency rather than on the basis of common needs of the whole set of people in the local body. The local bodies, in such situation, cannot visualize the long-term needs of development of the area and translate the long-term vision and goals into practice in the form of practical projects. The development strategy now followed is limited to allocate plan funds to different sectors and then distribute ward-wise rather than on the basis of any priority considerations in the planning process. As well, there has been inability to consider local body as a unit of planning by many elected functionaries and there is absolute lack of expertise at the disposal of local body to formulate long-term development strategy and development plan, based on a holistic agreed vision.

Formulation of a long-term vision has recently been made a compulsory step in local planning and the functionaries are to be trained in the creative task of developing a vision in accordance with the local situation.

The resultant production-increase visible in the primary and secondary sectors due to people's planning is minimal with stray islands of partial successes, against our expectations earlier. Formulation of plans for local economic development is a mandatory responsibility of local governments and hence local bodies should have engaged in promoting material production in agriculture and small-scale industries for increasing production and generating employment[3]. Agriculture sector should have gained more attention in the decentralisation process. Traditional sectors like coir, fishery, handloom, cashew etc. were left out of planning process. The projects aimed at local economic development did not show strong forward and backward linkages to make an integrated environment for production. Analysis and strengthening of micro enterprises, conducting entrepreneurship development programmes to upgrade skills and making the funding agencies accessible to local governments, are essential activities to be undertaken for shifting our focus from 'local development' to 'local economic development'.

The overall approach to local development in the decentralised planning was rapid, scientific and growth oriented one and hence sustainable and ecological local economic development based on indigenous knowledge and local resources has been more or less ignored in the process.

As part of local planning, the local bodies have not shown any initiative to sustain and manage natural resources and conserve environment. The local bodies should have engaged in identifying natural resources and common property resources while planning and implementing local projects. This has become a dire need in the context of ever-increasing environmental degradation.

Non-integration of spatial considerations in local economic planning is another problem. Construction of roads and buildings, provision of electricity and water supply etc. have critical spatial dimension. They should be planned not on socio-political consideration, but on spatial perspectives. In order to include spatial planning in the decentralised planning process, a clear binding provision in the legislation and proper training on spatial planning for the stakeholders are required. It is hoped that the watershed based agricultural planning will improve local spatial planning, raise environmental concerns, and introduce sustainability in the decentralised planning in the course of time.

Problems in Gender Empowerment

Decentralisation provides gender dimension in local government by earmarking ten per cent of the total plan funds, aiming at better quality of life for women and to enhance participation of women in overall development decisions. But, there have been serious lapses in women's participation in identifying and prioritising projects and many gender specific issues like health care, domestic violence, alcoholism etc. have been totally neglected in our decentralised planning process.

There is urgent need to include gender responsive budgeting in local governments in order to promote equality and social justice. Gender auditing should also be incorporated in the local governance. Development of skills in conceptualizing, preparing and implementing gender-based projects, should also be provided in the training for gender development to have a balanced growth.

Failure of Community Contracting

In the early years of people's planning, community contracting – doing public works by beneficiary committees—was encouraged to facilitate people's participation, social audit and to do away with the 'Contractor Raj' in local development. But the genuine beneficiary committees could not do much work as contractors masquerading as convenors of beneficiary committees took up work in many places making community contracting a big failure in the people's planning era. This has resulted in bringing the tender system for all works above an estimate of Rs. 25,000 as an interim measure. There is urgent need to explore ways to do away with tender system and to bring back genuine community contracting system. Provide leadership training to public-spirited local leaders and groom them for community work would be the probable solution.

Disinterest in Resource Mobilisation by Local Governments

The devolution of large amount of plan resources took away the interest of local governments in collecting their own resources, as they are comfortable with the sufficiency of plan grants earmarked to them. Local government can collect much higher taxes, tolls and fees than earlier at the current revised rates. Local governments need to improve their revenue by maximising the collection.

Local governments in Kerala enjoyed a continuous flow of plan resources due to the sustaining political will in the recent years, in spite of severe financial constraints. But weak credit linkages have been identified as a major weakness of local-level plans. "Both commercial and cooperative banks have by and large been unwilling to link official credit planning to the local planning projects.

Resources from voluntary labour, donations and beneficiary contributions have fallen short of anticipated levels. However, a number of panchayats did successfully mobilize sustainable resources from these sources indicating them as yet untapped potential (Fung and Erik, 2003). Local bodies should be motivated to bring their focus on resource mobilization from banks and outside sources.

Revitalization of Institutions—A Difficult Task

Grama Sabha

The Grama Sabha, endowed legally with enormous powers like prioritising development schemes, identification of beneficiaries, engage in social audit, right to know the statement of accounts, administration report and audit report and all development decisions/ rationale in arriving at that decision, is functioning in total deviation from its expectations, in spite of having detailed statutes, rules and orders.

Grama Sabha purported to enhance the quality of people's participation are now functioning as beneficiary determining mechanisms rather than a platform for meaningful dialogue on developmental priorities. The middle, upper and professional classes of people are not participating in our Grama Sabha meetings and majority of participants are the targeted beneficiaries of development projects. They attend the Grama Sabha for airing their needs and sharing the benefits. This is a significant threat to the deliberative character of the Grama Sabha.

Disinterest by the local functionaries to vitalize Grama Sabha, ignorance of the democratic rights relating to Grama Sabha by majority of the people, arbitrary decision making by local functionaries in total neglect of the Grama Sabha proceedings etc. lead to weakening of the institution. All pervading awareness building process and stable enforcement of legal provisions are needed to revitalize the Grama Sabha as a mechanism for direct democracy, deciding development priorities and for channelising public contribution for local development.

Ombudsman and Tribunal

A major threat to decentralisation is ever increasing and persistent malfeasance and corruption in execution of work, selection of beneficiaries and personally benefited projects. Devolution of sustained funds to local communities without proper safeguards will fuel rent seeking behaviour, community conflicts and corruption. There would have been irregularities from inexperience and haste rather than corruption in the initial years. But that may lead to absolute corruption unless checked properly.

The local government system is expected to deliver a faster and cheaper grievance redressal system in order to install the traditional virtues of public service like impartiality, neutrality, anonymity etc. and to deliver effective, efficient and equitable public services, devoid of corruption.

Ombudsman for state level redressal of grievances relating to corruption and maladministration and Local Government Tribunal at the district level for speedy and easily accessible redressal of grievances on wrong exercise of regulatory functions, are two institutional mechanisms envisaged for the purpose. The ombudsman, established initially with seven members, has been reduced to a one-member body recently and the Tribunal at the district level has not been established in spite of framing the rules governing it.

Inability of the single member Ombudsman to handle ever increasing complaints and the functioning of the Ombudsman like a court rather than an informal grievances redressal mechanism are problems which needs correction. Strengthening of internal grievances handling mechanism and ensuring exhaustion of all in-house remedial measures before approaching Ombudsman to minimise the number of complaints, are essential prerequisites to ensure effective functioning of Ombudsman. Revitalization and fine-tuning of Ombudsman and speedy creation of Tribunal are essential to combat decentralisation of corruption and possible mal-administration in local governance.

Need for a Decentralised System for Capacity Development

Capacity development of local government functionaries plays a very critical role for the success of decentralisation as the decentralisation process is engaged in creating new systems and procedures in local governance, transferring numerous key functionaries from development departments of the state to local governments with newer role and drawing newer elected functionaries in every election who are never exposed to the new systems of local governance. Our experience in the campaign type of training that dominated during the yester years shows that the initial focus on exposure, orientation and motivation has to move towards sound skill development of actors in local governments. Only an institutionalised system can take care of recurring training needs that emerge with introduction or change of procedures, functions or strategies and only decentralised systems can take care of the ever-increasing volume in the number of trainees.

For enhancing the quality of decentralisation we should have mechanism to train the elected representatives, especially women and Scheduled caste/scheduled tribe functionaries, with in a reasonable time frame on assumption of their elected offices. The elected representatives do not otherwise have the knowledge and skill to manage a panchayat, school or hospital. The existing institutional training available for them from training institutions like Kerala Institute of Local Administration (KILA), Institute of Management for Government (IMG), State Institute of Rural Development (SIRD) etc., are of general nature and lacks the rigorousness of intensive training. A mutually agreed upon overall strategy to be evolved is to provide uniform content or messages and to add quality to the training process for decentralisation in Kerala.

The capacity building should, not only focus on developing essential knowledge and basic skills but also change the attitude and values in favour of decentralisation in order to build the capacity to realize the development functions. The capacity development programmes for decentralisation should be able to motivate the relevant local functionaries to manage their responsibilities in tune with the procedures and practices of good local governance. Inclusion of spatial perspectives in every aspect of local economic planning should also be made a focus area in training for decentralisation.

In order to conceptualize, develop and implement capacity development programmes to support decentralisation, a systematic training system comprising of multi-disciplinary, multi-skilled trainers, and a network of training institutions including Non-Governmental Organisations (NGOs) designed with a two-tier cascading training scheme should be evolved for imparting need based effective training. All stakeholders in the decentralization process need to be exposed to training. Exposure training, intensive training, customized training, tailor made training etc. should be combined together to attack the problem in capacity development. We should evolve a training policy, with a binding framework for all capacity building activities by involving all major stakeholders, with clarity on the role of all actors and organizations.

Attempts should be made to identify the institutes, which can be involved in the capacity building of local government institutions. The problem of non-availability of quality training material on various subject areas needs to be addressed by engaging on the call experts. The problem of in adequate field exposure of the faculty available in the training institute like KILA, IMG, and SIRD etc. should be solved by engaging them in field studies regularly. Training of trainers should be a critical focus area in our capacity building exercise.

In short, development of a training policy, conducting a scientific Training Need Assessment (TNA) of all stakeholders of decentralisation, identification of training institution at the District and lower levels, evolving a training network, coordinated development of practical oriented curriculum and coordination of training implementation can address the problems in the area of capacity development to a very great extend.

Forging Civil Society Organisations with Local Governance

Civil society organisations are expected to have an increasingly greater role in development planning, mobilisation of people for participatory action, implementation of citizen's charter, social audit, entrepreneurship development and ensuring transparency in local government system. But the role played by civil society organisation in the decentralisation process in Kerala at the local government level is very limited. No systematic effort was made to encourage collaborative activities between both.

Absence of a formal mechanism to involve Non-Governmental Organisations (NGOs) in the decentralisation process and the total absence of trust between the NGOs and local governments are the reasons for the weak relation between the mutually essential organisations. Local government laws should provide a space to involve genuine civil society organisations in the decentralisation process in the state.

State Development Council and DPC

State Development Council (SDC), which is expected to act as the highest policy-making body on decentralisation in the State, has not been made an effective functional body in spite of our eight year old decentralisation efforts in Kerala. The SDC, consisting of all ministers, local body representatives, opposition leader, Vice-Chairman of State Planning Board etc., has not gained due value as a newly created platform, that could have pushed the pace of decentralisation much faster in a consensus oriented way. This institution is expected to take the lead in policy making and in sorting out operational issues in decentralisation.

The District Planning Committee (DPC), the coordinating body that integrates the rural and urban local body plans at the District, is not functioning as desired and needs to be vitalized. The District Planning Committee is composed of comparatively low profile leaders in the District Panchayat/Municipalities and is playing a very insignificant role in planning. The existence of District Development Committee (DDC) consisting of all members of the legislative body and sectoral officers in the District with collector as chairman plays a more crucial role and it undermines the DPC to a great extend. The District Planning Committee and the District

Development Committee need to be harmonized together, as the latter is an extended general body of the former, by legislation.

Conclusion

Kerala has made an excellent beginning and moved much ahead in the direction of decentralisation and development of third stratum of local governance with the goal of deepening and widening democracy and local development. But in order to make it efficient, effective and purpose oriented, it has to go a long way.

Since decentralisation is a curious phenomenon, which is preached by all, but practiced by a few, the sincere promoters of decentralisation should take all possible measures to push the decentralisation forward, inch by inch, to help solve the major issues by words and deeds.

NOTES

1. The 'reversals' include giving responsibility and then building capacity, giving powers and then creating procedures and systems and giving funds and then setting up accountability mechanism.
2. The stages followed in the People's Planning Campaign are identification of development needs in the gramasabha, preparation of a development report by task forces (renamed now as working groups) constituted by the local bodies, conduct of a development seminar for strategy setting, projectisation of the needs contained in the development report by the task forces (working groups, plan finalisation by the local body, plan vetting by the expert groups, plan approval by the DPC and implementation by beneficiary groups, agencies or functionaries of local bodies
3. Local governments had made only limited initiatives in creating employment opportunities for the unemployed and under employed due to complexity of problems, lack of multi-tier integration and absence of creativity and lateral thinking to formulate innovative projects.

REFERENCES

Bandopadhyaya, D. (1997): 'People's Participation in Planning: Kerala Experiment', *Economic and Political Weekly,* September 27: 2450-54.

Chathukulam, Jos and M.S. John (2002): 'Five years of participatory planning in Kerala: Rhetoric and Reality'. *Economic and Political Weekly,* 37(49) December 7: 4917-26.

Crook, Richard C. and James Manor (1998): *Democracy and Decentralisation in South Asia and West Africa: Participation, Accountability and Performance,* Cambridge University Press, Cambridge,

Franke, Richard W. and Barbara H. Chasin (2000): 'The Kerala Decentralisation Experiment: Achievements, Origin and Implication', Paper presented in the International Conference on Democratic Decentralisation, A.K.G. Centre, May 23-27, Thiruvananthapuram.

Fung, Archon and Erik Olin Wright (2003): *Deepening Democracy: Institutional Innovations in Empowered Participatory Governance,* Verso, London.

Gargan, John H. (ed), (1997): *Handbook of Local Government Administration,* Marcel Dekker, New York.

Government of Kerala (1996): *People's Campaign for Ninth Plan: An approach Paper,* Kerala State Planning Board, Thiruvananthapuram,

Government of Kerala (1988): *Committee on Decentralisation of Powers, Report on the measures to be taken for democratic decentralisation at the district and lower levels.* V.1and 2, Thiruvananthapuram,

Government of Kerala (1999): 'Committee on Decentralisation of Powers, Final Report Strengthening of Professional and Ministerial Support to Local Government' (Mimeo), Thiruvananthapuram.

Government of Kerala (2003): *Local Governments in Kerala: Reforms, Decentralised Development & Local Government Finances.* Background notes submitted to Twelfth Finance Commission (GOI) by Government of Kerala, October.

Heller, Patrick (2000): *Moving the State: The Politics of Decentralisation in Kerala, South Africa and Porto Alegre.* Paper presented in the international conference on democratic decentralisation, AKG Centre, May 23-27, Thiruvananthapuram.

Horvath, Tamas M. (ed), (2000): *Decentralisation Experiments and Reforms,* Local Government and Public Service Reform Initiative. Hungary.

Kannan, K.P. (2000): 'People's Planning: Kerala Dilemma'. *Seminar* (485), January.

King, Desmond and Gerry Stroker (1996): *Rethinking Local Democracy,* Macmillan, London.

Reguram, Sobha (2000): 'Kerala's Democratic Decentralisation: History in the Making', *Economic and Political Weekly,* 35(25) June 17: 205-07.

Stevens, Andrew (2003): *Local Government,* Politico's Publishing, London.

Thomas Isaac, T.M. and K.N. Harilal (1997): 'Planning for Empowerment: People's Campaign for Decentralised Planning in Kerala'. *Economic and Political Weekly,* 32 (1) January 4: 53-58.

Thomas, Isaac, T.M. and Richard W. Franke (2000): *Local Democracy and Development: Peoples Campaign for Decentralized Planning in Kerala,* Left Word, New Delhi.

Vijayanand, S.M. (2001): 'Issues related to administrative decentralisation and administering of decentralisation: Lessons from the Kerala experience', Paper presented in the workshop on Decentralisation organised by Institute for Social and Economic Change, Bangalore, May 31- June 1.

Watson, Douglas J. and Wendy L. Hassett. (ed), (2003): *Local Government Management: Current Issues and Best Practices,* M E Sharp, London.

16

The Institution of Grama Sabha and the Creation of Social Capital in Kerala

E.M. THOMAS

The introduction of decentralised planning in Kerala was an epoch making event, which brilliantly made use of the collective power of the people and government machinery to realise the so called goals of development planning. The devolution was unique in the sense that, 35 per cent of the plan fund was transferred to the local self-governing institutions. Such an unprecedented act was done by the government because of its confidence in the people. That is why the decentralised planning in Kerala was named as People's Plan. The unbridled enthusiasm and belief in the magical properties of people's participation in every aspect of development plan enabled the state to realise many tangible and intangible benefits. The tangible benefits are the physical achievements of planning and intangible ones took the form of 'social capital' and empowerment of people. Of all the various levels of people's participation, envisaged in the new system of planning, the participation in Grama Sabhas occupy the pivotal place. An attempt is made in this study to evaluate the performance of Grama Sabhas in the formation of social capital and empowerment of people, with the following objectives; (a) to examine the levels of people's participation in Grama Sabha meetings, (b) to analyse the extend of social capital created, (c) to examine the impact of people's planning on the empowerment of people, and (d) to analyse the reasons of the variations in attendance of people in Grama Sabha meetings.

The study is based on the primary data collected from four village panchayats, viz Alur, Melur, Nattika and Porathissery in Thrissur District. The four panchayats belong to Mala, Chalakudy, Thalikulam and Irinjalakuda development blocks respectively. The main occupation of people in the study area is agriculture. In Nattika panchayat a lot of people living in coastal areas earn their livelihood from fishing and allied activities also. During the study period from 1996-97 to 2000-01, Alur and Nattika panchayats were controlled by Left Democratic Front and Melur and Porathissery by United Democratic Front.

The chapter is divided into three sections. The first section discusses the conceptual and theoretical aspects of participatory planning, social capital and empowerment. The second section deals with the institution of Grama Sabha and decentralised planning in Kerala. The third section examines the impacts of decentralised planning on the participation of people and its impacts on the creation of social capital and empowerment.

I

PARTICIPATORY PLANNING, SOCIAL CAPITAL AND EMPOWERMENT

The importance and meaning of participatory planning may slightly vary according to place and time. Bhavan Bhatnagar (1992) defines people's participation as a process by which, people, especially the disadvantaged, influence the decisions that affect them. According to Cerna (1992), historically the issue of participation is intrinsic to public programmes. He believes that in many developing countries the need for popular participation in the implementation of plan projects, arose because of the following circumstances: (a) the enormously expanding role of public sector in launching development projects without a commensurate improvement of the mechanisms for the public's involvement, (b) the growth of international aid which amplifies financial resources, scope and number of government programmes while increasing the distance between the programme's "centre" and "periphery", and (c) the traceability of recurrent failure in public programmes to alienation from their own intended beneficiaries.

Hence the need for popular participation has become an essential precondition for the successful implementation of a plan project. In the words of Norman Uphoff (1992) participation can be regarded both as a means and as an end. People taking responsibility for their own development is a better way to achieve improvement in economic and social conditions; it is more likely to be successful, more cost effective and more sustainable. It is also desirable in itself, because it enlarges human talents and potential, the fulfilment of which is the most basic objective of development.

The effective practice of decentralised planning depends upon the interdependence and efficient performance of various institutions. In the words of Kurien (1996), institutions arise in the process of human interactions and once they emerge, they greatly influence motivations and actions. According to Bromely (1993), local institutions are effective because they permit us to carry on our daily lives with a minimum of repetition and costly negotiation. In the realm of decentralised planning in Kerala the institution of Grama Sabha emerged as the most important and powerful primary unit where people air and share their opinions about rural development. Hence any study on decentralised planning in Kerala becomes meaningless, if it leaves untouched the performance of Grama Sabhas.

The term social capital has nowadays become a matter of serious concern among social scientists as an indicator of the sum total of intangible benefits accruing to the society as a result of collective action and human interactions. In the opinion of Jules Pretty and Hugh Ward (2001), the term social capital captures the idea that, social bonds and social norms are an important part of the basis for sustainable livelihoods. Its value was identified by Jacobs (1961) and Bordieu (1986), later given a clear theoretical frame work by Coleman (1988, 1990) and brought wide attention by Putnam (1993, 1995).

According to Hang Blonkovist and Ashok Swan (2001), social capital theory proposes that, variations in the character of a social connectedness have a strong impact on our ability to co-operate.

Social capital facilitates coordinated action between individuals and is hence a means of making collective action problems, less problematic. It is in this theoretical and empirical context that, research on social capital ought to be understood. Social capital increases communication, since trust, networks and shared norms means precisely this.

Although there are numerous definitions of social capital, the central idea is constituted by the following aspects viz, (a) relations of trust, (b) reciprocity and exchanges, (c) common rules and sanctions, and (d) connectedness, networks and groups. The fulfilment of these conditions is so essential for the formation of social capital in any society.

According to James Coleman (2001) a prescriptive norm within a collectivity that constitutes an especially important form of social capital is the norm that one should forgo self interest and act in the interest of the collectivity. A norm of this sort, reinforced by social support, status, honour and other rewards is the social capital that builds young nations (and then dissipates as they grow older) strengthen families by leading family members to act selflessly in the 'family' interest, facilitate the development of nascent social movements through a small group of dedicated, inward looking and mutually rewarding members and in general leads persons to work for the public good. The norms of this sort are important in overcoming the public goods problems that exist in collectivities. People's planning in Kerala relies heavily on the collective action of people in realising the goals of planning.

Empowerment is perhaps one of the most important goals of decentralised planning. In the words of Norman Uphoff (1992) one of the objectives of popular participation may be empowerment—a more equitable sharing of power and a higher level of political awareness, and strength for disadvantaged people. If empowerment is the objective, the most important result of a development activity might not be an increase in economic production or incomes, but rather the development of people's capacity to initiate actions on their own or influence decisions of more powerful actors.

II

THE INSTITUTION OF GRAMA SABHA AND DECENTRALISED PLANNING IN KERALA

The Ninth Plan of Kerala was built upon the strong foundations of the concept of people's participation. Following the guidelines of S.B. Sen Committee Report, Kerala State Planning Board finalised the system and practice of decentralised planning in the state. Sen believed that, the true spirit of democracy lies in the participation of peoples in the functioning of the state, ranging from the stage of very inception of ideas and discussions to the stage of project implementation and evaluation.

According to Thomas Issac and Harilal (1997), the people's campaign for ninth plan represents an initiative to make use of the legacy of collective social intervention and strength of mass movements to meet the contemporary crisis of development. The decentralised planning programme, thus has become a part of the civic life of people in Kerala. They began to participate in this process, at various levels and capacities as responsible citizens by attending the Grama Sabha meetings, working as resource persons, task force members, monitoring committee members, beneficiary committee members and so on. That is why Richard W. Franke and Barbara H. Chasin (1997) opined that, Kerala's decentralised programme is probably the largest of its kind in the world at present. Three million people, 10 per cent of the state's population, took part in the Grama Sabhas that aired complaints and identified major problems in their villages and urban neighbourhoods in September and October 1996.

Grama Sabhas

According to the 73rd Constitutional Amendment Act, 1992, Grama Sabha means a body consisting of all persons registered in the electoral rolls relating to a village, comprised within the area of a panchayat. Thus all the voters in the ward of a panchayat are supposed to attend the Grama Sabhas. In the words of Thomas Issac (2000) through serious discussions in these assemblies people identify local development problems, analyse the causal factors responsible and put forward suggestions for possible solutions.

Powers and functions of Grama Sabhas in Kerala

The Kerala Panchayati Raj Amendment Act, 1999 (Act 13) envisages clearly the powers and functions of Grama Sabhas. Following are the important powers and functions of Grama Sabhas:

(a) Assist the panchayat in collecting valuable data and information which are essential for the preparation of development plans.
(b) Suggest the priorities for the preparation and implementation of development projects which are to be implemented in the panchayat.
(c) Selection and ranking of deserved individual beneficiaries for various beneficiary schemes.
(d) Extend all sorts of help to the panchayat in the implementation of various developmental projects.
(e) Provide necessary assistance to the effective implementation of developmental projects in the form of voluntary service, money or material.

These are the most important functions and responsibilities of Grama Sabhas regarding the formulation and implementation of developmental plans and projects. The above Act also envisages fourteen other functions to the Grama Sabhas, which encompasses various types of activities related to the provision of street light, water supply, village sanitation, social harmony among the villages, assistance to the beneficiary committees, provision of information to the people regarding pension and subsidy schemes, collection of detailed estimates of the projects which are to be implemented in the panchayat, providing details about the services of various government department officials to the people, observation of the logic behind the decision of the panchayat to implement a unique scheme to the area, finding the reasons for the lag and laxity in the execution of various decisions taken by the Grama Sabha, assist the employees of panchayat in the cleaning activities, finding the defaults and suggestion of solutions for the improvement in the service of public water supply system and street lights, assistance to the teachers and parent teacher associations of schools in the ward, assistance to the public health activities particularly family welfare programme, and other functions periodically suggested by the state government.

The 1999 Kerala Panchayati Raj Amendment Act also prescribed the quorum for Grama Sabha meetings and the number of meetings which should be organised every year as well. Accordingly Grama Sabhas should be convened once in three months every year and the quorum for the meeting is 10 per cent of the total number of voters in the concerned ward of the panchayat. In the case of a postponed meeting for the failure to satisfy the quorum of 10 per cent in the first meeting, the minimum number of persons is fixed at 50. According to Thomas Issac (2000) Grama Sabhas, the assemblies of voters in every Grama Panchayat or ward within the Grama Panchayat provide an ideal starting block for people's planning. In Kerala the average number of voters per ward is around 1500. Hence, it is practically impossible to facilitate effective discussion by each and every participant on various issues affecting their economic life. A practical solution to this problem is to adopt the small group approach. Instead of the Grama Sabha meeting as a general body of several hundred people; after a brief common gathering, the participants are divided in to smaller groups, each dealing with a particular development sector and discussing in depth the problems related to that sector. The small group arrangement made it possible for ordinary people, especially women, to be able to participate in the discussions. The resource persons and implementing officers transferred to the village Panchayat also helped the villagers to initiate discussions, thus making the Grama Sabha meetings very effective and meaningful.

III

PEOPLE'S PARTICIPATION IN GRAMA SABHA MEETINGS: SOCIAL CAPITAL AND EMPOWERMENT

In this section an attempt is made to examine the people's participation in Grama Sabha meetings based on the primary data collected from the four panchayats. Since Grama Sabhas provided the primary and fundamental opportunity for people's participation, the attendance ratio of people in such assemblies can be considered as the best indicator of people's participation in the new system of planning. An in-depth analysis of the participation ratio of people in the four panchayats, Alur, Melur, Nattika and Porathissery is made in this section. The Table 16.1 given below shows the total number of voters in the above Panchayats (1994).

Fearing the voluminous nature of the data, to be presented here, Grama Sabha attendance of people for only two years are analysed and compared here. Hence, the average attendance ratio of people all the wards in the Grama Sabha meetings during the years 1996 and 2000 are shown below in Table 16.2

From Table 16.2 it is evident that the percentage of people's participation in all the village panchayats, except Nattika in the year 2000, is below the statutory minimum of 10 per cent of the voters in each ward. In 1996 when the government launched the institution of Grama Sabha, people were attracted to Grama Sabha

Table 16.1: Total Number of Voters (1994) in Alur, Melur, Nattika and Porathissery Panchayats

Panchayat	*Male Voters*	*Female Voters*	*Total*
Alur	13578	14005	27583
Melur	8632	8772	17404
Nattika	6405	7789	14194
Porathissery	9900	11183	21083

Source: Documents from Alur, Melur, Nattika and Porathissery panchayats regarding voters.

Table 16.2: Percentage of People Participated in the Grama Sabha Meetings to the Total Number of Voters in the Sample Panchayats During 1996 and 2000

Panchayat	*Years*					
	1996			*2000*		
	Male	*Female*	*Total*	*Male*	*Female*	*Total*
Alur	9.11	2.22	5.60	5.15	4.12	4.62
Melur	10.21	2.65	6.42	5.34	4.82	5.07
Nattika	13.70	3.42	7.94	15.03	8.71	11.56
Porathissery	7.77	1.76	4.58	7.24	3.74	5.38

Source: Grama Sabha report books of Alur, Melur, Nattika and Porathissery panchayats.

meetings by the incessant activities of social workers, people's representatives and politicians. Various programmes like *Vilambara Jathas* (proclamation rallies), street plays, festival of development lamps and corner meetings were organised by the authorities for this purpose. Many people especially rural poor rushed to the venues of Grama Sabha meetings, expecting solid solution for their teething problems. But the solutions to the problems of a large number of people took the form of tiny and minor projects like distribution of seeds, seedlings, hen and goat. But after a short period of time, the beneficiaries understood the futility and worthlessness of such projects in improving their living conditions. The reflections of their loss of faith is evident from the decline in the percentage of people's participation in Grama Sabha meetings, (except in Nattika panchayat) in the year 2000.

Social capital formation in the form of increased cooperation of people, trust, reciprocity, collective action etc. could be observed from their eagerness and interest in attending Grama Sabha meetings. But the response of people to such meetings fell below the expectations of the governments. The formation of social capital would have been satisfactory, provided the percentage of Grama Sabha participation exceeded at least 20 per cent of the total voters in each ward. But since the attendance ratios in Grama Sabha meetings fell below the expected levels, the success of decentralised planning in generating a sizeable level of social capital for sustainable development of the area is doubtful. Empowerment of the weaker sections is one of the main goals of decentralised planning in Kerala. It may take the form of increased social awareness among the people regarding their rights, duties, roles and functions in the society. It starts from their convictions and beliefs in the system. The need for collective action to sort out the development problems haunting the local people both at the personal (micro) level and local (macro) levels emanates from their faith in the system. The participation of people in Grama Sabha meetings can be considered as the true reflections of people's attitudes towards this end. The comparative analysis of data presented above in Table 16.2, clearly shows two divergent trends.

The participation rate of male voters in Grama Sabha meetings declined considerably in all the panchayats. But at the same time there is a sizeable increase in the percentage of women's participation in such meetings. It can be considered as a clear indication of the formation of social capital and empowerment of women as a result of decentralised planning. Following factors are attributed to this trend: (a) the increasing awareness among women regarding the need for participation in Grama Sabha meetings, (b) the knowledge about projects for women, (c) the increase in civic consciousness among women, (d) the presence of women representatives in the panchayat executive committee, (e) the encouragement from women panchayat presidents, and (f) the success stories of women undertakings.

In short, the introduction of decentralised planning and the increased importance of women as elected representatives and as beneficiaries of various projects had resulted in a positive change in their approach to the various institutions of decentralised planning in Kerala like Grama Sabhas. Thus, it can be stated undoubtedly that decentralised planning have contributed to the empowerment of women in the state.

The low participation of people in Grama Sabha meetings can be attributed to the following factors:

(a) *Negative Social Capital*: The term negative social capital refers to the negative consequences of social capital. According to Alejandro Portes (2001), it includes exclusion of outsiders, excess claims on group members, restrictions on individual freedom and downward levelling norms. After a short period of euphoria and optimism many people understood that, the Grama Sabha had only a little to contribute towards the improvement in their living conditions. They conceived the idea of Grama Sabha as a programme for the poorest of the poor. They felt that only those people who are poor or below poverty line need to attend the Grama Sabha meetings. So they kept away from the Grama Sabha meetings.

(b) *Lack of Clear Awareness:* Lack of clear awareness among the people, about the real importance of Grama Sabha is another reason. Even though the campaign managers worked very hard to mobilise the villagers to the Grama Sabha, people looked upon them with an indifferent attitude. Hence the ignorance of the people regarding the real importance of Grama Sabha deliberations is another reason for the low level of people's participation.

(c) *Ignorance and Lethargic Attitude:* Coupled with the above factors, ignorance of the people, the lethargic attitude of the people especially well educated middle class, towards Grama Sabha meetings also has caused a decline in the number of people attending Grama Sabhas. They did not show any interest at all in the Grama Sabha deliberations. Even though they were aware of the importance of Grama Sabhas, they did not want to cooperate with the panchayat.

(d) *Lack of Interest after Getting Projects:* Another interesting factor is the response of the beneficiaries of various schemes, like housing, sanitation etc. Once their grievances are resolved, or after availing the financial assistance for their schemes, most of them did not care to attend further Grama Sabha meetings.

(e) *TV Programmes:* Sundays are the most preferred days for Grama Sabha meetings. But Sunday afternoons, were not convenient time for many people, because of the cinema telecasted by Doordarsan. Even on other week days, many people did not want to attend Grama Sabha meetings, in the afternoon by sacrificing the mega serials telecasted by Doordarsan. Many people opened their minds in this way.

From the above analysis, the Kerala experiment is certainly a brave new attempt to tackle the development problems of the state. The brand new experiment is a clear deviation from the age old paradigm of development planning with a strong bias towards centralised planning. The decentralised planning system relied heavily on people and people's participation through the newly formed institutions like Grama Sabha.

Suggested Policy Measures for Improvement

From the study, it is observed that the following policy measures can be taken by the authorities to improve the degree of people's participation and participatory planning system in the state. People's participation is at the core of decentralised planning and Grama Sabha is the soul of popular planning system. But the study revealed that, the concept of Grama Sabhas has not been taken seriously by a large number of rural people. Moreover, the Grama Sabhas were considered by many people as a forum for the free distribution of schemes to the poor people. The educated middle class constantly refrain from attending Grama Sabha meetings, and the quality of discussions in the meetings is dismally poor as well. All these must be changed. All the people must be attracted to the Grama Sabha meetings, either voluntarily or compulsorily. As responsible citizens, it is their duty to attend Gramas Sabha meetings. Hence, if people do not turn up voluntarily, it must be made compulsory, by attaching the attendance certificate in Grama Sabha meetings as a condition for enjoying all other facilities and services provided by the village panchayat. Hence, the denial of the services by the panchayat due to the absence of a citizen from Grama Sabha meetings, at least once in a year will certainly induce him to attend it.

Women empowerment is another dream of popular planning. This goal can be realised by motivating them to engage in productive occupations. This can be easily made possible by popularising micro credit systems through small groups of women in every ward of the panchayat. Promotion of *'Sthree Sakthi'* groups in every village panchayat is capable of producing good results. Likewise, when projects are formulated, especially for women, preference should be given to such production units, where the women members can do their jobs by remaining in their homes. For example, note books, safety match, readymade garments etc.

To conclude, the present study reveals a complex picture. The total participation rate in Grama Sabha meetings shows a declining trend. At the same time the trend in women's participation indicates a positive increase. The increasing participation of women in Grama Sabha meetings can be considered as an indicator of formation of social capital among them and their empowerment through the institution of Grama Sabha in the state. The general decline in the participation of people in Grama Sabha can be attributed to the strong presence of negative social capital and such other factors. Thus, decentralised planning in Kerala can be made more effective and efficient by eliminating the menace of negative social capital and ensuring the empowerment of people. This depends upon the vigorous and dynamic functioning of institutions like Grama Sabha. It will not only help to promote social capital but also accelerate the process of rural development based on the empowerment of people. It needs a holistic approach towards the realisation of the goals of planning backed by a strong political will.

REFERENCES

Alejandro Portes (2001): 'Social Capital: Its Origins and Applications in Modern Sociology'; in Eric L. Lesser (ed.) (2001), *Knowledge and Social Capital: Foundations and Applications.*

Bhatnagar, Bhavan, William Aubrey (ed.) (1992): 'Participatory development and the world bank-potential directions for change', book 183, *World Bank Discussion Papers*, World Bank Washington D.C.

Bromely, D. (1993): 'Common property as metaphor: Systems of knowledge, resources and decline of individualism' *The Common Property Digest*, 27 (1-8), Winrock and ICRISAT, Hyderabad.

Cerna, Michael (1992): 'The building blocks of participation—Testing bottom up planning', book 166, *World Bank Discussion Papers*, World Bank, Washington D.C.

Coleman, James (2001): 'Social Capital in the creation of human capital', in Eric L. Lesser (ed.), *Knowledge and Social Capital*, Butterworth and Heinemann, New Delhi.

Franke, W. Richard and Barbara H. Chasin (1997): 'Power to Malayalee people', *Economic and Political Weekly*, 32(48) November 29: 3061-3066.

Hang, Blonkovist, Ashok Swan (2001) 'Investigating Democracy and Social Capital in India', *Economic and Political Weekly*, 36(8), February – March.

Issac, Thomas T. M. (2000): *Campaign for democratic decentralisation in Kerala —an assessment from the perspective of empowered democracy*, Kerala State Planning Board, Thiruvananthapuram.

Issac, Thomas T.M. and Franke W. Richard (2000): *Local Democracy and Development—People's Campaign for Decentralised Planning in Kerala*, Leftword Books, New Delhi.

Issac, Thomas, Harilal K. N. (1997): 'Planning for empowerment - people's campaign for decentralised planning in Kerala, *Economic and Political Weekly*, January 4-11: 53-58.

Jules, Pretty and Hughward (2001): 'Social capital and environment', *World Development*, 29(2) February.

Kurien, C.T. (1996): *Rethinking Economics—Reflections based on a Study of the Indian Economy*, Sage Publications, New Delhi.

Uphoff, Norman (1992): 'Monitoring and evaluating popular participation in World Bank Assisted Projects', book 183, *World Bank Discussion Papers*, Washington D.C.

17

Social Capital in Kerala

Mixed Evidence from a Village Panchayat

JOS CHATHUKULAM AND M.S. JOHN

Introduction

This chapter examines the nature of social capital in Kerala drawing on empirical evidence from a village Panchayat in Kottayam District. After some introductory remarks, the paper first reviews the studies related to social capital already made, either focusing on the state alone or as part of countrywide studies, and then proceeds to state some general features of social capital in Kerala and its changing contours. The paper will then proceed to discuss the evidence from the study village and argue that there is no correlation between membership in associations and civic mindedness. It also makes a brief comparison between forums that have come into being organically and those engineered through statist initiatives as part of certain programmes related to development and participatory planning. The study also maps the five regions in the village on the basis of associational membership and civic mindedness and tries to account for the differential spread of social capital and civic mindedness in them. The data for the study were collected through a combination of methods, which include survey, focus groups discussions, selective observation, and interviews with key informants and leaders of the various associations. An earlier study was undertaken in the same Panchayat three years after the introduction of participatory planning to map the new institutions of social capital that had come in its wake by the same authors (John and Chathukulam, 2002). The present study is a continuation of the above with a view to exploring whether the observations made in the earlier study still hold good. Fieldwork for this study was undertaken during June-July 2002. As many as 420 persons collaborated in the study either as respondents or as key informants.

Social capital is now a widely discussed theme among the academic and policy circles. Why development and collective action takes place in some places and not in others, a point on which the tools of the economists failed to come up with answers, was the major factor accounting for the popularity of the term. For the academics, it has provided a new way of looking at the institutional and cultural aspects of development. For the policy-makers, social capital has become one of the areas in which public investment is found to be rewarding in the long-term in terms of its spin off effects on the formation of civic virtue and collective action. Some of the recent studies about social capital in India describe the Kerala society as representing the highest levels of social capital in the country in spite of low per capita income. While it was Kerala's model of development, which was at odds with the mainstream trajectory of development that drew the attention of the early commentators on development (Krishnan, 1998), it is the supposedly high levels of social capital that exists in the state and the participatory planning experiment known popularly as "People's Plan Campaign" (PPC) that the state witnessed in the last five years that have drawn the attention of recent scholarship.[1]

Social Capital in Kerala: Some Recent Studies

In his pioneering study of the performance of Italian regional governments, Putnam (1993) found that Northern Italy registered much better performance in view of the thick associational life that existed there, particularly in the form of choral societies, soccer clubs and cooperatives. Putnam had ignored associations like political parties and trade unions or even social movements. For Putnam, the dense network of secondary associations generates social capital and civic spirit through norms of reciprocity, trust that develops as a result of the networks of interaction that accompany membership in such associations. Trust among members of associations also is believed to have a radiating effect on society in general, leading to some form of generalised trust. This premise has been subjected to criticism by some commentators (Harriss, 2001). The existence of a civic community and the emergence of efficient and responsive government are inter-related according to Putnam. The Italian study found good governance positively related to factors like the number of persons who vote, who read newspapers, and who are free from patron-client relationships. Horizontally organised clubs and associations were the ideal sites for the generation of social capital. It has been suggested that one has to go beyond Putnam while analysing social capital in India. Putnam had concentrated on the outputs of social capital rather than outcomes, which alone can accommodate questions like distribution and equity (Mayer, 2001, p.685). Levels of education are an important factor contributing to social capital in India, according to Mayer. Blomkvist (2001) contests the argument of Kohli (1987) that "regime type" explains higher levels of performance in poverty reduction in the state of West Bengal compared to Karnataka and Uttar Pradesh. Making a comparison between Kerala and West Bengal, he says that, more than regime type, it is the existence of political mobilisation, civil society and social capital that contributed to the strong difference between these two states in poverty reduction.[2]

Serra (2001) studied sixteen Indian states in a comparative perspective and found that Kerala scored high on most counts making it the state having the highest stocks of social capital in the country. Secondary data were used for analysis in the study.[3] Kerala recorded a voting turnout of 74.6 per cent closely followed by West Bengal with 67.7 per cent. It may be noted that Putnam selected voting in national referendum on abortion and divorce rather than elections. In literacy, Kerala was ahead of all the states. The study found Kerala exceptional. It says that the state "exhibits the highest scores on almost all variables, and exhibits a quite unique profile with respect to all other states. Such findings attest the marked political consciousness of Kerala people, which has led, as it is widely recognised, to a highly effective state-citizens interaction and to a very democratic society. Kerala appears as the best Indian example of a society with high social capital" (Serra, 2001, p.698). However, it may be noted that Kerala ranked only third in respect of trust in state government as well as local government and sixth in trust in officials, which is close to the all India mean score. A study conducted in five states found that 31 per cent of the people have associational life, which varied between a high 51 per cent in Kerala and a low five per cent in Uttar Pradesh (Blomkvist and Swain, 2001). In a recent study of Kerala in the context of the people's planning programme, Veron (2001, p.609) says: "grass-roots environmental action tends to meet favourable conditions in Kerala because of its richness in social capital; people are politically aware and experienced with collective action". A study done by Morris (1998) on the relationship between social capital and poverty also ranks Kerala's performance high on the basis of the existence of social capital. Mayer (2001) says that a low level of corruption is associated with the existence of a civic community and that Kerala has the lowest perceived levels of corruption.

Harriss (2001) considers the class and mass organisations as the repository of social capital in Kerala and People's Plan Campaign is also moulded within the state-society synergy framework, within a political process and not within a framework that substitutes state action.[4] Heller says that civil society in Kerala, unlike in Putnam's thinking, had "distinctly political origins", which is the result of the communist strategy of "sponsoring mass organisations and by entrenching itself in civil society" (2000, p. 507). We agree that this political nature of large part of associational life in Kerala, does not find a place in the Putnamite vision. In Heller's (2000) understanding, Kerala stands apart from the Centre and all other Indian states on all key qualitative measures of democracy. Heller considers the alternating of the two political fronts, one led by the Indian National Congress and the other by the Communist Party of India Marxist or CPI (M), in power in Kerala as a stabilising factor. But this has also led to a kind of non-performance on the part of individual governments. Heller fails to notice the poverty of horizontal non-political civic associations in

Kerala. By saying that the horizontal forms of associations prevail over vertical forms in Kerala, which explains why democracy works better in the state, he has accorded the status of horizontal associations to the largely political associations that dominate Kerala's landscape. This is not true. They are largely vertical political organisations that have evolved new forms of clientelistic politics, although not of a particularistic kind. While it is true that democracy in Kerala evolved in the context of a history of conflict and social mobilisation, it is perhaps incorrect to designate Kerala democracy as effective on this count. While mobilisation may serve a particular role in the evolution of a democratic culture, it cannot produce civic mindedness unless conscious effort towards this end is also incorporated into it.[5]

The position of the Left in Kerala to the theme of social capital has not been free from controversy. The predominant view is that the idea of social capital was introduced by the World Bank in response to the challenges faced by the New World Order at the local level. This was done by incorporating and encouraging the role of NGOs and other non-political formations without questioning the power relations at the grassroots level (Baby, 2002)[6]. In other words, social capital is seen as the World Bank's own new determinant of development in line with its overall global agenda (Kunhikannan, 2002).[7] This is precisely what Harriss (2001, p. 5) also says. He adds that the enthusiasm for constructing social capital and building civil society is consistent with the neo-liberal agenda of reducing the role of the state and asking people to pull themselves together without outside help to deal with development needs. Isaac (2000) admits that democratic decentralisation can help mobilise social capital, but restricts his notion to those forms of social capital that can fit in with the state-society synergy framework. He is also wary of looking at social capital as "an ahistorical category independent of social relations" (p. 6). Participatory planning, which was organised in a campaign mode, sought to bank on the vaunted democratic consciousness of the people, their mutual trust and predisposition to co-operate. The Kerala Sasthra Sahitya Parishad (KSSP), the organisation which was in the forefront of the campaign, admitted that there has been a deterioration in the above qualities in Kerala in the last fifty years, initially due to the centralised nature of development, and more recently, due to globalisation. (KSSP, 2002, p. 21).

Counter Evidence

Certainly Kerala is well ahead of all other states as far as membership in associations is concerned, which is to a great extent, we feel, the result of years of mobilisation politics under left leadership. But the very same agitation politics has undermined respect for public property despite the leftist penchant for upholding the salience of the state in every sector. There is a disjunction between the high achievements in the social sector in Kerala and civic sense. The obsession of the people of Kerala with the public sector and a doctrinaire opposition to anything private had not led to a natural respect for governmental property. The law enforcing authorities usually do not act tough when public property is destroyed. Destruction of electrical machinery was common whenever, the electricity employees went on strike. During *Bandhs* (a protest aimed at cessation of all public activity) and *Hartals* (closing of shops and other institutions voluntarily either as a mark of protest or in observance of something) public property is routinely targeted for attack. Although smoking at public places has been banned with a court order, compliance has been difficult to achieve. There is no queuing system anywhere in Kerala except where there is a physical band bust. The sale of *Pan Masala* (grounded betel nuts mixed with tobacco and other intoxicants) or the addictive *Gutka,* which contains chemically processed tobacco, has been banned, but continues to sell as usual everywhere. Even the introduction of helmets in the state for those ride two wheelers has been resisted. Traffic rules are seldom observed by the public, and it is only when the law enforcing agencies are active that some thought is given to such rules. Driving in the night can be a nightmarish experience in Kerala since dimming of lights to facilitate the passage of vehicles from the opposite direction does not happen. The need for such civic sense and its cultivation has never occurred to the politicians. Use of mikes in public (sound blasting system) has been banned, but is widely used. Holding up of people and vehicles on the roads due to demonstrations by political parties and caste and communal organisations is very common in Kerala. Electricity pilfering is widespread by manipulating meters. Civic amenities like bus stands and waiting sheds are perhaps more common in Kerala than anywhere in the country. But they are very poorly maintained. Often they are used to paste graffiti and advertisements. Notice Boards have been set up in each Panchayat ward in Kerala following participatory planning in order to provide information to the public about Panchayat activities and services, which are now used for the same purposes. *Bandhs* and *strikes* are organised without giving any warnings, leaving women and children stranded by such sudden decisions. Very few hotels in Kerala have facilities for hygienic disposal of waste. There is hardly anything in the conventional educational curriculum that infuses civic sense and values.[8] Kerala police is featured as a corrupt force in the global tourist guide *Lonely Planet* and tourists are advised not to approach policemen if they have a problem but to seek alternative routes (quoted in *Malayala Manorama*, 4 August, 2002).

Associational life in Kerala is most pronounced in areas where the left had some support. The left strategy included expansion of the party-base through mass and class organisations, bargaining with government in an adversarial manner by these organisations when the Congress-led coalition is in power, and adversarial symbiosis when a left front government is formed. There has been a decline in the vigour of traditional leftist associations all over Kerala. The party, which used to provide some degree of certainty to the lives of the people, no longer is able to do it. Traditionally, all members protected interests of individuals in various organisations through joint action. Individual grievances are now seen as representing an individual problem requiring greater reliance on the resources possessed by the aggrieved party rather than the collective might of the organisation of which he/she is a member. New forms of associational life centred on particularistic loyalties are found to be undermining the traditional class-based associations in recent years. The thickness of associational life does not lead to the development of generalised trust or civic virtue as evidence from Kerala suggests. Several years of agitational politics has failed to create a work culture in Kerala, the reason for which can be gauged from the failure of the class-based organisations to cultivate or internalise civic values.

The poor condition of state-run buses and bus stations, indiscriminate use of government telephones and electricity in government offices, poor upkeep of the government institutions, misuse of government vehicles and so on clearly show a lack of civic sense. The public toilets of the bus stations, the hospitals and offices are in very bad shape. People drain their waste to roads. Leakage of public water taps without any one to attend to it is a common event in Kerala. Street lights are either not maintained or are often not switched off during day time. The Panchayat community hall, in most places, is dirty and poorly managed. There is a yawning gap between the personal and household hygiene of an average Malayalee and cleanliness and the concern for cleanliness in public places. Public institutions are seen as sources of private benefit. In other words, evidence from Kerala proves that higher levels of education and political consciousness need not automatically lead to higher civic mindedness.

Another noticeable feature of social capital in Kerala is its gendered nature. The social capital formed through political *agitation* had failed to include women. Even the non-agitational associations like clubs including recreational ones have also been male preserves. The library movement also had excluded women and libraries primarily serve as centres of male associational life. The very term youth stands exclusively for males in Kerala. Same could be said of the caste and religious organisations. It was only when the total literacy movement began in the late eighties that women got an entry into Kerala's public sphere. In other words, women's exclusion was glaring until recently in both horizontal and vertical associations. This lacuna was partially sought to be addressed through neighbourhood groups and women's self-help groups, brought into being by the state and local governments, particularly since the commencement of the participatory planning experiment (Chathukulam and John, 2000; John and Chathukulam, 2002).

Profile of the Study Area

Chempu Panchayat is located in Vaikom Block of Kottayam District with an area of 18.42 square kilometres and a population of 21087 as per 2001 census. There are 11 wards (electoral constituencies) in the Panchayat. The largest single caste group is Ezhava, closely followed by Dheevara, which together account for 62 per cent of the total population. The population of Scheduled Castes, Christians, Nairs and Muslims are roughly of equal size. Traditional artisan groups, mainly gold smiths, account for five per cent of the population. Associational life centred around each of these caste/ religious organisations exists in the Panchayat. The main association of the Ezhavas is the *Sree Narayana Dharma Paripalana Yogam* (SNDP). The *Dheevara* community has the Kerala *Dheevara Mahasabha* (KDMS). The Kerala *Pulaya Mahasabha* (KPMS) serves as the caste association of the Scheduled Castes. The Nairs associate with the Nair Service Society (NSS), the Muslims with *Jamat*, and the Christians with religious prayer and mutual benefit forums. The SNDP is known for its high level of associational ties among members. Barring the Muslims, all the other communities have women's wings (generally passive) in their associations.

Politically, the CPI(M) is the strongest in the Panchayat accounting for 247 members organised into 15 branches under two local committees. It also controls the Panchayat. The Communist Party of India (CPI) has 196 members under ten branches. The Congress has 636 members divided into 21 booth committees. The Bharatiya Janata Party (BJP) has 280 members from 11 booth committees. Since, the communist parties have a cadre type organisation, membership is restricted by selection. Its strength lies primarily in the support that it garners from its large number of followers and sympathisers. Other political parties with pockets of influence exist in the Panchayat. But since they are too insignificant, they have been excluded.

The party-affiliated youth organisations with considerable membership include the CPI(M) affiliated Democratic Youth Federation of India (DYFI) with 3521 members, All India Youth Federation (AIYF) of the CPI with 374 members, Youth Congress with 352 members and *Yuva Morcha* (pro-BJP) with 80 members. Barring the DYFI, which has a sprinkling of largely inactive female membership, males dominate all these youth organisations. Other party-affiliated forums with relatively weak associational ties and uneven spread in the Panchayat area have been excluded from the study.

There are 37 clubs (including voluntary organisations) and five libraries in the Panchayat accounting for 2220 and 1365 members respectively, most of whom are males. The forums sponsored in the wake of the "People's Plan Campaign" also constitute a major association form, particularly for the women of the Panchayat. Each ward in the Panchayat has a Ward Development Committee (WDC). There are 85 neighbourhood groups (NHGs) and 232 women self-help groups (SHGs). As many as 3640 women are members of the SHGs. In both the WDCs and NHG committees, women account for fifty per cent of the membership.

Of the five categories of associational membership, religious and caste organisations, political parties and party affiliated youth organisations have a vertical character, since they are linked up with organisations at higher levels. The clubs, voluntary organisations and PPC sponsored organisations are largely horizontal ones. People in the Panchayat, mostly males, hold overlapping memberships in several organisations, including those having implicitly contradictory goals. There is a variation between the different regions of the Panchayat in the level of vibrancy of each of these associational forms.

Chempu Panchayat has five geographical regions, each with its own natural boundaries. They are Kattikkunnu with roughly 800 households, Chempu with 1500 households, Thuruthumma with 220 households, Enadi with 560 and Brahmamangalam with 1400 households. Among the various associations in the Panchayat, cooperatives account for the largest membership with almost all families being covered. Cooperatives are organised along political lines. Such loose membership organisations do not promote any reciprocity or trust. The cooperatives are all brought under the state cooperative law supervised by officials of the state government. Apart from class and mass organisations like trade unions, the Panchayat has parent teacher organisations, farmer's forums, telephone and cooking gas users and other consumer associations, pensioners association, merchant association, prayer groups, clubs, libraries, voluntary organisations, hospital development committees, children's clubs, KSSP and associational forms revolving around worship of a family deity.[9]

Feudal land relations had existed in the Panchayat historically. Nearly 85 per cent of the people did not have legal rights over land. Their status was either *kudikidappu* (living in the landlord's land in a hut and working for him), or *pattam* (taking the land for lease for a stipulated period) or *varam* (cultivating the land and giving a share of the produce to the landlord, the share being dependent on a number of other factors). Most of them became direct beneficiaries of land reforms in the sixties following the *agitation* led by the communist parties towards this end. Many people had undergone hardships during this phase. The Panchayat also witnessed collective action of a similar kind against the attempt to transfer the *Palakkari* backwaters, a common source of fish for local fishermen, to a private party. The agitation in 1981 against the polluting of Muvattupuzha river flowing through the Panchayat by a news print factory situated on its banks with the participation of around ten thousand persons was another landmark. The factory management had to adopt pollution control measures following this agitation. In other words, the Panchayat is known for its record of collective action, and this factor had played a facilitating role in the mobilisation of people during the participatory planning phase (1997-2002).

That associational thickness and record of collective action of an adversarial kind do not always generate civic virtue is evident from the study Panchayat. The tendency to pay lesser building tax even for high-cost buildings by bribing the Panchayat officials is common throughout Kerala, as also in the Panchayat under study. The commons such as canals and waterways are often used as latrine outlets. There are two types of latrines, those that are directly constructed atop the canal without any pipes and those latrines located in houses which are drained directly to the waterways. Although a total sanitation programme was implemented in the

Panchayat, it could not prevent the draining of latrines to the canal.[10] Encroachment on the commons like the backwaters and village common land has been going on continuously although its intensity has increased in recent years. The people's groups and the local authorities seem to turn a nelson's eye to this.

Every time when floods come, four disaster camps are operated. It is usually the Panchayats and the political parties rather than the caste organisations or clubs which play a key role in organising these camps. When disputes between two communities take place, the leaders (mainly left supporters) are able to ensure some degree of moderation and resolve them through dialogue.

Social Capital in the Five Regions

(a) Kattikkunnu

The Kattikkunnu region can boast of several historical instances of collective action for local development. In 1953, a lower primary school was established under the aegis of the Panchayat the land for which was donated by a local family. A sum of Rs. 15,000 necessary for the construction of the school was mobilised by the people themselves. A local veterinary centre, a sub-centre of the primary health centre, a drinking water supply scheme etc., were also established in the region by people's participation. The patronising leadership of K. Sadananda Naik played a crucial role in the development of the region.[11] There are a number of non-political and non-community based horizontal organisations centred around the local library, which include six arts and sports clubs. The youth of this region and their families are more enthusiastic about their membership in these clubs than political parties. There is also some degree of healthy competition between these six clubs. All the six clubs are prepared to put their clout and resources behind the local library and reading room. For example, the *Onam* (a festival of Kerala) and annual day celebrations of the clubs were dropped during 2001 and the resources so saved were used for the construction of a new building to house the library and reading room. Two hundred and five households (25.62 per cent) in the area subscribe to vernacular newspapers on a regular basis. Although people from different communities live in Kattikkunnu, communal tension is rare. A committee consisting of representatives of all the ten Hindu sub castes found in the area administers the local Panakkal temple. In other words, representation is given to each caste regardless of the size of the population.[12] In Kattikkunnu region, holding of marriages are not burdensome to parents because the entire community shares the cost. All the families are invited to the marriage. This reciprocal burden sharing is vigorously practised only in this region of the Panchayat.

Kattikkunnu has a record of making even government sponsored associations function quite well.[13] Some efforts to protect the commons are found in this area. For example, when some people tried to encroach upon 55 cents of common land owned by the Panchayat, the local people protested and the land was finally retrieved. Full attendance is a regular feature in the meetings of the Ward Development Committee held every second Saturday of the month. It may be noted that partisan and competitive politics is less pronounced in the region. The region was isolated from other parts of the Panchayat until a bridge was constructed. This had motivated the people to come together to meet their development needs, partly by compulsion and partly also due to local leadership. In the last Panchayat elections held in 2000, the people of Kattikkunnu elected a member of the minority Muslim community without considering caste and political leanings, which is exceptional in Kerala. Vibrancy of associational life is most visible in this region and the score value obtained by the region as per the criteria used in this study is 44 out of the maximum of 60, which amounts to 73.33 per cent (Table 17.1).[14] Out of the five categories of institutions, it has been found that the PPC-related ones showed the highest degree of vibrancy followed by the category representing youth clubs, libraries and voluntary organisations (Table 17.2).[15] It may be noted that both the above categories are horizontally organised. The political associations of the youth showed the least score, which suggests a declining interest in partisan politics. During Panchayat level cultural and sports events, this region is represented by the largest contingent. People of other regions also do not have any hesitation in admitting that Kattikkunnu region can legitimately boast of the highest level of social capital and mutual trust.

Unlike other areas of the Panchayat, the institutions created through the PPC, namely NHGs, SHGs, Ward Development Committee etc., are generally very active in this region. Further, there is some degree of complementarity between the vertical (political/communal) organisations and the horizontal ones in this region with the former serving as a support to the latter rather than the other way round. In other words, the vertical associations have not sought to achieve predominance over the horizontal associations. Trust between members cutting across the communal and caste divide is found to be the highest in this region.[16]

(b) Chempu

Chempu region consists of three wards of the Panchayat. Chempu also has a record of people's mobilisation and collective action. It was in this region of the Panchayat that a successful *agitation* took place in 1972-73 period against granting ownership rights of a common fish resource of 160 hectares of backwaters to a private party by the state government. The persistence of the movement despite police brutalities finally forced the government to revoke its decision and restore the fish resource to the local fishermen community. K.S. Gopalan, a CPI (M) leader, led the movement.[17] An example of collective action for development is a kilometre long road from Murinjupuzha to Nadathuruthy IHDP Colony in 1982 constructed under the leadership of KSSP with people's participation. The people themselves gave the land for the road. This served as an inspiration for people of other regions of the Panchayat also to construct roads without looking for governmental assistance. In the sixties, a school was established in this region under the aegis of the SNDP Yogam with the support of the local people.

Earlier, loans used to be given to neighbours if available without interest being charged from them. Although loans are still given, interest is charged in most cases. In Chempu region, there were no anti-social activities earlier and any one engaged in them were ostracised. But now this is common. For example, as many as nine illicit outlets for the sale of liquor, are found in the above region.

Associational life in the region was found to be second to Kattikkunnu. It was found that the region got a score value of 40, which is 66.66 per cent (Table 17.1). Communal organisations in Chempu have been found to be the most active compared to all the other four categories and also the other four regions as Table 17.2 shows. As in Kattikkunnu, the politically allied youth organisations showed lower levels of associational vibrancy. But the PPC sponsored organisations got the same value as the communal organisations in terms of vibrancy. The youth clubs, libraries and voluntary bodies have been found to be quite inactive in Chempu, accounting for a score of 1.66 out of three. Five hundred and forty-eight of the households (36.53 per cent) subscribe to local newspapers.

(c) Enadi

Enadi also did quite well in collective action. The construction of the *Kuravanparambu* bridge by the people's committee was a major achievement. Since then, all Panchayat public works in the area have been carried by the people themselves through the *Grama Vikasana Samithi* (Village Development Council). This led to improvement in the quality of work and prevention of leakages accruing from giving contracts to private players. The farmers' forum of Enadi established the local school in the sixties drawing on their own resources. A reading room known as Tagore *Vayamasala* came into being in the early sixties and it serves as the main site around which associational life takes place. It is under the aegis of this reading room that sports and arts events are organised even now. A public television was installed in the reading room even before television had become popular. It is found that 25.53 per cent of the households of Enadi subscribe to newspapers. What we witness in Enadi is collective action above partisan considerations largely due to the existence of facilitative local leadership.[18]

Majority of the population (55 per cent) of Enadi are Ezhavas. Nairs constitute 25 per cent of the population. The Scheduled Caste population accounts for 13 per cent. Ezhavas have eight family groups under the Enadi *Sakha* (branch), each consisting of thirty to forty families. The activities of these groups include prayer meetings on every Saturday. It is the women's group that chants devotional songs during obsequies. The group disseminates information about death to members of the community. Money is collected from each family to help the bereaved family. Earlier, members of all social groups used to contribute. Now this has become an affair exclusive to the members of the Ezhava community. The SNDP *Sakha* operates a medical fund to assist needy members of their community, provides free notebooks, and has instituted five endowments for school going children. The traditional associational forms have been upset due to this caste consolidation and exclusivism. While trust within the community has increased, there has been a decline in generalised trust. The score of Enadi is close to the score of Chempu region. It is 37 or 61.66 per cent (Table17.1). The PPC-related organisations showed the highest level of vibrancy followed by voluntary organisations. Politically allied youth organisations showed the least score (1.25), which is evident from Table 17.2.

(d) Brahmamangalam

In 1915, a school was established at Brahmamanagalam exclusively with the support of the local people under the leadership of some local youths. The school was later upgraded to high school and subsequently to a higher secondary school. The school is managed by the descendants of the original families that had contributed 200 or more rupees for the construction of the school at that time. Local fishermen have established a fish market in Brahmamangalam nearly fifty years back drawing on their own resources.

Vivification of the caste-based associations has posed a threat to the political parties as well as the NHGs and SHGs in this region. There are as many as ten private financiers operating in the region.[19] It suggests that the credit needs of the poor people could not be adequately addressed through micro-credit organisations.[20]

A club known as Jawahar Arts Club has been functioning in the region for forty years. The original twenty seven persons retain its membership and they are all senior citizens now. They find themselves helpless to take up issues like the widespread plundering of the commons for fear of being isolated. Most of them are pensioners. They do not involve themselves in the neighbourhood forums.

There is another club known as Friends Benefit Forum set-up in 1999, which has 21 members as its founders. Most of them are employed. They do not solicit new membership. The forum was envisaged as a mutual benefit one. Members are drawn from all castes. Meetings were held at houses by rotation earlier. Now the forum has its own office and meeting place. Twenty five per cent of the income from the forums' earnings is spent for the benefit of the poor children who are from non-member families. They took the initiative to refurbish the local library and make it functional. It has been found that wilful defaulters of loans is highest in the Brahmamangalam region and the lowest in Chembu and Kattikkunnu regions[21]. The members of the Friends Benefit Forum, in a focus group, said that their region, although economically advanced, is poor in social capital compared to Kattikkunnu and Chempu regions. The reason they advanced through a focus group discussion was that people in the latter two regions engage in forms of work (e.g. fishing, coir, lime shell collection etc.) which necessitate greater co-operation and interactions between the participants. In Brahmamangalam, the SNDP branch is less vibrant. Most of the Brahmamangalam people seem to be sceptic about forums like the NHGs and SHGs. The secretary of Friends Benefit Forum claimed membership in another five associations, and stated that he is not a member of any political party. He values the membership in the Panchayat library management committee most, followed by SNDP and the Friends Benefit Forum. The region obtained a score of 34, which is 56.66 of the maximum (Table 17.1). In this region, institutions related to PPC have been found to be weak with political parties faring better in terms associational vibrancy. However, communal organisations, which have become active only recently, did much better in terms of vibrancy (Table 17.2). Although Brahmamangalam accounted for the largest percentage of households subscribing to newspapers (47.21), this has not been reflected in greater civic consciousness. It only reflects the relatively better off status of the people of the region in economic terms.

Local party leaders of the CPI(M), which is the dominant party in Brahmamangalam, hold membership in nine associations on an average. The women leaders of the party have membership of six associations, which includes membership in a local reading club. Party and party-affiliated organisations, cooperatives, PPC-related institutions and caste organisations are the forums in which party leaders have membership. In this region, the role of caste/communal organisations is confined mainly to marriage and such social ceremonies. The party rank and file involve in many non-political associations with a view to enhancing support for the party and to gain it respectability. There has been a decline in the public sphere in the region in recent years, a feature that is also noticeable throughout Kerala. Kerala's tea shops, barber shops, bus waiting sheds, pan shops etc., used to provide a site for discussion of public issues and local newspaper stories. This is no longer found.

(e) Thuruthumma

This is one region where instances of collective action are rare. The region has very little connectivity since it is an island cut off from the other parts of the Panchayat. The only public institution that exists in this area is a mother and child centre or *Anganwadi*. But the role of the political parties and the caste organisations is found to be the strongest in this region. Of the total households, 85.45 per cent are Ezhavas. A library with over two hundred books existed in the area for five years under the auspices of an Ezhava youth organisation. The books and the library no longer exist and the building has been converted into a place for community prayers. During the participatory planning phase, the Panchayat had supplied the same youth organisation a colour TV and a kiosk to house it. The TV was used for community viewing. An average of fifty persons used to watch the programmes every day. After a year, when the TV developed mechanical complaints, the kiosk was closed down. Electricians are locally available for repairing it. But the local people feel that repairing the TV is the responsibility of the Panchayat. This is the only area where the Ward Development Committees are not functioning. Same is the case of the NHGs and SHGs. Two non-governmental organisations consisting of more than a dozen people of the local youth have recently started functioning here.[22] However, there are no horizontal linkages between these organisations. The highest number of membership in associations is three and the average is around one. In terms of score value, the region accounted for the lowest level of associational vibrancy. But the public in this region discusses politics more often than the four other regions, using the teashops and the general provision shops as the main venues. Its score was the lowest in associational activity, a mere 28 which comes to 46.66 per cent (Table 17.1). Interestingly, as Table 17.2 shows, Thuruthamma is the only place where political parties scored better than all the other associational categories. Horizontal organisations have been found to be the weakest here, obtaining an average score of one only.

Table 17.1 shows the extent of vibrancy of selected associations in the five regions and the total scores. The relative level of vibrancy of each individual category in the five regions can be gauged from the Table 17.2.

The newly formed horizontal organisations under the auspices of the PPC are found to be the most active in the Panchayat as a whole obtaining a score of 2.19 out of a total of three, closely followed by communal organisations and political parties. But the youth organisations allied to political parties are the least active. The total average score for the Panchayat as a whole is 1.83. That people are keen to associate with the newly formed associations like the NHGs and SHGs as well as communal organisations compared to political parties and their youth wings suggests that the pull of politically organised associations is progressively on the decline. This also shows the fragility of forms of social capital brought into being through the intermediation of political groups. Even the PPC sponsored forums like the NHGs and SHGs have

Table 17.1: Vibrancy of Associational Life in the Five Regions of Chempu Village Panchayat

Category of Institution	a. Kattikunnu			b. Chempu			c. Enadi			d. Brahmamangalam			e. Thuruthumma		
	NA	*A*	*VA*	*NA*	*A*	*VA*	*NA*	*A*	*VA*	*NA*	*A*	*VA*	*NA*	*A*	*VA*
Communal Organisations															
SNDP		✓			✓				✓	✓					✓
NSS		✓			✓				✓	✓				✓	✓
AKDS		✓				✓		✓			✓		✓	✓	
Christian NHGs		✓				✓	✓					✓	✓		
KPMS		✓		✓				✓			✓			✓	
Muslim Jamath		✓			✓		✓			✓			✓		
Major Political Parties															
CPI (M)		✓				✓		✓			✓		✓		
CPI		✓			✓		✓			✓					✓
Congress		✓		✓			✓				✓			✓	
BJP		✓			✓			✓			✓			✓	
PPC Sponsored Institutions															
SHGs			✓			✓			✓		✓		✓		
NHGs			✓		✓				✓	✓			✓		
WDC			✓		✓				✓		✓		✓		

Contd...

Table 17.1 *(Contd.)*

Category of Institution	*a. Kattikunnu*			*b. Chempu*			*c. Enadi*			*d. Brahmamangalam*			*e. Thuruthumma*		
	NA	*A*	*VA*	*NA*	*A*	*VA*	*NA*	*A*	*VA*	*NA*	*A*	*VA*	*NA*	*A*	*VA*
Youth Organisation (Political)															
DYFI		✓				✓		✓			✓			✓	
AIYF	✓			✓			✓			✓				✓	
Youth Congress		✓		✓			✓			✓			✓		
Yuvamorcha		✓		✓			✓			✓			✓		
Others															
Youth Clubs			✓		✓			✓			✓		✓		
Libraries			✓		✓				✓		✓		✓		
Voluntary Organisations		✓		✓			✓			✓			✓		
Total Score Value	44 (73.33 %)			40 (66.66 %)			37 (61.66 %)			34 (56.66 %)			28 (46.66 %)		

NA: Inactive, A: Active, VA: Very Active

Source: Field Survey (420 Key Informants are contacted for Focus Groups Discussions and Personal Interviews).

Table 17.2 : Average Score Value of Vibrancy by Institutional Category and Regions

Category of Institutions	*Regions*					*Total average score value of institutio-nal-wise*
	a. Katti-kunnu	*b. Chempu*	*c. Enadi*	*d. Brahma-mangalam*	*e. Thuru-thumma*	
Communal Organisations	2.00	2.33	1.83	2.00	1.50	1.93
Major Political Parties	2.00	2.00	1.50	1.75	1.75	1.80
PPC Sponsored Institutions	3.00	2.33	3.00	1.66	1.00	2.19
Youth Organisations (Political)	1.75	1.50	1.25	1.25	1.50	1.45
Others (Clubs and Voluntary Organisations)	2.66	1.66	2.00	1.66	1.00	1.79
Total average score value	2.28	1.96	1.91	1.66	1.35	1.83

Source: Computed Data from Table 17.1

been found to be losing their vigour in three out of the five regions.

The above tables show that Kattikkunnu has the highest level of associational vibrancy followed by Chempu, Enadi, Brahmamangalam and Thuruthamma. It may be noted that the Panchayat under study is generally known for its relatively developed social capital. Hence, even a region like Thuruthamma in which associations are found to be relatively inactive, is far better than many rural areas in the District of Kottayam in absolute terms.

The associational characteristics of the different regions of the Panchayat can be seen from Map 17.1. Although Chempu region has the highest number of associations, this does not get reflected in associational vibrancy. With comparatively less number of associations, Kattikkunnu comes out first on this count. While this applies to Enadi and Brahmamangalam also, the experience of

Map 17.1: Associational Thickness of the Five Regions in the Chempu Panchayat

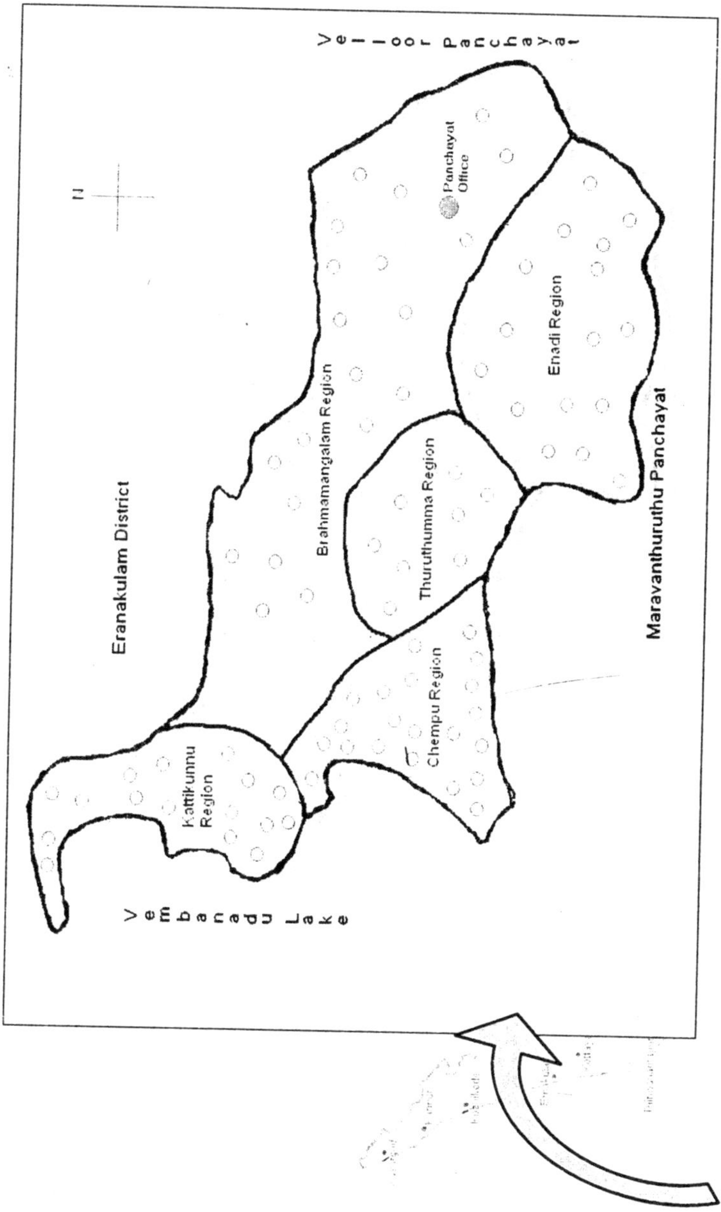

Thuruthamma suggests that it cannot be generalised any further.

Plundering the Commons—Decline of Social Capital?

Since the mid-nineties, plundering of the common property resources on an extensive and organised scale has been going on in Chempu Panchayat. The only exception to this is the Kattikkunnu region. The resources are fish, lime shell for both meat and shell and river sand. Increasing demand for all the three with modernisation and the enhancement in their prices made free riding in the exploitation of these resources attractive. It may be noted that the exploitation of these resources using traditional methods was replaced by more mechanised and large-scale modes. This has led to the generation of quick money. One thousand families in Chempu Panchayat as a whole earn their livelihood from fish and lime shell collection and sales, and another five hundred are engaged in sand mining. Many among them were displaced from agriculture, coir, mat weaving and so on, when these sectors became stagnant. While the first group gets a per capita daily income ranging between 250 and 300, the latter earn in the range of 800 to 1000 per day. Because mining is semi-mechanised, they get work for most of the days. This indiscriminate plundering of resources has not witnessed any sort of social action against it.[23] In other words, there has been an unholy alliance of all the local forces that matter for the sake of plundering the commons. Legal measures against such organised free riding or collective action to protect the commons are found lacking.[24] When plundering the commons emerged as a means to generate fast income, local youth clubs became inactive. There were six youth clubs in Chempu all of which are now defunct. Even the local KSSP unit, which was very active up to the eighties, is non-functional. Political parties have become the mediators of the interests of these free-riding groups. Sand mining is widespread throughout Kerala and this trade is "driven by the unholy nexus between contractors, politicians and trade union leaders, panchayat and revenue officials and corrupt policemen, making a mockery of the regulations imposed by the government" (Nandakumar, 17 July, 2002).[25] Political parties are forced to endorse the activities of the poachers because the latter are key vote banks in the Panchayat.[26]

Conclusion

Kerala's associational life is found to be the strongest in its agitational aspects aimed at securing what is seen by a group as their entitlement, but is found to be the weakest in generating civic consciousness concurrently. This makes social capital existing in Kerala strong on making claims on the political system and the society in general for securing entitlements but weak on creating conditions necessary for civic life. At no time in the people's planning phase, the class and mass organisations came forward to actively participate in the campaign effort as was hoped by the PPC managers. Such constructive efforts, except those mediated by the party mechanism, cannot be undertaken by the class and mass organisations because they are moulded within an agitational frame. It is predominantly through political associations that social capital in Kerala has been brought into being in recent decades. At the same time the failure of these groups to engage in collective action of a constructive kind has resulted in an imbalance, which can only be bridged if political groups work in tandem with associations of a horizontal nature. While rights/based political action has helped the weaker segments of Kerala society more than anywhere else in the country, the trust among members of groups undertaking such actions, is also found to be on the decline, particularly in the context of the weakening of the power of organised political groups following globalisation. PPC began at a time when these forces were in decline. This fact has been accepted and taken on board as one of the agenda of the KSSP in their latest review on the "people's planning" (KSSP, 2002).

The study shows that there is wide variation between different regions of Chempu Panchayat in terms of social capital. Where the political organisations are the strongest with lesser salience for non-political horizontal organisations, collective action seen from a developmental perspective is found to be weak, and *vice versa*. The existence of a large number of associations need not be correlated with effective governance. Even in the Blomkvist study

(2000), it was found that people in Kerala did not show much enthusiasm about the performance of the state government. Social capital is not a self-generative process and the role of agency particularly leadership is crucial in its formation and sustenance. It cannot be engineered from above in a mechanical fashion unless such initiatives are nurtured and sustained by local leadership. The nature of the leadership that is instrumental in the formation of social capital is crucial in defining its vigour and sustainability. The study found four varying types of leadership and of this social capital generated through horizontal organisations with suitable linkages with the local government to be the most vigorous and sustainable. This is precisely the type of social capital that is found to exist in the Kattikkunnu region of the Panchayat. The strength of Kattikkunnu is the primacy that the people of the region seem to attach to the social over the political, the horizontal organisations over the vertical.

The study also shows the complexities of analysing social capital in a state like Kerala. It also suggests the inadequacy of secondary data in understanding social capital. We need more representative large-scale studies to throw light on social capital in Kerala. One may wonder how plundering of commons can take place in a state like Kerala where the people are supposed to be politically conscious as secondary data tend to suggest. But it happens. There is high degree of difference between perceived levels of corruption and the actual extent of corruption. This happens because corruption takes place in an organised and synergistic form making it less crude and apparent. That the right to information movement in Kerala is still in a very low state compared to several other states also is suggestive.

NOTES

1. Kerala launched a participatory planning experiment of a scale not witnessed anywhere else in the country starting from the village level assembly upwards under the auspices of the Panchayats since 1996 when the Leftists came to power. It was organised as a campaign and therefore is popularly known as the "People's Plan Campaign" (PPC). The state government transferred approximately one third of all the development funds to the local bodies to be spent on the basis of priorities identified by the people

keeping in view some broad guidelines. A participatory methodology for data generation, plan formulation, implementation and monitoring were evolved as a result.

2. Ashutosh Varshney (2002) in his study talks about strong inter-religious civic engagement between the Hindus and the Muslims in Calicut (Kerala) reflected through political parties, business groups, trade unions, non-religious movements for social justice and land reforms compared to five other major cities such as Aligarh, Hyderabad, Lucknow, Ahmedabad and Surat.
3. One problem with secondary data is that such macro-level data often fail to reflect societal dynamics at the grassroots level. Many associations may exist only on paper. There are a number of other derivative memberships which come with membership in one association as exists in Kerala. In addition, such secondary data is never disaggregated making it difficult to bring out the gender dimensions of social capital (Kilby, 2002).
4. This theme has been developed by Heller (1996).
5. The idea that democratic traditions are more developed in the state compared to the rest of the country and the unprecedented verdict that the people of Kerala gave to the ruling Congress both in the Assembly and Parliamentary elections immediately after the emergency seem to send mixed messages about the type of civic culture that exists in Kerala. The verdict seemed to suggest that people of Kerala are prepared to place more value on effective government than on civil liberties, which is quite disturbing.
6. M.A. Baby is a member of the Central Committee and Kerala State Secretariat of the CPI (M) and one of the ideologues in the party
7. T. P. Kunhikannan is a former General Secretary of the Kerala Sasthra Sahitya Parishad.
8. The District Primary Education Programme launched in Kerala with World Bank assistance in the mid-nineties had a component on civic education. However, the new Congress-led government that came to power in 2001 decided to modify programme with a view to restoring conventional teaching content.
9. All these institutions have taken into consideration while mapping the thickness of associations in five regions of the panchayat. (See Map 17.1).
10. This practice is not found in other parts of the district including in regions where the topography is similar.
11. A number of leaders played a crucial role in fostering social capital in the village. The family of Sadananda Naik came originally from Goa and settled down in the region before three generations. He was Panchayat member from 1953 to 1972 and president during 1963 to 1972. He was elected in the first election without a contest. He has contributed to the development of Kattikkunnu region by patronising development initiatives using partly his own wealth and resources. (Interview with Naik, 12 July, 2002).
12. When a local coconut climber died following a fall from a coconut tree, the locals came together and mobilised Rs. 25,000 to help his family. Even

here, when a dog dies after being run over by a vehicle, people seldom care to bury it. While in the former case, the act has greater visibility, the latter case has not much visibility, but reflects greater civic mindedness. (Interview with Rajan K., an activist of library movement, 9 July, 2002)

13. The Kerala Samrakshana Samithi (Coconut Protection Council) is a ward level non-governmental organisation that has come into being under the Department of Agriculture in the late eighties. While in all the other wards of the Panchayat this body is dead, it is still active in Kattikkunnu with a membership of 700 persons. Each farmer is charged 5 rupees as annual subscription and ten rupees for registration. Every year they undertake a number of activities like spraying of pesticides on coconut trees. At least twenty five persons are available any time of the year for carrying out the Samithi activities.

14. The methodology adopted for calculating the score value is this. We have selected five broad associational forms found in all the regions as our point of reference. They are communal organisations, major political parties, institutions sponsored in the wake of "Participatory Plan Campaign", youth organisations and others (clubs, libraries and voluntary organisations). Each individual associational category coming within one or the other of the above five broad categories was ranked on a three point scale with inactive associations obtaining a score of one, active associations obtaining two and very active ones, three. Since the total number of individual associational categories covered is 20, the maximum that can be attained is 60, which is the possibility of all 20 of the associations being rated as very active. In order to make this a very simple exercise, no weightage has been given to individual associational forms. There are a number of other associational forms in some regions, but are found non-existent in others. Such categories have been excluded. (However, these organisations have been included in the map).

15. K. Mahadevan, a seventy two year-old school teacher in Kattikkunnu listed twelve associations in which he retains membership. Of these he considers the Ward Development Committee, which is an apex body of the NHGs at the ward level, as the forum which he values most, followed by Group Farming Committee and the Local Library. The Ward Development Committee, which engages his attention most, is a creation of participatory planning. He assigns the least priority to his community (caste) organisation. Mahadevan spends around 400 rupees from his pension for public activities every month. (Interview with K. Mahadevan, 12 July 2002).

16. We have come to this conclusion after discussions with a number of people and selective observation.

17. K.S. Gopalan is a communist leader who led most of the agitations in the panchayat and underwent police brutalities on this count. He was president of the Chempu Panchayat from 1978 to 1988. He was expelled from the CPI (M) in 1981. It was during the same year that he proved his

mobilisational skills by organising an agitation against the polluting News Print Factory with the support of KSSP. He was rehabilitated in the party in the year 2000. (Interview with Gopalan, 11 July 2002). K.K Ramesan, the current President of the Panchayat, is also drawn from Chempu. He was a Panchayat member from 1988 onwards and President from 1992. He is a CPI (M) area committee member. The Panchayat is known as one of the better Panchayats judged by its record of implementation of PPC, especially in ensuring people's participation. Even before the Kudumbasree, a state government initiative to bring all the SHGs under a governmental umbrella, came into being , an apex body for the SHGs was created at the Panchayat level as well as for two regions within the Panchayat due to his initiative. Ramesan also succeeded in making the Kudumbasree function keeping in view the Panchayat priorities and interests of the local SHGs, unlike most Panchayats where the Kudumbasree officials have largely been dictating the terms. He also succeed in forming Ward and Panchayat level development committees and NHGs and each of these were given some functions for selection of beneficiaries of projects, and also for monitoring. He has served a key role in strengthening the institutions that have come into being through state initiative. (Interview with Ramesan, 5 and 6 July 2002).

18. The lead taken by D. Mohanan Nair, a College Professor was instrumental in many of the achievements of Enadi. He founded the Village Development Council. When he shifted his residence to Vaikom, a town nearby, the verve and vigour of such collective action declined thereby suggesting the role of leadership as a crucial factor in the formation of social capital. (Focus Group Discussion 24 July 2002).
19. Of this one became bankrupt during 2001 leading to loss of 22 lakhs by the investors and another this year accounting for a loss of 65 lakhs of 124 depositors and 250 gold pledgers
20. In addition to ten private financiers, there is a village cooperative bank, urban cooperative bank and a branch of the Syndicate Bank. There are six groups of Tamilians who visit houses and provide loans notwithstanding the SHGs. The only impact is that the number of local informal moneylenders has come down, but the credit needs continue to be accessed by the private bankers and the Tamil peripatetic moneylenders.
21. This information was provided by Sasidharan P., Cooperative Bank Clerk, Brahmangalam on 23 July. 2002.
22. The President of one of the local youth organisations engages in illegal sand mining as his source of income.
23. That sand mining takes place recklessly is evident from the Murinjupuzha bridge falling in Chempu region. For example, poachers tie their country boats on to the bridge pillars and collect sand from around it during broad daylight knowing full well the illegality of and consequences of such mining on the bridge and the possibility of soil erosion. This has also led to the complete elimination of certain species of fish.

24. Illegal sand mining is found in all parts of Kerala. The woman Panchayat president of Chennithala in Alleppey District resigned recently following threats from the sand mining mafia and pressures from her immediate political bosses including the member representing the area in the State Legislative Assembly. (*The Hindu*, 6 August, 2002; *Madyamom Daily*, 5 August 2002). The Director General of Kerala Police stated that property offences showed an increase in Southern Districts of Kerala, and it is mainly due to the cases relating to illegal sand mining (*The Hindu*, 14 August, 2002).
25. According to one estimate 300 lakh to 400 lakhs of tons of sand is extracted from Kerala's rivers. It is worth Rs. 1000 crores of which hardly two per cent is legally accounted for. Wood smuggling by local forest gangs as well as encroachment on forestlands also is widespread in Kerala reaching alarming proportions. This is with the collusion of the state officials at different levels (Kuttoor, 2002). Recently it has been reported that poaching on wild life is also rampant in Kerala (Prabhakaran, 2002).
26. One Panchayat member and local leader of CPI (M) who had a brute majority in his ward in the Chempu region won the last election held in 2000 with considerably reduced margin even though his party followers were known traditionally for their blind support to candidates put up by the party. He is known for being not a very active supporter of the sand mining lobby, which explains his erosion of support. In one booth, he could get only limited number of votes, even though his party candidates for election to other tiers of local government could get support equal to the known strength of the party. The reason for this was the apprehension that if elected to the panchayat, he would become the president and the support of the Panchayat could not be taken for granted.

REFERENCES

Baby, M.A. (2002): 'Editorial Note', *Marxist Samvadam* (Malayalam), 6(21-22) October–March: 6-9.

Blomkvist, Hans and Ashok Swain (2001): 'Investigating Democracy and Social Capital in India', *Economic and Political Weekly*, 36(8), February 24: 639-43.

Blomkvist, Hans (2000): 'Social Capital, Associations, and Political Competition', paper for ECPR Joint Workshop, available from http://www.essex.ac.uk/ecpr/ jointsessions/Copenhagen/papers/ws13/blomkvist.pdf

—— (2001): 'Is Social Capital Good for the Poor?', Paper presented at the Poverty Conference, Sida, Stockholm, October 18, see http://www.sida.se/Sida/ articles/8400-8499/8428/Blomkvist.doc.

Chathukulam, Jos and M.S. John (2000): 'Empowerment of Women Panchayat Members: Learning from Kerala (India)', *Asian Journal of Women's Studies*, 6(4): 66-101.

Harriss, John (2001): 'Social Capital Construction and the Consolidation of Civil Society in Rural Areas', Development Studies Institute, London School of Economics and Political Science, Working Paper no. 16. available from http://www.lse.ac.uk/Depts/destin/workpapers/PUBLICATION PAPER.pdf.

Heller, Patrick (1996): 'Social Capital as a product of Class mobilisation and State Intervention: Industrial Workers in Kerala, India', *World Development*, 24(6): 1055-71.

Heller, Patrick (2000): 'Degrees of Democracy: Some Comparative Lessons from India', *World Politics*, 52(2): 484-519.

Isaac, T.M. Thomas with Richard Franke (2000): *Local Democracy and Development: People's Campaign for Decentralised Planning in Kerala*, Left Word Books, New Delhi.

John, M.S. and Jos Chathukulam (2002): 'Building Social Capital Through State Initiative: Participatory Planning in Kerala', *Economic and Political Weekly*, 37(20), May 18: 1939-48.

Kilby, Patrick (2002): 'Social Capital and Civil Society', available from http://www.fdc.org.au/files/pk-sc-cs.pdf.

Kohli, Atul (1987): *The State and Poverty in India*, Cambridge University Press, Cambridge.

Krishnan, T.N. (1998): 'The Route to Social Development in Kerala: Social Intermediation and Public Action', in Mehrotra Santosh and Jolly Richard (eds.), *Development with a Human Face*, Clarendon Press, Oxford.

Kerala Sastra Sahitya Parishad (2002): *Janakeeyasuthranam : Anubhavangalum Adyanthira Kadamakalum* (Malayalam), Cochin.

Kunhikannan, T. P. (2002): 'Vikasanathinte Rashtriyam', *Marxist Samvadam* (Malayalam), 6(21-22), October- March: 80-90.

Kuttoor, Radhakrishnan (2002): 'Wood Smuggling Rampant in Konni Forests', *The Hindu,* August 3:5.

Mayer, Peter (2001): 'Human Development and Civic Community in India', *Economic and Political Weekly*, 36(8), Feb. 24: 684-92.

Morris, Mathew (1998): 'Social Capital and Poverty in India', IDS Working Paper 61. available from http://www.ids.ac.uk/ids/bookshop/wp/Wp61.pdf.

Nandakumar, T. (2002): 'Ravaged Rivers', *The Hindu*, July 14: 17.

Prabhakaran, G. (2002): 'Poaching Posing Threat to Kerala Wild Life', *The Hindu*, August 5:5.

Putnam, Robert (1993): *Making Democracy Work: Civic Traditions in Modern Italy*, Princeton University Press, Princeton.

Serra, Renata (2001): 'Social Capital: Meaningful and Measurable at the State Level?', *Economic and Political Weekly*, 36(8), February 24: 693-704.

Veron, Rene (2001): 'The 'New' Kerala Model: Lessons for Sustainable Development, *World Development*, 29(4): 601-17.

Varshney, Ashutosh (2002): *Ethnic Conflict and Civil Life: Hindus and Muslims in India*, Yale University Press, Yale, NJ.

18

People's Planning and Kerala's Agriculture

The Missed Linkages

P.K. VISWANATHAN

Introduction

The launching of "Peoples' Planning" in Kerala has attracted wide scholarly attention, nationally and internationally. More striking aspect that captured scholarly attention is the fact that the campaign has been spearheaded by the state, that too in an era of policy changes driven by globalisation which essentially envisages the retreat of the state from its social responsibilities and welfare measures. A vast array of literature has already been made available by researchers by now lamenting on the gains as well as exposing the pitfalls of the "Peoples Planning" experiment in Kerala synonymously coined as 'democratic decentralisation', 'participatory planning' 'local level/grassroots level planning', etc. While a review of the literature with claims and counterclaims on the spectacular achievements or otherwise of the peoples' planning process as experimented in Kerala is beyond the scope of the present paper, the contents of the paper are essentially based on the insights drawn from the limited understanding of the process, enriched by a reading through some of the authentic and extensive studies on the thematic by Isaac and Franke (2000; 2002), John and Chathukulam (2002), Chathukulam and John (2002), Mohankumar (2002; 2003) and Sharma (2003).

The basic premise within which the chapter is conceived is the apprehension that the targets and goals of the much languished and celebrated participatory planning process has remained completely devoid of the objectives of growth in material production sectors, especially, agriculture. The planning process was aimed at effecting social mobilisation in the fields of education, healthcare and public distribution of food, as well as for introducing fundamental structural changes such as land reforms. It was seen primarily as a means to overcome the stagnation experienced in the commodity producing sectors in the state.

Given this backdrop, the important objective of the chapter is to initiate a discussion on the specific responses of the decentralised planning process towards addressing the persistent impasse confronting Kerala's agriculture sector ever since the mid-1970s, characterised by a paradigm shift in cropping pattern from food to cash crops due to a host of socio-economic, institutional and technological factors. The basic contention here is that the redistributive policies pursued by the state on the agrarian front especially since the late 1960s has invariably increased the risk of farming operations with respect to food crops, while the entire plantation agriculture was kept outside the ambit of ceiling legislations. More precisely, the agrarian impasse as discussed in the paper is a necessary fallout of the short-sighted agrarian policies pursued by the state and the launching of the peoples' planning programme could have been turned out to be a strategic intervention to overcome the stalemate through a host of structural and institutional reforms in agriculture.

The chapter is organised into four sections, including introduction. Section II reviews the agricultural development experience of the state, characterised by paradigm shift in cropping pattern from food to cash crops. Section III discusses the impasse confronting the crop production sectors in the state, which has become more pronounced in the context of globalisation with serious implications for sustainability of farming systems. The section also examines the interface between the decentralised planning process and the agrarian impasse and the missing links between the policies for decentralised governance of agriculture and the ground realities.

Section four concludes the chapter by highlighting some important issues for discussion and formulation of appropriate policy level interventions.

I. Agricultural Development in Kerala: An Overview

The process of agricultural development in Kerala, characterised by a paradigm shift from food crops, especially, paddy to perennial/ plantation crops has been a major source of debate in the development literature. The agrarian transition in the state is even described as necessary fallout of the implementation of the much-celebrated land reforms, which primarily expanded the agrarian base favouring the small/marginal farmers and landless labourers and exempting all plantation crops from land ceiling legislations (Varghese, 1970; Raj and Tharakan, 1983; George, *et al.*, 1988). While the switch over to a cash crop dominated agrarian system has been demonstrated in terms of peasant rationality dictated by market forces (Herring, 1991), the persistent stagnation in the agriculture sector especially since the mid-1970s has been attributed to a host of price and non-price factors. By and large, the important factors identified included: (a) loss of comparative profitability and high cost of production of food crops, especially, paddy; (b) perceptible decline in the size of operational holdings; (c) institutional and technological constraints in the development of land and water resources (Viswanathan, 2001); (d) changed agrarian relations; (e) labour market dynamics *vis-à-vis* high wage rates; (f) loss of interests in farming among farmers and neglect of less dignified farming operations by the labourers [George and Nair (1982); Pillai (1982); Narayana and Nair (1983); Kannan and Pushpangadan (1988, 1990); Francis (1990); Nair (1997); Kannan, (1998); Santhakumar and Nair (1999); Nair (1999); Thomas and Thomas (1999); Baby (2000); Eapen (2001)]; (g) relative profitability of the cash crops, especially, rubber (Thomas, 1999; George, 1999; Lakshmi and George, 2003) coincided with effective institutional support mechanisms (George, *et al* 1988), etc.

The trends in cropping pattern at the aggregate level indicate that the share of area under the eight major cash crops has increased from 38 per cent during 1960-61 to 64 per cent during 2001-02. Conversely, the share of area under annual/food crops has declined from 48 per cent to 18 per cent during the same period (Table 18.1). The trends in crop-wise area are much more revealing as it indicate substantial decline in the share of area under paddy from 33 per cent to less than 11 per cent over time. A notable feature of the crop shift has been the dynamic growth in area under two major cash crops, *viz.*, coconut and rubber and simultaneous decline

Table 18.1 : Trends in area under important crops in Kerala, 1960-61 to 2001-02

Crops	*1960-61*		*2001-02*	
	Area (000 ha)	*Relative Share (%)*	*Area (000 ha)*	*Relative share (%)*
Perennial/plantation crops				
Coconut	500.76	21.39	905.71	29.97
Rubber#	135.8	5.80	475.03	15.72
Coffee	16.8	0.72	84.80	2.81
Tea	37.61	1.61	36.90	1.22
Cardamom	28.68	1.23	41.33	1.37
Pepper	99.75	4.26	203.95	6.75
Cashew	54.32	2.32	89.72	2.97
Arecanut	24.26	1.04	93.19	3.08
Sub-total	897.98	38.37	1930.63	63.89
Annual/food crops				
Paddy	778.91	33.27	322.37	10.67
Banana*	44.42	1.90	106.05	3.51
Tapioca	242.2	10.35	111.18	3.68
Pulses	44.12	1.88	2.90	0.10
Ginger	12.00	0.51	10.70	0.35
Sub total	1121.65	47.91	553.20	18.31
Other crops	321.37	13.72	537.87	17.80
TCA**	2341	100.00	3021.70	100.00

Note: *Includes Plantation also; **Total Cropped Area.
Source: Directorate of Economics and Statistics, # Rubber Board 2002.

in area under paddy, tapioca and pulses. As a result, while coconut claimed the prime position with a relative share of 30 per cent in the total cropped area in the state, rubber has been elevated to the status of the second major crop with a relative share close to 16 per cent, relegating paddy to the third position (11%).

The changes in cropping pattern at the disaggregate level are examined so as to delineate the crop shift across districts over the past four decades (Table 18.2). The table brings out interesting contrasts of crop shift across districts. There was a substantial decline in the area under paddy in all the districts, the extent of decline being more than 85 per cent in Kozhikode (89%) and Kannur (86%) districts; more than 70 per cent in Trivandrum (77%), Malappuram (74%) and Idukki (71%); over 63 per cent in Kottayam (68%), Kollam (66%), 64 per cent each in Kasargode, Thrissur and Alapuzha districts; close to 50 per cent in Wynad (49%) and Pathanamthitta (48%); from 40 to 45 per cent decline in Ernakulam (44%) and Palakkad (42%) districts. The area under coconut has shown an overall increase of 16 per cent between 1975 and 1999 with spectacular increase in area in Wynad (181%), Palakkad (167%) and Idukki (87%) districts. However, there was notable decline in area under coconut in Kottayam (27%), Kollam (23%), Pathanamthitta (20%) and Alapuzha (20%) districts.

The area expansion under rubber has been 75 per cent at the aggregate level, with over 200 per cent increase in Trivandrum (241%) and Palakkad (229%) districts, followed by Ernakulam (167%), Idukki (139%), Kottayam (97%), Kannur (67%), Malappuram (64%), Kasargode (52%), Thrissur (46%); Wynad (33%) and Pathanamthitta (29%) districts. The exceptions were Kollam, Kozhikode and Alapuzha districts, where rubber area expansion was not of a significant scale. In fact, there was a decline in rubber area in Alapuzha to the extent of five per cent. While the decline in area under paddy has been the outcome of the growing conversion of paddy lands into coconut gardens in majority of the districts, the decline in area under coconut as observed in Kottayam, Kollam and Pathanamthitta districts may be explained as an outcome of replacement of coconut by rubber.

Table 18.2: Trends in area under major crops and relative share

District	*Paddy Area (ha) (1999)*	*% Change (1975-99)*	*Share in TCA (1999)*	*Coconut Area (ha) (1999)*	*% Change (1975-99)*	*Share in TCA (1999)*	*Rubber Area (ha) (1999)*	*% Change (1975-99)*	*Share in TCA (1999)*
TVM	9598	-77	5	91271	23	46	27472	241	14
KLM	17571	-66	8	75614	-23	36	36275	6	17
PTA	7497	-48	7	21994	-20	20	47570	29	43
ALPY	35125	-64	26	58621	-20	43	3722	-5	3
KTM	14393	-68	7	42571	-27	20	110548	97	51
IDKI	3846	-71	2	21444	87	9	38012	139	15
EKM	49730	-44	22	61719	22	28	56243	167	25
TSR	39215	-64	21	81171	60	44	13290	46	7
PLKD	107467	-42	35	45439	167	15	28550	229	9
MLPM	23818	-74	10	99276	41	40	28544	64	12
KKD	6843	-89	3	129536	33	57	17844	4	8
WND	15642	-49	8	10004	181	5	6337	33	3
KNR	13878	-86	5	95118	3	35	33554	67	12
KSGD	8010	-64	6	48596	39	35	21963	52	16
Total	352633	-63	11	882374	16	30	469924	75	16

With the crop shift as discussed above, there was significant change in the relative position of the three major crops in the total cropped area. Accordingly, paddy lost its dominance to coconut in the districts of Alapuzha, Ernakulam, Thrissur, Palakkad, Malappuram and Kannur districts. Rubber has consolidated its position as the second major crop in all the districts with few exceptions. Rubber became the single major crop in Kottayam (51%), Pathanamthitta (43%) and Idukki (15%) districts in terms of relative position in total cropped area. There has also been considerable expansion of area under rubber in Thrissur, Palakkad, Malappuram and Kasargode districts (Viswanathan, 2003a).

While a variety of factors have been attributed for the crop shift in favour of plantation/cash crops, *viz.*, coconut, rubber, coffee and pepper and the subsequent rise in output and yield of the crops over time, the most critical factor has been the definite price advantage enjoyed by these crops especially during the 1980s and 1990s.

Table 18.3: Economic significance of Cash/Plantation crops in Kerala

Crops	*Unit*	*1995-96*	*1999-2000*	*% Change*	*Kerala's share* (%)*
Output of crops					
Rice	(Lakh. Tons)	9.75	7.71	-20.92	0.86
Coconut	(Mil. Nuts)	5336	5167	-3.17	44.70
Rubber	(000 tons)	442.83	572.82	29.35	94.40
Tea	(000 tons)	60.72	71.3	17.42	8.11
Coffee	(000 tons)	46.24	60.47	30.77	22.10

Value of crops (Rs. crores)				**Share in state's agriculture SDP (%)**	
Crops	*1995-96*	*1999-2000*	*% Change*	*1995-96*	*1999-2000*
Rice	533	527	-1.12	7.68	7.37
Coconut	1766	1447	-18.09	25.42	20.21
Rubber	2304	1775	-22.97	33.17	24.80
Tea	291	513	75.93	4.19	7.16
Coffee	465	485	4.22	6.70	6.78
Sub total	5361	5760	7.44	77.17	66.32
Gross Agri. income	6947	7158	3.04	100.00	100.00

Note: Indicates Kerala's share in India.
Source: GOK (2001); Rubber Board; OPASI, Coffee Board

With this, the socio-economic significance of the cash/ plantation crops has become more evident in terms of value of output and income generated from agriculture (SDP) and employment in the state. Obviously, Kerala accounts for major share in the production of rubber (94%), coconut (45%), coffee (22%) and tea (8%) in India (Table 18.3). In the total agricultural income generated in the state, the four crops, *viz*., rubber, coconut, coffee and tea accounted for almost 70 per cent during 1995-96 though the share declined to about 60 per cent during 1999-2000 owing to the steep fall in the prices of these crops. Among the crops, though coconut is ranked first in terms of the share in total cropped area of the state, rubber ranks first in terms of the share in income from agriculture (25%), followed by coconut (20%).

From the foregoing discussion on the process of agricultural development and its current status in the state, it may be observed that commercial/plantation crops have been an important source of dynamism stimulating socio-economic development in the state with necessary linkage effects. Among the major crops, the case of rubber has been outstanding in terms of its emergence as a source of livelihood for more than one million population in the state, consisting of small and marginal growers and dependent labour households (Viswanathan, 2003a). Such a dynamism has been propelled by a host of favourable factors, which included: (a) self-sufficiency driven protected price policy regime especially in the case of rubber till 1991; (b) relative profitability of the cash crops; and (c) institutional interventions by the crop promotional agencies, such as the Rubber Board, Spices Board, Coffee Board, Tea Board and the Coconut Development Board (with varying performance efficiencies), which have been instrumental in making a breakthrough in production and productivity of the commercial/ plantation crops (George, 1999).

II. The Agrarian Impasse and Peoples' Planning

By and large, scholars tend to attribute the persistent stagnation in the material production sectors, especially, agriculture in the state to the dismal performance of agriculture, characterised by decline in area, production and productivity of crops with some exceptions. It may be observed that the agrarian impasse in Kerala's agriculture had its beginning ever since the mid-1970s when the shift from food to cash crops became more evident, eventually leading to the disintegration of the food crop production sector. Paddy and other wetlands have increasingly been converted on an extensive scale in the pretext of loss of profitability and the changing dynamics in the agricultural labour market in the state. The interventions made by the state to reinvigorate paddy production through participatory schemes, like Group Farming during the late 1980s and Group Approach for Locally Adjusted Sustainable Agriculture (GALASA) in 1998 have been less successful in strengthening the food crop sector. The extent of paddy land conversion continued unabated in spite of several legislations, such as the Kerala Land Utilisation Order (KLU) as early as 1967 regulating conversion of paddy lands. The issue has also not been brought into the agenda of the peoples' planning programme so as to explore various alternatives and action plans at the local level. There are instances reported from Palakkad, the rice bowl of the state, where farmers find paddy cultivation more profitable than cash crops ("Paddy cultivation more profitable: farmers", *The Hindu,* Jan 13, 2003) if the government procured it at the minimum support price and gave the promised subsidies on time. Farmers realised a profit of Rs. 1500 to Rs. 2000 per ha of paddy when the government's minimum support price was enhanced from Rs. 7.5 to Rs. 8 per kg. This sufficiently prove that the campaign that paddy cultivation was not profitable was a canard spread by vested interests, who wanted to convert paddy lands for real estate and other profitable land uses.

It is important to note that there have not been serious efforts made by the local planners to address the whole gamut of issues ranging from management of production and marketing of paddy as also to resolve the issues confronting the labour market through appropriate structural and institutional reforms and interventions. Though there are evidences of social capital formation achieved through mobilisation of local farming communities in terms of group farming in paddy cultivation and setting up of association of coconut farmers in some of the village panchayats, the potential of the existing committees of farmers to function as beneficiary committees was not fully explored in the plan campaign (John and Chathukulam, 2002: 1943). It is also important to note that though much have been acclaimed about the "Labour Bank Model" as experimented in the *Kunnathukal Grama Panchayat* (Mohanakumar and George, 2001) and similar other interventions in other panchayats, majority of such interventions have met with an untimely demise due to plethora of reasons that are self-explanatory. Mohanakumar (2003) indicated that the sole reason for the `contrived demise' of the 'Kunnathukal Model' has been a restriction placed on the formation of micro level institutions and the obstacles created in the path of implementation of development projects through such institutions. Resultantly, the Kunnathukal model could not be sustained on the one hand and prevented other Grama Panchayats from replicating the same on the other. Interestingly, Chathukulam and John (2002) bring out that the initial enthusiasm witnessed in the 'labour bank experiment' was waning. It has also been observed that the peoples planning process has miserably failed, as in many respects, it has been a replication of micro level initiatives to the state's broader context without much relevance to the specific characteristics of the stakeholders and specificities of the regions (Gopinathan Nair, 2000; Sharma, 2003).

Similar to the impasse as reflected in the labour market dynamics in general agriculture in the state, the rubber small holdings sector is also circumscribed by serious structural issues and operational level constraints confronting both the production sector and the labour segment, dominated by tapping labour. The rubber production sector in the state is dominated by the small holdings below two ha in area with a relative share of more than 95 per cent in the total number of operational holdings and 86 per cent of the area. The average holding size of rubber small holdings is less than 0.5 ha (Rubber Board, 2003). The growing sub-division and fragmentation of the small holdings has resulted in proliferation of holdings into non-viable and uneconomic units over time, which could have serious implications on the sustainability of the sector in the era of globalisation. The small holder sector is also characterised by increased dependence on hired labour for tapping and other related operations. An important outcome of the increasing sub-division and fragmentation of rubber holdings has been a steady decline in the number of trees available for tapping from a single grower and the resultant emergence of multiple grower dependence among the tappers so as to ensure comparable daily wages. However, even with multiple grower dependence, the average number of trees available for majority of the tappers is only 362 trees on a tapping day. Obviously, 86 per cent of the rubber tappers have been earning a daily wage of less than Rs. 100 across the rubber growing regions in the state. Resultantly, there has been significant withdrawal of tappers in the productive age group from the labour market coincided with aversion of younger generations to take up tapping (Viswanathan, *et al.*, 2003). The scenario points to the serious problem of tapper shortage in Kerala in the years to come. Though the rubber sector in the state is known for its institutional intervention operations through the Rubber Producers Societies (RPS) at the micro level, there have not been any efforts to address this serious issue.

Though the local level planning in the rubber growing regions could have been efficiently designed through a proper integration of the RPS with the planning process, the efforts in this direction had been totally absent. As a matter of fact, the planning process in the rubber dominant panchayats has been severely constrained by low levels of peoples' participation and inefficient use of financial resources (plan funds). Moreover, it has been evident from the Development Reports that the quality and success rate of implemented projects have been far from satisfactory in the rubber growing regions. The investment outlay earmarked for rubber sector during the Tenth Plan reveals that in Kottayam district (which accounts for almost half of the rubber plantations in the state), the share of rubber sector in the total outlay of the production has been hovering around 2 to 8 per cent (Mohanakumar, unpublished). This eventuality necessarily calls for more empirical investigations of the interface between the planning process and its responses with respect to the rubber dominated panchayats in the state.

In brief, there was not much appreciation of the fact that the stagnation in crop production sectors in the state has been mostly due to a host of operational level constraints in agriculture, broadly classified as: (a) institutional constraints; (b) socio-economic constraints; (c) technological constraints; (d) financial constraints; and (e) management constraints (Viswanathan, 2001). Some of the important institutional impediments that are most relevant in this regard are: (a) declining size of operational holdings leading to proliferation of small and marginal holdings across the major commercial crops, especially, coconut (0.25 ha) and rubber (0.42 ha); (b) fast disappearing full-time farming population leading to the emergence of absentee landlordism and growing dependence on hired labour; (c) shortage of skilled/unskilled labourers in the midst of growing rural unemployment; and (d) dwindling institutional support mechanisms in the post-reforms era. The cumulative effect of these institutional factors coupled with the persistent decline in the prices have been posing serious challenges to the pursuit of farming operations and the cash crop production systems in the state.

The technological constraints confronting the agriculture sector in the state mostly relate to the challenges posed by the available infrastructure facilities and level of technology adoption across crops and regions. It is important to note that given the technological possibilities for productivity enhancements within the existing institutional framework and scale of operations, most of the crops have serious agronomic limitations in the emerging scenario. As a matter of fact, the need for crop-specific interventions so as to enhance productivity levels through systematic replanting programmes as in the case of coconut have never been a serious agenda in the planning process neither at the state level or at the local levels.

In the case of coconut, the widespread attack of the pest, *Mandari* originating from central Kerala affected more than 590 lakh palms in the state leading to low productivity levels compared to rest of the country. Though the state accounts for 45 per cent of the area under coconut and 35 per cent of production in the country, the state's average productivity of 5747 nuts per ha is considerably lower than Maharashtra (15013 nuts/ha), Pondicherry (14182), West Bengal (13401), Tamil Nadu (10599), Andhra Pradesh (10342) and 7822 nuts/ha reported at the national level (CDB, 2001:31). Evidently, over 90 per cent of the holdings with 60 per cent share in total area are marginal and sub-marginal holdings (Rethinam and Thampan, 2001) and are incapacitated in terms of generating adequate income for the dependent households. Moreover, the tiny structure of the holdings along with lack of proper irrigation facilities has resulted in lower levels of adoption of inorganic fertilizers (40%), plant protection measures (30%) and other farm level secondary investments in the coconut holdings in the state. The contrast is that the crop-specific technologies developed are applicable only to coconut monocropping systems and appropriate technologies catering the requirements of the coconut homesteads are hard to come by (Nair and Rajesh, 2001). The technological constraints facing other crops, *viz.*, cardamom, arecanut and banana may also be regarded as similar to that of coconut given the tiny nature of the operational holdings and its distribution pattern in the state.

The most critical aspect of the impasse in the state's agriculture sector can be traced back to the early 1990s coinciding with major policy changes and trade reforms in the context of globalisation resulting in persistent decline in the prices of all the crops, especially, cash crops. The magnitude of decline in prices from the peak levels reported during the 1990s has been the highest for rubber and coconut (42% each), followed by coffee (37%) and tea (28%). It is important to note that the price of rubber has been hovering around Rs. 30 to Rs. 31 per kg during the last few years since 1997 with the peak level prices reported at Rs. 52 during 1995. The price of coconut has declined from Rs. 457 per 100 nos. in 1998 to Rs. 280 in 2000 (Viswanathan, 2003a). The decline in the value of output realised as a result of fall in prices has been more in the case of rubber (23%), followed by coconut (18%) during the period 1995 to 2000 (Table 18.3). The cumulative effect of the decline in prices of the major cash crops has been a decline in the income from agriculture in the state to the extent of 21 per cent from Rs. 31468 per ha during 1996-97 to Rs. 24736 per ha during 2000-01 (Viswanathan, 2003b). Though a recovery in prices is witnessed especially in the case of rubber recently, the sustenance of the same is rather questionable in the context of market integration in the era of globalisation. The issues become furthermore complex as Kerala has been losing its comparative advantage in the export of traditional commodities such as pepper, cardamom, ginger, cashew kernels, marine products, coir and coir products, tea and coffee (Jeromi, 2003) with the opening up of the economy and removal of quantitative restrictions (QRs) and imposition of non-tariff barriers (like sanitary control measures) on imports.

The argument that 'participatory planning becomes more difficult and less meaningful in the production of export commodities' as put forth by some scholars (Sharma, 2003), though appears to be illogical, needs further probing at length. In fact, the falling agricultural prices, especially, of the cash crops, has been the most burning issue during the heydays of the peoples' planning programme. Yet, apparently, there has not been any serious discussion on the issue supplemented with effective intervention so as to tackle the problem. An important paradox that looms large is the fact that the retail prices of agricultural commodities say, coconut, coffee, tea, etc. are much higher than the farm gate prices actually realised by the farmers. Though the extent of value added in the products is rather insignificant from the farm gate level to the retail outlets, the farmers stand to loose and deprived of the remunerative prices as a result of exploitation by intermediaries. This scenario points to the fact that the planning process could have been made as an appropriate platform through which local farmer initiatives could have been mobilised so as to tackle this issue in favour of the small and marginal farmers.

III. Issues for Discussion

The important concern of the paper has been to examine the interface between the impasse in Kerala's agriculture and the responsiveness of the peoples' planning process to address the same. The policy changes consequent on introduction of economic reforms in the era of globalisation add further to the impasse, as the state's agriculture sector is predominated by cash crops, having greater degree of external trade. The issues confronting the agrarian prospects of the regional economy is enveloped by a development crisis surmounting the crop production sectors, which are otherwise caught up in a stalemate caused by a host of operational level constraints, consisting of agronomic, institutional, technological, socio-economic, ecological issues. As a matter of fact, the decentralised planning process has been the rarest opportunity that the state ever had in its history, to address at least some of these issues and come out with realistic action plans and amicable solutions. Unfortunately, the entire planning process has been a missed opportunity especially in an era when serious questions are posed on the conventional role of the state in protecting agriculture, environment, resources and the rural livelihood systems. The issue assumes importance especially in the context of the dwindling levels of public investment for agriculture and allied infrastructure development activities, especially, irrigation development in the state. For instance, the share of agriculture and allied activities in the total plan outlay in the state has declined from 19 per cent during the First Plan (1951-56) to 14 per cent during the Eighth Plan (1992-97) and to 4.7 per cent in the Tenth Plan (2002-07).

Such an eventuality increasingly challenges the role and effectiveness of the state or governance systems in protecting the domestic agriculture sector and the common property resources (CPRs) from being subjugated by global competitors. The new tendencies emerge at the state level further bring out the irony that the state policies with respect to protection of common property resources, especially, land and water are diametrically opposing to the genuine interests of the farming community in the state. The move to lease out the paddy fields for banana cultivation to multinational companies as well as the much contested decision to sell the surface and groundwater resources to multinational beverage corporations are crucial as such moves would only augment the crisis confronting the agriculture sector in the state. In this respect, it is important to discuss some of the following issues at greater detail and come to consensus:

(1) To what extent the local level planning could be recast so as to address the crop-specific interventionist policies?
(2) How the participatory planning process could help reorient the crop production systems in the state so as to attain greater degree of resilience through crop/product diversification leading to higher value addition and realisation of higher net farm income?
(3) How the local level interventions could be assimilated to eliminate the prevailing asymmetries in the labour market across crops and regions?
(4) How the community oriented local institutions should be evolved so as to protect and conserve the natural resources (like water bodies, wetlands, paddy lands, etc.) of the state?

(5) How to evolve new forms of local institutional arrangements as also to integrate these institutions with the existing crop-specific and broad-based institutions for strengthening agri-business and thereby making the state's agriculture more competitive and rural livelihood systems more sustainable?

REFERENCES

Baby, A.A. (2000): 'The Dynamics of Agricultural Wage Formation in Kerala', Unpublished Ph.D. Thesis submitted to the Cochin University of Science and Technology, Cochin.

CDB (2001): 'All India Final Estimate of Coconut 1999-2000', *Indian Coconut Journal*, 32 (3), July.

Chathukulam, Jos and John, M.S. (2002): 'Five Years of Participatory Planning in Kerala: Rhetoric and Reality', *Economic and Political Weekly*, 37(49), December 7: 4916-26.

Eapen, M. (2001): *Rural Industrialisation in Kerala: Its Dynamics and Local Linkages*, Manohar Publishers, New Delhi.

George, K. T. (1999): 'The Natural Rubber Sector: Emerging Issues in the 1990s', in: B.A. Prakash (ed), *Kerala's Economic Development: Issues and Problems*, Sage Publications, New Delhi, pp. 186-199.

George, K.T., Haridasan, V. and Sreekumar, B. (1988): 'Role of government and structural changes in rubber plantation industry', *Economic and Political Weekly*, 23 (48): M158-M166.

George, P.S. and Chandan Mukherjee (1986): 'Rice Economy of Kerala: A Disaggregate Analysis of Performance', *Working Paper No. 213*, Centre for Development Studies, Trivandrum.

GOK (2001): *Statistics for Planning, Bureau of Economics and Statistics*, Government of Kerala, Thiruvananthapuram.

GOK (2002): *Economic Review*, Government of Kerala, State Planning Board, Thiruvananthapuram.

Gopinathan Nair (2000): 'Peoples' Planning in Kerala: A Case Study of Two Village Panchayats', *Discussion Paper No. 16*, Kerala Research Programme on Local Level Development, Centre for Development Studies, Thiruvananthapuram.

Herring, Ronald (1991): *Contesting the Great Transformation: Land and Labour in South India*, Cornell University (manuscript *as cited in Heller, Patrick, 1999)*.

Isaac, Thomas, T.M. and R.W. Franke (2000): *Local Democracy and Development: People's Campaign for Decentralised Planning in Kerala*, Leftword, New Delhi.

Isaac, Thomas, T.M. and R.W. Franke (2002): *Local Democracy and Development: The Kerala Peoples' Campaign for Decentralised Planning*, Rowman & Littlefield, Lawham.

Jeromi, P.D. (2003): 'What Ails Kerala's Economy: A Sectoral Exploration', *Economic and Political Weekly*, 38(16), April 19: 1584-1600.

John, M.S. and Jos Chathukulam (2002): 'Building Social Capital through State Initiative: The case of Participatory Planning in Kerala', *Economic and Political Weekly*, 37(20), May 18: 1939-48.

Kannan, K.P. (1999): 'Rural labour relations and development dilemmas in Kerala: Reflections on the dilemmas of a socially transforming labour force in slowly growing economy', *Journal of Peasant Studies*, 26 (2 & 3): 140-81.

Kannan, K.P. (1998): 'Political Economy of Labour and Development in Kerala', *Economic and Political Weekly*, 33 (52): L61-L70.

Kannan, K. P. and K. Pushpangadan (1988): 'Agricultural Stagnation in Kerala: An Exploratory Analysis', *Economic and Political Weekly*, 23 (39): A120-A128.

Kannan, K.P. and K. Pushpangadan (1990): 'Dissecting Agricultural Stagnation: An Analysis Across Seasons, Crops and Regions', *Economic and Political Weekly*, 25 (35 & 36): 1991-2004.

Mohanakumar (unpublished): 'Decentralised Planning and Natural Rubber Sector: An analysis of Natural Rubber Dominant Regions in Kerala', Rubber Research Institute of India, Kottayam.

Mohanakumar, S. and George, K.T. (2001): 'Agriculture Stagnation and Institutional Intervention in the Rural Labour Market: The Case of Kunnathukal Model in Kerala' in S.P. Jain (ed), *Emerging Institutions for Decentralised Rural Development*, National Institute of Rural Development, Hyderabad, Vol. 1, pp. 465-77.

Mohanakumar, S. (2002): 'From Peoples Plan to Plan *sans* People', *Economic and Political Weekly*, 37(16), April 20: 1492-97.

Mohanakumar, S. (2003): 'Decentralisation in Kerala: Peoples' Plan', *Economic and Political Weekly*, 38(30), July 26: 3214-16.

Nair, Sukumaran, M.K. (1999): 'Rural Labour Market in Kerala: Small Holder Agriculture and Labour Market Dynamics', *Economic and Political Weekly*, 32 (35): L-45-52.

Pillai, P.P. (ed) (1982): *Agricultural Development in Kerala*, Agricole Publishing Company, New Delhi.

Raj, K.N. and Tharakan, P.K.M. (1983): 'Agrarian Reform in Kerala and its Impact on the Rural Economy—A Preliminary Assessment', in Ghose, A.K. (ed), *Agrarian Reform in Contemporary Developing Countries*, Croom Helm, London and Canberra, St. Martins Press, New York, pp. 31-88.

Rethinam, P. and P.K. Thampan, (2001): 'Blue Print for Reviving Coconut Based Economy of Kerala State', *Indian Coconut Journal*, 32 (8), December: 1-9.

Rubber Board (2003): *Indian Rubber Statistics*, Vol. 26, Kottayam, Kerala.

Santhakumar, V. and K.N. Nair (1999): 'Kerala's Agriculture: Trends and Prospects', in M.A. Oommen (ed), *Rethinking Development: Kerala's Development Experience*, Vol. II, Concept Publishing Company, New Delhi, pp. 314-324.

Sharma, Rashmi (2003): Kerala's Decentralisation: Idea in Practice, *Economic and Political Weekly*, 38(36), September 6: 3832-50.

Tharakan, Michael (1997): 'History and Development Experience and Deconstructred Analysis of Kerala', Unpublished Ph.D. Dissertation, Mahatma Gandhi University, Kottayam.

Thomas, J. A. and T. A. Thomas (1999): 'Reaping before Sowing': Agrarian Relations in Kuttanad', in: B.A. Prakash (ed) *Kerala's Economic Development: Issues and Problems*, Sage Publications, New Delhi.

Varghese, T.C. (1970): *Agrarian Change and Economic Consequences: Land Tenures in Kerala 1850-1960*, Allied Publishers, Bombay.

Viswanathan, P.K. (2001): 'Economics of On-Farm Development: A Study of Major Irrigation Projects in Kerala', an unpublished Ph.D. Dissertation, University of Mysore, Mysore.

Viswanathan, P.K. (2003): 'Development Impasse in Kerala's Agriculture: The Emerging Crisis and Conflicting Paradigms in the post-reforms era', paper presented at the *National Conference on Economic Reforms in Kerala: A Critical Assessment*, held during 15-17 March, organised by CSDS, Thiruvananthapuram.

Viswanathan, P.K., George, K.T. and Joseph, T. (2003): 'Informal Labour Market and Structural Devolution', *Economic and Political Weekly*, 38(31), August 2: 3277-81.

SECTION–IV

LOCAL GOVERNANCE AT WORK: DYNAMICS AND CHALLENGES

19

The Functioning of Grama Panchayats in Karnataka

D. RAJASEKHAR AND SACHIDANANDA SATAPATHY

Introduction

Development is now regarded as a process that requires democracy (Mandal, 2003). If the essence of democracy is that people decide their own fate, then decentralisation is nothing but a first step towards fulfilling this process. In India, where large proportion of the population is poor and resides in villages, an enabling environment is required to make this vulnerable section involve in the process of democracy and development. The Centre-State led development has been criticised because it could not become responsive, cost effective, and develop local capability and self-reliance. With the failure of various state-led development programmes, attempts to improve people's participation in the decision-making and control of resources at the local level have been made. As a consequence, the local governance is now strengthening its base in the country with people-centred approach.

The issue of local governance has assumed more importance with the introduction of 73rd Constitutional Amendment. This amendment has sought to give space to the weaker sections and women to participate in the affairs of their own problems and development. It has also aimed at decentralising the power and removing gender imbalance in government institutions. The constitutional amendment has been hailed as revolutionary as it is expected to empower the poor, and marginalised (such as women and those belonging to depressed castes) and give them voice, feeling of solidarity and democratic politics (Bohra, 1997).

The main intention of the policy makers behind this decentralisation is twofold: one, democratic justice and the other, human resource utilisation (Jain, 1992). Local administrative agencies fall far short of the standard definition of local government having certain characteristics like separate legal existence, power to adopt its own budget, authority to allocate resources, comprehensive functions dealing with local development. One of the objectives of a well-developed local government system is to provide a two-way channel of communication between the local community and higher level government. It is also realised that the local government in countries like India is an eminently suitable mechanism to increase people's participation in policy formulation and implementation (Vajpayee, 1990). The Planning Commission, in the Second Five Year Plan itself, laid down the postulates like the Grama Panchayat (GP) at the village level should be organically linked with popular organisation at a higher level (Mathur, 1991; Mishra, *et al.* 1993).

The major premise of democratic decentralisation is that by building popular participation and accountability into local governance, the local level government will become more responsive to citizens' desires and more effective in resource delivery. The main rationale for this type of reforms arises from disillusionment with the performance of the state (Rajasekhar, 2004). Much of the decentralisation's strategy lies in its promise to include people from all walks of life in community decision-making, and reduction in poverty (Gaventa, 2003). As government comes closer to people, more people will participate in the process. Economic theories substantiate that decentralised decision-making optimises the outcomes and ensures the well-being of all those who are likely to be affected by such decision. Decentralisation helps identification of the local problems, takes an inventory of locally available manpower and resources, makes better estimates of financial resources, and locates the project properly. Thus, decentralisation is more responsive to the local needs and aspirations (Crook and Manor, 2001). More importantly, decentralisation creates institutions that are more amenable to the local needs and preferences that are able to empower new actors at the local level and create conditions for new lines of development.

Though the new Panchayati Raj system has constitutional legitimacy, structural shortcomings within the system may come in the way of PRIs undertaking the functions constitutionally assigned to them. Highlighting some practical problems, Mishra *et al.* (1993) point out that the lives of Panchayati Raj Institutions depend on the whims and policies of the state government. Regarding the bureaucratic intervention in the affairs of the panchayat, Bandyopadhay (2001) notes that in a democratic polity, power belongs to the people and it has to be exercised by their representatives. Unfortunately, deviation from these principles appears to be the norm rather than the exception. Studying from the perspective of how economic prosperity is required for making an effective participation, Diwan (2002) notes that the 73rd constitutional amendment on Panchayati Raj may not bring the needed transformation without economic liberalisation. The inclusion of backward castes in the decentralisation process assumes importance. *Dalits* or scheduled castes and scheduled tribes numbering 150 million form about 20 per cent of India's population. Backward castes as a whole (including *dalits*, tribes and other backward castes) form about 52 per cent of India's population. Exclusion of *dalits* from political, economic, social and cultural networks emerges from the crucial exclusion of them from the system of castes (Ghose, 2003)[1].

Thus, the issues relating to limited political, administrative and fiscal decentralisation have been cited to be main contributing factors for the less than optimal functioning of Grama Panchayats. It is in this context that an attempt is made to study the functions undertaken by the Grama Panchayats, and the factors contributing to undertaking and non-undertaking of functions.

The database for the paper is the primary data collected from presidents and secretaries of 74 Grama Panchayats in six districts [Belgaum (17), Bellary (5), Bijapur (4), Chitradurga (17), Gulbarga (18) and Kolar (13)] in Karnataka. We asked the panchayat presidents whether they had undertaken the functions that were constitutionally assigned to them. The responses were categorised into three groups: 'yes', 'partially' and 'no'. Such categorisation was also based on the qualitative information that was collected from presidents and secretaries.

Mandated Functions of Grama Panchayats in Karnataka

The Karnataka Panchayati Raj Act, 1993 was enacted to bring the functioning of Panchayats in Karnataka in line with the national pattern. This Act replaced the earlier Act, namely Karnataka Zilla Parishads, Taluk Panchayat Samithis, Mandal Panchayats and Nyaya Panchayat Act, 1983, consequent upon the changes proposed in the 73rd Constitutional Amendment. The new Act stipulated the following functions to the Grama Panchayats.

Grama Sabha

The Grama Sabha, according to the Act, shall consider the following matters and may make recommendations and suggestions to the Grama panchayat. Such matters are the annual statements of accounts of the Grama Panchayat, the report of administration of the preceding financial year and the last audit note and replies, if any. The Grama Sabha shall also mobilise voluntary labour and contributions in kind and cash for the community welfare programmes. It will also identify the beneficiaries for the implementation of developmental schemes pertaining to the villages.

According to a recent circular (GO No.RDP:222: GPA: 2001 dated October 10, 2001), the Grama Sabha shall be convened once in every three months. In the first quarter meeting, consideration and review of progress of previous year programmes, approval of the annual plan of Grama Panchayat and finalisation of beneficiaries list for all the beneficiary-oriented programmes shall be undertaken. In the second meeting, review of the work in the first quarter of the year shall be done. Third quarter's meeting shall consider the report of the Panchayat Jamabandi. Action taken on the points mentioned in the Panchayat Jamabandi report, half-yearly review of the approved Annual Plan of the Grama Panchayat, including monitoring of works, review of demand collection and balance and few others shall be discussed. The fourth meeting is to be devoted for, (a) initial discussions and preparatory work for the development of the subsequent year's plan for the Panchayat, (b) initiating the process of selection of beneficiaries, and (c) revision and review of new taxes and fees.

Meeting of Grama Panchayat

The *Adhyaksha* of GP has the power to convene the meetings of GPs. A grama panchayat shall meet for the transaction of business at least once in two months at the office of the Grama Panchayat and at such time as the *Adhyaksha* may determine. The seven clear days' notice for an ordinary meeting and three clear days' notice for a special meeting specifying the place, date and time of such meeting and the business to be transacted shall be issued to the members.

Development Functions Assigned to GPs

The first schedule of the Karnataka Panchayati Raj Act, 1993 has devolved 29 functions to the PRIs including GPs. These functions fall under the following broad categories:

(1) Agriculture, animal husbandry, fisheries, social and farm forestry
(2) Rural industries
(3) Rural housing
(4) Drinking water and sanitation
(5) Roads and buildings
(6) Rural electrification
(7) Non-conventional energy
(8) Poverty alleviation programmes
(9) Education (primary, secondary, adult and non-formal education)
(10) Markets and fairs
(11) Public health

(12) Development of women, child and welfare of weaker sections
(13) Public distribution system
(14) Maintenance of community assets

The working group on decentralisation (GoK 2002) has specified the functions in relation to each of the above broad categories. The same has been summarised below:

> There are several functions assigned to panchayat as specified in schedule one. The Panchayat should provide sanitary latrines to not less than ten per cent of the households every year and achieve full coverage as early as possible. Construction of adequate number of community latrines for the use of men and women and maintaining them are the other important functions. The local body has also been assigned the task of revision and collection of taxes, rates and fees periodically, and ensuring universal enrolment of children in primary school. Achieving universal immunisation of children, ensuring prompt registration and reporting of births and deaths, providing sanitation and proper drainage have also figured in the first schedule of the Panchayati Raj Act. The Panchayati Raj bodies have also been directed to repair and maintain public roads, remove encroachment on public streets or public places. Maintenance of all community assets vested in it, maintenance of records relating to population census, crop census, cattle census, census of unemployed persons and person below poverty line are also listed in the mandatory part of the Panchayati Raj Act.

Certain Powers Delegated by the State Government

The government may by notification and subject to such conditions as may be specified therein, transfer to any grama panchayat the management and maintenance of a forest situated in the panchayat area. It also makes over to the Grama Panchayat the management of wastelands, pasture lands or vacant lands belonging to the government situated within the panchayat area. The government can also entrust the Grama Panchayat with the collection of land revenue on behalf of the government and the maintenance of such records as are connected therewith. Every grama panchayat shall constitute a committee for performing functions relating to agricultural production etc. Power and duties of the *Adhyaksha* and *Upadhyaksha* include convening meetings of the Grama Panchayat, accessing the records of GP, exercising supervision and control over the acts of the officers and employees of the Grama Panchayat. The Grama Panchayat may do all things necessary for the maintenance and repair thereof and may lay out and make new roads, construct new bridges, widen, open, enlarge or otherwise improve any such roads or bridges.

Funds and Their Utilisation

Section 309 of the Karnataka Panchayati Raj Act, 1993 provides for the preparation and development of plans by Grama Panchayat, Ttaluk Panchayat (TP), Zilla Panchayat (ZP). This innovative step was taken to improve the functioning of the Panchayat. The concept of providing untied development grants to the Grama Panchayats was introduced (2001) in this direction. The statutory grant was meant for meeting electricity charges, maintenance of water supply schemes, sanitation and other welfare activities. The untied development grant was meant for the creation of assets like buildings, shopping complex, school and anganwadi buildings.

The Grama Panchayat fund includes the amount granted or passed on to the Grama Panchayat by government, Zilla Panchayat, or Taluk Panchayat. All sums received by the Grama Panchayat, by way of loans or contribution, the rent or other income from or sale proceeds of any immovable or movable property is counted as Grama Panchayat fund. The Grama Panchayat fund shall also be utilised for the following purposes: payment of salaries and allowances to the *Adhyaksha* and *Upadhyakshya*, officers and staff. It is also used for travelling allowances, daily allowances, and sitting fees to the members of the Grama Panchayat. The secretary has to prepare and lay before the Grama Panchayat at a meeting, a complete account of the actual and expected receipts and expenditure for the official year. The budget as passed by the Grama Panchayat shall be sent to the Taluk Panchayat.

Functions Undertaken by Sample Grama Panchayats

Annual Programme and Budget Estimation

Annual plan preparation is one of the important mandated functions of GP. As per the latest circular of Karnataka government, the planning process will commence in the last meeting of the Grama Sabha in a financial year. A final shape to the annual plan will be given in the first Grama Sabha meeting in a financial year. In the Grama Sabha, beneficiaries are to be identified and programmes have to be suggested. The identified programmes are discussed in GP meeting for final execution. In so far as budget estimation is concerned, it is to be passed by the GP and forwarded to the taluk panchayat for approval. If the GP fails in estimating the budget, the secretary will have to prepare a budget and pass it through the action plan. However, action plan does not reflect the panchayat planning process in its true sense. This is because such a plan is based on schemes sponsored by the State and Central Governments and the panchayat has nothing to do with this function except undertaking the function of recommendation.

When the question of whether GPs have undertaken the function of annual plan preparation and budget estimation, the presidents of GPs, as many as 35 out of 74 GPs, stated that they undertook this function as per the Act (Table 19.1). This means that about 47 per cent of the GPs had been able to prepare the annual plan and estimate the budget through Grama Sabha meetings and send to the Taluk Panchayat for approval. In some of these cases, GPs have called for general body meetings for discussing the matter. About 15 per cent of the GPs stated that they had partially undertaken this role. In these panchayats, the action plans were more or less prepared by the panchayat raj department and all that GPs had to do was only to implement the action plan as per the directions of the department. Over one-third of the GPs stated that they had not undertaken the function of annual plan preparation and budget estimation. In these panchayats, either the Grama Sabha meetings were not held or, even if held, the discussions in the meeting were only related to the beneficiary selection. Thus, these GPs did not discuss the agenda as per the directions provided to them.

Table 19.1: Distribution of GPs by whether they had undertaken the function of annual plan preparation and budget estimation

Responses of Presidents of GPs	*No. of GPs*	*Percentage*
Yes	35	47.30
Partially	11	14.86
No	28	37.84
Total	74	100.00

There are district-wise differences in the performance of GPs in so far as undertaking of this function. The performance of GPs in Kolar and Bellary was better than those from all the other districts. Ten out of 18 GPs in Gulbarga and 3 out of 4 GPs in Bijapur had not undertaken this function.

The contributing factors for the inability to undertake this function were as follows:

- In a significant number of cases, the proceedings of the Grama Sabha were confined to the selection of beneficiaries for different schemes[2].
- In other cases, the Grama Sabha meetings were not held regularly either because of strained relationship between elected and non-elected officials, or lack of interest in Grama Sabha meetings, leaders and the public.
- In most of the GPs, the untied grant was in the range of Rs.2 lakhs. However, most of this amount was deducted at the source for the payment of electricity charges towards water supply, street lights and office lighting. Further, in some of the GPs there were deductions

towards the supply of material for *Anganwadi* centres. This implies that the proportion of untied grant actually received to the total allocation was small in most of the GPs. This further implies that the GPs did not have sufficient autonomy in capturing the needs and preparing a plan on the basis of needs.

- As a result of the above, most of the GPs had to mainly implement the schemes sponsored by the State and Central Governments. These schemes authored a little scope for planning. This was because the schemes came with rules and regulations in-built. In other words, schemes specified for whom, where (sector) and how the funds were to be spent. Faced with this kind of situation most of the GPs did not have to do anything other than identifying the beneficiaries for the schemes.

Collection of Taxes

Section 199, of Karnataka Panchayati Raj Act, 1993, states that "every Grama Panchayat shall in such manner and subject to such exemptions as may be prescribed and not exceeding the maximum rate specified in Schedule IV levy tax upon buildings and lands which are not subject to agricultural assessment, within the limits of the panchayat area… A Grama Panchayat may levy water rate for supply of water for drinking and other purposes". Although a GP is empowered to levy taxes and fees on various other activities, property tax and water user fee are important means through which own revenue is mobilised. The GPs have powers to revise as well as collect these taxes and fees. We have, however, focused only on the collection of taxes.

We asked the presidents of sample GPs on whether they had undertaken the function of tax collection. About 35 per cent of the presidents had stated that they collected taxes while 16 per cent of them stated that they partially undertook this function (Table 19.2). These perceptions were cross-checked with data on the actual amount of taxes collected. Interestingly, nearly 50 per cent of the GP presidents stated that they had not undertaken the function of tax collection. In these panchayats, efforts to revise tax rates and preparation work such as listing of households, taxable sites, etc., were not made. Further, in some of these panchayats the tax collection was not regular.

Table 19.2: Distribution of GPs by whether they had undertaken the function of collection of tax

Responses of Presidents of GPs	*No. of GPs*	*Percentage*
Yes	26	35.14
Partially	12	16.22
No	36	48.65
Total	74	100.00

Nearly 50 per cent of the GPs have not been able to undertake the function of tax collection due to a number of factors. First, the staff was inadequate in some of the GPs on account of frequent transfer, placing two or more GPs under one secretary and large area of tax collection. Second, even if the staff was to be adequate, elected leaders did not have sufficient control over these staff members. It may be noted that the staff of GP include secretary, bill collector and water-men. While elected leaders had some control on water-men (including suspension), they did not have much control over the panchayat secretary. Third, the GPs did not have much capacity in terms of assessing property tax and periodic revisions[3]. Fourth, the services provided especially in the case of water supply were poor. As a result, GPs did not have any face to approach the households in its jurisdiction to contribute taxes. Fifth, the Grama Panchayats could not enforce the rule that the services would be disconnected if taxes and fees were not paid.

Immunisation of Children

Achieving full immunisation of children is an important mandatory function of GP. Generally, the immunisation process is understood as relating to administration of pulse polio vaccination only at the village level. But, immunisation should also include the administration of other vaccines through the staff from the health and women and child departments. The panchayat presidents generally feel that total immunisation is not the function of GPs. This itself indicates that the sample GPs have not undertaken the function of immunisation.

After explaining that immunisation of children has been indeed a function of the GPs, the presidents provided their responses on whether they had undertaken this function or not. Only about 23 per cent of the GP presidents stated that they had undertaken this function (Table 19.3). These panchayat presidents were generally educated and had longer experience in panchayats. They understood the immunisation both in terms of pulse polio and also administration of vaccines through health staff. On the other hand, nearly 42 per cent of the presidents stated that they partially undertook this function. In general, these presidents understood immunisation in terms of pulse polio campaign and they provided some support towards the campaign. This support included announcing the date of pulse polio through *dandora*, accompanying the health staff and providing boarding facilities to the staff visiting the GPs for pulse polio vaccination. It needs to be noted that about 35 per cent of the GPs had not undertaken the function of immunisation of children at all. An important reason for not undertaking this function was something to do with lack of awareness that this indeed was a mandated function of GPs and making the necessary provisions in so far as control over the staff involved in the immunisation of children at the panchayat level.

Table 19.3: Distribution of GPs by whether they had undertaken the function of Immunisation of children

Responses of Presidents of GPs	*No. of GPs*	*Percentage*
Yes	17	22.97
Partially	31	41.89
No	26	35.14
Total	74	100.00

Providing Sanitation and Proper Drainage

As noted earlier, it is the mandatory function of every Grama Panchayat to provide sanitary latrines for not less than ten per cent of the households every year. Further, the GP should achieve full coverage as early as possible by constructing adequate number of individual and community latrines.

Table 19.4 shows that nearly two-thirds of GPs were undertaking this function. The proportion was higher in Kolar, Chitradurga, Belgaum and Bellary. The evidence shows that the GPs had done well in providing drainage, individual toilets and in the employment of sweepers. It should be, however, noted that the track record in the provision of community latrines was not been good even in these panchayats. An important contributing factor for undertaking sanitation work was the allocation of funds under *Nirmal Grama Yojana*. Further, some of these GPs implemented the World Bank programme on integrated rural water and environmental sanitation programme and programmes with the support of other bilateral agencies such as Danida.

A small proportion of GP presidents stated that they had partially undertaken this function. In these GPs, the allocations under *Nirmal Grama Yojana* were not made. In about 30 per cent of the GPs, the function of providing sanitation was not at all undertaken. In poorer districts of Bijapur and Gulbarga, this proportion was quite high. An important contributing factor for not undertaking this function was cited to be limited fiscal decentralisation. Most of the GP presidents stated that they did not receive adequate funds on time to undertake the function.

Table 19.4: Distribution of GPs by whether they had undertaken the function of implementation of sanitation programme

Responses of presidents of GPs	*No. of GPs*	*Percentage*
Yes	47	63.51
Partially	5	6.76
No	22	29.73
Total	74	100.00

Maintenance of Community Assets

GPs are required to maintain roads, buildings, culverts, and bridges, etc. In fact, the first schedule of Karnataka Panchayati Raj Act uses the term 'maintenance' for maximum number of times. This implies that the maintenance of community assets is an important function of GPs. In most of the GPs in Karnataka, the maintenance is basically understood in terms of school building, panchayat office and roads in the villages. Table 19.5 shows that while 43 per cent of the GP presidents stated that the function of maintenance of community assets was undertaken; about 10 per cent of them stated that they had partially undertaken this function. These responses had come from those panchayats which had already provided community assets and received funds for the purpose of providing community assets. In such cases, they used the funds received for the maintenance.

As many as 35 out of 74 GP presidents stated that they had not all undertaken the function of maintenance of community assets. This was due to the following factors:

- The provision of community assets itself is an outstanding issue in these GPs. Hence, they have been mainly utilising the funds for the provision of community assets.
- In Karnataka, adequate provision has not been made in so far as the maintenance of community assets. Although JGSY grants in 2001-02 and SGRY grants in 2002-03 could be utilised for the maintenance of works, it was specified that only 15 per cent of the funds could be used for the purpose. Most of the GP presidents stated that these amounts were inadequate.
- As noted earlier, the untied grant of Rs.2 lakhs was mainly used for payment of electricity bills. This implies that most of the GPs did not have fiscal autonomy to undertake the maintenance work.
- Although the function of maintenance of community assets included natural resources such as tanks, most of the GPs have not spent any amount for this type of purposes.

Table 19.5: Distribution of GPs by whether they had undertaken the function of maintenance of community assets

Responses of presidents of GPs	*No. of GPs*	*Percentage*
Yes	32	43.24
Partially	7	9.46
No	35	47.30
Total	74	100.00

Maintaining Water Supply

In Karnataka, potable drinking water is provided through three types of schemes: (1) Borewells with hand pumps, (2) Mini water supply schemes, and (3) Piped water supply schemes. The responsibility with regard to the creation and maintenance of each of these sources is different. The first source will be created and maintained by public health engineering department. Mini water supply and piped water supply schemes can be provided and managed by Grama Panchayat (GPs)[4]. The government provides grants towards the maintenance of these water supply sources. GPs are also empowered to impose and collect water user charges from households having private connection for operation and maintenance of piped water supply schemes. Water cess is also collected by them for the maintenance of mini water supply and public stand posts. Thus, an elaborate provision is made in the Constitution in so far as the maintenance of water supply sources is concerned.

It is not, therefore, surprising that over 82 per cent of the GP presidents stated that they undertook the function of maintaining water supply sources (Table 19.6). Some of the activities undertaken in this regard were appointment of water-man, collection of water tax, undertaking of repair works, provision of electrical motors, co-operation with multilateral agencies such as World Bank and bilateral agencies such as DANIDA.

However, about 18 per cent of the GP presidents stated that they did not undertake the function of maintenance of water supply sources. An important reason for this was the presence of only borewells in the area of panchayat jurisdiction. It may be noted that it was the responsibility of the Taluk Panchayat to maintain the borewells and GPs did not have any mandate in this regard. Another important reason was that where only public sources of water supply were present, collection of water user charges became difficult and GPs, in such cases, depended mainly on inter-governmental transfers. In some of the cases, the transfers had not been made on time and in the case of others, they were inadequate. These factors contributed for not undertaking the function of maintenance of water supply.

Table 19.6: Distribution of GPs by whether they had undertaken the function of maintenance of water supply

Responses of presidents of GPs	*No. of GPs*	*Percentage*
Yes	61	82.43
Partially	0	0.00
No	13	17.57
Total	74	100.00

Concluding Observations

The foregoing discussion suggests that the functions that have been constitutionally assigned to GPs have not been fully undertaken by the sample GPs. This implies that there is hiatus between the vision of policy-makers and the extent to which the vision has been translated into practice. This is a very serious situation. If it continues, the goals of democratic decentralisation are difficult to be achieved. It is, therefore, important to understand the contributing factors for the inability of the GPs to undertake the functions assigned and discuss the areas where improvement in terms of policy and practice is to be made.

- Although 29 development functions have been constitutionally transferred to GPs along with functionaries, the GPs do not have sufficient control over the staff of line departments. Almost all the GP presidents state that they do not have disciplinary powers (such as sanction of leave, transfer, suspension, etc.) on the staff of departments of agriculture, veterinary, health, education and women and child welfare. As a result, it has become difficult for the elected leaders to undertake functions assigned to them in relation to development activities pertaining to these sectors. The sample GPs have control only on the staff appointed by them. This indicates that there is a need to place the development bureaucracy at the village level under the elected representatives or Grama Panchayat as a body. Viewed from this angle, the recent policy decision of the government to pay the salaries to teachers, etc., through Grama Panchayats is particularly welcome as this policy measure is likely to improve the accountability of development bureaucracy towards GP.

- Another important contributing factor is the creation of parallel bodies at the village level and patronage provided to them. It is to be noted that the multi-lateral agencies such as the World Bank and bilateral agencies of DfiD, DANIDA and so on insist that community based organisations (CBOs) are to be formed and entrusted with the responsibility of provision of benefits and services relating to water supply, watershed, tank rehabilitation, women development and empowerment. As a result, in most of sample GPs, community based organisations such as village water supply and sanitation committees, watershed committees, self-help groups, tank users associations and so on were formed under the programmes initiated both by external agencies and government. These organisations have been mandated with functions similar to those constitutionally provided to the GPs. A good case is water supply and sanitation. Rajasekhar and Veerashekharappa (2004) found that in 30 villages in Karnataka, the village water supply and sanitation committees formed by the World Bank programme was undertaking functions similar to the ones mandated to GPs. This led to duplications of functions and wastage of resources. The study suggests that all development functions should be entrusted to democratically elected bodies, which can take the help of community based organisations, if there is any need. It is suggested in the study that both GPs and CBOs have an important role to play in the development process. While CBOs can enhance the participation of the people by incorporating the interest of the weak and marginalised, the GP can undertake the functions relating to accountability, monitoring and in sustaining the benefits of development programmes. There is, therefore, a need to have a clear cut policy document on delineation of functions between GPs, CBOs and line departments.

- The GPs do not have fiscal decentralisation. Own revenue as a proportion of total expenditure is small. This is due to limited tax base and inability to collect taxes on account of capacity constraints, poor services provided and absence of institutional rules. The untied grant is insufficient and deducted at the source. Most of the funds to GPs come through the schemes sponsored by the State and the Central Governments. These schemes do not offer much scope for expenditure autonomy. In this context, there is a need to improve the capacity of GPs in own revenue mobilisation. However, one cannot expect that GPs will be in a position to undertake functions such as maintenance of assets with own revenue. This is because the funds required are really large. The National Institute of Rural Development estimates that Rs.225,731 crores are needed for the operation and maintenance of services relating to drinking water, rural sanitation, streetlights, primary education, primary health and rural roads for the period of 2000-05. It is, therefore, important to ensure that there are inter-governmental transfers in such a way that such transfers do not blunt the incentive structure in the PRIs.
- Grama sabhas which are important mechanisms to ensure that people participate in the preparation of annual

plans, identification of beneficiaries and enforcing accountability are not given due importance. In most of the cases, Grama Sabhas are not held. Even if they are held, the participation of women and persons belonging to depressed castes has been insignificant though the Act stipulates that Grama Sabhas should have mandatory representation of these sections. Further, it is well-known that Grama Sabhas do not undertake all the functions constitutionally assigned to them, and that, they only select beneficiaries. One of the reasons attributed for the limited success of Grama Sabhas is that they are not held by habitation. The working group on decentralisation in Karnataka has recommended that the Grama Sabha meetings should be held by habitations and also has incorporated provisions to ensure the participation of the weak and marginalised.

The complex write up of government circulars and Acts is another hurdle for the smooth functioning of the Panchayati Raj bodies. The circulars and Acts are very much jargonised and are in a form in which they cannot be easily understood by common people. Moreover, these local leaders are not able to get a clear picture regarding powers, functions and responsibilities from the circulars and Acts. In several sample GPs, the panchayat presidents stated that the functions constitutionally assigned to them were the responsibility of taluk panchayat. Therefore, the government should establish certain machinery to change these legal documents to common man's language for better performance.

NOTES

1. A recent study states that institutions and social capital work together in support of active participation of the poor and the effect of social capital is magnified when capable agents are also available (Krishna, 2002). Another study finds that human development position of the states is strongly determined by the position of the state in terms of education, awareness

on important issues, and the material possession it has (Pradhan 2002). The above indicate that decentralisation has the potential to empower the poor in their individual capacity as well as through collective bargaining. The linkages between grama panchayats and NGOs (and community based organisations formed by them) have been suggested to maximise the potential (Rajasekhar, 1999).

2. Raja and Hiremath (2001) have also found that this has been the widespread practice.
3. Rural development and panchayati raj department has realised that this is an important capacity constraint. Hence, it has prepared user-friendly method of property tax assessment and revision.
4. It needs to be noted that in the case of programmes of World Bank and Danida, piped water supply was provided and maintained by community based organisations in the initial phases of the projects. Nevertheless, the water supply schemes were transferred to GPs for maintenance.

REFERENCES

Bandyopadhay, D. (2001): 'What Ails Indian Bureaucracy', *Administrator*, 44(1): 15-18.

Bohra, O.P. (1997): 'Women in Decentralised Democracy', *Journal of Rural Development*, 16 (4): 637-83.

Crook, R. and J. Manor. (2001): *Enhancing Participation and Institutional Performance: Democratic Decentralisation in South Asia and West Africa,* Report, ESCOR, ODA of phase Research Project.

Diwan, G.R. (2002): "People's Participation in Decentralised Planning", *Indian Journal of Regional Science*, 34(1):17-29.

Gaventa, John (2003): *A Note on Citizenship and Governance*, Sources from IDS, www.ids.ac.uk.

Ghose, Sagarika (2003): 'The Dalit in India', *Social Research*, 70(1): 37-46.

GoK (2002): *Report of the Working Group on Decentralisation*, Bangalore: Department of Rural Development and Panchayati Raj, Government of Karnataka.

Jain, Devaki (1992): *Women: New Vision of Leadership* A Presentation at Global Forum, Dublin. Internet sources (www.onlinewomeninpolitics.org)

Krishna, Anirudh (2002): 'Enhancing Political Participation in Democracies: What is the Role of Social Capital', *Comparative Political Studies*, 35(4): 437-60.

Mandal, Amal (2003): *Women in Panchayati Raj Institutions,* Kanishka, New Delhi.

Mathur, P.C. (1991): *Political Dynamics of Panchayati Raj*, Konark, New Delhi.

Mishra, S.N *et al.* (1993): *Roads to Model Panchayati Raj*, Mittal, New Delhi.

Pradhan, Jaya Prakash (2002): 'Does Human Development Policy Matter for Economic Growth: Evidence from Indian States', *South Asian Economic Journal*, 3(1): 77-93.

Raja, Shoba and S.R. Hiremath (2001): *Panchayati Raj: Theory vs. Practice.* www.humanscape.org, 10(5).

Rajasekhar, D. (ed) (1999): *Decentralised Government and NGOs: Issues, Strategies and Ways Forward.* Concept, New Delhi.

Rajasekhar, D. (2004): *Poverty Alleviation Strategies of NGOs*, Concept, New Delhi.

Rajasekhar, D. and Veerashekharappa (2004): *Role of Local Organisations in Water Supply and Sanitation Sector: A Study in Karnataka and Uttaranchal States, India,* A Project Report Prepared for the World Bank, Institute for Social and Economic Change, Bangalore.

Vajpayee, D. (ed) (1990): *Local Government and Politics in Third World: Issues and Trends*, Heritage Publication, New Delhi.

20

E-Governance at the Grassroots

The Case of Belandur Grama Panchayat in Karnataka

MANGALA NAYAK, B.S. BHARGAVA AND K. SUBHA

Today, information technology is the basis of apt decision-making in all fields of life. So the role of computers in the area of local administration is quite crucial and can be used effectively from the point of view of getting timely information, accuracy, versatility and diligence. The so-called personal computer can be made use of in a small business unit and offices for programming database management, accounting, word processing and others. For computer operation there must be enough information to be fed. However, the computer is used in all fields of information dissemination from the multinational level to the local level. The emergence of the concept of e-governance has removed the barrier between people and administration at all levels of the functioning of a democratic government.

Belandur Gram Panchayat is one of the unique panchayats in the country in the sense of procuring a computer for computerising all the day-to-day activities intact. A centralised database is maintained for storing the detailed information about the panchayat including its administrative set-up. Recently, Kerala State Government has thought of equipping panchayats with at least one computer each and will be connected with a WAN (Wide Area Network).

Since many companies are using internet to conduct their daily business, communication, and provide support to their customers, advertise their services in their own website and look for valuable information to gain a competitive advantage, the former president and now the member of the Belandur Panchayat thought that for the panchayat internet would be very useful to get information of the market prices, agricultural information like prices of seeds, land value and related matters. In December 1999, the Belandur panchayat received Internet and e-mail connection. This panchayat has become outstanding and it got its uniqueness with this peculiar feature; and has become one of the fast developing panchayats in the whole country. There is a small background of getting a computer for this panchayat. There was a rural development committee constituted for smooth functioning of the panchayat. The decisions were taken in this committee to develop the village with the help of the community people. The committee consisted of the President, one Secretary and 10 members. The secretary was one of the members of the panchayat. The president of the panchayat was the president of this Rural Development Committee. The computer was donated by this committee.

The villagers were astonished to see a computer in their panchayat. They were thinking that the computer was a sort of television. First there was opposition from the village people but when it became useful for improving the village work and development, the people started supporting the initiative of the panchayat. In the discussion with the president, it was reported that the computer became very useful to the panchayat because, for three years they were facing the problem of getting a letter typed or photocopied, as they had to reach Bangalore city to get it done.

The president of the panchayat being young and active, was elected twice as president of this panchayat, and now continues to be an active member of the panchayat. His struggle and continuous efforts, close contact with the people, high hopes of improvement and cooperation from the people made him achieve this. During his tenure as president tremendous improvements and developments in the panchayat had taken place in many fields. The credit of getting computer for the panchayat goes to the president of this panchayat. The introduction of computerisation has led to this kind of developments and fame for this panchayat.

The discussion of this computerised panchayat has been made on television and newspapers worldwide. Then Compusol, a Bangalore based software company, came forward to provide additional help. The company gave them a software package free of cost and trained the staff and taught the Kannada keyboard operation and then followed by internet and e-mail facilities. But keeping a computer would not have served the purpose, unless they use it in a proper way. By just the press of a button the relevant information relating to the five villages; land holdings of each family, taxes due from them, the people and animals in the village, the death rate and birth rate, property details, government projects undertaken, pending projects, money sanctioned, government schemes, panchayat budget details, accounts, list of beneficiaries under housing schemes and other records can be obtained. In this panchayat every villager has been given an identification number. The Rotary Club has further donated two computers one to the panchayat and the other one to the school.

In Belandur, it has become easy for all the people to get information as to how much tax one has to pay. There is entry of the total population, property details, taxes, bank account, schemes, panchayat's income etc. But one cannot assume that everything is fine because there is a computer in this panchayat; it is facing problems like the problem of electricity, housing and roads.

Structural Aspects

The dream to change "Gramarajya" into "Ramrajya" is by putting more efforts and co-operation extended by hardworking people, to make their panchayat a prosperous one, is best seen in no other panchayat, but Belandur gram panchayat situated in Bangalore East Taluk of Vartur Hobli. The Belandur gram panchayat is located 30 kms from Bangalore City. The visit to this panchayat, itself looks different compared to other panchayats all over the State because of its outstanding features, i.e., the computerisation to maintain all the accounts, the only panchayat having underground drainage system and garbage collecting system from every house. One peculiarity of the panchayat is that there is no arrack shop.

The President reported that almost all people of that panchayat have stopped drinking alcohol. 100 per cent tax collection is also one of the features worth appreciating. So with all these special features, this panchayat has become one of the model panchayats in the country. There are 12 members with six female members and six male members. The co-operation from and the status of women members are reasonably satisfactory. There is no gender bias as such; equality in representation is maintained.

Demographic Details

The total area of the panchayat covers about 763.25 sq. kms, having a wet land of 25 per cent and 75 per cent of dry land. It has one of the biggest lakes in Karnataka, measuring about 950 acres covered with water plants. Totally five villages come under the jurisdiction of this panchayat. They are:

(1) Belandur (Panchayat headquarters)
(2) Amblipur
(3) Haralur
(4) Devarabisanahalli
(5) Kariammana Agrahara

Table 20.1: Area of Panchayat

Sl.No	*Name of Village*	*Area (in Hectares)*
1.	Belandur	167.56
2.	Devarabisanahalli	170.11
3.	Kariyammana Agrahara	54.46
4.	Haralur	264.85
5.	Ambalipura	106.27

The area of Belandur Gram Panchayat is spread out as given in Table 20.1. The area of Haralur is more than other villages though Belandur is the main village where the panchayat office is situated.

There are five wards and each village represents one or two wards like Belandur village consists of two wards; 4 members represent one ward and 3 members represent the other ward. Ambalipura and Haralur villages constitute one ward with 2 members representing it. Devarabisanahalli village is one ward with 2 members representing it and Kariammana Agrahara is one ward with 1 member representing it.

Table 20.2: Population (As per 1991 Census)

Total Popul-ation	*Rural Male*	*Rural Female*	*SC Population*			*ST Population*		
			Male	*Female*	*Total*	*Male*	*Female*	*Total*
4420	2326	2094	568	599	1167	96	111	207

Table 20.2 shows the total population as per 1991 census. The present statistics based on 2001 census are not available. The total population is 4420, out of which the rural male population is 2326 and rural female population is 2094. Scheduled caste population is 1167 where females are 568 and males are 599. Similarly, Scheduled tribe population is 207, wherein females are 96 and males are 111. There were 836 households in this panchayat as per the 1991 census. Today as per the survey made by the panchayat there are about 2030 households or so in total in all the 5 villages. In Amblipura there are more houses compared to the other 3 villages though Belandur has more number of houses as given in the table because the apartments are being constructed and there is no government land in Amblipura.

Table 20.3: Households

Sl.No	*Name of the village*	*Number of houses*
1	Belandur	700
2	Haraluru	325
3	Amblipura	525
4	Kariyammana Agrahara	180
5	Devarabisanahalli	300
	Total	**2030**

Source: Office of the panchayat.

Caste Structure

The people in the panchayat belong to different castes and sub-castes. The various castes and communities residing in the village are Reddy, Kshathreya, Brahmins, Lingayats, Thogata Viraru, Scheduled Caste (SC), Scheduled Tribes (ST), Mudhaliyars, Muslims, Dobhi, Acharya and Christians. Despite its mixed castes composition there is no apparent public discrimination. All of them extend cooperation and put efforts in the panchayat development.

Basic Facilities

There are primary schools, post office, veterinary hospitals, *Anganwadis*, agricultural service co-operative societies, *Grameena* bank, fair price Shop, telephone facilities, electric and street light facilities, national rural water supply, mini water supply, asphalted road facilities and under ground drainage system are available in Belandur village, but Haralur and Devarabisanahalli and Kariyammana Agrahara have primary school, *Anganwadi* centre, fair price shop, telephone facility, electric and streetlight facility, national rural water supply, mini water supply, asphalted road facility and underground drainage system is in progress. The developments in Ambalipura village are rapid in regard to construction of apartments though there are no basic amenities available. Only this village has telephone facility, electricity, streetlight and asphalted road facility.

Education

There are six schools. Five schools are government aided and one is private school. In Belandur village there are two schools. One is Urdu medium and the other is Kannada medium. Out of five schools three are lower primary schools (LPS), one upper primary school (UPS) and one LPS Urdu school. Two computers are donated by Lions Club to UP school. There are four *Anganwadi* schools with one teacher and an *Aaya.* The literacy rate is around 50 per cent. There are only primary schools. In Belandur from First standard to seventh standard, in Haralur, Devarabisanahalli and Kariyammana Agrahara from 1st to fifth standard.

Haralur has a school building where the desks and chairs are donated by villagers and Lions club. From 3rd standard onwards, desks and chairs are provided in all schools. All schools have toilets, water supply and electricity. Only in Ambalipura village there are no schools as there is no government land to construct school buildings and most of the families send their children to private schools. Houses are increasing in this village. From five houses in 1993, it has increased to 500 houses today. There is rapid development through construction of houses and panchayat has helped water supply by installing bore wells. However, there is no felt need for a school here at all.

Agriculture

The main crops grown here are vegetables, paddy and coconut. Only a few people have land and most of them are engaged in garment factories. 80 per cent of the ladies are working in the three garment factories. They get monthly salary of Rs. 1700 to Rs. 2,000. Men go for work in one small-scale transformer factory. The daily wages for farm workers—male is Rs. 80 and female is Rs. 60. For building construction workers—male is Rs. 150 and female is Rs. 50. Rupees one lakh has been spent on growth of roadside trees for shade. Since the lake water is polluted the crops are all spoiled. 100 per cent subsidy is given through agricultural department for farmers below poverty line (BPL).

There is one agricultural credit co-operative society covering 13 villages. There are no other societies like dairy cooperative society. The milk is sold in their particular village. The employment percentage in agriculture is 40 per cent, central/state and employees working in private concerns is 30 per cent, labourers and business is 20 per cent and migrated labour class is 10 per cent, and there is lot of labour class who have migrated from outside.

Health

Earlier there was one primary health care centre (PHC). However, for better medical facilities people had to visit the nearby panchayat or come to city and some of them even come to Bangalore. But now the Rotary Club has opened the dispensary and they have appointed a doctor and so the people of this panchayat are getting good health care. There is one veterinary hospital.

Electrification

Nearly 75 per cent of persons below poverty line have received *Bagya Jyothi* lights through the scheme. Almost all houses are electrified. There are 75 Sodium lights and 272 tube lights. They have project for electrifying houses for the persons below poverty line, to be implemented and it is in progress.

Drinking Water

The problem of drinking water is not severe because the president had taken care of the problem. There are about 700 taps. All people in this panchayat get equal quantity of water. An illegal connection attracts a penalty of Rs. 2000 or the tap would be disconnected for six months. This was followed so that there is proper use of water. It is said that this practice is not followed in any other panchayat in the State. There are six watermen who are in charge of drinking water supply and for monitoring the system. All the wards have a mini water scheme; 5 overhead tanks. Out of total 23 bore wells, Belandur has the highest number of bore wells (9). The Member representing a ward takes care of the water problem and is settled on a daily basis.

Employment

Though the families have lands, they are employed in factories. 15 per cent unemployed people are without any source of income. 85 per cent are engaged in factories like tailoring, ready made garments and some of them are self-employed. Main occupation of the people therefore is tailoring at home and at garments factory.

Underground Drainage

For the first time the underground drainage development (UGD) was introduced only in Belandur village. Then it was extended to other four villages. The underground drainage is completed in Haralur. In the other three villages Devarabisanahalli, Kariyammana Agrahara and Amblipur, it is in progress. Rupees 25 lakhs have been spent for drainage system. Through *Nirmal* 2000 scheme toilets are built for all persons below poverty line and general category people also. Every year 40 houses are getting the toilets built in their houses. The President viewed that the development is taken up village by village on priority basis and by the decision taken in the meetings, so that, the villages are provided with all development activities.

Transportation

The main roads of about 12 kms are tarred and rest of the sub-roads is jelly roads. The project work regarding improvement of the roads is also being undertaken as per the action plan in every village. Today the roads have improved and there are quite a number of buses plying to all these villages. The roads are maintained very well and trees are planted along the side of the main roads.

Sources of Income to the Panchayat

The source of income has tremendously increased from Rs. 61,000 in financial year 1994-95 to Rs. 1,76,09,000 in 2003-04. The reasons for this positive trend are many. The panchayat is getting tax from the sources like building and land tax, license fees, factories tax, and cess. The Government grant was Rs. one lakh and then it became Rs. 2 lakhs and now it is raised to Rs. 5 lakhs.

Out of the total amount collected from the taxes during the year 2001-02 i.e., about Rs.15 to 20 lakhs, 22.5 per cent of it was spent for individual benefits like housing, improvement of roads, development of SC/ST and drainage, 27.5 per cent for development purpose, 40 per cent was spent for administrative charges like salary, office expenses and stationeries. Ten per cent was kept as savings. The grants under centrally sponsored schemes and state sponsored schemes were also received by the panchayat. The Swarna Grama Swarozgar Yojana (SGRY), Indira Avas Yojana, of the 10th Finance Commission, Ambedkar housing scheme and the *Ashraya* housing scheme are all properly utilised. Under the housing schemes 10 or 11 houses are built every year. Under Ambedkar Scheme— 10 houses are built and under *Ashraya* Scheme—11 houses are built for people living below the poverty line.

The yearwise income expenditure statement of the panchayat is given below:

Table 20.4: Income and Expenditure Statement

Year	Income	Expenditure
2001-2002	Rs. 47,13,144	Rs. 47,06,158
2002-2003	Rs.1,39,01,878	Rs. 1,39,01,878
2003-2004	Rs.1,76,09,000	Rs. 1,76,09,000

Source: Data collected from office of the panchayat.

It is clear from the table that the income of the panchayat has been on the increase. In 2001-2002, the income of the panchayat was only Rs. 47,13,144 but year by year the income is drastically increasing. The income has increased to Rs. 1,39,01,878 in 2002-03 showing a tremendous increase whereas no other panchayat in Karnataka has such an income. No doubt, the panchayat has become a model for other panchayats as referred to earlier. The main reasons for this upper trend of income are cent percent tax collection, strategies used for collecting taxes and other fees, cooperation from the people and positive attitude of the people.

The total income from the taxes in the year 2002-03 was around Rs. 1,04,20,990 from property, building, land, water etc. In addition income from licence fees was around Rs. 5 lakhs. This shows the extractive capacity of the panchayat.

Political Composition

The leading party here is the Janata Dal. Majority of the members belong to the Janata Dal. There are totally 12 members including male and female; six are females and six are male. The lady members are given due respect; priority and co-operation is given for the issues raised by them and for all works. The members do not go according to political party system for doing development work. The election takes place very smoothly though the contestants belong to different parties. The members were elected mostly based on the person's ability, capacity, education and whether he/she will work devotedly for the panchayat. No doubt, the members can be categorised on the basis of party affiliations to all the 3 political parties viz., Janata Dal, Congress and BJP.

For the first term of 2½ years the Vice-President's position was reserved for a female, but for the rest of 2½ years it was reserved for a male. Similarly, in the case of President's term also the seat was reserved for male and so the former president was elected for the first term as well as in the second term of elections for 2½ years, but the second half of the term was reserved for a female, so a lady president was elected. In the course of two terms the president was there for almost nine years period because of his efficiency. Presently the President is a lady and she is also quite active. The ladies participation is quite favourable. The members do not have any discrimination of caste, creed or political party as far as the development works are concerned.

Works Done Under Schemes

Nearly 75 per cent of persons below poverty line have received Bhagya Jyothi Lights under the Bhagya Jyothi scheme. All the houses are electrified. During the period 2001-02 there were 162 streetlights in Belandur, in Devarabisanahalli 55, in Kariyammana Agrahara 41, in Haralur 52 and in Ambalipura 52. The project for electrifying houses for the families of BPL is also completed. This Panchayat does not have any drinking water problem. Through the water supply scheme all the five villages have one unit of mini water scheme; two overhead tanks in Belandur and one in each village except in Amblipura. There are motor pumps connected to overhead tank, five numbers in Belandur, two in Haralur, one in Devarabisanahalli and one in Kariyammana Agrahara. Under *Nirmal* 2000 scheme toilets have been built for all families of BPL. In 2001-02 totally 250 toilets were constructed in Belandur, and 30 in Devarabisanahalli, 43 in Kariyammana Agrahara and 42 in Haralur village under the scheme. There are nine hand pumps in Belandur, three in Haralur, nine in Devarabisanahalli, five in Kariyammana Agrahara and two in Ambalipura.

For Scheduled Castes and Scheduled Tribes the Panchayat has a number of programmes such as the *Saksharatha* programme, housing, free toilets, education etc.; under Housing Scheme houses have been constructed. All the schemes are fully utilised. In Ambalipura village, there are no government lands to build schools, burial ground, and drinking water supply. However, bore wells have been installed. Most of the buildings are in the form of apartments; hence the basic amenities are taken care of by the community. This may be taken as an instance of community initiatives in the process of development.

Impact of the Innovative Works on the Community

Among others, computerization facilitated various development activities in a major way.

(i) Under computerisation the gram panchayat is having a distinct character of achievement compared to the other gram panchayats in the state. It has really brought new aspiration among the people and the communities.

(ii) The basic facilities like drinking water supply, public works like underground drainage facility, open drainage system, road development works, streetlight facility and other infrastructure facilities provided by the panchayat has benefited the community to a great extent.

(iii) The participation of the people has increased to get more development work done and the people are voluntarily coming to the office and paying the tax.

(iv) The community is coming forward to donate chairs and desks and also school building.

(v) The underground drainage system, water supply, streetlights and development of roads have increased the value of the land in this village which has benefited the community to rent their houses. The rented value has increased from Rs. 50 to Rs. 500 per square feet.

(vi) The community is not coming forward with any major problems because the panchayat itself takes care of all the requirements for development.

(vii) The community is very happy about the cleanliness and general maintenance in villages through the resolution made for collecting door to door garbage.

(viii) The panchayat has earned the confidence and appreciation from the people since they are very much benefited by the avoidance of middlemen's corrupt deals.

Panchayat Office and Functioning

The former president belonged to the Other Backward Class (OBC) and former vice-president was a lady. The president was also the president of Belandur Rural Development Committee. From this committee, as referred to earlier the computer was donated to this panchayat which was very helpful to the panchayat to get the work done quickly and prosperity has increased to a great extent compared to any other panchayat. The E-governance at the panchayat level is the brainchild of the former president. The president was a committed person who took up all the civic, financial and developmental problems as a challenge and struggled very hard to overcome these problems by tackling one by one, initiating with the collection of local taxes to raise the income of the panchayat. He then took up other issues and brought the panchayat to this level. The real credit goes to the president. Today after completing his two terms of presidency, still as a member, he is supporting the present lady president.

The main problems after having the computer was that there was often failure of electric power and the telephone cable would always be under repair. Naturally operating the Internet and e-mail would be a problem.

The panchayat is having its own panchayat building. The administrative set-up of the panchayat is reasonably good. There is one secretary appointed by the Government and the other staffs like one computer operator, one typist cum clerk, three bill collectors, six watermen, one peon and seven sweepers are appointed by the panchayat and their salaries are also paid by the panchayat. The president, vice-president and 10 members are collectively doing the works for the panchayat's development. Development of the roads through JRY scheme, gutters, cleaning the environment, construction of toilets, educational facilities are all done to increase developmental activities.

For SC/ST category people the *Saksharata* programme, housing, free toilets, education etc., exclusively benefiting them are undertaken. The members are of the opinion that for smooth functioning of the panchayat, a person should have capacity, strength, energy, intelligence, physical strength and development goal orientation.

Grama Sabhas

The Grama Sabhas are effectively conducted every six months and if necessary special meetings are also convened. At the time of field study three Grama Sabhas had been already conducted; two were held in year 2001-2002 and one Grama Sabha in 2002-2003. The Belandur grama panchayat has convened the Grama Sabhas from time to time as stipulated under the Act. The beneficiaries for all the beneficiary oriented prgrammes are selected in the Grama Sabhas ensuring transparency in the process of selection.

Since all the voters are members of the Grama Sabha the selection process of beneficiaries is transparent and very little scope is left to cause either injustice or for any biases to creep in. The gram sabha is held also to prioritise the development oriented programmes required for the village to produce a concrete action plan for the beneficiaries and for the infrastructure required for each year. The review of the progress is done from time to time. So the beneficiaries list prepared for various schemes through Grama Sabha, the proceedings of the gram sabha and the action plan are available on the computer.

Grama Sabhas were conducted twice every year but now they are convening four Grama Sabhas as per the recent Government order. Other than the Grama Sabhas the panchayat conducts monthly meeting. In the Grama Sabha every person is asked to place their problems in the Grama Sabha individually because if the problems are collected by the member of that ward and forwarded to the Grama Sabha, there will be poor attendance in the Grama Sabha, so this panchayat has made it compulsory that anybody who has problems should only give application in the Grama Sabha personally. The attendance of women was also more before the live telecast of the Grama Sabhas on televisions. Now nearly 25 per cent of the ladies attend the Grama Sabha and the quorum is maintained.

Secretary writes the minutes of the meeting and also presents the agenda and proceedings of the previous meeting. He also reads out the income expenditure statement of the previous month and the copy of it is circulated among the members and to public also. The transparency in accounts is maintained to a greater extent, which has prevented corruption. The monthly income and expenditure statement is distributed to all the members to maintain transparency.

Participation of Women

Participation of women in the panchayat meetings and grama sabha was 70 per cent to 80 per cent before they were relayed on television. Today since the panchayat meetings are relayed on the television the people are able to view live telecast of the meetings.

Hence the attendance of women is declining as observed during the Grama Sabha meetings.

In the previous Grama Sabha (26-12-2002) the attendance was very less (30%) because there was live telecast of the Grama Sabha on televisions otherwise the attendance would be more. There was a drastic decrease in the attendance of the members in the meetings. The president has now planned to record the complete proceedings of the panchayat meeting and then telecast it on the next day to improve the attendance in Grama Sabha.

The participation of women is quite effective. Two women have been elected for the second time, and they have experience in giving their ideas and are very much aware of the problems. The other 4 women members are also quite articulate because the former president would see that they reveal the problems of their respective areas. He also shoulders responsibility for them to see that the development works are done. He makes them responsible for the works of their respective wards. Because of the good leadership qualities and commitment, the president was able to monitor and inspect the work and also gets information of any problem faced in all the five villages. He used to tell them to collect all the issues relating to their area and produce them in the Grama Sabha. According to the requirements demanded by the members of their area they will be allocated funds based on priority. Now apart from all development works, major work of Underground Drainage is taken up in all villages. The women members also co-operate well in every development work.

Tax Collection

The bill collectors collect the taxes. The bill collectors go house to house for collecting the tax. Collection of tax in this panchayat is cent-per cent as it has been mentioned earlier. The idea behind collecting 100 per cent tax is that when one person comes to panchayat to get no objection certificate (NOC) then they tell him that unless he pays the tax till date he cannot get the NOC. Similarly, if a person comes for getting records of rights (*Katha*) transfer, he is also told to pay the tax otherwise he will not get the transfer, so he pays the tax in order to get the transfer. This is one method they are following to collect tax. The people get their work done on time without delay. The people are also made aware that if they do not pay the tax it will be a burden for them and that the tax is used for development works only. So they also come voluntarily to pay the tax. There are certain strategies to collect tax like if the bill collector collects more tax he is given incentive; if the tax is paid regularly they do not have to pay for the garbage collection every month.

Identification and Implementation of Works

The process of identification of the problems was made by spot inspections, through panchayat meetings, grama sabhas, and complaints from the people. The planning was done by discussing the issues in the meetings and depending on the funds the works were taken up for implementation.

Due to the limited revenues for some time, there was a problem to give salaries to the panchayat staff. Thus the taxes were raised from Rs. 5 to Rs. 10. Since the yearly fair, street lights were maintained through the tax collected and the money collected from the people, the problem was solved. Cash was collected from the houses that required the repairs of bore wells and street lights. The panchayat and public works had no link. The people believed that the taxes would go to the government. But after they were aware that the tax collected would be utilised for development works the people voluntarily came forward to pay the tax to the panchayat office. Gradually the source of income in the panchayat increased. Then sweepers were appointed to clean the roads and streetlights were installed. The people came to know that development of the village was the major concern of the panchayat and it would be useful and thus voluntarily came and paid the tax. The then CEO encouraged the panchayat to take up the sanitation works, since the roads were blocked by the overflow of open drainages, bad smell, polluted air and the stagnant water that polluted the lake. So the former president took up this work seriously and people co-operated to get the work done. The first stage of Under Ground Drainage system (UGD) started in 1993-94 stagewise. It was taken up first in Belandur village, based on the demand by the villagers. Now the underground drainage system is completed in Belandur and Haralur villages, and the first stage is in progress in other three villages.

There was no proper drinking water supply to all the houses. The people were taking water by cutting the pipes and stopping the further flow of water to other houses. Since it became a very major problem the stages were increased from two stages to twelve stages for increasing the pressure of water. 200 taps were fitted for each stage. Today there are 600 to 700 taps only in Belandur village. Now there is no problem of water supply because if anybody takes illegal connection of water they are fined for that and the tap will be disconnected for six months so there is proper water supply. The monthly water tax is increased from Rs. 10 to Rs. 50 that has also accounted for the increase in source of income of the panchayat.

Utilisation of the Computer

Extensive training course for 3 months for operating the computer was given to the clerical staff. The training on how to maintain and enter the data related to the panchayat was given. The main data maintained in the computer are the *Kathas* (RR), Tax Assessment Registers, Mutation Registers, Property details, Daily Collection Registers, Water Tax and other taxes. The details of Grama Sabhas, yearwise budget, income and expenditure statements are also maintained. Through the computer the panchayat can issue computer generated birth and death certificates, property certificate, tax assessments, demand notices and water bills. Around 2,500 and above households across 5 villages are getting benefits from these services.

The panchayat is not free from problems either. Two major issues for illustrative purposes are given below:

Issue of the Belandur Lake

The lake covers an area of over 950 acres. Nearly 45 species of birds depend on the lake for survival. Over 5000 water birds arrive here every year, making the lake conservation very important. The Belandur lake was to be selected for the Asian Games but due to green water plants being more in this lake, it was not selected. The lake was very advantageous for this panchayat, as it was the main means for living of the poor people. They were leading their livelihood through fishing, but when the sewage of the nearby factory was let out to this water, it became poisonous and all fishes died and as a result of this they stopped fishing. The bore well water (drinking) was also contaminated. It became a problem for all those farmers who depended on this water for growing of crops. The paddy crop was also spoiled and had to face huge loss. So the former president took initiative to notify and then filed a suit to control the water pollution, which has become a big issue for the panchayat.

This matter was also discussed in the Grama Sabha and then decision was taken to file a case in the High Court and it is still unsolved. The court has given order to get the lake cleaned in given time and every two months the government should submit the progress report. After the verdict of the High Court, it has been given to the Lok Adalat to take necessary action. The case is being attended to for further settlement. The process of cleaning is going on and very soon the panchayat may get good returns in near future through this lake.

Issue of Land Acquisition

The acquisition of land is one of the issues in this panchayat. The extent of land required for Infosys was nearly 100 acres of land, but the government wanted to acquire more than 600 acres of land keeping Infosys in the forefront for which there was opposition from the farmers and also the panchayat though the farmers were proud of the achievements of Infosys. Since they were acquiring the wet land, the farmers wanted them to take dry lands and make use of it. The question raised by the farmers is that, can the State government dictate the land acquisition terms without consulting the panchayat? The farmers have thought of this because they were getting lesser price for which they cannot make their livelihood. The panchayat was held responsible for this. So the former president along with the farmers' support, agitated to stop the land grab and now the problem is in the process of its solution.

Contributions of the Community in Development Works

Underground Drainage System

For the construction of the underground drainage there was lot of controversies by the people of this village and also by the government. The former president took up the initiative and solved all the problems with great difficulty. The community was first convinced by the president and other members because they were the ones who were complaining about cutting of the roads, trees in front of their houses. Then after they gave their consent, the consent by the higher authorities became easy. The community contributed upto the tune of 20 lakhs for the UGD. They also gave full cooperation and voluntarily helped to complete it. The former president and other members had discussion in the panchayat meeting that the UGD would be completed village by village and so decision was taken to start from Belandur village, then Haralur and so on. The work is going on smoothly and is in the process of completion in the three villages and in the other two villages it is completed.

Development of Roads

The roads were in a very bad situation, so the first development of the village started with the development of roads. In the initial stage while getting the roads widened there was no cooperation by the people. So the panchayat members started working part by part where people cooperated and agreed to get the roads done. Where there was objection by the community and no cooperation the roads were left undone. And again for the repairs and development there was controversy in the beginning. The former president and other members took a strong step in convincing the people from house to house and also gave notice. Then slowly the people who objected also gave cooperation after they became aware that the development was for the whole *panchayat* area and it was not an individual benefit. The contribution here can be noted in terms of kind. For further improvement of the road and extending of roads also, the community extended their cooperation. Today the roads are done in every street and the *panchayat* looks more like a town.

Overhead Tank

The water problem was taken up as the crucial work, which is one of the basic necessities for the people. The public also contributed around one lakh rupees for the construction of the overhead tank. The water problem was also solved by cooperation from the panchayat members and the public. All the wards have one mini water tank. The panchayat has 5 overhead tanks. There are 23 bore wells and Belandur has the highest number of bore wells. 700 taps have been installed and all are getting equal amount of water. If there is any illegal pipe connection then penalty will be upto Rs. 2000. This is one method of controlling the water theft in the panchayat. The panchayat has evolved some of its own strategies for controlling the misuse of anything in the panchayat area.

Collection of Garbage

The panchayat started the system of collecting garbage from house to house. The people are paying Rs. 10 every month for collection of garbage. The panchayat has appointed 2-3 persons to collect the garbage from every house. Through this, the panchayat has been able to maintain cleanliness and environment pollution free. The people are also cooperating in this regard. There are trees planted along the roadside in the village, which has helped the people to get fresh air and good atmosphere.

Identified Local Needs in the Panchayat Area

(i) The siteless people are more in number and there is a need for allotting sites for them and to build houses under any housing scheme.

(ii) Due to migration of people from outside, the population is increasing and there is problem of drinking water supply.
(iii) The pollution of the lake is still an existing problem.
(iv) Need for metalling of roads.
(v) To put fencing between the Iblur military camp and the Haralur village.
(vi) Need for burial ground.

The Future Plans of the Panchayat

(i) Solving problems of the people through 'Phone In' programme.
(ii) Providing free sites to the poor people.
(iii) To clean the Lake and convert it into a Tourist place with boating facilities.
(iv) To provide High Schools, Health Centre, Police Station.
(v) To collect tax for all facilities provided for the houses constructed in the revenue lands like water, electricity etc.
(vi) To promote dry land through INFOSYS to get greater value for that land.
(vii) To create the city atmosphere in the village by providing all facilities available at the city level.

Concluding Observations

Computerisation leading to smooth functioning and the efforts made to increase the source of income and becoming self-sufficient and sustainable has helped this panchayat to be a model among all 5659 Grama Panchayats in the state. Also the special features like the effective leadership of the former president and a member, efficiency in functioning, motivation, hard work and commitment have also led to its becoming a model for others. Last but not the least, the Panchayat has changed from rural setup to urban setup and it has taken a step towards bridging the digital divide. The innovative ideas and practice as mentioned earlier has led the panchayat to maintain its accountability and transparency which is most important for any level of governance. These changes are due to the E-governance at the grassroots that has attempted to transform administration into a people friendly, transparent, efficient and accountable proposition. Ultimately, E-governance concept can deliver a variety of services to the community. In fact, the panchayat has become so resourceful that computers have been donated to two other Gram Panchayats. E-governance is the best option to remove barriers between the people and the administration to attain good governance at the grassroots.

21

The Role of Panchayats and Bureaucracy in Rural Development

D.V. GOPALAPPA

Introduction

In India, 'Rural Development' has become a major slogan of almost all political parties since independence. Even the main objective of Indian Five-year Plans has been the rural development as a majority of the population lives in villages and their main occupation is agriculture. However, there is an increasing realisation among the political parties, planners and policy makers that rural development can no more be a vote or a fund fetching slogan but it is the key issue for national progress. The Planning Commission in the Five-Year Plan document, defined rural development as the "Economic betterment of people as well as greater social transformation." The document further emphasises that economic betterment is possible through the development of agriculture and allied activities and social transformation through improvements in health, education, drinking water, energy supply, sanitation and housing. The Indian experience reveals that with the top down approach at the State and the Centre, the rural development could not be achieved up to the expected level (Bhagwati, 1998). The magnitude of the task of rural development demands organisational and educational efforts on the widest possible scale, geared to location-specific planning and intensive utilisation of local resources. In all these respects Panchayati Raj Institutions have a significant contribution to make (Mishra, 1981).

Towards this end, the 73rd Constitutional Amendment has made a basic framework that it is obligatory for all the states to have three-tier Panchayati Raj Institutions (PRIs). The Panchayat Raj system is adapted basically to facilitate the local people in decision making and involve actively in making rural development a reality. The elected representatives of these Panchayats are expected to take appropriate decisions according to the needs of the people and act in the interest of the general public (Mathew, 1986; Inbanathan, 1992; Inbanathan, *et al.* 1997; Crook and Manor, 1998). Besides people's representatives, the officials of the panchayats are also responsible for giving appropriate information and implementing the decisions of the representatives. If, both the representatives and officials work together with greater co-ordination and understanding, the efficiency of the PRIs would be enhanced (Gurumurthy, 1988). In this context, an effort has been made here to understand the interface between the elected representatives and the bureaucrats to achieve the goal of rural development.

Mainly, case study method has been followed to carry out this study. The respondents include officials of the PRIs, line departments and elected members. Totally 25 officials of PRIs working as Chief Executive Officer (CEO) of the Zilla Panchayat (ZP) and the Secretaries of the Grama Panchayats (GPs) were interviewed. About 250 elected representatives, consisting of Presidents, Vice-Presidents, members of ZPs, Taluk Panchayats (TPs) and GPs were interviewed. The panchayats (all the three-tiers) selected for the study are Mandya, Gulbarga and Dakshina Kannada (DK) ZPs. The TPs were selected within these districts. Within these TPs, GPs have been selected for the study based on the representative sampling method. To select the TPs and GPs the reservation of President and Vice-President has been followed. The paper is divided in to four sections. The first three sections discuss the role of officials and representatives in GPs, TPs and ZPs respectively and the last deals with summary, conclusions and policy suggestions.

General Profile of the Study Districts

The three districts are different in terms of various socio-economic parameters. The difference in the socio-economic status is something to do with the performance of the PRIs. Therefore, the district profile is given to understand socio-economic status of the districts. There are 7, 10 and 5 TPs and 233, 336 and 208 GPs in Mandya, Gulbarga and DK districts respectively. The density of population is 416 per sq. km. in DK district, 355 in Mandya and 193 in Gulbarga district (Census, 2001). The actual rainfall in 2000 is highest in DK district with 3975 mm. compared to Mandya with 967mm. and 805 mm in Gulbarga district. In DK district the per capita net sown area is 0.21 acres when compared to the Mandya district 0.35 acres and Gulbarga 1.13 acres in 1999-2000. The literacy rate in DK district has been the highest (83.47%) followed by Mandya district (61.21%) and the least literacy rate is noticed in Gulbarga district (50.65%). Even the female literacy rate is 77.39 per cent in DK, which is much above the other two districts.

I

THE PERFORMANCE OF THE OFFICIALS AND THE REPRESENTATIVES IN GPs

In GPs there is a full time personnel designated as secretary. However, a GP can have other staff like bill collector, waterman and others on temporary basis appointed and paid by the panchayats themselves. The members of the GP are directly elected by the people. The President, Vice-President are indirectly elected from among the members by the members. The experience of the sample GPs reveals that in Mandya district three patterns emerge in terms of exercising the power in the GPs. In a few GPs the secretary plays a major role in the panchayat administration as he is the only government official. The elected members in these GPs by and large are ignorant, illiterate and poor. Therefore, the panchayat is dominated by the secretary. For instance, in Haradanahalli GP of Nagamangala taluk the secretary takes decisions on matters relating to the works to be done in the panchayat. He identifies the work and allots them to some contractor and gets the work certificate from the junior engineer. In this process, the works executed in the villages are substandard and not worth the money spent on them. The main reason for this is the fact that the president of the GP is an illiterate woman. Several times we met her for discussion and almost all the time she was grazing the sheep in the open fields and she could not answer our questions and the usual answer was "you ask my husband." Though her husband keeps track of the on-goings in the panchayat, he does not bother about panchayat's development as he is sufficiently bribed by the secretary.

In contrast to the above, in Maddur taluk, there is a Grama panchayat called Kadlur, which is a small panchayat compared to the other GPs in Nagamangala and Maddur taluks of the same district. In this panchayat the president is from general category, rich and he himself is a contractor. The president is supreme in the GP and his decisions are final. A large number of developmental works have been implemented in this panchayat. The president has taken initiative to construct the houses under Ashraya, Ambedkar and Indira Awas Yojana schemes. About 600 houses have been constructed over a period of seven years and there is hardly any single thatched roof house found in the panchayat. The panchayat has provided street lights, good drainage facilities, drinking water and dairy cooperative society. All these could happen because the president is non-corrupt and has the ambition to climb up the ladder and hence he is working towards rural development. As the researchers observed within five years' term, a lot of developmental activities were taken up in the panchayat. The secretary does not have any role except sanctioning the amount for the development works in the village. The secretary does not interfere in the panchayat matters as he was afraid of the president to indulge in malpractices. However, for minor works like road repair, repair of small bridges, etc., the members take a small portion as bribe for which the president does not come in the way as he requires their support also. Hence, in this panchayat the role of government official is very minimal and the panchayat is dominated by the president and the elected members.

Other extreme cases are Bellur GP in Nagamangala Taluk and Kestur GP of Maddur taluk. In these panchayats around 50 per cent of the total elected representatives are stronger when compared to the presidents of both the GPs. The president belongs to minority (Jain) community in Bellur and is a women (general category) in Kestur GP. The stronger group takes decisions on their own and asks the president and the secretary to implement the programmes and schemes. However, the Kestur GP is better in terms of development as there is strong opposition in the Panchayat and there is a *de facto* president who is able to lead and guide the GP members. Where as in Bellur GP, the resources are more, but most of the works are in the court and as such there are no sufficient funds to implement the development programmes. In this GP more than 50 per cent of the members are strong and they are misguiding the president who is not able to take concrete decisions which resulted in poor development of the village GP in general. In both these panchayats the secretaries are just facilitators and they do not have own decision making power.

The experience in northern Karnataka is something different. In these panchayats neither elected representatives nor the officials take much interest in the development of the panchayat. In all the GPs the dominant members or the president or the village elite try to have control over the GPs. The secretaries have to obey and follow the directions of these functionaries. Out of the six sample GPs, four GPs are dominated by one or the other caste or political party. This caste or political party have nexus with the officials and get away with the panchayat funds. The other members do not have either economic strength or physical strength to question these leaders and officials. As against this the young boys aged around 25 years have been raising their voice against these leaders. However, they are snubbed by their parents, relatives and caste leaders. For instance, in Udagi GP of Sedam taluk, a boy aged about 24 years had plans to contest election against a dominant caste old man aged about 65 years. The few village headmen wanted the old fellow to win. Therefore, they tried their level best to select him unopposed, but this boy resisted and decided to contest the election. Therefore, in the beginning his parents and relatives did not encourage him, only his friends of similar age group supported him. Of course, gradually, the parents and relatives came to his rescue and helped him financially. Ultimately he won the election and he is happy for this achievement. This special incident has to be explained because when the boy was asked the purpose of contesting the elections he said "the present members and the president have nexus with officials (secretary) to swallow all the panchayat funds with out any developmental works." He has given the example of poor drainage facilities, poor drinking water available in the village, bad roads and the pathetic condition of the houses constructed under various government schemes. Since he being an educated, studied up to PUC, wants to take up some development works in the village (his own GP). If the new blood of this kind moves in this direction definitely the existing pattern of panchayats changes in the Gulbarga district. Here and there we find similar people who have taken initiative and acted as opposition leaders, which have resulted in the partial development of such GPs.

There are extreme cases in Gulbarga district where the entire GP is controlled by a single family that have relations with high profiled politicians. One best example is Athanur GP in Afzalpur taluk of Gulbarga district consisting of only women. The women members were selected unopposed by a single family residing in that village. Their relative is an MLA and, therefore, they do not want to lose the power in the entire village. The members of the family could sense that there is an opposition to their family in the village. Therefore, they decided to make it an all women GP by saying that they will get Rs. one lakh extra grant for their panchayat (this is proved to be only a wrong impression when it was cross checked with the officials of the Election Commission). When we met two aspirants for the GP election they said "we wanted to contest for the election this time but we could not as the family decided to make it an all women panchayat". They could not go against the wishes of that family as even these are depending for financial and other material help. Totally, it is the question of surviving in the village and the village people cannot antagonize them. As a result these aspirants kept quiet, including the reserved categories, during the selection of women candidates. In this panchayat the role of official is very much neglected as the members of dominant caste take all the decisions regarding the panchayat matters. The secretary and the office bearers get some benefit from the family directly as they behave like obedient servants. Hence, in Gulbarga district we have extreme situations of this kind.

One more example is Chamanal GP in Shahapur taluk. In this panchayat two members control the panchayat. They belonged to dominant caste and relatives of ex-MLA of the taluk. Therefore, secretaries fear to work in this GP due to dominant attitude of such members. For this reason, during the past six years, many secretaries were changed. Present secretary expressed difficulty to work in such a panchayat. He told that, during previous time, these leaders used to manhandle the secretary. In one instance a secretary was dumped inside the office and locked when he did not listen to their orders. Hence, in Gulbarga, the GPs are in the hands of local dominant people, which resulted in the less power in the hands of secretaries or any official. However, it cannot be generalised that such extreme situations are there every where in Gulbarga. But one thing is clear that the secretaries have more pressure and difficulty in carrying out the activities. The factors which are responsible for the situation are: social hierarchy, concentration of political power with some sections of the society and higher rate of illiteracy among the people.

The experience of GPs in DK district reveals a different kind of situation. Here, the members, office bearers and the officials work collectively for the overall development of the community. Most of the members, presidents and vice-presidents think that it is an honorary job and it is an opportunity to work for the development of people. They have service motive rather than profit. There are so many examples where the elected representatives spent the money from their pockets for the panchayat works. For instance, in Aranthodu GP of Sulya taluk, a member called Bhavani Shanker has spent lot of money from his pocket and also brought money through various means to develop his constituency and also the panchayat as a whole. The major works undertaken by him were; laying 5 kms. metal (tar) road in the forest area and getting power connection for the first time for the village in 1998. Interestingly he has not taken power connection to his own house as it is located in an interior place. For these, he has not taken support either from the village secretary or the executive officer of the TP. However, he was helped by the MLA of Sulya taluk. The ex-president (Madhava Patel) of the same GP is economically sound due to arecanut garden he owns. Therefore, the entire budget of the GP is very much negligible and he does not bother about it. Therefore, he spent the money from his own pocket for the development of the GP instead of misappropriating the GP resources. His major achievements in the GP were construction of a big meeting hall, a bridge (the bridge is not an ordinary one), school rooms, laying road and facilitating quite a few houses to get drinking water through mini water supply schemes. The secretary has been co-operative and he was getting information about the development programmes through taluk and zilla panchayats and persuading the president to make effort to get programmes for the development of the panchayat. He never tried to take bribe or misutilise the panchayat funds. He was acting according to the advice of the president and vice-president. At the grassroots level, local level bureaucracy and Panchayati Raj Institutions, the two decentralised agencies, are mainly responsible for successful implementation of development programmes. But in most of the rural areas lack of proper coordination and absence of motivation have mainly been responsible for shoddy performance of these two institutions, (Mishra 1986). However, DK district's GPs are something different and therefore better developed.

Another GP, viz., Ujire GP of Belthangadi taluk has some peculiarities. Here we have a female secretary who has links with a powerful leader like Sundaragowda. He was responsible for her to come to Ujire as GP secretary. She has good relationship with all the members. She herself awards contracts and in certain cases the members themselves take up contract works in *benami* names. We were told that the secretary takes about five per cent as bribe to service the guests, auditors and other miscellaneous expenditure. This was admitted by herself and she swore that she does not save any single rupee out of this. In case some amount is left over she distributes the same among the temporary staff of the panchayat.

Therefore, the secretary has been appreciated by most of the members and other powerful leaders in the GP. They do not compromise with the quality of the GP works to be done. They see that a minimum of 85 per cent of the funds are really invested in the panchayat works.

One more good example is Malavanthige GP of the Belthangadi taluk. Here the president and the secretary are the final authorities in taking decisions regarding the panchayat functioning. The other six members do not bother about the panchayat as the president and the secretary are taking care of the panchayat without any problem. We have got some information about the collective corruption of both the secretary and the president. However, the quality of the works done is not questionable as the percentage of their corruption is very minimum. This is happening in this GP because of no opposition members in the panchayat and the members have good faith in secretary and the president.

GPs' Financial Planning

The planning at the grassroots level is only notional. The GPs prepare action plan for the funds available through various schemes and the same is forwarded to TP for approval. The authorities in the TP scrutinize the action plans and approve the same with or without asking for modification. The secretaries and the members of the GPs say that they never get the resources according to their requirement. We take up the works based on the availability of funds but not *vice versa*. The GPs receive grants from various sources like Central Government, Swarna Jayanthi Grama Samruddi Yojana (SJGSY), 10th Finance Commission (till 2000-01), state government grant and their own tax and non-tax revenue. Among these sources SJGSY and 10th Finance Commission grants are tied ones where they specify the activities to be taken up by using these funds. The GPs have restricted freedom only in the state government grants (the GPs are supposed to spend on 3-4 specified projects) and they have freedom on their own resources. Out of these, they have to spend on the salaries, electricity charges and the remaining resources will be minimal and they will be used on streetlights, water supply and the repair of roads and drainage. The GPs are always at the receiving end and they cannot demand the resources according to their plan. However, the healthy trend developed in the panchayats as the elected representatives started discussing the financial requirement in the GP meetings and also in the Grama Sabha meetings. The activities will be taken up according to the availability of the funds. This being the case one can say that planning is done at the grossroots level.

II

RELATIONS AT THE TALUK PANCHAYATS: MANDYA DISTRICT

Like Grama Panchayats, in Taluk Panchayats also similar trends are noticed in all the three districts. However, we find little variation in terms of official involvement in higher tier panchayat. Two Taluk Panchayats in Mandya district have been taken up for the present study. These TPs are Maddur and Malavalli. In both the TPs, apparently, the dominance of members is noticed in terms of power as they have patrons of high profiled politicians like MLAs, MPs, block level party bosses and other local elite. Even a few members identify themselves as the staunch followers of ex-Prime Minister (H.D. Devegowda) and the former Chief Minister (S.M. Krishna) of the state. However, the officials control the members through paper work as they receive all the correspondence from their respective ZPs and the state government. The officials are supposed to convey the details regarding the programmes, funds available and the modalities to implement the programmes. But, the officials try to avoid the transparency of the official documents and give only oral information to the members so that the members will be in regular touch with them. This, the officials say, helps them to maintain their status and in turn can get some reward. Therefore, ultimately the officials' hand is stronger when compared to the elected members. The officials are capable of obtaining approval of certain works from the Standing Committees and the General Body meetings of the Taluk Panchayats. Even they try to keep good relations with the local MLA to protect themselves from the elected members of the panchayat. This results in the nexus between the officials and the elected members in the Taluk Panchayats, which led to corruption. As the researchers observed from the field about 60 per cent (rough estimation) of the funds allotted for rural development dry before reaching the villages as it is shared among the officials, representatives and the contractors. The elected members in these TPs agree to this point.

There are a few instances where the members gained upper hand in decision-making. In Maddur taluk the members who belong to Raithasanga party strongly condemned the officials' mal-practices and they were mainly responsible for the suspension of an Executive Officer who has misused the funds available in the Housing Scheme. And, there are instances of this kind which mainly responsible for the non-cooperation between the members and officials in Maddur Taluk Panchayat. Therefore, at present both the members and officials will see that kickbacks are distributed equally.

In Malavalli TP understanding between the members and the officials is lacking as majority of the members belong to Janata Dal (S) party and the local MLA belongs to Janata Dal (U) party. The members said that the MLA has brought the Executive Officer (EO) who was his follower. Therefore, there has been always friction between the members on the one hand, MLA and the officials on the other. In one instance, the members could stop the decisions of the EO and the MLA. For example, out of the SC/ST funds about Rs. 5 lakh was saved for the construction of Ambedkar Bhavan.. Even after the lapse of two to three years nothing materialised in concrete terms. However, even before getting the site from the revenue department, the EO had sanctioned the money to the land army to construct the Bhavan with the support of MLA. The members took strong objection to this and said the money should be distributed to the constituencies of the members to carry out pending works. Therefore, the construction of Ambedkar Bhavan was stalled. The EO has issued a deadline to lay the foundation stone to construct the Bhavan. In case he does not get the site within the dead line the understanding was reached that the funds will be released for the development of the members' constituencies.

Hence, in Mandya district both the officials and the elected members are strong and sometimes the elected members proved stronger when compared to the officials.

Taluk Panchayats (TPs)—Gulbarga District

In Gulbarga district, Shahapur and Chitapur TPs have been studied. In these TPs two groups of members are strong as they have support of their own party, communities, castes, civil societies and the officials. However, most of the other members do not have the strong support of either the politicians or of their own community or any civil society. The last category of the members is women belonging to general, SC/ST and BC categories and few male members of the same groups. These members are representing the panchayats because of the reservation. Normally, they don't speak in the Standing Committees and general body meetings. The officials do not care for either personal or official works of these members. However, these members also take bribe *(mamool)* from the contractors who get works in their constituencies by having nexus with the officials to sanction the works. The contractors bribe both officials and the members to make as much as possible from the works sanctioned.

In general, in the Taluk Panchayats, ultimately the elected representatives are strong and the works have to be carried out as per their advice. However, the officials try to manipulate certain issues as they are responsible for all the official files and they are the first to know the Government programmes and sometimes they don't inform the same to the body. Though the body decides everything, the programme implementation has been through the officials and also the cheque signing authority rests with the Executive Officer of the Taluk Panchayat. Therefore, a kind of nexus exists between the officials and the members and hence only 30 to 35 per cent of the funds allotted to development projects reach the rural areas and the remaining dry on the way. The executive officer of one of the TPs says "if we do not nod our head for the demands of the members, we will be transferred to either a useless department or a remote area where we have to face practical problems to survive".

Taluk Panchayats—DK District

In Dakshina Kannada (DK) district Sulya and Belthangadi taluks were studied. In these taluks the members and also the officials are strong, sincere and take part in development works seriously. The officials and elected representatives attend the panchayat office regularly. The president and the vice-president attend the office daily and stay for longer time in the office. They listen to the grievances of the public and also the officials. There exists a good co-ordination between the officials and the elected representatives in these TPs compared to their counter parts in Mandya and Gulbarga districts. The officials of various departments and the elected representatives of panchayats are dedicated themselves for development of their constituencies. Therefore, the question of superiority or inferiority does not arise. The officials in TPs are prompt enough to inform the general body about the programmes and available funds for the specified work. The standing committees and the General Body take decisions appropriately for the development of the panchayat. More transparency in the functioning of the panchayat has been mainly responsible to solve many problems between the officials and the elected members.

In Belthangadi taluk, the local MLA is mainly responsible for the development of the area. He, for various programmes, mobilises money and asks the officials and the members to implement them. Therefore, he got a good name and has become a popular leader in the taluk. Hence, he is respected by not only the members and the officials but also the common man. However, corruption element has been noticed even in this TP. The nexus between the officials and the contractors helps the officials to get a portion as commission. The officials get commission regularly as they have cheque signing authority. If they do not release the cheque in the right time there will be a great loss to the contractor. Therefore, to minimize the loss the contractor bribes the officials. A very few members also take some bribe who are responsible to get works sanctioned to their constituencies. In total the rate of corruption does not exceed around 15 per cent and the contractor keeps profit margin of about 10 per cent. The quality of works has been high in the study area as around 75 per cent of the funds actually spent on the development projects. Therefore, the literacy rate, awareness among the public, the dedication of the officials and the members towards the area development and the attitude of the members towards the poor and the needy have been playing a major role in DK district.

Planning Process at the TP Level

The chief planning officer of ZPs helps the TPs to prepare the plans as there are planning personnel in the TPs. The Executive Officer of the TP asks all the line departments to indicate their financial requirement for the next financial year. Accordingly, the line department heads enhance about 10 per cent with reference to current year budget and forwards the same to the TP. (A copy of this will also be sent to their respective department heads at the district level). The TP will consolidate all the plan documents of the line departments and put it in Finance and Planning Committee. After taking approval of this Standing Committee it will be placed before the General Body meeting of the TPs. The members have to discuss the plan document in the meetings and they have to approve it. They have to do it within the grants allocated and according to the guidelines of each sector. Once the plan is approved at the TPs, the executive officer has to send the same to ZP for scrutiny and approval. If the ZP approves the plan it will be included in the district plan or ZP plan. As the EOs of Maddur TP of Mandya district and Chitapur taluk of Gulbarga district say the members of the Standing Committee and General Body do not alter the plan much as they do not show much interest in planning. What they are worried is whether the programmes which they have asked for are reflected in the document or not. In case they are not reflected they ask the EO to include it. However, in DK the scenario is different. Even in GPs the members discuss the plan document in detail and send it to the TPs. In TPs the plan document will be discussed in detail before sending it to the ZPs. The members' opinion will be greatly respected and suggestions will be incorporated in the plan document. The EOs of Beltangadi and Sulya taluks of DK district felt that whether higher authorities consider the views of TPs or not they follow the formality and they are serious about it. Therefore, the plan document at taluk level has been *pucca* in DK unlike the TPs of Mandya and Gulbarga districts.

III

RELATIONS IN ZILLA PANCHAYATS

As mentioned earlier the three ZPs, namely, Mandya, Gulbarga and Dakshina Kannada ZPs were studied. One can find a slight variation in terms of the relations between the officials and elected representatives of the ZPs in the respective districts. The main reason for this is the members are much above the TPs level and little below the MLA in terms of power and the status. Most of the members have close relations with the MLAs, MPs and even with the ministers through patron client relations or belong to their own caste or party. Therefore, the officials are a bit careful with the ZP members.

Zilla Panchayat—Mandya

According to the Council Secretary, out of 39 members in Mandya ZP about 45 per cent are very strong as they have strong political links, money power and their caste background (most of them belong to Vakkaliga community). When these members ask some favour from the officials, they will be considered without delay. One more category of members is moderate. These members are well aware about the Panchayat Act. They persuade the officials by exhibiting their knowledge and get their works done. Sometimes, the persuasion leads to corruption. The third group of members is those who belong to the reserved category like women, SC/ST and BCs. These categories of members are taken for granted and on behalf of these members the officials and the contractors take decisions and the members are just channels to get the projects to their constituencies. These members get lower percentage of kickbacks. Therefore, in general, in Mandya district about 40 per cent of total funds are invested in the field and the remaining is being misappropriated by the officials, members and contractors in the range of (20%), (15%) and (25%) respectively.

Gulbarga ZP

We get slightly different scenario in Gulbarga district. In Gulbarga district we get four categories of members. The members of dominant caste (lingayat) who are also economically sound, the members of SC/ST community, the members of BCs and the women who come under reservation. The members who belong to first category are powerful as they are the leaders of their community and financially sound. There is no bar for these members either in the government office or in their own villages. They are the deciding authority in all the matters. The officials by and large will have very good relation with these members. The members from SC/ST categories can be divided into two groups viz., male and female. A few male members of this category are strong as they have support of the high ranking politicians and also the Dalit Sangarsha Samithi, through these, they try to achieve their goals. Whereas the remaining members and the women are very weak as women do not dare to look at their own men in the village and also the officials. They are weak in all respects and therefore, the officials do not care for these members. The third category is the members who belong to the reservation under BCs. The members from this category can also be divided into two groups. The first group of members is those who belong to the dominant caste like lingayat. They are very powerful in terms of money and political links. The second category of members is the worst sufferers. These members carry out the works through persuasion. Here, the officials try to dominate and make money. The last category is the women who got elected under the reservation. It is difficult to get women who are strong in terms of power in this district. Most of the members have their husbands, family members or some other close relatives as *defacto* members. These *defacto* members are only responsible for their contest and winning the elections. However, as the members' achievement is minimal the officials do not care for these members but the *defacto* members get some respect from the officials. There are instances where these members have attended the panchayat meetings and public functions. Due to the objections raised by few members of the panchayat, these *defacto* members temporarily stopped attending the meetings. However, the members could not stop them from taking panchayat related works indirectly.

One of the officers of Gulbarga ZP felt that the members are power mongers and every member tries to make money as much as possible. Therefore, the development in the district is not up to the expected level. The Chief Executive Officer (CEO) says that as long as the members follow the stipulated procedure he does not interfere in any matter. In case he gets any complaint he will attend to it. As the CEO says "In some cases the members try to deviate from the existing procedures. Under such circumstances I try to guide the members to follow the panchayat rules and regulations. Even then if the members deviate from the guidelines I write to the government." The CEO says that as for as possible he tries to compromise with the members, the Vice-President and the President. In case the situation goes beyond the control then only he writes to the government. However, he feels happy that such a situation did not arise in his tenure and his advice has been taken positively by the president and the members of the ZP.

ZP-DK District

In Dakshina Kannada district we can classify the members into two groups. The first category consists of the members of general group, BCs and the women. The second category of the members is those who belong to SC/ST community both male and female. The first category of the members belong to forward caste owning land, where arecanut, coconut, coffee and other plantation crops are grown. These members contest elections with the purpose of serving the public and they do not mind if their opponents get elected after their term. As most of the members are economically sound they do not bother much to make money after becoming the member of the ZP. However, there are a few members in this category who make money by taking about five per cent of the project cost as commission from the contractors. However, they rarely charge from the general public for doing individual favours. Instead the members will be happy if the customer bears the transport and other expenses. The officials take bribe to the tune of 10 per cent from the contractor, the contractor's profit margin is about 10 per cent and the members' share will be 5 to 10 per cent. Therefore, in general about 25 to 30 per cent being shared by these functionaries and 70 to 75 per cent is really being spent on the development projects. The interesting feature of the DK-ZP is that there is less number of members practicing contract in benami names unlike Mandya and Gulbarga where a majority of the members themselves are contractors. Therefore, in DK, the development can be noticed in terms of increasing per capita income, literacy rate, establishment of roads and other infrastructure facilities specially the construction works in the district.

The second category of the members is those who belong to SC/ST. These members are not economically sound but they have service mind and do not try to misappropriate the funds meant for development. Though, they act like dummies in the hands of their patrons, they do not compromise with the development works to be implemented in their constituencies. However, the members have some interest to accept the commission but the percentage is minimum constituting about five per cent. Compared to Mandya and Gulbarga districts the personal status of these members is low.

Planning Process at the ZP Level

The Chief Planning Officer in consultation with members and departmental officials prepares the plan and the members have to discuss about the plan in the concerned standing committee meetings before its approval. Finally, the ZP consolidates the three-tier plans before sending it to the State Planning Department. As the Zilla Panchayat prepares its own plan it is called as bottom up planning or decentralized planning. The senior officials of Mandya, Mysore and DK district said that the final plan document with specified resources will not be approved by the State Planning Department. Funding will be according to the estimates of the State Planning Department (off the record). Before getting the plan documents from the districts the State Planning Department advises the ZP as to how much they can increase in the next financial year. Based on that, the ZP can increase about five per cent compared to last year's. Beyond this, the State Planning Department does not consider further enhancement. Given the situation there is no significance for the plan document prepared by the ZP says the official.

The senior officials who take part in the preparation of plan document of Mandya and Mysore districts opine that the participation of the members is very minimal as they do not show interest. Only they are bothered about the works to be done in their constituencies. For this they take part in the preparation of action plan where they can include the works to be taken in their constituencies. Therefore, the plan preparation and finalization of the same is purely the officials' domain but not the members'. In DK, while preparing plan document the development works will be kept in mind based on the suggestions of the members and they do not spend on unnecessary projects like Mandya and Gulbarga districts where petty projects, viz., mud roads, filling the pits and padding (the members and the officials collude and certify that the project has been carried with out doing it), will be taken as major ones. The members of DK will have thorough discussion about the plan document and then only they give consent to it.

IV

SUMMARY AND CONCLUSIONS

To conclude, the understanding between the elected members and the officials in Mandya district is poor as the members and officials compete with each other to make money as much as possible. They are not bothered much about the development work in the panchayats. There are instances where the houses, buildings and bridges constructed are in poor condition and in some places they have collapsed. All this is due to lack of sincerity among the officials and the members to maintain quality. The officials try to overtake the members and members bring political pressure on the officials to get the work done. The members themselves are contractors and they try to swindle the money. We have the examples where the members keep the receipt books of various companies to claim the money. This reveals that the morality has gone down among the members in the panchayats. The officials and members always quarrel for petty things and try to show their power through various means. This has reflected in the poor development of their constituencies. Therefore, in Mandya district, in the sample GPs, TPs and even in ZP the percentage of amount spent on development works is around 40 per cent of the total budget (a rough estimation). Interestingly, majority of the members of various parties, castes and communities are powerful due to the support from their parties, groups and castes.

The scenario in Gulbarga district is not totally different from Mandya. However, in Gulbarga district the rate of corruption is too high due to illiteracy, ignorance of the people as they think of immediate gains like liquor and minimal cash benefits from the elected representatives. The elected representatives at GP level give respect to the secretary as he is responsible to award works, which have to be taken up in their constituencies. After getting the work awarded they see that the secretary does not visit the work spot. Even the secretary also does not bother as long as he gets benefits out of the work awarded to a particular member. Of course there is a specified percentage for all the officials starting from bill-collector and secretary at the GP level to clerk, junior engineer and the executive officer at TP level. According to the available information, out of the total budget of a project only around 35 per cent will be spent on the work and the remaining will be swindled by concerned authorities, elected representatives and the contractors (a rough estimation). Therefore, the quality of work done in Gulbarga district is poor compared to the Mandya district. Interestingly, the members of Mandya and Gulbarga districts try to win the elections again and again as they do not want to lose power and financial benefits. However, due to reservation policy we can see majority of the members are new to the panchayats.

The scenario in DK is quite different from the other two districts. The officials and the elected members have future vision about the works to be done in the panchayats as they have good co-ordination in understanding the issues. The members also have good education and knowledge about their constituencies and moreover, they can understand the public problems. Personal supervision of the works is very much predominant in this area. In certain situations the president, vice-president and the members spend from their own pocket for certain works to be done in their constituencies. Basically, the members are rich as they have income yielding arecanut and coconut gardens. Therefore, they try to be non-corrupt as much as possible. The members have service motive rather than profit motive. The members, vice president or president do not want to stick on to their positions instead they try to give chance to others to serve the public after serving one term. Among the officials also the rate of corruption is less and they co-operate with the elected office bearers to the maximum extent. That is why the rural development is noticed which has reflected in the establishment of educational institutions, good transport facilities, drinking water, bus-stands, better roads, drainage facilities, street lights, etc., in all the sample panchayats. However, there is a lacuna even in DK district. The members who belong to SC and ST categories do not have any say in the panchayat matters as most of them are casual labourers. They are mostly dependent on the landlords for their lively-hood. For instance, Ayathappa (30 years old) and Chennamma (28 years old) are members of the Aranthodu GP and they are working as casual labourers even after becoming the members of panchayat. They say that there is no question of working against the general category of members who hire them for wage labour regularly. In Halatti GP, which is dominated by the ST population who are mostly agricultural labourers are controlled by the other members who are economically strong. The women president of the ST category is controlled by a dominant member belong to Vokkaliga community. Though, she is a president, even now, she is working as casual labour in the Gowda's gardens (the secondary data, which are available reveal that in DK there is only one SC farmer who has more than ten acres of land). When these members were consulted they said that it is not possible for them to work against their patrons who are instrumental in getting elected and also providing economic security. Therefore, it may take longer time to change their attitude. Except this, in DK, the GPs, TPs and even the ZP are doing better compared to PRIs in other two districts. The panchayat members in DK have service motive rather than profit motive and it is *vice versa* in the case of Mandya and Gulbarga districts.

REFERENCES

Bhagwati, Jagdish, N. (1998): 'Poverty and Public Policy', *World Development*, 16(5): 539.

Crook, R.C. and James Manor (1998): *Democracy and Decentralisation in South Asia and West Africa: Participation, Accountability and Performance*, Cambridge University Press, Cambridge.

Gurumurthy, K.G. (1988): *Rural Development and Factional Politics,* Reliance Publishing House, New Delhi.

Inbanathan, Anand (1992): '*The New Panchayat Raj in Karnataka*' (Manuscript Report 6), Institute of Social Sciences, New Delhi.

Inbanathan, Anand, T.A. Bhagyalakshmi and R. Doraiswamy (1997): 'Democratic Local Governance: The Case of Panchayati Raj in Karnataka', Paper commissioned by United States Agency for International Development, Center for Development Information and Evaluation, Washington D.C.

Mishra, S.N. (1981): *Rural Development and Panchayati Raj,* Concept Publishing Company, New Delhi.

Mishra, S.N. (1986): *Panchayati Raj Bureaucracy and Rural Development*, Indian Institute of Public Administration, New Delhi.

22

Differences and Identities

Women and Political Participation

V. VIJAYALAKSHMI

Affirmative action and the reservation of seats in the institutions of local government (panchayats) in India has enhanced the potential for participation of women in grassroots politics. With the enactment of the 73rd Amendment to the Constitution, one-third of the total seats are reserved for women as well as one-third the posts of president and vice president[1]. Provisions were also made for the reservation of seats for women belonging to other disadvantaged sections of the population, such as Scheduled Castes and Scheduled Tribes, and some states also made provisions for Backward Castes[2]. The inclusion of women in positions of leadership raised expectations of change in gender relations in the political space. However, the limited power that women wield and their marginal participation[3] do not correspond to their numerical presence. While the opportunity provided for the representation of women from different sections of the community, there are no clear indications of consolidation of their presence by the women. The authority of women representatives was not converted into power. Men used their power as individuals and elites to maintain differential power structures and women legitimised male power. The paper examines factors contributing to women's marginalisation in the functioning of the panchayats and why do women support ideologies that sustain their subordination.

The dynamics of gender relations in local governance assumes significance in the context of increase in the number of women representatives. One-third of the total seats have been reserved for women in the three tiers of panchayats. Their inclusion in local governance, in all its diversity is potentially important not only for women's status in society but also for the nature of the polity. The restructuring of gender composition in panchayats affects women differently according to their position in the class and caste structures. Similarly, the significance of the 'gender regimes' (Walby, 1997) in the lives of most women has consequences for their political participation. This paper discusses some of these issues. The analysis is based on in-depth interviews with elected representatives, members of different communities, and officials. The elected representatives were from the Gram Panchayats, Taluk Panchayats, and Zilla Panchayat of Mandya district.

The analysis of women's political participation is carried out in three stages. First, the chapter briefly examines the socio-economic and political profiles of women members. This includes the nature of women's entry into politics. Second, the participation process and a typology of women's participation in panchayats are discussed. Finally, the constraints that made women's role in local governance less effective are analysed. The differences between women, powerlessness and dependence of women representatives are examined to understand their constraints. Interviews with elected representatives of rural local governments in two districts of Karnataka (Mandya and Udupi) were used to examine these issues. Analysis is based on interviews with 261 elected representatives (from 2 district councils, 4 sub-district councils and 11 village councils) in Karnataka, of which 145 are men and 116 are women. Mandya district is a politically sensitive place mainly because of its proximity to the state capital and also because several prominent politicians were from this district. The Vokkaligas are the dominant caste group in Mandya and are well represented at different levels in politics. Although an economically developed district, the gender indicators of Mandya are rather low.[4]

II

WOMEN IN LOCAL GOVERNANCE

The reservation of seats for women is a positive step to provide them an opportunity in politics. In practice, however, the reservation of seats has turned out to be inefficacious in nurturing a political culture among women, producing one timers who went into political obscurity once their term was completed. The results point to a pattern in electoral participation of women. First, women in a majority of cases were elected to reserved seats. Their election to the posts of president and vice-president was also determined by the reservation of seats.[5] Second, five years as members in local government did not enable women to develop political contacts or a political base that could have facilitated their continuation in politics. With less than three per cent of the women representatives contesting for a second term, the development of individual capabilities and overcoming constraints in political participation are important issues in the context of women's interests. And lastly, *de facto* politics negatively affected women's political participation, and also the scope of addressing gender interests.

The widely held view among representatives and the constituents was that general seats were exclusively for men. Although male representatives accepted the likelihood that women needed the reservation of seats to be represented in panchayats, there was disagreement on the percentage of seats to be reserved. They were of the opinion that the reservation of one-third of seats for women and the process of rounding off of proportions of reservation to different categories of women have resulted in over 40 per cent of seats in panchayats being occupied by women.[6] In their opinion the reservations in panchayats were excessive, and also restricted the choice available to the electorate. Quotas were seen as antithetical to an efficient system of representation where qualified individuals were elected to institutions of governance. There was a strong view that reservations lead to *de facto* politics where women were elected as proxies of male family members or elites. The widely shared perception among both men and women was that although women were elected to *panchayats*, men controlled the functioning of women representatives.

There were perceptible differences in the socio-economic profiles of the women representatives of the three-tiers. Among others, there were differences in their education levels and economic status. Women at the higher tiers were comparatively better educated than women at the Gram Panchayats. Women representatives in the Taluk and Zilla Panchayats were also from a better economic background. Variations in education and economic status existed between women at each tier. There was no instance where a Scheduled Caste woman representative got elected contesting a women (general) seat. Vokkaligas contested in both OBC and general constituencies.[7]

Gram panchayat women representatives were poorly educated, with 69 per cent having studied less than 6th standard. Twenty-two per cent of the women representatives were illiterate and 9 per cent were educated above the high school level. Among the Taluk and Zilla Panchayat members, a much smaller section was illiterate (seven per cent), while fifty eight per cent of the women had completed schooling and the remaining attended school for six years. Men were comparatively better educated and fewer male representatives than women were illiterate.

Low education levels of women representatives were perceived as a possible factor in women representatives' marginal participation. The t-tests show that there is a significant difference in the political interest levels and participation among representatives who were illiterate and those above school level (see Table 22.1). The political construction of women was closely tied to the family status, economic and political standing of the male members of the family, and not the individual capabilities or personal achievements of women. The representatives (both men and women) emphasised the importance of education in effective political participation. We asked the women about their perception of the importance of education in their functioning as representatives. Except for 4 per cent of the women, the rest of them considered being literate important for the representatives. Women who were illiterate stated that there were times when they felt greatly handicapped because they were not literate. While acknowledging the importance of education to improve their functioning as representatives, 40 per cent of the women stated that the main objective of reservation is to bring women into politics. Hence, educational qualifications need not be a criterion in the choice of candidates. Twenty-two per cent were of the opinion that there should be a minimum level of education as a selection criterion.

Table 22.1: Relationship of education, interest in politics and participation

	Illiterate/lapsed into illiteracy	*Above school level*	*t-value*
Political interest	23.63	26.85	-2.629*
Participation in panchayats	20.96	23.55	-2.951*
Number	57	84	

*Significance at 1 per cent

The views of elites who were also involved in the selection of the candidates are particularly interesting in this context. They were of the opinion that political parties could use educational levels as a criterion to select party candidates. Generally, the factors in the selection of candidates were the caste composition of the constituency, and the support the candidate was able to mobilise. Education was never a consideration in the selection of the candidates. The selection process rarely considered merit as a sole criterion. A minimum education criterion comes in for criticism mainly on two grounds. First, the low female literacy level in rural areas would disqualify a large section of women; and second, the level of participation was not always better among literate members. That there were better educated representatives who performed poorly should not, however, be construed as evidence suggesting that education is not a significant factor in political participation.

Gram panchayats had women representatives who worked as wage labourers. It was difficult for these women to be actively involved in panchayat affairs while simultaneously earning their living. At taluk and zilla panchayats most women representatives were from a relatively secure economic background. The economic status of the women candidates assumed greater importance in the higher tiers since it had a bearing on their selection as candidates, the exception being Scheduled Caste women candidates. Election expenses to Taluk and Zilla Panchayat seats were high, and candidates had to spend substantial amounts on political campaigns.

Barring a few representatives, women were unwilling candidates. They entered politics either as surrogates for male family members who could not contest as the constituency was reserved for women, or contested at the behest of male incumbents of political/ party positions. As a result most of them could not function independently. They owed their allegiance to caste leaders, local elites and party functionaries, without whose support they would not have contested and won elections. Such loyalty to the members of the elite did not in any way help the political careers of women members, as patronage was not extended to contest for seats not reserved for women. When women members were asked who would have contested if there had been a choice, most of them said that some male member from the family would have been the first option.

In the political ethos of the panchayats, women members had a less significant position. With a few exceptions, the interaction of these women with patrons, constituents, and officials was minimal. The level of participation can be gauged from the attitude of officials and constituents who were more comfortable interacting with the male family members rather than with women representatives.

Selection of Women Candidates

Personal attributes such as higher levels of educational qualification and an inclination towards political activities were not factors in the selection of women as candidates. The political construction of women was closely tied to the family status, economic and political standing of the male members of the family, and not the individual capabilities or personal achievements of women.

Gender difference in the election to panchayats was evident from the fact that the overwhelming majority of the women were elected to the panchayats only on seats reserved for women. The crucial nature of affirmative action to ensure women's election to the panchayats was evident in both Mandya and Udipi districts.[8] The position of the women based on their caste and class contributed to the variations in women's political participation. There were greater constraints on the participation of women belonging to scheduled castes, and often in the case of scheduled tribes too. There were no instances in our study where any Scheduled Caste or Scheduled Tribe woman was elected to a woman (general) constituency. At all levels of local government, there was little evidence of political parties supporting women candidates to contest general seats, which were considered as a male domain.[9] Nineteen per cent of the women elected in the 1993 Grama Panchayat election and 1995 Zilla and Taluk Panchayats elections wanted to contest panchayat elections in the year 2000. They could not contest in the elections as the party did not support their candidature to general seats (seats that are not reserved for women), and they did not have any chance of winning elections as 'independents'. In the case of 97 per cent of the women representatives their political representation was a one-time affair. The remaining three per cent had a longer tenure in politics as they had earlier either contested panchayat elections or had been panchayat representatives. The alienation that women experienced was because of their marginal participation in the larger political space, in political parties and civil society.

At least two factors were important in the selection process of women candidates: affirmative action and choice of the candidates. Women representatives of all panchayats stated that if it were not for the reservation system they would not have contested in these elections. They were sure that they would most likely lose if they contested against male candidates. The fact that there was no instance where women candidates were preferred over male candidates indicates that, given the social circumstances, reservation of seats was the only way to enable women to get elected to the panchayats.

In panchayats, one of the reasons for the limited participation of women was in the selection process itself. Women who belonged to the families of male incumbents in political positions/elites were often the first choice.[10] In the case of the constituency being reserved for Scheduled Castes/Scheduled Tribes greater conformity determined the choice. While selecting women candidates, their abilities and positive personality traits were rarely a requisite factor. The most common route to becoming a panchayat member was through belonging to a political family or being docile to the demands of male elites and faction leaders. The choice of candidates was a precursor to the inequality in local governance. There was little effort to select women candidates who were educated and were in a position to devote time for panchayat matters. Despite this manner of selection there were a few women representatives who acquired administrative and political skills and wanted to function without interference. This transformation from docile women to active functionaries was perceived as an affront to their 'mentors'. These women had to face a backlash as they were seen as jeopardising the interests of the dominant male individuals.

While selecting candidates for Grama Panchayats, the factors contributing to greater dependence on male members and/or party representatives was considered. These factors included women candidates who were economically backward; the numerical preponderance of the caste to which the candidate belonged; and the political background of the family. Women from the families of party workers who would not go against the views of dominant individuals were preferred. Also, it was mentioned that it was easy to keep weaker candidates dependent. At the taluk and Zilla Panchayat levels the selection of candidates was based on considerations such as political influence and higher economic status of the family of potential women candidates.

The selection of relatively weak candidates should not be construed as a lack of stronger women candidates. It only indicates that elites (male), political party functionaries and incumbents of political positions influenced the selection process. Such a selection process proved to be disadvantageous for women who may have been better candidates. Evidence suggests that male elites were concerned about ways of controlling power, even when they are not representatives of panchayats. Male respondents were asked if they would support a woman candidate who was assertive and independent. A majority of them were against supporting such candidates. Although less importance was given to the capabilities of the women, it was often suggested that the solution to avoid such a situation was to have education as an eligibility criterion for women candidates. It is an irony that male members of the elite who were involved in selecting weaker candidates also made this suggestion.

Political parties played a significant role in the selection of candidates at all levels of local governance. Women representatives automatically followed the political party affiliation of prominent male family members. Women from the families of party workers were chosen as candidates irrespective of their interest in politics. Political parties build their local base by ensuring that their 'supporters' are elected to panchayats. The intention behind such a practice was to have control over panchayat matters and funds and expand the local base of the political party. Ignoring their ability and interest in politics was an important factor in the poor performance of women members.

III

FUNCTIONING AS ELECTED REPRESENTATIVES

Institutional factors such as the reservation of seats and rotation of executive positions were factors facilitating women's representation. The change in the proportion of women in local governance, however, did not result in any corresponding transformation in the perception that 'politics is a male bastion'. The difficulty for women stemmed from the fact that they were new to the political arena and as a consequence inexperienced in politics as well as administration.

Very few women representatives had a significant role in the functioning of the panchayats. Further, even the executive position of president did not necessarily confer power on the incumbent (except in the minimal sense of mechanically signing cheques without having any role in the financial dealings of the panchayats)[11]. Power was related to the person who occupied the post of president, rather than to the post itself. In the panchayats that we studied, there were cases where the post of president was reserved for women in the categories of Scheduled Caste and Scheduled Tribe, and Backward Classes. Usually, it was the vice-presidents and officials who influenced or controlled the functioning of the panchayats in these cases. *De facto* politics, as can be seen in the three models reduced the power of the representatives. It was moderately significant when estimated for both men and women, and was significant at 0.05 per cent when estimated for women. In the case of men too it showed a negative relation to power although it was not significant. It was found that the *de facto* politics were high in the case of women elected for the first time to the panchayats, and it needs to be pointed out that over 94 per cent of the women representatives were first timers. In the power regression for women, being first timers significantly reduced their power. In the case of men it was not negative although not significant.

The question most often asked is: Are women members perceptive of the problems of women? Although women representatives were sympathetic to the problems women faced, there was considerable difference in the issues that were taken up at the three levels. At the Grama Panchayat, women were concerned with immediate and basic necessities.[12] The concern of women about the 'basic needs' before proceeding to address other issues was often not seen in the right perspective by male representatives. Women were ridiculed for limiting themselves to the water problem and not being concerned about wider issues.

For a majority of women, representing gender interests was untenable in practice since the elections are constituency based and the representatives have to take into consideration the interests of the constituency (which include different groups) that voted them to power. The problem here is not about giving more attention to the constituency's needs, but about the notion that pursuing gender specific interests is antithetical to the interests of the constituency. Although the institutional mechanisms do not give the elected representatives much choice to follow a particular course of action or to take up group specific issues, there is always a possibility to mobilise support on what should form a part of planning and budgeting.[13]

There was no effort made by women representatives to organise women and work for women's development. Women were represented in the Social Justice Committee and Village Education Committee at the Grama Panchayat. At Taluk and Zilla Panchayats they were represented in the Social Justice Committee.[14] There was a perception that unless mandatory, women members were never a natural choice for the Standing Committees. Women executives, because of their position, were chairpersons of different committees. As per the requirements each committee should have six members and no member should be in more than one committee. So women cannot be excluded even if the men so desired. Women were not usually the first choice for the Finance Committee. Also, women who were in the Standing Committees because of their executive positions had a token status. In the assessment of women representatives, over a period of time there was a difference in their understanding of the various issues concerning the functioning of panchayats. But the short tenure of 20 months for presidents and vice-presidents (in Zilla and Taluk Panchayats) was insufficient to acquire skills and use them.

Women in panchayats were entangled in identities (such as class, caste to a large extent and party to a lesser degree) and the manifestation of any particular identity of women is situational. They did not consider themselves as a group, where despite differences, common concerns can be addressed. The conditional and relational nature of the identities makes it untenable for women to acknowledge interests which are related to only one group of women. Representatives who belonged to different groups, whether political parties or caste or class categories, expected that their individual benefits would be adversely affected by an appeal to women's interests. They were of the view that their bargaining power would be considerably reduced if they took up gender specific issues which were not supported by other members or political functionaries.

The nature of participation of women draws our attention to the importance of the social and political environment. It was evident that various forces predetermined the nature of women's participation in panchayats. Women representatives did very little to overcome such a predetermined role for them. To begin with, most women members had a low self-esteem. They were of the opinion that men were better administrators. Dependence on men was perceived as inevitable if women were to be in politics. The belief among most women was that it was a disadvantage being a woman in male dominated politics, which made transition into the political sphere more difficult. One perception was that affirmative action alone could not enhance their status in politics. Women's political role was perceived as antithetical to the family and there was no attempt to balance both the roles.

Women's own perceptions about their limited abilities adversely affected their performance in panchayats. Women's political performance was assessed using the following indicators: women's assessment of how successful they considered themselves; their effectiveness in the functioning of panchayats, public relations; decision-making ability; and their role in meetings and committees. This was gauged through in-depth interviews and a scoring method where the respondents made a self-assessment of their performance. As indicators of success, women were asked to respond on their negotiating capability, political manoeuvring skills, conflict resolution, crisis management, information gathering, problem solving, organising ability, overcoming opposition and taking new initiatives (in the panchayat). They considered themselves as less efficient on these indicators, and the reasons for not being successful varied. A large section considered socio-cultural constraints as discouraging them from fully participating in the panchayats. A few of them attributed political inexperience as the important reason and were of the opinion that a longer training period might help them overcome their shortcomings. These perceptions were found across all the panchayats.

The indicators for effectiveness in development work include perception of the situation, prioritisation of issues, innovative initiatives and completion of projects. Some of these indicators were not found to be relevant in the case of gram panchayat members. The women representatives in Taluks and Zilla Panchayats admitted that male family members managed the panchayat activities on their behalf. Gram, Taluk and Zilla Panchayat executives considered that their lower effectiveness was related to their limited role in the panchayats since they were not allowed to function at all. However, these women were not particularly concerned that they were not involved in development work. They attributed preoccupation with their family, and administrative inexperience as reasons for keeping away from development work. There was a small section of representatives at the Taluk and Gram Pànchayats who took an active interest in development work. We tried to ascertain the traits that distinguished these women from others. It was found that they were better educated, willing entrants to politics, were keen to learn, and wanted to create an impact. Most importantly these women were interested in a political career. It was also a pertinent fact that their male family members were not politically inclined. The families extended their support to further the political interests of these women members.

Considering the importance of public relations in the political sphere an assessment of women representative's relations with other members, officials, elites, patrons, members of the upper tiers, MLAs and MPs, and the general public was sought. They considered themselves, as having 'good public relations' which according to them was the avoidance of controversies and conflicts. They tried to build a favourable image by adopting an approach that enabled compromise. It was in a way a reaction to the demands of the gender norms, which discouraged individualism. We also observed that, barring a few, the interaction of most women with officials, elites, and constituents was very low. Officials discussed panchayat matters with the male family members who in turn informed the women members. Similarly, the elites/patrons did not directly interact with women members. Such a pattern was seen at all the levels of local governance, the only difference being that women in the Zilla Panchayat were better informed even though they did not actively participate in panchayat activities.

The interaction or the lack of it should not be interpreted as only the shortcomings of women. It highlights the rigidity of the gender norms. Irrespective of the tiers, women were constantly concerned about how they were perceived by others and what impact that would have on their domestic life. There was no demarcation of their political and private lives and both were seen as related. It was considered improper and not respectable for a woman to visit the panchayat office unescorted. Both men and women held such a view. Since the officials and elites were men the constraints were even more. A few women members who ignored prevalent gender norms and practices were not 'respected'.

A related pattern was seen in the organisational effectiveness of women. The indicators used to assess their organisational effectiveness were awareness of rules and regulations, involvement in the panchayat activities and standing committees, participation in the meetings, budgeting and fund management, selection of beneficiaries and problem solving. They were, by and large, less effective in organisational matters. On indicators for decision-making, the role of women representatives was limited. There were various reasons for their non-involvement. For most it was their first term as representatives and they were politically inexperienced. There were a few women members who thought they had a choice whether to participate or not. The reason for such an attitude was the acceptance of the functioning of male family members on behalf of women representatives.

There were women representatives and executives who were competent and effective although their number was small. The self-esteem of these women was high and they were of the opinion that women can be good leaders and administrators. Being a woman was not a major handicap for them, and they were of the opinion that woman's active role in panchayats should get wider acceptability. They had a sound understanding of the functioning of the panchayats, financial management, and other administrative procedures. These women were regular in attending panchayat meetings. Their involvement in the activities of the panchayats was without any intermediaries, although at times they sought the suggestions of others. They had firm views on issues and they did not let others persuade them to vote against their inclinations. There were instances where women executives in Taluk and Grama Panchayats took the initiative to bring in changes that brought positive benefits to the panchayats. In one case, the woman taluk president issued cheques to the beneficiaries, to minimise commissions at various stages. Some at the grama panchayats and Taluk Panchayats carried out road repairs, electrification of streets, and made arrangements to lessen the drinking water problem. One of the Grama Panchayat executives was involved in organising women's thrift groups. Although this did not come under the purview of panchayats she was of the opinion that women should be more involved in group activities to be able to actively participate in panchayats.

An important indicator of the level of involvement was the lack of interest to attend panchayat meetings. Women representatives were neither regular nor interested to attend *panchayat* meetings. At the Grama Panchayat the sitting fee was the motivating factor for a few who attended the meetings. These were the only occasions when most Grama Panchayat women representatives went to the panchayat office. At taluk panchayats the reason given by most women for not attending meetings was the lack of transport facilities. Women found it difficult to get transportation to their village when the meetings were delayed (late evenings).

Not all women participated in the deliberations of the panchayat. Some of them raised issues related to their wards. Women at the three levels of panchayats participated in discussions only if they were related to their own constituency. The panchayat meeting was one of the sites where gender inequalities and differences came to the fore. The rigid gender ideologies were apparent in these meetings. Women who actively participated faced disapproval. The 'token' presence of women was appreciated and representatives who did not participate were cited as examples to emulate. In exceptional cases when the panchayat had an active woman representative, very little was done to encourage her. The irony was that it was the other women representatives not favouring active participation who sought to silence her. The problems of dalit women were even more problematic. Their active participation in deliberations was often considered offensive by both men and women. The dominant perception of how women should behave was always from the men's point of view. The actions and behaviour of women were guided by the dominant ideology that women should not talk back, contradict men, and do anything that might adversely affect family prestige. The panchayat role of women was entwined with 'womanliness' and 'family prestige'. The notion of 'honour' (*'gourava'* or 'dignity' and *'maryade'* or 'decency') was so strong that several women opted out of active participation.

Perceptions About Women Representatives

There were no major variations in the perceptions of women representatives across the Zilla, Taluk, and Gram Panchayats. Their perception was that women were neither confidant in their newly acquired political role nor did they make any effort to acquire administrative skills. Men and women respondents were of the view that women representatives were indecisive and dependent on men. This was attributed to the political and administrative inexperience of women. Women rarely took independent decisions, as they did not want to risk making a mistake and disconcerting their families. Women were considered as easily subject to persuasion when compared to men. Family, social, and political compulsions influenced the decision-making of women, whereas men were more influenced by their own political considerations.

The carry over of gender role expectations into the political life of women was evident in most responses. It was expected that women remained subservient to men within and outside family and such an expectation came from both the sexes. For women who did not attach importance to their political role (the number of such women being significant), the situation was not conflicting. However, for those representatives who wanted to work out a balance between their dual roles, the carry over of the asymmetry in the private sphere to the political realm posed problems. These women walked a tight rope, being fully aware of their limitations in a male dominated political culture.

It was also evident that gender differences were taken for granted in the participation on panchayat matters. Although there were several male representatives who did not participate in the deliberations it remained under an assumed unity of male experiences. Unless it was probed their performance was not evaluated. On the other hand, the political experiences of women were constantly scrutinised and linked to their domestic roles. Women's limitations in political participation were seen as the result of the demands of their domestic roles. However, the representatives (men and women) underplayed the consequence on the political roles of the gender asymmetry in the private sphere. The imbalance of power in the private realm affected the political experiences of men and women representatives in different ways.

The contradiction in being 'feminine' and 'politically shrewd' were explicit in the responses of the representatives. If women adhered to the gender role conventions as expected of them by their family and community, it would be hard for them to be politically astute. On the other hand, active involvement in the functioning of panchayats was perceived as unfeminine. Most women liked to be identified as 'feminine'. This is a consciously adopted strategy by many women representatives to avoid giving an impression that they challenged the prevailing gender hierarchies. For most women this was very important, as their political managers were men from their family.

Men considered it natural that woman should comply with the gender norms. The widely held attitude was that politics is not an appropriate career choice for women. The reason for such a belief was that politics involves spending more time in the public sphere, and greater interaction with men, which was not desirable. The lack of respectability of politics when it concerned women was evident in most responses. The solution to this in their view was encouraging women to follow a dependent role in panchayats. In such a situation women representatives did not fully relate themselves to panchayat achievements or problems, as they perceived their role as nominal. The alienation that women felt has other consequences too. Women executives in particular did not hold themselves accountable for panchayat mismanagement.

Women representatives reported the contradictions in the role expectations of male and female members. Since women did not display the behaviour or traits that were traditionally associated with politics they were perceived as not effective. The very traits that made men representatives successful in panchayats had negative consequences for women. Therefore, a predominant section of women representatives expressed a preference to blend with the gender culture in panchayats without questioning the asymmetries of power.

V
TYPOLOGY OF WOMEN REPRESENTATIVES[15]

A typology of women representatives has been developed on the basis of how women coped with the contradictory expectations on them in the private realm and the political role. Women representatives are classified as 'traditional', 'progressive' and 'in transition'. The paths women took during their panchayat tenure depended on their awareness of the matters related to panchayat management; the degree to which women accept, conform or reject the gendered segregation within the political system which also includes their understanding of equality; the extent to which they were able to draw a balance between their domestic and political roles; their ability to transcend the barriers in the 'male dominated politics;' and finally the socio-cultural expectation of women's role and priorities shaped their political participation.

Women who belonged to the 'traditional' category were the larger group (62 per cent). They accepted the prevalent gender norms about 'women's place' in the family, community, and society. They considered the total involvement in male dominated politics of panchayats as challenging the existing gender structure. Equality was perceived as opposing male authority within the family and community. Conforming to the existing gender structure and traditions was important because male family members often managed the panchayat functions on behalf of the women. These women were uneasy about 'effective participation of women', as they did not see the need for it. In their view, others (male members from the family) effectively carried out their responsibilities in the panchayats and their non-participation was not an issue.

Women representatives who were 'traditional' did not believe that as elected representatives and executives it is essential that they participate in the panchayats. They justified their non-participation stating that the male surrogates managed the panchayat functions better and there was no need for their involvement. Most women who belonged to this category contested because their husbands could not do so as these constituencies were reserved for women. A similar reason was attributed to women contesting for executive posts. Women presidents in all tiers admitted that they could contest for executive posts because male members were not eligible as the posts were reserved for women. The opportunity to participate in local governance, however, was not seen as a learning process. By being dependent on others, women perpetuated the asymmetric power relations in local governance. Thus, they also indirectly supported the gender structure that encouraged male dominance in politics.

These women representatives did not want to pursue a career in politics. Their awareness of the panchayat functioning was also limited. There was a modicum of unity among women representatives sharing the traditional viewpoint. They were extremely critical of women who were active participants. Among the women who were traditional, there were a few who had a fairly good grasp of the situation and who gave an impression that they could have been good administrators if the male family members and panchayat representatives allowed them. They justified their non-participation by giving priority to their family roles.

'Progressive' women members comprised hardly six per cent. Nevertheless, they were significant as a category because of their urge to participate in the panchayat with minimum support of male (family and panchayat) members. They did not like being passive spectators in the panchayat management. They were clear about their dual roles and were able to balance both. These women were aware of the disadvantages of being a woman in the political sphere. There were certain common features among these women. What distinguished them from other women was that while identifying the reasons for women's subordinate position they simultaneously tried to overcome them. These women were keen to contest future elections and considered politics as a possible career. They had the support of their families to pursue a career in politics.

Women who were unconventional and progressive succeeded in making a dent in the stereotypical image of women representatives, i.e., being docile and compliant. They were analytical and reflective in describing what differentiated men and women in the participation process. The differences in decision-making between men and women were attributed to earlier gender inequalities in panchayats. Women's approach concerning various issues was perceived as unprofessional, less calculative, and sometimes emotional. Women were considered as over cautious in the panchayats because they were more concerned about how they were perceived by others. Women's limitation in grasping the implications of their decisions was the reason for taking the help of male members. These women tried to overcome these shortcomings.

'Progressive' women representatives were of the opinion that awareness of their disadvantaged position was important to overcome their difficulties. Although in most cases they lacked the support of other women members, they did not like the idea of just 'being there'. It was a painful realisation for these women that the traits of independence and assertiveness of women representatives were not always accepted. Women presidents at Grama Panchayat and Taluk Panchayats had unpleasant experiences of their patrons (male politicians) trying to weaken their position by bringing in a motion of no-confidence against them. Their experience of non co-operation from both men and women representatives made them realise that idealism is not always practical.

Having recognised the inequalities in panchayat politics these women evolved strategies to overcome them. Some of their strategies were: developing contacts with powerful patrons and acquiring administrative skills. Although they realise the vital role of patrons in their political career they do not want to succumb to the often-generalised powerlessness of women. They made an effort to contest the stereotypes of women representatives being passive. Unlike the traditional women, progressive women gave importance to their identity as panchayat members. In the process, some of them were perceived as defying the norms of womanhood. By attaching equal importance to their political role they often risked being branded as unfeminine. Non-compliance of these members to the gender structure within the panchayat was perceived as contesting male authority. The backlash was evident in three cases where women resisted male dominance. Women presidents were usually pressurised through male family members to support the dominant members. In the event that these women held an independent view there was a possibility that they would face a no-confidence motion and lose their post.

Representatives 'in transition' (32%) were an ambiguous category. They were of the opinion that being a woman was a disadvantage in politics and were pessimistic about the future of women in panchayats. The ideal situation for them would be equality of power among men and women in local governance. Although they owed their presence in panchayats to the reservation policy, they also pointed out its disadvantages. They considered reservations as one of the reasons for women being perceived as less competent and as secondary members.

The dilemma between the primacy of domestic and panchayat roles was also evident. These representatives were from families that discouraged their active participation. A nominal representation of these women was acceptable to their families, but they did not support active participation. These women were unhappy about the non-cooperation of the family members. To them, encouragement from the family and community was an important factor in the effective political participation of women. Reservation *per se* would be of little help if there were no corresponding change in the attitude of the family and community. Since they did not see any future in politics, they gave priority to their domestic role.

VI

WHY DIFFERENCES MATTER

Gender inequality in panchayats is only one among the many constraints that were responsible for differential participation. Women representatives had to reconcile themselves to other differences such as the manifestation of caste and class in the public sphere. The way women's role in local governance was perceived and constructed was to a large extent also influenced by caste and class factors. To begin with, there were certain perceptible divisions among women representatives which were difficult to reconcile. First, in all the tiers of panchayats, women members were never united as a single group. Gender interests were not important enough to bring them together. Second, women perceived caste and class factors as having a direct bearing on their status and the power relations in panchayats. Conscious of these differences, they did not consider the interests and goals of all women as identical. Third, the perception of women members about these differences and how they dealt with them was distinct. The social reality of the plurality of women also included the reality of living as women. Each of these differences is discussed here.

Women representatives are broadly seen as belonging to dominant caste, backward caste, and scheduled caste and scheduled tribe. The problems of *dalit* women representatives were intense, as they had to confront not only structural differences of gender but also the hegemonic caste relations. The marginalised status of most *dalit* members was reflected in their scepticism that reservation alone will improve their position in local politics. They were of the opinion that dominant caste women representatives commanded respect because of their caste. The usage of language was also stated to be different, as women belonging to scheduled castes were addressed in a less polite manner. The identification of scheduled caste women with their caste group did not give them enough leverage to change the power relations in their favour. They were always perceived as different, inexperienced, and ill equipped for the post they occupied. The discrimination was particularly pronounced in the case of scheduled caste women occupying executive positions. In a few instances where these women (ordinary members) were 'independent', the backlash was evident. We found that the male respondents used abusive language while referring to these women.

The significance of caste in political participation can be discerned in the entire process. It influenced their nominations, actual election, contesting for executive positions and participation. There were many instances where dominant caste and prominent family women who had no noticeable attributes that distinguished them from others, succeeded in getting support for their candidature and won elections in constituencies reserved for women (general). *Dalit* women under similar circumstances found it difficult to secure candidature for such constituencies, sometimes even when they were better equipped. The problem could be the reservation of seats. When a seat was reserved for 'scheduled caste woman' there was less inclination to encourage a scheduled caste woman to contest for a women (general) seat.[16] In unusual cases we found women succeeding despite the caste disadvantage. Such women needed many things to favour them in order to win against women from a dominant caste.

Politically inclined individuals (men) who could not contest because of the reservation system consider women representatives as weakening the institution of panchayats, while the optimists regarded it as justice being done to those who were hitherto kept out of the realm of political power. Although they were disappointed at the inequality of power sharing, the women representatives from disadvantaged sections were optimistic about the statutory provision to effect their inclusion. They expected upward social mobility for the group over a period of time.

The experience of inequalities in the panchayat influenced the relations among women representatives in panchayats. It is a paradox that identifying these concrete differences did not unite members belonging to marginalized castes into a single group. The division among the scheduled castes into 'left' and 'right' was one of the constraints in uniting them as one group. In an instance where a 'left' scheduled caste woman was a possible candidate, another woman belonging to the 'right' category was preferred.[17] The substantive differences between various castes, and the unequal status of scheduled caste women representatives prevented the challenging of the dominant caste members or structures of power. On the contrary, they joined different factions to consolidate their personal positions and maximise the profits of office even if it meant a subordinate status in the panchayat power structure.

The advantage of the convergence of class and caste positions that was evident in the case of dominant caste men was not seen favouring women. Although, in principle, all members irrespective of the social hierarchisation of class have an equal status as representatives of panchayats, there was considerable disparity in the distribution of power. An analysis of the data revealed that the weak members (from a participatory point of view) in panchayats often belonged to these disadvantaged groups. It is a possibility that the incumbents of higher ranked political positions would want to support 'weak candidates' so that they could have control over the functioning of panchayats (Inbanathan, 1999). The choice of candidates from the wage labour class and scheduled castes for reserved seats followed a similar pattern. Educated and assertive women of the scheduled castes were not preferred, as it would be difficult to get their easy compliance in the management of the panchayats.

This predicament of having authority and not sharing in the power was found to be common among both men and women of the wage labour class. These representatives interpreted the 'authority' and 'being there' as social mobility, which they perceived as the first step to achieve social mobility. Panchayat members belonging to disadvantaged caste and class groups attributed the 'outward equality' to their political status. The relatively higher caste members and incumbents in political positions allowed the Scheduled Caste members to enter their houses and there was less hesitation among those of his/her class/caste to visit the colonies of Scheduled Caste and wage labour members.

The consequences of such mobility were different at the Grama Panchayat compared to Taluk and Zilla Panchayats. This is because the economic disparities were greater at the Grama Panchayat than at higher tiers. Social mobility through politics was more demanding for some members particularly in gram panchayats. A woman gram panchayat president who had earlier earned a living as a wage labourer stopped going for wage work, as it was perceived to be below the dignity of her panchayat status. She intended to take up wage work after her term in the panchayat ended.[18] Male representatives were also emphatic that it would be difficult to accept as President one who worked in an occupation that was considered low.[19]

There were also other differences among women of different classes. First, most women belonging to the 'better class' had the advantage of the socially prominent status of their family, economic position, and political background of the male members of the family. On the other hand, women representatives belonging to the wage labour class had to spend a major portion of their time in earning a living. Second, the occupations in which these women were engaged were low in prestige. Third, most of the 'upper class' women representatives were there to consolidate the political position and power of male representatives from their own families. Women from the wage labour class were often victims of manipulations in local and factional politics.

There was no similarity in women's approaches in dealing with differences and disadvantages. Although women members perceived the differences, the idea of organising as a single group did not appeal to them. To put it in the words of one of the women members, "there is no benefit in collaborating with women who are generally powerless." Instead it would benefit them if they individually collaborated with powerful male patrons. Scheduled Caste women representatives expressed similar views. In the construction of political realities the importance of their gender, caste, and class identities did not matter to most women. Instead, most women found it advantageous to relate to identities such as the political party or the faction they supported.

VII

BEYOND PLURALITIES: POWERLESSNESS AND DEPENDENCE

Viewing women's success in local governance in terms of representation alone would be inadequate. As the foregoing sections suggest non-participation of women is a consequence of many interrelated factors. First, the socio-cultural constraints, which were, manifested in the gender inequalities, differences among women, and how they deal with their multiple identities. The differences pointed to the problems of women belonging to disadvantaged caste and class groups. The multiple identities of women and the resulting dilemmas contributed to limiting their participation in panchayats. Second, the constraints were also related to their multiple roles as women in private and public spheres. The significance of the private sphere for all women representatives resulted in the construction of an identity with non-political activities. Third, the individual constraints originating from their family background, lack of interest in politics and poor political abilities were factors that restricted their political participation. Women representatives more often had a weak orientation to 'power' and 'authority'; and adopted a greater willingness to compromise in their style of functioning, which did not help them to effectively participate in panchayats matters. Since women considered their presence in politics as a short-term one they did not see the necessity to develop administrative and political skills.[20] And finally, males in political and elite positions and dominant roles were responsible for women's limited participation. Women faced the predicament of having to be 'different' to fit the male dominated politics. The need for such a transformation was conflicting to most women representatives, as it did not have societal acceptance. Although nominal representation of women has been acceptable, their total participation is yet to find societal endorsement.

The social roles women performed in non-political areas (private sphere) promoted a value system that did not act as a facilitator in their political role. Women members found it difficult to comprehend faction politics and the intricacies of power brokerage. As they did not perform any decision-making role in community life, associations or other areas of civil society, they found it difficult to adjust to the newly acquired political role. Power equations in panchayats were perceived as between faction leaders, members of the rural elite, political parties, and male family members. The lower quantum of power for women members stemmed from within and outside family. Leaders or dominant members had a patronising relation with women members. To begin with, they encouraged women to contest elections, assuring their support to the women. However, the motive behind supporting their candidature was to place their own followers in the local institutions and thereby control panchayat activities. Although not stated, the precondition of extending support was that the woman representative would accommodate the interests of the dominant member/and or local leader who supported her candidature. The economic and social status of the women representatives also determined how far the 'mentors' would go to get the work done their way. The powerlessness arising out of such a situation also contributed to women refraining from participation.

Another source of power inequality was from within the family itself. Women were supported because male family members could not contest elections as the constituency was reserved. The motive was similar as in the case of patrons. Men were interested in politics and wanted to have say in the functioning of the panchayats. Although they may claim legitimacy based on their wife's/mother's membership to be involved in panchayat affairs, it was not in the interest of women's status or local governance. Most women neither found such a situation disturbing nor did they perceive it as powerlessness. They considered men's involvement as benefiting the panchayats since their performance was better. While it was loyalty to patrons that made women accept the powerlessness, it was political aspirations of male family members that made them compromise on their own (women's) political career. They were relieved that they did not have the burden of the political role. Power was not considered as forfeited as it was within the family. The notion of 'individuality' or 'I' was not important in the evolution of 'political women' in local governance. They thought and acted in terms of 'we' which represents the family, political party, faction leaders, and others. Women members are yet to progress from 'we' to 'I' which is important if they are to have a distinctive and significant participatory role.

The distribution of power indicated that women did not have any role in the decisions taken. There was a gender order that approved the role of intervening forces in decision-making and effecting the dependency of women. The practice of the husband or any other male member of the family being involved in local governance was tolerated and supported. A small section of women representatives expressed some unhappiness about their token role in the panchayats. But the predominant view and attitude of both men and women disapproved women's involvement in politics. Claiming a greater role invited a backlash in the form of no-confidence motions, allegations of corruption, and talking disrespectfully about those women. The gender norms and values not only discouraged participation but also located women outside the realm of politics.

To a certain extent, lack of resources to contest elections perpetuated the asymmetry in power relations. In the reserved constituencies, faction leaders and political parties supported candidates who lacked resources, which resulted in a dependency relationship. Contesting elections needed funds, which many could not afford. While supporting a woman candidate a crucial criterion was woman's pliability to the sponsor's wishes. A higher degree of compliance was one of the ways of getting support. When women representatives were expected to be a 'figure head' or 'approvers', their participation in governance was bound to be inefficient.

Women members did not want to transcend the gender norm in order to maximise their power position. Idealising their role in the private sphere was common among most women representatives. They considered their term in the panchayats as a transitory one and did not want to disrupt their family relationships. Men talked of women as all-powerful, and symbolised them as *'shakthi'*. The symbolic power, however, was a construct of the private realm. It was the perception of most men that women would be 'honoured' if they exercised their power in the private sphere. Exercising power in the public sphere or in politics would bring dishonour to women and family. 'Women power'—a power of the private realm was not seen as complementary to political power. The symbolic power ascribed to women was of an informal nature unlike the institutional authority that gives them more visibility. Men and women venerated the 'symbolic power' of women in the private sphere and justified male hegemony in governance and politics. In a social construct that viewed male dominance in politics as natural; women representatives have only two options. One, is to come to terms with the powerlessness despite having the authority, and two, to assume roles and identities that are germane to political participation.

A wider conceptualisation of women's participation should therefore recognise the constraints that women faced. In the process of strengthening the political participation of women, it is important to emphasise the two categories of differences, i.e., between men and women, and between women arising out of their social status. The differences in the positions of women have implications for women's disinterestedness and exclusion from the political power structure. We conceptualise that the solution to limited political participation of women lies in reducing these constraints and initiate ways to enable fuller integration of women in local governance.

This entails a change in the perspective that political functioning is thinking and doing like men. There should be a reversal from the stance that an active political role is unfeminine. The solution to gendering of the political participation as masculine does not lie in the mere entrance of women into local governance. The solution lies on an alternative discourse to authority and actual power sharing in local governance that would enable effective participation of women. It would mean that we should work towards producing a politics of honour and respectability that would enable the active participation of women in local governance, without being called unfeminine.

NOTES

1. The 73rd Constitutional Amendment enacted in April 1993 has certain important features such as the reservation of one-third of seats for women and reservations for Scheduled Castes and Scheduled Tribes. Reservations were also effected for the executive positions in the panchayats, i.e. for President. The subsequent Karnataka Panchayati Raj Act, 1993 in addition to the provisions made in the 73rd Constitutional Amendment also reserved one-third of seats for Other Backward Classes (OBCs). Karnataka has also made similar provision for reservation of seats for the post of Vice President in the similar proportion as that of the president. Some states did not provide for reservations in the post of vice president.
2. Scheduled Castes and the castes which in the past were stigmatised due to their low position in the caste hierarchy, and are predominantly among the very poor, and which are now listed in the government schedule for special benefits. Scheduled Tribes are the tribes which are among the poor, and also listed in a special schedule for benefits to help them raise their socio-

economic position. Backward Castes are those which are considered as economically poor, and listed as such to improve their position through government provided benefits.

3. This paper does not make a comparison of men and women representatives, and it does not suggest that all men are effective participants either.
4. Human Development in Karnataka, 1999, Planning Department, Government of Karnataka.
5. Through a recent amendment to the Panchayati Raj Act, Grama Panchayat presidents and vice-presidents would have a thirty-month tenure. Five of the gram panchayats studied had women executives i.e., president and vice president. At the Taluk and Zilla Panchayats, where the rotation system has been in force, the election to the executive position was conducted thrice during the entire five year term. Women were elected thrice to the post of vice president at the Zilla Panchayat. They were elected once to the posts of president and vice presidents at each of the selected taluk panchayats. Each president and vice-president has a tenure of twenty months. The conventional reservation principle for different groups works here too, and the post is not reserved for the same group for two successive twenty month terms.
6. The higher percentage of women in local institutions than the mandatory one-third of seats reserved for women was due to the rounding off of the seats reserved. For example, if one seat was reserved for Scheduled Caste it became a women's seat as there is a requirement that one-third of seats should be reserved in each category.
7. Vokkaligas (men and women) comprise 56 per cent of the Grama Panchayat seats in the district. *Source*: State Election Commission.
8. The rare case was a woman representative in Udipi Zilla Panchayat who had contested a general seat and won. It was a significant win because she defeated the other contestant by a margin of 2989 votes.
9. Although political parties were not officially involved in Grama Panchayat elections, their role was significant in the selection and support of candidates.
10. The term 'elite' is used in a broad sense in this paper. 'Elite' includes all those who occupied privileged positions in hierarchies, whether in terms of wealth or prestige (Aron, 1970, p. 154)
11. With the large proportion of illiterate persons among the representatives, particularly women, they had to give a thumb impression—making it even less likely that the women knew what they were endorsing.
12. It needs to be noted that the functions and money related to Grama Panchayats are local and on a small scale. The representatives therefore took up the problem of water supply (drinking water) which was limited to drilling bore wells. At the taluk and zilla panchayats, these issues were on a much larger scale and involving a much wider area.
13. This raises questions related to the autonomy of panchayats and whether local institutions always have to rely on the state and central funds.

However, whatever the source of funds, the members cannot do very much for their own group because of the top down planning.

14. Social Justice Committee for example requires at least one woman member in the gram panchayat. There is no such reservation or requirement of a woman member in taluk and zilla panchayats.
15. The typology developed at this stage is not meant to be restrictive of the possible patterns that might emerge in the course of the study.
16. And the same applies to the reservation of seats for women in general. Women were not considered as candidates for unreserved seats.
17. There is a social categorisation (not by the government) of the castes included within 'Scheduled Castes' as belonging to 'right hand' and 'left hand'. The castes belonging to the 'right hand' are considered ritually superior.
18. Wage labour was an indication of the lowest economic level. As such those who were in this position were not respected due to their poverty.
19. There were reports of similar instances elsewhere too. There was a press report about a gram panchayat president who was actively engaged as a sweeper, which was considered as demeaning to the office of president.
20. Such indifference can be better explained with game theory. If the game were an ongoing one, women would be interested to learn skills, develop strategies and even form a group. Since they see it as a one-time game (single shot one) it is a hit or miss kind of an approach. There is no long-term commitment that would sustain their interest in local governance.

REFERENCES

Afshar, Haleh (1998): 'Strategies of Resistance among Muslim Minority in West Yorkshire: Impact on Women' in Nickie Charles and Helen Hintjens, *Gender, Ethnicity and Political Ideologies*, Routledge, London.

Afshar, Haleh, and Mary Maynard (eds.) (1994): *The Dynamics of Race and Gender: Some Feminist Interventions*, Taylor & Francis, London.

Aron, Raymond (1970): 'Social Class, Political Class, Ruling Class,' in Marvin E. Olsen (ed.), *Power in Societies*, Collier-Macmillan, London.

Allen, Sheila (1998): 'Identity: Feminist Perspectives on Race, Ethnicity and Nationality' in Nickie Charles and Helen Hintjens (eds.), *Gender, Ethnicity and Political Ideologies*, Routledge, London.

Barrett, Michele (1988): *Introduction to Women's Oppression Today*, Verso, London.

Bradley, Harriet (1996): *Fractured Identities Changing Patterns of Equality*, Polity Press, Cambridge.

Charles, Nickie and Felicia Hughes-Freeland (1996): *Practising Feminism: Identity, Difference and Power*, Routledge, London.

Charles, Nickie and Helen Hintjens (1998): *Gender Ethnicity and Political Ideologies*, Routledge, London.

Charles, Nickie (1993): *Gender Divisions and Social Change*, Harvester Wheatsheaf, Hemel Hempstead.

Cockburn, Cynthia (1991): *In The Way of Women: Men's Resistance to Sex Equality in Organisations,* Macmillan, London.

Cunnison, Sheila and Jane Stageman (1995): *Feminising Union—Challenging the Culture of Masculinity*, Avebury, USA.

Einhorn, B. (1993): *Cinderella Goes to Market: Citizenship, Gender and Women's Movements in East Central Europe,* Verso, London.

Eisenstein, Z. (1993): 'East European Male Democracies: A Problem of Unequal Equality,' in N. Funk and M. Mueller (eds.), *Gender, Politics and Post-communism: Reflections From Eastern Europe and the Former Soviet Union*, Routledge, London.

Hartmann, Heidi (1986): 'The Unhappy Marriage of Marxism and Feminism: Towards a More Progressive Union,' in L. Sargent (ed.) *The Unhappy Marriage of Marxism and Feminism*, Pluto, London.

Hooks, B (1991): *Yearning,* Turnaround, London.

Inbanathan, Anand (1999): 'Decentralisation and Affirmative Action: The Case of Panchayats in Karnataka', *Journal of Social and Economic Development*, 2(2), July-December: 269-286.

Jones, Kathleen B. (1993): *Compassionate Authority, Democracy and Representation of Women*, Routledge, New York.

Lovenduski, Joni and Vicky Randall (1993): *Contemporary Feminist Politics*, Oxford University Press, Oxford.

Maynard, Mary (1994): 'Race, Gender and the Concept of Difference in Feminist Thought', in Haleh Afshar and Mary Maynard (eds.), *The Dynamics of Race and Gender: Some Feminist Interventions*, Taylor & Francis, London.

Mies, Maria (1986): *Patriarchy and Accumulation on a World Scale,* Zed Books, London.

Mohanty, Chandra Talpade (1992): 'Feminist Encounters: Locating the Politics of Experience,' in Michele Barrett and Anne Phillips (eds.), *Destabilising Theory: Contemporary Feminist Debates*, Polity Press, Cambridge.

Ortner, Sherry B. (1974): 'Is Female to Male as Nature is to Culture?' in M Z Rosaldo and L. Lamphere (eds.), *Women, Culture and Society,* Stanford University Press, Stanford.

Pateman, Carole (1988): *The Sexual Contract,* Polity, Cambridge.

Poornima and Vinod Vyasulu (1999): 'Women in Panchayati Raj Grass Roots Democracy in India' Paper presented at the Meeting on Women and Political Participation: 21st Century Challenges, UNDP.

Rosaldo, Michelle Z. (1974): ' Women, Culture and Society: A Theoretical Overview,' in M.Z. Rosaldo and L. Lamphere (eds.), *Women, Culture and Society*, Stanford University Press, Stanford.

Rowbotham, Sheila (1989): *The Past Is Before Us: Feminism In Action Since 1960s,* Pandora, London.

Segal, Lynne (1987): *Is the Future Female?,* Virgo, London.

Srinivas, M.N. (1987): *The Dominant Caste and Other Essays*, Oxford University Press, New Delhi.

Srinivas, M.N. (1996a): *Village, Caste, Gender and Method Essays in Anthropology*, Oxford University Press, New Delhi.

Srinivas, M.N. (1996b): *Caste: Its Twentieth Century Avatar*, Viking, New Delhi.

Subha, K. (1997): *Karnataka Panchayat Elections 1995*, Concept Publications, New Delhi.

Walby, Sylvia (1997): *Gender Transformations*, Routledge, London.

Weeks, J. (1990): 'The Value of Difference', in J. Rutherford (ed.), *Identity*, Lawrence & Wishart, London.

23

Party Politics and Functioning of Panchayati Raj Institutions in a Tamil Nadu Village

S. RAJENDRAN

Introduction

People centred civil society organizations make a considerable change in the traditional Indian societies. In fact India has a long tradition of community oriented voluntary contribution of physical labour for undertaking developmental activities. During the pre-independence era, the Britishers successfully involved the state-centred administration in taking up developmental programmes. At that time slowly but consistently the local communities were made to depend on the government machinery for the designing of development programme and subsequently implementing the same. The introduction of 'Top Down' (UNDP, 1993) philosophy for development made people disregard precious natural resources only to depend on the government for every sphere of activity and in the process this has destabilized the people's participation. Despite this community organizations including non-governmental organizations (NGOs) started either independently or jointly to develop rural development programmes and successfully implementing such schemes (Rajendran, 2004). Theoretically and empirically it is reported that voluntary agencies including civil society organizations have made considerable contribution to development across the world (Muttalib, 1987 and Brett, 1993).

Across the country after independence states favoured development programmes through their departments and some selfless organizations especially in the countryside joined hands with them on a large scale. However, people's democratic institutions that have been operating since centuries have considerably influenced the identification and execution of development programmes in the country. Over the years the Panchayati Raj Institutions (PRIs) have encountered a number of amendments to provide various provisions which enable the local panchayat members and office bearers to independently and confidently take-up development programmes. Similarly, both union and state governments provide financial aid and resources to PRIs. As a moderate provision, members of PRIs contest in party based elections at least upto taluk level.

As per the recommendations of the Santhanam Committee (1963) and Ashok Mehta Committee (1977) participation of political parties in the panchayat elections was suggested for better implementation of development works at grassroots level. It was felt that this would bring more dynamism in the functioning of PRIs and undertaking development works rigorously. Hence, for the first time in the Indian history, the panchayat elections were held on the party lines in West Bengal in 1978 and later the states like Karnataka, Andhra Pradesh and Kerala followed that suit. Empirical studies on the functioning of PRIs found that such system worked moderately well in delivering the desired goods at local level. However, there are issues like non-cooperation of opposition party members, wilful blocking of development works and so on which have been hampering development works.

In fact when a particular party governs a state government, it is extremely difficult for the chiefs (belonging to opposition parties) of PRIs to function smoothly especially on availing grants and sanctioning and executing crucial development projects. Secondly, the state government either put barriers or prolongs intentionally the sanctioning of development works, wherever the office bearers of opposition govern the PRIs. Thirdly, at local level, opposition members give resistance merely as their rival party chair brought development programmes, whether they help the stakeholders or not. Thus it is a herculean task to get resources, sanction development works and ultimately execute them successfully in the interest of the stakeholders—people. In this context it is worth examining the dynamics of party based PRIs and the present study makes a moderate attempt in this direction with two-fold objectives. Firstly, it is intended to examine the structure and component of the PRIs and secondly, to examine the development works initiated and executed with a case study.

Methodology and Data Source

Required data have been collected from the village panchayat office, president, ward members, village elders and block development officials. Wherever possible cross checking was done to bring down the bias of a particular source. Data have been collected for two periods i.e., 1996-2001 and 2001—March 2004. The present chairman of the panchayat under study was elected consecutively for two terms of the above mentioned periods. Comparative analysis for two periods would give clear picture in understanding the magnitude of the development works and other issues and hence it was decided to have information for these periods.[1]

The grassroots information was collected from Nadur—a village panchayat in Orathanadu block[2] of Thanjavur district. This village is the second largest in size (areawise) and located very close (10 kms) to Thanjavur town and only 15 kms away from the block headquarters of Orathanadu (village map). This village was selected mainly for the reason that the researcher had ground knowledge in the area and it is a large panchayat in the block. Since long the researcher has developed good rapport with the surrounding villages for field studies pertaining to livestock enterprise and well acquainted with the functioning of the grassroots organizations including PRIs and NGOs. This has helped the investigator to intensively and extensively probe the dynamism of party politics[3] and functioning of the PRIs in the village for executing the development works.

Relevant information was collected from the panchayat office in the village and some information was gathered from the block development office. A cross section of people like the panchayat president, ward members, village elders and people from diverse social and economic groups was also contacted for eliciting detailed information. Observation technique was used for getting information regarding the deliberations of issues in the village meetings and during the execution of development works in the field.

Profile of the Village

The village Nadur is located in Orathanadu taluk but has very close proximity to the district headquarters—Thanjavur. This is the border village to the district headquarters on the southern side of Thanjavur taluk. It has a population of more than 3500 as per the 2001 census and is the second largest in size in Orathanadu taluk. Very interestingly, though it is just 10 kms away from the district headquarters, this village has not been exposed to urban culture till recently. However, the laying of tar roads and the introduction of public bus transportation in 1989 has contributed towards adopting urban environment to a considerable extent. Not only this, the villagers have better access to health, market (for buying and selling) and entertainment today. The general profile of the village is given in Table 23.1.

Table 23.1: Profile of the Selected Village

Sl. No.	*Particulars*	*Numbers*
1	Total households	750
2	Hamlets	3
3	Population	3500
4	Voters	1900
5	Ponds/tanks	7
6	Public buildings	9
7	Schools	4
8	Ward members	9
9	Post office	1
10	Road length (kms)	12
11	Panchayat revenue (Rs. annum)	25000
12	Primary agriculture and credit cooperative society	1

Source: Village Panchayat Office, Nadur, 2003-04

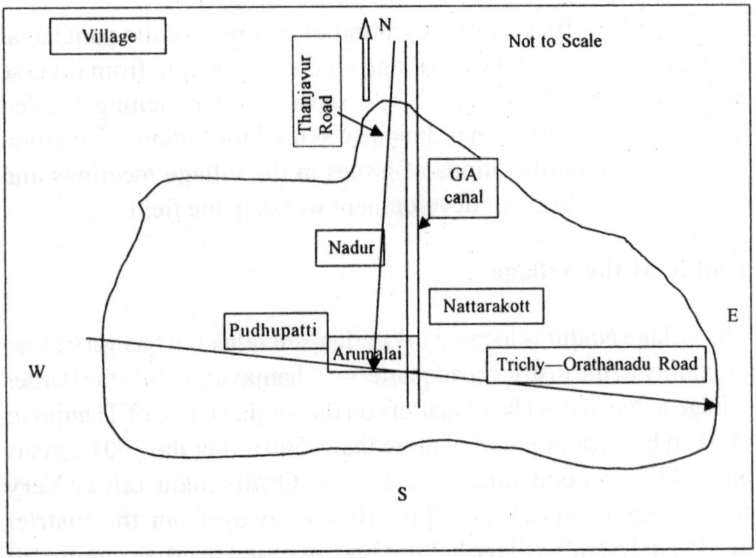

Though it is a large village, this panchayat has limited Common Property Resources (CPRs) to generate its own income. Three major village ponds, five temples, more than two dozens of fruit yielding trees and temple lands that generate a few thousands of rupees as its annual income. Besides, Nadur panchayat generates around rupees 25,000 from house tax, professional tax, water tax and library tax. For the past three years due to erratic rainfall and non-release of water from Mettur dam, the farmers could not undertake farming and no income was generated from private and lands of CPRs. Due to shortage of canal water farmers could not harvest even a single crop and for many farmers paddy crop withered for want of water. From dry land, villagers get income from mangoes and cashew and unfortunately, these crops either yielded less or failed to fetch good price due to glut in the market. This has forced the locals not to pay the taxes and hence the panchayat is unable to clear the mounting electricity bills of more than rupees one lakh. It is like any other Indian village that is rural in nature with farming, livestock and forest-based income sustaining the economy to a large extent. Livestock—sheep—rearing is a major activity at least in more than 25 households from all castes.

This supplements the farm income and also provides organic manure for crop cultivation.

Basically, there is no big political leader in this village though it has some local leaders from two regional parties—DMK and ADMK. Perhaps, this village does not have any farmer who has a feudal character in terms of land and land based asset holding. But there are a few rich farmers who own around 50 acres of land and many of the villagers including scheduled castes and others are landowners. They own both wet and dry lands. There are three major communities—*Kallars* (backward community), *Valayars* (most backward community) and scheduled castes (*Parayars* and *Pallars*). More than 90 per cent of the households from Kallar community own agriculture land and it is found that less than 10 per cent of the households from the scheduled castes own and cultivate lands. It is to be noted that while households in Kallar community owns their land, households of Scheduled Castes mortgage/lease in land from others in the neighbouring and own villages. A few households from Valayars own land and some of them work as agriculture labourers on others' fields.

It is interesting to note that though there is no higher educational institution in this village more than 50 graduates got their degrees in various disciplines. Three got their doctorate, five obtained M.Phil and around 10 received their master degrees. Many of these graduates entered into jobs in higher learning institutions like Regional Engineering College and the University. At the same time it is to be remembered that many of the old generation in this panchayat do not possess even primary education and perhaps, this would have influenced them to send their wards for higher education. The young educated of this village, albeit work elsewhere shows considerable attention in the development of the village.

This village has three hamlets—Natarakkottai, Arumalai and Pudhupatti. It has a middle school, three primary schools, a post office, two outlets for PDS, five middle level grocery shops, two *Anganwadi* buildings, panchayat office, and six water tanks. Very notably, two hamlets (Arumalai and Pudhupatti) are located very close to main roads that connect major district headquarters of Trichy and Thanjavur. By and large there is no major conflict either within a particular community or across communities or across hamlets on any issue. In other words people live harmoniously in the panchayat and this gives indication that with regard to undertaking development activities people support wholeheartedly.

Discussions

It was found that the present panchayat president belongs to DMK, main opposition in the state assembly and one of the most powerful and committed regional parties in the country. Though the DMK is a regional party in the country it played crucial role in forming coalition government at the centre and for this the DMK had to change its political ideology especially with regard to secularism in the previous general elections. This party unlike many regional and national parties has unique feature of periodically conducting party elections for its office bearers from village level to the state level. It shows that this party has been adopting the democratic principle of electing its members at various levels. The president of the Nadur village panchayat is one of the committed and long time members of the DMK. Recently in 2003, he was appointed a member of party's central committee. The present chairman was elected to this panchayat two consecutive times, firstly, in 1996 and later in 2001. However, he secured more number of votes (more than 1100) in the previous election as compared to the later one (secured around 910). In other words, albeit he does not have any corruption charges against him and did considerable development works during the earlier phase, he was preferred by a less number of voters during the second time. Surprisingly, the person who contested earlier belonged to ADMK (the main political rival in the state) also pitted this time and his popularity increased though he lost to the DMK member.

The chairman studied upto SSLC, aged 43 and belongs to fairly rich—Kallar agricultural family. He owns more than 25 acres of wet and dry land and he has his father, a brother (younger) and a sister. While his father and brother take care of the farming activities the chairman devotes much of his time in the village development works and party assignments. His family has the tradition of controlling locals including many labourers belonging to Valayars and SCs mainly by providing agricultural works on his farms under traditional Indian *jajmani* system. In many occasions, this clout helped him to successfully undertake development works without much hassle. The ward members of nine belong to the DMK (3), ADMK (5) and Congress (1) and this shows that he has to face the opposition members especially from the archeival—ADMK. Notably many of these members belong to his own community—Kallar and also found that some of them are his relatives that help the chairman to undertake development works in smooth manner.

The details of development works, undertaken during the previous and present phases as chairman of the village panchayat are given in Table 23.2. A cursory look indicates that the chairman could manage to mobilize resources on a large scale during the previous regime, when his party—DMK—was in power in the state. Also due to his strong clout with the officials, taluk and district panchayat council members, ward members and villagers he could do more development works[4]. This is mainly due to the reason that the ADMK government is hesitant to allocate and release funds (due to resource constraint and political unwillingness) to Panchayati Raj institutions let alone the selected village panchayat under study.

During the first phase the chairman could do substantial development works and welfare based programmes in the village. He could successfully undertake these cutting across communities, wards and hamlets in the panchayat. Major among them is laying of roads and this helps the villagers to transport the agriculture products from the fields to their homes without difficulty. In other words, laying of roads, and connecting the fields with village roads, gave fillip to the villagers to undertake their agriculture activities. Such roads were either mud filled or gravel filled and were not in usable form earlier.

To lay the roads, state government provided fund and also under union government's special programme cement road was laid for a colony belonging to the scheduled castes—*Parayars* in the panchayat. In fact earlier there was no *pucca* connecting road to this habitation.

Table 23.2: Development works undertaken in the village

Particulars	*1996-2001*	*Since 2001*
1. Road length in kms		
(a) Gravel	1	1
(b) Metal	1	600 (meters)
(c) Tar	12	—
(d) Cement (meters)	100	—
2. Threshing floor	—	1
3. Desiltation of tanks	2	1
4. Buildings		
(a) Self-help groups	—	1
(b) *Balwadi*	1	—
(c) School	2	—
(d) Pump shed	4	—
(e) TV room	1	—
(f) Houses	50	—
5. Others		
(a) OAP (number of beneficiaries)	16	—
(b) SHGs (numbers)	12	12
(c) Electricity (high power line)	1	—
(d) Toilet (number)	—	1
(e) Free clothes (households)	700	—
(f) Power connection to huts (households)	40	—
(g) Ration shop (part-time)	1	—
(h) Bus service (routes)	2	—

Source: Village Panchayat Office, Nadur, 2003-04.

Another major development work was that the construction of group and fire-proof houses for the households belonging to MBC and SC. There were 15 group houses constructed for the SCs and 35 houses for the households of MBC and SCs. It is to be noted that none of these beneficiaries belong to his own community – Kallar, thereby the president is liked by other castes as well in the panchayat. However, when fire destroyed two houses, belonging to Kallars, the president helped the concerned households to get compensation from the government. More importantly, during the earlier phase, the primary school was upgraded to higher primary and for this the local MLA helped the panchayat in getting sanction. Now the school children need not trek five kms to get their education upto eighth standard.

There has been enough discussion and initiation to encourage forming of Self-Help Groups (SHGs) to create confidence in village business venture to promote economic development in rural India. In this direction with the help of the villagers and ward members, there were 12 SHGs each formed during two phases. However, during the field survey it was noted that the women SHGs function well as compared to men SHGs. Mainly SHGs meant for dairy enterprise is doing well in this panchayat and bank officials are convinced about the transactions of such SHGs.

Drinking water supply is crucial for PRIs to foster their track record for contesting subsequent elections and this panchayat was having drinking water scarcity. Realizing the gravity of the problem, the president undertook digging four bore wells and got pump set connections. Two bore-wells—one each—for socially disadvantaged groups—MBC and SC (*Pallars*)—were dug and this attracted the beneficiaries to a great deal especially women in the panchayat as reduced their drudgery.

In addition to these a number of other welfare-based works was also undertaken based on the needs and requirements without any partisan approach. Earlier only 250 beneficiaries were receiving free clothes during scheduled festivals like Deepavali or Pongal and the president with the fullest cooperation of revenue and block development officials, increased the numbers to 700. However, the present state government headed by the ADMK due to financial crunch as a policy stopped distribution of free cloths.

In spite of such successful development works there are a few aspects that could not be either completed in full or undertaken at all. For instance, there is a need for developing library in the village and it would not only bring awareness but also enrich the general knowledge of the locals. During the previous state government headed by the DMK, it started libraries in all villages in the state and this had not taken much root due to the problem of accommodation (building) and fund and the case study village is not an exception to this.

During the course of two phases, the present chairman of this village panchayat could do fairly enough development works. This was possible as admitted by the chairman, ward members and villagers due to strong cooperation of the locals despite a few conflicts (difference of opinion). These were enumerated in Table 23.3 and it clearly shows that by and large all sections extended cooperation. Except partial cooperation from the ward members of opposition parties there was sufficient cooperation from other quarters.

It appears that though the unsuccessful candidate from the ADMK for the village panchayat was defeated by the DMK man, he is either active in local issues or participates in the village panchayat meetings. However, it was pointed out that some of the villagers with vested interest and ulterior motive raise some issues

Table 23.3: Details of cooperation and conflict

Particulars	*Cooperation*		*Conflict*	
	1996-2001	*Since 2001*	*1996-2001*	*Since 2001*
Within the party	Fully extended	Fully extended	Not found	Not found
From other party	Partly extended	Partly extended	Partly found Not found	Partly found Not found
Within villagers	Fully extended	Fully extended	Not found	Partly found Not found
From officials	Fully extended	Fully extended	Not found	Not found
From other castes	Fully extended	Fully extended	Not found	
Within hamlets	Moderately extended	Moderately extended		
From the district panchayat council members	Fully extended	Fully extended	Not found	Not found
From taluk panchayat council members	Fully extended	Not extended	Not found	Fully found Not found
From ward members	Fully extended	Fully extended	Not found	

Source: Personal communication with president and ward members from Nadur Panchayat.

in regular panchayat meetings just to embarrass the president. At the same time while the president prefers to listen to the suggestions and constructive criticisms from the villagers often maintain maximum patience without provocation.

Despite this, officials in the revenue and block development offices extended their full cooperation during the project sanctioning and execution of the same. It is a common feature that unless officials are bribed sufficiently the work would not move and in the present case, it was pointed out that such practice was completely absent. Perhaps, the clean character of the chairman would have influenced the officials for not accepting any influence in the form of money. Wherever possible, the president used his influence to get the works done purely within the rule of law.

It was observed that the taluk panchayat council member, belongs to opposition—ADMK—is unwilling to cooperate with the president. According to the president, the post of taluk and district panchayat council members is waste and unwanted as the district and Taluk Panchayat chairmen and district development council have powers to allocate resources and sanction development schemes. In fact this would help the village panchayats to function smoothly.

There is a mandatory situation for the village panchayats specially to convene twice a year to hear the perception of the public on January 26th and August 15th. In addition to this, there are regular meetings where the ward members and villagers participate and deliberate. In this village panchayat, besides regular meetings, the special meetings attract persons who are employed elsewhere to provide their comments and observations, which have helped the panchayat to undertake development activities more rationally. However, many villagers and ward members revealed that there is poor participation of women to put forth their ideas. Even if they participate, they do not actively participate in the deliberations. The dynamic and young people of this village do show keen interest in articulating in the panchayat council not only issues of panchayat but also other aspects including these socio-cultural in nature. On many occasions like drought and floods, this section of the villagers, stood by the panchayat council for providing relief measures without partisan manner as confessed by a large section of the villagers.

Despite the fact that the two rival regional parties have some second rank leaders in the village they confine themselves to their party works without adversely influencing the development activities in the panchayat. However, if the rival political parties do think only about the welfare of the village there is enough scope for further developing it as a model village at least within the taluk panchayat.

During the filed survey it was observed that the local people sometimes either misuse or waste the resources like drinking water and CPRs. For instance, though protected water is supplied through taps, people do not take adequate care to use it rationally and water flows on the roadside. Similarly, some of the households got private tap connection for their houses and use the water for growing crops in kitchen gardens. This puts heavy pressure on the panchayat council to equitably distribute the precious water especially during the summer, when water table recedes drastically. Unless the people cooperate to use the water rationally the panchayat council would not provide it to all equitably and sustainably.

At times as reported by nature lovers in this village though saplings were planted on the common land, the locals do not pay much attention to prevent them from cattle grazing and hence the growth of such plants affected thereby the income to the panchayat. Strip plantations of local species on the roadsides and around ponds have been taken up only to be spoiled by the livestock in the village due to gross negligence of the cattle tenders.

Conclusion

Thus from the above discussion it is evident that the party based elections to PRIs have made some influence over the development programmes. Though village panchayat is exempted from party based elections, in reality it is other way round in Tamil Nadu. This is evident from the case study village. Also it is observed that when the rival parties respectively enter into panchayat and state assembly, there are incidents of misunderstanding and stalling of projects merely for political ends without considering the economic viability and social adaptability. It is found that if the panchayat leadership is free from corruption and nepotism, the officials support and encourage the development works, meant for the rural folk. The public in the Nadur village panchayat demonstrated maximum cooperation with the council to design and execute the development programs despite some differences from a few corners.

There are incidences where opposition members in taluk and district panchayat councils have helped the village president to get funds for development works. Also they extended support in the identification and execution of the project. However, there are few cases where the council members did not cooperate with the village panchayat merely for the pressure from the higher authorities like MLAs, MPs and Ministers, who belong to their political party. In the interest of the stake holders political parties should bury their differences while bringing development works. Also the villagers should extend full support to protect and manage the development programmes including the CPRs in their larger interest. Perhaps if the village panchayat council, taluk panchayat council, district panchayat council and the locals join hands for development works it is not difficult to realize the dream of *Grama Swaraj* of Mahatma Gandhi.

NOTES

1. During the first period the DMK was in power at state level and in later period the ADMK is in power.
2. Orathanadu is also taluk headquarters for the selected village Nadur.
3. The elections for PRIs are held on party lines for Municipal Corporations, Municipalities and Town Panchayats except for village level. However, in almost all cases the contestants for village panchayats identify themselves with political parties and the president of Nadur panchayat belongs to the DMK.
4. The elected representatives of state assembly and parliament belong to his party during the first phase and during the later phase only parliament member belongs to his party and assembly member belongs to rival – ADMK. It was noted during the field visits that there have been frequent tussles between the panchayat president and the present member of state assembly over getting development works and availing welfare schemes obviously for gaining ground level support.

REFERENCES

Brett, E.A. (1993): 'Voluntary Agencies as Development Organizations: Theorising the Problem of Efficiency and Accountability', *Development and Change*, 24(2):269-303.

Muttalib, M.A. (1987): 'Voluntarism and Development–Theoretical Perspectives', *The Indian Journal of Public Administration*, 23(3):399-419.

Rajendran, S. (2004): 'Non-governmental Organizations and Sustainable Agriculture Development', paper presented at the Sixth International Conference of the International Society for Third Sector Research at Toronto, Canada from July 11-14.

UNDP (1993): Human Development Report, New Delhi.

SECTION–V

THE EMERGING PARADIGM OF LOCAL GOVERNANCE

24

The Panchayat's Raj over Global Capital[1]

PRADEEP NARAYANAN

The Government of India adopted the New Economic Policy (NEP) in the year 1991 enunciating the process of liberalization, privatization and globalization of the Indian economy. There was a perceptible change in the relationship between the state and the market. The private investments began to be regarded as the engine of the economic growth. The State no longer held a monopoly position in terms of investments even in the infrastructure sector. There was a growing pressure on the State to withdraw from the business of doing business, as well as to stop policing the market. In this changed economic climate, the negotiations between the State and the Multinational Corporations (MNCs) became a crucial factor for the State as well as the community in general. The factors in the negotiations* included resources such as ground water, forest and land, which hitherto were under the command of the local communities.

During the same period, the historic Panchayati Raj Act, 1992 also came into existence. The Act devolved a few important powers to the local self-governments[2]. Hence, the negotiations disembarked into the functional domain of these local-self-governments as well. However, there is no built-in mechanism that could ensure the participation of the local self-government in important policy decisions that influence the negotiations. Therefore, the two

*Here onwards the State-MNC negotiations are referred by *negotiations*.

simultaneous processes of liberalization and democratic decentralization appear to be contradictory. This paper analyses the 'bargaining' models available in the existing development literature to show that, according to these models, the local government has no space in the negotiations. The case of the agitation by villagers against the Coca-Cola Plant at Plachimada, Kerala is presented here to strengthen the claim that the two main actors cannot ignore the power of the village community and the Village Panchayat. The paper further examines the feasibility of institutionalizing the Village Panchayat as the 'guardian of community rights' in the negotiations.

State-MNC Bargaining Models

Rational Bargaining Model

According to Streeten (1976: 298), the negotiations are of 'rational' nature. There are clearly defined upper and lower limits of the bargaining range for each actor. The bargaining range behaves in a step like function, where upper and lower limit of the range is determined by the special monopolistic advantages (Capital, Technology, Research and Development) enjoyed by the TNC and policies of the host country like creation of advantageous investment climate, guarantee against expropriation, political stability and rivalry between MNCs[3]. This rational model has two important presumptions. One, the host government has the power to negotiate and enforce the final settlement; and two the government represents the national interests of the host country (Nixson, 1988: 381)[4]. If negotiations are purely of rational nature depending on the respective endowments, the State should have an upper hand as it controls the huge domestic market, raw materials and skilled and cheap human resources and also the national economic policies. Despite, these advantages, the State (in most of the developing countries) has been unable to help itself obtain a good deal in the negotiations. Therefore, the model and especially its presumptions were criticized for being over-simplistic[5].

Political Economy Perspective of the Bargaining

Nixson (1998 : 381) argues that the forces other than the rational economic ones also influence the negotiations. Analysing the negotiations from the political economy perspective, Nixson indicates that there are underlying forces in the form of national capital which influence the negotiations, and therefore, the interactions are among the forces representing the State, the national capital and the foreign capital[6]. The existence of a very powerful and vocal lobby for globalization in the local capital represented by traders, industrialists and Non-Resident investors cannot be ignored. While the traders have financial interests in opening up of trade, the local industrialists find MNCs as sources for new business ventures[7]. Although, the model captures the role of the national capital in the negotiations, it fails to explain the apparent shift that has taken place since 1991 in the general attitude of the Indian Government towards MNCs, and the reasons thereof. It does not explain the influences of external forces on the negotiations.

Two-tier, Multi-party Bargaining Process

Ramamurti (2001:24) views the negotiations in the form of a two-tier, multi-party bargaining process. The tier-1 bargaining occurs between host (developing) countries and home (industrialized) countries through bilateral negotiations or through the multilateral institutions, and these negotiations form the basis for the tier-2 bargaining between the host countries and individual MNCs[8]. The liberalization of various regulatory norms and introduction of new incentives to attract FDI are the result of the tier-1 bargaining. Due to these policies, the State is already left with little to bargain. Further the State itself is no longer a homogenous entity. Various provincial governments provide 'competitive' concessions to MNCs in terms of cheaper access to natural resources and labour and greater returns to their investments. MNCs also play not only countries against each other, but also provinces against each other and derive multiple concessions. Along with reduction in tax rates, provision of tax holidays and subsidies, MNCs even get its primary raw material at concessional rate.[9] Incidentally, due to mergers and acquisitions happening among MNCs all the time, the ability of host government to pit MNCs against each other also gets restricted[10].

Shifting Attitude Towards Global Capital: A case of Indian State

The Congress Government, which implemented the new economic policy of 1991, lost the subsequent elections held in 1996. Since 1996, political parties of diverse socio-economic ideologies have been part of the ruling coalitions. The left oriented Communist Party of India (CPI) was a part of ruling coalition (United Front Government) along with many other socialist parties for two years (1996-1998). The Bharatiya Janata Party (BJP) with *Swadeshi* ideology led the ruling coalition for six years (1998-2004). After the 2004 general elections, the Congress Party formed the government again after 8 years. The new government was formed through an outside support of the Left Parties. Similarly, in all the states, the political parties belonging to diverse political and economic ideology have been part of the ruling establishment[11]. However, all through the changes in the governments at the centre as well as the states, the liberalization and globalization agenda that formed the basis for the NEP neither got derailed nor slowed down. The establishment did not deviate from the basic notion of the economic globalization. The 'necessity' of attracting and retaining foreign capital has been recognized and politically legitimized by these political parties.

The unhindered continuation of the policy changes based on NEP was construed by some as presence of a 'political consensus for the policy changes'. It was said that all the major ruling alliances since 1991 have unanimously carried out the national consensus of 'economic reforms' and globalization to attract foreign investments"[12]. However, if the election results are the basis for measuring the support of the common people for the changes, then the fact that the governments at central as well as state level were voted out of power in almost all elections since 1991 suggests that the people in general have shown their discontent with the policies.

Although the link between the loss of the ruling party in the election and its economic policies cannot be easily established, there is no substantive reason to presume that there is a 'political consensus' on the NEP. At best, it can be said that there is a consensus amongst the major political parties on these economic changes.

Irrespective of the presence or absence of a political consensus on the NEP, the apparent presence of a political consensus amongst the major political parties prevents the emergence of a credible alternative economic policy. The very adoption of the neo-liberal economic policies has strengthened the market forces, which cause the 'capital accumulation' need of the State getting the primacy over the need for the government to seek legitimacy from the people through a distributive nature of economic programmes. With the standard of measuring the achievements of government itself being the amount of foreign investment brought-in during the tenure, the elections result in mere rotation of ruling classes that favour the same economic policies, and as a result the interests of the excluded sections never get manifested in the policies.

Adding to that, in the new economic regime, all pre-1991 policies involving grant of subsidies and concessions were subjected to the feasibility and sustainability test in respect of the macro-economic indicators. While the concessions given to the industrial capital were construed as investments, the subsidies given to consumers and small producers including small and marginal farmers were considered as growth-distortions. The concessional loans given to farmers and rural artisans were curbed because of latter's inability to repay them, but the increasing NPAs owing to the non-repayment of loans by industrial forces were analyzed in a different platform of the economic sickness and the enhanced competition from the global economy. With such a policy system in place, the MNCs receive the support not only of the policies that favour the national capital but also of a major section of the political and administrative leadership of the State that favour the entry of global capital 'at any cost'.

The powerful multilateral institutions and bilateral donors played an important role in cementing the new attitude of the State towards the global capital. They react positively to the market-oriented policy changes, and thus strengthen the hold of the market forces over the political actors, while contributing to the erosion of the legislative and the administrative capacity of the government. The incremental policy changes emanating from the State appeared to be less of voluntary nature and more due to pressure from the donors, the three powerful multilateral actors[13] and the agreements[14], which have, in tandem, strengthened the bargaining power of MNCs (Ramamurti, 2001: 28).

The Synergy Model

The above-discussed bargaining models focused on the entry stage relationship between the State and an MNC and therefore assumed a conflictual-adverserial relationship between them. The models ignored the after-entry or operational stage relationship. Yadong Lou (2001: 409) examined the nature of 'cooperation' that exists between the State and MNCs. He incorporated sociological and strategic perspectives to the political economy analysis[15]. He argued that the cooperation between the two actors can create synergies in areas where the interests of the State and MNCs are compatible, for example both actors desire a speedier economic growth, a favourable investment environment and a better and robust infrastructure. It was felt that such an approach helps MNCs in fostering the adaptation and legitimacy to mitigate the burden of its foreignness.

It is also in the interest of the State to have a cooperation-based relationship with MNCs. Only then, the State can attract foreign investments in infrastructure sectors, where the public sector is said to have an efficiency problem and the domestic capital are reluctant to invest owing to the low levels of anticipated returns on investments. The State needs foreign capital to ease potential balance of payments constraints on the growth. The cooperation-based negotiations on the one hand will provide a greater scope for profit for the MNCs, and on the other hand will also strengthen the macro-economic parameters of the State. Therefore, the approach is said to produce a win-win situation for both the actors.

This model too rests on certain presumptions. The interests of the dominant elites represented by political and non-political officials in the government shall have to be identical with that of the State as an institution. The interests of the State as an institution also need to match with the needs and requirements of the excluded sections in society. The absence of the reflection of interests of the marginalized communities in the negotiations may lead to appropriation of profits by the powerful interest groups.

MNCs form informal network-based, personalized exchanges with officials in the political organizations and bureaucracy to safeguard operations during distress. This informal network actually results into a nexus among corporate officials, politicians and bureaucrats, which is the root for any devastating impact on the people[16]. The State will emerge a loser in the long run if the plights of the marginalized communities who do not have any institution to safeguard their interests are ignored. Such marginalized communities are forced to resort to agitations to safeguard their interests. They mobilize themselves. These movements start as localized, but could also become highly influential when they receive support from other influential actors such as the media, organized politics and other national and international advocacy organizations. A powerful movement can, at a later stage, jeopardize the operations of MNCs. Eventually, a win-win situation gets transformed into a lose-lose state of affairs.

The issue again reduces to the question how the marginalized people can participate in the negotiations. A case is described below, where a so-called successful negotiation ended in a failure for the State, the MNC and the local community.

Agitation Against the Coca-Cola Plant in Plachimada, Kerala[17]

The Coca-Cola Company established its bottling plant at Plachimada in the year 2000. Within two years of the company's operation, a couple of thousands of local inhabitants, mostly farmers, started organizing blockades and picketing outside the plant. They demanded the closure of the Plant. The agitators have at least four grievances.

First, they assert that the factory has come up at an arable land violating the Kerala Land Utilisation Act. Secondly, they allege that the Plant extracts more than one million litres of water daily. As a result, their wells have dried up. Thirdly, they have noticed deterioration in the quality of groundwater. Finally, they accuse the company of selling their waste to the farmers as fertilizers. The company, however, claims that it extracts only 600,000 litres of water daily. It argues that it has not violated any federal or State laws, but has instead installed an advanced rainfall harvesting technology. It says that the depletion of the aquifers is due to the 60 per cent fall in rainfall and that it complies with standards set by the Kerala State Pollution Control Board. The company also claims that local communities have welcomed their business as a "good corporate neighbour."

The absence of support from the organized politics did not prevent the marginalized people from organizing and building a mass-movement by gathering support from various non-State actors. Through continued agitation and mobilization of masses, the affected community was able to pressurize the local Panchayat to initiate action against the Plant. Finally, on April 7, 2003, the 15-member Perumatty Grama Panchayat Board decided not to renew the licence issued to the plant as the company was "causing shortage of drinking water in the area through over-exploitation of groundwater sources."

When the Kerala Government set aside the Panchayat's decision, the latter filed a writ petition in the High Court. On December 16, 2003, the Kerala High Court held that groundwater was a public property held in trust by a government and that it had no right to allow a private party to overexploit the resource to the detriment of the people. The Single Bench said that the company should henceforth be allowed to use only a quantity of groundwater equal to that used by a resident owning an equivalent area (34 acres) and directed the Perumatty panchayat and the state government to ensure that it stuck to this rule after a grace period of one month. Significantly, the court also said that the panchayat should not interfere in the functioning of the Coca-Cola unit if the company could find alternative sources of water for its use. The court also questioned the action of the panchayat ordering the closure of the unit and said that the panchayat could at best only say that it would not allow the company to extract groundwater and that the company should find alternative sources for its production requirements.

The State as the Protector of the Community Rights: A Case of Water Rights

It need to be understood that the State, through acquiring functions such as making policies, framing and promulgating laws, planning and executing projects for the welfare of people, has already contributed in creating an unequal power relationship between the State as provider and the community as recipients[18]. The unequal representation of interests of various groups in the political power gets reflected in the State's relationship with the community. It is not that the pre-1991 State had adequate representation of vulnerable communities. In fact, the domination of elites over the vulnerable communities was cemented through the process of the institutionalization of Welfare State when the rights of many a marginalized group over land and water were transferred to the State. (Narsalay, 2003).

Let us take the example of water rights. The Constitution of India lists 'water' as a state subject[19] and has allowed the state governments to acquire the power to legislate on issues relating to water. The growing pressures of irrigated agriculture, disputes between states with respect to sharing water, growing presence of private water supply lobbies and depleting groundwater compelled the Central Government to establish a Ministry on Water Resources and to adopt national policy on water in the years 1987 and 2002 (Narsalay 2003). The State formulated the National Water Policy (1987), which requires the "governing of water resources by national perspective"[20]. The policy, however, does not define what constitutes the national interest, which may be the welfare of the affected community or may be the necessity of maintaining macro-economic stability. Hence, the 'national interest' can be used to justify the priority that the State assigns to the needs of a multinational company. Further, the State has also retained the space for itself for altering the priorities in special cases. In special cases, the State can justify fulfilling the needs of the industry even though the villagers' need for water for drinking and irrigation remain unfulfilled.

The new National Water Policy, 2002, which came in the post-1991 era, emphasises the need for the involvement of water users association and local bodies in the operation, maintenance and management of water facilities[21]. It also encourages the participation of private sector in planning, development and managing of water resource projects. From the implementation of the National Water Policy 2002, it is clear that there is enough space for the corporate sector to claim control over water rights, but the role of the village community and local bodies in shaping the water policy and to effectively execute the principle of social equity in the region remains ambiguous as ever. Further, the State engages in the bilateral and multilateral platform for negotiations in respect of issues relating to water, but in preparation to the meeting, there is little involvement of civil society groups and local bodies in the decision-making process of the Government while deciding what to offer and what to request for in the negotiations (Narsalay, 2003:7)[22]. As a result, there is actually no mechanism in the hands of community and the concerned civil society groups to challenge and influence the negotiating position of the Centre in water-related issues at international negotiations[23].

Moreover, the Central Government sponsored policy environment leaves the governments of states with little option but to "embark on the project of corporatisation of water resources to showcase their progressiveness" (Narsalay, 2003 : 13). In the case of Sheonath River project of Madhya Pradesh Government, the decision of granting the right of extracting of groundwater to the company was taken without consulting local farmers who are dependent on the river for water and livelihood. (Shiva, *et al.* 2003: 25) The Groundwater Department of Kerala Government did not even assess the groundwater position in the region before the decision was taken, as it was not mandatory under the law (Surendranath, 2003). Such many decisions prove that the interests of the village community rarely get reflected in the policies and negotiations. In other words, the State has not been able to safeguard the interests of local communities.

Village Panchayat as the Guardian of Community Rights

The Constitution of India, formally, provides for the involvement of Local Governments in matters relating to water and land use by incorporating subjects like water management, drinking water, minor irrigation, land improvement and land consolidation[24]. In addition, different state laws provide space for the local self-governments to intervene in issues relevant to local people. But can the Panchayat exercising these powers, challenge the State-MNC cooperative bonding?

It was seen that the Perumatty Grama Panchayat Board, Kerala refused to renew the license of operation of the Hindustan Coca-Cola Beverages Limited.[25] This decision, it can be argued, was a milestone because of three reasons. Firstly, it was an outcome of a mass movement organized by the *adivasis*, one of the most vulnerable sections of the society. The movement that demanded recognition from the authorities of their problems was supported and organized by local inhabitants. Local and international NGOs working on rights-related issues joined the agitation later. There was little support from the organized politics, which are generally considered as facilitating force for mobilizing people in the pursuit of the power situated in the State. The decision proved that a community movement by vulnerable groups could be successful, working independently or even in opposition to the organized politics. Secondly, the decision is against Coca-Cola, a mighty corporate giant. The decision, in a way, symbolizes the assertion of the authority and control of local community over corporate power, and a warning to industry not to disregard the interests of the local people in their operation. Thirdly, and most importantly, the decision questions the authority and legitimacy of the decisions made by the State without involving the local government especially in matters regarding establishment as well as operation of the company located in its jurisdiction. Through such decisions, the village panchayat becomes a part of the village community rather than a mere extension of the

State to the local level. Even if it functions as an arm of the State, at least this arm could be co-opted by the mass-movement. In other words, under the pressure of the village community, the village panchayat can act independently of the higher levels of the government.

The key issue for a strong local government is the fiscal autonomy of local governments. Firstly, one of the ways by which the State retains control over Panchayats is through the control of fiscal powers and resources. There are legislative provisions for the devolution of financial resources to Panchayats either by devolving power to raise their own revenues through local taxes or by 'mandatory' grants from the Central and State Governments. However, various study of Panchayat finances suggest that their ability to mobilize funds is constrained by various factors such as low local revenue base, willingness to tax local voters, project-tied grants, lack of political will on the part of state governments to devolve revenue powers and a 'resistant' bureaucracy[26]. The share of its own revenue in total income of Grama Panchayat in Kerala declined continuously from 61 per cent in 1995-96 to 15 per cent in 1999-2000 (de Souza 2000:153). This reflects increasing reliance of them on the state government[27].

Secondly, a presence of very big corporate entity in a small village can at times make the village panchayat completely reliant on the company, as the company will be the highest single contributor to the Panchayat finances. For example, a decision of revoking of Coca-Cola plant's licence cost the Perumatty Panchayat a major portion of its annual income (Vallely, *et al.* 2003). According to the Perumatty Panchayat president, the company failed to explain even the amount of water being extracted by it (Krishnakumar, 2003). In all such cases, the ability of the local government to control the company is inhibited.

What about the inherent social, economic and political inequalities in the village community? Can the village panchayat transcend those inequalities? The Panchayati Raj Act, 1992 tried to address the issue of marginalization of hitherto excluded groups like women, *dalits* and *adivasis* through an in-built mechanism of their representation through reservation of seats for underprivileged sections[28]. Formal representation need not necessarily be an indication of participation, because factors like poverty and economic dependence of the excluded section on other sections prevent the former from enjoying autonomy even after getting elected into formal positions. Some commentators rightly view that the voices of *dalits, adivasis*, traditional fisherfolk and other lower level groups were buried under the apparently spectacular achievements of the middle level groups, communities and castes (Kurien, 1995: 2)[29].

There are a large number of cases where the male relatives of women *Panchas* (head) become the real Headmen. Similarly, there are cases where a person from dominant caste ensures victory for a particular lower caste person in the local election and runs a puppet government at village level. These cases of proxy-rules, even after a decade of existence of these institutions, are not exceptions. However, local government elections with reservations for hitherto excluded may be one of the best available institutional mechanisms to recast hierarchies in favour of excluded in a hierarchical society. The articulation of issues by elected representatives belonging to the excluded sections in Panchayati Raj Institutions (PRIs) and their participation is bound to broaden the agenda of the PRIs by including issues like reproductive health, education and drinking water that have major impact on the vulnerable. In the long run such participation will create alternative discourses and power structures. The fundamental transformation of the Panchayat from being the tool for the marginalized people to becoming the institution of the excluded sections remains as an important condition for protecting the interests of the marginalized people in the negotiations.

It is interesting that there are commentators who reject decentralization project for its anti-capital nature. The decentralization project is viewed as another strategy for the Kerala Government to continue to encourage the path of campaigns and mobilization by pressure groups advancing particular vested interests[30]. Such a step, it is argued by them, would reproduce the same political environment that is hostile to capital and entrepreneurs instead of addressing the issue of 'aborted- industrialization'[31]. The democratic decentralization might actually reduce the influence of vested interests and increase the loudness of the unheard voices of marginalized communities, but the meaningful involvement of the marginalized sections in participatory institutions necessitates a degree of empowerment of the hitherto excluded sections (Narayanan, 2003: 25).

A cooperative relationship between the State and an MNC, generally leads to a confluence of interests of political and corporate elites, who can through political influence and money power garner the support of dominant elites in village communities. One can also not ignore the social and economic inequalities inherent in a village community, which might not allow the community to project a united face against the onslaught of this State-corporate nexus, in case of exploitation by an MNC. Therefore, it can be argued that for a village panchayat to guard the community's rights over its resources, there requires an empowerment of the marginalized sections, so that they can contribute to the decision-making process. In the absence of genuine participation of all sections of society, the Panchayat functions as just an extended arm of the State. Hence, the institutionalization of village panchayat in the negotiations can result in protection of interests of marginalized communities, if certain preconditions are addressed.

Conclusion

Throughout this chapter, I have highlighted three main issues. Firstly, since the launch of economic reforms, the relationship between the State and MNCs is gradually emerging into a cooperation-based relationship and a relationship in which the State's bargaining power appears to be declining. Secondly, the decline of State's administrative and legislative capacity has an adverse impact on the marginalized sections of the society. Finally, the village panchayat, despite the mentioned constraints, appears to be in a better position to represent the interests of the community in the negotiation process than the higher levels of government.

It may be unmerited to generalize any conclusion through one case study, but this case has been put across to show that while focusing on macro-economic stability, the State is increasingly in loggerheads with the interests of the local community. The State of Kerala that is exemplified by the world community as one that has focused on demand-led development by facilitating political mobilization of vulnerable groups has been unable to assimilate the interests of *adivasis* as is visible from the case of agitation against the Coca-Cola plant. The decisions to allow MNCs to operate in a region are predominantly a product of in-camera discussions of bureaucrats, politicians and corporate officials. The events show that such decisions are not merely economic decisions. They are political settlements, in which every actor represents an interest group. Hence, in the absence of institutional actors who can represent the interests of marginalized communities, deliberations in an open public platform could emerge as a possible means for safeguarding such interests.

Despite the above-mentioned constraints, the institution of village panchayat, by virtue of its closeness to people and the vastness of its influence, appears to be an important political institution that can be used as a platform where the problems of the marginalized people can be discussed and negotiated *vis-à-vis* concessions to the industries. As discussed, the village panchayat can represent the interests of the poor only if the institution in itself is provided financial and executive autonomy from the influence of the higher levels of administration, and if the excluded section within the local community is sufficiently mobilized to influence the community decision-making process. There needs a degree of empowerment of the excluded for their real participation in the institutional framework.

The amalgamation of globalization and democratic decentralization is a difficult process because the aim is to see that the space provided for the global capital is not at the cost of the opportunity of marginalized sections to create a space for them through the democratic decentralization project. It would be difficult for the State to frame policies that could clearly demarcate the vested interest from the 'genuine' interests and then curb only the vested interests. However, that is the reason why the State should exist.

NOTES

1. This chapter is based on the earlier work of the author for the School of Oriental and African Studies titled "Institutionalization of Village Panchayat in the bargaining process between the State and an MNC" (unpublished).
2. In 1992, the Indian Parliament passed the 73rd and 74th Constitutional Amendment Act, popularly known as Panchayati Raj Act, making it mandatory upon states to set-up local self-governments at village and municipality levels and devolves powers to them in subjects mentioned in Schedule XI of the Constitution.
3. The model explains the negotiation as a rational process without giving due importance to the role of other actors.
4. According to Nixson (1988 : 381), the presumptions made by the model has been criticized by Streeten (1971), who question the will, ability and political power of the host government to bargain with/control MNCs. Lall and Streeten (1977: 221-222) also argue that the policies may correspond to particular dominant section of society and that the right policies will be adopted only if they conform to the underlying forces operating in particular LDCs.
5. Read Nixson, 1988.
6. Nixson (1988:381) argues that these three groups are neither homogenous nor they have identical interests.
7. It may be noted that when the Perumatty village panchayat, Plachimada, Kerala refused to renew the licence of the Coca-Cola plant, the local industry groups appealed to the state government against the order as they argued that such a step would scare away prospective investors. The Kanjikode Industries Forum, Kerala, India had issued statement on detrimental effects of the cancellation of licences of Coke and Pepsi. Read Gopakumar (2003).
8. According to Ramamurti (2001:24), tier-1 bargaining has weakened the hand of host governments in tier-2 bargaining.
9. For example, as a part of the deal between the government of Kerala and the Coca-Cola Company, the latter was given the right to extract millions of litres of groundwater everyday to produce its product (Shiva, *et al.* 2003: 25). The company draws water from the ground almost free of charge. The total cost for the Coca-Cola Company in Plachimada comes out to 2.25 paise (US$0.00047) per kg. for spraying and cooling, 3 paise (US$0.00062) per kg. for domestic use and 7.50 paise (US$0.0016) per kg. for processing (Ninan, 2003).
10. In an industry like Cola, where there is a global duopoly, governments have little power to play them against each other.
11. Although the communist parties have publicly been against the new economic policy 1991, the economic policies of their governments in Kerala and West Bengal were no different from the central government's economic policies.

12. Sheo Narayan Singh (2003), "Deconstructing the hegemony of the State: Dialectics of Domination and Resistance", NMML Monograph, p. 43.
13. The International Monetary Fund (IMF), the World Bank (WB) and the World Trade Organization (WTO).
14. The Foreign Direct Investment (FDI) was linked to the agendas of multilateral institutions meant for other purposes, such as development aid from the WB or loans from the IMF for financing BOP crises or negotiating trade deals in WTO.
15. Read Luo, Y (2001:401-419) analysis of the relationship between the Chinese government and MNCs taking the cases of entry and operation strategies of 131 MNCs in China. The author incorporated sociological and strategic perspectives to the political economy analysis on the Negotiations.
16. The synergy model perceives cooperation in a positive manner, and hence does not capture the role of corruption in an MNC's efforts to derive unfair and illegal concessions. For example, the Perumatty Gram Panchayat in the case of the Coca Cola plant in Plachimada Kerala had written to various departments of government on "unauthorized" functioning of the company such as its violation of Kerala Land Utilization Act, statutory provisions of Health Department, illegal drawing of electricity and for detailed study of the toxic sludge that the company has been giving to the farmers as fertilizer. Such gross violations cannot occur without the 'cooperation' of corporate officials with those in the administration.
17. See Narayanan (2003a).
18. In a democracy like India, there are checks on the state-authoritarianism in the form of institutions like legislature and judiciary, and processes like elections and litigations, through which people retain some power to check abuse of power by the government. However, it is also true that there are limitations in these institutions and processes, owing to which the State retains its position as an undisputed authority.
19. The List II of the Seventh Schedule of Indian Constitution lists the responsibilities of the provincial governments. The Entry 17 of this List is "Water, that is to say, water supplies, irrigation and canals, drainage and embankments, water storage and water power". This is subject to the entry 56 of List I (Union List), which provides power to regulate and develop inter-state rivers and river valleys in the public interest.
20. The Policy lays down priorities for water-allocation as "first priority be for drinking water, with irrigation, power, industrial and other uses following in that order" with the proviso that "these priorities might be modified if necessary in particular regions with reference to area specific considerations." The policy also seeks regulation of exploitation of groundwater with reference to recharge possibilities and considerations of social equity.

Read India, Ministry of Water Resources, *National Water Policy 1997,* New Delhi, available at http://wrmin.nic.in/policy/default4.htm

21. India, Ministry of Water Resources, *National Water Policy 2002,* New Delhi, available at http://wrmin.nic.in/policy/default4.htm.
22. Narsalay (2003:7) argues "Ministry of Commerce (Government of India) remained disinterested in consulting the Grama Panchayats who have been empowered and mandated by the Constitution to chart out the financial and the political character of development on issues like water."
23. The international negotiations are important because once an issue forms part of international agreement the legislative and administrative capacity of national and sub-national governments in respect of that issue gets reticent. With the constitutional recognition of the local bodies, ignoring the local body institutions in respect of matters allotted to them defies the spirit of the Panchayati Raj Act, 1992.
24. The Schedule XI of the Constitution of India lists subjects identified for devolution to the grassroots level government.
25. The Panchayat passed Ext.P.1 resolution on 7-4-2003, deciding not to renew the licence of the factory. The translation of that resolution reads as follows: "As the excessive exploitation of groundwater by the Coca-Cola Company in Plachimada is causing acute drinking water scarcity in Perumatty Panchayat and nearby places, it is resolved in public interest, not to renew the licence of the said Company". There were other similar actions by local governments in recent times. Pudussery Gram Panchayat in Palakkad district, Kerala revoked the water-use licence of the Pepsi bottling plant. Similarly, about one hundred Municipality Governments throughout India sought explanation from the Coca-Cola plant on presence of pesticide in its bottles within one week of the investigation report of Centre for Science and Environment, New Delhi becoming public. Pradeep Saha. Personal communication. Activist in Centre for Science and Environment, New Delhi. August, 2003.
26. See Oommen (1999:145) and Johnson (2003:22)
27. de-Souza (2000:154) prefers expenditure decentralization to fiscal autonomy "in the prevailing circumstances", but it could also be argued that such a step would make the local institution merely as an executive arm of the state to execute its programmes, rather than a self-governing institution.
28. As per the constitutional requirement, one-third of seats have to be reserved for women. The *dalits, adivasis* and the backward castes have to be represented to the extent of their share in the population. Similarly, the posts of Panchayat President and Chairperson have also been reserved for the marginalized people.
29. Kurien (1995) identified Dalits, Tribal people, and traditional fisherfolk as "outliers" to Kerala development experience.
30. Tharamangalam (1998) feels that the goals of mobilization and organized activities centred on extracting benefits from the patronizing state

government, due to which the government is unwilling to address long-term goals of the state like industrialization, and the activities of trade unions and political interference have undermined the efficiency of economic enterprises.

31. It is presumed that there is a nexus between the state and anti-capital vested interests. But it is not clear whether these vested interests include the interests of the vulnerable communities.

REFERENCES

Barlow, M. and Clarke, T. (2002): *Blue Gold: The Fight to Stop the Corporate Theft of Water*, New Press, New York.

Brown, P. (2003): 'Coca-Cola in India: Accused of Poisoning Lands', in *The Guardian,* July 25.

Centre for Science and Environment (2003): 'Analysis of Pesticides Residues in Soft Drinks', available at www.cseindia.org

Coca-Cola (2003): 'Coca-Cola India Addresses Water Issues at Kerala', available at http://www2.coca-cola.com/presscenter/viewpointsindia.html

de Souza, P (2000): 'Multi-State Study of Panchayati Raj Legislation and Administrative Reform', *World Bank Background Papers*, New Delhi. Available at http://www1.worldbank.org/wbiep/decentralization/saslib/Volume%20III%20Rural%20decentralization%20in%20India.pdf

George, K.K. (1998): 'Historical Roots of Kerala Model and Its Present Crisis', *Bulletin of Concerned Asian Scholars* (now renamed *Critical Asian Studies*), 30(4).

Gopakumar, K.C. (2003): 'High Court sets aside Coca-Cola's plea', in *The Hindu,* May 16.

India, Ministry of Water Resources (1997): *National Water Policy 1987,* New Delhi, available at http://wrmin.nic.in/policy/default4.htm

India, Ministry of Water Resources (2002): *National Water Policy 2002,* New Delhi, available at http://wrmin.nic.in/policy/default4.htm

Isaac, T. and Franke, R.W. (2000): *Local Democracy and Development: People's Campaign for Decentralized Planning in Kerala,* Leftword Books, New Delhi.

Jananeethi Report (2002): 'Amplitude of Environmental and Human Rights Ramification by the Hindustan Coca-Cola Beverages Private Limited at Plachimada', available at www.jananeethibulletin.org/archives/cocacola.htm

Jayaraman, N. (2002): 'No Water? Drink Coke!', *CorpWatch India*, available at http://www.corpwatchindia.org/issues/PID.jsp?articleid=1603

Johnson, C. (2003): 'Rights, Claims and Capture: Understanding the Politics of Pro-Poor Policy', *ODI Working Paper 199*, Overseas Development Institute, London.

Kaliyadan, R. (2002): 'India: Coca-Cola swallows villagers' fresh water', in *Green Left Weekly*, May 22.

Krishnakumar, R. (2003): 'On the Defensive: Coke and Pepsi', in *Frontline*, June 07.

Kurien, J. (1995): 'The Kerala Model, Its Central Tendency and the Outlier', *Social Scientist*, 23(1-3).

Luo, Y. (2001): 'Towards a Cooperative View of MNC-Host Government Relations: Building Blocks and Performance Implications', *Journal of International Business Studies*, 32(3):401-419.

Narayanan, P. (2003): 'Empowerment through Participation: How Effective is This Approach?', *Economic and Political Weekly*, 38(25).

Narayanan, P. (2003a): 'Invitation to Coke and Privation to Villagers' in *The Hindu*, October 8.

Narsalay, R. (2003): 'Who Controls Rights Over Water in an Unfolding GATS Regime? A Case Study of India', Paper prepared for the Research Project on 'Linking the WTO to the Poverty Reduction Agenda'.

Ninan, A. (2003): 'Private Water, Public Misery', *Corp Watch India*, available at http://www.corpwatch.org/issues/PID.jsp?articleid=7528

Nixson, F. (1988): 'The Political Economy of Bargaining with Transnational Corporations: Some Preliminary Observations', *Manchester Papers on Development*, 4(3): 377-390.

Oommen, M.A. (1999): 'Panchayat Finance and Issues Relating to Inter-governmental Transfers', in *Decentralisation and Local Politics: Readings in Indian Government and Politics*, edited by S.N. Jha and P.C. Mathur, Sage, London, 142-172.

Ramamurti, R. (2001): 'The Obsolescing 'Bargaining Model'? MNC-Host Developing Country Relations Revisited', *Journal of International Business Studies*, 32(1):23-39.

Roddick, A (2002): 'It's the Real Thing- Thievery and Corruption', available at http://www.alternet.org/story.html?StoryID=14623

Shiva, V. *et al.* (2003): *Corporate Hijack of Water*, Navdanya, New Delhi.

Singh, K. (1994): *Managing Common Pool Resources: Principles and Case Studies*, Oxford University Press, New Delhi.

Singh, Sheo Narayan (2003): 'Deconstructing the hegemony of the State: Dialectics of Domination and Resistance', NMML Monograph, p. 43.

Streeten, P. (1976): 'Bargaining with Multinationals', *World Development*, 4(3).

Subramanian, K.K. (1990): 'Development Paradox in Kerala', *Economic and Political Weekly* 30(37): 2053-58.

Surendranath, C. (2003): 'Coca-Cola: Continuing the Battle in Kerala', *CorpWatch India*, available at http://www.corpwatch.org/issues/PID.jsp?articleid=7528

Swaminathan, V. (2002): 'Indigenous People Launch Struggle against Coca-Cola', *Transnational.org*, available at http://forums.transnationale.org/viewtopic.php?p=4058

Tharamangalam, J. (1998): 'A Rejoinder', *Bulletin of Concerned Asian Scholars* (now renamed *Critical Asian Studies*), 30(3).

Tharamangalam, J. (1998a): 'The Perils of Social Development Without Economic Growth: The Development Debacle of Kerala, India', *Bulletin of Concerned Asian Scholars* (now renamed *Critical Asian Studies*), 30(1).

Vallely, P.J., Clarke and L. Stuart (2003): 'Farmers Fighting to Stop Drinks Giant', in *Independent*, July 25.

Venugopal, P. (2003): 'Plachimada: Water vs. Coca Cola', *The Hindu Survey of Environment*, 87-89.

25

Democratic Institutions in the Water Sector of Kerala*

A Case Study about Water Users Associations and Participatory Irrigation Management from Kerala Community Irrigation Project

JOS C. RAPHAEL

Participatory Irrigation Management (PIM) refers to participation of farmers at all levels and aspects of irrigation management. It can include the initial project formulation to all further irrigation developmental activities like construction, supervision, financing, resource mobilisation, decisions, operation, maintenance, conflict resolution, joint management with officials, monitoring and evaluation of irrigation system. The levels can be from the field channel to the entire system (Groenfeldt, 1998).

Irrigation Management Transfer (IMT) is another term used in this paper that refers to "a process of shifting a number of basic irrigation management functions from a public agency to a private sector entity, a non-governmental organisation, local government or to a local level organisation with farmers at its base"(Svendsen,

---

* This paper is generated out of author's dissertation entitled "Participatory Irrigation Management in Kerala, India" submitted as a partial fulfilment for the Degree of MSc Social Policy and Planning in Developing Countries", at London School of Economics and Political Science, University of London, 2000. Author is grateful to the comments of Prof. Peter Townsend and Dr. Anthony Hall of London School of Economics and to Dr. B. S. Bhargava of Institute of Social Sciences, Bangalore.

1997). For instance, irrigation management responsibilities can be shifted from a centralised government irrigation department or agency to a self-managed and autonomous local organisation controlled by the farmers. Irrigation Specialists of International Irrigation Management Institute, Colombo, Sri Lanka defines the IMT as "the expansion of the role of farmers and the private sector and the reduction of the role of government in irrigation management" (Vermillion, 1994). It conceives that IMT can reduce the government expenditure on irrigation system operation and maintenance while responding to the broader democratisation and privatisation policies and programmes.

IMT is attempted currently in many parts of the developing countries of Asia, Africa, Latin and Central Americas, and the Pacific. Efforts to this turn over began in USA followed by France and Taiwan between 1950s and 1970s. IMT became a national strategy in developing countries during 1980s and 1990s, with Chile, Peru, Mexico, Brazil, Dominican Republic, Haiti, Senegal, Mauritania, Niger, Zimbabwe, Tanzania, Sudan, Somalia, Madagascar, Turkey, Pakistan, India, Sri Lanka, Bangladesh, Laos, Vietnam, China, Indonesia, the Philippines and several other countries tried to adopt similar turn over programmes. This development change has been referred as "turn over" in Indonesia and the Philippines, "management transfer" in Mexico and Turkey, "privatisation" in Bangladesh, "disengagement" in Senegal, "post-responsibility system" in China, "participatory management" in India and Sri Lanka, "commercialisation" in Nigeria and "self-management" in Niger. In South Asia this reform is more of augmenting the role of farmers than replacing the role of governments in irrigation management as seen in the other parts of the developing world especially in Mexico, Turkey and China (Geijer, *et al.* 1995).

Irrigation Concerns

Seventy-three per cent of all water withdrawals in the world are for irrigation. In most developing countries irrigation constitute a higher percentage than the global figure of 73 per cent. In many countries the water is supplied at heavily subsidised prices and users seldom pay more than 10 per cent of operational cost (World Development Report, 1992). In India, irrigation accounts for 93 per cent of present gross water use and in Indian Punjab it reaches up to 95 per cent (Salman, 1997).

The total area put under irrigated agriculture grew threefold between 1950 and 1980 than from the past that resulted in the dramatic increase in the quantity of food grains produced especially in developing countries of Asia. In India, Pakistan, Indonesia, Philippines, Sri Lanka, and Thailand this development revolution is clearly evident especially with rice production. A massive agricultural output increase between 50 per cent and 60 per cent was recorded during 1960 to 1980 in the developing countries (Ostrom, 1992).

Donor agency emphasis on modernisation in the agriculture sector made substantial investment for irrigation dam projects. The World Bank alone provided nearly $ 12 billion in loans for irrigation projects between 1947 and 1985. Other bilateral agencies and regional banks have followed the same. However, the lack of sustainability of many large-scale irrigation projects in economic terms and several other related problems gave various starting troubles in the beginning. Timely water availability in required quantity at right locations is the primary need of a farmer and the large-scale dams are not always helpful to attain this primary need. Poor maintenance and lack of related inputs became the sickness of the irrigated agriculture (Ostrom, 1992). Eventually, the farmers who make use of water do not have any control on water available through the dams and canals. Rather irrigation engineers have the final authority on water and the irrigation sector continued to be governed by the irrigation agencies of the government (Uphoff, *et al.*, 1991).

The causes for disappointing irrigation sector performance generally are associated with under utilisation, poor performance of irrigation bureaucracies, poor system management, inadequate maintenance etc. (FAO-RAP, 1995). Then the missing ingredient i.e. 'participation' kept its promises in the irrigation sector too as a panacea. The countries like Philippines, Mexico, Turkey, India, Pakistan and Sri Lanka started to invite farmer participation in irrigation management. However, in the absence of essential pre-conditions of PIM and official commitments, the participation was rather rhetoric or manipulative participation (Midgley, *et al*., 1986). For facilitating the participation of farmers in the irrigation sector, Water User Associations (WUAs) were formed by government orders in many developing countries including India. The WUAs thus organised did not sustain and remained as organisations on paper, as happened in India and Pakistan. However, in some countries like Philippines, Community Organisers (social planners) were appointed by National Irrigation Administration (NIA) to help farmers and found successful. Inadequate leadership and management capacity was the problems for some WUAs and party politics afflicted on few others. Besides this, farmer participation arises only after the implementation of the project and not in the formulation stage of irrigation projects (Maloney, 1994). Thus problems engulfed with PIM are many.

Looking Back

Traditional forms of PIM were prevalent in India before British rule, for instance, *warrabandi* in North India and *kuhls* in Himachal Pradesh. The modernisation and advancement of technology in the last century embraced large-scale irrigation dams for water supply and power. In 1974, Irrigation Commission of India after learning the inadequacies with large-scale dams and irrigation management, recommended formation of Command Area Development Authority (CADA). As per this, 'farmer organisations' under the command area of medium and major dams were recommended to manage the irrigation systems. Later, National Water Policy Statement in 1987 repeatedly recommended the same farmer's participation in the irrigation management. It says that "...Efforts should be made to involve farmers progressively in various aspects of management of irrigation systems, particularly in water distribution and collection of water fees. Assistance of voluntary agencies should be enlisted in educating farmers in efficient water use and management...." (National Water Policy, 1987). However, the policy does not go much beyond this conceptualisation and the states are expected to evolve their action plans on PIM. Only few states like Andhra Pradesh, Maharashtra, Gujarat and Tamil Nadu pushed considerable efforts to move as per the policy recommendations. And in the other states of the country, still farmers either depend upon vagaries of monsoon or decision of irrigation bureaucracy who mainly control the irrigation water to farmers. Thus for the country, effective farmer participation in irrigation management is more of a need for planning a strategy to make use the optimum utilisation of basic natural resources through all other forms of capitals such as social capital, human capital etc. (Navalawala, 1995).

Kerala faces drought even after receiving average rainfall of 3000 mm throughout the state that tells the story of inadequate rainwater conservation practices in the State. There are 14 rivers that flow towards west to Arabian Sea and three rivers that flow to the east and several distributaries of the rivers cut across the landscape. As per the 1991 Census of India figures, 97 per cent of the total agricultural land is below one hectare. Average land holding of households is 0.34 hectare in the state. The fragmentation of land holding is being increased at higher rate in the recent years due to high population density and preference of the people for separate homestead-cum-agricultural plots. Such human agro-eco systems of habitat pattern are a peculiar feature of the Kerala state in comparison with other states in the country (Babu, 1999). These human agro-eco systems separated by compound walls normally consist of a house, coconut trees, kitchen garden, vegetables, pepper,vines, mango tree, jack fruit, tamarind and other wild varieties of trees. Houses within rubber estates and spice gardens are common in many parts of the state especially in the eastern hilly areas.

After Independence, so far 28 medium and major irrigation projects have been started and 14 among them were commissioned. Several mini projects also have been completed in the state and so far nearly Rs.1000 crores has been spent for this purpose. As per the statistics of 1990, only 24 per cent of the total arable land (250,000 hectare) has been irrigated with this amount (GOK, 1990).

Though the Kerala state made increase in the cultivable area under irrigation, it could not increase the production correspondingly. Similarly, irrigation water is mainly made use for paddy cultivation and the production of paddy remains at the rate of 1.7 tonne per hectare (GOK 1989). The studies show that even after supplying irrigation water, only four quintals of paddy could be increased. The main reason behind the gap is that the farmers who make use of the irrigation water are not involved in the management of either dams or any bodies' stand for dam water. Neither the bureaucracy who controls the dam water has much connection with usage of water. It is not enough that water is flown through the canals, but the water should reach the farm fields of farmers in time at right location adequately (Chackacherry, 1994).

The Command Area Development Authority was established in the state by 1986, through CADA Act that envisages the farmer participation in irrigation management. The Kerala CADA constituted a 3-tier management structure, which comprise of Farmers' Association, Canal Committees, and Project Committees from the grassroots to the dam project level. These organisations are made up by a Kerala Government Order and brought them under nearly 14 irrigation dams that cover about 75,000 hectares of irrigated areas. According to the state model, farmers' organisations are registered bodies under the Societies Act. The Committees of CADA system allows the membership from local governments and state governments at three levels. However, the CADA Act is so restrictive in which most powers are not vested with farmers' associations than the higher command area authority. Also, they are not allowed to raise their own finances (Maloney, 1999).

As per the statistics of 1995, 3431 farmers' associations have been registered in the command area of 14 major irrigation projects. The study by Chackacherry (1994) shows that these CADA associations are not functional other than for its namesake since the farmers do not know much about such associations to get involved in the activities. The study covered more than 100 associations and it revealed that though the farmers believe that working of water distribution has been improved, its reliability is not yet ensured and consequently output of the agriculture has not improved. Though CADA conducts several training programmes and seminars, 80 per cent of farmers interviewed have not participated in any of such activities. Community organising is a weak component in CADA. Inadequacy of co-ordination and departmental compartmentalisation within CADA system also have affected its functioning (Babu, 1999).

Odd attempts from State Agriculture Ministers paved the joint efforts of paddy farmers in the vast tracts of paddy fields in the form of collective action known as Group Farming. Also it can be seen as a modified version of traditional co-operative farming of farmers who own land in the vast low land areas with some state back-ups. Traditional social capitals of collective action known as Padasekhara committees for purchasing pump sets to pump water into the paddy fields during summer and pump out the rain water from logged areas, is also seen in many parts of the state. Kerala Community Irrigation Project (KCIP) aided by The Netherlands government and Minor Irrigation project implemented with assistance of European Union are the recent examples of attempts toward PIM in the state. KCIP focuses on cash crops and Minor Irrigation project exclusively is set for paddy cultivation.

It can be seen from the above discussion that PIM/IMT are attempted in many developing countries during the past three decades. Emphasis of overseas development assistance for stakeholder participation and social planning in several development projects are being tried for, including in India. One such attempt took place for KCIP and the relevance of participatory approach coupled with social planning component deserves attention. Hence, the present study intends to analyse the benefit of participatory approach of irrigation management from KCIP through a micro level study of a sample Water User Association (WUA). The sample WUA selected for this purpose is from Kurumal community that fairly represents the other community irrigation schemes under the KCIP. The study also focuses on how replicable is the participatory approach adopted in the project for social policy implications in Kerala State. And this objective is mainly based on author's own working experience in the implementing agency, a Kerala

Government Undertaking called Kerala Samuhya Jalasechana Samithy (KSJS), as Social Scientist for a period of 5 years from the beginning of the project.

The main concept associated with PIM is obviously "participation". The kind and level of participation reflects the degree of farmers' freedom in decision making of irrigation activities. Pseudo participation of imposed and centralised nature is quite common in the blue print approaches. During the 70s and 80s, manipulative participation in various development projects in the developing countries was quite common including in irrigated agriculture (Rondinelli, 1994). On the other side, there are projects planned by the needs of people and implemented by the people from the bottom. In such bottom-up approaches, interaction process with stakeholders are seen and there project planning will be modified with flexibility through the process of learning the contexts and needs. Such participatory approach is generally known as learning process approach (Korten, 1980; Hall, 1986). Ideally, the social planners would suggest the people-participation in the four stages of planning process as local people's participation in the project formulation, implementation, monitoring and evaluation. But in practice a combination of such four-stage participatory process approach and blue print approaches are seen especially in the donor aided development projects under government departmental set-up. Perhaps non-governmental organisations (NGOs) may be successful in practising the learning process approach by the help of flexible NGO procedures (Uphoff, 1991).

In the irrigation scenario, why participation? What are the potential benefits of participation? Why should the government be involved in irrigation? The answer is that farmers may not be able to make heavy investments in constructing large-scale multi-purpose dams for national interest whereas the government can do it with its resources, access, departments, agencies, trained staff etc. Then why to re-invent the wheel and ask farmers to organise to construct the dams? The comparative advantage of farmers is in the incentives to manage irrigation water in a productive and sustainable manner at field level with their intimate local knowledge that most dedicated government staff cannot equally offer. Similarly, while designing irrigation projects the farmers' traditional knowledge and the demand needs can be taken into consideration for better construction, maintenance, cost-saving and fine delivery (Groenfeldt, 1998). On the other hand, farmers who are on the verge of dire poverty cannot afford to divert resources to short-term or seasonal irrigation benefits for uncertain long-term benefits of dam constructions. Neither can a public official be expected to be assigned a project location for not more than few years with long-term commitment for improving capital structures at field level (Ostrom, 1992). Therefore the physical apparatus of an irrigation system and the social structure for its use are necessarily intertwined. If the projects overlook the social structure it may not be successful (Coward, 1991).

Another concept associated with PIM is 'management'. The management component of PIM can be divided into two models as 'traditional irrigation management model' and 'farmer initiative model'. The difference is that former is dominated by the state and bureaucracy and later is initiated by farmers. Traditional irrigation model comprises of irrigation engineers without any involvement of farmers whereas the farmer initiative model consists of social planners, agronomists and irrigation engineers with managerial role for farmers at the higher level in decision-making. This farmer initiative model is adopted in KCIP and farmers are managers of projects and not beneficiaries.

Uphoff (1991) assesses the benefit of participatory development in irrigation sector in terms of (i) efficiency (ii) equity and (iii) empowerment. According to him, better efficiency in managing the irrigation activities at field level is by the user organisations than the government irrigation departments. In the same way, equity consideration for all rich, poor, big farmers, elite, masses and tail-enders are seen when user organisations take the responsibilities to do so. Empowerment of WUAs and authority on water make the government less burdensome on the distribution and maintenance of irrigation systems. Evidence from Mexico and Turkey suggests that farmers can manage irrigation efficiently and cheaply than their predecessors when WUAs are empowered (Groenfeldt, 1998).

Water Resources Management Policy Paper of the World Bank enlists the benefits of user participation in irrigation management as follows: (a) better maintenance of irrigation facilities (b) spread of community cohesion and empowerment for related developmental activities and (c) reduction of financial and management burden of government in irrigation sector as its main benefits. It further adds that "in irrigation projects, user participation helps promote sustainability by ensuring that design choices and operational practices are consistent with local crop requirements and farmer capacities. Such projects are more likely to be valued and maintained by the local population than projects without these elements. ... Governments are finding that by involving strong WUAs in project management and fee collection at local level, they can use the capacity of community members to exert social pressures on their neighbours to pay. Equally, because associations-managed systems have a consumer orientation, they are likely to provide services and improve willingness to pay" (World Bank, 1993).

While discussing about PIM, the vital component of PIM i.e., WUA has to be carefully examined. In fact, WUA is the bedrock of PIM. The term WUA is used mainly in South East Asia. And they are known by different names in different countries such as farmer organisations (Sri Lanka), water associations/water user group (Nepal) etc. The WUA generally refers to a grouping of farmers usually in one hydraulic unit, command or irrigation district, with one formal body for the purpose of managing irrigation system (Salman, 1997). Farmer managed local and traditional irrigation systems can be found in almost every country where irrigation is important. *Zanjeras* of Philippines, *warrabandhis* of North India, *kuhls* of Himachal Pradesh, local irrigation systems of Tamil Nadu (South India), and Peruvian Andes are some of the examples of such social capitals (Putnam, 1993; Coward, 1991; Aggarwal, 2000) with mutually acceptable roles and undertaken responsibilities among farmers endowed with traditional local knowledge.

By the onset of modernisation and large-scale dams, the importance of such traditional social capitals (or call it 'original social capital') was ignored. Much later NIA in Philippines had ignored the *zanjeras* during 1970s (Yabes, 1993). Now the modern social capitals or scientific social capitals (author's own expressions) replace the original social capitals. The wave of various newly built user organisations and WUAs are some of the examples of scientific social capitals. The distinction is original social capitals are originated within the people for a common cause whereas the scientific social capitals are organised by community organisers/ village animators or extension workers or they are constituted by government order to implement certain government schemes with the help of the beneficiary group. No doubt, if there is no original social capital, some new form of social capital has to be created. Uphoff observes that "unless the intended beneficiaries are already organised and accustomed to involvement in formal development programmes, some procedure for introducing participation should be explicitly worked out. ... procedures will be needed to acquaint beneficiaries with the project from the beginning, to elicit their ideas and suggestions, to encourage and assist appropriate modes of organisation for institutionalising participation and to monitor progress so that changes in the approach can be made whenever problem arise or better means can be identified" (Uphoff, 1991). Moreover, project implementation is a social process that follows various rules and is conducted by individuals or people occupying specific roles in various associations (Coward, 1991).

Again the paper organisations or imposed associations by a government order are not enough to facilitate the farmer participation in PIM. These associations have to be endowed with powers, water rights, controls, autonomy and authority on irrigation water and related development sectors of agriculture. Recognition for farmer organisation and responsibility to raise local funds to manage its affairs are some of the other sets of pre-requisites of PIM. Enabling laws from the national government, byelaws and the political will to support the PIM will determine the quality of outcome from it (Maloney, 1994; Salman, 1997). The role of social planner as community organiser (Philippines NIA) and trained extension workers with social planning orientation (many other parts of the world) is also decisive in the catalysing process of community organisation (Maloney, 1994).

According to Ostrom (1992), crafting institutions for self-governing irrigation systems such as WUAs require skills in understanding how rules, combined with particular physical, economic and socio-cultural environment produce incentives and outcomes. Such rules must be devised, tried, modified and tried again, in building the institutional framework. Time and resources need to be invested in learning more about how various institutional rules affect participant's behaviour. Neither there is one best way to organise irrigation activities nor choice of institutions is one-shot decision in a known environment. Rather it is an ongoing investment in an uncertain environment.

The World Bank technical paper on Legal Framework for WUA—A Comparative Study" by Salman (1997) holds that for WUA to be established as a legal entity, there has to be a law authorising its establishment such as comprehensive national/state water laws. The National Water Act in Mexico, Water Resources Act in Nepal, 'Implementing Rules and Regulations on the provisions of Republic Act No.7607' on small farmers in Philippines are some of the examples of such laws. In India in the absence of such enabling laws other than a National Water Policy (1987), each state has issued or followed its own laws and regulations on water. For example, the state of Andhra Pradesh enacted 'Farmers Management of Irrigation Systems Act, 1997' under a big-bang approach for irrigation management transfer. In Maharshtra, WUAs are established and registered under Co-operative Societies Act. In Tamil Nadu and Orissa they are built through Societies Registration Act. In Kerela, WUAs are registered under Charitable Societies Act, 1955.

The second legal instrument for the establishment of WUA is the byelaws. The byelaws explain the basic facts and objectives of WUA, criteria for becoming a member, structural organisation and internal management of WUA, election of office bearers, rights and obligations of members etc. This legal entity status makes the WUAs capable of contracting, operating bank accounts and instituting and answering suits (Salman, 1997).

The third component of the legal requirement is 'transfer agreement' between irrigation agency/state and WUAs /users. As per this agreement the responsibilities of irrigation, operation and maintenance of certain part or some part of the irrigation system is transferred from irrigation agency to WUAs. Also it is an agreement of responsibilities between the two management systems.

Robert Chambers divided the relationship between state and users in irrigation sector to four types of irrigation management structures (FAO RAP, 1995). It starts from individual tube well to irrigation systems entirely run by government agency. In between there are systems managed entirely by farmers known as 'Farmer Managed Irrigation Systems' and those managed by irrigators' associations and government agencies commonly referred as 'Jointly Managed Irrigation Systems'. Nearly 20 years later, Groenfeldt (1998) explained this relationship between state and users under paradigms ranging from 'government does everything' to 'farmers do everything' as given below:

Paradigm 1: Government Does Everything

In Malaysia, the Department of Irrigation and Drainage operates and maintains the main and secondary canals. And the government sponsored farmer organisations undertake the activity of supplying water to individual farmers. Here, the farmers do not have the responsibility hence no management decisions are taken at field level. Largely, the situation in India is similar to it.

Paradigm 2: State Dominates; Users Help

In this case the state takes responsibility of operation and maintenance of major headwork of irrigation such as dam or river and the main, secondary and larger tertiary canals. And the farmer group that comprise of 10 to 15 farm families manage the water distribution and maintenance along the lower level canals with responsibility. NIA and community irrigation management of Philippines can be put under this category.

Paradigm 3: Users Dominate, State Facilitates

In some countries like Mexico, WUAs enter contractual agreement with irrigation associations for the provision of water facilities and services. The National Water Commission of Mexico does the major works of dam and main canals. WUAs employ their own technical staff for the management of secondary and tertiary levels of the canal networks. Farmers approach WUAs for water and paying fees. A small portion of fees is passed to National Water Commission.

The other part of the fact that Mexico's approach to WUAs is a positive impact of structural adjustment programme in the debt crisis. In the mid-1980s, Mexico was under great pressure of debt burden and the irrigation maintenance works suffered major set-backs that were further worsened by anarchy in the irrigation department. Out of necessity, Mexican government created National Water Commission hurriedly with a mandate to turn over the management of irrigation districts to WUAs created especially for this purpose. This move of the government reduced the burden of irrigation activity from the government to the shoulders of farmers. It was then known as Big Bang approach in IMT. Andhra Pradesh State in India adopted the same strategy. Whereas many parts of the world mentioned above, followed learning process or gradual approach.

Paradigm 4: Farmers do Everything

In the hilly regions of Nepal, local communities construct and manage their own canal system for tapping the small streams. Such original social capitals in the irrigation sector are seen in many parts of the world as discussed already.

But in practice, powers, responsibilities and relationships of the state and users keep swinging between paradigm two and paradigm three. Groenfeldt asserts that "in between these two ends of the continuum is a very large grey (blue) area where a government agency performs some management functions and farmers perform other functions."

Kerala Community Irrigation Project (KCIP) is implemented with the assistance provided by the Netherlands Government. The overall objective of KCIP is, "to determine a replicable method for self-sustaining improved productivity and living standards for small and marginal farmers, and for women, through community management of irrigation schemes" (KCIP Inception Report 1994). The pilot project is initially confined to Trichur (Thrissur) District of Kerala State and is scheduled to run for five years. Based on the success of the project, it might be replicated to the other districts of the state. The project period started from 15th December, 1993 as per the records. But the project with nearly full strength of staff started actually by October 1994.

The project assists small farmers to form WUAs to construct and operate bore-wells (tube-wells) for their joint benefit. The project is implemented in the unirrigated garden lands where coconut, arecanut, banana, pepper, cashew and other horticultural crops are cultivated. The water from the bore well is pumped and distributed to each household plot with separate hydrants using plastic pipes. It was proposed for drilling bore wells in 210 communities, of which about 152 are likely to have sufficient yield for irrigation (10,000 litres per hour). In the interest of flexibility and efficiency, KCIP is implemented by an autonomous society, Kerala Samuhya Jalasechana Samithy, (KSJS) (local language version meaning Kerala Community Irrigation Society), which has been legally registered as a Society with District Registrar, Trichur on 17th May 1994.

An important objective of the project is that KSJS should become institutionalised and increasingly sustainable during the course of the project. In the same way it is envisaged that WUAs also should become institutionalised and entirely sustained by the farmers. Accordingly, project would directly benefit nearly 5000 families or about 26,000 persons.

> "The main importance of the project, however, is not the number of bore wells, nor the persons directly affected, nor the direct agricultural production increase, but the approach and the method" (KCIP Inception Report, 1994).

KCIP adopts Farmer-Initiative Approach to achieve sustainability of the irrigation system and its organisation, starting from farmer and ends at farmers with profit and better life style. Traditional Irrigation Management Model mainly managed by technocrats and still virtually a monopoly of the engineering profession even though it is a socio-economic activity. KCIP has learned from the experimental projects in India and from examples of farmer irrigation management in many other Asian countries, and so has adopted the farmer-initiative approach. KCIP is the first irrigation project in the state to be implemented with the help of Community Organisers—COs (Social Planners). "It is the vision of this Project that the farmer-centred approach, if successful, will ultimately be adopted both in groundwater and in other minor irrigation, and then in all irrigation in Kerala" (KCIP Inception Report, 1994).

The implementing agency, KSJS has three Wings: Water Development Wing (WDW), Agronomy Development Wing (ADW) and Social and Organisational Development Wing (SDW) for respective functions. These wings implement the community irrigation schemes with the participation of WUAs. Once a scheme is completed, it is handed over to the WUA and it has to maintain the system. The Consultancy Section of the project provides Technical Assistance (TA). A mix of local and expatriate consultants stationed at Trichur for nearly three-quarter project period of five years. Thus, regular consultation is provided to KSJS staff especially in the beginning part of project when the majority of the project staff is deputed from various Kerala Government Departments such as Ground Water, Irrigation, Social Welfare, Rural Development and Agriculture. Consultants for SDW and ADW mainly are local experts than expatriate consultants. Nearly one-third of the staff is recruited on contract basis. Project Director heads KSJS and Team Leader leads the Consultants. The Director is appointed by the Government of Kerala and is responsible for administration and implementation of the project through the three Development Wings. Enough provision for establishment, development, foreign study tours, training, vehicles etc. has been given under the project. The budgeted outlay for the project is about US$ 2.1 million.

Steps for Implementation

As per the steps of implementation of the scheme, the COs under the SDW identify the feasible communities suited for the implementation of schemes in the ground water potential zones located by the WDW. Once a feasible community is identified, an informal water group meeting is held in which all community members are invited to take part. Details and conditions of the scheme are explained and the same will be discussed with the farmers in this meeting. If conditions of the scheme are found acceptable to farmers, an informal water group is formed in the same session. The President, Secretary, Treasurer and four members are elected in this meeting. Nearly 30 per cent of the total members normally have to be women. This group is not a registered organisation. The water group is meant to follow up the works related with the drilling of the well. It is insisted that all farmer members have to attend the consecutive meetings held especially during the implementation stage. This assures the participation of farmers in the plan formulation stage.

The bore-well is drilled in the presence of community members with joint supervision of farmers and project staff of WDW. Once a successful well is drilled with sufficient water for irrigation, the informal water group will be promoted to a WUA in the second meeting in which office bearers are elected and byelaws and memorandum of association are discussed. WUA is registered under the Travancore-Cochin Cultural, Scientific and Charitable Societies Act, 1955. Baseline survey and Participatory Rural Appraisal are conducted after WUA formation.

After the formation of WUA, the scheme area is surveyed (Engineering Survey) and Engineering Section under the ADW prepares layout maps. Pipeline is marked on the location and materials required for constructing distribution system are assessed. Detailed budget estimates are prepared and discussed in the Community Planning and Budgeting (CPB) meeting. As per the norms of schemes, farmers have to share 10 per cent of the total cost. Farmers contribute their labour, cash and raw materials to the scheme. During the implementation stage, farmers' participation is also in trench making for the laying of under ground pipe lines, inviting quotation for the purchase of pipes and pump, construction of pump shed, application and availing of electricity etc. Monitoring meetings like mobilisation meetings are held if any lethargy is noticed. These activities bring participation of farmers in the scheme implementation. Farmer tours are held from the WUAs of implementation stage to commissioned schemes. Once a scheme is fully functional and commissioned, the staffs of the ADW conduct training on rotation and scheduling of water for WUA members. Based on the training and discussions held afterwards, WUA members finalise a schedule for water distribution. Further training is also given for irrigated agriculture.

Participatory training for office bearers of WUA is given by SDW, which is meant for the effective and sustainable management of irrigation system. The main content of this training is accounts and record keeping and co-operation and social relationships among farmers involved in the Participatory Irrigation Management. Participatory techniques are made use in this training. Monitoring and evaluation are regularly held in the general body meeting of WUAs, in order to confirm that farmer's PIM is sustainable. After commissioning the irrigation scheme, the system is handed over to WUAs and farmers manage the scheme completely. Neither irrigation engineers nor any government departments have power over these associations.

Micro Level Study from Kurumal

Kurumal community is located at the northern part of Trichur headquarters about 20 kms away. It is predominantly an agricultural area but the farmers do not depend wholly upon agriculture and majority of them are part time farmers. Arecanut, coconut, pepper, cashew and banana are the main cash crop grown in the area. Rice the staple food in the state is also grown in vast tracts of paddy fields. Men-folk work with secondary and tertiary sectors except few agricultural labourers. Womenfolk are either agricultural labourers or housewives. Kurumal community is a compact area of 8.5 acres that comprise the plots of 28 farmers. The houses in each plot are connected with water supply hydrant. Average land size in the community is 0.30 acre. The CO in charge identified the community as per the ground water potential indication of WDW in 1995. The CO and the interested farmers in the area visited all plots of the community and shaped a feasible size suited to the implementation of the scheme. After 'transects and group walks' and 'oral histories' (these tools of PRA are not considered as PRA in KCIP) with farmers, CO recommended the site for further feasibility from three wings of the KSJS.

As per the green signals of all wings, an informal water group meeting was organised in which all farmers had to attend the meeting. And in the initial stages of KCIP implementation, night meetings were conducted in order to facilitate the participation of all concerned farmers. The first water group evening meeting at Kurumal community was not successful due to the alcoholic addiction in the evening and consequent unruly nature of farmers in the evenings. This experience from Kurumal and few other sites defeated the notion of conducting night meetings in KCIP. The second water group meeting was conducted during daytime in which the attendance of farmers was made compulsory. After the successful second meeting, hydro geological and geophysical surveys were conducted to locate the potential bore well site. The participation of farmers was insisted during these surveys and their contributions were recorded to add up the 10 per cent share of the total cost. A bore well was drilled on 4-6-95 just before the rainy season at a depth of 112 metres. And after the rain, pump test was conducted in which an optimum yield of 12,000 litres per hour was recorded.

An official PRA exercise was conducted in the community on 21-3-95. It was conducted after lunchtime at a convenient time for farmers as well as to the official from KSJS. Since the period of conducting PRA was after the paddy harvest, all farmers took part in the PRA exercise. The tools used for PRA were community mapping and drawing of graphs. Drawing of graphs was common sense for farmers and not new learning for officials. Ironically, participatory meetings, transects walks and oral histories were not recorded as PRA in Kurumal community.

Community Planning and Budgeting (CPB) for Kurumal community could not be done in an appropriate way and as a serious implementation procedure. Since Kurumal was the third well drilled in the project, several steps and procedures were under trial and error method. This method during the pilot phase is a part of learning process approach of participatory implementation of irrigation projects. A joint bank account in the name of Civil Engineer (CE) and President of WUA was opened in a nearby Service Co-operative Bank. Engineering surveys and pipeline marking of distribution system with the participation of farmers was undertaken in the community. The baseline survey that includes various socio-economic parameters of the community was completed on 25-8-95. A WUA meeting was organised on12-9-95 in which the office bearers were elected and WUA was registered under District Registrars Office, Trichur. Installation of distribution system was completed by 15-1-96 and the irrigation system was commissioned on 31-3-96.

Thereafter, series of agriculture training and water rotation training were conducted for scientifically scheduled distribution of water, improved farming practices and cropping pattern. A pump operator was appointed from the farmers who have the responsibility of operating the motor, valves and allied accessories and a minimum salary is paid to this person. The total cost for the system is Indian Rupees 3,70,000 (nearly £ 5000). 10 per cent of this total cost was borne by the farmers through labour, construction of pump shed, assistance for surveys, stand post support, land for constructing well and pump shed.

Analysis on Benefits of Participatory Approach from Kurumal WUA

Kurumal WUA has conducted eight Executive Meetings and six General Body Meetings from 14-5-96 to 31-12-99.(Table 25.1) Nearly 90 per cent attendance was recorded in the Executive Meetings whereas it was 82 per cent in the General Body Meetings. Men and women farmers actively take part in these meetings. (Table 25.2) Several subjects have been discussed in the meetings such as hike in user fees, pump operator's salary, maintenance, and other related WUA members needs and problems. The data for the same was availed from well-maintained Minutes Book of the WUA.

Table 25.1 : General Body Meetings

Dates	*No. of WUA members participated (out of 28 total number of farmers)*	*Female*	*Male*
29-12-96	25	12	13
02-11-97	20	08	12
28-12-97	21	07	14
03-01-99	28	11	17
28-02-99	22	07	15
26-12-99	21	05	16

Source: Minutes Book of Kurumal Water User's Association, 2000.

Table 25.2 : Items discussed in the General Body Meetings

Items	*Nos.*
Hike in user fees	3
User fees	4
Installing lock for each hydrant	1
Pump Operator's salary	2
Election and change in the office bearers of WUA	2
Presentation of Annual Report	5
Insurance for Motor and Pump Operator	2
No hike for user fees	1
No hike for Pump Operators salary	1
Support for Women-in-Development forum	1
Leave for Pump Operator	1
Festival Allowance for Pump Operator	1
No increase in the number of leaves for Pump Operator	1
Payment of electricity bill	2
Tuition class for children in the corridor of Motor Shed	1
Maintenance of distribution network	1
Submission of Pumping time accounts	1
Starting Primary Health Centre – availing free land	1

Source: Minutes Book of Kurumal Water User's Association, 2000.

The records of Kurumal WUA show that Kurumal WUA has conducted annual general body meetings with 75 per cent attendance of its members with fairly adequate representation of women members. The WUA members have actively taken part in the deliberations of the meetings. User fees and the provisions for pump operator are seen the prominent issues discussed in the General Body Meeting as shown in the Table 25.1. The pump operator being a key person in the distribution of water at the outlets, the provisions of this position such as salary, leave and other emoluments have emerged dominantly from pump operator. Considering the increase in the maintenance cost and hike for pump operator's salary, corresponding hike in the user fees is reflected in the items for the discussion in the General Body meeting.

A brief summary of comparison between the result of baseline survey conducted in 1995 and an impact study conducted in the year 2000 reveals that families having the land area between 0.50 and 1.10 acre (25% of the total number of farmers) have either doubled or tripled their cultivation by new planting. The farmers having the land area between 0.25 and 0.50 acre have shown moderate success in improving their existing crops and planted new crops depend upon the availability of cultivable land for new planting, manpower available in the family and interest shown by the farmers for new cropping. Table 25.3 forty-three per cent of the farmers have the land below 0.10 acre. Three plots having nearly 0.10 acre without house in those have tried to cultivate banana. The other farmers among this category do not have enough space to cultivate any new plants and benefit from water for domestic use.

The income from the crops could not be analysed since the farmers have planted more perennial crops that take few years to give yield. Considering the number of trees newly planted, the result is not very encouraging. Partly it is a result of pests and diseases attack especially on cash crops and partly it is due to the attitude of part-time farmers who do not depend much upon the income from crops because of the small size of agriculture plots. The encouragement from the project office to give boost upon the crop is fading because the agronomists work with the project had the

Table 25.3 : Cropping Pattern before the Project and After at Kurumal

Farmer	Area in Acre	Coconut BP	Coconut AP	Arecanut BP	Arecanut AP	Banana BP	Banana AP	Pepper BP	Pepper AP	Cashew BP	Cashew AP	Mango BP	Mango AP	Vegetable BP	Vegetable AP
1	0.60	30	30	50	250	10	10		6					3	
2	0.06	2			5					1		1	1		
3	0.60	3	25	50	250	50	100		6				1	1	1
4	0.21	4	8	30	75			2		1			1	1	1
5	0.20		7		50		10					2	1	1	1
6	1.01	35	30	100	255	20	30		20		3	2	1		1
7	0.65						5								.5
8	0.38	24	25	15	70		15				3	3	5		1
9	0.06					5	6								.5
10	0.05						4								
11	0.18	18	20	20	100	60	100	5							.5
12	0.04						4						1		1
13	1.00	20	30	150	300	70	200	5	40	1		1			
14	1.00	75	50	300	150	105	50	75	50			15	15	1	1
15	0.28	5	18	10	50	5		5	25				2		
16	0.18	2	8		15	7	4		8				2		1

Contd...

Table 25.3 Contd ....

Farmer	Area in Acre	Coconut BP	Coconut AP	Arecanut BP	Arecanut AP	Banana BP	Banana AP	Pepper BP	Pepper AP	Cashew BP	Cashew AP	Mango BP	Mango AP	Vegetable BP	Vegetable AP
17	0.17		9		35								2		1
18	0.08	2	1				6					1			
19	0.09		2			2	3				2				.5
20	0.70	30	35	100	100	25		20	20						.5
21	0.04		1				13						2		
22	0.20	3	3				60								
23	1.01		25		225		50		15		5		4		1
24	0.07		13		3										
25	0.18		20		105		100			60		4	4		1
26	0.04														
27	0.08														
28	0.04														

Note: BP-means before project implementation and AP-notes after the project implementation.

Source: Data compiled from Baseline Survey of Kurumal Community and Impact Survey conducted in 2000.

duty of CE, in the absence of CE for several considerable different periods.

The benefits derived to this community is analysed by the variables of efficiency, empowerment and equity (Uphoff, 1991). One of the variables of efficiency is measured in terms of availability of water for drinking, domestic and agriculture purpose adequately, in time and in right location. From the field survey all respondents were found satisfied with the distribution of water according to their needs and demands. Other variable to measure the efficiency is financial situation of WUA. The Accounts Book of WUA indicates that even after meeting the recurrent expenditures and maintenance of water distribution, a balance of more than £ 200 recorded every year. A third variable of efficiency can be the additional income from crops in the community that currently cannot be measured till the new plants start yielding. Apart from these, social benefits to the women especially in the reduction of time required for fetching water, health benefits of potable water and other developmental activities undertaken by WUA profit have to be taken into account as positive benefit of PIM.

Socio-economic survey conducted by KCIP in about 18 communities reveals that gross incomes from agriculture increased by about 55 per cent, which is considerably high. Another result according to this survey is social cohesion achieved through formation and strengthening of WUA by the KCIP. Land value in these communities has also increased in these WUAs (KCIP, 1999). This social cohesion and increase in the land value are also observed in the present study and forms a boost for similar development activities of the Kurumal community area.

Regarding equity, it is learned from the survey that water equitably distributed at the rate fixed by the WUA that is applicable to all farmers in the WUA. The common problem seen in the irrigation schemes i.e., availability of water to the tail-enders was never experienced in the project. Empowerment of farmers as managers rather than as beneficiaries is the unique feature of this project. Empowerment of women members into the executive committee with 30 per cent reservation is another positive landmark seen in this project. A sense of collective ownership was created with 10 per cent of total cost sharing for construction of distribution system. Such joint responsibility and sharing to maintain the system leads to sustainable irrigation management in Kurumal that can be replicable. Pump operator is not government servant and is appointed and paid by the WUA. Whereas if the government agency controls the water perhaps none of the above mentioned benefits may accrue to the Kurumal farmers. And, therefore, it can be established that the PIM is beneficial indeed as seen in the Kurumal community where IMT takes place in real situation than rhetorically.

Analysis of KCIP Participatory Approaches

The participatory approach adopted in KCIP is unique since it has learnt lessons from several in-country and international projects. The merit part of these projects and value of original social capital from different parts of world have been blended in KCIP by the first Team Leader of the project who happened to be an international irrigation sociologist. The following analysis on KCIP participatory approach is based on the author's own first hand experience by working in KCIP and discussion with farmers and WUA representatives from nearly about 75 WUAs.

Community Identification

Community identification is the second step in the project implementation. As shown by the WDW, COs visit the new locations, discuss with farmers, move around and assess the need of the community. Also, farmers from various parts of district approach KSJS office with the demand of implementing the scheme. Accordingly, WDW and COs visit the locations and a feasible compact farmer group will be marked off suited to the project. And thus community identification is need based, demand driven and participatory. Whereas, in the irrigation department office the post of CO do not exist and no social planners deal with the projects.

Water Group Meetings

Water group meeting before drilling the well is a participatory meeting at project formulation stage. Such meetings for assessing the needs and knowledge of farmers often do not take place in many irrigation projects in developing countries (Ostrom, 1992). Again the participation in divining a feasible bore well site and their labour contribution is well recorded and added to the 10 per cent of the total cost of the scheme. Entrance of drilling rig through the plots with tree crops and wild woods often invite resistance from families. Water group office bearers have to sort out such problems at field level by themselves.

Farmer Tours

Farmer tours from new communities to commissioned communities is an another participatory approach in the participatory learning process for learning from other farmer groups regarding the implementation, WUA office management, water rotation, sharing of contribution and new cropping pattern.

PRA

Various tools used in the PRA exercise were community history, community mapping and few time series analysis occasionally and an exercise on gender access to facilities. The initial enthusiasm in learning about the community undoubtedly was beneficial to the officials or outsiders than to the farmers. Several communities in certain ground water potential locations, which are very close, and the inferences drawn from these communities are very similar and repetitive. Considering the steps of implementation of the project, PRA is inevitable sociology component recommended by the donor agency. And unfortunately, transects walks, oral histories, participatory meetings in the scheme implementation were not considered as PRA. Before conducting PRA, a rehearsal is often required the day before the PRA play. Apart from PRA, complete information about the community is collected through household base line survey. The poor farmers and agricultural labourers are compelled to attend such colourful exercise while loosing their work for daily bread and therefore, 'time' factor deserve very high attention in PRA. It seems that PRA became a fashionable development jargon in the development projects without looking into the suitability of the projects (Shepherd, 1998). Often it is observed that PRA means mapping and drawing diagrams. In KCIP, this issue was raised in the Mid-term evaluation review and PRA was ultimately dropped.

Community Planning and Budgeting (CPB)

Community Planning and Budgeting is a participatory method of involving the farmers in the planning and budgeting of the distribution system, in which decisions are taken regarding the cash contribution according to the land size, procuring quotations for supply of materials, quotations of plumbing etc, implementation activities. In the beginning of the project, CPB was not a serious meeting and was a component of PRA. Later, after enough experience and experiments, project staff especially SDW and ADW together shaped this tool suited to the project. Though this may not come under the tools of Chambers' PRA model, definitely it is a participatory implementation methodology suited to the needs of the project to make it transparent between farmers and officials. Implementation Committee that includes the concerned COs, CE and office bearers of WUA, open the tendered quotation in a priorily fixed meeting and thereby the mal practice and temptations of the suppliers are done away with. However, such developments are recent phenomenon (after 1997) in the refining process of implementation. Still, new community approach for drilling the wells is sought since the drilling operations in the project are under the mercy of contractors in the absence of a drilling rig in the project.

Joint Bank Account

The Joint Bank Account is operated jointly by the president of WUA and an officer in charge of the account from KSJS office. Normally it is done through CE or in his/her absence Junior Agronomist will be given in charge. The bureaucracy role of Engineer and other departmental staff in the procedure of joint operation of this account has created innumerable problems. CEs involved in the process often are not happy with the loose method of operation in the absence of proper government order and guidelines that are different from the usual government procedures. Consequently, Engineers leave the post and it takes a minimum of 3 to 4 months to get another person for reappointment. Moreover, the CE has to be deputed from the government and the post cannot be filled up on contract since the person will be dealing with payments and work approvals. Absence of personnel in this post has created considerable delay in the project achievements. Frequent change or termination of duties of CEs deteriorated the situation.

Participatory method in the joint bank operation is of course advisable in sociological principles but practically participatory implementation is a time consuming and often frustrating process in the government set up irrespective of its transparencies in the joint operation where project target approach may not be suitable. Perhaps NGOs may be better equipped to do it in the absence of government formal procedures. Whereas similar schemes under the Ground Water Department of Kerala, are implemented much faster and steadily by supplying the pipes and pumps directly from the government stores. Currently, pipes and pump for the distribution system are procured locally from Trichur town or nearby stores by tendering quotations from the local suppliers and this activity is done by the WUA. And the farmers have to be taught government tendering procedures and purchase. This takes considerable time. Occasionally the WUAs are trapped in receiving high commission from the suppliers and accepting low quality goods without knowing the facts of standard goods. During the third year of the project such ignorance of WUA and traps of suppliers were brought to the notice of new communities by the COs. Thus it is likely that participatory approach in implementation takes more time than regular bureaucratic approach and also the participatory approach is not suitable in certain crucial stages of implementation.

Most unfortunately, change of party politics at the state assembly during the middle of project affected the process adversely. The State Legislature did not show timely willingness to pass necessary orders to support joint bank operations through WUAs.

Therefore, CEs cannot be blamed for their reluctance with joint bank operation. It took four years to pass a simple official formality to back up this participatory implementation of scheme. Donor's warning to the state government with the suspension of drilling was not enough for the state government to pass this important order. Eventually, contract staff that depends upon the project for their livelihood put pressure on state politicians to pass the required orders. Here too, social planners have legitimate lobbying role.

Participatory Monitoring and Evaluations (PME)

Participatory Monitoring and Evalution in the commissioned communities and communities at the stage of implementation take place in the General Body Meeting of WUA. In such serious meetings, PRA type tools of PME are of no importance where appraisals of various real situations are discussed and find solutions. Every decision of the meetings are recorded in the minute's book and read to the audience. The same has to be approved, signed and sealed by the office bearers of WUA in the midst of General Body meetings. Members are informed of the holding of general body meeting or executive committee meetings through Notice Book at least seven days in advance. And thereby the people are well informed about the meetings. The lack of dissemination of such information neglects the local people's participation in the planning process (Raphael, 2000).

Participatory Training

In the initial phase of the project, method for giving training to the office bearers of WUA was lecture method with some facilitation of discussion among the participants. Later, after learning from several experiences, this training was shaped to the needs of the office bearers of new WUAs, those who are going to take up joint implementation of schemes. For example, book keeping and accounts of the WUA office management is an important capacity building need of office bearers of WUAs. In the absence of such skills, social tensions and complaints within the WUAs have been experienced in some communities. And in the light of such experiences, loopholes had to be filled up in the implementation process and beyond. In certain communities social relationships within WUA broke up and reached the courts. And such instances led the project staff to give training on systematic writing of Minutes Books and other records like accounts, receipts, vouchers etc. Distribution of pipelines cut across the plots of each household to reduce the cost of the system instead of laying the same along the roadside. The process occasionally invites tension among WUA members. Such issues are given to the training participants (in-groups) as riddles to solve and to come up with feasible solutions. Discussions on social relationship and sharing of traditional skills are another component of training with game plays. Rural men and women office bearers of WUA take part in these training. And finally, SDW developed participatory training schedule and training manual suited to the project needs and training needs. As Korten (1980) says, a sort of learning process approach is required till a concrete project implementation methodology developed. Still if the KCIP is wound up after the completion of project period, all experience from learning process approach will be in vain.

Success and Failures of KCIP Replicable Model

From the analysis on the potential benefits derived from the PIM in comparison with traditional state paradigms (Paradigm 1) it is evident that participatory approach in irrigation management is undoubtedly beneficial if it is undertaken and controlled by the farmers than bureaucracy as seen in Kurumal. The analysis of the participatory approaches adopted in the KCIP, shows that the project has adopted a participatory learning process approach while establishing a concrete irrigation system that is replicable in the similar projects in Kerala. Community identification methods, water group meetings, farmer tour, WUA office management, CPB, Implementation Committee Meetings and Participatory Training are other examples of such participatory learning process that are designed suited to the project needs by the project staff.

The failure part of the project is centred on with KSJS structure and its physical and financial achievements. As per the project targets, 210 WUAs with successful wells required to be implemented. And so far the project could dig only 131 wells in which only 100 wells are successful either for irrigation or for drinking water. Nevertheless, 3223 families have been benefited against a target of 5250 families. Regarding the financial front, achievement is nearly 50 per cent. The reasons behind this lag are beyond the scope of the study and leaves further scope for study.

A comparative study on PIM projects (Maloney, 1999) in Andhra Pradesh, Kerala and West Bengal highlights that joint bank account operation and implementation between WUA and bureaucracy reduced the cost of installation of the system from over 4 lakhs to about 2.5 lakhs in KCIP. But the truth remains that reduction in the cost is due to the intervention of social planners against corrupt bureaucracy. The high cost of the scheme was a form of bribe that usually had to go the profit part of suppliers and some officials. The similar schemes executed by the Ground Water Department however cost only nearly half of this scheme. Here, the supply of material for distribution system is from the government store and therefore, there is no delay whereas in KCIP when the farmers are taught to do the tendering procedures of government and procuring materials, it takes long time that gives enormous delays in the scheme implementation. Therefore, it reaches the conclusion that in certain crucial stage of the implementation, participatory approach may not always be feasible if it is under project approach with targets. The Inception Report of the project asserts that the main importance of the project, however, is not the number of bore wells, nor the persons directly affected, nor the direct agricultural production increase, but the approach and the method. In this meaning, participatory method of procuring the materials and its delays can be justified. And this can be replicated elsewhere in the state and it forms as the success part of the project than the physical and financial achievements in comparison with targets.

Are GONGOs Replicable?

The failure part of the project is rooted in the structural gaps of governmental NGOs (GONGOs). These organisations particularly set up for implementing foreign aided project seem to work as a government department though GONGOs are envisaged to have the flexibility of NGOs and the authenticity of government. Such blending however has been proved a failure in several projects in the developing countries that eventually made an issue in the World Social Summit in 1995 at Copenhagen (Todaro, 2000). The following is a quotation about KCIP from the comparative study mentioned above, "KCIP is supposed to be an autonomous agency, but for lack of autonomy it suffered many of the problems of line government agencies. The government changed the director many times, and some other staff, partly for political and personal reasons. It took 4 years and repeated pressures to get Government Orders for permission for the WUAs to procure their own equipment and implement the works, for formal recognition of the joint bank accounts, for more autonomy for KSJS and for orders for priority electricity connection. Government rules prohibit building in incentives for good work of the staff. Political changes, social stress, labour unrest and resource constraints tend to paralyse such projects. Government staff quite often find problems in adapting to different concepts and requirements of projects with a clear social dimension… Traditional resistance of technical personnel, and their inability and reluctance to grasp social concerns are well known… government staff used to working under rigid rules and procedures seem reluctant to change these days. This difficulty to accept social dimensions precludes effective co-ordination among the staff drawn from different disciplines" (Maloney, 1999). This shows that GONGOs are not replicable. The same author and the first team leader of the project holds that organisational models adopted for PIM in the three states mentioned, KCIP is the least productive among the three since the government cut the freedom of autonomous body with subsequent reintegration back in to the government. Whereas West Bengal shows "how minor irrigation management can indeed be managed in the context of tiered panchayats (rural local governments)" (Maloney, 1999). On the other side, Andhra Pradesh has gone far ahead by enacting laws for IMT to affect uniformly through out the state under Big - Bang (transformation) approach. Adopted strategy till Mid-Term

Evaluation period for identifying the communities without looking in to the ground water potential locations certainly over emphasised the sociological variables over hydro geological variables that took valuable man-days of the project staff. Lethargic attitude of communist led left government over foreign aided project brought by the opposition party in the state legislature is also responsible for unstable project management.

Recommendations for Policy Implications

The state legislature needs to pass the laws for enabling WUAs and farmer organisations throughout the state for IMT. KSJS an autonomous government body with social planners and already successfully tested learning process model of participatory approach may be approved for implementing irrigation projects in the future in the state (except participatory purchase). Similar approaches can be adopted in CADA schemes and the schemes of minor irrigation department. Political support, staff stability, funds, flexibility, and Big-Bang approach without over-emphasising physical targets and achievements are crucial for KSJS as an autonomous organisation in paving ways for democratic decentralisation and IMT in the future. And if the state government is not conscious about these serious efforts on PIM, all learning process are in vain and this novel irrigation system may die down once the project closed in December 2000. Or rural local governments as noted in the West Bengal's case on PIM could take up KCIP participatory approach. As Uphoff already pointed out NGOs may be more successful in practising this approach.

The social planners have multifarious roles in PIM as catalysts -+ grassroots level organising, as social scientists in the project, and as in the role of lobbying persons for passing the enabling laws in favour of IMT. Social planner COs, the catalyst in the scheme has to work out practical approaches at the grassroots levels according to real field contexts of the area. Further, from the implementation stage and to commissioning and beyond, social planners have rigorous and often tedious roles and responsibilities in the social engineering. In the present farmer initiative approach adopted in KCIP, the SDW is fully dedicated for social planning roles in a multidisciplinary organisation. The foregone discussion in section 3 invariably proves the importance of social planning in irrigation management that can reap positive benefits. Yet governments in the developing countries often show lukewarm response on social planning components of development projects.

REFERENCES

Aggarwal, R.M. (2000): 'Possibilities and Limitations to Co-operation in Small Groups: A Case of Group Owned Wells in Southern India', *World Development*, August: 1481-97.

Babu, M.N. (1999): 'Participatory Irrigation Management in Kerala: A Guideline', paper Presented in Regional Conference on PIM, February, Thiruvananthapuram.

Chackacherry, G. (1994): *Farmer Participation in Irrigation Management*, Kerala Community Irrigation Project, Trichur.

Coward, W. (1991): 'Planning Technical and Social Change in Irrigated Areas': in Cernia M. (ed) *Putting People First,* World Bank, Washington D.C.

FAO, RAP (1995): *Irrigation Management Transfer in Asia*, Bangkok.

Geijer, J. *et al*., (1995): 'Irrigation Management Transfer in Asia'; in FAO RAP, *Irrigation Management Transfer in Asia,* Bangkok.

Government of Kerala (1989): *Eighth Five Year Plan 1990-95: Report of the Task Force on Command Area Development Authority,* Kerala State Planning Board, Thiruvananthapuram.

Government of Kerala (1990): *Community Irrigation Projects in Kerala: An Evaluation Study,* Kerala State Planning Board, Thiruvananthapuram.

Groenfeldt, D. (1998): *Electronic Learning Guide Book for PIM*, Environment Natural Resources Division, World Bank Institute, available at http://www.worldbank.org/wbi/pimelg/pim.htm

Hall, A. (1986): 'Community Participation and Rural Development', in J. Midgley et al, *Community Participation, Social Development and the State*, Methuen, London.

KCIP (1994): *Kerala Community Irrigation Project: Inception Report*; Trichur.

KCIP (1999): *KCIP Socio-Economic Impact Study*, Main Report, Vol. I, Trichur.

Korten, D. (1980): 'Community Organisation and Rural Development: A Learning Process Approach', *Public Administration Review,* September-October: 480-511.

Maloney, C. *et al.* (1994): *Managing Irrigation Together*, Sage, New Delhi.

Maloney, C. (1999): 'PIM Projects in Andhra, Kerala and West Bengal: Policies to Scale Up Support Services', paper presented at National Conference on PIM, January, Hyderabad.

Midgley, J. *et al.* (1986): *Community Participation, Social Development and the State*, Methuen, London.

Navalawala, B.N. (1995): 'Participatory Irrigation Management in India : Status, Issues and Approaches', in FAO RAP, *Irrigation Management Transfer in Asia*, Bangkok.

Ostrom, E. (1992): *Crafting Institutions for Self Governing Irrigation Systems*, ICS Press, C.A. USA.

Putnam, R. (1993): *Making Democracy Work*, Princeton University Press, New Jersey.

Raphael, J.C. (2000): *Decentralised Planning in India*; Anmol Publication, New Delhi.

Rondinelli, D. (1993): *Development Projects as Policy Experiments*, Methuen, London.

Salman, A. (1997): *Legal Framework for WUAs*, World Bank, Washington DC.

Shepherd, A. (1998): *Sustainable Rural Development*; Macmillan, London.

Svendsen, M. *et al.* (1997): 'Participatory Irrigation Management: Benefits and Second Generation Problems', paper presented at International Workshop held at Centro Internacional de Agricultura Tropical (CIAT), 9-15 February, Cali, Colombia.

Todaro, M. (2000): *Economic Development*, Longman, London.

UNDP (1992): World Development Report, New York.

Uphoff, N. (1991): 'Fitting Projects to People', in M. Cernia M. (ed) *Putting People First*, World Bank, Washington DC.

Uphoff, N *et al*, (1991): *Managing Irrigation*; Sage, New Delhi.

Vermillion, D.L. (1995): 'Irrigation Management Transfer: Conditions for Success', in FAO RAP, *Irrigation Management Transfer in Asia*, Bangkok.

World Bank (1993): *Water Resource Management*, World Bank Policy Paper, Washington DC.

Yabes, R.A. (1993): 'The Zanjeras and the Ilocos Norte Irrigation Project', in D. Ghai and J. Vivian, (ed) *Grassroots Environmental Action*; ODI Publication, London.

Disaster Management and Role of Local Institutions in India

SUSANTA KUMAR JENA

Disasters always affect mankind and will probably continue to perturb as long as life exists on this planet. Their wraths prevail all over the world and the developing countries are the most vulnerable regions. The lack of required human and material resources in the developing countries poses a serious challenge in handling disasters effectively. Even when adequate resources are ensured, experiences show that improper management does not allow these countries to tackle disasters effectively and which ultimately leads to severe loss of human as well as material resources. These irreparable damaging consequences of disasters in the last few decades have made these nations to reassess and recuperate not only their disaster management strategies but also redesign their communitarian approach to face these challenges.

Local Governments and Disaster Management

Developing countries started to accommodate the local institutions and non-governmental organisations in disaster management with a centralized approach, which are considered inefficient for a number of reasons. The governments of these countries find it convenient to operate from a centralized position rather than to have a shared programme framework with grassroots. As a result, most of the disaster management programmes adopt a top-down approach, with local level involvement serving mainly as an aid to implement such programmes instead of being a part and parcel of the system itself (UNDP 1994: 44).

However, centralised approach often results in more casualties and increasing the case of vulnerability. The long-drawn bureaucratic procedures associated with centralised system are very slow to save the life and properties of a large number of citizens under such circumstances. It also fails to address disaster management properly, because of the complex relationships that exist between people and their social, physical and economic environment. It is not possible for a centralised authority to take into account the uniqueness of the culture of a particular region and the enormous range and variety of local needs and priorities. Therefore, very often, even well intentioned programmes turn out to be counter-productive for the people. In addition to this, the centralised system is not adequate enough to handle emergency situations because of the necessity to take immediate decisions on the spot as per the demand of the circumstances.

As the centralised approach to disaster management failed in checking losses and bringing local community participation in preparing and managing disasters, the focus shifted towards the involvement of local level institutions. Thus, local government initiatives in disaster management have received a renewed thrust in the last decade of the twentieth century. In fact, the United Nations Organizations declared 1990-2000 as the "International Decade for Natural Disaster Reduction" (IDNDR). In Yakohama in May 1994, it adopted the famous guideline known as 'the Yakohoma Strategy', emphasizing on local communities and considering them as primary actors in the design, adoption and implementation of disaster reduction policies and measures. So the concept of community participation emerged as one of the central ingredients of disaster management. An institutional arrangement of this nature not only facilitates smooth implementation of disaster management initiatives but also provides scope for greater interaction and empathy to absorb the shock and trauma induced by the catastrophe. It also provides a level playing field to all sections of the society for participation and assertion of their choices.

Disaster Management: Indian Experience

Under Constitution of India, disaster management is a state subject. The responsibility for undertaking preparedness, response, recovery and mitigation measures in the event of disaster is the concern of the state governments. The role of the Central Government is to support the State Governments in terms of physical and financial resources. Until 9th Finance Commission's guidelines for Disaster Management came into effect, the Centre supplemented the efforts of the State Government by providing additional resources in the name of 'Margin Money' on the recommendation of the Finance Commissions. The Eleventh Finance Commission (2000-2005) has suggested the creation of National Calamity Contingency Fund (NCCF), where the share of the Central and State Governments is 75:25 per cent. The Department of Agriculture and Cooperation in the Ministry of Agriculture, New Delhi is the nodal agency for natural disaster management in India. The response of Central Government to a natural disaster depends on (i) the gravity of the calamity, (ii) the scale of the relief operation, (iii) the requirement of Central assistance for augmenting the state governments (NCDM 2001:92).

In the year 1999, Government of India established a High Power Committee to oversee the disaster situations in India and it recommended disaster management in a holistic manner in the year 2001. It recommended management in central, state, district, block, village and family level and the coordination among these agencies. Though, it did not provide a clear-cut functional guideline as to how these institutions can be involved into disaster management in a coordinated manner, it made enough room for the participation of local government and institutions in the process of disaster mitigation.

In the Indian context, the effectiveness of the local government institutions in disaster management can be analysed on four important parameters; such as decision-making, human resource management, resources and technical efficiency.

Decision-making

Soon after independence, India introduced a centralised administration and centralised planning of economy with the objective of achieving fast growth in the same pattern as ex-Soviet Union did. However, this failed in several fronts and resulted in administrative inefficiency, red-tapism, sluggishness, corruption and wastage of public resources. The failure of top down planning gave way to decentralization and importance on bottom up approach. The experiments on decentralization started with Balwant Rai Mehta Committee to push forward the much-needed local participation in the development sector. However, it was only in 1993 that the 73rd and 74th Constitutional Amendments to the Constitution of India were legislated, pointing towards a serious policy initiative for decentralization and legitimising the rural and urban local bodies to participate in decision-making process. Decision-making entails the local bodies a greater degree of freedom to take important decisions in various developmental activities.

Decision-making is a kind of participation and centres on the generation of ideas, formulation and assessment of options, and making choices about them. Three types of decisions can be distinguished: initial decisions, ongoing decisions, and operational decisions (Cohen and Uphoff, 1980: 218); (a) Initial decision generally described as 'project identification', needs to be carefully distinguished and focused upon followed by (Strategies for Small Farmer Development 1976: 95-107), (b) Participation in ongoing decisions occurs after the initial decisions, may be more critical to project success than such participation in the initial decisions, (c) We conceive of operational decisions as relating to specific local organizations, which have been established by the project or linked to the project in an effort to involve people in the delivery aspects of the enterprise.

For the analysis of decision-making in disaster management FEMA's (Federal Emergency Management Agency) systematic approach in four functional phases as preparedness, response, recovery and mitigation has been taken. Let's substantiate each of them for greater understanding.

Disaster Preparedness: Preparedness entails "... the activities closest to the onset of a disaster which minimises disaster damage and enhances disaster response operations" (National Governors' Association 1979: 237). It includes the formulation of viable emergency plans, the development of warning systems, the maintenance of inventories and the training of personnel. Disaster preparedness assumes the occurrence of disaster in future but mainly focuses on emergency response to disaster. It is a multi-sectoral approach in which the local institutions can be effective in performing its role. The local institutions allow the communities to respond effectively before the disaster occurs. It provides emergency health or life saving and specialised training in communication or information skills for the persons actively engaged in disaster. The local institutions provide basic ideas to understand what to do before a disaster. On the onset of disaster the local government delivers the work to the employees (those who engage in disaster management programme) and the volunteers to do the preparedness work like preparedness plan, warning, information, and evacuation. Local institutions' participation in decision-making has knowledge of local safe and vulnerable areas, survival experience in face of disaster loss and understanding of the hierarchical local system circumstances.

Disaster Response: Response includes the activities to be undertaken most closely after the disaster occurs. These activities may consist of evacuation (although evacuation may also occur prior to the disaster), mobilization, and emergency assistance for victims. This phase requires emergency management for the people in disaster-affected areas. In this period the role of 'ocal government is more important for executing the work. The local government helps in setting up control rooms, putting the contingency plan in action, issuing warning, rendering medical aid and evacuation etc. Simultaneously, it also renders relief to the homeless, (food, drinking water, cloth etc.), restores communication, and disburses assistance in cash or kind to the needy.

Disaster Recovery: The third phase of management is recovery—both short and long-term. The activities undertaken during this phase are designed to return the affected community to normal condition existing prior to the advent of disaster. These activities may either short-term restoration or long-term reconstruction efforts. Recovery is used to describe the activities that encompass rehabilitation and reconstruction programmes. The local government is more useful in these activities.

Rehabilitation: Rehabilitation includes the provision of temporary public utilities and housing as interim measures to assist longer-term recovery. In collecting the information on the needs of local people and the damage assessment the local authority helps to provide the basic need at that moment and helps to construct temporary makeshift shelters. Also the local authority distributes compensation to the people on partial or fully damage house and other losses. The local government also involves in providing psychological counselling for the traumas.

Reconstruction: The local government can attempt to bring back the people to their normalcy. It includes the restoration and construction of buildings, infrastructure and lifeline facilities so that long-term development prospects are enhanced rather than reproducing the same conditions which made an area or population vulnerable in the first place.

Disaster Mitigation: The final phase is mitigation. This entails "those activities undertaken before the disaster to lessen its effects" (Drabek, 1983: 9). Mitigation involves modifying the causes of the hazard, or the vulnerability to the event, or distributing the losses. In addition to these physical measures, mitigation also aims at reducing the economic and social vulnerability. Therefore, mitigation activities divided into structural or non-structural activities.

Local institutions' participation in disaster mitigation accepts the fact that some events may occur but it will try to reduce the impacts and damages. Local institutions can participate in housing, plantation, education or the training of homebuilders to improve the quality and performance of houses, financial incentives as an inducement to communities to use hazard resistant construction technique and insurance of their properties. Public information and education at local institutions level are the most effective steps in mitigation phase. Typical public awareness activities include radio and film programmes, additional school curriculum that covers lessons about mitigation, comic books and hand outs for general distribution and posters around the community to state about the measures available to reduce the impact and the actions to take when the hazard strikes (Kumar, 1992:100). All these approaches are possible only when initiative is taken at grassroots level by local government with proper cooperation from the state government.

It is necessary to constitute a local body to constitute a permanent "Disaster Management Committee" to implement the programmes the committee is supposed to be represented by local government and other government offices and NGOs will help them for preparedness. The Committee will devolve a plan for disaster preparedness for the area specific. An office, for example, a Local Disaster Management Office should be created in the targeted local government units and staffed with trained and qualified disaster management personnel. Here, the focus is on voluntary associations, co-operatives, traditional associations and other organisations involved in substantive activities of the project.

Human Resource Management

Another important area is of human resource management and it is here the local institutions and communities can play a crucial role both in preparedness and mitigation of disaster. It is essential for the technical staff to assess the risk, analyse the vulnerability and discuss it with the local people. In this activity they will have to identify the hot-spot areas or the areas of prime concern. In the period of assessment the local community should be involved into exercise to express their views because they are better aware about the locality. A comprehensive vulnerability analysis should be undertaken in all hazard prone areas, taking into account the post disaster events, the socio-economic conditions of the population living in the area. Along with the risk assessment, resource mapping should also be undertaken. This is a useful tool in identifying the strengths, weaknesses and opportunities, threats to a community in terms of resources available and its level of preparedness for disasters. In carrying out this resource mapping, potential targets of a disaster should be identified. These targets would include both public and private infrastructure and property.

One of the most critical components of the management strategy is the training to be imparted to the local government members and the volunteers involved at the local institutions level. Education about disasters and its preparedness should be given to the public. ·And people are to be educated through mass media, like radio, television and from other sources.

Technical Staff: Public information at local government level is the most effective step in disaster management. Like District Information Officer at district level, there should be a post of Block Information Officer (BIO) at block level. His role as an information officer is more important before and after a disaster that reduces the impact of disaster strikes. His activities in preparedness period include film programmes or documentary on disaster; disaster drills and rehearsals; school curriculum that covers lessons about hazard mitigation; comic books and posters for general distribution around the community. He provides information to the local people before a disaster. After the disaster he informs the local government and outsiders for viable situation in monitoring the distribution of relief and other materials. He appraises the situation according to the instruction and situation regarding disaster and provides information to the people at local government level.

Field Official: He is an expert in the locality. He prepares the list of safer places in the locality according to nature of disaster. He prepares safer route for communication, if a disaster strikes. He presents the vulnerable areas of the locality and people at risk in that locality. He prepares the hazard map of each village and the local areas for first hand information to provide a schematic representation of the village or the local institutions. He updates data in to data bank in providing accurate information. He collects information on number of vulnerable people in an area, weaker section people, old age people, women with pregnancy, women without anybody and the handicapped people. He trains the local people on disaster map and data bank of their locality.

Village Preparedness Committee: For effective preparedness all section of the community has to be mobilised and integrated: the government and its institutions, the Panchayats, local voluntary organisations and the people of the community. The roles of the various sections have to be clearly defined so that every unit can work on its defined task, and together achieve a common outcome. A task force comprising of certain village members can develop a contingency plan and identify and assign roles and responsibilities to various individuals or groups to be undertaken both in normal times and in times of disaster.

The committee consists of volunteers and rescue staff to help the people in the period of disasters. The village preparedness committee is equipped with proper training, which could be geared up in the time of disaster. The over all responsibility of this group to evacuate the people before disaster, rescue those are trapped in disaster and help in relief programmes after the disasters. The other activities include bringing the people to dispensary for their first aid, sanitation of the areas after the disaster, clearance of the debris and other helps.

Coordination with Local NGOs: The need for action and intervention in a disaster situation is at multiple levels and cut across various sectors. The quality of intervention depends a lot on the inter-sectoral, inter-departmental coordination and efficient teamwork. Local organisations, which are well equipped with local knowledge and indigenous methods of dealing previous disasters, can save the life and properties of the people. In addition, the local population and their leadership, who are useful assets in dealing disasters, can deal the problems in an efficient manner.

Financing

The local authorities remain constrained by a lack of adequate resources mainly financial and material. Whatever accesses they do have towards funds are spent on personnel needs and other recurrent expenditures. It is rare to find local authorities exercising significant power over major projects. In such a scenario adequate fund at local level becomes a key ingredient in effective disaster management.

Allocation of Expenditure: There are no specific provisions made in the state plans for allocation of funds to local government for disaster preparedness. However, the 73rd Constitutional Amendment Act 1992, makes a provision to constitute a State Finance Commission [Article 243-(I)] to deal with the distribution of funds between the State and the Panchayats on the net proceeds of the taxes, duties, tolls and fees levied by the state. On the recommendation of successive Finance Commissions, the Central Government and State Governments are providing grants-in-aid to the Panchayats.

The system of state allocation of this fund to local government should be on the basis of priority of disaster prone areas. It can be utilised on two distinct categories: recurrent and development activities. The recurrent activities include the salaries of the experts, office expenditure and the development activities include the preparation of projects.

Income Sources: The second question on finance is how to raise income sources at local level. Though in the 73rd and 74th Amendment Acts, there is a provision to earn income through taxes, the state governments have not yet empowered the local authority to raise their own revenue. Despite the increased proportion of resources having spent at the sub-national level, own-source revenues of local institutions are comparatively small and remained heavily dependent on state and central funds. The local institutions should be allowed to collect and increase tax net.

In addition to the taxes, local institutions should be allowed to take loans and credits for sustainable development from multilateral and bilateral agencies with state as a guarantor. But the question arises if local decision-makers are allowed to allocate their funding, will they make better decisions than central decision-makers and accountable to the funds they use? The response is affirmative in the sense that the local institutions are better aware about their problem. Accountability in policy-making exists as locally elected representatives are presumed to be more closely in touch with the public than their regional or national counterparts.

Like *Grameen* Banks in Bangladesh, Self-Help Groups (SHGs) and micro-insurance groups can contribute a small sum of money to community funds. This community fund can be used for disaster management. Additional funds can also be raised from funding agencies, both at national and international level.

Technical Expertise

Awareness and expertise in handling technologies to advantage during the disaster are absolutely essential priorities. Community consciousness about technologies is necessary to prepare them for facing natural disasters. Effective measures for protection against disasters can be achieved to a greater extent through the accessibility to policies in science, research and technology. Most of the methods for improving disaster resistance and preparedness are available by the application of technological gadgets. However, significant gaps exist in the application of modern and old technologies to disaster reduction and the understanding of natural processes in disaster management practice because of lack of knowledge at local level. One can blend old and modern technologies in the following ways for the local advantages.

Space technologies such as remote sensing, satellite communications and global positioning system are widely used in monitoring the occurrence of different types of disasters and in evaluating the losses and the impact on development process (Sahni, 2001: 6). The Geographic Information System (GIS) software plays a crucial role in the process of gathering and analysing information needed for disaster preparedness

Space Technology: Space technology plays a crucial role in efficient mitigation of disasters and help to: minimise potential risks by developing early warning strategies; preparing and implementing developmental plans; mobilising resources including communication and tele-medical services and helping in rehabilitation and post disaster reconstruction. Local institutions can use the information provided by remote sensing application centres in disaster management for focusing on priority areas. It also becomes easy for them to identify areas of potential exposure to hazards, so that measures can be taken to reduce the social and economic impact of potential disasters in the planning process. It can give higher quality of results than the manually drawn results. It facilitates decision-making and improves coordination among agencies at local government level for better management.

Disaster Mapping: Disaster mapping or hazard map is a tool for assessing, storing and conveying information of the geographical location and spread of the effects, or probable effects of disasters. It is essential for disaster preparedness activity in local governmental level for its accuracy and comprehensive information. It will provide the level of hazard prone areas, the socio-economic conditions of the local population living in the area, the infrastructure and other facilities for natural hazards. Information from several sources can be combined in a single map to give a composite picture of the magnitude, frequency and effect of hazards. The next stage is identifying vulnerable population and properties/assets in the local level. With the help of these maps the community can assess the groups and people who are at risk in the advent of a disaster and can take proper action.

Data Bank: It is essential in planning and execution of disaster preparedness programme at local institutions level. It indicates a widely recognised need for improved data bank concerning resources and capabilities and the information systems necessary to make these available to disaster managers. Such database and information systems have direct relevance in planning and preparedness at local level.

Use of Internet: Internet sites are providing an increasing array of information related to various hazards, as well as providing more information about the growing number of organisations and professional disciplines addressing them. It also establishes electronic communications with the outside world effectively, which is of utmost importance for risk management at prior, during and the aftermath of disasters.

Communication: Communication has been a lifeline for millions of disaster stricken people. Warnings, reports about the current situation and the coordination of response activities can be communicated through the use of transistor radios, cell phones, etc. A HAM radio is a low cost and low frequency radio and can be operated from a point-to-point or multi-point basis over a fixed geographical area to provide information to affected people. It is suggested that HAM systems be made a part of regular disaster management exercises.

Conclusion

After the implementation of 73rd and 74th Amendment Acts, local government institutions have started taking active interests and initiatives in most of the subjects under their jurisdiction, whereas disaster management as an area has not yet captured their attention so far. However, with the increasing frequency of disasters and their effects, local government institutions have to involve themselves in disaster management. Their involvement is necessary to take important measures in the aspects of decision-making, human resource management, financing and technical efficiency. The institutions' role in decision-making is to reduce disaster risk as well as to build up their strength through sharing ideas, transfer of basic knowledge and training on disaster programmes. The disaster management experts in local institutions have to train the village preparedness committee members and the community on disaster. The state should revamp the fiscal condition of the local government institutions and allow them to generate funds from different sources to take adequate steps to manage disasters.

The local governmental institutions, with their grassroots level contacts with the common people, can make a substantial contribution to the process by ensuring active people's participation in disaster management activities. They are the ideal channels to conduct any disaster management programme, right form relief, recovery and rehabilitation to planning for mitigation and prevention. However, the success of disaster management depends upon above mentioned parameters and the active involvement of local institutions in disaster management.

REFERENCES

Cohen, J.M. and N.T. Uphoff (1980): 'Participation's Place in Rural Development: Seeking Clarity through Specificity', *World Development*, 8(2): 216-.228.

Drabek, E. Thomas *et al.* (1983): *Earthquake Mitigation Policy: The Experience of Two States*, Institute of Behavioural Science, Boulder, Colo.

Kumar, Pawan (2000): 'Role of Community Participation in Natural Disaster Management', *Dialogue*, 2 (4): 96-104.

National Centre for Disaster Management (2001): *Manual on Natural Disaster Management in India*, NCDM (IIPA), New Delhi.

National Governors' Association (1979): *Emergency Preparedness Project: Final Report*, National Governor's Association Office of State Services, Washington, D.C.

Sahni, Pradeep *et al.* (2001): *Disaster Mitigation: Experience and Reflections*, Prentice Hall, New Delhi.

Strategies for Small Farmer Development (1976): *An Empirical Study of Rural Development Projects*, Westerview, Beulder.

United Nations Development Programme (1994): *Disaster and Development*, Disaster Management Training Programmes, Geneva.

Synergetic Action for Participatory Development

SITAKANTA SETHY

Introduction

'Poverty is considered as a threat to prosperity' is also applicable to India. It is so because; in India itself we find a lot of disparity among and within the states. While formulating the five-year plans for the states by the Central Government 'growth with social justice' to all sections of society and backward areas are given due weightage. In India, the other side of development is large-scale poverty[1], deprivation and misery in rural areas. For alleviating poverty, the development agencies, institutions and local organizations including the government and NGDOs (Non-Governmental Development Organisations) implement a number of development programmes but with a different approach.

In this regard, literature developed by the Institute of Development Studies (IDS), United Nation's Development Programme (UNDP) and the World Bank and the authors such as Myrdal (1968), Cernia (1985), Sen *et al.* (1989), Korten (1981) and Chambers (1995) are noteworthy. In the latest literature developed by the World Bank, poverty is linked not only to material deprivation but also deprivation of human resources, social contacts, voice against injustice and exploitation and power[2]. Rural poverty is perpetuated due to lack of skill and adequate resources with very low and uncertain returns. The poor households suffer due to lack of access over public goods and services and even poverty of social relationships (Kozel *et al.* 2003)

Redefining and Measuring Poverty

Defining and finding a permanent solution to poverty and development is a contentious and debatable issue. Development scientists and grassroots activists think that it is non-measurable. However, innumerable attempts have been made to define the problem and measure it. The workable definition to poverty is that 'it describes the condition of people lacking the basic necessities of life'. It could be due to a number of disadvantages including lack of income, lack of adequate and inappropriate food intake resulting in shortage of calorie required for leading a healthy life. The old definition of poverty says that due to lack of income only people face a number of inter-related problems in their day-to-day life. Estimates of poverty that rely exclusively on income and consumption measures may fail to capture significant aspects of deprivation experienced by the poor.[3]

In India, taking the physical requirement of human beings, the need of food intake that would provide at least 2400 calories and 2100 calories for the rural and urban people has been set respectively. Indian Council of Medical Research (ICMR) in 1981 prescribed 2400 calories for light workers, 2800 calories for moderate and 3900 calories for heavy workers. After conversion of the calories requirements, Rs 11,000 has been fixed as the annual per capita income of a family of five. The family having less the amount is considered as below poverty line (BPL). While calculating the income for family under BPL, current prices of the food intake that provides energy has been taken into account. The concept is criticized on the basis of dependants on the sole earning member of a poor family. Adding to this, availability of productive assets, physical (biological and structural) weakness is also responsible for prevalence of poverty with rural households. The above calculations for identifying a BPL family hardly take these factors into consideration.

Poverty is structurally determined by taking into consideration the other facts such as availability of reliable and authentic information and the communication facility through which a household could have access over power. The other reality is that, even a household would cross the BPL line; there is fair chance that it may come back to the same state again. This is possible because in numerous ways the BPL families are vulnerable to low income and exploitation in society. Powerlessness indicates the poor household's lack of power to represent and secure their interest and even raise voice against any exploitation and injustice against them.

Understanding 'the concept of poverty' has been changed to a great extent during the last two decades. Especially, Haq (1996) on Human Development Index (HDI) and Gender Empowerment Index (GEI) brought in a paradigm shift towards the analysis of poverty and its eradication especially in the underdeveloped and developing countries. The concept of Physical Quality of Life Index (PQLI) by Morris *et al.* (1982) and Participatory Rural Appraisal (PRA) by Robert Chambers are considered as the path breaking exercises in the said field. While measuring poverty, generally income of a household is taken into consideration. However, lack of income *per se* is not poverty. Lack of productive assets such as land, skills, animals and birds are also responsible to enhance the income, self-esteem and social status of a poor household.

Adding to the above issues physical weakness, isolation, powerlessness, health and vulnerability are also responsible to keep a household below poverty line for a pretty long time. The poor households stay isolated due to lack of access over information regarding the different individual, community and local area development programmes, health and sanitation facilities, education, infrastructures, market, communication system and mass media. The other side of the story is that, counting the number of BPL families becomes very difficult for government due to a number of reasons. Some states take the possession of TV, dwelling unit/ house, telephone and land as the indicators of households to be counted above the poverty line and others take food habit as one of the criteria. These are the visible indicators of poverty, whereas the invisible indicators are left altogether while identifying the BPL families.

If this were the case with the government, then it would be wise to analyse what the poor thinks? The studies undertaken by

Narayan *et al.* (2000) and Kozel *et al.* (2003) reveal that the rural poor consider the possession of low quality and non-irrigated land, begging, lack of adequate wage employment, illiteracy, job skills, limited or no access over social networks outside the village, desertion by male spouse, family with many daughters, disability and long illness of the sole bread earner, low caste, mud wall and thatch or no house and sometimes natural calamities and unproductive expenditures make families poor. All these distinctiveness do not help them to overcome poverty easily.

Need for an Integrated and Holistic Approach Towards Reducing Rural Poverty

After independence, to ensure rural development in India a number of programmes were launched with different objectives and approach. Soon after independence, the Community Development Programme was launched to involve local people in the development process. However, due to lack of people's participation in the rural development programmes, the government failed to achieve its goal. As the Food and Agriculture Organization (FAO) of the United

Table 27.1: Characteristics of selected development approaches

Development approach	*Broad based development*	*New technology*	*Local initiative*	*Government initiative*
Community development	****	–	****	***
Green revolution	*	***	*	***
Basic minimum needs	**	–	*	****
Integrated rural development	****	*	**	****
Farming system research	**	****	***	***
Training and visit-extension	*	***	*	**
Farmer centred resource management	***	**	***	**
People's participation	***	*	****	*
Structural adjustment	**	–	–	**

Notes: * Week, ** Intermediate, *** Strong, **** Very strong
Source: Adopted from FAO, 1994.

Nations observes 'the local people with government collaboration could have initiated and implemented the programmes at the grassroots' (Table 27.1).

In case of green revolution programme, the rural elite exploited the resources more than the poor did. At the same time, the Integrated Rural Development Programme (IRDP) in India was supposed to be implemented by adopting an integrated approach; however, it failed to involve the target people in the implementation process. The other programmes like the farmer centered agricultural management, training and extension and promotion of basic minimum needs again failed to initiate the target group's participation to the expected level. All these programmes were planned and implemented by the government agencies including the District Rural Development Agency (DRDA) and the development administration in the district (Table 27.1).

In development literature, mainly three terms are used such as poverty alleviation, poverty reduction and poverty eradication. Generally, poverty alleviation as a concept is used by the government development agencies that intend to take the poor households out of the vicious circle of poverty. Swarnajayanti Gramin Rojgar Yojana (SGRY) and Jawahar Gramin Swarozgar Yojana (JGSY) implemented by the government come under this category. Whereas, poverty reduction aims at a more lasting solution by implementing integrated area development programmes, providing subsidized productive assets, skill training in different areas for different jobs and providing gainful employment at the local level.

The most suitable solutions to the problem of isolation could be providing information in right time and right place so that the vulnerable sections of society can be well aware about the different avenues for earning more income, fighting for their rights. Providing ample development choices and alternatives can help them to lead a happy life like others in society. Rural people's participation in local development decision-making process, asserting themselves through protests may help them to voice against exploitation and injustice. A participatory planning and development process can aim at building the rural poor household's capacity and capability with better education, healthcare, building knowledge and strengthening the entitlement of the poor and helping them to exercise their rights as well. If done properly then the rural poor may lead a happy life and be self-reliant in managing its own affairs.

Poverty could be absolute as well as relative. Development agencies including the NGOs always aim at reducing the number of households living under absolute poverty. Eradication of relative poverty is accepted as a utopian concept. It is not just possible to eradicate poverty from any society because it is a relative concept. To enhance the income of the poor households, both the government and NGOs do employ a number of methods whereas along with higher income they need education, health and productive assets etc, urgently. In India, the poor are not a homogeneous group with different social, behavioural and economic characters (Sethi, 2003). So, there is an urgent need to formulate rural development policy and programmes keeping an eye on these characters.

NGO's Intensive Intervention at the Grassroots

India is a vast country with numerous problems that varies from state to state and region to region. Adding to this culture, geographical conditions and language vary from place to place. Communicating development information from Central Government to the regional and rural local self-governments becomes a challenging task. In this regard the role of the local self-governments becomes vital to identify the local needs, priorities and plan along with the local people accordingly and make the poor families self-reliant. The other reality is that what is true for one village may not be applicable in case of its adjoining village.

Taking enormity of the problem into consideration, there is a need to properly identify the problem and find out the most appropriate solution. Decentralization of the delivery of goods and services can solve the problem of information asymmetry; reduce transaction/implementation cost as well as the social, economic and political structure of our society. It can solve the multiplication of the local problems. Along with a decentralized mechanism to act for the purpose, the receiving system has to be made aware, active and responsible for the failure of any local development intervention.

Development agencies could be governmental, non-governmental and informal and formal local organizations. Formal organizations include NGOs, Panchayati Raj Institutions (PRIs), government line departments; DRDAs and the Integrated Tribal Development Agencies (ITDAs) are the formal organizations. Whereas, all the Community Based Organizations (CBOs) or People's Organizations (POs) are known as the informal organizations. These agencies implement rural development programmes all over the country. From this line of reasoning, growth of vast number of NGOs doing developmental activities is a boon. It is difficult to define an NGO, however, a working definition could be NGOs as 'the agencies facilitating the implementation of development programmes without aiming to attain the self-serving ends'.

The available information about the number of NGOs say that there are about 30,000 NGOs in India that each are working at least in five villages with five motivated, skilled and dedicated workers. The number of NGOs in a district varies from 100 to 500 (Rajasekhar *et al.* 2002). Taking the number into confidence it could be presumed that the sector provides employment to a good number of people and infrastructure for working towards promoting people's participation in rural development. Grassroots development NGOs' role in promoting participatory planning and development for poverty eradication is praiseworthy (Sethi, 2000).

The idea that any organization other than government is an NGO is a wrong view. NGOs could be categorized according to their functions and area of specialization. It could be charity based to serve people during natural calamities, disasters and misery. Providing free food, dress and educational expenditures are some of the other functions of the charity NGOs. Next comes the social action oriented NGOs that give emphasis on mass campaigns, struggles and protest rallies etc. NGOs advocating for the exploited and disadvantaged section of society come under this category. The other categories of NGOs always act for capacity building and empowerment of the community and families at the grassroots. These NGOs prefer to facilitate than directly implement the rural development programmes for the poor families.

All the above NGOs can be categorized under operational NGOs. Development NGOs also undertake support, networking, funding, action research and research action in a number of fields at the grassroots level. A study of fifty selected NGOs, undertaken by one among the leading NGOs in Bangalore, SEARCH found that the agencies need management training. The NGOs that had undergone such a training to promote professionalism in their organization were observed that the management trainings had played a critical role for growth of their organization (Stephen *et al.* 2002). Taking the growth of the NGOs, coverage of their developmental activities and above all their providing employment to a substantial section all over India it is truly considered as the 'third sector' in government.

There is a need to act collaboratively with the government and develop these agencies as more efficient institutions. The strength, weakness, opportunity and threat to these organizations have to be studied to bring their activities in to limelight and scaling up. The sector has to intensify its activities to build social capital and civil society effectively. Though, Government has a favourable policy towards these agencies, it has to be intensified, information has to be shared, strategies towards joint planning, policy formulation and action based on comparative advantage has to be evolved (Coston, 1998).

Need for Synergetic Action Among the Development Agencies

Synergetic action by the development agencies can be the most effective action towards reducing rural poverty because it can build the poorest of the poor's capacity to fight out poverty. The government and non-governmental development agencies need to come together and involve the poor in planning and implementation of education, forestry, health, sanitation, credit, asset development, food security and gainful employment programmes in an integrated manner. Partnerships in specific fields that would bring out mutual benefit and maximum utilization of the resources have to be given priority to promote grassroots development.

Building mass awareness and education for all is one among the major challenges. By doing this the NGOs begin their intervention and end up with capacity building and empowerment of the poor and disadvantaged communities. Motivating the rural poor to participate in the local level development decision-making process, organizing training and orientation programmes and exposure visits; identifying the individual household problems and prospects are their other activities. Solving problems with local people's active and direct participation helps the rural poor and disadvantaged families to overcome powerlessness, isolation and low income. The poor households are organised, educated and critical awareness is built so that they ask the government development agencies for their entitlements such as subsidized food, fertilizer, free house and house sites etc.

The power to bargain for better life and higher income can be made possible through the intensive intervention from the NGOs. Participatory planning for local area development approach gives the rural poor an opportunity to participate in the local development decision-making process (Sethi, 2003). It helps the rural poor to identify the local needs and its prioratisation, identification of the potential resources, planning small projects to solve the locally identified and prioratised problems, implement the projects, monitor, evaluate and also undertake necessary follow up activities.

Through active and direct participation, the local people own the development programmes and contribute and maintaining such programmes in long-run. Most of the NGOs argue that they have the capacity to identify the right people for development intervention, in right time and with the most appropriate programmes so they succeed to reduce poverty. NGOs with a dedicated and motivated work force claims to succeed in their endeavour towards community empowerment and social transformation. However, their success needs to be simulated in the other backward areas.

To make such a vast and difficult task easier there can be a strategy to bridge the gap between the government development personnel and the poorest of the poor in remote rural areas. Building a strong linkage with the local banks, cooperatives and government agencies including DRDAs, ITDAs and the indigenous community specific agencies. It is a challenging job to motivate these communities without any dedicated and motivated personnel. Therefore, it makes a case for collaborative action among the local organizations, grassroots NGOs, institutions and government agencies for participatory planning and rural development. Instead of building parallel local organizations, there is a need to amalgamate such organizations with the local self-governments (Powis, 2003).

The non-governmental development agencies build local leadership who can make the local self-governments responsive to meet the local needs and aspirations most effectively. Good governance demands maintaining transparency, accountability, and people's participation and check corruption. For building a strong civil society, social capital and good governance, collaboration with NGOs is essential. Strengthening the service delivery system with the government could be possible by organizing participatory trainings for the personnel involved in the programme implementation, monitoring and evaluation process of the rural development programmes.

Before initiating such a process, it is most essential to undertake ground works that include constant interaction, linkage with different local development programmes, build cooperation and operational coordination (Riley, 2002). At the same time through collaborative action only NGOs could be made accountable for any misdeeds. Building strong and active federations among the local development agencies and keeping their horizontal and vertical linkages could also be one among the solutions. Black listing the NGOs for their wrong doings or misappropriations would not solve the problem. Building mass awareness about the NGOs' development approach and activities can reduce such problems to a great extent.

Along with accountability to the local people, the role of the multilateral donor agencies is imperative to change the approach of the development agencies. Collaborative action among the government and non-governmental development agencies is expected to solve the social, economic problems. At the same time the successful and genuine NGOs can intensify their activities to bring in all the agencies to work collaboratively and maintain transparency. Making quick money form the development projects should be exposed and discouraged. The sector can be popular as the 'third sector' in government provided they work more collaboratively with other agencies, the PRIs, local banks and co-operatives.

For NGOs, working in few selected areas with little or no managerial ability may not serve the purpose. So, it is high time that the sector should be recognized, regulated and provided wider publicity. Utilization of information technology on building better organizational structures and processes, maintaining co-operation and global lesson sharing can help the sector to grow. Above all, emphasis on local resource mobilization and participatory planning with enhancing the government and non-governmental development agencies, institutions and local organizations collaborative action at the grassroots can reduce rural poverty.

NOTES

1. Defining poverty and poverty line is not discussed at length in the paper since it is not directly under the purview of the paper. Dandekar and Rath first time defined it as an expenditure of Rs. 15 per capita per month for rural and Rs. 18 per capita per month for urban areas in India at 1960–61 prices. ICMR's prescription is termed as second and the third poverty line was constructed by fixing Rs. 49 and Rs. 56 per capita per month for rural and urban areas respectively. The Government of India certified it in 1993. International poverty line is defined as a purchasing power of $1 for per capita per day at 1985 and $ 1.08 per capita per day at 1993 prices. For details see http:/www.infochangeindia.org/povertylbp.jsp. Web site visited on August 20, 2003.
2. The work done at the Social Development Department, World Bank in this regard is noteworthy. For details see Narayan *et al.* (2000).
3. For detail analysis on the subject see http://www.worldbank.org/indiapovertyworkshop

REFERENCES

Cernia, Michael (ed) (1985): *Putting People First: Sociological variables in Development Project,* The John's Hopkins Press, Baltimore.

Chambers, Robert (1995): *Poverty and Livelihood: Whose Reality Counts?* Discussion Paper No. 347, University of Sussex, Institute of Development Studies, London.

Coston, Jennifer M. (1998): 'A Model and Typology of Government—NGO Relationship', *Non-profit and Voluntary Sector Quarterly*, 27(3).

Haq, Mahboob ul (1996): *Reflections on Human Development*, Oxford University Press, Oxford.

Korten, David C. and Norman Uphoff (1981): *Bureaucratic Reorientation of Participatory Rural Development*, NASPAA Working Paper 1, National Association of School for Public Affairs and Administration: Washington D.C.

Kozel, Valeie and Barbara Parker (2003): 'A Profile and Diagnostic of Poverty in UP', *Economic and Political Weekly*, 38(4), January 25.

Morris, D. Morris (1979): *Measuring the Conditions of World's Poor,* ODC, Washington.

Morris, D. Morris and Micelle B. McAlpin (1982): *Measuring the Conditions of India's Poor*, Promilla, New Delhi.

Myrdal, Gunnar (1968): *Asian Drama*, Penguin Books Australia Publication.

Narayan, Deepa *et al.* (2000): *Voices of the Poor: Can You Hear Us,* World Bank, Washington D. C.

Powis, Benjamin (2003): 'Grassroots Politics and Second Wave of Decentralization in Andhra Pradesh', *Economic and Political Weekly,* 38(24), June 28:.2617-22.

Rajasekhar, D. and R.R. Biradar (2002): *Pecple, Government and the NGOs,* Working Paper 114, Institute for Social and Economic Change, Bangalore.

Riley, John M. (2002): *'Stakeholder's Participation for Rural Development: Critical Collaboration in State NGO Partnerships*, Sage, New Delhi.

Sen, Amartya and Jean Dreze (1989): *Hunger and Public Action*, Oxford University Press, New Delhi.

Sethi, Sitakanta (2000): 'Participatory Planning and Development: NGO Initiatives in Orissa, *Madhya Pradesh Journal of Social Science Research,* 5(2), July-December.

—— (2003): 'People's Participation in Local Level Planning and Development', *Kuruksetra,* January.

Stephen, F. and N. Rajasekaran (2002): *Management Practices Among NGOs in India and Bangladesh: An Empirical Study Focusing on HRD*, SEARCH Publication, Bangalore.

28

Paradigm Shift in Local Governance

The Synergy between State and Non-State Actors in Kerala

T.M. JOSEPH AND JOS CHATHUKULAM

The institution of State has been, traditionally, held in high esteem by the people of Kerala. This, in turn, had the effect of keeping private initiative and volunteerism at a reasonable distance from the public realm. The people, by and large, looked towards the intervention of the government for the betterment of their living conditions and infrastructural development. This is evident from the fact that the private sector undertakings and large scale business establishments were still not given a prominent place in the Kerala society. Even in the education and the health sectors, where Kerala is lauded for its longstanding contributions, private initiative was not encouraged till recently. The delivery of welfare measures was considered to be the exclusive domain of the state. One of the probable reasons for the large prevalence of this sentiment could be the influence of the leftist political parties in Kerala.

But the advent of the new economic order, manifested in the form of globalization, liberalization, and privatization has slowly but steadily changed this scenario. It is being increasingly realized that the state, though still dominated by the leftist ideology, cannot withstand the global current towards economic integration. As a result, the government has started receding to the background from many of its traditional areas of operation and the non-governmental organizations, community based groups and multi-national development agencies have stepped in to fill that void.

This new paradigm of governance is in consonance with the increasing trend towards globalisation, privatisation and liberalisation which is making the state to loose its pre-eminence as an agency for development. The new system unfolding on the nation in the last one decade or so entails following new and previously uncharted paths for realising our developmental goals. The thrust of the new approach appears to be one of maximising the growth potential by unleashing outward looking and market driven forces by making necessary adjustments in the structure of the economy and the manner of exercise of control over power and resources (Government of India, 2002).

The emergence of this new paradigm of governance has serious implications for both developed and developing nations (Chandhoke, 2003). In the developed countries of the west, the role of welfare state has been declining under the influence of the neo-liberal Reagan Thatcher ideology, which advocates a drastic cut in the public spending on welfare activities. In the developing countries, the state is being forced to give more scope for other actors in development with the introduction of globalization and structural adjustment programmes. As a result, there is a growing pluralisation of state with multiple actors or agencies spread over from local to global level trying to both supplement and supplant the conventional state in its basic role of development.

Development is now perceived to be delivered by multiple agencies including the state. Pluralisation of state basically means the pre-eminence or even centrality of the state is lost. The state has to limit itself or contract its role so that other players like market and civil society are given adequate space and scope to contribute for development (Shylendra, 2004). The pluralisation has been necessitated as the state alone cannot respond to the diverse needs of development. The different actors who come into picture for development include state agencies like local, state and national governments, and multilateral agencies; market agencies like local traders, national and multi-national companies; and civil society institutions like Community Based Organisations (CBOs), and national and international NGOs (Table 28.1). Thus, governance as a paradigm includes real multiplicity or plurality of institutions which are supposed to be acting in unison to influence development at and from different levels. All these actors are to co-ordinate and network with each other more through horizontal linkages which are both non-hierarchical and non-bureaucratic (Chandhoke, 2003). Through such a linkage, the sharp difference between the state and non-state is to be blurred or rendered irrelevant for development.

Table 28.1: Actors in development under governance paradigm

Reach/ Jurisdiction	*State*	*Market*	*Civil Society*
Global	Multilateral Agencies (UN, WB, WTO etc.)	Multi-National Companies (MNCs)	International NGOs
National	National/ Regional Governments	Domestic Companies/ MNC Branches	National/ Regional NGOs
Local	Local self-government	Local Traders/ Businessmen	Local NGOs/ CBOs/Citizens

Source: H.S. Shylendra (2004): 'The Emerging Governance Paradigm and its Implications for Poverty Alleviation and Equity', Working Paper 182, Institute of Rural Management, Anand.

In the state of Kerala which has demonstrated a high degree of social and political development, the role of this multiple actors is even more pronounced. Along with the state, the other actors involved are the local government, Community Based Organisations and Non-Governmental Organisations. It is the purpose of this chapter to examine what kind of synergy and harmony is achieved among these multiple players. It also looks into the impact this new paradigm has created in solving the problems of the rural people. The chapter concludes by making some suggestions for making these multiple players to become more active and accountable.

One of the reasons for the increased role of these multiple players in development process, in fact, is the decentralization drive that was unleashed in the country for the last one decade. The historic 73rd Constitutional Amendment Act, 1992 which came into being on April 20, 1993, was intended to improve participation of people in the process of development and to transform Panchayati

Raj Institutions into institutions of self government for rural areas. The PRIs are provided with new opportunities for planning based on local needs and priorities, empowerment of women, SC/ST development, mobilization of local resources, generation of demand for services, participation of women in decision-making etc. The Kerala Legislature in follow-up to the 73rd Amendment enacted the Kerala Panchayati Raj Act in 1994 which provides for a three-tier Panchayati Raj system in the state. The Panchayati Raj Institutions are Grama (village) Panchayat, Block panchayat and District panchayat. The basic unit of Panchayati Raj system in Kerala as stipulated by the Kerala Act is a general body of all persons registered as voters in each of the wards (constituencies) of a Grama Panchayat termed as "Grama Sabha" (Village Assembly). The Grama Sabha is a fundamental participatory unit of PRIs in Kerala, constituted at the ward level and there are a total of 13,259 wards. There are 991 Grama Panchayats with an average population of 21,600, 152 Block Panchayats with an average population of 1,80,900 and 14 District Panchayats with a population of 15,24,000.

The focus of this paper is further limited to the emerging pattern of governance in Kerala with special attention on the drinking water sector. It has now been experimented in Kerala to address the drinking water problem with an increased involvement of the people and civil society organizations. The experiment is called *Jalanidhi*, a project implemented with the support of the World Bank, Village Panchayat, Beneficiary Groups and NGOs.

Background of the Project

Kerala is one of the smallest states in India—covering only 1.3 per cent of the total area of the country. However, it has a total population of over 29 million. The population density, at 747 per sq. km, is much higher than the national average of 267 per sq. km. Geographically, Kerala can be divided into three distinct natural divisions—viz., Sandy Coastal Region (< 7.6 m above MSL), Midland region (7.5-75 m above MSL) and the Western Ghats (> 75m above MSL). Kerala gets on an average of 307 cms rainfall, the bulk of which (70%) is received during the South-West monsoon which sets in by June and extends upto September. The state also gets rains from the North-East monsoons during October to December. Blessed with an abundance of rainfall of about 3000 mm annually, Kerala has 44 monsoon-fed rivers with a minimum length of 15 kms. However, given the terrain conditions, run-off is also quite high. The state experiences severe summer from January to May when the rainfall is minimal. Thus, it is an irony of sorts that a green, verdant state like Kerala has a lesser than average per capita availability of potable water, even lesser than that of Rajasthan.

Most of the families depend on private water sources, which are usually open wells. Most of these wells dry up by early March and remain so till the monsoons, which are in May. Sanitation coverage is only 51.36 per cent in the urban areas and 44 per cent in the rural areas. Only 32 per cent of families below poverty line have latrines.

It is estimated that the Government of Kerala has already invested Rs.50,000 crores in the drinking water sector. Despite the more than adequate investment made by the Government on the water and sanitation sector over the years, only one-third of its population is having access to safe drinking water. Some of the reasons cited for this dismal performance were: an unacceptable top down approach to planning, non- involvement of the users, highly inadequate levels of cost recovery, depletion of sources due to overdrawal, frequent breakdowns due to poor operation and maintenance, etc.

In this context, the policy-makers in the state have been influenced by the success of a drinking water scheme that was going on in the Olavanna Panchayat in Kozhikode district. Popularly known as the Olavanna model, this single project stands testimony to the success of a programme that is carried out with people's participation. Taking cue from the Olavanna model, the Kerala Rural Water Supply and Sanitation Project (*Jalanidhi*) is designed and implemented by the users themselves as against the "top-down approach". This will be owned, operated and maintained by the users themselves on a total cost-recovery basis. The major objective of the organisation being the sustained provision of adequate quantities of safe drinking water to the rural poor, the focus on ensuring sustainability of source, sustainability of operations, adequacy of water and quality of water are equally important and are designed into components within the project design.

Jalanidhi Project

The Kerala Rural Water Supply and Sanitation Project (*Jalanidhi*) is supported by the World Bank and is being implemented in four districts: Kozhikode, Palakkad, Malappuram and Thrissur. The Government has also created an autonomous institution "Kerala Rural Water Supply and Sanitation Agency" to implement this project. The project is implemented through Village Panchayats. The total outlay of the project is Rs.450 crores out of which Rs.350 crores are to be repayed to the World Bank within 35 years. The project is implemented in six years (2001-2006) and expected to cover three lakh households, benefiting a population of over 15 lakhs in 4 districts through 2500 piped water supply schemes.

Philosophy of the Jalanidhi Project

Demand Driven Approach—Unlike the supply driven approach hitherto followed, this project is based on the need of the people. The Project will be introduced only in areas where interested groups of people show their willingness to participate in the project and abide by the conditions of cost-sharing. The group then gets a legal entity by registering themselves and only then proceeds with the rest of the planning. The source selection, technology selection, purchase, contracting and implementation is done by this registered body, the beneficiary group, with technical help from Support Organisations. This inculcates a sense of ownership in the people.

Cost Sharing—To ensure stake holding of the project, 15 per cent of the capital costs is borne by the beneficiary community. Of the remaining, the Grama Panchayat bear 10 per cent and 75 per cent is the share of the government.

Cost Recovery—The beneficiary groups themselves meet 100 per cent of the recurring costs of operations and maintenance.

This lightens the burden on the state exchequer, thereby helping the government to utilise this money for other priority needs.

Integrated Approach—The objective of the Project being sustainable supply of safe drinking water, sustainability of source, sustainability of operations, regularity and adequacy of supply and quality of water needs to be ensured. This is being met through other well-integrated components. Sustainability of source is ensured through point-source recharge measures. Quality is ascertained through a mix of Sanitation and Hygiene promotion and provision of infrastructure like latrines, compost pits etc. Sustainability of system is ensured through community empowerment, capacity building, women empowerment and social mobilisation.

Pro-Poor Approach—Special efforts have been taken in the project design to include the poor and vulnerable while selecting the user groups. The project has been so designed to incorporate the beneficiary contribution of 15 per cent of capital costs either through cash or in kind, as labour. Intra-group subsidisation and even inter-group subsidisation is permitted at the behest of and under the total responsibility of the beneficiary groups. Thrift and Credit schemes are promoted in the Beneficiary Groups as "Self-Help Groups" which are operated by the women of that group.

Women Development Initiatives—Women are the most affected both directly and indirectly, during water shortages. The project makes conscious efforts to mainstream the women users in the planning and decision-making activities. Apart from this, they are also encouraged to form "Thrift and Credit Groups" to help them make the payments towards the recurring expenditures of the water supply system. Income generation activities are also designed in the project where groups of women are given financial assistance and skill development training to start viable micro-enterprises of their choice.

Community Empowerment—Capacity building and equipping the community to operate the project is a major thrust area of this project as this is planned, designed, implemented, owned, and operated by the users themselves. This will not only ensure the involvement of the people but will also chart a new path to community-based approach for meeting any local needs.

Community Contracting—The users themselves are fully involved in all the activities right from identifying their sources, deciding on the technology to be utilised, community contracting and implementation till the operations and maintenance aspects of the schemes. All contracting of goods, works, and services will be done at the user level itself for which adequate training will be provided and guidelines made available.

Utilization of Available Resources—The Schemes already operational in these project areas, will also be rehabilitated, and handed over to the User groups. This will ensure efficient utilization of investments made.

Dovetail with Decentralised Planning—This project will be operationalised through the Grama Panchayats and the beneficiary groups, thereby acknowledging and strengthening the efforts of decentralised planning in Kerala.

Implementation

Government of Kerala has overall responsibility for implementing the state project and the national component with the Government of India's Rajiv Gandhi National Drinking Water Mission (RGNDWM). The main implementing agencies are:

Table 28.2: Division of Responsibilities under the *Jalanidhi* Scheme

Activity	*Implementing Agency*
Component A (Institution Building)	KRWSA on behalf of its General Body
Component B (Community Development & Infrastructure Building)	Beneficiary Groups, Grama Panchayats, Support Organisations, and KRWSA
Component C (Statewide Sector Development)	Secretary (Irrigation and Water Supply), Govt. of Kerala and KRWSA
Component D (National Sector Development)	Govt. of India's Rajiv Gandhi National Drinking Water Mission

Source: website; www.jalanidhi.com/components.htm

The Project will be implemented in 80 Grama Panchayats (GPs) in 5 successive but overlapping batches consisting of 5, 15, 20, 25 and 15 GPs respectively. Each batch will follow a 27 month scheme cycle consisting of four distinct phases—

Table 28.3: Plan of Implementation under the *Jalanidhi* Scheme

1. Pre- Planning Phase	-	3 months
2. Planning Phase	-	12 months
3. Implementation Phase	-	8 months
4. Post-Implementation Phase	-	4 months

Source: website; www.jalanidhi.com/design.htm

The main activities and outputs of each phase are as summarised below:

(1) *Pre-Planning Phase:* The main activities during this phase are GP selection, Pre-qualification of Support Organisations and signing of a Planning Phase Tripartite Agreement between the KRWSA, GP and SO.

(2) *Planning Phase:* The main outputs during this phase will be orientation and capacity building of GPs and SOs, BG registration, formation of beneficiary committees, resource mapping and pre-feasibility studies. These will be done in the first four months of this phase. Subsequent activities are technology selection, preparation of engineering designs and community empowerment plans and finally, a GP level Implementation Phase Proposal. The GP, BG and BC capacity-building, sanitation and hygiene promotion and women's development programmes are held as parallel activities during the planning phase. The planning phase concludes with the signing of the Implementation Phase Quadrilateral Agreement (IPQA) between the KRWSA, GP, BG and the SO. There is one IPQA per BG. A separate Implementation Phase Tripartite Agreement (IPTA) is signed between the KRWSA, GP and the SO for managing SO contracts.

(3) *Implementation Phase:* The main activities during this phase deal with the actual implementation. They are procurement of materials, construction of schemes as per agreed plans and procedures and management of project funds.

(4) *Post-Implementation Phase:* During this phase, the GPs will provide advisory support to the communities in efficient operation and maintenance of services, on collection of water tariff and book- keeping. The signing of the Implementation Completion Reports (ICRs) in public gathering by KRWSA, GP and BCs mark the formal exit of KRWSA from a project GP. Sustainability monitoring and impact assessments will be conducted by the KRWSA to assess the project outcome.

FUND FLOW

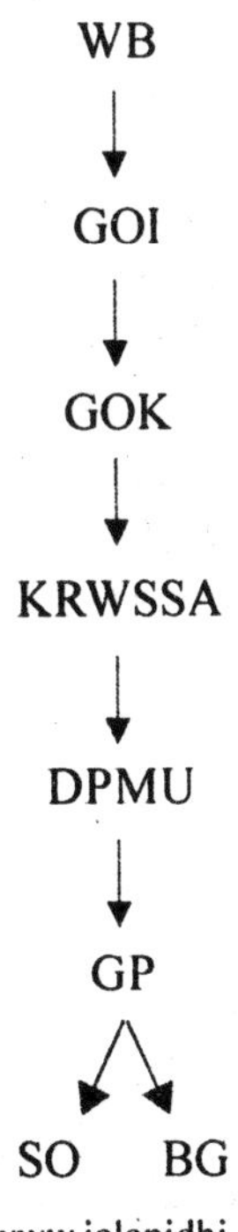

Source: website; www.jalanidhi.com/fundflow.htm

The Multiple Actors Involved in the Project

Grama Panchayat

The Grama Panchayat (GP) will be the focal point for project activities in the GP area. GPs will be mainly responsible for seeking project assistance following a self-selection process, preparing the implementation phase proposal during the planning phase, and for facilitating project implementation by BGs during implementation phase. GPs will provide counterpart funding to BGs as a percentage of infrastructures building costs. During the post-implementation phase, the GPs will monitor the sustainability of scheme operations and ensure that the BGs satisfactorily discharge their O&M management function including levying and collecting user charges from the beneficiaries to fully recover the recurrent O&M costs.

Beneficiary Groups

The Beneficiary Groups (BGs) will be responsible for planning, technology selection, and constructing their RWSS facilities, providing their part of the capital cost contribution, managing O&M of the improved facilities, and levying and collecting sufficient user charges. Representative Beneficiary Committees (BCs) will be set up by each of the participating BGs. Their composition, functions, method of selecting members and relationship with the GP and KRWSA have been agreed. The project would make vigorous efforts to maximize women's representation and management role in the BCs. The project rules require that membership of BCs would be at least 50 per cent women, and 20 per cent from socially disadvantaged groups. At least one of the top management position of the BC (President or Treasurer) will be held by a woman.

Support Organisation

The NGOs and private sector consultants will play an important role in the projects. There will be three categories of Support Organisations (SOs). The first will support the GPs, BGs and Beneficiary Committees on a day-to-day basis in planning and implementing the project's activities, and provide brief support to BGs during post-implementation stage to stabilize scheme operations.

The second will be a range of programmes or providing specialized assistance—such as in the preparation of groundwater recharge schemes, water quality monitoring, or in developing strategy and materials for sanitation and hygiene promotion programmes.

The third category will be private sector consulting firms which would provide assistance in computerized financial management systems, audits and accounts, design engineering of multi-panchayat water supply schemes, independent construction quality monitoring, and management of information systems.

COSTFORD

Centre of Science and Technology for Rural Development (COSTFORD), established in 1985 by a group of scientists, technologists, educationists, professionals and social workers led by Shri C. Achuta Menon strives to change the social, economic and political position of the poor, the deprived, the oppressed and the weak. The strategies followed are mobilization and developmental and social change. COSTFORD is involved in sustainable development based on Gandhi's and Laurie Baker's vision through field application of the philosophy, by leading an example

COSTFORD team of experts consists of architects, engineers, advocates, economists, sociologist, geo-physists, accountants, agricultural scientists, veterinary doctors, medical practitioners, industrial consultants, educationists, artisans, and other construction management people apart from specialists of cost-effective architecture and building technologists.

District Project Management Unit (DPMU)

The District Project Management Unit (DPMU) is set up as the district office for the KRWSA project. The main activities of the DPMU are:

- Capacity-building of the SO through appropriate training and guidelines.
- Capacity-building of the BGs through training organised in support with the respective SO.
- Orientation to the GP, members and staff.
- Confidence building of the BGs through field visit and attending BG meetings by DPMU officials.
- Monitoring of the project activities of SOs and BGs.
- Liaison with the other agencies for effective convergence of various government programmes for the benefit of the BGs.

The Setting of the Study

The study is conducted at the Mundathicode Panchayat in Trichur District of Kerala. The importance of Mundathicode is that it is the panchayat in which the *Jalanidhi* project is first launched. Severely affected by the drinking water shortage, the Panchayat received this project with lot of enthusiasm and expectations. As many as 28 beneficiary groups (BGs) were formed in the panchayat and efforts were made to implement the project. All the BGs were studied in detail. Profiles of the BGs were given in Table 28.4.

The field level data were collected at two levels. First is at the leadership level and then at the beneficiaries' level. The leadership level information was collected from the leaders of Panchayat, Beneficiary groups, Support Organisation and the KRWSSA. The beneficiary level information is collected through an intensive field work done among 230 beneficiaries of all the 28 BGs.

It has been found that the water use patterns of the villagers have changed after the launching of the *Jalanidhi* programme. Though the number of people who used to take less water before the implementation of the scheme has reduced after the programme, the number of those who take more water has increased. This indicates that the people have got more access to drinking water after the introduction of the scheme (Table 28.5).

Table 28.4: Beneficiary Groups under the *Jalanidhi* Scheme at Mundathikode Panchayat

Sl. No.	*Name of the Beneficiary Group*	*Total No. of Households in the B.G.*	*No. of Households Surveyed*
1	Aiswarya	52	05
2	Anugraha	47	04
3	Athani Medical College Development	163	15
4	Bhageeratha	98	10
5	Gandhinagar	38	04
6	Gramasira	105	10
7	Gamasree	94	10
8	Irunnamkallu	41	04
9	Jawahar	147	15
10	Kallidathuchira	57	06
11	Kiliathuchira	64	06
12	Kottakunnu	49	05
13	Manakulam	68	07
14	MKKVS	43	37
15	Navajyothi	51	05
16	Peringandoor	87	09
17	Pheonix	70	07
18	Pratheeksha	65	07
19	Puthuruthy Sudhajalam	74	07
20	Puthuruthy Vadakkummury	48	04
21	Safron	53	04
22	Samrudha	148	14
23	Sangamam	58	06
24	Sanjeevani	94	09
25	Souhrudha Nagar	37	03
26	Subiksha	87	09
27	Theerthadhara	56	05
28	Yuvajana Sangam	34	03
	Total	2115	230

Source: Field Survey.

Table 28.5: Water use patterns before and after the launching of the Jalanidhi scheme.

Usage of water (in litres)	*Before Jalanidhi* No.	%	*After Jalanidhi* No.	%
100-300	67	29.13	57	24.78
301-500	132	57.39	121	52.60
501-750	31	13.48	52	22.61
Total	230	100	230	100

Source: Field Survey.

Though the water intake has changed, majority of the respondents were not happy with the volume of water they got. As many as 157 people said that they did not get the volume of water that they expected at the launching of the programme. 123 people have opined that there was no sufficient water at the source, while others have attributed certain technical problems like insufficient tank, lesser width of pipe etc. for the inadequate supply of water.

The technical aspects of the project implementation were supposed to be looked after by the Support Organisation (SO). In the case under study, the SO involved is COSTFORD, an organization which is widely acclaimed for its commitment to the cause of Rural Development. As it is the purpose of the study to examine the synergy between various state and non-state actors in pursuit of rural development, the performance of the Support Organisation is brought under close scrutiny. The degree of acceptance of the SO among the beneficiaries is taken as one of the indicators in this regard.

A question was posed to all the sample beneficiaries that "are you aware about the existence of a support organization in this project?" It is surprising to note that only 28.70 per cent beneficiaries are aware that a support organization does exist at all. This is supplemented by another answer which revealed that only 30.87 per cent beneficiaries have positive opinion about the job done by the COSTFORD. It has been made clear in the survey that the SO could not effectively integrate with the society in which it is put to work. On a specific question whether the SO has made its presence felt in the Panchayat, only seven per cent of the beneficiaries replied in the affirmative. No wonder in 76 per cent of the beneficiaries saying that there is no need for any support organization in this kind of a project.

The apparent problem with the SO is that they did not trust the villagers. On many aspects of the project, the common people had their own ideas about the implementation process. But the staff of the COSTFORD strictly went by the text of their technical knowledge. The local circumstances and wisdom were completely ignored. Shri Ajith Kumar, a member of Gram Panchayat, for instance, said that the COSTFORD actually worsened the situation. They have constructed the water tank at a much lower terrain, ignoring the views of the Beneficiary Groups. The common men knew that the tank should be kept at a higher plane, to make water available in the remote areas. But since such local wisdom was not heeded to, most of the beneficiaries do not get water at all. Shri Ajith Kumar even suspected financial irregularities in the project. He said that Rs. 35 lakhs were given to the SO in the Mundathikode Panchayat itself. He is of the opinion that the entire project could be completed with half of this amount.

It is made known in the study that the Village Panchayat, another actor involved in the project was not given the due role in the project implementation other than contributing 10 per cent of the total project expenditure. It did not have any regulatory authority over the SO in designing and implementing the project. But the beneficiaries always view the Panchayat as their sole authority in terms of rural development. It has become evident from the high degree of acceptance that the Panchayat as an institution has got among the beneficiaries.

As many as 208 people (90%) said that they got good support and encouragement from the village panchayat. In fact, none of the beneficiaries had even a minute complaint against the Panchayat. It was an irony that when people put their trust in the Panchayat, it was found itself in a helpless situation. One Panchayat member who does not want to reveal his identity said that the Panchayat has no control over the SO. "In fact, the Panchayat and the SO work at parallel levels. The SO is just a temporary installation of people with no practical experience. They are not competent to carry out this kind of work. They were giving just 1000 rupees to those girls who supervised the work. How much sincerity and commitment can we expect from a diploma holder in civil engineering with such a meagre amount of salary", he asked.

One of the indirect aims of this kind of a project is to generate the right kind of trust and cohesiveness among the beneficiaries. Therefore, more attention was given in the study to ascertain the level of social capital that has been created as a result of this *Jalanidhi* project. The major idea emerged from the study is that the objective is not met. In fact, some of the ideas shared by the leaders of beneficiary groups reveal that the social capital generated was of negative nature.

Shri Gopi (a traditional Ayurvedic physician by profession), the president of the Bhagiratha Beneficiary Group, for instance, said that this project actually cheats the people. It could not solve the water needs of the people. The people were not giving the user fee regularly. He had to spend money from his pocket. He lost his public acceptance even as he took up this responsibility.

The leaders of beneficiary groups were, by and large, not satisfied with the degree of co-operation they got from the beneficiaries. It was difficult for them to collect the users' fee in time. In case someone doesn't get water he/she used to rush to the houses of the president or secretary of the BG with complaints. It becomes a headache for the BG leaders to address these issues. Sheela, an unmarried girl of 22 years who heads the Puthuruthi Sudh Jal, said that she had to suffer a lot of humiliation on account of these complaints. Her parents were not happy with creating such unruly scenes in the house. Even good marriage proposals were called off as this girl is 'a public figure'. She wants to get rid of this responsibility at the earliest. But nobody seems to be willing to take over.

Most of the complaints were due to the forcible opening of locks that regulate the water flow to various outlets. The beneficiaries have a tendency to break open these locks to access more water. The beneficiaries have an understanding among themselves that they should not indulge in such malpractices. But the frequent violations of such understanding indicate the lack of trust that exists among the beneficiaries.

One general trend that has been seen in the survey is that those who are in the leadership positions do not want to continue any longer. On the other hand, nobody seems to be interested in taking over. This has been made clear from the data collected. In most of the BGs, the leadership positions were not changed since the launching of the scheme. Voting has not been taken place in any of the BGs to choose the office bearers. It indicates the BGs have not yet become vibrant associations.

The general body meetings of the beneficiaries were held rarely. Only seven respondents have said that the general body is held 2-4 times so far. Twenty-three respondents have said that it has been held once. The remaining 200 respondents said that the general body is either not held or they have no idea about it. As many as 226 respondents do not know anything about the executive committee meetings of their BGs. They have no idea of what they are discussing in the executive committee meetings.

One interesting thing noticed in the survey is that the political identification of beneficiaries does not affect the smooth functioning of the scheme. As many as 219 respondents were identified with one political party or the other. But only two respondents have said that political identification adversely affected the scheme. Majority of the respondents have said that the problems emerged in the beneficiary groups are settled within the group amicably. All problems are related to the inadequate availability of water. In any case, the internal disputes and quarrels have not disturbed the implementation of the scheme.

Beneficiaries' identification with the project has been another concern of the study. To ascertain this aspect, questions were asked to test their knowledge about the source of funding for the project. It is noted that 56 respondents had no idea about the sources of funding. Of the total 230 respondents, 174 knew that money comes from the World Bank. But only 82 respondents knew that this money has to be refunded. Even among them only 30 people know that it is the government which should refund this money. But nobody knows the period of repayment and the rate of interest. As many as 217 beneficiaries justified the act of seeking foreign money, since it is a problem of drinking water. The low level of knowledge about the project among the beneficiaries again indicates that the project could achieve only limited success in activating the rural community.

The *Jalanidhi* project in Kerala has to be seen as an attempt to achieve rural development through an interface between state government, panchayats, Community Based Organizations (CBOs) and non-governmental organizations (NGOs). Among these, government and panchayats are state actors and CBOs and NGOs are non-state actors. The study has been focused on ascertaining the effectiveness of the synergy between the state and non-state actors as it is an emerging pattern of development governance.

The inference drawn from the study is that there is no proper coordination between panchayat, CBO and the NGO. While the CBO believes that the panchayat is the main actor, the panchayat takes NGO as the main actor. In fact, as per the script, it is the NGO which has to supervise and implement the project. Therefore, the panchayat is not supposed to interfere in the day-to-day administration of the project. But the people do not know this. There is a wide divergence between the perception of the beneficiaries about the role of the panchayat and its assigned role. On many occasions when the beneficiaries do not get water, the beneficiaries rush to the houses of panchayat members with complaints. But the panchayat members were helpless as they were not given any meaningful role in the design of the scheme. The designing of the scheme is left exclusively with the SO. But the SO is neither accountable to the panchayat nor to the people. After the completion of the project, the SO withdraws from the scene and the project is to be then managed by the beneficiary groups themselves. At this stage the people look towards the panchayat as the sole savior of all their problems.

One of the implications is that there is a gross sidelining of the panchayat in the whole process, though the people lend legitimacy and credibility to the institution. The panchayat's role is limited just to select the SO from the list of SOs approved by the state government and provide 10 per cent financial assistance to the project. It has no control over the SO in the process of designing and implementing the project. At the same time, all complaints against the SO are to be settled by the panchayat. This dichotomy is not visualized in the *Jalanidhi* project.

The SO on the other hand, takes this opportunity to exert their authority over the beneficiaries. Having bestowed with technical knowledge and expertise, they tend to ignore the indigenous knowledge and wisdom of the local people. On many occasions, the local people have convincingly argued for a different design and method of implementation. But they, in turn, were cajoled for their lack of modern knowledge and experience. This had the effect of lessening the credibility of the SO in the eyes of the public.

The beneficiary groups have the good intention of running the project effectively, and thereby solve their water problems. But they were found without proper guidance and discipline. Driven with their self-interests, they had least concern for the interests of their fellow users. This caused unnecessary tension and non-cooperation within the beneficiary group, defeating the much desired objective of generating social capital within the society. The study reveals that the already existing amount of social capital is at a loss as they got a new space to quarrel over sharing the facility offered by the project. This makes one to conclude that any good intended programme may result in generating 'negative social capital' if it is poorly designed and implemented.

REFERENCES

Chandhoke, Neera (2003): 'Governance and the Pluralisation of the State: Implications for Democratic Citizenship,' *Economic and Political Weekly,* 38(28): 2957-68.

Government of India (2002): *Tenth Five Year Plan (2002-2007): Dimensions and Strategies,* Vol. I, Planning Commission, New Delhi.

Jayal, Niraja Gopal and Sudha Pai (eds) (2001): *Democratic Governance in India: Challenges of Poverty, Development, and Identity*, Sage, New Delhi.

Rajasekher, D. and R.R. Biradar (2002): People, Government and the NGOs, Working Paper 114, Institute for Social and Economic Change, Bangalore.

Riley, John M. (2002): *Stakeholders' Participation for Rural Development: Critical Collaboration in State NGO Partnerships*, Sage, New Delhi.

Shylendra, H.S. (2004): 'The Emerging Governance Paradigm and its Implications for Poverty Alleviation and Equity', Working Paper 182, Institute of Rural Management, Anand.

World Bank (1994): *Governance: The World Banks Experience*, World Bank, Washington D.C.

INDEX